WALKERS'
BRITAIN

Acknowledgements

DRAWINGS

The black and white drawings are by **Andrew Hutchinson**, with the exception of the milestone, which is by **Nigel White**.

PHOTOGRAPHS

The Automobile Association would like to thank the following photographers, libraries and associations for their assistance in the preparation of this book:

Malcolm Boyes 198 Sproxton Church, 199 Strensall New Bridge, 201 River Wharfe, 202 Milestone, 203 Ilkley packhorse bridge, 203 Ilkley Moor, 205 Rowley Church, 207 Brantingham, Steamboat, 209 Wintringham, Wharram Percy, 210 Ganton Hall, 211 Filey Bay

Countryside Commission for Scotland 233 Bridge of Orchy, 234 Dumgoyne and Strathblane, 237 Crianlarich, 239 Loch Tulla, 240 Meall a'Bhuiridh, 242 Lundavra

Bill Dawes 110 Langleys, 111 Coggeshall, 112 Essex Way

E T Archive 179 Battle of Preston (Harris Museum & Art Gallery, Preston), 215 John Ruskin

Jeremy Evans 56 Watership Down, 116 Newgale, 117 Porthgain, 118 Solva, 119 Caerfai, 121 Whitesands Bay, 122 Pwllcrochan, 124 Tredegar House, 125 Fourteen Locks, 126 Mynydd Machen, 127 Coed y Llanerch, 128 Display board, 130 River Usk, 131 Prioress Mill

Frank Haskew 98 Stoke Talmage, 99 Rycote Chapel, 102 River Cherwell

Julian Holland Publishing Library 10 Leland Trail, Ilchester, 28 Lodge Hill, 29 Logo, West Camel Church, 30 King Alfred's Tower, 31 Castle Cary, 32 River Yeo, 33 Ham Hill, 62 Beeding Hill, 65 Monk's House, 69 St Botolph's Church, 71 Christ's Hospital School, 72 Itchingfield, 73 St Martha's Church, Wey & Arun Canal, 75 St Peter's Church, Hambledon, 76 Pitch Hill, 77 Duke of Kent School, 78 Jevington, 80 Great Buckland, 85 Chiddingly Church, 93 River Thames, White Horse, 145 Caldon Canal, 146 Mow Cop, 147 Froghall Wharf, 148 Alton Station, 149 River Churnet, 178 Dolphin Inn sign, 181 River Ribble, 183 Helwith Bridge Hotel

Tony Hopkins 9 Deer Play, 11 Great Shummer, 220 Alston, 221 The Cheviot, 222 Castle Nook, 223 Killhope, 225 Crag End, 226 Padon Hill, 227 Catscleugh Reservoir, 228 The Cheviot and Hedgehope, 229 Auchope

George Keeping 95 Icknield Way, 96 Princes Risborough

Brian Pearce 12/13 Bull Point, 14 Hollow Brook, 18 Baggy Point, 20 Dart Valley, 21 Clapper Bridge, Blackface sheep, 22 Leftlake, 23 Petre's Cross, 24 Hameldown Cross, 25 Soussons Farm, 26 Bennett's Cross, 27 Castle Drogo

Roger Smith 248 Strathspey Railway, 250 Feith Musach, 251 Glen Conglass

Colin Speakman 185 Pen-y-ghent, 193 Dent, 195 Bowness

All other pictures are held in the Association's library (**AA PHOTO LIBRARY**), with contributions from:
M Adleman 91 Wayland's Smithy, 206 Brantingham Dale **M Allwood-Coppin** 129 Usk **A Baker** 91 Avebury, 142 Monsal Dale, 178 Ribchester Church, 179 River Ribble, 186 Linton Falls, 189 Grassington Bridge, 191 Kettlewell **P Baker** 105 Henley-on-Thames, 142/3 Monsaldale **J Beazley** Title page Hotbanks Crags, 120 Ramsey Island, 121 St David's Cathedral, 152 Matlock, 180 Clitheroe, 199 Castle Howard, 208 Londesborough Church, 224 Cuddy's Crags **M Birkitt** 94 Ewelme, 108 Greensted Church, 147 Rudyard Reservoir, 150 Peveril Castle, 153 Mam Tor, 213 Whinny Brow, 218 Latrigg **E A Bowness** Cover Above Grasmere, 217 Hill Top Farm, 219 Carlisle Citadel **J Carney** 243 Ben Nevis **P Enticknap** 50 Portsdown Hill, 53 Bat and Ball **R Eames** 177 Settle, 182 Giggleswick **D Forss** 51 Alresford Fulling Mill, 53 Hambledon Church, 54 Alresford, 64 Poynings, 70 Bramber Castle, 81 Tonbridge, 82 Tonbridge Castle **S Gibson Photography** 235 Balmaha **V Greaves** 144 Abbots Bromley **D Hardley** 232 Loch Lamona, 236 Inversnaid Falls, 243 Glen Nevis **T Hopkins** 136 Symonds Yat, 176 Horton in Ribblesdale **B Johnson** 51 Inkpen Beacon, 88 Hackpen Hill, 90 Hackpen Hill in snow, 92 Uffington **S King** 187 Windermere, 219 John Peel's grave **A Lawson** 15 Ilfracombe, 16 Cliff Railway, 17 Combe Martin, 19 Braunton Burrows, 23 Buckfast Abbey, 25 Widecombe in the Moor, 35 Stanway House, 101 Blenheim Palace, 179 River Ribble **S & O Mathews** 43 Alum Bay, Stag Rocks, 44 Osborne House, 45 Newtown Estuary, 47 Needles, 48 Ventnor, 49 Whitecliff Bay, 49 Bembridge, 59 Birling Gap, 61 Harting Hill, 75 Leith Hill, 77 Leith Hill Tower, 81 Kent orchards, 83 Ashdown Forest, 84 Chiddingly, 97 Ivinghoe Beacon, 103 Ot Moor, 104 Chiltern beechwood, 107 Cloth Hall, Dedham, 109 Pleshey, 111 Paycocke's, 113 Dedham café, 154 Holkham Gap, 155 Sheringham, 156 Brettenham Heath, 158 Castle Acre Priory, 159 Peddars Way, 160 Hunstanton, 161 Brancaster Marshes, 163 Wells-next-the-Sea, Wells & Walsingham Light Railway, 164 Cley next the Sea, 165 North Norfolk Railway, 166 Hickling Broad, 168 Cromer, 170 North Walsham Church, 171 Swan, Hickling, 183 Stainforth Bridge, 184 Horton in Ribblesdale Churchyard, 188 Strid Gorge, 189 Bolton Priory, 192 Ribblehead Viaduct, 194 Friends' Meeting House **C & A Molyneux** 141 River Wye **J Morrison** 190 Upper Wharfedale **R Newton** 89 West Kennet, 149 Gladstone Pottery Museum, 153 Monsal Dale Viaduct, 196 Helmsley Castle, 197 Low Petergate, York, 200 Skeldergate Bridge, York **G Rowatt** 204 River Humber **P Sharpe** 174/5 Derwentwater, 195 Steamboat Museum, 212 Coniston, 216 Tarn Hows, 217 Skelwith Bridge, 230/1 Pass of Glencoe, 241 Pass of Glencoe **T Souter** 36 Chipping Campden, 162 Holkham Hall, 169 Blickling Hall, 172 Thurne windpump, 173 River Thurne **F Stephenson** 37 Sudeley Castle, 38 Winchcombe, 100 Bourton-on-the-Water **R Surman** 215 *Gondola* **M Taylor** 40/1 Windover Hill, 246 Spey Bay, 249 Aberlour Bridge, 252 St Andrews Cathedral, 253 Crail, 254 Earlsferry, Elie, 256 Forth Rail Bridge **M Trelawny** 58 Cuckmere Valley, 63 Fulking, 66 Glynde Place, 68 Steyning, 79 Wilmington Priory, 85 Fireback, 86 Michelham Priory, 87 Beachy Head, 203 Otley Memorial **W Voysey** 33 Montacute House, 46 Tennyson Down, 55 Brown Candover Church, Mid Hants Railway, 57 Combe Gibbet, 109 Chelmsford Cathedral **R Weir** 244 Tomintoul, 245 River Spey, 247 Fochabers old station, 247 Aultdearg Pillars, 248 Craigellachie **H Williams** 34 Hailes Abbey, 52 Langstone Harbour, 60 Iron Age Farm, 61 Weald & Downland Museum, 65 Clayton windmills, 67 Seven Sisters, 97 Ashridge, 114 St David's Head, 132 Tintern, 134 Chepstow Castle, 135 Tintern old station, 137 Olde Ferrie Inne, 137 Forest of Dean, 138 River Wye, 139 Hereford Cathedral, Bulmers advertisement, 140 Kilvert's grave **T Woodcock** 106 Epping Forest **J Wyand** 39 Painswick Church, 67 Long Man of Wilmington

The publishers acknowledge the assistance given in the preparation of this book by **Hugh Westacott**, of the Outdoor Writers' Guild, and by **Iain Liddell**, of the Long Distance Paths Advisory Service.

AA

WALKERS'
BRITAIN

BRAMHOPE CROSS 4
OLD BRAMHOPE + 14.
OTLEY SCHEVIN 2
CARLTON BAR 17
GUISELEY CHURCH 57
KIRSKILL HALL 1 L
ARTHINGTON HALL 2 4
CASTLEY FORD LANE 8
ARTHINGTON STATION 5

Conceived, designed and produced by Julian Holland Publishing Limited,
Somerset, and published by AA Publishing (a trading name of Automobile
Association Developments Limited, whose registered office is Norfolk House,
Priestley Road, Basingstoke, Hampshire RG24 9NY; registered number 1878835).

Edited by Susan Gordon.

© The Automobile Association 1992
Maps © The Automobile Association 1992

First published 1992. Reprinted 1999.

ISBN 0 7495 2091 4
ISBN 0 7495 2103 1

A CIP record of this book is available from the British Library.

The contents of this book are believed correct at the time of printing. Nevertheless,
the publishers cannot be held responsible for any errors or omissions or for changes
in the details given in this book or for the consequence of any reliance on the
information provided by the same. The opinions expressed by the comntributors
throughout this book are not necessarily those of the Automobile Association.

Typesetting by PCS Typesetting, Frome, Somerset.
Colour reproduction by Scantrans PTE, Singapore.
Printed and bound by Graficromo S.A./Spain

THE AUTHORS

EBOR WAY/WOLDS WAY

Malcolm Boyes has walked extensively in all
parts of Britain and is the author of some 20 books
on walking and the north of England, including
AA Village Walks. **Hazel Chester**, his wife, is co-
author with him of several of these, and is also an
illustrator. They live in North Yorkshire.

ESSEX WAY/ISLE OF WIGHT COASTAL FOOTPATH

Bill Dawes has walked most of the country's long
distance paths since completing his first at the age
of 16 and is a freelance watersports and sports
writer living in Sussex.

CUMBRIA WAY/RIBBLE WAY

Charlie Emett took early retirement and now
devotes most of his time to his favourite hobbies,
walking and writing, mainly in the North. Born
on the banks of the Eden, he devised and wrote
the guide to the Eden Way.

PLANNING A LONG DISTANCE WALK/COTSWOLD WAY/LIMESTONE WAY/PEMBROKESHIRE COAST PATH/SIRHOWY VALLEY WALK/ SOUTH DOWNS WAY/ USK VALLEY WALK/WAYFARER'S WALK

Jeremy Evans is a writer, journalist and
photographer living in West Sussex. His many
books include *Classic Literary Walks*, *Offroad
Adventure Cycling* and *Camping and Survival*.

LELAND TRAIL

Julian Holland is a book designer, living and
working in Somerset. In his spare time he enjoys
walking, photography and travelling by train.

PENNINE WAY

Tony Hopkins is a writer, illustrator and
photographer, specialising in countryside and
wildlife subjects. He has written several books,
including the official Countryside Commission
guides to the Pennine Way, and contributed to
AA Country Walks.

PEDDARS WAY & NORFOLK COAST PATH/STAFFORDSHIRE WAY/ WEAVERS' WAY

Charles Hurt is a freelance writer of books
and articles on country matters. A lover of music
as well as walking, he lives on the north
Norfolk coast.

RIDGEWAY

George Keeping has walked many of the long
distance paths of Britain and in 1984 became the
first person to traverse all the British 3000ft
mountains in one continuous journey. He now
works for Lincolnshire Rights of Way Team. He
contributed to *AA Village Walks*.

OXFORDSHIRE WAY

Helen Livingston was born and brought up in
southern England and her love for walking in the
region dates from her school days. As a freelance
writer, she combines her interests in the
countryside, history and literature.

WYE VALLEY WALK

Les Lumsdon has researched several regional
walking books and writes a regular outdoors
column. He is Associate Editor of *Getting About
Britain* and is Senior Lecturer in Tourism at
Staffordshire Polytechnic.

SOUTH WEST COAST PATH/ TWO MOORS WAY

Brian Pearce is Interpretations Officer for
Exmoor National Park and has contributed to
several books on walking, including *Walkers'
Britain* and *AA Village Walks*.

DOWNS LINK/GREENSAND WAY/WEALDWAY

Ben Perkins has lived and worked in the
Brighton area all his life. A keen conservationist,
he is Vice Chairman of the Society of Sussex
Downsmen. He devised and co-wrote the guide
for the Sussex Border Path and contributed to
AA Village Walks.

FIFE COAST WALK/SPEYSIDE WAY/ WEST HIGHLAND WAY

Roger Smith is a freelance writer and editor
living in Scotland. He has written a number of
books about walking and was formerly editor of
the walkers' magazine *The Great Outdoors*.

DALES WAY

Colin Speakman is a freelance writer and
transport consultant, and was one of the
originators of the Dales Way. He is the Secretary
of the Yorkshire Dales Society and lives at Ilkley,
Wharfedale. He contributed to *AA Village Walks*.

INTRODUCING LONG DISTANCE PATHS/A–Z OF LONG DISTANCE PATHS

Hugh Westacott is the author of *The Walker's
Handbook*, *The Illustrated Encyclopaedia of Walking
and Backpacking* and several footpath guides. He
also contributed to *AA Village Walks*. He serves on
the committees of the Outdoor Writers' Guild and
the Long Distance Paths Advisory Service.

Contents

Map and List of Paths

Introducing Long Distance Paths

IN BRITAIN, a long distance path, known colloquially as an LDP, is usually defined as a route of at least 20 miles (32km) that has been given a distinctive name, and for which a guide exists. Sometimes shorter routes are also referred to as long distance paths, especially if they provide a link between two other long distance paths. The term 'wayfarer' is applied to a person who walks a long distance path, as in 'Pennine wayfarer'.

It is likely that the Schwarzwaldverein (Black Forest Association), formed in Germany in 1864, was the first organisation to promote and develop long distance paths. The first was the 450-mile (280km) West Way from Pforzheim to Basle, opened in 1900, which was followed in 1903 by the 145-mile (233km) Middle Way (Pforzheim – Waldshut), and the 148-mile (238km) East Way (Pforzheim – Schaffhausen). Sweden established the Kungsleden in Lapland before World War I, and James Paddock Taylor founded the Green Mountain Club and began to carve out the 265-mile (427km) Long Trail from Massachusetts to the Canadian border in 1910. In 1921 Benton MacKaye first proposed the establishment of the 2113-mile (3400km) Appalachian Trail down the eastern United States from Maine to Georgia which was completed in 1937. In England, Tom Stephenson first publicised the idea of establishing a long distance path along the watershed of northern England in an article in the *Daily Herald* in June 1935. This led to the formation of the Pennine Way Association, but long distance paths were not formally established until the implementation of the National Parks and Access to the Countryside Act 1949, which followed the publication of the Hobhouse Report. Scotland and Northern Ireland had to wait much longer for legislation. Long distance paths have been established in most European countries as well as in other developed nations. There are now a number of European international long distance paths that criss-cross Western Europe, and it is likely that the political events of 1989 will ultimately lead to links with the long distance routes in eastern Europe.

There are two kinds of long distance path in the United Kingdom: official routes and unofficial routes. There is no uniform legislation governing rights of way and long distance paths in the United Kingdom and each constituent country has its own distinctive laws. England and Wales have many more LDPs than Scotland and Northern Ireland.

In England and Wales, official routes, now known as national trails, were first established under the provisions of the National Parks and Access to the Countryside Act, 1949. In England, the following national trails are the responsibility of the Countryside Commission: the Cleveland Way, the North Downs Way, the Peddars Way and Norfolk Coast Path, the Pennine Way, the Ridgeway Path, the South Downs Way, the South West Coast Path, the Thames Path (this route still awaits official designation but is included here as it is walkable throughout its length), and the Wolds Way. I Wles, the Countryside Council for Wales, is responsible for Offa's Dyke Path and the Pembrokeshire Coast Path. Unofficial routes may be devised by local authorities, rambling clubs or individuals (in England and Wales, the Countryside Commission and the Countryside Council for Wales now refer to them as 'regional routes'). This is a better term, although it has not gained wide currency, because all long distance paths created by local authorities are, in a sense, official routes in that they are normally waymarked and maintained as part of the local authority's countryside management programme, and the guide to the route is unlikely to go out of print. Some long distance routes created by individuals, rambling clubs and other organisations are well established but there is a risk that if the route does not prove popular, the guidebook will go out of print and, in effect, that particular long distance path will no longer exist.

In Scotland, provision for the creation of long distance paths was included in the Countryside (Scotland) Act, 1967, which also established the Countryside Commission for Scotland (now Scottish Natural Heritage), the body responsible for the Southern Upland Way, the Speyside Way, and the West Highland Way. The concept of LDPs has not been received enthusiastically by many Scottish walkers, who fear that their existence may compromise the traditional freedom that exists in Scotland to roam in open country.

The Ulster Way is the only official long distance path in Northern Ireland and is the responsibility of the Sports Council for Northern Ireland.

It should be noted that a footpath guide is normally necessary to follow a long distance path because rights of way in this category are not plotted distinctively on Ordnance Survey maps, except those sections of national trails that appear on Outdoor Leisure maps. National trails and some other LDPs are named at points along their route on Ordnance Survey Landranger maps but not in a manner that enables the walker to follow the exact route.

A number of organisations concern themselves with long distance paths. The Long Distance Paths Advisory Service (Administrator: Gerald Cole, The Barn, Holme Lyon, Burneside, Kendal, Cumbria LA9 6QX) maintains a register of routes in an attempt to record all long distance paths, and to prevent the duplication of routes which can result in erosion and other environmental damage. The register is kept on a computer database, and the routes are recorded on Ordnance Survey Landranger maps. Anybody contemplating devising a long distance path may consult the register and will be advised of the proximity of any other routes, and whether the area is subjected to heavy use. Note that the register acts primarily as an advisory service for authors, publishers, local authorities etc. The answers to most of the requests for information made to the LDPAS and outdoor magazines could be supplied very quickly by any public librarian.

The Long Distance Walkers' Association (Hon. Secretary: Alan Castle, Wayfarers, 9 Tainters Brook, Uckfield, East Sussex TN22 1UQ) exists to further the interests of those who enjoy long distance walking. It promotes organised challenge walks, pioneers new walking routes and receives and publishes information on all aspects of non-competitive walking, and is now recognised as the governing body for the activity of long distance walking.

The Ramblers' Association, 1-5 Wandsworth Road, London SW8 2XX, is the national organisation that looks after the interests of all walkers. It aims to help all to a greater love, knowledge and care of the countryside and works hard to keep open and protect rights of way, including LDPs.

Using this Book

The book describes in detail 30 long distance paths in Britain. The country is divided into six regions, as shown on the Map and List of Paths on page 6. The description of each walk starts with a general introduction, accompanied by a map of the path or, in some cases, the section of it covered in this book. Also on these introductory pages is a list of detailed guides and the Ordnance Survey 1:50,000 Landranger maps which it is recommended walkers take with them. Other long distance paths that cross or coincide with the route are also listed and marked on the map, making it possible to plan further walks.

A detailed route description follows the introduction, divided into sections that may generally be walked in an average day. Precise starting points are given, with grid references, as well as details of car parking places. 'Escapes' are suggested (shown on the map with a corresponding Ⓔ symbol) for those who may wish to leave the path and return to the start point using a different route or, in some cases, public transport. Grid references are given for the break-out point, but full details of these 'escape' routes are not given in the text, or on the map, and readers will need to refer to the relevant Ordnance Survey map or local guides.

To help in planning the walk, whether it be an afternoon's outing or a full week's hike, a Guide Box lists places to visit on or near the path and includes concise information on car parking, public transport and accommodation along the route. The Tourist Information Centres listed will provide further details of accommodation and public transport (or, in the case of buses, may refer the reader to the relevant local bus company or enquiry line). They will also give detailed opening times for the suggested places to visit. Note that, although a place may be described in this book as 'open all year', it may be closed over Christmas, and that 'open Easter' may mean 1 April or Easter, whichever is the earlier. It is always advisable to check current details in advance to avoid disappointment.

MAP SYMBOLS

Symbol	Meaning	Symbol	Meaning
- - - -	Route of LDP	⚱	Country park
▬▬▬	Route of LDP described in this book	🐻	Theme park
Ⓔ	Suggested 'escape' point	🐘	Zoo
Minster Way ◄►	Link point with other LDP	🦏	Wildlife collection - mammals
Coniston	Section start/finish point	🦅	Wildlife collection - birds
═══	Motorway	🐬	Aquarium
▬▬▬	Primary route	🦫	Nature reserve
———	A road/B road	RSPB	RSPB site
———	Railway line	🌿	Nature trail
- - - -	Vehicle ferry	☀	AA viewpoint
·—·—·	National border	♣	Picnic site
◆	Urban area		Hill fort
◉	Village/hamlet	🌾	Roman antiquity
≡≡≡	Marsh	Ⅱⅳ	Prehistoric monument
⌒	Sandy beach	✕ 1461	Battle site with year
▲	Hill	🚂	Preserved railway/ steam centre
ⓘ	Tourist Information Centre	⌒	Cave
ⓘ	Tourist Information Centre (seasonal)	✗	Windmill
♠	Abbey, cathedral or priory	⚑	Golf course
⋏	Ruined abbey, cathedral or priory	🏏	County cricket ground
♙	Castle	🏃	International athletics stadium
🏛	Historic house	🐎	Horse racing
Ⓜ	Museum or art gallery	⬥	Coastal launching site
🏭	Industrial interest	⛷	Ski slope - natural
✳	Garden	⛷	Ski slope - artificial
🌳	Arboretum	★	Other places of interest

Abbreviations used in the text
LDP Long distance path
NT National Trust
EH English Heritage
Cadw: Welsh Historic Monuments

THE MAPS

The maps show the path and its immediate surroundings, with places of interest marked in red. Suggested 'escape' points off the route and other linking long distance paths are also shown. All maps are orientated north but are shown at different scales. Refer to the scale bar on each map.

GRID REFERENCES AND HOW TO READ THEM

Grid references are given in this book for specific points of interest. These may be used with Ordnance Survey and other maps which make use of the National Grid.

The National Grid divides Britain into 100km squares, each of which is identified by two capital letters, such as SO. Each 100km square is in turn divided into 10km squares, which, on the Ordnance Survey 1:50,000 Landranger and 1:25,000 Outdoor Leisure and Pathfinder walkers' maps, are further sub-divided into 1km squares. The vertical lines dividing the 1km squares are known as Eastings, while the horizontal lines

dividing the 1km squares are called Northings.

Each grid reference in this book has six numbers. The first two numbers refer to the Eastings vertical grid line read from left to right across the map, while the third number refers to each 10th of a kilometre (100 metres) from left to right. The fourth and fifth numbers refer to the Northings horizontal grid lines read upwards from the bottom of the map, with the sixth number referring to each 10th of a kilometre upwards. Using these numbers, draw an Eastings line up or down the map and a Northings line across; the intersection of the two lines is the point in question. The reverse procedure is used to provide the grid reference for any point. Eastings must always be quoted before the Northings.

Planning a Long Distance Walk

Planning a long distance walk can be almost as much fun and as rewarding as the walk itself. It can involve many evenings poring over guides and maps, working out daily itineraries, accommodation and transport.

Bear in mind the following guidelines.

CLOTHING AND BOOTS

What to wear for walking will depend on the weather and the terrain. Over lowlands in summer, trainers and light clothing, such as shorts and a T-shirt, may suffice if the weather is guaranteed settled. However, 15 miles or more can be a full day's walking, and that gives the British weather plenty of time to change its mind.

Much greater care needs to be taken in colder weather or when walking in the hills, where rapid changes in temperature can be brought about by the onset of mist, wind or rain. Extra clothing should be carried, to be put on or taken off in layers, which provide insulation by trapping the air between them. For instance, two middleweight sweatshirts are better than a single heavy pullover.

So for a long distance day walk in summer consider clothing which includes T-shirt, sweatshirts, shorts or possibly breeches, long thick socks which can be rolled down or pulled up as required, and lightweight walking boots or possibly trainers if the terrain allows. If there is any chance of rain carry waterproofs. A jacket made in a brightly coloured, lightweight, breathable material is to be preferred; most of these are designed to fold up into a small bag which can conveniently be worn on an elasticated belt.

For winter, or for generally cold and wet weather, a heavier duty, fully waterproof coat and overtrousers become necessary, along with waterproof boots and gaiters to keep water out of the top of the boots. Breeches or polycotton trousers which dry quickly are usually worn, with extra layers of main body insulation provided by pullovers over a shirt or thermal vest. Waterproof mittens provide the most effective protection against cold hands, while a woolly hat prevents heat loss from the head.

A good pair of boots is vital for happy long distance walking, although in warm weather, if the ground is dry and you are not carrying much weight, a pair of trainers with a thick sole and a good grip may prove more comfortable. Proper walking boots are a must for rough or rocky terrain, and steep downhill walking. In the old days it was considered necessary to 'walk boots in', but with a well-designed modern boot that fits properly this is no longer necessary. When buying new boots, always try them on with thick walking socks, and check there is enough length in the boot by sliding your index finger down behind your heel and wiggling your toes. The lacing can then be adjusted to hold the boot rigidly.

Generally, lightweight boots are the most comfortable, but ones with canvas panels should be treated with caution. If you make an early start after camping overnight, the grass underfoot may be wet, even in summer, and the canvas panels will soak up water. In no time at all your boots and socks will become saturated, and your feet will soften up and become prey to blisters. Fully waterproof boots, with sewn-in watertight tongues, are much to be peferred for British long distance walking.

EXTRA EQUIPMENT

A long distance walker has to compromise between what is needed, and what can comfortably be carried. For those who are not carrying camping gear, a lightweight daysack should suffice for basic necessities: extra clothing, including waterproofs and spare sweaters, and items such as hat and gloves if the weather warrants it; a map and compass to show the way; a watch to tell the time; a whistle to summon help if lost or injured; a pencil and notebook to keep a note of your progress; food and drink as necessary; emergency rations such as chocolate bars, nuts and raisins, or mint cake.

Those who choose to backpack have the option of staying in their own tent whenever possible, which can be both convenient and cheap. However, it requires a long list of extra equipment, the most important item being a comfortable, waterproof nylon backpack, mounted on an internal or external frame. The rule of thumb is that the weight of the pack should be no more than a quarter of the weight of the person carrying it. The heaviest items should be carried as high up and as close to the shoulders as possible. Another golden rule is last in, first out, which makes packing a backpack a thought-provoking exercise.

Depending on individual requirements, the kit needed for backpacking may include: a tent of sufficient size; an insulated sleeping mat; a sleeping bag; a torch; extra clothing for sitting around in on a cold night; a stove; food and drink; mug, plate and cutlery; water container; basic materials for washing up; tin opener; first aid box; complete change of clothing; and personal washing gear.

HOW TO NAVIGATE WITH A COMPASS

A compass is an invaluable aid to navigation which should be carried on a lanyard round the neck at all times. Despite the fact that most long distance paths are well signposted, when visibility is bad and no landmarks can be seen, the compass may be the only means there is of finding the way. Most modern walkers' compasses are based on the Swedish-made 'Silva' which is low-priced, lightweight, tough, and easy to use. Principal components are the compass base, fitted with direction-of-travel arrow and a magnifying glass, and the rotating compass dial with orienting arrow, enclosing a red compass needle which naturally points to magnetic north. (The vertical lines, or Eastings, on an OS map point to grid north, which may be a little different from magnetic north, though by an insufficient margin to affect navigation.)

The 'Silva' method of navigation

Long distance walkers on the Pennine Way at Deer Play, Northumberland

combines following a compass-bearing while walking towards a landmark. First place the compass flat on the map with one of its edges aligned with the route. Turn the dial until the letter N points to north as shown on the map; then pick up the compass, and turn round until the red end of the compass needle points to N on the dial. The direction-of-travel arrow then points in the direction you should be walking in; if possible, pick a landmark and walk towards it.

ESTIMATING TIME AND DISTANCE

The time taken to complete a section of a long distance path will to some extent depend on your own experience and level of fitness, prevailing weather conditions, and the type of terrain to be walked – for instance, on a hard track it is possible to walk at a high speed, but that speed may be halved when crossing rough moorland.

The main governing factor of speed and time taken is likely to be the number of hills encountered on the way. Naismith's Rule is a formula used by walkers to estimate how long it will take to cover a particular distance and height. It suggests you should allow 15 minutes for every kilometre covered on flat ground, plus four minutes for every 30 metres of height to be climbed. Changed into miles and feet, which were the measurements originally used by Naismith, this means you should allow one hour for every $2^1/_2$ miles over flat ground, plus one hour for every 1500 feet to be climbed.

The daily mileage covered on a long distance walk should be less than one normal day's walk a) to take into account the extra weight carried in a backpack and b) because it is more taxing to walk for consecutive days because the body has little time to recover from the previous day's exertions.

A right of way may run straight across a field: below, on the Leland Trail in Somerset

SAFETY

Ten principal rules for safe LDP walking are:
1. Choose a route that reflects your walking experience – do not attempt the Pennine Way, for instance, if you have never walked in wild terrain. Always plan out each section of your route. Be sure to take a compass and map, and make sure you know how to use them. When walking on high ground, avoid low cloud and mist on the hills if possible. If you are not sure where you are, do not be afraid to ask other walkers.
2. Check what clothing and equipment you should take with you. Always carry a watch, a pen or pencil and some waterproof card to write on, and coins for telephoning. Take snacks as necessary. In hot weather it is important to carry sufficient drink. Carry information about public transport and taxi services in case of emergencies.
3. Tell someone responsible where you are making for, and when you expect to arrive. When estimating how long a particular walk will take, never risk getting caught by nightfall, especially on hills or mountains. In winter, always carry a torch with spare batteries. If you are caught by nightfall, make your way slowly and carefully to the nearest road. Book accommodation in advance.
4. When walking on the road, walk towards oncoming traffic. Wear bright clothing so you are easily spotted. At night swing a torch in your roadside hand so that drivers will be sure to see you.
5. Listen to the weather forecasts, or watch them on television. If high wind, heavy rain, fog or mist are forecast, do not commit yourself to a long distance. Keep an eye on the weather while walking and, if it turns bad, decide in plenty of time whether to turn back or to look for an escape route to lower, safer ground.
6. If it starts raining, put on waterproofs immediately. Do not risk getting wet and cold.

7. Keep your party together, and always wait for anyone who is slow.
8. A whistle is easily carried, and useful for signalling in an emergency. The international distress signal is six long blasts, followed by a pause of one minute. The answering signal is three long blasts. The same signalling technique can be used with a handkerchief or clothing, or with a torch if it is dark. If you are being rescued by a helicopter, the ground to air signal is a Y.
9. If you are competent at first aid, a small kit should also be part of your equipment. This should at least contain plasters, dressings, bandages, safety pins, antiseptic cream, small scissors, and forceps to remove splinters.
10. In case of an accident check the map to see where the nearest telephones or mountain rescue posts are. If there is a serious accident, one person must stay with the injured person while another, who should be a competent map-reader, goes off to find help. The first aid guidelines for helping a severely injured person are: prevent further injury; make the injured comfortable without unnecessary movement; maintain breathing and circulation; control bleeding; treat for shock; get help.

When setting out to walk long distances, be aware also of the potential dangers of excessive heat or cold. When walking in a cooling breeze, the effects of sunburn may not be felt until it is too late. In very hot weather always protect your skin with a suitable sun block; wear light, loose-fitting clothes; and protect your head, if necessary, with a wide-brimmed hat that shades your neck.

When it is hot you will also sweat a lot, especially if you are climbing. It is important to keep drinking liquid to prevent dehydration, and on a very hot day you should expect to drink several litres. If you fail to drink a sufficient amount, dehydration can result in dizziness and fainting. A short rest with your head down and knees up, followed by a drink, normally cures this. Severe dehydration may result in headache, vomiting and collapse. This can be cured by resting in the shade and cooling the upper body by sponging and fanning.

Exposure is another dangerous condition which can result from walking fatigue combined with freezing temperatures, strong winds, or driving rain. When the body becomes dangerously cold and exhausted, a condition known as hypothermia develops. Symptoms include shivering, lack of interest in what is going on and, as the condition worsens, blurred vision, slurred speech, irrational behaviour and eventual collapse. Hypothermia is prevented by keeping warm and dry, and keeping your energy up. A victim of hypothermia must be sheltered from the wind and protected with as much extra clothing as possible.

WALKING TECHNIQUES

The first thing to do before setting out is to check your toenails! If they are too long, trim them down. You can experiment with what type of socks suit you best; a wide variety of purpose-made walking socks is available; most walkers prefer a thick sock which can be pulled up to the knee. The socks must fit as well as your boots, with no wrinkles or hard edges that may cause blisters. If you do get a blister, take off the boot and sock immediately. Protecting the affected area with a plaster will normally suffice for the rest of the day.

Try to maintain a steady walking rhythm which is neither too fast nor too slow, and preserves your energy. Try to keep to the same speed on all ground by lengthening or shortening your pace. Walking uphill is obviously most tiring; take deliberate steps, keeping the soles of your feet flat on the ground, and stop for frequent rests. Keep your hands free to aid balance. When going downhill, shorten your stride and dig your heels in, taking care not to slip or fall over backwards. If necessary, tighten your boot-laces to hold your feet more firmly and stop your toes digging into the toecaps. If the slope becomes very steep you may need to zig-zag, but paths will normally be cut into the hillside to show the way. Sprained ankles usually occur when walking downhill, as the boot gets turned on its side and the tissues around the ankle are damaged. In this case, if you are wearing an ankle-high boot, do not take it off – it may not be possible to get it on again, and leaving it on will contain the swelling. In warm weather, try soaking your foot in a stream to ease the pain.

EROSION

Some of the most popular long distance paths are badly eroded due to too much use. The Pennine Way has become a victim of its own popularity, and only continual upkeep by volunteers is maintaining the condition of its paths. The imprint of thousands of heavy boots kills the grass and other vegetation that binds the soil together. Once the surface vegetation is killed, the rain washes away the loose surface, and will eventually cut deep channels or make the path too boggy to walk on. Walkers then walk on the good ground on either side of the path, extending the eroded area still further. If the paths and tracks are also used by horses and four-wheel-drive vehicles, the problem becomes considerably worse.

To prevent erosion, wear lightweight boots and, where possible, walk on stony ground rather than on peat or grass, treading carefully and walking slowly when going downhill – never run down or set loose stones rolling. Avoid cutting corners on a path, and walk in single file when in a group, respecting any diversions around badly worn areas which are being repaired.

THE COUNTRY CODE

The Country Code is a voluntary code of behaviour which applies to walking on most long distance paths:

•
Do not damage hedges, fences or walls.
•
Always secure gates as found.
•
Keep to footpaths, bridleways and other rights of way.
•
Keep dogs under close control.
•
Protect wildlife, plants and trees.
•
Guard against fire.

The basic rule of walking in wild places is 'Leave only footprints; take only photographs'. Under the Wildlife and Countryside Act, it is illegal to uproot any wild plants without the permission of the landowner. It is illegal to kill, injure or take any wild bird, as it is to take or destroy the nest or eggs. It is also illegal to disturb listed vulnerable bird species when they are nest-building, brooding or caring for their young (and this applies to taking photographs of a nest). Many vulnerable mammals are protected, including all bats, shrews, badgers and dormice. Protected invertebrates include several species of butterfly, moth, beetle, dragonfly and cricket.

RIGHTS OF WAY

All long distance paths run along rights of way and across common access land, with routes that in some cases have been specially negotiated with landowners. Rights of way include footpaths, open to all walkers; bridleways, open to walkers, cyclists and horseriders; and byways or green lanes, which are also open to motorised vehicles. A right of way is part of the Queen's Highway, and subject to the same protection in law as all other highways. In most cases the surface of a right of way is considered to belong to the highway authority, while the soil beneath remains the property of the owner of the surrounding land. Maintenance of stiles and gates on a right of way is primarily the landowner's responsibility, but the highway authority must contribute if requested. If an owner fails to maintain his/her stiles and gates, the authority can do the job and forward the bill.

Erosion in the Yorkshire Dales, at Great Shummer

Rights of way are marked on walkers' Ordnance Survey maps. Highway authorities have a duty to signpost them at all junctions with metalled roads, and long distance paths and other pathways are usually signposted or waymarked off the road, using the standard colour code of yellow for a footpath, blue for a bridleway, and red for a byway. A right of way may only be ploughed up if it runs across a field, but must be made good within 24 hours, or within two weeks if the disturbance is the first for a particular crop. If a right of way is not made good, the highway authority may serve notice and prosecute the person responsible.

A farmer also has a duty to prevent any crop other than grass making a right of way difficult to follow, and must allow a minimum width of 1 metre for footpaths across fields, and 1.5 metres round the side of fields. If crops obstruct a path, you have every right to walk through them, but do report the problem to the highway authority. Similarly, if a right of way is illegally obstructed, you can remove the obstruction as much as is necessary to get through, or walk around the obstruction if this is easier. This should also be reported to the highway authority. Most bulls are banned from fields crossed by a right of way, though certain safe breeds are allowed if accompanied by cows or heifers. No landowner can close or divert a right of way, unless ordered by a local authority or central government.

As well as rights of way, the public also have access to some areas defined as 'open country' which consist of mountain, moor, heath, down, cliff, sea foreshore, beach or sand dunes. The most extensive access land in England has been made available by agreements between landowners and local authorities, covering large areas of the Peak District, Yorkshire Dales and Lake District National Parks through which some of the best-known long distance paths pass. In Scotland, the laws of trespass and landowners' attitudes have generally been much more relaxed than in England and Wales. There now seem to be a growing number of exceptions, but generally you are free to roam over countryside and wilderness so long as you use your common sense and respect other people's property.

THE
WEST
COUNTRY

The north Devon coastline at Bull Point

South West Coast Path

COMPLETE ROUTE
MINEHEAD TO POOLE HARBOUR
594 MILES/956KM

SECTION COVERED
LYNMOUTH TO BRAUNTON
42 MILES/68KM

Detailed guides
There are a number of publications which cover the whole route or just this part of it. The South West Way Association regularly update their guide *The South West Way*, which contains many practical hints. Full of facts is *Along the South West Way, Part 1: Minehead to Bude* by A G Collings (Tabb House). The 'National Trail Guide' to the Minehead to Padstow section of the path is by Roland Tarr (Aurum Press in association with the Countryside Commission and the Ordnance Survey). The Exmoor National Park Authority publishes *Coastal Walks*, a guide to their section of the path, including circular routes. Another excellent guide is *The South West Way, A Walker's Guide to the Coast Path* by Martin Cullins (Cicerone Press) and an amusing account of the whole walk is *500 Mile Walkies* by Mark Wallington (Arrow).

Maps
OS Landranger 180

Links
The Two Moors Way (see pages 20-7) runs from Lynmouth across Dartmoor to Ivybridge.

FORMERLY known as the South West Peninsula Path and sometimes as the South West Way, the South West Coast Path is the longest official long distance path in Britain. Estimates of its full length vary between 560 and 600 miles, as it is incomplete in places, contains alternative routes and is continually being adjusted and improved. It runs from Minehead in Somerset to South Haven Point at Poole Harbour in Dorset. After more than 20 years of negotiations with landowners it was opened a section at a time between 1973 and 1978. For administrative ease it is divided into sections – the Somerset and North Devon, Cornwall, South Devon, and Dorset Coast Paths. It is waymarked with the acorn symbol and local councils along its route are grant-aided by the Countryside Commission to maintain it.

This publication covers a 42-mile section of the Somerset and North Devon Coast Path, which runs from Minehead to the Devon/Cornwall boundary at Marsland Mouth. The route between Lynmouth and Braunton has been chosen because it offers great contrasts from the high cliffs of the Bristol Channel to the Atlantic surf and sand and the sheltered Taw estuary. The Bristol Channel coast is relatively sheltered – it faces north and the prevailing winds are south-westerly. In the lee to the east of the head-lands woods often cloak the cliffs. These are fairly undisturbed and contain a great variety of wildlife, including rare whitebeam trees. Red deer can be found in the wooded combes and cliffs all along this part of the coast. Atlantic grey seals breed on Lundy Island and are frequent visitors to this coast.

The coastal heaths in some of the more exposed areas are a blaze of colour in late summer with deep purple bell heather and bright yellow western gorse. Look out for the pink-flowered parasite dodder on the

Hollow Brook, near the start of the walk

gorse. Baggy Point has some Cornish heath, possibly introduced. Braunton Burrows claims over 400 species of plants. It is particularly resplendent with orchids in June and July, along with marsh helleborine and round-leaved wintergreen in the dune slacks.

Seabirds nest all along the higher cliffs. Gulls and fulmars are found throughout, shags and cormorants in places, and guillemots, razorbills and kittiwakes at Martinhoe and the Valley of Rocks. Jackdaws and ravens are common, although choughs ceased to nest early in this century. Peregrine falcons are making a comeback after disappearing as a breeding bird in the 1960s. The Taw estuary abounds with wintering waders.

The cliffs are largely of sedimentary rocks – sandstones, shales and thin limestones – of Devonian age. The headlands and bays of the west-facing coast are largely due to the erosion of alternate beds of relatively hard and soft rocks. The beds generally dip towards the south, a factor which contributes towards the 'hog's-back' shape of the Exmoor cliffs. The seaward slopes of these were largely shaped by frost weathering and soil creep in the colder phases of the Ice Age, when the sea did not touch the cliffs. Since the Ice Age its level has risen and the sea is

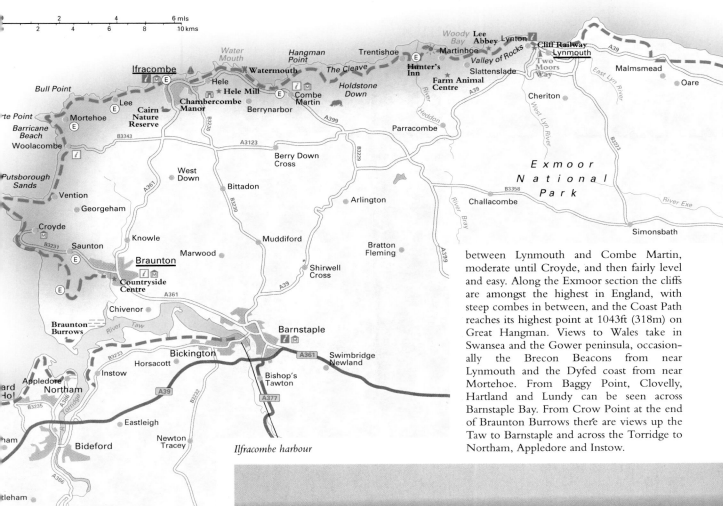

Ilfracombe harbour

between Lynmouth and Combe Martin, moderate until Croyde, and then fairly level and easy. Along the Exmoor section the cliffs are amongst the highest in England, with steep combes in between, and the Coast Path reaches its highest point at 1043ft (318m) on Great Hangman. Views to Wales take in Swansea and the Gower peninsula, occasionally the Brecon Beacons from near Lynmouth and the Dyfed coast from near Mortehoe. From Baggy Point, Clovelly, Hartland and Lundy can be seen across Barnstaple Bay. From Crow Point at the end of Braunton Burrows there are views up the Taw to Barnstaple and across the Torridge to Northam, Appledore and Instow.

eroding the base of the cliffs. This rise has caused the drowning of river mouths, particularly at Combe Martin, Watermouth and Ilfracombe, creating natural harbours. The solid bed of the Taw is 150ft below its present mouth, which has silted up, forming Braunton Burrows and Marsh on one of its terraces. At times during the Ice Age the sea level rose above its present level, as indicated by raised beaches at Lee near Lynton, and the southern sides of Baggy Point and Saunton Down. Terraces on the Down are Saxon cultivation terraces, not natural features.

The sandstones naturally give rise to sandy beaches, although much depends upon the degree of exposure. Those at Woolacombe, Croyde and Saunton are most popular with bathers. Those on the Bristol Channel coast tend to be pebbly and less accessible. The Channel has the second highest tidal range in the world – over 30ft at times – and even where beaches are accessible they may be cut off as the tide rises – a frequent safety problem. Landslips can be a problem also in that the route may be diverted around them, but are not usually a risk to the walker as long as diversion notices are obeyed and barriers are not climbed.

The route can be described as strenuous

Ilfracombe harbour

Lynmouth

Ilfracombe

OS Landranger 180
Start at grid reference SS 723 494
Start point: Lyndale Bridge at Lynmouth.
Ample parking beside bridge and at far end
of Esplanade.

Lynmouth is an attractive village at the confluence and mouth of the East and West Lyn
Rivers. It is noted mainly for the disastrous
flood which occurred in 1952. Reminders of
this are at the Glen Lyn Gorge (charge for
walk along the West Lyn River) and Flood
Memorial Hall on The Esplanade. Although
much was rebuilt after the flood, the village
retains its Victorian character, with some
older cottages above flood level on Mars Hill
and around Shelley's Cottage, near where
the poet lived for a while.

Walk to the Cliff Railway at the far end of
The Esplanade, passing the Exmoor National
Park Information Centre. The path lies up
some steps between the two, zig-zagging
across the Cliff Railway and eventually
turning right along the level North Walk to
the Valley of Rocks. To save the climb one

The Cliff Railway at Lynmouth

can use the railway, turning left at Lee Road
at the top, then left again at the church and
down to North Walk.

The Valley of Rocks is a famous sight – a
dry valley with a rugged, pinnacled ridge

Looking down on to Lynmouth

GUIDE BOX

Places to visit
Lynton and Lynmouth Cliff Railway, at The
Esplanade, Lynmouth or via Lee Road, Lynton.
When built in 1890, its 1 in 1³/₄ gradient made
it the steepest railway in the world. It has kept
going without accident or breakdown ever since.
It is gravity powered – the downward car pulling
the other up, using water as ballast. The tanks are
filled with water at the top and are emptied
when the car reaches the bottom. It operates
daily from March to December.

Exmoor Farm Animal Centre, at Mannacott Farm,
1 mile south of the Coast Path between
Martinhoe and Hunter's Inn, is a working farm
with many rare breeds of sheep and cattle, old
farm implements and sheep-shearing
demonstrations. Open afternoons Spring Bank
Holiday week and mid-July to early September,
Sunday to Thursday.

Combe Martin Wildlife and Leisure Park, at Higher
Leigh Manor on the A399, a mile from the
Coast Path on the eastern outskirts of Combe
Martin, is well-known for its otters, seals,
monkeys and meerkats. It also has gardens and
children's activities, including rides. Open Easter
to end October, daily.

Hele Mill, on the A399 at Hele Bay, on the
eastern outskirts of Ilfracombe, is a restored 16th-
century corn mill with an exhibition of milling.
Wholemeal flour ground on the premises can be
purchased. Open Easter to end October,
Monday to Friday and Sunday afternoon.

Car parking
There are large car parks in Lynton and
Lynmouth. Other main parking areas along the
route are at Valley of Rocks (grid ref. SS 707
497), Hunter's Inn (SS 655 480), Combe Martin
(SS 577 474) and Ilfracombe, which has several,
particularly in the harbour area.

Public transport
The nearest British Rail station is at Barnstaple,
from where there are bus connections to Lynton,
Combe Martin and Ilfracombe.

Accommodation
Lynton and Lynmouth, Combe Martin and
Ilfracombe are tourist resorts with no shortage of
guesthouses and hotel accommodation. There
are youth hostels at Lynbridge (grid ref. SS 720
486) and Ilfracombe (SS 525 476) and camp sites
in the Lynton, Combe Martin and Watermouth
areas. Exmoor National Park Authority (tel.
0398 23665) produces the free *Exmoor Visitor*
paper, which includes an accommodation guide.

dividing it from the Coast Path and cliffs. It
is the home of wild Cheviot goats and,
according to the story of Lorna Doone, the
witch Mother Meldrum.

The route continues along the toll road
(free to walkers) past Lee Abbey, a Christian
retreat which has an interesting natural
history museum, near Lee Bay. Follow the
narrow road upwards towards Woody Bay
Hotel, near which the path drops through
woods. It then ascends the Woody Bay road
for a short distance and turns off to the right
at a hairpin bend in the road. One can
detour down the road to the bay, with its old
cottage, limekiln and base of a pier which
was demolished in 1903 after a futile attempt
to develop Woody Bay as a tourist resort.

Alternatively, detour uphill to the road towards Martinhoe and turn off at the next hairpin bend along a path running parallel with the main Coast Path to Hunter's Inn. This passes the site of Martinhoe Roman Signal Station, a fine viewpoint.

The main path continues through oak woods and out into a dramatic section of open cliff from Hollow Brook waterfall to the Heddon valley. From this path an eccentric Victorian vicar of Martinhoe, the Reverend James Hannington, made paths to view caves on the shore below, now only visible from the sea. The path descends from Highveer Point to the River Heddon. Here a detour can be made downstream to the pebbly beach with its limekiln or upstream to Hunter's Inn (refreshments and toilets).

Ⓔ *From the Heddon valley (grid ref. SS 654 489) one can return to Lynmouth on an inland route, via Hunter's Inn. A road runs steeply uphill beside the inn to the Exmoor Farm Animal Centre at Mannacott Farm. A path runs through the farm up to the road at Martinhoe. The road can be followed to Slattenslade, from where a path leads to Croscombe Barton and Lee. From Lee a path overlooking the Valley of Rocks can be taken to Lynton along South Cleave.*

The main path crosses the river a short distance upstream, then zig-zags up the Cleave and out to Peter Rock and an exposed section of the route. It then follows the cliff along the heads of various 'guts' or gullies to Holdstone Down. This heath-clad hill is known to many who believe it to have mystical qualities and reports of UFO sightings here are common.

The path continues along the estate drive, known as Sea View Road, down into Sherrycombe and up towards Great Hangman. A detour can be made along an old miners' track to Blackstone Point, where there were iron mines in the last century. Return to the main path, which continues over Great Hangman to Little Hangman and descends Lester Cliff to the car park and Information Centre at Combe Martin.

Ⓔ *From Combe Martin (grid ref. SS 577 473) one can return to Hunter's Inn and the Heddon valley via the main street. This passes the 18th-century Pack of Cards inn, built like a card house, to the crossroads near the church. Continue up the street to Combe Martin Wildlife and Leisure Park or turn left up Corner Lane and past the old silver mine, then right along minor roads and path to Holdstone Farm, Trentishoe and Hunter's Inn.*

COMBE MARTIN

ILFRACOMBE

APPROX. 6 MILES/9.5KM

OS Landranger 180
Start at grid reference SS 577 473
Start point: Kiln car park, adjacent to Combe Martin beach.

Combe Martin never fully developed its harbour despite several ambitious plans. It was quite important, however, in the 19th century for the export to South Wales of iron and copper ores from Exmoor mines and the import from that area of limestone and coal. The lime was burnt in kilns, now demolished, near the beach. This was used for making cement and plaster and for dressing the acid Exmoor soils during moorland reclamation. There are old silver workings in Lester Point at the far end of the beach.

The path keeps to the edge of the bay as closely as possible, passing the small local history museum at Newberry beach. At the far side of this beach some rough steps cut in the rocks are said to have been made by Phoenicians coming to trade for local silver. The path climbs the lane at the back of the beach and up to the main road. After a short ascent it diverts seawards to cut off a bend in the road and rejoins the road as far as the Sandy Cove Hotel. A track alongside the hotel takes the route past the steep access to Broad Sands beach, shortly after which it diverts right and down over fields to rejoin the A399 at Watermouth.

The path continues alongside the road to a gateway opposite the entrance to Watermouth Castle. This leads down to Watermouth harbour. The main path leads along the road and into the woods, but a diversion can be made along the beach at low tide to some steps up to the woods.

The Combe, Combe Martin

Keep to the coast around Widmouth Head, with its old coastguard lookout, to Samson's Bay, Rillage Point and the present coastguard station. Continue alongside the road to Hele, with its Old Corn Mill, to which a diversion can be made up the road towards Ilfracombe. The path skirts the small bay and ascends steeply to the summit of Hillsborough, with fine views of Ilfracombe. On the way down to Ilfracombe harbour it passes through the double rampart which defended Hillsborough as an Iron Age promontory fort.

This part of the route ends at the quayside car park at Ilfracombe.

Ⓔ *For an inland route back to Combe Martin, take the road that leads from the eastern end of Ilfracombe car park (grid ref. SS 527 477) up to the A399. Cross this road and ascend Chambercombe Road to Chambercombe Manor. A track continues past the manor, through Comyn Farm and up to Trayne. It then crosses a road and the waymarked route descends into the Sterridge valley. From here minor roads can be followed through Berrynarbor and back to the Coast Path just west of Combe Martin. By linking this route with the two 'escape' routes mentioned above, a complete return route to Lynmouth can be made.*

WATERMOUTH

Here the drowned mouth of the River Sterridge forms a small landlocked harbour. There is access to this and the Warren – the narrow neck of land separating it from the sea – via the Coast Path. Parking is for the nearby caves or castle, for which there are charges. Watermouth Castle is a Regency mock castle, originally home of the Basset family. It now contains a museum of mechanical music, pier machines and bygones with many games and items for children. The castle is open from Easter to early November, most days except Saturdays.

Ilfracombe

Braunton

OS Landranger 180
Start at grid reference SS 523 477
Start point: Quay car park on southern
edge of Ilfracombe harbour.

Ilfracombe is a large, mainly Victorian resort
with some Regency and Georgian terraces.
The harbour, now used mainly by pleasure
craft, was formerly the most important
refuge on the northern coasts of Devon,
Cornwall and Somerset. The ancient
mariners' chapel of St Nicholas has a lantern
at the western end of the roof and it has
acted as a lighthouse for centuries. There is
a substantial herring fishing industry in the
18th and 19th centuries. Boat trips are available from the pier or inner harbour, according to the tide.

Walk along the Strand – the inner harbour
beach – to the 18th-century Royal Britannia
Hotel, patronised by Admiral Nelson and
novelist Henry Williamson, who lived near
by. From the front of the hotel take
Capstone Crescent opposite and round
Capstone Parade to Wildersmouth beach.
Then follow the Parade around to
Ilfracombe Museum, originally the laundry
for the enormous Victorian Ilfracombe
Hotel, now demolished to make way for a
car park. The path ascends through gardens
behind the Museum to the Granville Hotel
and then along the coastal road. One can
look down to the Tunnels beaches with their
bathing pools exposed at low tide. Access to
the beaches is via tunnels cut through the
cliffs by Welsh miners in 1836, when a Bath

House was built at the entrance and a small
sea-water pool was heated.

Keep as close to the coast as possible along
the road, then take a right turn by a National
Trust sign for Torrs Walk. The path leads
back to the cliff, from where it zig-zags up to
the highest point of the Seven Hills. This
was once a private path for which walkers
had to pay and the remains of turnstiles can
be found.

From the summit keep on the path nearest
to the coast. Cross a stile and turn inland,
then right along a track wide enough for
vehicles. This was the old road to Lee over
Lee Downs and is easy to follow to the Blue
Mushroom bungalow, where it becomes a
tarmac road descending to Lee. Here it
meets the road by the Lee Bay Hotel, where
refreshments can be obtained, or a detour
can be made up the road to the left to the
14th-century Grampus Inn, near which is
the Post Office shop and picturesque Old
Maids' Cottage. Many fuschias grow here,
but once there were whole hedgerows of
them, giving Lee the title of Fuschia Valley.

The route continues on the road around
Lee Bay Hotel and the beach, at one end of
which is an old mill and at the other end the
17th-century Smugglers' Cottage. Smuggling
was said to be rife in the area in the 18th and
early 19th centuries.

Ⓔ *From the car park near the beach at Lee (grid
ref. SS 479 465) it is possible to return inland to
Ilfracombe. A track runs up the valley to the
Grampus Inn, before which one can take a path
on the right which follows the Borough valley.
From here a forest track forks left to Shaftsboro
Farm and continues to the B3230. Pass under the
road bridge on to the former Ilfracombe-to-
Barnstaple railway line, which can be followed
into Ilfracombe via the Cairn Nature Reserve.*

Below *Baggy Point, from Barricane Beach*

GUIDE BOX

Places to visit
Chambercombe Manor is reached from
Chambercombe Road off the A399 on the
eastern outskirts of Ilfracombe. It is a farmhouse
which is mainly of the 16th and 17th centuries,
but dates back to 1162 and was formerly a manor
of the Champernowne family. It contains period
furniture and has an infamous ghost story. Open
Easter to end September, Monday to Friday and
Sunday afternoons.

Croyde Gem Rock and Shell Museum, in the centre
of Croyde, is a shop and small museum with a
collection of gem rocks and minerals, both cut
and in their natural state. It also has a large
collection of shells from all over the world.
Open March to end October, daily.

Braunton Burrows National Nature Reserve is
accessible by car via Sandy Lane, off the B3231
Braunton-to-Saunton road or toll road via the
A361 at Wrafton. At roughly 3 miles long by 1
mile wide and over 100ft high in places, it is one
of the most extensive sand dune systems in
Britain. It has been noted for its flowers from the
17th century and is the only location in Britain
for several species. There is a boardwalk from the
end of the toll road, and several trails. Open all
year, except for occasional military training
exercises in some areas.

Braunton Countryside Centre, at the old railway
station near Caen Street car park in Braunton,
contains displays about the wildlife and
conservation of Braunton Marsh, Burrows and
Great Field. There is an Information Centre and
guided walks are available. Open Easter to end
September, daily except Sunday, mornings only
from Easter to Whitsun.

Car parking
Principal car parks along the route are at
Ilfracombe, Lee (grid ref. SS 479 465),
Woolacombe Marine Drive (SS 458 433),
Croyde (SS 436 396) and Braunton (SS 486
366).

Accommodation
There are large numbers of guesthouses, hotels
and camp sites in the Ilfracombe and
Woolacombe areas. Ilfracombe, Woolacombe
and Croyde Publicity Associations produce their
own guides and the *Devonia* guide, produced by
North Devon District Council, covers the whole
area.

Public transport
The nearest British Rail station is at Barnstaple,
from where there are bus connections to
Ilfracombe, Woolacombe, Croyde and
Braunton.

BOAT TRIPS

The bases of Exmoor's towering cliffs are often
invisible from the Coast Path and beaches are
only accessible at a few points. A boat trip
gives a different perspective of the coast and
enables one to get better views of seals and
seabirds. The motor boat *Devonia,* (tel. 0271
862299) sails from picturesque Ilfracombe
harbour frequently in summer months. The
steamers *Balmoral* and *Waverley* (tel. 0446
720656) call occasionally at the pier for cruises
along the coast and to Lundy Island and South
Wales.

Climb the road past the cottage and fork right at the National Trust sign for Damage Hue. The path is easily followed along the coast to Bull Point. Here the original lighthouse was replaced by an automatic one in 1975 after landslips threatened to carry it away. Keep close to the coast and round Morte Point, so named from the death it and the infamous Morte Stone off it have caused by shipwreck. There are strong tidal currents off the Point.

⊕ *It is possible to return from Mortehoe (grid ref. SS 454 448) to Lee by following the lighthouse road. Half a mile from the village, a path to the right of the road crosses a small valley to the minor road which descends to Lee from Borough Cross.*

Descend towards Woolacombe and the road between Woolacombe and Mortehoe. Pass Barricane beach, renowned among Victorian shell-collectors. There are no great rarities to be found there now, but its sand is largely composed of shell fragments.

From here the route follows the side of the road along the coast to the large car park on the former military road backing on to the dunes. When the tide is low enough, it is possible to take a short cut across the beach and up one of the paths through the dunes, or to walk along the beach all the way to Putsborough.

WOOLACOMBE

BRAUNTON

APPROX. 15 MILES/24KM

OS Landranger 180
Start at grid reference SS 458 433
Start point: Marine Drive car park, which runs behind the sand dunes at Woolacombe.

Woolacombe (which means 'valley of wolves') did not begin to develop until the end of the last century. It is now an unattractive resort surrounded by camping and chalet developments but the sandy beach is popular, particularly with surfers. The National Trust, who own Woolacombe Warren, have struggled to help the sand dune system to recover from the erosion caused by tourists.

The route runs to the end of the Marine Drive, where it becomes a bridleway following the contour above Vention to Putsborough Sands Hotel. Vention has several buildings now, but the name refers to the old limeburners's cottage next to the kiln and is supposedly derived from the description of lime-burning as a 'new invention' in 1630 by Devon historian Tristram Risdon. The route follows the lane for about 200yds beyond the hotel, then forks right over a stile.

The path continues through fields above the cliff-top to Baggy Point. There is a large cave, Baggy Hole, in the end of the point, not visible from the path, and the area is popular with climbers. The path rounds the Point and descends towards Croyde. The cliff is covered with patches of mesembryanthemum, known as Hottentot Fig – an

introduction from South Africa. About 300yds after the National Trust car park turn right by a caravan site. The path follows the edge of the dunes at the back of the beach. After crossing the stream half-way along, a detour can be made inland to Croyde village for refreshments at the Carpenter's Arms, or a visit to the Gem Rock and Shell Museum.

At the end of the beach the path ascends to a wartime blockhouse, rounds the end of Saunton Down and crosses the road. It then runs above the road to Saunton Sands Hotel, where it drops through the hotel grounds to the dunes. A detour can be made to the beach to examine the fossilised Ice Age dune system in the cliff and the pink granite boulder below it, brought by ice sheets travelling down the Irish Sea. The path continues inland to the road at Saunton, taking the first turning right after the entrance to the golf course.

⊕ *A short cut to Braunton can be made from where the Coast Path joins the American Road on Braunton Burrows (grid ref. SS 463 346). Fork left here, past a car park to the road at Sandy Lane. Turn first right and after ¹/2 mile take the lane to the left. This crosses Braunton Great Field, a relic of the medieval open field system, and enters Braunton near Caen Street car park.*

The path skirts the golf course and continues behind Braunton Burrows dunes to a dirt road known as the American Road – made by US forces in World War II when the area was used for tank training prior to the Normandy landings.

⊕ *One can return inland from Saunton to Woolacombe by following the bridleway over Saunton Down which starts opposite the entrance to the golf club (grid ref. SS 457 377). It joins the road at Forda, following it to Georgeham, once home of novelist Henry Williamson. Fork left by the church along the lane through Pickwell and on to the Coast Path at Woolacombe Warren.*

Continue along the road for a mile to a car parking area. A detour can be made along the boardwalk to view the Taw/Torridge estuary. The path continues through the car park to the White House, a former ferry house, and along a flood bank to the Taw and Caen estuaries. The dyke was built in the 1850s as part of the reclamation of Braunton Marsh and canalising of the Caen to allow cargo vessels to reach Velator Quay. The original route of the river can be seen on the inland side of Horsey Island and the new channel starts opposite the end of the main runway of Chivenor airfield. Cargo vessels used the Quay until the 1950s, exporting river gravel and farm produce to South Wales and returning with coal and limestone for the kilns.

After the Quay the path joins the road at Velator Bridge. Follow the road for 200yds and at the former level-crossing turn left along the old railway line to Braunton Countryside Centre and car park. The line was closed in 1970 after a 96-year history. It forms the Coast Path to Barnstaple.

Braunton Burrows

Two Moors Way

COMPLETE ROUTE
IVYBRIDGE TO LYNMOUTH
102 MILES/163KM

SECTION COVERED
SEQUER'S BRIDGE TO YEOFORD
43 MILES/70KM

Detailed guides
The official guide to the Two Moors Way is published by the Devon Ramblers' Association, c/o J R Turner, Coppins, The Poplars, Pinhoe, Exeter, EX4 9HH. It is regularly updated, and has a supplement for accommodation (both are also available from Tourist Information Centres on the route). Dartmoor National Park and Exmoor National Park publish guides to walks in their areas, often overlapping with the Two Moors Way. They also publish free visitor newspapers with details of places of interest, guided walks and accommodation. Dartmoor National Park publishes a separate accommodation leaflet.

Maps
OS Landranger 191, 202

Links
The Two Moors Way links with the South West Coast Path at Lynmouth and meets three unofficial long distance routes along the way. These are the Abbot's Way, along which monks used to walk between Buckfast, Buckland and Tavistock Abbeys; the Mariner's Way, a 106-mile route once used by seamen between Bideford and Dartmouth; and the Tarka Trail, following the wanderings of Tarka the Otter in Henry Williamson's novel.

THE Two Moors Way was opened in 1976. It is the creation of members of the Devon Ramblers' Association and, despite some pressure, has not been recognised by the Countryside Commission as an official long distance footpath. As a result it tends to be a quiet walk, although most walkers take just the Exmoor or Dartmoor sections of the route.

At present the Two Moors Way is 102 miles long, but there are alternative routes and diversions for accommodation or sites of interest. It is planned to extend the route from Ivybridge to the mouth of the Erme to make it a coast-to-coast walk, linking with the South West Coast Path at each end. At the time of writing negotiations have not been completed, but this guide covers the area south of Ivybridge from Sequer's Bridge, where public footpaths already exist, and details a 43-mile section north from here to Yeoford.

The route follows public footpaths, bridleways, roads and open moor. The Dartmoor Commons Act gives the public right of access to commons on Dartmoor, where much of the route is not on rights of way. The same freedom of access does not apply to other parts of the walk. In mid Devon much of the walk is on minor roads which can be narrow, twisting, and with high banks, making it difficult to be seen by traffic. Both roads and paths in this area are, however, well signposted and waymarked.

The Two Moors Way is usually distinguished by the symbol of an M over a W on the uprights of the signposts. There are large sections of open moor where the route is deliberately not marked to avoid intrusion, and where map and compass proficiency is essential.

Although it is easy going in places and avoids the bleakest parts of Dartmoor, it is not generally an easy walk. The route is

The Dart valley, towards Holne Chase

undulating, muddy in places and can be exposed, so proper equipment is essential. The route reaches a maximum height of 1737ft (529m) at Hameldown Tor. In the higher areas it is generally along ridges, avoiding the boggier parts of the moors.

Public transport to and from the route presents some difficulties. The nearest railway station to the start is at Plymouth and Ivybridge is served by bus from Plymouth, Torquay and Exeter. There is only a small lay-by at Sequer's Bridge and those wishing to leave cars for long periods should start at Ivybridge. There is a bus link to Lynton (for Lynmouth) from Barnstaple, which has the nearest railway station to the end of the walk. The Barnstaple-to-Exeter railway line has a halt at Yeoford, where the section of route chosen here ends.

The two moors themselves are contrasting. Dartmoor is half as big again as Exmoor and more open. Its valleys are wider, with concave hill slopes culminating in rocky tors. Its centre is granite, a once molten rock which cooled deep underground and has since been exposed. Surrounding it are slates, sandstones and shales, some altered by contact with the granite when hot in what is known as the metamorphic aureole. The dark Culm Measure sandstone and shales of mid Devon are briefly punctuated by the Permian sandstones which give rise to the famous red soils and dairying country. Exmoor is on Devonian sandstones and shales. Its landscape has a more enclosed feel

A drovers' clapper bridge over the Avon, built using huge slabs of granite

than Dartmoor's, with smoothly rounded convex slopes and deep combes.

Much use has been made of granite in Dartmoor's buildings and this durable material has aided the survival of many farms and cottages built between the 15th and 17th centuries. For similar reasons it has the greatest concentration of prehistoric remains in Europe. The sandstones and shales elsewhere on the route make poor building materials and rubble and cob were generally used in mid Devon and Exmoor. Cob is a mix of clay, dung, straw, hair and small stones. It was used to make thick walls for thatched cottages. It is not very durable and is generally rendered and whitewashed to prevent rain and frost from disintegrating it.

Everywhere along the walk are Devon banks – hedges built on banks made of turf faced with stones. Plants grow between the stones, binding the whole together and providing wonderful shows of wild flowers, particularly primroses. On the moors the hedges are often of beech, introduced in the 19th century, but in mid Devon the variety of tree species shows the great age of most hedges.

Birds such as wheatear, curlew, stonechat and raven are common on the moors and everywhere are buzzards. The moors are also famous for their ponies. Those on Dartmoor are more numerous and widespread, but are usually crossbreds, while those on Exmoor are frequently purebred and as close to prehistoric wild horses as one is likely to find in Britain.

Blackface sheep grazing near Grimspound

Sequer's Bridge

Scorriton

SEQUER'S BRIDGE

IVYBRIDGE

APPROX. 3½ MILES/5.5KM

OS Landranger 202
Start at grid reference SX 632 518
Start point: Sequer's Bridge, where the A379 crosses the River Erme. Parking is limited to a small lay-by on the western side of the bridge.

Sequer's Bridge is a lovely old bridge at the head of the Erme estuary. Cross the bridge and turn left where the footpath is sign-posted. Cross the field to Sexton Farm and follow the track beyond. Cross two stiles, keep to the edge of the wood and drop to the river bank. Follow the waymarks to the left of the buildings at Fawns. Take the road opposite and walk up past Strode, with its ornate gateway. This was home to the Strode family from the 13th to 15th centuries and traces of their mansion remain at the farm.

Just past the next junction turn left through the gateway with the footpath sign. Continue downhill towards Thornham Bridge, passing a barn. Before the bridge turn right and follow the track across the fields to the road. Keep ahead, then left at the next bend to the bridge at Keaton.

Ⓔ *Here (grid ref. SX 640 545) it is possible to return to Sequer's Bridge (approximately 2 miles) by crossing the bridge and following the road around to the left to Ermington. Just before the village is a trout farm and Ermington Mill Craft Centre. Here in old mill buildings are a tea shop and workshops for fishing flies, furniture, engraving and pottery. Ermington Church is known for the crooked spire of its 13th-century tower. Inside is much beautiful woodwork, both old and new. The latter was carved by the daughter of a former vicar. Turn left after the church and descend to the B3210. Turn right and follow the road to Ermewood House Hotel, taking the footpath opposite. Follow the path alongside the river, crossing stiles by the sewage works and returning to Sequer's Bridge.*

To continue to Ivybridge from Keaton, do not cross the bridge, but turn right up the track with the footpath sign. Pass the weir and continue through a field and along a track to a road by a bungalow. Continue up the road and pass through the field by the Tennis Centre. Pass through two subways under roads and follow the river bank to the car park by the Leisure Centre.

IVYBRIDGE

SCORRITON

APPROX. 11½MILES/18.5KM

OS Landranger 202
Start at grid reference (SX 636 561)
Start point: Ivybridge, on the A38, 14 miles east of Plymouth. Car park near the bridge.

Ivybridge was a hamlet around its 13th-century bridge until the late 19th century, when it grew with mills and the coming of

the railway. Its church was built in 1882. It still has some light industry, including a mill making high quality paper.

From the car park join the main street to the east of the bridge. Keep upwards along Harford Road, passing the paper mill and school. Follow the signs for Harford, crossing the railway bridge. Just before the bridge a stone marks the beginning of the Two Moors Way. The bridge crosses the former Great Western Railway of Brunel, who designed the viaduct just to the west.

Continue for a few hundred yards and turn right along a lane signposted 'Bridleway to the moor'. A left turn takes one up a lane to the moor. Continue ahead through gorse to a cairn beside a track. The Two Moors Way follows the track northwards for several miles, although in dry weather it is easier to follow the ridgeway above. The track is the

The old tramway track beside Leftlake

bed of a tramway used between 1910 and 1932 by the isolated Redlake china clay works, 6 miles further north. There are views westwards to the huge modern china clay works at Headon and Lee Moor.

Follow the track up to Spurrell's Cross on the ridge. Although recently restored, only the head of the cross remains. Most such crosses are medieval and mark routes over the moors used by local abbeys.

Ⓔ *From the Cross (grid ref. SX 658 600) it is possible to return to Ivybridge by following the track down the valley to the left. This passes through a small car park on the edge of the moor and down a lane to Harford. The little 15th-century church has two 16th-century brasses to Thomas Williams, former Speaker of the House of Commons. Take the footpath by the farm opposite the church. This crosses a bridge and fields to the road at Broomhill. Follow the road downhill to Ivybridge (a circular route of about 6¹/₂ miles).*

From Spurrell's Cross return to the tramway and continue along it. Running alongside to the left is one of Dartmoor's longest stone rows, over 1¹/₂ miles long. Hobajon's Cross is inscribed on one of its stones, although the name may refer to a former cross. The purpose of most Bronze Age stone rows is unclear. This one is extended by more recent boundary stones dividing Ugborough from Harford Commons.

The route passes above Piles Copse in the Erme Valley. The copse of stunted oaks covered in ferns, mosses and lichens is one of three much studied relics of Dartmoor's pre-historic forest cover. Later it passes the flooded pit of Leftlake china clay works, closed in the 1920s. Above, on Western White Barrow, is Petre's Cross, one of several erected in the 16th century to mark the boundary of Sir William Petre's property on Brent Moor.

After a sharp right-hand bend, the route leaves the tramway by some ruins and continues ahead on the Abbot's Way down the Avon valley to Huntingdon Warren. This was a rabbit enclosure with many 'pillow

mounds' in which the rabbits burrowed. The route keeps to the south of the river, fording it beyond the 16th-century Huntingdon Cross, but a diversion can be made to the medieval clapper bridge and the north bank followed to the Cross. A diversion can also be made up the Western Wella Brook to an old mine. Next to it are the remains of a blowing house (tin-processing mill) used as a chapel by the Reverend Keble Martin, the well-known flower painter.

Beyond the Cross the route ascends Hickaton Hill and continues beyond Pupers Hill to cross the River Mardle by a foot-bridge at Chalk Ford. A track climbs the hillside opposite and becomes a broad lane descending to Scorriton.

Ⓔ *From the Square at Scorriton (grid ref. SX 703 684) a return can be made to Spurrell's Cross. Take the road opposite the war memorial. At the bottom of the hill turn right for Hawson Cross, next to Stumpy Oak, an ancient oak pollard bound with iron rings. Take the next right turn after the cross. Continue over Cullaford*

Above *Sir William Petre's Cross, a 16th-century boundary stone*

Bridge and up a sunken lane. Turn left along the road at the top and right down the bridlepath at the next crossroads. At the ford turn left, skirting the edge of the moor. From Skerraton Gate the path is signposted over fields and down a lane to Moor Cross.

Turn right down the road and over Gidley Bridge. At the top of the hill turn right along the bridlepath to the moor. Continue ahead over Dockwell Ridge to the bridge over the Avon and down the drive to the car park at Shipley Bridge, site of a former works making naphtha (inflammable oil) from peat.

Do not cross the bridge but continue along the road for ¹/₄ mile and take the bridlepath to the right. At Ball Gate, with its ornamental pillars, continue along the moorland boundary past a Neolithic long barrow showing its collapsed burial chamber. Ford two streams and continue ahead up the hillside to Spurrell's Cross. This makes a circular route of approximately 20 miles.

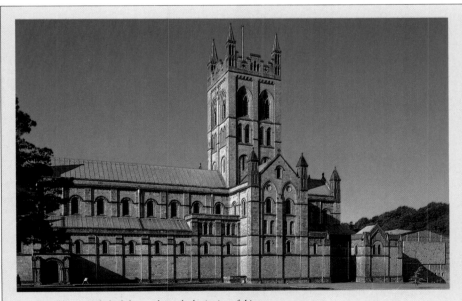

Buckfast Abbey, mostly built by monks at the beginning of this century

BUCKFASTLEIGH

Just off the A38, 3 miles south-east of the Two Moors Way at Scorriton, this former market town grew with the woollen industry and there are old mills and weavers' cottages. The church, on a hill pitted with limestone caves and quarries, has the tomb of Richard Cabell, connected with the Hound of the Baskervilles legend. The town is terminus for the Buckfast Steam Railway, near which are the Buckfast Butterfly Farm and Dartmoor Otter Sanctuary. The town's most famous attraction is, however, Buckfast Abbey. On a Saxon abbey site, this became a Cistercian abbey from 1147 until dissolution by Henry VIII in 1539. Little remains of the medieval buildings. The site was bought in 1882 by French Benedictine monks, who built most of the present structure between 1907 and 1932, with the addition of a chapel in 1966. The monks are famous for their beekeeping and tonic wine, sold in the souvenir shop. There is also a tea room and free audio-visual presentation. The abbey is open all year, except during services.

Scorriton
Bennett's Cross

SCORRITON

HAMEL DOWN

APPROX. 8 MILES/13KM

OS Landranger 202, 191
Start at grid reference SX 703 684
Start point: Scorriton village square.
Scorriton is on an unclassified road about 3
miles north-west of Buckfastleigh.

Scorriton is a small farming community with
the Tradesman's Arms pub and chapel built
in 1904. It is surrounded by the enclosed
strips of medieval open fields.

From the square turn down the road
opposite the war memorial. Turn left at the
bottom and cross the Holy Brook. Originally
the Northbrooke, this stream joins the Dart
at Buckfast Abbey and formed the boundary
of part of the abbey's property. At the next
bend take the lane ahead and ascend to the
road at Holne. Continue ahead through the
village, passing the church and inn. Continue
uphill to the road junction at Butts Cross.
The Butts is an adjacent field where archery
practice took place in Tudor times.

Turn left, then immediately right over a
stile. Crossing further stiles, the path
descends over fields with good views up an
isolated part of the Dart valley, clothed in
ancient oak woodland. It then passes through
the National Trust's Cleave Wood and along
the river bank to New Bridge. Cross the
bridge to the car park.

Follow the river downstream along the
path which starts under the bridge. The river
here is on slates but contains some granite
boulders washed down from several miles
away by floods, some possibly from meltwater during the Ice Age. Leave the river
where the path meets the road. Turn uphill
on the road then take the path to the right
leading up through the bracken to Leigh
Tor. The tor is made of attractively streaked
metamorphic rocks. Turn left and cross two
roads, heading for a car park in an old
quarry. Turn upwards to the track above the
quarry. Turn left along the track, known as
Dr Blackall's Drive.

Dr Blackall bought the 18th-century
Spitchwick Manor in 1867 and so became
lord of the manor. When his wife became
unable to walk on the moor he had the track
made for her pony and trap so that she could
still enjoy the fine views over the Dart
valley. The track continues past Aish and
Mel Tors to the car park at Bel Tor Corner.
Cross the road and keep ahead over the
moorland to the next road. Turn right to
Lock's Gate Cross and take the road signposted to Ponsworthy. Descend the hill to
the ford.

The cottages by the ford include the
former smithy with its double door. One can
make a short diversion over the ford to the
old bridge with its datestone of 1666.
Miller's House is next to the mill. The mill
wheel is behind the building and can be seen
from further on along the route.

Turn left by the ford along the footpath
signposted to Jordan. The path follows the
West Webburn River, which is crossed by
footbridge at Jordan Mill. Turn right by the
mill, then left at the road. Keep uphill across

A manorial boundary stone, Hameldown Cross,
set among Bronze Age barrows on Hamel Down

GUIDE BOX

Places to visit
Holne is a small and attractive village. The
Church House Inn is believed to date from
1329. The Old Forge tea rooms serve cream teas
and are open from Easter to October. Holne
Court was the manor house until the 18th
century, when the Wrey family, lords of the
manor, built a new house in their hunting
grounds at Holne Chase. Near by is Venford
Reservoir, built in 1907 to supply water for
Paignton. It has a car park and toilets and is
surrounded by remains of prehistoric settlement.

The River Dart Country Park is 2 miles east of
Holne on the Ashburton-to-Two Bridges road.
It has a bathing lake, woodland adventure
playgrounds, pony rides, nature trails, café and
shops. Open April to September daily. Self-
catering accommodation or camping.

New Bridge dates from the early 15th century and
crosses the River Dart on the Ashburton-to-
Two Bridges road, 4 miles north-east of
Ashburton. There is a car park, toilets and
National Park Information caravan (open Easter
to October, daily). The river bank is popular for
picnicking and downstream are several deep
pools popular with bathers. Near by is an ancient
animal pound.

Buckland in the Moor is 2 miles north of the Two
Moors Way at New Bridge. It is best known for
its picturesque group of thatched cottages. The
church dates from the 12th century and its clock
has numbers replaced with the words 'My Dear
Mother' by a local landowner. The same man
also had the Ten Commandments inscribed on a
stone on nearby Buckland Beacon.

Car parking
The main car parks on this part of the route are
at Holne, next to the village hall (grid ref. SX
705 694), New Bridge (SX 711 718), Bel Tor
(SX 694 731) and Bennett's Cross (SX 681 817).
On the alternative route is a large car park at
Widecombe in the Moor (SX 718 768).

Public transport
The nearest British Rail stations to this part of
the route are at Newton Abbot and Totnes.
Closest bus routes are through Buckfastleigh and
Moretonhampstead.

Accommodation
The nearest centres for guesthouses and hotels
are at Buckfastleigh, Ashburton,
Moretonhampstead and Chagford. There is little
of this sort of accommodation along the route.
There is basic self-catering accommodation and
camping at Holne Court and camp sites at the
River Dart Country Park, Cockingford near
Widecombe in the Moor, and Poundsgate.
There is a youth hostel 4 miles north-west of the
Two Moors Way at Jordan.

the next crossroads to the crossroads on the
edge of open moorland. Cross this then
strike ahead up the moorland ridge. After a
mile one comes to a crossing of tracks on the
crest of the ridge (grid ref. SX 706 774). For
Widecombe (a mile south-east), where
accommodation is available, go over the
ridge and down the track to the right.

Ⓔ *One can return from here (grid ref. SX 706*
774) to New Bridge by crossing the ridge and
descending the track to the right. This follows the
edge of the moor and becomes a lane leading down
to Widecombe in the Moor. At the village centre

turn left by the Church House, opposite the inn. Walk down the road and over the clapper bridge across the East Webburn River. Pass the Rugglestone Inn, named after a large logan or balancing stone in a nearby field. Pass Venton and Shilstone Rocks Stud and turn uphill. At the open moor turn right along the edge of the moor and keep ahead to the next road. Cross this to the bridlepath which becomes Elliot's Hill road running down to the road at Buckland in the Moor. Turn left and then right after the church down an unsigned road which leads to Buckland Bridge. Cross the bridge and follow the road alongside the river back to New Bridge (a circular route of some 9 miles).

Soussons Farm, below Hamel Down

HAMEL DOWN

BENNETT'S CROSS

APPROX. 4 MILES/6.5KM

OS Landranger 191
Start at grid reference SX 706 774
Start point: The crossing of tracks on Hamel Down, 1 mile north-east of Widecombe in the Moor, where there is a large car park.

From the crossing of tracks the route continues uphill along the crest of the ridge for 2 miles to its highest point at Hameldown Tor. It passes a number of Bronze Age barrows. Some of these were excavated in the 19th century and were found, uniquely on Dartmoor, to be of the Wessex culture. They are mainly of earth within a ring of small stones. Underneath is a small cairn, with cremated human remains under that. Single Barrow revealed the bronze blade and amber pommel of a dagger.

Hameldown Cross was a manorial boundary stone. Other such stones on the barrows were erected in 1854 and bear the initials of the Duke of Somerset, then lord of Natsworthy Manor.

The route descends through Grimspound, a 4-acre Bronze Age enclosure with the remains of 16 hut circles and 8 other buildings. The entrance is through a large, paved stone gateway. The huts were made by building a double-skinned circular stone wall with a filling of earth. The floor was dug out inside and a central pole held a conical roof of branches covered with turf.

Pass straight through Grimspound and over Hookney Tor on the far side. Descend to cross a road. Keep straight ahead over the next hill to the B3212 road and Bennett's Cross car park.

ⓔ To return to Hamel Down, descend the West Webburn valley from Bennett's Cross (grid ref. SX 681 817). A number of tracks lead to the remains of Vitifer mine. Follow the broad track alongside the river and through the gate into the forest at Soussons Down. Take the bridlepath to the right, signposted to Soussons. Follow the path signs to Soussons Farm. Take the farm drive to the road. Turn left and keep ahead at the next junction. After a mile at a T-junction take the gate ahead and the uphill track signposted to Widecombe. Take the gate on to the moor and continue up to the crest of the ridge.

WIDECOMBE IN THE MOOR

This is the village (on the B3387, 7 miles west of Bovey Tracey) famous for its popular song, as is reflected in the carved granite village sign. The Fair is held on the second Tuesday in September. Once for cattle, sheep and ponies, it is now commercialised. St Pancras' Church is known as the 'Cathedral of the Moor' for its 120ft-high tower and was partly built with profits from tin mining. Plaques commemorate the time it was struck by lightning in 1638, injuring many of the congregation and killing four. By the entrance to the church is Church House, a former ale house and school dating from 1537. Part, called Sexton's Cottage, is a National Trust information centre and shop.

'All along, down along, out along' – Widecombe in the Moor

Bennett's Cross

Yeoford

BENNETT'S CROSS

CHAGFORD BRIDGE

APPROX. 5¹/₂ MILES/9KM

OS Landranger 191
Start at grid reference SX 681 817
Start point: Car park at Bennett's Cross, beside the B3212, 2¹/₂ miles north-east of Postbridge.

Bennett's Cross dates from the 13th century, when it marked the route from Tavistock to Chagford. It was later used as a boundary stone for Headland Warren; hence the initials WB (Warren Bounds) carved on it.

Cross the road and head across the moorland, keeping slightly to the left to skirt the rather boggy area at the source of the North Walla Brook. After this veer right, down the spine of Hurston Ridge. Hurston comes from the Saxon hare or hoar stone, meaning a boundary stone. A large prehistoric stone once stood here, marking one of Dartmoor's most important ancient trackways and later the boundary of the Royal Forest. An impressive double stone row with tall menhirs at each end still survives on the ridge.

Keep downwards along the ridge to the road between Fernworthy and Chagford. There are views to Fernworthy with its reservoir, completed in 1942, and forest, begun in 1919, which hides many prehistoric remains. Turn right down the road and over a cattle grid. Turn left along the Mariner's Way down the drive to Yardworthy. Follow the signposts and orange waymarks for the Mariner's Way, crossing the South Teign River by footbridge and a road between Teignworthy Hotel and Frenchbeer. Continue across field to Teigncombe and turn right, leaving the Mariner's Way, which continues through Gidleigh. At a sharp right-hand bend continue ahead down a lane to Leigh Bridge, where the South and North Teign Rivers meet.

Cross the bridge and continue along the road towards Chagford. At the next cross-roads turn left to Chagford Bridge.

Bennett's Cross, placed here 700 years ago

GUIDE BOX

Places to visit
The Miniature Pony Centre is on the B3212, 3 miles west of Moretonhampstead and 3 miles south of the Two Moors Way at Chagford. Suited to children, there are many ponies, pony rides, adventure playground, shop, restaurant and picnic area. Open March to October, daily.

Fernworthy, belonging to the Forestry Commission, lies on minor roads 3 miles south-west of Chagford. The reservoir belongs to South West Water. There is a picnic area and toilets, a nature trail around the reservoir and waymarked trails in the forest. There is a bird sanctuary with two hides at the south-western end of the reservoir.

Chagford, is a former stannary town, where tin was brought for weighing and stamping in medieval times. Its Square has a quaint market house known as the Pepperpot, built in 1862. The 15th-century church contains the tomb of Elizabethan judge Sir John Whyddon, whose family lived in what is now the Three Crowns Hotel, a 13th-century thatched inn and scene of Civil War fighting. The Cider Press Museum in the Square has a collection of cider-making equipment (open all year).

Spinsters' Rock is at Shilstone, 2 miles west of Drewsteignton and 2 miles north of Chagford on minor roads. It is a dolmen, or burial chamber consisting of three upright stones surmounted by a huge stone weighing 16 tons. The mound which covered it has long since disappeared and the stones have been reconstructed since their collapse in 1862. Legend has it that it was originally raised by three spinsters before breakfast.

Car parking
There is a car park at Bennett's Cross (grid ref. SX 681 817) and parking space in the Squares at Chagford (SX 701 875) and Drewsteignton (SX 736 908). There is on-street parking at Yeoford (SX 783 989) particularly in the cul-de-sac beyond the railway station. On the alternative route at Drewsteignton there are parking areas either side of the bridge at Fingle Bridge (SX 743 900).

Public transport
There are railway stations at Exeter and Yeoford. Buses serve Chagford and Drewsteignton.

Accommodation
There are guesthouses and hotels at Chagford and Moretonhampstead. There are camp sites at Clifford, 2 miles downstream of Fingle Bridge; just west of Whiddon Down; just west of Crockernwell; and at Hittisleigh. The nearest youth hostel is at Steps Bridge, 4 miles west of Drewsteignton (open March to September). The hostel at Gidleigh, still shown on most maps, is now closed.

Ⓔ *One can return from here (grid ref. SX 694 879) to Bennett's Cross via Chagford. At the crossroads turn right for Chagford instead of left for the bridge. The return route forks right in the village at the next junction, but one may detour ahead to explore Chagford. After forking right, turn left at the next junction and up the hill to Meldon Common. At the top bear downhill to the right. Keep ahead at the next two junctions and return to the junction with the Mariner's Way.*

Turn left here along the Mariner's Way, over fields and down the drive to Lower Shapley. Follow the signs across fields and between thatched farmhouses at Hurston. Turn left down the farm drive, then right as signposted along fields through Lingcombe to Jurston. Look out for medieval gate posts, slotted to take removable poles instead of hinged gates. Cross the road at Jurston and the green to the clapper bridge, taking the track to Lettaford with its old longhouse, opposite which the path leads through a farmyard. Follow the Mariner's Way across fields and across the B3212 to Coombe. Here the Mariner's Way used to pass through a house, presumably one of the rest houses which were spaced every 8 or 10 miles along the way. Turn right along the bridlepath up the combe to join the Two Moors Way below Hookney Tor. Continue ahead, crossing the road and hill to Bennett's Cross. This makes a circular walk of about 13 miles.

CHAGFORD BRIDGE

YEOFORD

APPROX. 10½ MILES/16.5KM

OS Landranger 191
Start at grid reference SX 694 879
Start point: Chagford Bridge, just west of Chagford, where there is parking in the Square.

Both Chagford and Rushford Bridges are narrow packhorse bridges built in the 17th century when Chagford was a thriving woollen centre. There was a woollen mill close to Chagford Bridge.

Cross the bridge and turn right on the footpath through fields along the river bank. At Rushford Bridge turn left along the road, then right, between buildings at Rushford Mill. Keep ahead along the river bank to Dogmarsh Bridge. Cross the road, not the bridge, here and continue along the river bank. After ½ mile cross a small stream (grid ref. SX 722 895). Here there are alternative routes to Drewsteignton via the Fisherman's Path along the River Teign or Hunters' Path above the Teign gorge.

The route along the Fisherman's Path follows the river bank to Fingle Bridge, another 17th-century packhorse bridge and popular beauty spot. The Angler's Rest pub and shop is open from Easter to October and

lunchtimes in winter. Do not cross the bridge, but turn left up the road to the parking area. Take Hunters' Path up through the woods to the left. This rises to the top of the Teign gorge and follows the edge for ½ mile until a right fork is made, joining the main route to Drewsteignton.

The main route ascends a small combe from the river to join a farm drive. A short distance up the drive, double back to the right along Hunters' Path. This passes under Castle Drogo to Sharp Tor, where a detour left can be made to the house. After Sharp Tor take the next turn to the left signposted Drewsteignton. The road is joined by a stone commemorating the opening of the Two Moors Way. Turn right, then left for the Square. For anyone wishing to leave or join the walk at Drewsteignton, there is parking in the Square.

Drewsteignton is a pretty village with thatched cottages and the unspoilt 18th-century Drewe Arms inn. This was once called the Druid's Inn, after an association of Druids with Spinsters' Rock. It was renamed after the return of the Drewe family this century, one Drogo or Dru having been given the manor by William the Conqueror. The church has a tall 15th-century tower and a wagon roof with carved bosses, one of which has a face said to be a self-portrait of one of the builders. The Church House also dates back to the 15th century and served as a hall and ale house for members of the congregation.

From the Square pass the Post Office shop and turn right down the road beyond. Keep downhill past two junctions to Veet Mill. Take the track ahead at the road bend and follow it past Winscombe to a road. Turn left, cross the flyover over the A30 and turn right down Hask Lane. Turn left along a path which passes down over fields, through

woodland and crosses a ford to a road by Forder Farm.

Turn right, then left over a stile by the gateway to Forder Cottage. Continue up fields to Hill Farm. Take the lane to the right of the farm and continue ahead down to a bridge over a small stream. Continue up between some trees and, keeping Whitethorn Farm to your right, take the gateway to the farmyard. Follow the farm drive to the road and turn right. Keep ahead at Hittisleigh Cross to the small hilltop settlement of Hittisleigh.

The Church of St Andrew is mainly 14th-century and its granite arcaded aisle has a wagon roof with carved bosses. There is a Norman font of black marble. A sparsely populated parish, Hittisleigh provided the poorest church income in Devon.

Continue along the road for 2 miles, where the Two Moors Way forks down a farm track to Newbury. Instead of making this left turn, continue down the road for 1½ miles to Yeoford. Here is a railway station, Post Office shop and the Mare and Foal pub.

Ⓔ *To return to Drewsteignton, walk up the road and turn left along a road just after the turn for Newbury (grid ref. SX 758 972). Turn right after the bridge, then left at the crossroads at the top of the hill. Turn right at the T-junction and after 300yds take the footpath to the left through two sets of double gates. The path passes under the A30 and along a lane past Lambert to Crockernwell. Turn right at the road, then left down the side street.*

Crockernwell, now by-passed by the A30, grew on the old Exeter-to-Okehampton road. It is a hamlet in the parish of Cheriton Bishop. It was a Saxon manor and has had a chapel since 1390.

Turn right along the lane signposted public footpath. The lane passes Budbrooke and Narracott, and at Coombe Hall forks right up the drive to a road. Take the road nearly opposite and at the next bend take the farm drive ahead to Burrow Farm. Follow the footpath signs to the left of the farm buildings and down to a stream. Keep ahead uphill, following the yellow waymarks along the edge of fields to a lane returning to Drewsteignton (making a walk of about 6½ miles from Newbury).

CASTLE DROGO (NT)

The granite castle is on the Two Moors Way, 1 mile west of Drewsteignton. It was built between 1910 and 1930 by architect Sir Edwin Lutyens. He built it for Julius Drewe, founder of the Home and Colonial Stores, who wished to return to his family's roots at Drewsteignton. It is austere yet comfortable and has its own hydro-electric power supply and internal telephone system. It has extensive landscaped grounds and formal terraced gardens, protected by high yew hedges. There is a croquet lawn for visitors' use and National Trust café and shop with plant sales. Open Easter to October, daily except Friday.

The Teign gorge, overlooked by Castle Drogo

Leland Trail

KING ALFRED'S TOWER TO HAM HILL

28 MILES/45KM

THE Leland Trail, completed during 1989 by the South Somerset District Council, crosses the lowlands of South Somerset, linking several villages, towns and historical sites. It uses definitive rights of way, tracks and lanes that follow in the footsteps of John Leland, who travelled on horseback through this area during the 16th century. A well-educated scholar who worked for King Henry VIII as a keeper of the royal libraries, he was commissioned in 1533 to produce a survey of England's antiquities and 'peruse the libraries of all cathedrals, abbeys, priories, colleges etc, and also all places wherein records, writings and secrets of antiquity were reposed'. He reached South Somerset, some time between 1535 and 1543, and after visiting Bruton travelled south-west through Castle Cary, North and South Cadbury, Ilchester, Montacute and Stoke-sub-Hamdon.

Detailed guides
South Somerset District Council produces a beautifully packaged booklet on the Leland Trail which comprises a very detailed and clear description of the walk, with maps printed on waterproof laminated cards. Contact the South Somerset District Council, Tourism and Marketing Unit, Brympton Way, Yeovil, Somerset BA20 1PU (tel. 0935 75272) or a Tourist Information Centre (see pages 30 and 32).

Maps
OS Landranger 183, 193

Links
No other long distance paths link directly with the Leland Trail, but the West Mendip Way and the Dorset Coast Path are within 20 miles or so.

The modern-day Leland Trail, if one opts to travel in a south-westerly direction like John Leland, starts at King Alfred's Tower (NT) which is just inside the Somerset county boundary and is close to the National Trust property of Stourhead in Wiltshire. It is not an arduous walk and although most of the trail is fairly level there are opportunities for wonderful views of South Somerset from several vantage points along the route. At no point is the walker more than 3 miles from a town or village with refreshments and, in most cases, some form of public transport.

The Leland Trail is very well waymarked, with its own logo depicting John Leland, and the route is relatively easy to follow throughout. The guide produced by South Somerset District Council, does, however, make a valuable companion.

From King Alfred's Tower it is a pleasant walk down through Penselwood to Redlynch, then along an old coach road to the picturesque and historical town of Bruton, nestling in the valley of the River Brue and famous for its school, dovecot (NT) and packhorse bridge.

From Bruton to Castle Cary the walk zigzags and tends to be more undulating than the first section, with glorious views of South Somerset from several vantage points. On the way it passes the small village of Wyke Champflower, famous for its unusual and tiny church, and then follows a winding route through the village of Cole (where remains of the closed Somerset & Dorset Railway can be seen), past Castle Cary vineyard and down into the unspoilt town of Castle Cary.

Castle Cary is a good stopping-off point on the walk, with several places worth visiting, including the Old Market House, the lock-up and the High Street's interesting bookshops. There is a good choice of inns and public transport.

From Castle Cary the Trail climbs up to nearby Lodge Hill, another wonderful viewpoint, where the earthworks of ancient Cary Castle can just be seen, and then descends through lush farmland, following several

The panoramic view from Lodge Hill over Castle Cary and north Somerset

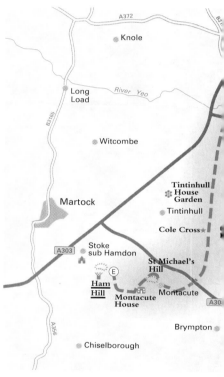

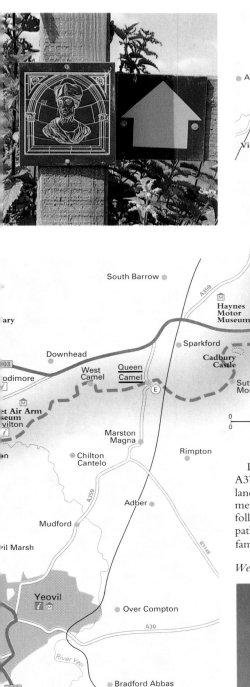

by the National Trust. The Trail also passes close to the village of Chilthorne Dormer. After a short climb, Montacute House (NT) and Ham Hill, the final destination, can be seen in the distance.

Passing through the Montacute Estate, the Trail goes to the south of the famous Elizabethan house (which is the property of the National Trust and well worth a visit if time allows) to the picturesque village of Montacute. From the village the route is on a defined footpath, on National Trust land, to St Michael's Hill, where a short detour to the top and a climb up the folly tower will be rewarded with superb views. Following a series of footpaths through woodland, the Trail eventually ends on Ham Hill, site of an Iron Age settlement, Roman fort and famous stone quarry, and now designated as a Country Park.

The views across Somerset from the outer ramparts of Ham Hill are stunning and along with a trip to the Prince of Wales Inn, which is situated on the top of the hill, make a fitting end to the walk. A short descent to the village of Stoke-sub-Hamdon will bring the walker back to modern-day amenities and transport.

Beyond Ilchester the Trail crosses the busy A37 Fosse Way and, traversing level farm-land, passes the site of the abandoned medieval village of Sock Dennis before following a series of enclosed tracks and pathways to come close to Tintinhull House, famous for its modern garden, now managed

West Camel Church

streams and small rivers, to the village of North Cadbury. It then crosses the busy A303 trunk road to the ancient village of Compton Pauncefoot and reaches South Cadbury village, where a short detour will take the walker to the top of Cadbury Castle, site of one of the most famous ancient hillforts in England. The route of the Leland Trail rounds the base of Cadbury Castle to the picturesque village of Sutton Montis. For the next 8 miles the route is across flat farmland.

The Trail follows this level route, over many waymarked stiles, through the villages of Queen Camel and West Camel, then skirts the southern perimeter of Yeovilton RNAS airfield, with its famous Fleet Air Arm Museum. It continues past Yeovilton village and weir and on to the ancient town of Ilchester, now just a shadow of its former importance in Roman and medieval times.

King Alfred's Tower

Queen Camel

KING ALFRED'S TOWER

CASTLE CARY

APPROX. 9 MILES/14.5KM

OS Landranger 183
Start at grid reference ST 745 351
Start point: King Alfred's Tower, about
100yds inside the Somerset county
boundary, adjacent to the unclassified road
from Redlynch to Kilmington and north-
east of Stourhead. Car parking is available
next to the Tower, which is the property of
the National Trust.

King Alfred's Tower, on the western edge of
the Stourhead Estate, stands on Kingsettle
Hill on the edge of an escarpment 656ft
(200m) above the Somerset Plain. It was
conceived in 1762 and built in 1772 for Sir
Henry Hoare, of Stourhead House, to commemorate peace with France and the succession of George III two years earlier. The
160ft tower, with 221 steps, can be climbed.

Walk from the Tower for a short distance
down the adjacent metalled lane and turn left
on to a track waymarked with the Leland
Trail logo to Aaron's Hill. Follow the usually

King Alfred's Tower, site of one of his battles

muddy track down through Penselwood.
After 500yds turn left on to a forestry track,
then turn right down on to a metalled road
which skirts the edge of the forest for
250yds. Following the signpost to Redlynch,
the route now leaves the road on to a track
through natural woodland, where wild deer
can occasionally be seen, and eventually leads
on to a wide path through the woods to a
stile. A succession of waymarked stiles is now
crossed until a farm track is reached. Cross
this and continue through several fields to
Coach Road Farm. Cross the metalled road.
The Leland Trail is now following the route
of an old coach road which will eventually
lead to the gates of Redlynch House on the
B3081 road.

At the gates turn right on to the B3081
road and walk to the nearby crossroads,
turning left down a metalled lane, past
several cottages to a stile and gate signposted
to Bruton. Cross over a series of stiles and
fields and pass Dropping Lane Farm on your
right, eventually coming out at a metalled
road on the outskirts of Bruton. From this
point the roofless dovecot and the church
tower can be seen nestling in the valley of
the River Brue. Follow the road that leads to
the left of the dovecot passing an old, ivy-
clad wall on the right. Bruton Dovecot (NT)
is worth making a short detour to visit if
time permits.

Once past the dovecot, turn right into
Godminster Lane over a railway bridge, then
right into Silver Street and past King's
School to the one-arched, 15th-century
packhorse bridge over the River Brue. Cross
the bridge into Patwell Street and turn left
into the High Street, where refreshment can
be taken at the Sun or Castle Inns.

Bruton has much to offer the visitor and
time should be allowed to explore its narrow
streets. Bruton was an important Saxon town
and by the 12th century an abbey for
Augustinian canons had been founded – little
now remains. By the end of the 14th century
Somerset produced a quarter of all the wool
in England and Bruton prospered as one of
the main producers.

Ⓔ *To return from Bruton to King Alfred's
Tower by a different route, walk along the A359
Frome road for a short distance then take the
unclassified road towards the village of North
Brewham. Before the village, turn right to South
Brewham. After ²/₃ mile turn left up the hill to
King Alfred's Tower.*

From Bruton the Leland Trail continues
from the bottom of the High Street in
Trendle Lane at the side of a garage
workshop. Walk up the sunken lane, lined
with sycamores, to the top, where there are
good views across Bruton to the dovecot.
Follow the track through a cool and leafy
tunnel of trees which eventually opens out
on a hill, with magnificent views of
Somerset. The Trail is now downhill across

several waymarked stiles and fields, with the
railway line visible on your left and, beyond
it, apple orchards and Castle Cary Vineyard
nestling beneath Ridge Hill. Emerge on to a
metalled lane in the village of Wyke
Champflower. Turn left on to the lane and
walk past the unusual 17th-century church,
which is attached to the Manor House.

Staying on the lane, cross a disused railway
bridge and then turn left into Wyke Lane,
following it for about 1 mile. The route
passes under a rather forlorn railway bridge
which once carried the much lamented
Somerset & Dorset Joint Railway on its way
from Bath to Bournemouth and which was
closed in 1966. Passing under a second
railway bridge, which carries the main line,
and crossing over the River Brue, reach the
small village of Cole. Turn right at the road
junction and walk up the lane past Cole
Farm to a stile and signpost to Ridge Hill.

Follow the waymarked path across a field, up through apple orchards until Ridge Hill is reached. From here there are wonderful views of the valley below. The path now follows the ridge of the hill over several stiles and down steps to a metalled lane, where a left turn followed by a right turn will bring you into a bridleway named Solomon's Lane and signposted to Ansford. Follow this shady bridleway until the main road at Ansford is reached. Turn right for a short distance and then turn left down Ansford Road into Castle Cary High Street.

Castle Cary, like Bruton, owed much of its prosperity in the Middle Ages to the woollen trade. However, it owes its name to a castle which was built on nearby Lodge Hill in the early 12th century and eventually stormed by King Stephen in 1138. The centre of the town is well worth exploring, particularly the many old shops and houses in the High Street. The Market House, rebuilt in the 19th century, now houses a fine museum and behind, on Bailey Hill, is an 18th-century lock-up which resembles an old beehive. Castle Cary is amply stocked with old inns and is also well provided with rail and bus services.

Ⓔ *To return from Castle Cary to Bruton walk the short distance along the A371 to Castle Cary railway station for a train back to Bruton.*

CASTLE CARY

QUEEN CAMEL

APPROX. 9 MILES/14.5KM

OS Landranger 183
Start at grid reference ST 641 324
Start point: The George Hotel, Castle Cary. Street parking.

From the George Hotel in Castle Cary walk up Paddock Drain and into a narrow footpath signposted to Lodge Hill. At the top cross the stile into a field and walk up and over Lodge Hill 505ft (154m), site of the former castle with earthworks of a large keep just visible from the path, to a bench on the top of the hill. From here there is an uninterrupted view over Castle Cary towards Glastonbury Tor and the Mendip Hills. Continue along the top of the hill over several waymarked stiles and passing farm buildings on the right. Follow the waymarked path across several stiles and fields to an electricity sub-station and turn left along the A359 road for 100yds to a gate and stile, signposted to Woolston (2 miles). Do not take the bridleway immediately before this.

The Trail now passes through several fields down a small valley, with the hedge on the right. Continue on to a farm track, following this for about 1 mile to a metalled lane. Walk down this lane for about 200yds to a stile and gate, signposted Brookhampton (1 mile). Crossing the stile into the field, the Leland Trail now passes through some very tranquil and beautiful Somerset countryside. Follow the waymarked path over a succes-

sion of stiles and fields into a metalled lane in the hamlet of Brookhampton. Turn left along the lane, past a working waterwheel and several cottages for $^1/_4$ mile until a waymarked stile is reached. The route now parallels the winding River Cam before gaining the lane again. Cross into the lane and turn left over a bridge and up some steep old stone steps and stile into a field. The path soon reaches North Cadbury School playing field, which it crosses, and eventually leads into the pretty village of North Cadbury, where there is an inn and village stores.

Passing through the village, turn right at an old corrugated iron hut along a track to a waymarked stile signposted Compton Pauncefoot (1 mile). Several fields are then crossed, with views of North Cadbury Court and Church to the right, until the extremely busy A303 trunk road is reached. Great care must be taken when crossing this motorway-like road to the stile in the hedge on the opposite side. (To avoid this, take Parish Hill out of North Cadbury, cross the A303 by the road bridge at Chapel Cross and continue on the road to South Cadbury.) A short walk up a metalled lane will lead to the beautiful and ancient village of Compton Pauncefoot, passing the late 15th-century St Andrew's Church on the right. Continue on up the lane to a road junction and turn right, signposted Sparkford (A303). Follow this lane past an unusual quarter circle of five cottages, to the neighbouring village of South Cadbury, nestling beneath Cadbury Castle hillfort.

Cross the road by the Red Lion pub to Folly Lane, which then continues as a track. Crossing over a succession of waymarked stiles and fields, the Trail skirts· around the massive bulk of Cadbury Castle, with distant views to the north-west of Glastonbury Tor, and eventually leads to a metalled lane and Sutton Montis. On reaching the small 13th-

The Old Market House, Castle Cary

century Holy Trinity Church, walk up the steps, carefully following the waymarked path across the churchyard, across a stile and into a field behind the church. The Trail now crosses over a series of waymarked stiles and fields, crossing a narrow metalled lane *en route,* until the tall blue-lias stone tower of Queen Camel Church comes into view. Before reaching the village of Queen Camel, the Castle Cary-to-Weymouth railway line is crossed on the level and great caution must be taken when crossing the track. A narrow, enclosed footpath soon reaches the village, coming out into the main street (A359) by the side of the church. Turn left along this road into the centre of the village.

Ⓔ *To return from Queen Camel to Castle Cary by a different route take the series of lanes via the villages of Weston Bampfylde, South Cadbury, North Cadbury and Galhampton. Alternatively, there are several buses a day from Queen Camel back to Castle Cary (except on Sundays).*

CADBURY CASTLE

This can be reached from South Cadbury village as a detour from the Leland Trail, turning left at the crossroads by the Red Lion Inn. Walk up Castle Lane which can be muddy and is very steep.

This major Iron Age camp covers some 18 acres on the top of the hill. It is a three-sided fortress guarded with four huge banks and ditches. It is the largest prehistoric camp in Somerset – and one of the finest in the whole of Britain. Excavations have found both Neolithic and Late Bronze Age domestic occupation of the hilltop. The hillfort defences were erected in Iron Age times but were eventually destroyed by the Romans. About AD500 it was the most formidable fortification of its day and is identified in folklore as the possible site of Camelot, seat of the legendary King Arthur's Court.

In late Saxon times King Ethelred the Unready founded a royal mint here, which was later destroyed by King Canute. From the top of Cadbury Castle it is possible to see King Alfred's Tower in the north-east and Ham Hill in the west.

Queen Camel
Ham Hill

QUEEN CAMEL

ILCHESTER

APPROX. 4³/₄ MILES/ 7.5 KM

OS Landranger 183
Start at grid reference ST 595 248
Start point: Queen Camel High Street.
Street parking.

Queen Camel is a well-cared-for village, built of blue-lias stone and dominated by the late 14th-century, tall tower of St Barnabas Church. The village flourished in the 16th century, when there was a market trading in the locally made linen and woollen cloths. The size of the church is an indication of this prosperity, but in 1639 there was a disastrous fire which destroyed many houses, and the village never fully recovered.

From the village High Street turn down England's Lane, leading into Dark Lane, and then turn right into Green Lane, signposted West Camel (1 mile). At the end of the lane cross into a field through a gate, then go across several further fields until a kissing-gate is reached. Walk past a riding school along a track which eventually leads into a metalled lane. This ends at the crossroads, dominated by a grand old spreading horse chestnut tree, in the tiny hamlet of Wales. Walk over the crossroads, through the hamlet and at the end of the lane continue through a farmyard. There then follows a succession of waymarked stiles across fields to the village of West Camel. Keeping the early 14th-century All Saints' Church on the right, turn right on to the main road to the village stores.

Turn left at the village stores down Back Lane for just over ¹/₄ mile, past Frog Lane to a stile signposted Chantry Lane. Cross the field to Chantry Lane, turning left along the lane to a road junction, then turning right and second left to a lane signposted to Chilton Cantelo and Mudford. After approximately ¹/₂ mile, where the lane turns sharp left, cross over a waymarked stile into the field on the right.

Yeovilton Royal Naval Air Station can now be seen and the Leland Trail follows the southern perimeter of the airfield for some distance to Yeovilton village. On days when the base is operating, noisy Harrier jump-jets can be seen going through their paces. With the airbase radar on the left and the River Cam on the right, follow the metalled track across several fields, through a disused wartime camp. Crossing over a small bridge and still following the perimeter fence, reach the River Yeo. Yeovilton village's St Bartholomew's Church can now be seen on the right.

A detour from the Leland Trail would take you to the Fleet Air Arm Museum at Yeovilton (see Guide Box).

On reaching the metalled road turn left over a bridge, with Yeovilton Weir to the left, and then turn right over a waymarked stile, signposted to Limington, into a field. The path now crosses two further stiles and fields to an old mill stream which it then follows along the east bank, crossing a sluice gate bridge on the way, to a bridge. Cross the bridge and follow the waymarked signs over a series of stiles and fields until the ancient town of Ilchester can be seen ahead. The path goes downhill over several more stiles and fields until the River Yeo is reached at Ilchester. Walk into Free Street to

Below *The River Yeo, near Yeovilton*

GUIDE BOX

Places to visit
Yeovilton Fleet Air Arm Museum, on the B3151 road just off the A303 between Sparkford and Ilchester, houses a very large collection of naval aircraft tracing the history of the Fleet Air Arm from World War I to the present day. Also includes the supersonic Concorde 002 prototype aircraft. Open all year, daily.

Lytes Cary Manor (NT) is near the village of Charlton Mackerell, to the north of the A303 Ilchester bypass. This manor house has a 14th-century chapel, a 15th-century Hall and a 16th-century Great Chamber. It was the home of Henry Lyte, translator of the *Niewe Herball* in 1578, and the manor bears the name of the Lyte family who lived there for 500 years. Open April to end October, Mondays, Wednesdays and Saturdays.

Ilchester Museum. Located in part of the Town Hall, Ilchester, this small, well laid-out museum traces the history of the Roman and medieval settlements in the town. Open all year, Thursdays and Saturdays.

Tintinhull House Garden (NT) is situated in the village of Tintinhull, 5 miles north-west of Yeovil, just off the A303. The 20th-century formal garden surrounds a 17th-century farmhouse (not open to the public). Garden open April to end September, Wednesdays, Thursdays, Saturdays and Bank Holiday Mondays.

Stoke-sub-Hamdon Priory (NT), North Street, Stoke-sub-Hamdon, just off the A303 west of Ilchester, is built of Ham Hill stone. The 14th-century building formerly housed the priests of the chantry of St Nicholas in a nearby manor house, Beauchamp, which no longer exists. The great hall and screens passage of the chantry, and the dovecot are all that remain. Open all year, daily.

Car parking
Street parking is available in Queen Camel, Ilchester, Montacute village and Stoke-sub-Hamdon. There are car parks for visitors to Yeovilton Fleet Air Arm Museum and Montacute House, and there is parking space in the Ham Hill Country Park.

Accommodation
See information on page 30.

Public transport
The nearest British Rail stations to this part of the route are at Yeovil Junction/Pen Mill and Crewkerne. Bus services operate to North Cadbury, Yeovilton and Stoke-sub-Hamdon.

the B3151 main road and turn left along this road into the town. Ilchester is a good place to break for refreshment and has a hotel. It is on a bus route back to Bruton.

Ⓔ *A return from Ilchester to Queen Camel by a different route unfortunately involves some road-walking and retracing of steps. Follow the B3151 out of Ilchester past the RNAS Yeovilton Airfield, turn right to the village of Speckington and then retrace your steps on the Trail back to Queen Camel. The other alternative is to retrace your steps the whole way.*

ILCHESTER

HAM HILL

APPROX. 8½ MILES/14KM

OS Landranger 183, 193
Start at grid reference ST 522 226
Start point: Car park near the church.

Looking east from Ham Hill at the end of a walk that has several spectacular viewpoints

Ilchester was once the important Roman town of *Lendiniae*, positioned strategically on the Fosse Way (A37). In medieval times it was also a town of some importance with walls and gates, a friary, a hospital and a county gaol, as well as a thriving market and mint. In the 18th century it was the county town of Somerset but all that remains of its past now is one church, St Mary Major, and a medieval bridge.

From the car park, walk south along the main street towards the roundabout with the A37 Fosse Way, crossing over this road at the traffic island to the stile in the fence opposite. From this point the waymarked Leland Trail crosses several fields and drainage ditches for about 1 mile to Sock Dennis Farm. Sock Dennis was named after the ancient family of Dacus and is a deserted medieval village. Some earthworks are visible in a field where the Leland Trail passes the eastern edge of the site.

Cross a stile past the farm buildings and follow the path ahead into a field. Cross a further stile into a wide, grassed lane. Follow this lane, crossing several more waymarked stiles and fields to a footbridge and two bridlegates to a leafy enclosed footpath. A short climb leads to Cole Cross, about 1 mile from the village of Chilthorne Domer. From Cole Cross the route crosses the metalled road into Kissmedown Lane, signposted Windmill Lane. Walk uphill along Kissmedown Lane, a bridleway which eventually gives a good view of the approach to Montacute House and Ham Hill. The bridleway gives way to a metalled road at Windmill Farm, which is passed on the left, and shortly after this a road junction is reached. Cross straight over into a leafy, enclosed lane to its end, where the busy A3088 road is crossed (with care).

Follow the waymarked signs across a stone millstream bridge to the grounds of Montacute House (NT). Bear left over the small hill and follow the waymarked path over a succession of stiles, with good views of Montacute House, to the main road at the southern end of Montacute village.

Picturesque Montacute, with its fine Norman St Catherine's Church, is built of locally quarried Ham Hill stone. It was originally named Bishopston after the Norman, William of Mortain, who founded a Cluniac priory here in 1102. The village has a main square called 'The Borough', which is surrounded by pretty 17th- and 18th-century houses. The entrance to the magnificent Montacute House is just off this square.

Walk through Montacute village along the main street and past the church and the King's Arms Inn to the village recreation grounds. Turn left through these grounds, towards St Michael's Hill, go through a kissing-gate and follow the permissive path up the hill to the stile at the edge of the wooded hilltop. From here the Leland Trail turns right and skirts along the lower edge of the wooded hill, but a short detour to make the steep climb to the top of St Michael's Hill is worthwhile.

Originally Montacute Castle, built in 1068, stood on this hill. The name of Montacute is derived from the Latin *mons acutus*, which means pointed hill. Now it is topped by a 60ft high circular folly tower, built in 1760, which affords wonderful views over the Somerset countryside.

The Leland Trail also affords good views, towards the Blackdown and Mendip Hills in the distance. The path crosses a waymarked stile, goes down a sloping field towards a sunken path, which was once a Roman road, then uphill and right into the woods on Hedgecock Hill. The waymarked path through the woods and around the ramparts of the Iron Age hillfort on Ham Hill soon leads to the final destination.

Ham Hill was a large fortified settlement and is a dominating landmark visible for many miles around. It covers an area of nearly 200 acres and has been shown by archaeologists to have been in continuous occupation from the New Stone Age times up to and beyond the Roman occupation. The Romans occupied the site most intensively by strengthening the prehistoric earthworks. The honey-coloured Ham Hill stone which was quarried on the hill for centuries was used to build large houses, including Montacute House, chapels and cottages in the area.

Ham Hill was made a Country Park in 1970 and now boasts car parks, barbecue areas and a toilet. Fine views over Somerset can be had from the ramparts. On a clear day King Alfred's Tower, the starting point of this walk, can be seen to the north-east. A fitting end to the walk is a visit to the Prince of Wales Inn, situated on the top of Ham Hill, before descending the short distance to the village of Stoke-sub-Hamdon, which nestles beneath the Hill and lies just off the busy A303 trunk road.

Ⓔ *To return from Ham Hill to Ilchester by a different route descend to East Stoke from the footpath from Ham Hill, then take Marsh Lane to the village of Tintinhull. From here another footpath leads back to the Leland Trail at grid ref. ST 511 195, where the route back to Ilchester can be retraced.*

MONTACUTE HOUSE (NT)

Montacute House is one of the finest mansions in the West of England. The magnificent Elizabethan house, built of locally quarried Ham Hill stone, was begun in the 1590s by Sir Edward Phelips. During the early 20th century the house was in a decayed state and by 1931 was valued at only £5832 'for scrap'. Ernest Cook, grandson of Thomas Cook (founder of the travel agency) then purchased the house for presentation to the National Trust.

Montacute has a fine collection of heraldic glass, tapestries, panelling and furniture. The National Portrait Gallery has a permanent exhibition in the 172ft Long Gallery of Elizabethan and Jacobean portraits. There are also fine formal gardens and a park.

House open April to end October, daily except Tuesday. Garden and park open all year daily except Tuesday.

Cotswold Way

COMPLETE ROUTE
CHIPPING CAMPDEN TO BATH ABBEY
98 MILES/158KM

SECTION COVERED
CHIPPING CAMPDEN TO PAINSWICK
47 MILES/76KM

THE Cotswold Way is a regional long distance route stretching the length of the Cotswold hills between Chipping Campden in the north and Bath Abbey in the south. It covers some 98 miles and, as well as giving some great views from the top of the Cotswolds limestone ridge, visits many delightful villages and small towns along the way. The 47-mile section described here, covers the northern part of the route, between Chipping Campden and Painswick.

The name Cotswold is derived from a man called Cod who set up a farm near Winchcombe some 1500 years ago. This came to be known as Cod's Wold, meaning Cod's 'High Land'. The name is now used to describe a much wider area, but the Cotswold heartland which contains the best of the peace and charm of the area remains the northern section, covered by this walk.

The Cotswold Way came into being in 1970, some 17 years after the Gloucestershire Ramblers' Association suggested a route using existing rights of way. The area is well endowed with footpaths and bridleways, and the route has been skilfully constructed to visit as many prime attractions of the Cotswolds as possible. Sometimes this means it meanders in a slightly frustrating manner, but the route can be modified to pursue a straighter course if desired, and of course the advantage of all these diversions is that it is easier to make a return to the start point.

The attractions on offer are many and varied, and are generally monuments to the more civilised people who have occupied the Cotswolds over the millennia The Neolithic people left behind numerous long barrows, which were used as burial mounds for their important tribal members. Their size and careful construction have ensured that many remain well preserved and prominent today.

The route is also rich in hillforts, the most notable being that at Crickley Hill. Built in high defensive positions with concentric circles of ramparts and ditches, these forts preceded the Roman invasion, which brought some security to the area. The Roman legacy is most obvious around Bath – the important villas at Chedworth and Woodchester are well off the Cotswold Way. The Normans left many fine churches many of which have been modified over the centuries, and they also paved the way for the building of religious institutions such as Hailes Abbey near Winchcombe.

Following the Norman invasion, England was also able to build itself to a position of pre-eminence in the export of woollen cloth. It is estimated that this provided half of England's revenue in the 14th century and the Cotswold's half a million or so sheep in their turn provided at least half of England's wool. For some time this brought great wealth, and the leading wool merchants were able to use the mellow Cotswold stone to build fine houses for their own lifetimes, as well as endowing the 'wool churches' for their after-lives. The more philanthropical also provided for almshouses and market buildings. Chipping Campden and Painswick, at the beginning and end of this walk, are wonderful examples of this legacy. Dog-owners should note that the northern part of the Cotswold Way is still sheep country and only dogs which can be kept under close control will be welcome.

The Cotswolds suffered in the Civil War and its wool industry then went into irreversible decline. For the peasants this meant great hardship, but the advantage for us today is that the northern part of the Cotswolds was preserved in a kind of rural time-warp, being spared the developments of the Industrial Revolution. The area remained undisturbed until it was 'discovered' by William Morris and fellow artistic Victorians, while today the age of the car has opened it up fully, at the same time seriously jeopardising its tranquillity.

The prime season for tourism in the Cotswolds is of course the summer, though the walker following the limestone ridge can rise above the parking problems and crawling traffic which besets the area. With

The ruins of Hailes Abbey, near Winchcombe

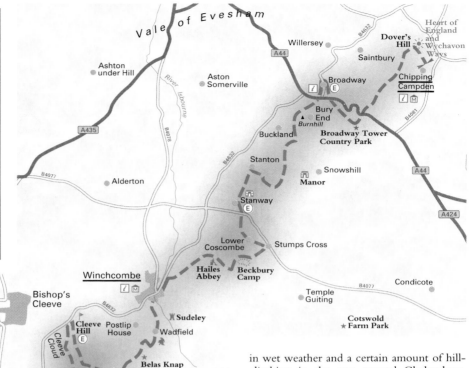

in wet weather and a certain amount of hill-
climbing in the area around Cheltenham.
Fog also besets the area in autumn, and
though the route never rises above 1000ft
(300m) and is always close to towns or
villages, a compass and OS map should be
carried, together with one of the excellent
pocket guides which provide more detail on
points of interest. Signposting is generally
very good. There are occasional 'Cotswold
Way' signs but more usually a white circular
blob is set into the standard yellow or blue
waymarks for footpaths or bridleways.
However, here and there both markers and
signposts are missing, making it important to
follow progress on the OS map.

The south gateway to Stanway House

so much on offer, the best time to walk the
Cotswold Way may be in spring or autumn,
when tourism is less intrusive, many of the
attractions for which there is an entrance fee
are still open to the public, and the beech
woodlands which form an important part of
the route are at their best. There is plenty of
bed-and-breakfast and hotel accommodation
in the towns and villages along the way, but
camp sites are few and far between and any
camping on private land will have to be
negotiated with the landowner.

With so much to see and do, it is
impossible to put a time on how long the
route will take to walk, and careful planning
is necessary to fit in with opening times of
places to visit. Generally, the going is very
easy, though there may be quite a bit of mud

Chipping Campden
Winchcombe

CHIPPING CAMPDEN

BROADWAY

APPROX. 6 MILES/9KM

OS Landranger 151, 150
Start at grid reference SP 155 394
Start point: St James's Church. Car parks signposted in village.

'Chipping Campden' is derived from 'ceping', meaning a market, and 'camp-denu', meaning a valley with enclosures. Its church is a magnificent pile, built on the prosperity of the wool merchant William Grevel in the 15th century. Next to it is the gatehouse to Campden House, built by the 'mercer', or textile dealer, Sir Baptist Hicks in 1615 and burned to a shell by its retreating Royalist garrison in 1645. Sir Baptist also built almshouses for 12 poor people of Chipping Campden, which can be seen in almost original condition on the road leading down from the church via a raised pavement. Beyond the almshouses, Campden High Street is without a doubt very splendid. Look out for Grevel House, built by William Grevel in 1380, the Market Hall, built by Sir Baptist Hicks in 1627, and the 14th-century Woolstaplers' Hall, which houses a museum and information centre.

Past Market Hall, the first Cotswold Way signpost points right up a lane by the side of St Catherine's Church. The route follows Hoo Lane uphill, past a number of affluent Cotswold stone cottages, joining a track which goes straight ahead uphill. This crosses a level field, and emerges on the top of Dover's Hill from where there are fine views, on a clear day, over the Vale of Evesham and the Malvern Hills. The hilltop area is now owned by the National Trust. It was named after Robert Dover, a local 17th-century lawyer who organised a series of famous annual games which continued to be held, on and off, until the mid-19th century. In more recent times they have been revived in a modified version.

Past the car park the route turns left along the road, and then right at the next crossroads, by Weston Park Farm. A short way along on the right, the Kiftsgate Stone is set just inside Weston Wood, marking the meeting point of the Saxon hundred court. The route turns off the road by the side of Campden Woods, following the Mile Drive track in an area that was landscaped in the 19th century by the Earl of Gainsborough. Crossing a road, the route leads past a small hillock surmounted by the Panorama Dial, close by the Fish Inn which is on the A44. This building has an interesting history: it was granted a licence by Royal Charter from Charles II, and then, in the 18th century, was rebuilt as a gazebo.

Crossing the A44, a track leads through woodland, and then across grassy hollows and small valleys towards Broadway Tower, which is straight ahead. This magnificent folly was built in 1799 by the Earl of Coventry, and later let to two Oxford tutors who used it to introduce the delights of the area to such worthies as William Morris and

The Jacobean Market Hall, Chipping Campden, built by a wealthy benefactor

GUIDE BOX

Places to visit
Broadway Tower Country Park. Attractions of the Country Park include Broadway Tower, wildlife walks, a children's farmyard and a restaurant. Open April to end October, daily.

Snowshill Manor (NT), 3 miles south-west of Broadway, off the A44. This house contains Charles Wade's extraordinary collection, which ranges from Samurai armour to bicycles. The gardens, where no chemicals are used, are also worth seeing. Open May to September, Wednesday to Sunday; April and October, Saturdays and Sundays. The hamlet itself is charming, with many fine Cotswold stone buildings, a church by a green and a pub. Teas are served from the village hall in season.

Hailes Abbey (EH and NT), near Winchcombe. The ruins of this Cistercian abbey and place of pilgrimage are set in a quiet location. Museum and shop. Open all year, daily. The 12th-century church opposite is notable for its medieval wall paintings.

Car parking
Principal car parks are at Chipping Campden, Dover's Hill (grid ref. SP 138 396), Broadway Tower Country Park (SP 120 370), Broadway, Snowshill, Hailes Abbey (SP 051 301), Winchcombe.

Public transport
Bus services operate between Chipping Campden, Broadway and Winchcombe.

Accommodation
There are hotels and bed-and-breakfast establishments in Chipping Campden, Broadway and Winchcombe.

Dante Gabriel Rossetti. The tower has now been renovated as part of the Broadway Tower Country Park, and is open to the public. On the first floor there is an exhibition devoted to sheep and wool production, both old and new, while the second floor is devoted to William Morris, the Pre-Raphaelite craftsman, artist and socialist. The tower stands some 55ft above Beacon Hill, which at 1024ft (312m) is the second highest point of the Cotswolds.

From the tower, a path leads steeply downhill to the village of Broadway, emerging near the top of the High Street. This is the picture-postcard Cotswold village *par excellence,* its single street lined with impressive buildings that now house antique shops, cafés, pubs and hotels. This unusually wide street was created to accommodate the twin streams that ran down its length, with willows on either side, giving the village the name of Broadway. It became prosperous due to its importance as a staging post for coaches *en route* between Worcester and Oxford. The famous Lygon Arms Hotel was once the much more humble White Horse Inn, until the ex-butler to General Lygon bought it, changed its name, used the general's coat of arms to promote it as a coaching inn, and made his fortune. Even when coaches were replaced by the railway, Broadway continued to prosper, having been established by William Morris and his friends as a fashionable artistic retreat.

Ⓔ *To return to Chipping Campden (grid ref. SP 095 375), follow the footpath north to Willersey, and from there on to Saintbury Church. A footpath leads due east to the Dover's Hill car park from where the Cotswold Way can be followed back down to Chipping Campden.*

BROADWAY

WINCHCOMBE

APPROX. 12 MILES/20KM

OS Landranger 150
Start at grid reference SP 095 375.
Start point: Broadway Green. Car parks signposted in the village.

The Cotswold Way continues from Broadway near its oldest house, the Abbot's Grange, which is sited below the green. The route turns off on to a footpath opposite the church. Crossing the lane, the route climbs through the woods of Broadway Coppice, passing along the side of a field and crossing the Worcester/Gloucestershire border to go through a complicated series of gates and stiles. A long, straight track leads on above Burnhill, with views to Broadway Tower.

This leads to a rather messy farmyard where the Cotswold Way signposting may be confusing. The correct route follows a sometimes muddy track that doubles back to the right, before bearing left on a much firmer track by the side of woods and on along the ridge past solitary hilltop farm buildings. A short way on it passes a disused quarry on the left, and then comes to a crossroads, with the Cotswold Way signpost by a cattle grid. Here you may wish to divert to Snowshill, a quaint hamlet with an interesting manor house in the valley. To do so, take the left-hand track by the side of the woods, and then bear left on to a footpath

down through the woods. At a lane turn right, and then left and left again for Snowshill, about a mile distant.

To continue along the Cotswold Way, follow the track straight on along towards Shenberrow Farm, where the hillfort at the top of the hill is sited in what must have been an impregnable position, though little remains of it today. From the farmhouse a track leads downhill through woods, bearing left on to a narrow path to cross an equestrian eventing ground and pass close by Stanton's small reservoir before entering the village. Stanton has splendid Cotswold buildings lining its main street, without the tourist trappings and massed cars which spoil Broadway and Chipping Campden. Most of its buildings were built in the 17th century, and restored to their current condition by architectural enthusiast Sir Philip Stott in the early 20th century. For the walker it also boasts a pub at the eastern end.

From Stanton the route crosses fields, before entering the fine parkland of Stanway House. It joins a lane by a most unusual, thatched cricket pavilion standing on staddle stones. The fine stately home is passed immediately on the left (occasionally open to the public during the summer season). It was built by Sir Paul Tracey in the early 17th century, and was also the home of Dr Robert Dover, grandson of the Robert Dover who organised the games at Chipping Campden. Notable is its magnificent south gateway in the style of Inigo Jones, just past the much restored 12th-century church. Beyond the south gateway the route bears left on a footpath past estate cottages, going through a wooden gate with a beautifully carved duck's head.

Ⓔ *For a return to Broadway, walk east from Stanway and take the bridleway (grid ref. SP 068 320) through Lidcombe Wood towards Snowshill. From there either follow the road due north to Broadway, or take the footpath via Great Brockhampton Farm and Buckland Wood towards Bury End.*

The path leads on across the B4077, with

the Cotswold Way taking an indirect route to Hailes Abbey in order to visit Beckbury Camp. At the small hamlet of Wood Stanway it bears left up the hillside above sheep pens, crossing fields, towards the imposing farmhouse at Lower Coscombe (where the signposting leaves something to be desired). The route crosses a large ladder-stile, and then follows the contours of the hillside to the road junction at Stumps Cross. However, it is easy to make the mistake of wandering on to the old route, which joins the farmhouse drive and leaves the walker with a dangerous stretch of road to negotiate, leading up to Stumps Cross. It is probably safest to cross to the other side.

From here the route leads via a track to the imposing hillfort of Beckbury Camp, where again the signposting is confusing. The walker should go steeply down the hill by the stone pillar, and follow the path across level ground beneath the fort's ramparts, joining a track and turning downhill towards Hailes Abbey. This is a good spot, by the church, to stop and rest awhile, before the route turns left across a field giving fine views of the abbey ruins, crossing fields towards Winchcombe along the Pilgrims' Way. A track leads down to join Puck Pit Lane, entering Winchcombe by the A46. An optional footpath route which avoids the main road follows the east side of the River Isbourne to enter by Castle Street.

SUDELEY CASTLE

Sudeley Castle has royal connections going back to the 10th century. Once the property of Ethelred the Unready, it remained in the hands of the Crown during the early Tudor Age. Granted to court favourites, Sudeley became the palace of Queen Catherine Parr, who died there and is buried in the chapel, St Mary's Church. Henry VIII, Anne Boleyn, Lady Jane Grey and Elizabeth I stayed in the castle, which for Charles I and Prince Rupert became their headquarters in the west during the Civil War, resulting in its effective destruction by the Commonwealth. The castle remained a ruin for some 200 years, before being rebuilt and brought back to life in the 19th century. Open April to end October, daily.

Winchcombe
Painswick

WINCHCOMBE

THE DEVIL'S CHIMNEY

APPROX. 16 MILES/26KM

OS Landranger 163
Start at grid reference SP 025 283
Start point: Winchcombe Town Hall. Car parking signposted in town.

Winchcombe has grown from the Saxon settlement of 'Wincel Cumb'. Much of its early importance was due to its prosperous abbey, which played host to pilgrims paying homage to the shrine of St Kenelm, a young Saxon king murdered in mysterious circumstances in the 9th century. The abbey was dissolved in 1539, and today nothing of it remains, though its stone was used for building in the town.

Winchcombe missed the wool boom which had made other parts of the Cotswolds wealthy and, once it had lost its abbey, it became a poor town. Nevertheless, there are many fine buildings in Winchcombe, notably the Jacobean King's School House, attributed to Inigo Jones. St Peter's Church, opposite, was built in the 15th century and is notable for marks of shot in its walls dating from the Civil War, an organ case attributed to Grinling Gibbons, a magnificent collection of gargoyles, and a weathercock which is reckoned to be one of the finest in Britain.

The Cotswold Way leads down Vineyard Street, bearing off across fields by the west entrance to Sudeley Castle, which is well

worth a diversion. From here it heads uphill, passing close by the imposing farmhouse at Wadfield and coming to Humblebee Cottages, with fine views over Sudeley Castle behind. The Wadfield Roman Villa, on a small site to the right here, has remains of walls and a mosaic pavement. The route joins the road, and then follows a track signposted towards Belas Knap, a massive and very well preserved Neolithic long barrow burial chamber of the Severn-Cotswold type.

From Belas Knap paths and trackways head across to Cleeve Common, passing beneath overhead power lines by Wontley Farm. These power lines seem to dominate this part of the route, as it goes in a great circle via Cleeve Hill. It crosses the only remaining moorland of the Cotswolds, giving some idea of what the terrain might have been like in days before the enclosures. For a time the landscape is quite wild, but after a steep climb this illusion is shattered by finding a golf course at the top of the hill.

Ⓔ *From here (grid ref. SO 987 269), the B4632 leads directly back to Winchcombe, less than 3 miles distant. Alternatively, it is possible to follow a bridleway towards Postlip House, with a footpath heading on by the River Isbourne into Winchcombe.*

The golf course also poses some route-finding problems as the Cotswold Way dodges the bunkers, following the west side of the ridge with fine views of Cheltenham sprawled on the plain below. Cleeve Hill Camp is well worth looking out for here, as is Cleeve Cloud, a large rock formation on

The mellow Cotswold stone of Winchcombe

GUIDE BOX

Places to visit
Cotswold Farm Park, Temple Guiting, near Winchcombe, has an extensive collection of rare breed farm animals, including descendants of the original Cotswold sheep. Open Easter to end September, daily.

Painswick Rococo Garden, Painswick House, in Painswick, is a unique rococo garden which is the only complete survivor of the short period in the 18th century when gardens in this style were fashionable. The garden was abandoned in 1960 and planted as a wood. Restoration commenced in 1984 and is still under way. Open February to mid-December.

Car parking
Principal car parks are at Winchcombe, Cleeve Hill (grid ref. SO 989 270), Leckhampton Hill (SO 951 189), Crickley Hill (SO 929 163), Barrow Wake (SO 931 153), Cooper's Hill (SO 893 146) and Painswick.

Public transport
The nearest British Rail station is Cheltenham. Bus services operate to Winchcombe, Cheltenham and Painswick.

Accommodation
There is a youth hostel at Cleeve Hill. Cheltenham and Painswick have a choice of hotels and bed-and-breakfast establishments.

the hillside. Beyond the prominent radio masts the route heads along the hillside, joining a lane and then heading across fields towards Colgate Farm, close by the overhead power lines which sing oddly as the Way passes under them once again. A path leads downhill by the side of Dowdeswell Wood, which has a pleasant mixture of trees being grown for commercial purposes. At the bottom of the hill the path leads out by the side of the Dowdeswell reservoir, built by the Victorians in suitable heavy style.

The reservoir could be a pleasant place to stop, but is spoilt by the proximity of the A40, which must be crossed near the pub here. A track leads uphill over what was once a part of the Great Western Railway, heading through Lineover Wood, the 'lime tree hill'. This is pleasant undulating walking through quiet woodland, a foretaste of the extensive beech woods to come nearer Painswick. Past a solitary farmhouse in a fine position, and an improbable bed-and-breakfast sign in the middle of nowhere, a narrow track leads diagonally up to the top of the steep hill, from where there are magnificent views over Dowdeswell Reservoir and towards Cheltenham. Passing through a narrow belt of trees, the route crosses a field to reach the busy A436 where there is an optional bridleway route by the side of Chatcombe Wood. This is approximately twice as far as walking along the road, but if one has the time is much to be preferred.

Both routes lead to the Seven Springs roundabout, named after the springs which are the source of the River Churn, a short

way down the A436. The Cotswold Way turns off the main road here, following a lane northwards to join a ridgeway footpath along the top of Hartley Hill, above Charlton Kings' Common. From here there are immense views over Cheltenham, as the route leads to the highest point at Leckhampton Hill Fort where there is a trig. point to confirm your position. From here it is worth walking to the cliff-edge to see the Devil's Chimney, an impressive rock tower left by the quarry workings which eventually ceased here in 1925.

THE DEVIL'S CHIMNEY

PAINSWICK

APPROX. 13 MILES/21KM

OS Landranger 163, 162
Start at grid reference SO 948 184
Start point: Trig. point near Devil's Chimney, on top of Leckhampton Hill. There is a car park off the lane to the south of the hilltop.

From the Devil's Chimney the Cotswold Way heads southwards, crossing a lane where there is a convenient small car park for Leckhampton Hill, and following a bridleway downhill towards Ullenwood, which is now used as a training centre for young disabled people. The route crosses the B4070, following a lane past the Nissen huts of an old military camp and passing Shurdington Long Barrow to the left. At the top of Shurdington Hill the route turns on to a footpath, following the ridge with fine views over unspoilt ground to the west, looking as far as the mountains of South Wales.

The path soon enters Short Wood where there are wonderful mature beech trees on either side, keeping to the side of the ridge before emerging on open ground at Crickley Hill. This is a famous hillfort site in a magnificent position, though it has to some extent been spoilt by quarrying on one side. Founded in the Neolithic period 4000 – 3000BC, it became an Iron Age camp around 600BC, suffering destruction at the hands of enemy tribes several times.

From the summit of Crickley Hill the route heads downhill, entering more beech woods and emerging at the road by the Air Balloon roundabout. This is the busy intersection of the A46, A436 and A417 and can be something of a nightmare for the walker, with the route continuing on pavement up by the side of the A46 past the Air Balloon public house. Thankfully it soon bears off on a hillside path below Barrow Wake, with the fine views over to Crickley Hill marred by the din of traffic roaring up the hill. The route follows the contours just below the hilltop, entering more beech woods. A 75yd diversion leads to the top of a small hillock known as The Peak, giving a magnificent viewpoint to the west. Unfortunately the expansive plain below is made ugly by modern development, and on

a still day the traffic noise is still pervasive, despite the remoteness of the situation.

From The Peak the route leads downhill through beech woods to Birdlip Hill, crossing the road and entering Witcombe Wood, from where there is a long stretch of woodland walking. The woods here are very fine in spring and autumn, but the wide track can be muddy. The mass of tracks is also confusing, but there are Cotswold Way waymarks, painted on trees with the customary white blob at all intersections. With pheasants much in evidence, the route passes a sadly overgrown entrance gate to Witcombe Park, and further on a track to the right leads downhill to the Roman Witcombe Villa.

The route leaves the Witcombe estate by a small cottage in a fine hillside position, passing another cottage named The Haven, in an equally fine position, which has the double bonus of acting as an informal café for passing walkers and being staffed by a Cotswolds Warden who helps administer the route. A lane continues through the hamlet of Witcombe and then past the bottom of Cooper's Hill. This is where the famous annual cheese-rolling event takes place, in which cheeses have to be chased down the near vertical slope. The hillside is suffering from erosion and has now been fenced off, and the footpath is a diverted route which bears left up through woods to reach the top of Cooper's Hill. Here the tall maypole is surmounted by a creaky weathercock. Its wide-ranging views make this an excellent place to stop.

Ⓔ *From Cooper's Hill (grid ref. SO 893 147) footpaths lead via the Roman Villa to Witcombe Park, from where footpaths lead on to Cold Slad by Crickley Hill.*

The main route enters Brockworth Wood, where there are information boards and nature trails, going on to Buckholt Wood to cross the A46 to Prinknash Park and Abbey. The park is open to the public, and the Benedictine monks are famous for their pottery and their modern abbey. From here the route passes the back of a modern Cotswold mansion, joining a bridleway track across an extensive golf course all the way to the outskirts of Painswick. The walker

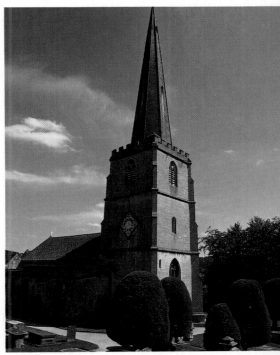

Painswick Church, famous for its yews

should divert to the highest point of Painswick Beacon, off to the right. From the trig. point there are magnificent views over the surrounding countryside, and one can also see the extensive ramparts and ditches of the ancient hillfort, which has now been commandeered by golfers.

Coming to a lane, the route follows a footpath along the hillside, passing Catsbrain Quarry and rejoining a track across the golf course behind the club house. It continues by a stone wall, reaching the far end of the golf course where the official route follows the road into Painswick. However, a path through the woods ahead is signposted as being available to 'Walkers Only' and leads directly to the front gate lodge of Painswick House, where the Rococo Garden is well worth visiting and scarcely off the route into Painswick. Painswick itself is a fitting end to this part of the Cotswold Way, having been largely built on the profits of the wool trade. Its fine buildings are dominated by St Mary's Church. Dating from the 14th century, it has a 174ft tower and spire, and is surrounded by over 100 carefully clipped yew trees.

COTSWOLD STONE

The houses and churches of the Cotswolds are built of limestone, or oolite, meaning the egg stone. The newer layers of Great Oolite lie over the older Inferior Oolite, and have been quarried over the years to provide an easily cut building stone which hardens on exposure to the elements. Thin layers of oolite were split by the frost to provide the Cotswold slates used for roofing, with the heaviest 'tilestones' at the bottom requiring massive oak beams to support their weight. Nowadays Cotswold stone continues to be used for building, but the original Cotswold tilestones are virtually unobtainable and modern copies are often used instead.

SOUTH
&
SOUTH EAST
ENGLAND

Sussex downland, seen from Windover Hill

Isle of Wight Coastal Footpath

RYDE TO RYDE
68 MILES/109KM

Detailed guides
The Coastal Footpath is described in four leaflets, each with sketch map and directions for walking the route in a clockwise direction. Available from the Isle of Wight Tourist Board or the County Surveyor, County Hall, Newport, Isle of Wight PO30 1UD.

Maps
OS Landranger 196

Links
By using the ferry from Yarmouth to Lymington, a link can be made with the Solent Way and the Bournemouth Coast Path at Milford on Sea. The Solent Way can also be picked up from the Ryde-to-Portsmouth ferry.
On the island itself, there are eight trails that link with the coastal footpath. The Vectis Trail is another round-the-island walk.

'ENGLAND in Miniature', they call the Isle of Wight – and not without reason; the variety of terrain and panorama offered by this coastal footpath must surely make it one of the most varied and enjoyable long distance paths in the country. The great thing about a coastal footpath on any island is that it is circular – walk for long enough and you are bound to end up back at the starting point. 'Long enough', in this case, can be anything from three days to a week, depending on how fast you want to go and how lightly you are travelling.

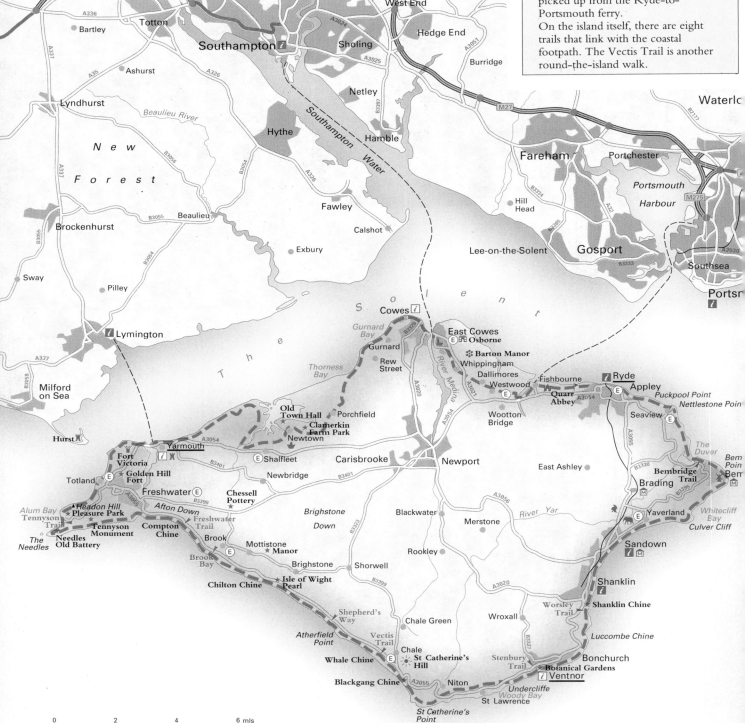

he path is detailed here in an anti-clockwise direction. There are advantages in walking it either way, but the anti-clockwise approach does seem to offer more appreciation of the scenery. The logical starting points for anyone arriving from the mainland are the ferryport towns of Cowes, Ryde and maybe Yarmouth. Both the Ryde and Cowes ferries are easily accessible from the motorway network – the Portsmouth ferry is at the bottom of the M275, while the Southampton ferry can be easily reached from the M271. Both are also well connected to public transport, particularly the Portsmouth-Ryde ferryport, which is right beside Portsmouth Harbour railway station, making this an ideal walk for those not wishing to use a car.

Ryde has been chosen as the start point because this disposes of the less scenic parts of the route on the first day. The going is generally fairly easy, nothing too steep to climb or descend, and plenty of fine open cliff-walks with excellent views in all directions. Due to the island's fame as a Mecca of the British yachting fraternity, and its general appeal as a summer holiday location, a fair amount of walking towards the beginning and end of the route will be on tarmac, and in some quite densely populated areas. However, the exhilarating hikes along the cliff-tops in the south do more than make up for this.

One of the most unique aspects of this particular long distance path is the large number of options available at so many places for overnight stops and for breaking out from or re-entering the main route. Wight is blessed with a regular and efficient bus service and, because the island is so small, there is only minimal travelling time between locations. The walk passes through or close to a dozen or so major towns, all offering accommodation and links to public transport. It is quite feasible to break the route down into day-long stages, returning to the comforts of a hotel each night. In case of injury or bad weather, it is simple and speedy to escape from the path and return to the ferryports from anywhere on the island. There are few routes in the UK offering such versatility to the walker.

The route almost forces the walker to take an interest in the geological structure and history of the island. The multi-coloured sands of Alum Bay, the dinosaur-rich shales of Chilton Chine, the breathtaking chalk faces of the Needles and cliffs under Tennyson Down – so huge and impressive but slowly and surely being destroyed by the sea – the walk passes through it all. If history is of interest, then this 68-mile stroll provides everything from 1500BC, through Henry

VIII to the Industrial Revolution.

It is hard also not to wax lyrical about the flora and fauna of the Isle. For the serious ornithologist the Newtown estuary on the north-west shore will be paradise, being home to over 170 different species of bird (and 300 plant species), while the seabirds along the southern cliffs pander to both enthusiast and casual observer alike with their wonderful displays of aerobatics and soarings on the updraughts. The botanist will find much to enthuse over, particularly in the chalky upland soils. Pocket flower and bird books would be useful travelling com-

The multi-coloured cliffs of Alum Bay

panions for this particular ramble.

One last warning, due again to the built-up nature of much of the coastal region, and also to the large inlets and creeks opening on to the Solent, much of the coastal path is not, in fact, anywhere near the coast at all. On the first day the walker will be positively thirsting for a glimpse of the sea! Rest assured, however – all will be put right.

Stag Rocks, Freshwater Bay: the white chalk is in stark contrast to Alum's sandstone

Ryde
Yarmouth

RYDE
EAST COWES
8 MILES/13KM

OS Landranger 196
Start at grid reference SZ 594 929
Start point: The entrance to Ryde Pier, Ryde seafront (also Ryde railway and bus station, and the ferryport). Car parks in St Thomas Street.

The town of Ryde is famous for its Victorian architecture and associations, a theme which continues throughout the island. The walk starts in St Thomas Street, and picks its way through quiet streets to Spencer Road, and thence to the footpath to 'Binstead and Quarr'.

This pleasant footpath descends gradually for about ¹/₂ mile, bordered on both sides by the links of Ryde golf course, and then ascends to reach Binstead Church. The elegant and ordered appearance of this building belies its eventful history; part Norman, part Victorian, and part early 1970s (after an unfortunate fire destroyed much of the old nave roof). The seat in the graveyard is well placed for the first breather of the day.

The path continues westward along a bridleway and Quarr Road. Soon the towers of the new Quarr Abbey come into view.

The route to the new abbey takes the walker through the grounds of the old one; those low-lying walls to the right are all that is left of the original Abbey of Our Lady of The Quarry, founded in 1311 and built in the local Binstead limestone. The new abbey is hidden by trees to the right of the path, but is worth a quick detour. This abbey was built early this century by a Benedictine order of monks, and is constructed of bright red bricks from Belgium. (The old abbey had been dissolved by Henry VIII in 1537.)

The track continues westward and, just when the walker is getting used to the peace and quiet of the countryside, emerges rather unexpectedly by the new Fishbourne Ferry Terminal, with all the hustle, bustle, noise and smells of modern 'civilisation'. Turn left on to the main road here, and then take the path to the right beside the telephone box, which leads to a tree-lined lane and eventually the A3054. Turn right here and descend to Wootton Bridge.

Ⓔ *From this point (grid ref. SZ 548 919), it is a simple matter to catch the bus either back to Ryde, or ahead to East Cowes.*

The next 4 miles are all road, and there would be no shame in hopping on to the next bus straight to Cowes. The official route follows a tortuous path up through a housing estate to the top of the hill at Wootton to join the minor road that passes through Westwood and Dallimores, heading towards Whippingham. Apart from a few views across the Solent there is little to distract walkers from their pace.

Once the main A3021 road is reached, there is a choice. Although busy with traffic, this road has a wide pavement and offers a quick march into East Cowes. Alternatively, take the first left to view the Church of St Mildred at Whippingham. Built in 1860 to the specifications of Prince Albert, it occupies the site of an 11th-century church and is now a popular tourist attraction, even boasting public toilets in the cemetery.

The road from the church continues straight into East Cowes, passing an attractive line of almshouses on the right. Make your way down to the 'Floating Bridge' ferry, resisting the temptation to stop for provisions in East Cowes – the shops and restaurants across the river are much better.

Ⓔ *Being mainly residential, this area is not particularly well served with footpaths that might provide an alternative route back to Ryde. Bus services, however, operate regularly.*

COWES
YARMOUTH
APPROX. 16¹/₂ MILES/26.5KM

OS Landranger 196
Start at grid reference SZ 500 956
Start point: West Cowes 'Floating Bridge' chain car/foot passenger ferry across the River Medina. Parking in town.

Osborne House, dear to Queen Victoria

GUIDE BOX

Places to visit
Quarr Abbey. As this is right on the route it would be a shame not to spend a few moments within its walls. The church is open for viewing and all may attend the services. There is also a small bookshop on site. The monks all seem very willing to chat and pass the time of day.

Osborne House (EH). This fascinating house should not be missed by anyone with any interest in the life and times of Queen Victoria. The entrance fee includes admission to the private state rooms and the grounds, plus the Swiss Cottage Museum, where the children of the Queen occupied their days learning the skills of cooking, housekeeping etc. Open Easter to October, daily.

Barton Manor, close to Osborne House, is also open to the public. Of particular interest are the vineyards and winery. Open May to mid-October, daily, plus April weekends. The entrance fee includes wine-tasting and souvenirs.

Clamerkin Farm Park, near Newtown on the Shalfleet-to-Cowes road is a large show farm estate on the banks of the estuary, with craft shows, 30 acres of land to explore and various animals to meet. Open Easter to October, daily.

Car parking
Public car parks in Ryde (grid ref. SZ 593 929), Cowes (SZ 504 962), Yarmouth (SZ 354 895), Also at Osborne House (SZ 514 945), Shalfleet (SZ 414 895) and between Bouldnor and Yarmouth, on the A3054 (SZ 368 899).

Public transport
Bus services are good and connect Ryde, Cowes, Newport, Shalfleet and Yarmouth.

Accommodation
Ryde, Cowes and Yarmouth have many hotels and guesthouses, although you would be well advised to book ahead in the summer months, particularly if in or around Cowes during Cowes Week. The Isle of Wight Tourist Office has an accommodation listing nearly 200 pages long – contact Quay Store, Town Quay, Newport, Isle of Wight PO30 2EF (tel. 0983 524343). Camping is a little more tricky; there are few open pitches and just a couple of camp sites, one just south of Shalfleet and another by Cowes.

The town of Cowes is steeped in history – from the ferry can be seen the premises within which the J S White Company built and launched their first sea-plane. Close by is the home of the British Hovercraft Corporation, from where the first-ever hovercraft came.

Notwithstanding these technological achievements, Cowes is first and foremost a yachting town, home of the National Sailing Centre, the Royal Yacht Squadron, Cowes Week and the Admiral's Cup. Be warned that in July and early August it will be very busy indeed.

Walking west from the ferry, head for the pedestrian precinct area. Here in summer one finds a curious mix of holidaymakers and serious yachting types, blocks and shackles rubbing shoulders with buckets and spades. Continue through the pedestrian zone until the start of the Esplanade walk. This runs for a good few miles to the city limits, passing in front of the Royal Yacht Squadron HQ and Egypt Point, the most northerly point on the island and site of an anti-submarine boom that during the war stretched right across the Solent to the mainland.

The path eventually leaves the road, and reaches a sailing club with a slipway. Turn uphill here and take the footpath up to the right between black bollards. Be sure to take note of the sign here advising 'Strictly no mining'. Follow the path into Worsley Road and then first right, downhill to Gurnard Bridge.

After the bridge turn immediately right on to a track. For the first time since leaving Ryde, the walker is now on a proper coast path. The low-lying shaley cliffs here are in stark contrast to the splendour of the chalk Needles waiting ahead.

When it reaches the sandy beach in front of the Thorness Bay Holiday Camp, the route turns inland to pass through the camp to the entrance gate. From here the footpath leads across a number of fields to the village of Porchfield. The route is now well inland, avoiding the marshy tributaries of the Newtown River – a nature reserve and famous haunt for birdwatchers. Porchfield to Newtown is another 3 miles of road walk, finishing with a short cut across the fields, via a stile just after Old Vicarage Lane, picking up the route of Newtown's Nature Trail.

Newtown is well worth a few moments' pause, especially for a look at the estuary and quay, where ships of up to 500 tonnes used to dock. The walk continues up the road past the Old Town Hall and along towards Shalfleet, branching left up a small track and over the bridge by Shalfleet Mill and thence to the New Inn at Shalfleet, a hostelry much acclaimed for its excellent seafood.

Above *The estuary at Newtown*

Ⓔ *From Shalfleet (grid ref. SZ 414 893) it is possible to turn back to Cowes along footpaths through Parkhurst Forest, along the road, or to catch the bus either straight ahead to Yarmouth or back to Cowes changing at Newport.*

Turn westwards to pass the Church of St Michael the Archangel. The church tower was constructed just a few years after the Norman conquest and, ironically, was often used as a place of refuge from further French harassment in the following centuries.

Continue to the first footpath signed to the right, around a large field to a small and rickety footbridge over a muddy stream and into some dense woods. The path then joins a wider and well-signposted track – follow signs for Lower Hamstead farm. Pause for a moment while passing Pigeon Coo Farm to hear why it is so named. The track eventually reaches the waterside, back on to the Newtown estuary with all its wonderful birds and plants. This is a particularly popular haunt for yachtsmen, not surprising as it is a very beautiful and idyllic spot.

The route now skirts inland around a large tributary and then turns north-east across some low-lying fields and a long wooden bridge to reach the coast briefly again. The concrete ramp and debris here all date back to the intense activities of World War II – training, defence and D-Day preparations. The track soon turns back inland, joining a

lane which leads to Hamstead Farm, and then proceeding west across a couple of fields. After passing Cliff Cottages, Greenacres and one or two other houses and farms, the route plunges back into some very pleasant forest, home to many red squirrels and a variety of other flora and fauna.

Diversions and route-changes abound here due to the movements of the cliff – if in doubt keep as close to the cliff-side as is safely possible. Occasional views over the Solent keep the walker occupied and the first sign of approaching civilisation is the sight of Yarmouth pier sticking way out into the ocean. The path does at one point reach sea level, and then climbs again past Bouldnor Battery, barely recognisable as anything other than a ruin nowadays.

The path eventually surrenders to tarmac about a mile short of Yarmouth. This last stage could be done by bus, but walking it offers the enjoyable finale along the sea-wall leading straight into the High Street. Yarmouth is one of the prettier towns on the island and has its fair share of history, earning its charter in 1332. The castle by the pier was one of a number commissioned by Henry VIII to keep the French at bay, and is worth a visit. The adjoining hotel was apparently once owned by Admiral Sir Robert Holmes, best remembered now for his naming of the small and unimportant American town of New York.

NEWTOWN VILLAGE AND OLD TOWN HALL (NT)

This ancient borough is well worth an exploration. Now a quiet little backwater, 600 years ago Newtown was a thriving and important community, the capital of the island and sending two members to Parliament for over 200 years, until the 1832 reform Act put a stop to such practices. Originally called 'Francheville', it was ironically sacked by the French in 1337, and then rebuilt as Newtown. While little remains of this former glory, the Old Town Hall is worth a visit, and the street names (Gold Street, Silver Street etc) give some hint of the prosperous past. Old Town Hall open Easter to September, Mondays, Wednesdays, Sundays; July and August also Tuesdays, Thursdays.

45

Yarmouth

Ventnor

YARMOUTH

FRESHWATER

APPROX. 9 MILES/14.5KM

OS Landranger 196
Start at grid reference SZ 354 897
Start point: Yarmouth Pier. There is a large car park at River Road, on the A3054.

From the pier, walk west across the bridge, and then along the sea wall, turning left up into the woods as soon as the wall ends. The path then briefly meets a road before entering Fort Victoria Country Park. The wide and straight wooded trail is actually the site of an old military road. History students may well wish to detour here down to Fort Victoria, built in 1853 and twin sister to Hurst Castle across on the mainland.

Emerging from the park, the route passes through Brambles Chine holiday camp to the beach, and then stays by the waterside all the way to Totland. Cast a glance over your shoulder back at the fort, and across the Solent to Hurst Castle. The scenery is now improving all the time.

Ⓔ *From Totland (grid ref. SZ 323 873) it is possible to cut the corner and short-cut straight to Freshwater Bay, removing some 4 miles from the route. Alternatively, there is a bus route straight back to Yarmouth or ahead to Freshwater.*

At the end of the sea wall the route climbs through Totland, and then breaks out into open heathland as it climbs Headon Hill. Head for the Bronze Age tumulus at the summit, where you should pause to enjoy the views in all directions – this is the highest point so far, and gives a good look at the interior of the island. Walk to the westward end of this sea-pink infested ridge to view The Needles and then descend to the road and the noise and the congestion of the Needles Pleasure Park.

Now a busy tourist location, it is strange to think that this was once an important scientific site. From the cliff-top here, Guglielmo Marconi made his first wireless transmissions.

Beyond the car parks, a wide track leads out to The Needles, the visually dramatic end to the spine of chalk that runs right across the island to Culver Down on the eastern side. Look back at the multi-coloured sands of Alum Bay Cliffs, and the contrast between those pastel shades and the stark white of The Needles up ahead. For the ultimate view, you can pay to enter the Needles Battery, but there are plenty of fine clifftop views to be had without handing over your cash.

From here on the walker can really open out. The path continues along the cliff-tops for the next 15 miles – open, airy walking right at the cliff-edge. This is what coast paths are all about.

As one strides along from The Needles, the 500ft Tennyson Monument seems the obvious next stop. Alfred Lord Tennyson lived in Freshwater for many years, hoping for peace and quiet, but even in those days suffering from his superstar status as Poet Laureate. Pause here to enjoy the views, and then descend to Freshwater for some well-earned refreshment.

Ⓔ *Anyone wishing to return to Yarmouth from Freshwater (grid ref. SZ 347 857), could take one of the footpaths straight across the neck of the peninsula, along the River Yar or up the Freshwater Way, to its west.*

Below *Tennyson Down, above Freshwater Bay*

GUIDE BOX

Places to visit
Golden Hill Fort, on the hill above Totland, is one of the major tourist developments on the island. Originally the site of a Victorian fortress, the location offers excellent views right across the island, and the building now houses a variety of entertainments including art galleries, craft centres, a military museum and a period doll collection. The displays are mainly indoors and it is open all year round, daily.

The Alum Bay Needles Pleasure Park. Although Alum Bay is very touristy, its multi-coloured sands make this place worth a visit, especially if you have any interest in geology. You can make your own 'Alum Sands Souvenir' from the different coloured sands available, and see some interesting glass-blowing demonstrations. Cable-car rides to the beach, boat trips and funfair. Open Easter to end October, daily.

Chessell Pottery. Two miles north of Brook, the home of Chessell porcelain is housed in a large converted stone barn. Open to the public all year round, daily, except Sundays May to September. Every stage of the creation of the porcelain may be observed.

Mottistone Manor (NT). The gardens to this fine manor, 1 mile north of Chilton Chine, are open to the public from April to September, Wednesdays and Bank Holiday Mondays.

Isle of Wight Pearl. An interesting insight into the world of jewellery-making, this craft centre is also just by Chilton Chine, and open all year round. Jewellery can be created to your own design while you watch.

Blackgang Theme Park. Featuring Smugglerland, Frontierland, Dinosaurland and Jungle-land amongst others, the park is set in Victorian gardens which have been public since 1842. There is also an interesting sawmill museum. Open from March to late October, daily, with floodlit evenings from end May to September.

Ventnor Botanical Gardens, Tropical Bird Park and Rare Breeds Park are situated in the Undercliff between St Lawrence and Ventnor. The Botanical Gardens (admission free) is a 22-acre site by the cliff-edge, teeming with plants from South America, Africa and the Antipodes, all growing happily outdoors. The Tropical Bird Park contains over 300 species of brightly coloured ornithological interest, Finally, the Rare Breeds Park has 40 or so species of grazing animals and 100 types of waterfowl and poultry. All three centres can be visited from the footpath, or the 16b Ventnor-to-Niton bus.

Car parking
There are plenty of public car parks on this stretch of the walk, both in the towns and at several other points such as Compton Chine (grid ref. SZ 370 851), Brook Bay (SZ 385 835), Chilton Chine (SZ 409 822), Whale Chine (SZ 470 782) and Blackgang Chine (SZ 490 768).

Public transport
Buses run regularly all along the coastal road.

Accommodation
There is plenty of accommodation in Yarmouth, Freshwater, Niton and Ventnor, but rather less in between, other than the very pleasant Clarendon Hotel in Chale. Camp sites abound along the southern cliffs and there are many spots for an overnight backpacker pitch (although be warned that much of the land is National Trust property), but bed-and-breakfast or hotels will require either a bus-ride or a hike inland.

FRESHWATER

VENTNOR

APPROX. 17½ MILES/28KM

OS Landranger 196
Start at grid reference SZ 347 857
Start point: Freshwater Beach. There are large car parks directly opposite the bay, and also up on Afton Down, just to the east.

This section of the route is virtually uninterrupted clifftop path, wide and very pleasant throughout, with minimal human habitation. The path is clear and simple to follow, and is never more than ¼ mile away from the main coast road which is regularly patrolled by buses.

From Freshwater beach climb the wooden steps to the cliff-top, and pause to look back at The Needles and Tennyson Down. From here to Compton Chine, the path runs very close to the main A3055 road, known as the Military Road because it served purely military purposes for almost 100 years until it was opened to the public in 1933. The cliffs along this most exposed south-westerly section suffer constant erosion from the winter gales, which is why the footpath has in places been pushed inland.

Notice the colour change in the cliffs where the road diverges from the coast. The chalk is replaced by a darker rock, another sedimentary product known as Wealden marl, rich in palaeontological artefacts.

There is now little along this entire stretch to distract the walker from the basic pleasures of walking beside the sea. The only thing to upset the continuity of the coastline is the occasional 'chine', originating from the Saxon 'cinan', meaning yawn or gap. Chines are deep ravines that cut into the cliff-edge, often extending some way inland. Many are completely impassable, and require a lengthy hike inland to skirt round them. Brook Chine is the first of these, necessitating a detour into the village to get past it.

Brook is a hamlet with a history. In the last century it was an important lifeboat station; some 260 lives were saved during the 76 years it was in operation, but now the building lies in ruins.

Ⓔ *From Brook (grid ref. SZ 385 835) it is possible to return to Freshwater by walking inland towards Shalcombe and taking the Tennyson Trail along East Afton Down (a circular walk of about 8 miles).*

Chilton Chine is next, also requiring a detour to the Military Road. Grange Chine offers a choice; either descend within and climb the other side, or walk to the road once again. Grange is the half-way point of this stage, and the pleasant village of Brighstone is just ½ mile inland, offering refreshments and overnight accommodation.

After negotiating Cowleaze Chine and Shepherd's Chine, both requiring detours inland, the walker reaches Atherfield Point, not a popular spot with mariners. This piece of coastline is notoriously bad, with hundreds of ships having met their doom on the reef here. The cottages just inland are for the coastguards, who must have had their work cut out in days of yore.

Take a look over the edge at the lobster and fishing boats pulled some way up the cliff-face; not an easy way to make a living. The next chine to be encountered is Whale Chine, a classic and completely impassable fissure leaving absolutely no option but to head inland to the Military Road once again.

Soon after this is another big one; Walpen Chine. The path goes inland once again, to Chale, nestling under St Catherine's Hill. Head for Chale Church, where smugglers hid their contraband inside the tombs.

Ⓔ *From Chale the bus can be caught either straight back to Freshwater or ahead to Ventnor.*

From Chale Church, with its graveyard full of bodies pulled from the sea, the route proceeds south-east towards the rather more cheerful environs of Blackgang Chine Theme Park. Blackgang got its name from a particularly ruthless gang of smugglers, and is still an impressively deep and dark gash in the cliff-side, even after the years of slumping and erosion that has occurred.

Walk through the Chine car park to the stile, and then climb the steps and path to the top of Gore Cliff. The first views from here of the area down below, known as the Undercliff, are magnificent. This lush fertile area, caused by years of landslip is now a

haven for wildlife – with some very desirable human residences too. There is also a lower-cliff with its own cliff path, but for various reasons the higher route has been chosen as the official long distance footpath route.

While rounding St Catherine's Point, look out to sea at the horrendous tidal race. Even on a flat, calm day this can be a swirling maelstrom, caused by a variety of different tidal flows and currents. The tides of the Solent and surrounding areas are the most complex in the United Kingdom.

Look also inland to the top of St Catherine's Hill, where there appears to be a rocket about to take off. This is known as the 'Salt Pot', and the odd building adjacent is the 'Mustard Pot' or 'Pepper Pot', depending on whom you ask. Both are the remains of medieval lighthouses – the octagonal Pepper Pot dating back to 1320, while the Salt Pot was begun in 1800 but never finished. The up-to-date lighthouse can be seen down on the lower cliff.

The path continues onwards along the cliff-top around the southernmost point of the island, following a well-defined track. After passing the large radio station, the route then descends down Boxers Lane, which eventually reaches the main road at Niton. Crossing this, the path soon re-establishes itself at the top of the upper cliff, offering yet more tantalising views down into the Undercliff.

The path eventually opens out, and descends slightly towards a seat. Here it drops rapidly seawards into St Lawrence, crossing the path of the old railway line, which was closed in the early 1950s.

Descending through St Lawrence, the walker is eventually reunited with the lower cliff path. Passing Woody Bay and Orchard Bay, the path then continues to seaward of the Botanical Gardens and it makes for an interesting diversion to walk amongst llamas and exotic flora.

The coastal path, signposted Steephill Cove, eventually leads into Ventnor, former spa town and now a busy holiday resort.

THE NEEDLES AND THE OLD BATTERY

The Needles are probably the most famous example of sea stacks, where the continual erosive action by the sea on a headland creates first a cave, then a sea arch, and finally the roof of the arch caves in completely, to leave the stack. Whilst stacks are not uncommon around our coastline, it is rare indeed to have so many stacks in succession as with the Needles.

The Old Battery is a Victorian Fort, right on the path, and worth a visit just for the views. Built in 1862, it was opened to the public by the Prince of Wales in 1962, and is certainly the best way to see The Needles if you have the time (and pennies) to spare. A 200ft tunnel takes you through the rock and right to the very outer edge of the mainland, giving superb vistas over The Needles, and also inland towards Lymington and the mouth of the Solent. Other objects of interest include an original gun barrel mounted on a carriage in the parade ground, the laboratory and searchlight positions, all restored to their former glory.

Ventnor

Ryde

VENTNOR

BEMBRIDGE

APPROX. 11 MILES/17.5KM

OS Landranger 196
Start at grid reference SZ 563 773
Start point: Ventnor Pier. Parking is extremely limited on the esplanade, but there is plenty further up the hill.

The walk starts off with an easy mile along the shore to Bonchurch, following the new sea wall, opened in 1988. Above are the Winter Gardens, an attractive sight when in full bloom.

Bonchurch is a small waterside hamlet – a few houses, a church and a pottery. Once past the pottery, take the next path uphill, over a small stream to the church. Bonchurch Old Church is a delightful little building, appearing in *Domesday Book* as 'Bonecerce' – 'Bone' being a contraction of Boniface, an 8th-century monk reputed to have performed missionary work in the area. The architecture is the usual mix of many styles and eras. There is a strong Norman influence, but artefacts include a medieval painting on the north wall. From here the path enters the Landslip, a lush area of dense foliage once again caused by unstable ground slowly but inexorably making its way towards the sea. The route is well maintained throughout this area, with wooden duckboards and steps over the more tricky bits of path. There is not much contact with the sea, however.

After passing through some incredible hydrangea plantations, the path emerges on to a lane by Luccombe Chine. Although this part of the coast has numerous footpaths, the coastal route is well signposted throughout. Luccombe tea gardens make a good resting point before the slow descent into Shanklin and the start of a fairly long stretch of tarmac-pounding.

Past Shanklin Hospital, turn right into Popham Road, and then go through the gardens down to the sea. After a short section along the beach, the main promenade is reached. Here the route takes the road back up past Shanklin Chine Inn to regain the upper ground, and also to bypass all the frenetic tourist activities happening along the seafront strip.

From here it is tarmac all the way to Sandown, although a fairly pleasant stroll throughout with fine views of Sandown Bay and Culver Cliff away in the distance. While both Shanklin and Sandown may appear little more than holiday resorts, there is history and interest to be found in both. The lift to the beach in Shanklin has been in place for over 100 years now (although the present version was built in 1956) and played an important part in the preparations for PLUTO, World War II's famous Pipeline Under the Ocean.

Further along you may well see or hear a train pass by – the last remaining section of Isle of Wight railway line runs close to the path. In its heyday the island had a busy and comprehensive rail service, but now only one line survives, the trains being redundant London Underground stock.

Sandown Zoo is actually on the site of an old fort which is why the walls are so thick. On a rainy day the Geological Museum is worth visiting, but for sunny days the next part of the path offers rather more enjoyment.

Ventnor's sheltered position under St Boniface Down makes it a popular resort

GUIDE BOX

Places to visit
Shanklin Chine. Take a walk through the gorge-like chine, with waterfalls, a huge variety of plants and the usual tea-rooms, gift shops etc. In the evenings the special lighting does look rather good. Entrance fee. Open Easter to end October, daily.

Sandown Geology Museum, Sandown High Street, helps to tie together all that the walker sees on the island circumnavigation. Not surprisingly, much is made of the incredible fossil collection that the island has produced. Open all year, Monday to Saturday.

Bembridge Windmill (NT), is the only windmill to survive on the island, and much of its original wooden machinery can still be seen. Open Easter to beginning November, Sunday to Friday.

Brading Roman Villa is a mile or so inland of Yaverland and was once the site of a large and prosperous Roman farming estate. Many mosaics remain and much of the site is now under cover, with displays of Roman artefacts found on the site. Open April to end September, daily.

The Lilliput Antique Doll Museum, also at Brading, just inland of Yaverland, is one of Britain's finest collections of dolls. There are over 1000 on display, some nearly 4000 years old. Open mid-March to Mid-January, daily.

Car parking
There are plenty of public car parks all along this part of the coast, including Bembridge Down (grid ref. SZ 625 860), Culver Down (SZ 635 855) and the Duver (SZ 637 892).

Public transport
Again, most places on this section of the route are well served by buses. The Isle of Wight Railway runs between Ryde and Shanklin, stopping at Brading, Sandown and Lake.

Accommodation
There is a fair spread of hotels and guesthouses all along this stretch of coast, plus a good number of camping sites. Overnight back-packing pitches are a little more difficult to find, however.

Ⓔ *From the zoo it is simple to catch the bus either back to Ventnor or ahead to Bembridge. Alternatively the Bembridge trail cuts out the stretch around Culver Cliff, to go straight to Bembridge.*

From Sandown pier continue along the esplanade to the very end, the path up Culver Cliff easy to see up ahead. This is the last bit of climbing and decent cliff on the walk, so enjoy it. The path leaves the road to begin the climb up Culver Down at Yaverland, the site of another Wealden marl outcrop, equally rich in dinosaur artefacts. The large obelisk on top of the Down is clearly visible, and the path heads towards it. The name 'Culver' apparently derives from the Saxon 'Culvre', meaning pigeon.

Walk right up to the obelisk, and take a moment to read the inscription. 'Raised by public subscription' to commemorate the Earl of Yarborough, it goes to some length to extol the virtues of the fine naval architect

nd First Commodore of the Royal Yacht Squadron.

From the monument the path leads down towards the large and unsightly caravan site at Whitecliff Bay, with views of Bembridge airfield to the left. Rejoining the cliff-edge, the route continues through another area of serious slumping and the path is continually being re-routed due to landslips. It soon emerges beside the playing fields of Bembridge School, which houses the famous Ruskin Gallery, featuring the works of John Ruskin, 19th-century writer and artist.

From here until Bembridge itself, the path becomes more and more interrupted by civilisation, eventually being swallowed by a large residential area. The occasional signpost keeps one on approximately the correct track, which should eventually lead down past a small golf course to the lifeboat station. If the tide is out, there is also the option of walking along the beach for some way.

From the lifeboat station the path continues along the shore, and then turns inland on a woodland path. Once again in a quiet residential district, the route proceeds along cycleways and metalled footpaths, eventually emerging at Bembridge Point, by the harbour.

———— · ————

BEMBRIDGE

———— · ————

RYDE

———— · ————

APPROX. 6 MILES/9.5KM

———— · ————

OS Landranger 196
Start at grid reference SX 642 877
Start point: The entrance to Bembridge harbour by Bembridge Point, where the road doubles back on itself. Large car parks are situated at Silver Beach and the Point.

Although there is a ferry across the harbour mouth, it is more fun to walk around the harbour and look at the variety of houseboats moored along the waterfront, some very plush, others in considerable decay. Bembridge is in direct contrast to the tourist traps of Shanklin and Sandown passed earlier on; it is definitely more about boats than buckets and spades. The road skirting the harbour is Embankment Road, built in 1878 for a quarter of a million pounds, a princely sum in those days.

After crossing the (second) River Yar turn right into Latimer road and make your way through the buildings of St Helen's Tide Mill to the Old Mill Dam Wall. The walk across the dam gives good views back across the harbour and of the old mill workings.

The dam takes the walker to The Duver, once a golf course, now a National Trust property designated a Site of Special Scientific Interest because of its population of 250 or so different and sometimes rare wild plants. Walk straight across here towards the red-roofed building.

The official path does not connect with the shore, but a short detour to the site of St Helen's Old Church is worthwhile. Now only the tower remains, built in the reign of Henry III (1216-72). The church began its

Whitecliff Bay as seen from Culver Down

seawards disintegration in about 1550 and was eventually bricked up in 1703 and painted white for use as a seamark. Legend has it that the nautical phrase 'holystoning the decks' originated from sailors using the rocks from this church to scour their decks.

Heading back inland from the church, the route proceeds north-west over a couple of fields to a road, and then turns left into the drive of the Priory Hotel. It soon forks left again along the edge of a wood, to a sharp right-hand corner and a track leading right down to the sea. Turning left by the public toilets, the track leads into the attractive little village of Seaview. Once another thriving Victorian holiday town, Seaview used to have a 1000ft pier and receive regular shipping from Portsmouth.

————————————————

Ⓔ *From the High Street it is possible to catch a direct bus either back to Bembridge or ahead to Ryde.*

————————————————

At Nettlestone Point the sea wall can be reached from the yacht club, and from here on it is sea wall all the way into Ryde; the ¹/₂ mile-long pier can even be seen away in the distance. The best views now are across the Solent towards busy Portsmouth and the granite forts out in the middle of Spithead.

There are four of these forts in all, built on Palmerston's orders in the 1860s when we really were not friends with the French. They were built so well that they are now pretty much indestructible and no-one knows quite what to do with them. A property speculator has recently renovated one as a 'desirable residence'.

The last half-hour of the walk passes to seaward of the pleasant gardens of Puckpool Park and Appley Park. Appley House can just be seen through the trees, as can St Cecilia's Abbey, home of the Benedictine Order of Ryde Sisters.

After passing the large boating lake (watch out for the 'Dotto Train', which runs up and down this section of the esplanade), it is roadside all the way to the pier from which the walk started. You have now completed the 68-mile coast path of the Isle of Wight – Ryde Pier makes a very prominent and suitable final destination.

————————————————

Ⓔ *For a return to Bembridge, take the train or bus from Ryde to Brading, from where the Bembridge Trail is a 2¹/₂ mile walk across the Yar estuary to Bembridge.*

————————————————

BEMBRIDGE MARITIME MUSEUM

After much close involvement with the coastline of this island, which has such an important maritime history, a visit to this splendid and historical collection of discoveries from the depths certainly does not go amiss.

The museum houses a large collection of marine artefacts and photographs, ranging from pirate gold to logs and ships' bells retrieved from wrecks throughout the centuries. Everything has been salvaged by a professional diver who specialises in the very rich pickings around the island's shores. A visit to this place really does bring home how much the history of the island is connected to the sea, and what it must have been like in years gone by. Open March to end October, daily.

Wayfarer's Walk

EMSWORTH TO INKPEN BEACON
70 MILES/113KM

THE Wayfarer's Walk is Hampshire's principal long distance footpath, stretching from south to north across the country. In the south it starts close by the West Sussex border, at the harbourside town of Emsworth; while in the north it finishes just over the Berkshire border at Inkpen Hill, popularly known as Inkpen Beacon. The route has been skilfully designed so that it shows off the best that rural Hampshire has to offer, leading through quiet farmland on little-used footpaths and bridleways, passing through occasional villages, and generally avoiding long stretches of road or too much modern civilisation.

For the walker who might overlook Hampshire, preferring the more obvious delights of the Lake District or Cornwall's coastal footpath, the Wayfarer's Walk is a walk of surprises, and very pleasant it is too. Away from the towns and villages with their customary dog-walkers, it is possible to cover several miles at a time without seeing another soul.

The walk is generally easy, with the route covering mainly flat country for most of its distance until it suddenly heads steeply up towards Watership Down and a fine high-level finish along the chalk downs that lead towards Inkpen Beacon – and from where the views are as splendid as anywhere in the country. At this northern end the path is mostly on grass and chalk, which provides a good walking surface, but further south one can encounter a lot of mud and undergrowth, and in wet weather the going could be quite heavy and waterproof footwear would be advisable.

This begs the question, when is the Wayfarer's Walk best attempted? Passing through so much heavily cultivated farmland, there seems little doubt that this is a walk for spring or summer when the crops look at their best and the going is firm underfoot. At other times of the year there may well be stretches of ploughed fields and heavy mud, though some parts of the route, such as the Meon Valley and Abbotstone Down can look their most attractive in their autumn colours.

There is no particular reason to prefer starting this walk from its southern or its northern end. The excellent official guide to the Wayfarer's Walk starts from the north. This way most of the high ground is covered first, and the walker is heading into the sun. The views over the sea from the top of Ports Down come as a pleasant surprise near the end of the walk, but this enjoyment is slightly diminished by a long fiddly section by the side of the M27 towards Langstone, before it finishes with a very pleasant 2 miles along the side of Chichester Harbour and into Emsworth. By contrast, finishing the walk at Inkpen Beacon means ending literally on a high, with the views and the countryside getting better and better over the last 12 miles. The finish point by Combe Gibbet is a wonderful place to stop and meditate on

the achievement of a 70-mile walk. Here the Wayfarer's Walk is described travelling in a south-to-north direction.

Connections at each end may be a consideration. If you are relying on public transport, Emsworth's main line railway station is close to the start of the walk and has frequent fast services to London. Inkpen Beacon is much less well served. The nearest station is around 4 miles distant by road and footpath at Kintbury, where there is an unmanned station with direct connections to Reading and London.

Despite the fact that the walk passes through or close by several villages, accommodation is not so obviously available as on some of the more popular long distance footpaths. When it is time to finish the day's walking, the next hotel or bed-and-breakfast may be a long way on, and anyone contemplating this walk would be well advised to obtain full accommodation lists from the relevant Tourist Information Centre and plan the walk accordingly. There are no official camp sites actually on the route, though there are numerous possible sites on farmland if the permission of the owner can be obtained.

Most of the route is easily followed. The general direction is indicated on the relevant

Portsdown Hill, near Cosham

Detailed guides
Along and Around the Wayfarers Walk, the excellent official guide, is available from Hampshire County Council Recreation Department, Tower Street, Winchester, Hampshire. The 96-page paperback gives a full route guide. It also details six circular walks off the Wayfarer's route. It may also be ordered through bookshops.

Maps
OS Landranger 174, 185, 196, 197

Links
At Inkpen Beacon the Wayfarer's Walk connects with the Test Way, a 44-mile walk that ends at Southampton. At various points along the route it also connects with the Sussex Border Path, the Solent Way, the South Downs Way extension to Winchester, the Inkpen Way and King Alfred's Way.

The old fulling mill at Alresford: it straddles the River Alre, whose waters were once put to use to harden cloth

Approaching the end of a wintry walk, near Inkpen Beacon

OS maps, and the route itself is waymarked with a WW symbol, sometimes with an accompanying arrow, and occasionally by a full signpost showing the distance to or from Emsworth or Inkpen Beacon. Only on the early part of the route, going west from Langstone, are the waymarks in short supply, but elsewhere they may be faded beyond recognition or missing altogether, depending on when they were last checked by the local authority. This makes the official guide a vital back-up to finding your way along the Wayfarer's Walk. All you then have to do is go and enjoy it. For those feeling energetic, the route could be covered in three days of fairly intense walking. It would be considerably more relaxing, however, to take four or five days to complete the walk.

Emsworth

Kilmeston

OS Landranger 197, 196
Start at grid reference SU 755 055
Start point: The Quay, Emsworth, off the A259, about ¹/₂ mile south of the railway station. Ample car parking available near by.

Emsworth is a small and rather charming town on the shores of Chichester Harbour, boasting an old quay and a nearby marina. It came of age in the Middle Ages, rapidly overtaking nearby Warblington and becoming an important centre for corn milling in the early 18th century. The Wayfarer's Walk starts from the Quay (close by the renowned restaurant, 36 On The Quay), near the start/finish of both the Solent Way, which follows the same route west for some distance, and the Sussex Border path, which heads north on its 150-mile circuit of the Sussex border.

From the Quay the way follows the edge of the old mill pond, passing moored boats and the marina over to the left and soon coming to the Emsworth Slipper Sailing Club which is housed in one of the town's old tidal mills. Just past here, look out for the bollard with the commemoration plaque to Lord Mountbatten, a past Commodore of the club. The path goes by the front of some harbourside houses, and there are fine views over the mudflats and sandbanks of the harbour as the route heads towards Hayling Island in the distance. Turning inland, it passes through woodland before heading towards the tower of Warblington Castle, all that remains of a mighty 16th-century building.

The route crosses a stream, heading for St Thomas à Becket's Church at Warblington. It is worth taking time to stroll through the ancient graveyard here. It boasts a yew which is thought to be 600 years old, and has a grave-watcher's flint hut in the corner, used at a time when corpses were stolen for medical students. From here the route crosses the modern graveyard, rejoining the shores of Langstone Harbour where the ominous black turret of the 18th-century mill built out over the water comes into view. Beyond it is the Royal Oak pub.

Past the Royal Oak the route goes straight ahead to cross the busy A3023 Hayling Island-to-Havant road, crossing over the quiet grassland of South Moor near the huge IBM building, and passing close by IBM's cinder track and endurance course. Heading towards the sewage works ahead, the Wayfarer's Walk here separates from the Solent Way, which continues for another

Langstone Harbour

GUIDE BOX

Places to visit
Denmead Pottery and Glassworks, Forest Row, Denmead, is located on a 20-acre estate. Visitors have the opportunity of seeing every part of the production process from mould-making to kiln-firing and unloading. There are also extensive landscaped grounds, farm and other animals, forest walks, a shop and a pub.

Old Winchester Hill Fort, approximately 3 miles from Droxford, is an Iron Age settlement on high ground with rings of protective ditches and banks. The area is a sanctuary for wildlife and flowers, administered by English Nature.

Car parking
Principal parking areas on this section are at Emsworth (grid ref. SU 755 055), in Denmead (street parking, SU 658 122), and in Kilmeston (SU 590 258, parking on village roads).

Public transport
British Rail at Emsworth and Cosham. The Mid Hants Steam Railway at Alresford connects with British Rail at Alton. Bus services do operate through most of the villages on the route, but somewhat infrequently.

Accommodation
Bed-and-breakfast accommodation is available in Emsworth, Denmead, Droxford and Kilmeston.

60-odd miles along the coast towards Milford on Sea. The signposting for both walks is poor here, and some care with the OS map is needed to find the way as it heads inland and over the A27 by the footbridge (passing over a surprising area of green fields close by the railway) and crosses the old railway bridge into Bedhampton. Now it is no more than a suburb of Portsmouth, but in its day Bedhampton was a village in its own right, which John Keats visited in sad circumstances. A plaque at Lower Mill House records 'In this house in 1819 John Keats finished his poem "The Eve of St Agnes" and here in 1820 he spent his last night in England', while *en route* for Italy where he died.

From Bedhampton the route crosses the A3(M) on the B2177, passing thoughtful signs provided by the Samaritans on each side of the bridge. Past a fine Strawberry Hill gothick house on the far side, it continues due west along the top of Portsdown Hill, a chalk ridge which is high above the coastal plain, though you are not aware of any undue uphill walking. This ridge stretches for 6 miles from Bedhampton to Fareham, and on a clear day there are fine views past Portsmouth to the Solent and the Isle of Wight beyond.

After a long but not unpleasant road section, the route follows a footpath round the back of the redbrick Fort Purbrook, sunk low into the hilltop, with a dry moat and keep which is preserved today. This was one of six hilltop forts built to defend Portsmouth from the French in the late 19th century, all part of a massive, unused defensive system.

Ⓔ *For a return to Emsworth from Fort Purbrook either retrace your steps, or continue westwards along the road to Fort Widley (grid ref. SU 663 066), and then turn back to walk down the hill, following the A3 southwards to Cosham railway station, just over a mile distant. From here there are regular services to Emsworth.*

Past Fort Purbrook, the route continues west beside the golf course before turning north on to a signposted footpath. Following the back gardens of a terrace of houses downhill, the path leads out across fields to a quiet country road at Purbrook Heath. Here it once again heads west for ¹/₂ mile or so, before turning north on to a track which leads into woodland on the corner where the road bends left.

These woods are one of the pitiful remains of the Forest of Bere which once stretched from Southampton to the Sussex border. Under the Enclosure of the Forest Act 1810 the trees were felled and the land was sold and turned to agricultural and other use. The route emerges at the road by Sheepwash Farm, leading by road and footpath past Closewood Farm and Glenfield Farm to the outskirts of Denmead, a modern village which has grown from a collection of scattered farms over the last 100 years. Here a Wayfarer's Walk signpost points the way back to Emsworth for those bound north to south. The White Hart is on the green.

DENMEAD

KILMESTON

APPROX. 14 MILES/23KM

OS Landranger 196, 185
Start at grid reference SU 658 122
Start point: The village green of Denmead. Parking in the village.

The most urban section of the Wayfarer's Walk follows, as it makes its way through Denmead's modern housing estates to the cemetery. Here it once again enters peaceful countryside, following a footpath along the side of a field across Anthill Common to Rookwood Farm. Following the route onwards for another couple of miles, footpaths lead to the hangers, or wooded hillsides, above Hambledon, a charming Hampshire village nestling in the valley.

Hambledon is an excellent place to stop and rest awhile (with a choice of three pubs). It has a famous history as a cricketing village and just to the north is Hambledon Vineyard, whose dry, white wines are among the most successful of English vintages. The vineyard is no longer open to the public, but its wines are on sale in the village. At the bottom a lane leads down past some fine Georgian houses to the road.

Ⓔ *From Hambledon (grid ref. SU 645 149), a 4-mile return may be made to Denmead by taking a footpath eastwards to Denmead Mill. From here a lane leads south back to Denmead.*

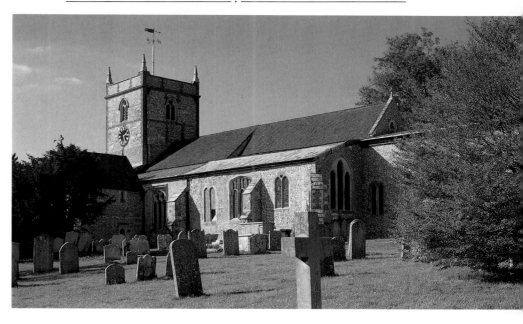

Hambledon's large parish church

To continue the main walk, walk up towards the church, which is of 11th-century Saxon origin, and then follow the footpath across fields to the B2150 Droxford road, with fine views back to the church. Cross the road by modern houses, and then follow the woodland path uphill and across a field, crossing a minor road near East Hoe Manor, from where there are distant views to the sea.

The route enters woodland, joining OS map 185 as it approaches the village of Soberton. Here the White Lion pub is in an attractive setting on the corner of the village green, while on the far side of the green the route passes St Peter's Church, whose tower has some unusual carvings featuring a man's head with a key and a woman's head with a pail. The Walk crosses a disused railway line, once part of the Meon Valley Line, built between Alton and Fareham in 1903 and finally closed with so many others in the 1960s. The route then turns right on to a footpath across fields, following the course of the River Meon in a very pleasant setting, passing a horse chestnut copse with beech trees on the hillside to the right and water meadows to the left, before entering the village of Droxford via a narrow footbridge.

This village, with its attractive Georgian houses is where Izaak Walton, of *Compleat Angler* fame, spent much of his later life. Of the Meon Valley he wrote that it 'exceeds all England for swift, shallow, clear, pleasant brooks and store of trout'. The route continues west, passing through wooded countryside with larch, hazel, beech and old oak trees, before turning north via Steynes Farm and St Clair's Farm. Here it passes through a large clearing amid Norway spruce and Canadian pines, passing the strangely named Betty Munday's Bottom. Though there is nothing to see, the name is from the folklore story of a local lady who got up to no good, luring passing travellers to her house before murdering them and throwing their bodies down her well.

Beyond here a route skirts a tennis court at the end of a track from Preshaw, carrying on towards Lomer Farm with a view across to the site of Lomer, a medieval village which died out and disappeared due to bad harvests and plague in the late 14th century. Heading west once again along the road, the route passes Wind Farm before crossing the Winchester-bound extension of the South Downs Way, at a point where there are fine views down the hillside and over the low-lying land ahead towards New Alresford. Dropping down over Kilmeston Down, the Way leads to the attractive hamlet of Kilmeston with its imposing manor, pretty church, and one of the few obvious bed-and-breakfast signs along the route.

CRICKET AT HAMBLEDON

Hambledon Cricket Club (1750-1787), was the birthplace of English cricket, in the days when two forked sticks were used for stumps. It boasted a team which won 23 out of 29 matches against All England teams, and their cricket ground was on Broadhalfpenny Down (grid ref. SU 678 167) to the north-east of Hambledon. The Bat and Ball pub was used as their pavilion and clubhouse, and John Nyren, England's leading cricketer of his time, was landlord. A stone memorial was placed in front of the pub in 1908 to commemorate the Hambledon Club.

Kilmeston
Dummer

KILMESTON

ABBOTSTONE DOWN

APPROX. 9 MILES/14KM

OS Landranger 185
Start at grid reference SU 590 258
Start point: By the roadside telephone box
on the corner next to Kilmeston Moor.
Limited parking.

A footpath leads northwards through
Kilmeston, passing by magnificent beech
trees and giving fine views of Dean House
over to the right. It emerges on the north
side of the hamlet, where it is worth walking
up the lane to the left for a look at St
Andrew's Church and the 18th-century
Kilmeston Manor, before carrying on along
the footpath which leads over a small hill
towards Hinton Ampner. This is believed to
be the old Winchester-to-Petersfield coach
road, although one can scarcely believe it
today. It gives fine views of the south side of
Hinton Ampner House ahead, entering
parkland and heading up by the side of the
ornamental gardens before emerging by the
small church of All Saints.

From Hinton Ampner, which is really no
more than a hamlet formed by one very
large house and its collection of associated
buildings, the route leads downhill past the
Old Rectory, with more fine parkland to the
left. If you wish to stop for a drink here, a

footpath deviates diagonally across the park,
leading almost directly to a pub by the side
of the A272 Winchester-to-Petersfield road.
Continuing on the main route, cross straight
over the A272 by a Wayfarer's Walk signpost
which points straight ahead up a track, saying
there are 42 miles to go to Inkpen Beacon.
Turn left at a bridleway crossroads, as shown
by a Wayfarer's Walk waymark, and then
carry on towards the village of Cheriton.
The waymarking is a little vague here, so
care must be taken in following the route to
ensure you emerge in the right part of the
village.

Despite being described by William
Cobbett as a 'hard, iron village', Cheriton is
now a pretty little place with a green and a
pub that is called simply the HH (or
Hampshire Hunt) – surely the shortest name
for a pub in Britain. To the north-east is the
site of the Battle of Cheriton, where the
Royalists were defeated by Cromwell's
forces in 1644. From here the route follows
a footpath along water meadows by the
source of the River Itchen to the west of the
village, coming out on to the road by
Cheriton Mill. It crosses the B3046 to join a
track which runs up the side of a field,
turning left at a crossing track and continuing
through trees to emerge on the road once
again by farm buildings opposite Tichborne
Park.

A Wayfarer's Walk alternative route leads
into Tichborne, and from there on to New
Alresford. Tichborne is a hamlet which
boasts a church of Saxon origins with a

Alresford's Broad Street

GUIDE BOX

Places to visit
Hinton Ampner (NT) Bramdean, near Cheriton.
A house was originally built here in the 16th
century. It was replaced by a Georgian house in
the late 18th century, which in turn was restyled
as a Victorian house in the 19th century. Ralph
Dutton remodelled it in Georgian style in 1937,
but it was gutted by fire in 1960. He rebuilt and
re-furnished it, before passing it on to the
National Trust soon after. Open April to end
September, Gardens Saturdays, Sundays,
Tuesdays, Wednesdays; House Tuesdays,
Wednesdays, plus Saturdays and Sundays in
August.

Avington Park, Itchen Abbas, some 3½ miles
west of New Alresford, is a great 17th-century
mansion in wooded parkland. Tours include the
ballroom and state rooms. Open May to
September, Saturdays and Bank Holidays.

Car parking
Principal parking places for this section are in
Kilmeston (grid ref. SU 590 258) on village
lanes, New Alresford car park (SU 585 325),
Abbotstone Down car park (SU 583 362) and in
Dummer (roadside, SU 587 462).

Public transport
The Mid Hants Steam Railway (Watercress
Line) at New Alresford connects with British
Rail at Alton. Bus services operate through New
Alresford and Cheriton (A272).

Accommodation
Overnight accommodation is available in
Kilmeston, New Alresford and Dummer.

Roman Catholic side chapel. It is be
known for the Tichborne Dole, a custor
that originated during the reign of Henry
Sir Roger Tichborne, who does not soun
the most pleasant of men, promised h
bedridden wife flour for the needy from
much land as she could crawl round! Sh
eventually managed 20 acres, an area know
as The Crawls.

Ⓔ *For a 2½-mile return to Kilmeston from
Tichborne (grid ref. SU 572 303), a bridleway
leads south-west to Gander Down (SU 556
276), swinging south-east to Lane End (SU 56-
256) where a footpath and lane lead via
Beauworth to Kilmeston.*

The main route misses Tichborne, follow
ing a track through woodland befor
dropping downhill to a golf course on th
outskirts of New Alresford. Follow the sigr
across the golf course and on to the foo
bridge which crosses the A31, turning righ
and then left uphill, and following the roa
along the east side of New Alresford. Pa
the railway line, you come out on to th
B3047 road. In the centre, turn right dow
the rather grand Broad Street. Because c
serious fires in the 12th, 15th, 17th and 18t
centuries, the architecture is predominantl
Georgian, and very pleasing too. At th
bottom of Broad Street the route bears le
on a narrow lane as shown by a Wayfarer
Walk waymark. This heads along a track b
the side of Alresford's complex waterwork

the creation of the 12th-century Bishop de Lucy of Winchester, who dammed up small local streams to provide enough water to make the River Itchen navigable by boat as far as Southampton.

The route passes a pretty waterside cottage by the side of the River Alre, and further on there is a stone monument with a difference: 'Here lies Hambone Jnr, faithful friend of the 7th Infantry Regt, 9th Division US Army, May 1944'. Keep on along this track which leads out of Alresford, ignoring a 'Private' sign by some houses on the left, until it brings you out on to the road. Cross over at the bend, and follow the wide grassy track ahead. This frequently has a large gypsy encampment with fine working horses tethered along the track, which is known as Drove Lane. In its day it was a busy route for driving sheep to Alresford's sheep market, which eventually died out in the 1970s. The track crosses a road about a mile on, carrying on along a leafy way through quiet countryside before turning right at a bridleway crossroads, as indicated by a Wayfarer's Walk waymark.

The route passes Abbotstone, a now non-existent village which once covered 15 acres and boasted a church and a 100-room mansion built in 1719. Incredibly nothing survives. It continues along a track through fields, passing a barn by a footpath/bridleway crossroads and coming to the wildlife reserve at Abbotstone Down by a notice board next to the car park. This 32-acre area is managed by the County Council as natural downland, preserving much local wildlife when there is intensive farming all around.

ABBOTSTONE DOWN

DUMMER

APPROX. 9 MILES/14KM

OS Landranger 185
Start at grid reference SU 583 362
Start point: Free car park at
Abbotstone Down.

From the Abbotstone Down car park, carry straight on over the road ahead, following the route as it bears left by Oliver's Battery, an Iron Age defensive settlement where the earthworks can still be seen. The route continues along a wide track known as Spybush Lane, going due north, with fine views over farmland and woodland to the east. Passing by a belt of trees it joins a hard farm track heading north downhill between fields, in open country, on the way towards Brown Candover.

However, as it reaches the farm buildings ahead, the route turns left along a track to divert towards Totford, though the more direct route to Brown Candover is to turn right and left, coming out on the road not far from the church. The track to Totford is called the Lunway which connected Old Sarum, Stockbridge and Crawley, and is now also part of the modern road system. At Totford's Woolpack Inn sheep were penned on their way to market, and beyond here the

The village church in Brown Candover

route follows a bridleway which joins a lane on the outskirts of Brown Candover, coming to the B3046 which it follows as far as St Peter's Church. Set back from the road on a green, it is notable for a fine Flemish altar rail. Brown Candover is one of three Candovers, the others being Chilton and Preston, originally small valley settlements.

Ⓔ *For an alternative return route from Brown Candover (grid ref. SU 578 392) follow the road to Preston Candover (1½ miles), and turn south via Down Farm to join the Ox Drove which rejoins the Wayfarer's Walk to the south of Brown Candover, some 2 miles away.*

Cross the green and join the footpath by the west side of the church. The route bears right over a stile and then left up the side of a field, coming to a large modern barn in a clearing, which is part of Church Lane Farm. Church Lane continues straight ahead, but is well hidden as it is enclosed by the thicket that runs between two fields. The Wayfarer's Walk waymark is easily missed here, and care should be taken not to continue along the main track which bears off to the right. Follow Church Lane down to a gate, going ahead by the side of Lone Barn, now converted to residential use.

Bear right here as indicated by the right of way sign, following the track by the side of the remains of Micheldever Forest across

Becket's Down. This area was once full of chalk pits, a few of which can still be seen. The chalk could be used to make lime, linoleum, plaster and putty, to whiten paint, and to fertilise the soil. The Wayfarer's Walk waymarks show the way through woodland past Breach House with its modern driveway and Breach Farm beyond, going on to the road ahead by Breach Cottage and turning left for a short way uphill. The route then turns right down the long, straight driveway that leads past Dummer Grange Farm to Dummer Grange, bearing left to follow a track round the side of the house, which remains well hidden.

The track ahead gives good views over the surrounding countryside, eventually coming to the road on the outskirts of Dummer with just a faint hum of a reminder that the M3 is close by. Dummer Down Farm, a mile or so to the south-west, was the home of the present Duchess of York, and the village itself, despite its proximity to the motorway, is interesting. Turn right and then left opposite the 12th-century All Saints' Church, which has a pretty entrance gate to the churchyard and a 14th-century pulpit, said to be one of the oldest in England. A short way on, past a fine, stone-built house on the right, the Queen Inn is a popular pub which makes a welcome place to stop.

MID HANTS RAILWAY

The Mid Hants or 'Watercress' Line between Alton and Winchester operated from 1865 until it was closed by British Rail in 1973. It was re-opened as a private steam railway between Ropley and New Alresford in 1977, with help from the Mid Hants Railway Preservation Society. The line now extends to Alton, where it connects with British Rail. Visitors can watch restoration work in the engine sheds at Ropley. The line operates throughout the year.

Dummer

Inkpen Beacon

OS Landranger 185, 174
Start at grid reference SU 587 462
Start point: The Queen Inn, Dummer.
Roadside parking.

From the pub at Dummer turn left downhill and walk on through this picturesque village. Beyond the village the road heads up towards the M3 roundabout. Here there is a long footpath detour which follows a sweeping driveway by the side of the motorway, passing corporate-style buildings well hidden by trees before crossing the motorway by a footbridge.

On the other side the path bears left through trees by the side of the Kemshott Park Estate which has now been developed as a golf course. It emerges on the roadside at the A30, which splits here and needs to be crossed twice before you can turn on to a minor road signposted to East Oakley. On the corner here there is a footpath sign in a completely overgrown tangle, so – unless it is clear – follow the road on ahead as far as the bend, where the footpath goes straight ahead over a stile, by the side of New Cottages and next to the farm driveway. The route follows the path along by the side of South Wood towards Bull's Bushes Farm. It passes through Bull's Bushes Copse to join the road on a bend.

The route bears left here, joining a track which follows the side of a field and by the side of trees to pass under the railway, emerging on the road by Cheesedown Farm.

Ⓔ *To return to Dummer from Cheesedown Farm (grid ref. SU 548 497) (a walk of about 2¹/₂ miles), follow a lane southwards to Steventon, and then turn south-east through North Waltham. Continue to the Sun Inn where a lane passes under the M3 and into Dummer.*

To continue on the Wayfarer's Walk, turn right past Deane Gate Farm, crossing straight over at the B3400 by the Deane Gate Inn, and going up the lane ahead with lovely views of All Saints' Church, which is set in Deane House's parkland. Follow the road to the right just opposite the entrance lodge to Deane House, turning left by Deane Cottages a short way on, as directed by the Wayfarer's Walk waymark. Do not go through the gate ahead, but bear right round the back of the houses and then left up the side of a field as directed by another sign, crossing the railway and coming out on the road by Deane Down Farm. The road here is part of the Harroway, a prehistoric route

connecting Pilgrim's Way in Kent to Salisbury Plain.

Past Little Deane Wood the route crosses Summer Down, passing Great Deane Wood and Frith Wood, with much of the woodland felled in the 1960s to make space for the intensive cereal farming which characterises this area – and though the views are extensive, they are bland indeed. Past Freemantle Farm the route emerges on the road at North Oakley by the Manor Farm. Turn left here opposite a fine, black barn and at the bend go straight ahead on the track past Warren Cottages, before turning right down an overgrown track as directed by the Wayfarer's Walk waymark. This track climbs up For Down with fine views behind.

The lane ahead is part of the Portway, a Roman road which connected Salisbury with Silchester, an important Roman centre to the north of Basingstoke. The Portway crosses the countryside in a straight line, and when it leaves the modern road its course can be followed by a long line of trees to the west known as Caesar's Belt, as it makes its way towards Andover. Cross over here, and go straight ahead up the side of a field to a gate where there is a wonderful view of the route ahead, looking towards Watership Down. The track heads downhill, emerging on the B3061 by the White Hill car park. From here on, as the walk enters its final stages on OS map 174, its character changes. The intensive farmland of central Hampshire

The cornfields of Watership Down

GUIDE BOX

Places to visit
Highclere Castle is the largest mansion in Hampshire, with grounds laid out by Capability Brown for Henry Herbert in the 1770s. In the 1840s it was converted into a Victorian castle by Sir Charles Barry on behalf of the 3rd Earl of Carnarvon. The 5th Earl discovered the tomb of Tutankhamun with Howard Carter. The 7th Earl became racing manager to the Queen in 1969. Open July to September, Wednesday to Sunday and Bank Holiday Mondays.

The towpath of the Kennet and Avon Canal can be joined at Kintbury for a pleasant walk westwards to Hungerford (3 miles) and a possible return by train.

Car parking
Principal car parking places on this section of the route are at Dummer (roadside, grid ref. SU 587 462), White Hill car park (SU 515 565) and Inkpen Beacon car park (SU 382 641).

Public transport
There is a British Rail station at Kintbury, about 4 miles from Inkpen Beacon. The unmanned station is opposite a pub in a very pleasant canalside setting, which makes it a reasonable place to wait for a train on a summer evening. The nearest British Rail stations to Dummer are Micheldever or Basingstoke. The British Rail station at Quidhampton, convenient for the youth hostel at Overton, is approximately 3 miles distant from Deane. Bus services are patchy.

Accommodation
There is a youth hostel at Overton, 2 miles west of the Walk at Deane. Basingstoke has a choice of hotels and guesthouses and bed-and-breakfast accommodation is available at Dummer, Oakley and Kingsclere.

is left behind, and the chalk downland of the North Hants Ridgeway takes over, with the route following a prehistoric track which stretches from Basingstoke to the Vale of Pewsey in Wiltshire.

WHITE HILL

INKPEN BEACON

APPROX. 12 MILES/19KM

OS Landranger 174
Start at grid reference SU 515 565
Start point: Small car park at the top of White Hill on B3051, 1¹/₂ miles south of Kingsclere.

From the White Hill car park the route follows the Portway westwards, following a track uphill on chalk and grassland. The chalk drains away any rainwater, so it is never too wet for walking and is equally suitable for the racehorse gallops which are either side of the route on Cannon Horse Down.

Watership Down inspired Richard Adams' bestselling book of that name, so look out for friendly rabbits. The Downs here are also notable for ancient barrows and hillforts. Passing the trig. point at 777ft (237m) on the top of Watership Down, the route follows a narrow track downhill by the side of trees, crossing a lane and following a fine avenue of beech trees, before turning right across open grassland. From here it bears westwards again to reach the great hillfort on top of Ladle Hill, an Iron Age fortification which, together with the fort on nearby Beacon Hill, defended the ancient route which is now the A34.

Ⓔ *For an escape back to White Hill, take the bridleway past Ladle Hill (grid ref. SU 478 568) going north to Old Burghclere. Follow the road through Sydmonton to the outskirts of Kingsclere where the B3051 leads back up to White Hill (a circular walk of about 5 miles).*

The route bears south downhill on a wide grassy track dividing two fields, with the A34 in the valley below and fine views of Beacon Hill on the other side. The track twists and turns and needs to be followed with care as it descends Great Litchfield Down, eventually joining a narrow, overgrown tarmac track which heads downhill to the A34, crossing under overhead powerlines. Go through the old bridge that marks the disused railway and cross the dual carriageway with great care.

The road here divides seven ancient barrows, a number of which can be seen on the west side, as well as a memorial to the aircraft builder, Geoffrey de Havilland, who flew his model planes here as a boy. The track climbs uphill through pretty woodland along Lower Woodcott Down, coming out by the side of a field and passing a copse with good views north to Beacon Hill. From here the route swings north along the grassy hillside of Upper Woodcott Down, heading for a belt of trees and then joining a hard track coming up from the right. All the way along here the views to the north look out over the 6500 acres of the Highclere Estate, with the rounded top of Sidown Hill in the foreground.

The route joins a woodland track through Grotto Copse, passing a pretty, castellated gatehouse to Highclere Castle before emerging on the A343. This has to be crossed on a blind bend, so take care. The continuing track is about 75yds to the left uphill, heavily overgrown, with fields on either side obscured by trees and hedges. Over a lane the route continues along

Above *The final panorama, from Combe Gibbet*

another very overgrown and sometimes very muddy track as it follows the North Hants Ridgeway, joining a lane by the side of woodland. As the Walk turns right here, there are fine views of Highclere Castle surrounded by trees in the distance. The route then bears left, on to a waymarked track, as the road starts to head downhill.

At the top of Pilot Hill this track passes a trig. point at 938ft (286m). A little further on, after just over 67 miles through Hampshire, the Wayfarer's Walk crosses Berkshire's border for the last 3 miles. The track joins a quiet road which continues westwards along the top of the Down, coming to the car park at Westbury Hill. From here a hard, chalk track leads on by the side of Walbury Camp, a prehistoric hillfort on top of the highest chalk hill in England, marked by a trig. point at 974ft (297m). It is a massive fortification, covering some 82 acres, with a mile-long ditch and rampart.

The track leads on to the car park on the top of Inkpen Beacon, where you are rewarded with brilliant views of the countryside to the north and south, and the sight of a twin signpost marking both the beginning and end of the Wayfarer's Walk and the Test Way. However, Combe Gibbet on top of Gallows Down, the official end of the route, is ¹/₂ mile or so further west on the chalk track that lies ahead. This is a modern replica of the hanging post first erected here in the 17th century. Despite its grim associations, on a clear evening this is the finest possible place to end the walk.

SANDHAM MEMORIAL CHAPEL (NT)

Built in the 1920s as a memorial to H W Sandham, who was killed in World War I, the chapel in Burghclere, near Newbury, is notable for the 19 frescoes by Sir Stanley Spencer. The allegorical paintings are based on his own experiences, both in Salonica and as a hospital orderly. The poignant scenes include soldiers dealing with laundry, rubbish, wound-dressing and kit inspection. Open Easter to end October, Wednesday to Sunday and Bank Holiday Mondays; November to March, weekends only.

South Downs Way

COMPLETE ROUTE
WINCHESTER TO EASTBOURNE
106 MILES/171KM

SECTION COVERED
QUEEN ELIZABETH COUNTRY PARK TO EASTBOURNE
80 MILES/129KM

Detailed guides
Recommended guides include: *Guide To The South Downs Way* by Miles Jebb (Constable); the National Trail Guide, *South Downs Way* by Paul Willmore (Aurum Press, in association with the Countryside Commission and The Ordnance Survey); *Along The South Downs Way To Winchester,* by and available from Eastbourne Rambling Club, 254 Victoria Drive, Eastbourne, East Sussex BN20 8QT; *The South Downs Way* by and available from the YHA.

Maps
OS Landranger 197, 198, 199

Links
The Sussex Border Path, the Downs Link, the Lipchis Way, The Wey-South Path, Vanguard Way, The South Coast Way and the Wealdway, all link into the South Downs Way.

THE South Downs Way was designated as a long distance footpath by the Countryside Commission in 1972, passing along the length of the South Downs of Sussex from the Sussex – Hampshire border, a few miles south of Petersfield in the west, to Eastbourne in the east (where the route divides into two to include the Seven Sisters Loop for those who prefer to follow the coast). At the western end of the South Downs Way the Downs also extend beyond Sussex into Hampshire, which is why there is a South Downs extension route as far as Winchester, adding some 25 miles (this section is not covered in this book).

Most walkers content themselves with the 80 miles or so of the original South Downs Way which spans both West and East Sussex, generally taking around a week to traverse its length. This route is a bridleway, with the exception of the Seven Sisters Coastal loop near Eastbourne, which is footpath. The bridleway alternative follows the Downs inland. Therefore you can expect to meet horses and mountain bikes, though thankfully no motorised vehicles are allowed.

There is no obvious reason to prefer walking from east to west or west to east, but since the prevailing wind is normally from the west or south-west, we have chosen to follow the South Downs Way starting at the western end. Eastbourne as a start or finish point has the advantage that it is a big town well served by railways and public transport, while at the other end the route is more easily served by car. Otherwise, it will be necessary to rely on infrequent buses, or to walk from Petersfield railway station.

The South Downs Way is an undulating

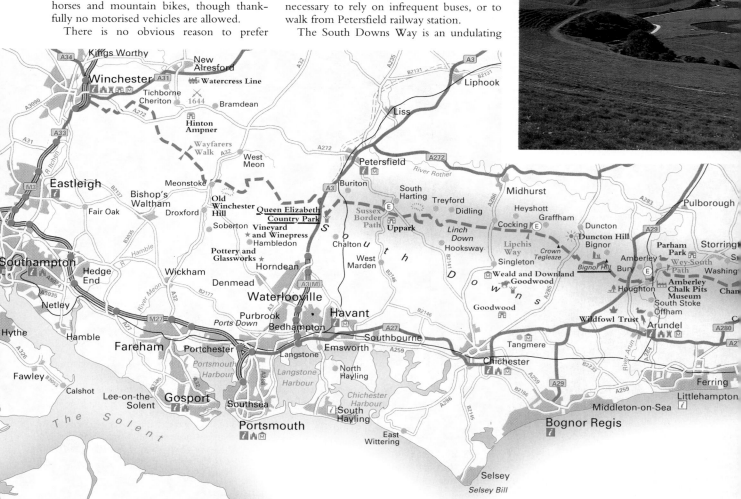

route, following the high chalk ridges of the Downs and dipping in and out of valleys and combes. If the weather is kind, the views are magnificent, ranging out across mainly unspoilt English countryside, with frequent glimpses of the English Channel beyond. The route is largely untouched by the urban sprawl that links Brighton, Littlehampton and Bognor Regis along the south coast, and with a few noisy exceptions is infrequently crossed by roads. Its character changes along its length. The first half of the route from the Sussex – Hampshire border as far as Steyning is less touched by modern farming, with delightful woodland sections, plenty of wildlife, and the prettiest villages, while the second half is more given to open grassland and can be bleak when walking in the face of lashing rain or a strong headwind.

The South Downs Way, compared to some other long distance footpaths, is friendly and forgiving. The highest point of the route is under 900ft (300m), which means the walker will not suffer from any dangerous extremes of weather due to height

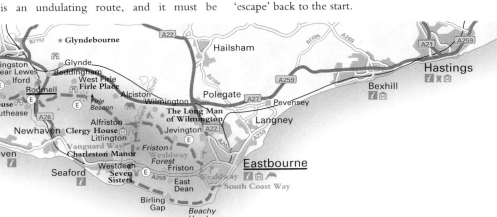

Looking west from Birling Gap

The Cuckmere valley at Exceat

and, since the surrounding country is mainly flat, the impression of height is maintained. There are frequent access points along its length which are easily reached by car with convenient parking on the top of the Downs, and with the aid of an OS map it is possible to bite off chunks of the South Downs Way at a time and devise personalised circular routes which will be invariably well served by the local villages and other attractions.

Most of the route is easily followed, with the traditional acorn LDP sign showing the way. There are one or two points where it is possible to err off the track which we have highlighted in the text that follows (though this is more likely to be a problem for mountain-bikers who speed by without checking the signposts). Much of the going is on hard chalk paths which are easy underfoot but require proper walking boots for covering extended distances; some parts of the route can also be muddy after wet weather, with horses turning the narrower paths to wet, squelchy quagmires.

We have said that the South Downs Way is an undulating route, and it must be

accepted that there is plenty of uphill walking, a fair amount of level walking on the top of the Downs, and an equal amount of downhills to cover. The hills are no better or worse to walk up whether covering the route from west to east or east to west; they are all easy, steady climbs, never very steep but usually quite long. If tiring of these climbs, there are many interesting things to see along the length of the South Downs Way, but mostly they demand diversions that take extra time and miles, and sometimes it is necessary to leave the Downs and then climb back up to rejoin the route. The same is true of pubs, cafés, camp sites and other accommodation – if diversions are made to the various pretty villages within reach of the South Downs Way, there is plenty to choose from, but there is very little which is actually on the route itself.

Numerous footpaths and bridleways lead down from the Way, both south and north, into the various villages, several of which are on bus routes, enabling the walker to 'escape' back to the start.

Queen Elizabeth Country Park

Bignor Hill

QUEEN ELIZABETH COUNTRY PARK

COCKING

APPROX. 11 MILES/18KM

OS Landranger 197
Start at grid reference SU 718 185
Start point: Queen Elizabeth Country Park on the A3, 5 miles south of Petersfield. Ample car parking available for which there is a modest charge. From November to February, when the Information Centre is closed, make sure you have the correct change to get out of the car park (£1.00).

The Queen Elizabeth Country Park, where there is a Forest Information Centre and café, is a convenient place to start walking the South Downs Way, just on the Hampshire side of the Hampshire – Sussex border. An alternative start point is the village of Buriton, where Edward Gibbon, author of *The Decline and Fall of the Roman Empire,* lived in the Elizabethan manor house when he returned from Switzerland in 1758. Buriton is served by buses from Petersfield

The reconstructed Iron Age farm at Queen Elizabeth Country Park

and Portsmouth, and has an old-fashioned pond and a friendly pub named the Maple Inn.

The Queen Elizabeth Country Park is *en route* for those extending the walk to and from Winchester. A large map on a notice board sends walkers off on the South Downs Way via dense woods until the top of the hill is reached by War Down, the first of many climbs on this route. From there the Way drops down to the south of Buriton, following both lanes and track to the east past Coulters Dean Farm. The next stage of the walk leads to Sunwood Farm, the original official beginning and end of the South Downs Way on the Hampshire – Sussex border.

From here the South Downs Way acorn signs point the way along chalk tracks, with some severely muddy stretches in wet weather conditions, towards Harting Downs.

Ⓔ *For a circular walk back to Queen Elizabeth Country Park, leave the South Downs Way here (grid ref. SU 772 192), heading south and then turning south-west along West Harting Down to join the Sussex Border Path. This leads to Chalton, beyond which a bridleway turns up Chalton Down towards Queen Elizabeth Country Park, a distance of around 8 miles.*

The first village encountered is South Harting, notable for the church's green copper spire, and once the home of Alexander Pope and later of Anthony Trollope, who was said to shock the village with his weekend parties. A footpath leads down the hillside to the left, and the village is about 20 minutes distant by foot.

Alternatively, on the south side of the Down, make a diversion to the National Trust mansion of Uppark, built in the Wren style by William Talman in 1685-90 and partly destroyed by a fire which was caused during restoration on the roof in 1989. This gutted most of its interior and damaged many of its treasures, and the rebuilding programme which started in 1990 was estimated to take ten years.

A short way on one emerges at the top of Harting Downs by a car park, to experience the first of many fine views that the South Downs Way offers from here on. To the south-west the views extend uninterrupted across Chichester Harbour to the Isle of Wight; to the south-east one looks out across the city of Chichester itself, with its elegant, mainly Norman cathedral and rather more modern Festival Theatre in the foreground. Here the route follows a fine grassy trail along the top of the Downs, a popular location on fine days, for both hang gliders and model aircraft enthusiasts, who launch their craft over the flat countryside to the north.

The ancient signpost at Cross Dykes is the next landmark, with the much smaller South Downs Way signpost giving the option of a

stiff climb straight up Beacon Hill (with its ancient Iron Age hillfort, of which virtually nothing remains at the top) or the more popular gentle climb, skirting the hill to the south and east. Although clearly signposted, this is one of the few places along the Way where it is possible to wander off the route, which takes a sharp left turn before a small

The view north from Harting Hill

ountry estate to the right, named Telegraph House. As an alternative diversion, this track eads to The Royal Oak pub at Hooksway a mile or so on, a popular stopping-place for walkers.

The South Downs Way drops towards Buriton Farm – far from the village of the same name – before a long climb to the top of Linch Down leads past The Devil's Jumps. These are five Bronze Age round barrows that have been excavated and are maintained by the Society of Sussex Downsmen. The nearest villages are Treyford and Didling, the former with two churchyards but no church and the latter with an isolated, 13th-century church boasting original pews. A short way on the route passes through ancient woodland, bearing round the back of Monkton House, the cottage once owned by the late Edward James, the surrealist art collector who filled it with priceless works by such notables as Salvador Dali. Sadly his collection has been dispersed, and the house, which cannot be seen from the track, is now surrounded by a high security fence that is out of tune with its pastoral surroundings.

Linch Down is heavily wooded and here one may sometimes hear the rustling of pheasants in the undergrowth, and see the occasional rabbit hop across the path. After a couple of miles of walking through these peaceful glades, which afford excellent protection against both wind and rain,

agricultural land reasserts itself once again and a magnificent view opens to the east, looking to the next great hill of Graffham Down and beyond to the twin radio masts on top of Burton Down which dominate the surrounding country. Cocking village is about 1/2 mile to the north, complete with church, duckpond, and choice of two public houses (overnight accommodation available).

COCKING

BIGNOR HILL

APPROX. 7 MILES/11KM

OS Landranger 197
Start at grid reference SU 878 177
Start point: From Cocking on the A286, 3 miles south of Midhurst. Limited roadside car parking in the village; limited roadside car parking 1/2 mile south of Cocking, where the South Downs Way crosses the A286.

From the pleasant village of Cocking one can rejoin the South Downs Way via a bridleway past the church. By Hill Barn Farm is one of the few public water taps for walkers along the entire length of the route. A plaque set in a flint cairn dedicates it to the memory of 'Peter Wren aged 14 years. He loved the English countryside and walked

the South Downs Way in the summer of 1978'.

Fill up your water bottle as the track heads steeply uphill past Manor Farm Down and Heyshott Down. To the south is Goodwood Park, while far beyond on the coast is the former RAF Hurricane and Spitfire fighter station at Tangmere, where one may now visit the commemorative museum. Along the top of the Down the views are shrouded by dense woodland. One passes the village of Heyshott to the north, where 53 acres of downland are conserved by the Society of Sussex Downsmen as a Site of Special Scientific Interest. Some way on one passes Graffham, also to the north and shrouded by trees, the village where the Victorian free trader Richard Cobden once lived.

Ⓔ *For a circular 7-mile walk back to Cocking, turn north off the South Down Way at grid ref. SU 927 162 to follow the bridleway track downhill to Graffham, and then follow the lanes and footpaths that lead due west to Heyshott and Cocking, a pleasant walk across flat country.*

Off to the right a little way on is the highest point of the Sussex Downs, Crown Tegleaze (836ft/255m), at the top of Littleton Down.

Another long downhill stretch leads to the A285 Petworth – Chichester road by the side of Littleton Farm. Turning left, to the north, here, the road leads to the car park at the top of Duncton Hill, from where there are fine views towards Blackdown, the house built by Alfred Lord Tennyson, with Seaford College at the foot of the hill below.

A stark white chalk track wends its way up to the top of Burton Down, homing in towards the two radio masts. The South Downs Way passes some way to the south of them along a narrow and sometimes muddy track, crossing National Trust land. Soon the walker comes to the car park at Bignor Hill. This part of the route is usually well filled by Sunday afternoon walkers in summertime, congregating at the Bignor Post. This ancient signpost shows the way along Stane Street, built by the Romans to connect London Bridge with Chichester's East Gate in the 1st century AD.

The nearest overnight accommodation is about 2 miles away in Sutton.

OPEN AIR MUSEUM

The Weald and Downland Open Air Museum is about 3 miles south of the South Downs Way on the A286, just past the village of Singleton. It is a fascinating collection of rescued historical buildings in beautiful surroundings, set on a hillside. The buildings date from the 14th century onwards and include blacksmith's, carpenter's and plumber's workshops, as well as a village school and working watermill. A restaurant serves lunch and teas by the millpond, and there are frequent demonstrations of rural crafts and open days such as the annual Rare Breeds Show. The museum is open daily March to end September, and on Wednesdays and Sundays in winter.

Bignor Hill

Fulking

BIGNOR HILL

WASHINGTON

APPROX. 10 MILES/16KM

OS Landranger 197, 198
Start at grid reference SU 973 129
Start point: Free car park at the top of Bignor Hill, reached by road from Bignor.

From the top of Bignor Hill, the South Downs Way follows a hard, chalk track to the east, along the top of the Down, with fine views southwards over the coastal plain as far as Bognor Regis and Littlehampton. Ahead lies Chanctonbury Ring.

The route zig-zags steeply downhill to old farm buildings in a spot which can frequently be muddy at the bottom of Westburton Hill, before taking the walker uphill on a narrow chalk track, passing a trig. point at 584ft (178m) to the left and soon reaching the busy A29 Worthing road.

From here there is a splendid view of the route ahead, as the landscape dives down into the Arun Valley, with dramatic chalk hills beyond Amberley.

Cross the A29, and the bridleway that continues the route will be found a short distance to the south.

The South Downs Way carries on steeply downhill by the side of Coombe Wood on another chalk track, bringing you to a lane a short way to the north of the hamlet of Houghton. Turn right here and then left on to the B2139 to continue towards Amberley. Alternatively Houghton repays a visit. The George and Dragon pub is a few hundred yards uphill to the right and is well thought of, not least because Charles II is reputed to

have stopped there while making his escape from near Brighton to France in the 17th century. After his time this was also an important trading place, with a long-gone wharf down by the river where barges were loaded with locally quarried chalk. The river was part of the Wey and Arun Navigation Canal system which closed down in 1871.

The B2139 is a narrow road with no pavement and care should be taken when walking into Amberley. On the far side of the old bridge that crosses the River Arun there is a riverside café with outdoor seating, as well as a pub, restaurant, small shop, and water trough with drinking tap. Upriver are the Amberley Wild Brooks, a scheduled nature reserve stretching as far as Greatham Bridge, to the east of Coldwaltham.

Ⓔ *An interesting diversion follows a footpath south from Amberley (grid ref. TQ 025 118) along the banks of the River Arun. This leads to South Stoke, Offham, and on past the Swanbourne Lake nature reserve into Arundel itself, where there is plenty of accommodation (a distance of some 4 miles).*

To complete a circular route, footpaths can be followed north-east through Arundel Park, to the junction of the A284 and the A29 at Whiteways Lodge (where there is a large car park at the roundabout, grid ref. TQ 004 119, convenient for a pick-up by car), and on through Houghton Forest to Bignor Hill.

The South Downs Way route follows the road past Amberley railway station and the famous Chalk Pits Museum, turning off to the right, steeply uphill on High Titton Lane, by the side of a large Victorian house. There are fascinating glimpses of the Chalk Pits Museum below, before the route emerges on the open Downs, away from

The Way as it crosses Beeding Hill

GUIDE BOX

Places to visit
Parham House and Gardens are on the A283 west of Storrington. The house is a fine Elizabethan mansion dating from 1577. Its features include over 300 Elizabethan and Stuart paintings, a 158ft Long Gallery, and what is claimed to be the finest collection of needlework in any house in England. Beyond the walled gardens, the park is extensive with deer roaming free. Open from Easter to early October, Wednesday, Thursday and Sunday.

Arundel Castle, the ancestral home of the Dukes of Norfolk for over 700 years, dominates the town of Arundel. Most of the castle was rebuilt in the late 19th century, but the 11th-century keep and ancient barbican are preserved, with furniture, paintings and armour on view. Open April to October, afternoons Sunday to Friday.

Arundel Wildfowl Trust encompasses some 55 acres between the River Arun and Swanbourne Lake, on the outskirts of Arundel. Landscaped pens, lakes and paddocks contain geese, ducks, swans and wildfowl from all over the world. Open every day except Christmas Day.

Car parking
Principal car parks are at the top of Bignor Hill (grid ref. SU 973 129), Whiteways Lodge (TQ 002 108), Amberley Station (TQ 027 118), the top of Chantry Hill (TQ 087 121), and Steyning Bowl (TQ 162 094).

Public transport
The nearest British Rail stations to this part of the route are at Amberley and Shoreham-by-Sea. Buses operate between Upper Beeding, Bramber, Steyning, Washington and Storrington.

Accommodation
Most of the downland villages and towns have bed-and-breakfast and hotel accommodation, in particular Arundel and Steyning. Refer to *Along The South Downs Way To Winchester* (see page 58) for detailed information which includes limited camping facilities. There are also youth hostels at Arundel (grid ref. TQ 033 073) and Tottington Barn near Fulking (TQ 221 106).

built-up civilisation. A fenced track leads steeply uphill on grass away from Downs Farm towards Amberley Mount, and on to the top of Rackham Hill.

With few trees on the hillsides, from here on the views are mostly unobstructed all around. To the west is Amberley Castle, once a 14th-century fortified manor house belonging to the Bishops of Chichester, and now a luxury country house hotel. To the north lies Parham House, an Elizabethan mansion with wooded deer park. To the south is Arundel, an ancient town built on a hillside, with its own fine castle and Roman Catholic Cathedral of St Philip Neri.

At the top of Chantry Hill there is a car park, with a tarmac lane leading downhill to the busy village of Storrington. Nearby Sullington has a Saxon church ringed by old yew trees below. The South Downs Way then divides to give two optional routes. The direct way goes eastwards and downhill, passing by a drinking tap to cross the A24 on a busy dual carriageway section. The much

safer option is to divert to the north-east downhill past Rowdell House, to where a footbridge leads over the A24 and into Washington by the side of its church. Further on is the old London Road now known as The Street, and The Washington Inn. Guesthouse accommodation is available.

WASHINGTON

FULKING

APPROX. 10½ MILES/17KM

OS Landranger 198
Start at grid reference TQ 123 128
Start point: Washington, on the south-east side of the intersection of the A24 and A283. Roadside parking.

From Washington a footpath leads steeply up the wooded hillside to rejoin the South Downs Way at the top of Chanctonbury Hill. Beyond a dewpond the route passes a trig. point at 780ft (238m) and heads east along the top of the Downs towards Chanctonbury Ring, a mystic circle of trees which broods over the whole area. Originally an Iron Age hillfort on which the Romans built a temple in the 3rd-4th-century, the ring was planted with trees in the late 18th century. Many of the trees were felled by the great gale of 1987, but replanting has taken place. Just over 2 miles to the south of Chanctonbury Ring lies another great ancient landmark of the Downs. The Iron Age hillfort of Cissbury Ring can be clearly seen, and is sited in an area of extensive Neolithic flint mines with panoramic views over the English Channel.

The route turns south-east, with Wiston Park and the 16th-century Wiston House to the north-east below. It follows a wide chalk track on a slight downhill, crossing open grassland with fine views ahead and the urban sprawl of Shoreham and Worthing in the distance.

Steyning comes into view at the bottom of Steyning Round Hill, where a Bronze Age burial site was excavated in 1949. By a trig. point at 620ft (189m) a footpath leads steeply downhill to this small, interesting town. Close by is Bramber, which boasts the remains of an 11th-century Norman castle that is open to the public. This was a busy port in medieval times, before the Adur estuary became too silted up for navigation.

On the top of the Down above Steyning and Bramber, the South Downs Way joins a narrow road for a short distance, passing by Steyning Bowl on the left. This is a magnificent natural amphitheatre cut into the hillside, which with its small car park is a popular launching place for hang gliders.

Ⓔ *From Steyning Bowl (grid ref. TQ 162 094) a track may be taken south and then west to Cissbury Ring, which is accessible by car and has a car park. From here a bridleway leads due north, back to Chanctonbury Ring, where the South Downs Way may be rejoined to return to Washington, a distance of about 6 miles.*

About ½ mile on, the route turns left off the road, crossing a grassy field by the side of Annington Hill, with the valley of the River Adur coming into sight ahead. This is the first river crossing of the South Downs Way, signalling the start of the much more open country of the eastern part of the route.

A hard track leads downhill, joining a narrow road by Annington Farm, and heads east towards St Botolph's Church, on the riverside near the site of a Saxon farmstead. A hundred yards or so before the church, a track turns left to cross the river by a footbridge; here there is a water tap to drink from, as well as a notice board indicating the southern end of the Downs Link (see pages 68-73).

On the east side of the River Adur the route follows the A283 Shoreham road for a couple of hundred yards to the north, before turning right on to a track which heads up the side of Beeding Hill. This leads to a narrow road on the top of the Downs with a panoramic view of the valley behind and, far beyond to the south-west, the magnificent 19th-century chapel of Lancing College, built on a hill. The school's founder, Canon Woodward, decreed that his chapel must be seen from the sea and all around, and he indeed created a remarkable landmark.

Above *The pub at Fulking, beneath the Downs*

The road leads east along the top of this bleak Down, passing Tottingham Barn with its few protective conifers, the only youth hostel directly on the route of the South Downs Way. From here the road becomes a track, passing the radio masts and trig. point at 709ft (216m) on Truleigh Hill, and crossing National Trust land by the earthwork remains of an ancient Norman motte-and-bailey on Edburton Hill. Here one can look over to Thundersbarrow Hill to the south, an important site of Roman and Iron Age settlements. Beyond the electricity pylons, as the route follows an undulating track towards Fulking Hill, a footpath leads left down into Fulking village, where the picturesque Shepherd and Dog inn has a fresh water spring gushing from the hillside. Bed-and-breakfast available.

AMBERLEY CHALK PITS MUSEUM

Close by Amberley railway station, Amberley Chalk Pits Museum is sited in a 30-acre chalk quarry. It is a working open air museum, where the industrial history of south-east England is being studied and preserved. Attractions include the massive outdoor lime kilns, a narrow-gauge working railway, country brickworks, a smithy, print works, and a carpenter's shop; plus displays of developments in transport, canals, engineering and radio communications. Open April to end October, Wednesday to Sunday and daily during the school summer holidays.

Fulking

Rodmell

FULKING

DITCHLING BEACON

APPROX. 6¹/₂ MILES/10KM

OS Landranger 198
Start at grid reference TQ 248 114
Start point: Fulking, on a minor road
between Upper Beeding and Pyecombe.
Considerate roadside car parking.

From the Shepherd and Dog inn at Fulking,
a footpath joins a bridleway which leads
diagonally up the hillside to rejoin the
South Downs Way. Beyond Fulking Hill the route
goes over open grassland towards the isolated
Dyke Hotel (public house) at the top of
Devil's Dyke, above the village of Poynings
and its 13th-century church. The Devil's
Dyke, a natural phenomenon, got its name
because, according to legend, the devil dug a
dyke in the hillside in order to flood the
surrounding country and its churches, but
was interrupted and never finished the job!

The route joins the narrow road which
connects the hotel to the outside world, with
the dyke below to the left. A funicular
railway used to bring tourists to the hotel,
where a large direction board shows the
many viewpoints that can be seen on a clear
day from the summit.

The road leads on to a car park set in an
area of shrub and woodland, where the route
turns left downhill into the hamlet of
Saddlescombe, once the site of a Knights
Templars house. Although signposting for
the South Downs Way is generally excellent,
this turning is not obvious and care needs to
be taken not to miss it.

At the bottom of the hill a path leads off
to the right past farm buildings, coming to a
sunken track that heads up towards open
downland above West Hill. The National
Trust's Newtimber Hill, a popular viewpoint
rich in downland flora and fauna, is about ¹/₂
mile to the north. Carrying on along the top
of the Down, the route then heads downhill
on a bridleway, joining the A23 Brighton
road by the Plough Inn at Pyecombe.

Having crossed the main road, the South
Downs Way is signposted left, past the
church, which has an unusual lead font. Near
by is the smithy, renowned for the
manufacture of Pyecombe shepherds' crooks
in the days when sheep rather than cereals
dominated the Downs. The route turns right
to cross the A273 Haywards Heath road,
turning off eastwards through the entrance of
Pyecombe Golf Club a short way uphill.

Past the club buildings, the route follows a
fenced track along potentially muddy
ground, keeping to the side of the golf
course and then following the headland.
Beyond New Barn Farm the twin Jack and

Jill Clayton Windmills come into view
above Clayton village, one of the famous
landmarks of the Downs, but now no longer
working and converted for domestic use.

The route carries on eastwards, passing the
Keymer Post on the top of the Down at
764ft (233m), then coming close by
dewponds and across grassland as it drops
down to the trig. point at the top of
Ditchling Beacon (745ft/227m). One of the
highest points of the South Downs Way, this
is the site of an ancient hillfort, where fires
were lit to warn of the Spanish Armada four
centuries ago. From here the North Downs
can be seen on a clear day and, closer to
hand, Ashdown Forest and Crowborough
Beacon. A steep, narrow road connects
Brighton with the village of Ditchling on the
north side of the downs. It was once a Saxon
royal estate and has some interesting houses,
including one known as Anne of Cleves'
House, though there is no proof that she
ever lived there. The village has attracted
many artists and craftsmen, including the
eccentric Eric Gill. There is a choice of bed-
and-breakfast accommodation.

Ⓔ *For a pleasant circular walk back to Pyecombe*
or Clayton, (from where buses run to Brighton)
head south from Ditchling Beacon down Heathy
Brow west to the farmstead in the valley at Lower
Standean, then crossing the Sussex Border Path
which divides the east and west parts of the
county. A final climb up to Clayton Windmills
makes a distance of around 3 miles and from here
it is a short distance into Clayton, on the A273..
Alternatively, turn left on the South Downs Way
again to return to Pyecombe.

Poynings, from the Devil's Dyke

GUIDE BOX

Places to visit
Danny, near Hurstpierpoint to the north of
Pyecombe, is an Elizabethan brick mansion of
1595, which was enlarged and restored in 1728.
Open May to September, Wednesdays and
Thursdays and by appointment in winter
months.

Lewes, is well worth a visit, boasting an 11th-
century castle and 14th-century Barbican (open
to the public on weekdays throughout the year
and Sunday afternoons from April to October).
The old town has a large Cluniac priory, and a
300-year-old bowling green that was once the
scene of medieval jousting. There are timbered
cottages and elegant Georgian houses, with
another Anne of Cleves' House, which contains
a museum of local history, in Southover High
Street (open Easter to end October, daily).

Brighton is the largest town along the South
Downs Way, an important year-round holiday
resort with some magnificent Regency
architecture. Most notable is the Chinese-style
Royal Pavilion, built in 1822 for the Prince
Regent. With its pier, beaches, shops, art gallery,
museum, squares and terraces, Brighton is a town
where there is plenty to see and do.

Car parking
Principal car parks are at Devil's Dyke (grid ref.
TQ 257 111), Saddlescombe (TQ 258 112),
Clayton Windmills (TQ 303 136), and Ditchling
Beacon (TQ 332 131).

Public transport
The nearest British Rail stations are at Hassocks
and Southease. Buses run into Brighton from
Pyecombe and Clayton, between Lewes and
Plumpton, and Westmeston and Hassocks, and
through Rodmell between Lewes and
Newhaven.

Accommodation
Refer to local Tourist Information Centres or
Along the South Downs Way To Winchester (see
page 58) for detailed accommodation lists
showing bed-and-breakfast establishments,
hotels, and camp sites.

DITCHLING BEACON

RODMELL

APPROX. 10 MILES/16KM

OS Landranger 198
Start at grid reference TQ 332 132
Start point: Ditchling Beacon, at the top of
the minor road running due south from
Ditchling to Brighton. Car park at top.

Cross the narrow road from the Ditchling
Beacon car park with care. There is a blind
bend near the top. From here the South
Downs Way continues eastwards over the
grassy top of the Downs, passing a V-shaped
plantation which commemorated Queen
Victoria's Jubilee. Beyond lonely Streathill
Farm the view looks north across Plumpton
towards the famous race course, with
Plumpton Church and Agricultural College
close by the foot of the Downs. To the
south the enormous mass of Brighton, its
marina jutting out into the sea, dominates
this part of the coast.

Just over 2 miles from Ditchling Beacon,
the South Downs Way takes a major change
in direction, following the line of the Downs
to the south-east. However, first it turns to
the south-west, leaving the bridleway which
goes straight ahead at a clearly signposted
gate. This is just before the track reaches
Ashcombe Bottom, the only extensive patch
of woodland on this part of the Downs.
Beyond is the 676ft (206m) trig. point at
Blackcap, and almost a mile further on the
electricity pylons which march across the
Downs.

The route turns down a track with wire
fences on either side, before bearing left to
head south-east down the side of a field,
passing beneath the overhead electricity
cables. From here there are clear views over
Lewes and its disused race course, looking
out over an area where the Battle of Lewes
was fought between King Henry III and
Simon de Montfort in 1264. Along Balmer
Down the Way crosses the site of an
important Roman settlement where remains
of a cemetery have been found, and heads
downhill towards woods. Here it enters the
Ashcombe Plantation, and soon comes to the
A27 Lewes-Brighton road.

With dual carriageway and no bridge, this
is the trickiest road crossing of the South
Downs Way. On the far side is the
Newmarket Inn and a petrol station. The
route carries on past them, going through a
railway arch and uphill on a chalk track,
climbing the side of the valley by Loose
Bottom. At the top of the Down the South
Downs Way turns left by the Newmarket
Plantation, a grove of beeches badly
damaged in the 1987 gale, and left again by
the side of Castle Hill, before turning right
to resume its south-easterly course towards
Eastbourne, above the village of Kingston
near Lewes.

Past a large dewpond, the route crosses
Swanborough Hill with views over
Swanborough Manor below. Once the
grange of Lewes Priory and later owned by

Jack and Jill Windmills, near Clayton

Sir Philip Sidney, the manor has fine carved
griffons in the driveway, a 13th-century hall
and chapel with 15th-century dormitory.

Ⓔ *By taking the track at grid ref. TQ 391 069,
down past Swanborough Manor, and crossing the
road, an escape can be made, by a path along the
east side of the road, into Lewes (2 miles).*

Heading on along the top of the Down,
the route eventually comes to a concrete
track that runs straight as a die along Ilford
Hill and Front Hill. From here a narrow,
enclosed track leads along the side of woods
at Mill Hill by a large house in a fine
position on the right, emerging with views
towards Newhaven to the south.

An unmade road leads down to the village
of Rodmell (overnight accommodation
available), once famous for its silk industry.
Many of the older houses have an 'A'
marked on them, in homage to the Marquess
of Abergavenny, who was the landowner
until 1919. Beyond lies the River Ouse.

Ⓔ *From Rodmell, footpaths follow close by the
east side of the road via Ilford, north to Lewes
(approx. 3 miles).*

THE MONK'S HOUSE (NT)

The Monk's House in Rodmell was the home
of Leonard and Virginia Woolf from 1919
until Leonard's death in 1969. They
entertained many writers and artists of the
Bloomsbury Group there, and both the house
and Virginia's writing hut are full of
memorabilia. The gardens, which were tended
by Leonard, are pleasant, with fine downland
views. Open Easter to late October,
Wednesdays and Saturday afternoons.

Rodmell
Eastbourne

RODMELL
ALFRISTON
APPROX. 9 MILES/14.5KM

OS Landranger 198, 199
Start at grid reference TQ 418 059
Start point: Rodmell, on the minor Lewes-to-Newhaven road. Car parking at eastern end of village.

From Rodmell the South Downs Way crosses the River Ouse, where Virginia Woolf drowned herself when she feared impending madness in 1941. The route follows the road south towards Newhaven, turning into Southease, a village with a green, some 17th-century cottages, and a round-towered Norman church, which has some 13th-century murals. A bridge leads over the Ouse, with the route skirting Southease railway station to reach the A26 Newhaven Road by Itford Farm.

Turning right for 100yds or so down this road, the route then bears left up the side of Itford Hill on a chalk track, which curves its way up the hillside to head east past Red Lion and White Lion ponds, dried-up dewponds in an area where a complete Bronze Age farming settlement was discovered. The Downs here are dominated by the enormous radio mast on the top of Beddingham Hill at 623ft (190m), while below is Beddingham itself, where a Roman villa was discovered as recently as 1987, part of the important network of old trading routes which criss-crossed the region.

To the north is Mount Caburn, an Iron Age hillfort. Below it is the village of Glynde, where John Ellman, who developed the local breed of Southdown sheep, is buried and, near by, Glynde Place, a 16th-century courtyard house. A mile or so further north is Glyndebourne, the Elizabethan mansion which hosts the annual world-famous Glyndebourne Opera season.

Further on along the top of the Down, the route meets with the road coming steeply uphill from West Firle. Firle Park is at the foot of the Down, with its house, Firle Place, built for George Gage in 1557 and rebuilt in 1730. Carrying on past the car park towards the trig. point at Firle Beacon (712ft/217m), the route passes a maze of tumuli with extensive panoramic views.

ⓔ *From Firle Beacon (grid ref. TQ 485 059) an interesting 4-mile route can be taken to Glynde Station, on the Lewes-to-Eastbourne line, by following a track down to Firle Park, a footpath east to Little Dene and then the lane and road north to Glynde.*

Turning to the right to head south-east, the South Downs Way continues along the top of the Downs, passing Charleston Farm to the north below, once the home of the artists Vanessa and Quentin Bell and now open to the public. While heading up Bostal Hill past Bopeep Farm and Jerry's Pond, the route passes small villages of Saxon origin at the foot of the Downs. Alciston boasts a 170ft-long timber-framed barn, while Berwick Church has murals painted by the Bells and their friend Duncan Grant.

More tumuli give an interesting variation to the landscape, before the route heads downhill on a fenced track via Long Burgh towards the village of Alfriston, on the banks of the Cuckmere River, where there is overnight accommodation. Here the South Downs Way emerges in the main street by the ancient Star Inn. Beyond, by the river, is a large church, known as 'the Cathedral of the South Downs'. Its handsome green makes it an excellent place to stop and rest.

ALFRISTON
EASTBOURNE
APPROX. 9 MILES/14.5KM OR APPROX. 11 MILES/17.5KM

OS Landranger 199
Start at grid reference TQ 521 030
Start point: The church green at Alfriston, on the Seaford road. Car parking on the north side of Alfriston.

From Alfriston the final section of the South Downs Way divides, either continuing inland over the Downs on a fairly direct route, or following the coastal path along the cliff-tops of the Seven Sisters Country Park. The first option is bridleway, and must be followed by horse-riders and mountain-bikers, the second is footpath and can only be used by walkers, who will relish the close proximity to the sea after so much inland walking.

The Inland Route
The inland route crosses the Cuckmere River above Alfriston, heading steeply up

Left *Glynde Place, built of knapped flint*

Windover Hill on a hard, chalk track. On its northern slope the Long Man of Wilmington can be seen on the hillside, a gigantic figure, some 226ft long, cut into the turf, and first recorded in the mid-18th century. At the top of the hill there is a wonderful view over the huge bowl of Tenantry Ground. Neolithic remains include tumuli and a long-barrow burial chamber, one of 12 found in Sussex. To the north lies Wilmington, with the remains of its fine Benedictine priory.

From here the route crosses open grassland, with direction markers showing the way as it passes other tumuli and curves round to the south. Here it enters woodland above Jevington, descending to this peaceful hamlet, which was once favoured by smugglers such as Jevington Jack Jigg, and joining the road by the Saxon church with its unusual tapsell gate mounted on a central pivot.

Ⓔ *From Jevington (grid ref. TQ 562 012) a track can be taken south-west through Friston Forest to Westdean, from where the alternative South Downs Way footpath can be followed back to Alfriston (approx. 5 miles).*

The route continues up a track by the side of the Hawthorn Lodge tea-rooms, heading up the last climb of the South Downs Way for those going west to east.

As the Way crosses Wealdway at the top of Willingdon Hill, there is a view north over Combe Hill, a large Neolithic causeway camp. The route continues along a hard track across level ground, passing Eastbourne golf course to the right, with Eastbourne itself laid out at the foot of the Down to the left. On reaching the A259, this track continues straight ahead, before sweeping eastwards downhill into Eastbourne and appropriately finishing on the outskirts of the town at Paradise Way. Here there is a sign, sometimes disfigured by graffiti, marking the end of the South Downs Way.

The Coastal Route

After crossing the bridge over the River Cuckmere at Alfriston, the footpath route leaves the bridleway at Plonk Barn to head south to Litlington. Continuing on past Charleston Bottom, one can glimpse Charleston Manor with its 12th-century hall, and then the route skirts the western end of the 2000 acre Friston Forest to reach Westdean. Its pretty village church and the walls of a medieval dovecot stand among the remains of a manor House.

Ⓔ *From Westdean (grid ref. TV 525 997) a return can be made to Alfriston by heading north-east into Friston Forest, to Snap Hill, and then turning north-west through Lullington Heath Nature Reserve.*

By the A259 Seaford-Eastbourne road, the route enters the Seven Sisters Country Park by the Park Centre at Exceat, once a medieval village, which ceased to exist in the 14th century due to the depradations of plague and attacks by the French. The Seven Sisters themselves are known as Haven Brow, Short Brow, Rough Brow, Brass Point, Flagstaff Point, Bailey's Hill and Went

The Long Man of Wilmington

Hill, and the route passes them on its way along the cliff-path across some 770 acres of National Trust land to Birling Gap, once famous for both smugglers and wreckers. Inland the old part of the village of East Dean has an attractive green and the 13th-century Tiger Inn.

After a diversion due to erosion of the path as the cliffs slide into the sea, the route comes back to follow the cliff-top by the old lighthouse of Belle Tout, built in 1831 of Aberdeen granite and now converted to use as a house. From here it heads round the southernmost part of the coast at Beachy Head (a name derived from the French *beau chef,* meaning fine headland) where the lighthouse at the foot of the cliffs was built to replace Belle Tout in 1902. Finally, the route turns north by the playing fields of Whitebread Hole, entering Eastbourne on the seafront by a refreshment kiosk to complete the South Downs Way.

SEVEN SISTERS COUNTRY PARK

The Seven Sisters Country Park covers 700 acres, including the estuary of the River Cuckmere. There are trails and valley walks within the Park, and a permanent exhibition in a converted 18th-century barn. There is free parking at Exceat. Other exhibits include the Living World exhibition of butterflies, bees, spiders, snails, ants and marine life. Open from Easter to end October daily, and during winter and school holidays at weekends.

Downs Link

SOUTH DOWNS WAY (ST BOTOLPH'S CHURCH, NEAR BRAMBER)
TO
NORTH DOWNS WAY (ST MARTHA'S HILL, NEAR GUILDFORD)
33 MILES/54KM

THE Downs Link was developed as a joint venture between the County Councils of West Sussex and Surrey in conjunction with Waverley Borough Council. Between them, these three local authorities, own much of the old railway line which forms most of the route. The Downs Link is not one of the Countryside Commission's designated long distance paths (or 'National Trails' as they are now renamed). It does, however, serve the important purpose of linking two of these official trails, the South Downs Way from the point where it passes through Botolphs, north of Shoreham-by-Sea, and the North Downs Way at St Martha's Hill, west of Guildford.

The guides to the Downs Link listed below describe the route from north to south. In this book, we travel in the opposite direction, a decision which, as well as offering a choice, does have advantages. In most seasons and at most times of day, you will have the sun behind you or on your flank, and the final climb to the 573ft (175m) summit of St Martha's Hill provides a very real climax, something which is not experienced by walkers arriving at the southern terminus and the flat acres of the Adur valley.

The South Downs Way is the only officially designated long distance bridleway. It is, therefore, particularly useful that the Downs Link, too, is open to horseriders as well as walkers. For 'through' riders, the 12-mile section of the North Downs Way between Guildford and Ranmore is also on legally defined bridleways.

Cyclists, too, may use the Downs Link. The gentle gradients and the smooth and generally well-drained surface of the track bed (there may be a few muddy stretches at the southern end) make it an ideal route for the ordinary bicycle as well as the more

Church Street, Steyning, an ancient town with a rich heritage of vernacular buildings

Detailed guides
Downs Link, the official guide (in the form of a detailed leaflet or a 20-page route guide), is available from West Sussex County Council Planning Dept., County Hall, Chichester, West Sussex, PO19 1RL (tel. 0243 777100). West Sussex County Council also publishes leaflets describing shorter circular walks, based on the Downs Link.
The South Downs Way and the Downs Link, Kev Reynolds (Cicerone Press, 1989).
Railway Walks GWR and SR, Jeff Vinter (Alan Sutton, 1990) includes a description of a walk along the Downs Link.

Maps
OS Landranger 186, 187, 198

Links
The Downs Link intersects with three other 'unofficial' long distance routes. The Greensand Way (see pages 74–7) crosses the route near Shamley Green. The Wey-South Path, another route across the Weald, following as closely as possible the line of 'London's lost route to the sea', the Wey and Arun Canal, coincides with the Downs Link between Bramley and Run Common. On the county boundary, the 150-mile Sussex Border Path, linking Emsworth and Rye, crosses the Downs Link above Baynards Tunnel.

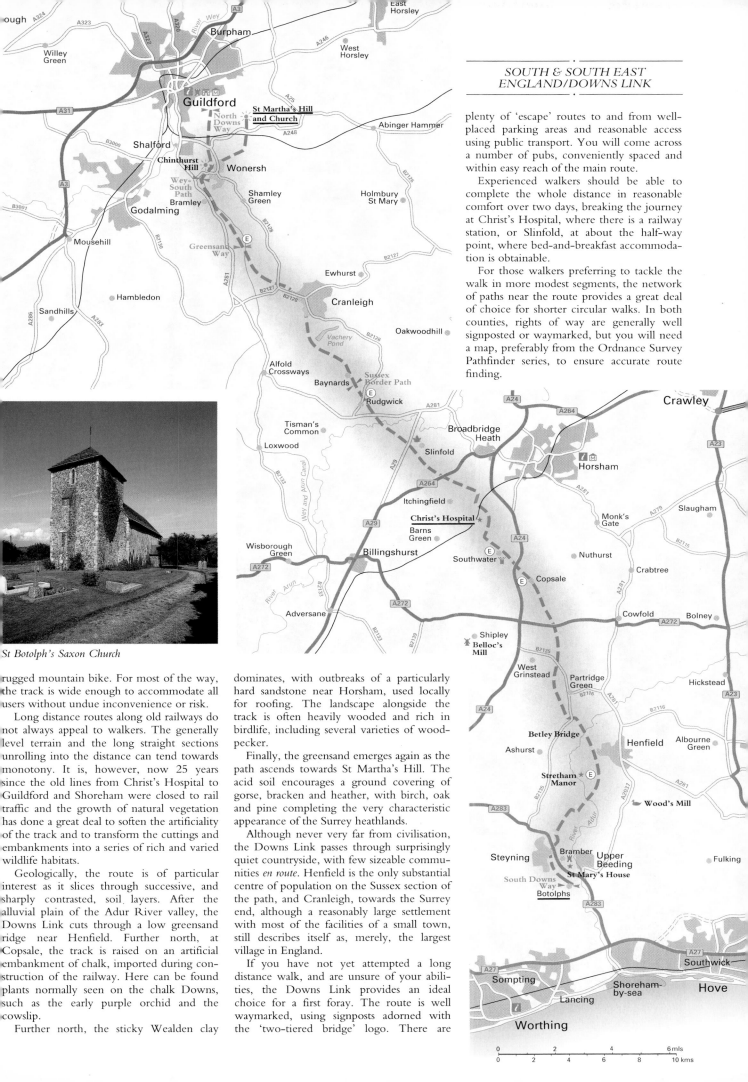

plenty of 'escape' routes to and from well-placed parking areas and reasonable access using public transport. You will come across a number of pubs, conveniently spaced and within easy reach of the main route.

Experienced walkers should be able to complete the whole distance in reasonable comfort over two days, breaking the journey at Christ's Hospital, where there is a railway station, or Slinfold, at about the half-way point, where bed-and-breakfast accommodation is obtainable.

For those walkers preferring to tackle the walk in more modest segments, the network of paths near the route provides a great deal of choice for shorter circular walks. In both counties, rights of way are generally well signposted or waymarked, but you will need a map, preferably from the Ordnance Survey Pathfinder series, to ensure accurate route finding.

St Botolph's Saxon Church

rugged mountain bike. For most of the way, the track is wide enough to accommodate all users without undue inconvenience or risk.

Long distance routes along old railways do not always appeal to walkers. The generally level terrain and the long straight sections unrolling into the distance can tend towards monotony. It is, however, now 25 years since the old lines from Christ's Hospital to Guildford and Shoreham were closed to rail traffic and the growth of natural vegetation has done a great deal to soften the artificiality of the track and to transform the cuttings and embankments into a series of rich and varied wildlife habitats.

Geologically, the route is of particular interest as it slices through successive, and sharply contrasted, soil layers. After the alluvial plain of the Adur River valley, the Downs Link cuts through a low greensand ridge near Henfield. Further north, at Copsale, the track is raised on an artificial embankment of chalk, imported during construction of the railway. Here can be found plants normally seen on the chalk Downs, such as the early purple orchid and the cowslip.

Further north, the sticky Wealden clay

dominates, with outbreaks of a particularly hard sandstone near Horsham, used locally for roofing. The landscape alongside the track is often heavily wooded and rich in birdlife, including several varieties of woodpecker.

Finally, the greensand emerges again as the path ascends towards St Martha's Hill. The acid soil encourages a ground covering of gorse, bracken and heather, with birch, oak and pine completing the very characteristic appearance of the Surrey heathlands.

Although never very far from civilisation, the Downs Link passes through surprisingly quiet countryside, with few sizeable communities *en route*. Henfield is the only substantial centre of population on the Sussex section of the path, and Cranleigh, towards the Surrey end, although a reasonably large settlement with most of the facilities of a small town, still describes itself as, merely, the largest village in England.

If you have not yet attempted a long distance walk, and are unsure of your abilities, the Downs Link provides an ideal choice for a first foray. The route is well waymarked, using signposts adorned with the 'two-tiered bridge' logo. There are

Botolphs

Christ's Hospital

BOTOLPHS

HENFIELD

APPROX. 5³/₄ MILES/9KM

OS Landranger 198
Start at grid reference TQ 194 094
Start point: The tiny hamlet of Botolphs on the narrow unclassified road running along the west side of the Adur valley between the A27 coast road and Steyning. There is very limited parking space beside the narrow road which heads north from the A27 between Lancing and Shoreham-by-Sea at grid ref. TQ 193 094, within yards of the start of the path.
Alternatively, catch a bus from Shoreham to a bus stop on the A283, ¹/₄ mile north of the cement works, and use the South Downs Way bridle bridge to cross the river. To walk to the start from Shoreham-by-Sea, use the path along the west bank of the Adur.

The Downs Link starts where the South Downs Way crosses the line of the old railway. This point is identified on the map as Botolphs, now no more than an isolated church and a handful of houses. The archaeological evidence in surrounding fields suggests that this was once a thriving community, brought down, like so many other lost villages, by a combination of the Black Death, famine and a general decline in prosperity. The tiny church retains features of its Saxon origins, including a chancel arch and a window in the south wall of the nave.

Start the Downs Link walk along the old railway track. After a little over ¹/₂ mile, turn left along the Bramber bypass, where there is a wide grass verge. At a roundabout follow Castle Lane, opposite.

Bramber Castle, to the right, deserves a detour. The 11th-century castle was demolished in 1641, during the Civil War. The site is now dominated by an 80ft wall fragment. In its heyday, the castle overlooked the Adur Gap, at a time when the water came right up to the foot of the castle mound.

After 500yds along Castle Lane, turn right into King's Stone Avenue. This ends at a junction with King's Barn Lane. To visit Steyning, a delightful village, turn left.

To continue the walk, turn right. After about ¹/₂ mile, a bridge takes the track across the line of the old railway, here restored to

Bramber Castle: its remains still hold a
commanding position over the Adur Gap

GUIDE BOX

Places to visit
St Mary's House, Bramber is a timber-framed house dating from the 15th century. The interior includes a Painted Room, decorated for a visit by Queen Elizabeth I. The house is open afternoons on Sundays, Mondays and Thursdays during the summer months.

Wood's Mill, headquarters of the Sussex Wildlife Trust, can be reached along a public footpath which heads eastwards from the Adur River bank just south of Stretham Manor at grid ref. TQ 202 135. It incorporates a nature trail and a small museum, and is open to the public during the summer months.

Shipley Mill is only infrequently open to the public, usually about one weekend in every summer month.

Southwater Country Park, alongside the Downs Link at Southwater, is a 54-acre site under the management of Horsham District Council. A visitor centre is open at weekends from April to October. It contains information displays and offers light refreshments.

Car parking
Car parking is possible at Bramber, near the castle (grid ref. TQ 185 106), at Henfield (TQ 207 162), at West Grinstead in the old station yard (TQ 183 227), at Copsale opposite the Bridge House pub (TQ 171 249), at the Southwater Country Park (TQ 161 259), and at Christ's Hospital Station (fee) (TQ 148 292).

Public transport
British Rail stations at Shoreham-by-Sea (connected by bus to and from Upper Beeding) and at Christ's Hospital. Bus services connect with Brighton and Horsham from Henfield and Partridge Green. There is also a bus linking Southwater and Horsham.

Accommodation
Shoreham-by-Sea, Steyning and Bramber all provide accommodation convenient for the start of the Downs Link. Tottington Barn youth hostel is on Truleigh Hill, 2 miles eastwards along the South Downs Way (grid ref. TQ 220 106). The George hotel in Henfield offers bed-and-breakfast. The latest *Downs Link* route guide leaflet provides some accommodation information (available from West Sussex County Council, see page 68 under Detailed Guides).

farm use and available for walkers and riders. Shortly, go ahead along Wyckham Lane. After Wyckham Farm, the track climbs gently, the only significant incline on the Sussex section of the route.

After another 200yds, turn right along a grassy path which brings you back to the old railway. Turn left along the track bed. For the next 2 miles you can enjoy the most open section of the whole route, through the flat and wide Adur valley. Cross the river at Stretham Manor, near the point where the Romans, in the 1st century AD, also established a river crossing.

Ⓔ *From here (grid ref. TQ 200 137) there is a choice of river bank paths, either back to Botolphs along the west bank of the river, or northwards, along the east bank for 4 miles to Betley Bridge where the Downs Link crosses the river.*

On approaching Henfield, the old railway crosses a track and enters a deep cutting. For a short distance the line of the railway is occupied by a housing estate, appropriately called 'Beechings'. Use Lower Station Road, a few yards to the east, to reach the Cat and the Canary pub. A right turn by the pub takes you into the centre of Henfield, a small but bustling community with food shops, accommodation and a bus to Brighton or Horsham.

HENFIELD

CHRIST'S HOSPITAL

APPROX. 9 MILES/14.5KM

OS Landranger 198
Start at grid reference TQ 206 162
Start point: There is a small parking area for Downs Link users to the west of the Cat and the Canary pub.

From the car park, head north along the line of the railway. After a mile, beyond the northern river crossing at Betley Bridge, a bridle gate leads into a field, where the line of the railway is less clearly defined. After a second bridle gate, the track is again enclosed between two hedges.

After another ³/₄ mile, turn left on a crossing track. At the B2135, turn right and walk towards Partridge Green (where buses connect with Brighton and Horsham). Just short of the bridge over the railway, fork left on a narrow path down to rejoin the railway track bed.

After a mile or so the Downs Link crosses the B2135 and shortly enters a pleasant wooded cutting and then passes under the A272. To the north of the road, you will come to the overgrown platforms at West Grinstead Station. The station yard is being converted to a parking and picnic area. The Tabby Cat pub, marked on some older maps, is no more, but has been replaced by a 'Little Chef', on the A272, immediately to the west of the bridge.

Shipley Mill can be found about 2¹/₂ miles to the west of here. It can be reached by road or on footpaths from the Downs Link at grid ref. TQ 183 214, past West Grinstead Church and through Knepp Park. The mill was built in 1879 and is the last working smock mill in West Sussex. It was once owned by the writer Hilaire Belloc, an early long distance walker who described a journey on foot across the country.

To the north of the A272, the Downs Link enters a more varied landscape – an attractive patchwork of small woods and fields, perhaps the most appealing

Christ's Hospital School

countryside on the whole of the Sussex section of the path. The footpath network to the east of the old railway is well marked and provides excellent opportunities for return circuits linking West Grinstead, Southwater and Copsale.

Another 1³/₄ miles on the track bed brings you to Copsale, where the Downs Link crosses the road next to the Bridge House pub, a welcome refreshment stop with a garden alongside the old railway. On the south side of the road there is a car park for Downs Link users.

Ⓔ *For an escape from here (grid ref. TQ 171 249) back to West Grinstead, start east along the road then head south.*

After another ¹/₂ mile, the route burrows under the Southwater bypass and continues along a lane, parallel with and to the right of the line of the railway. After crossing another road, the Southwater Country Park is to your left and there is another large car park. At the turn of the century, the 54-acre site of the park was occupied by the brickyards of the grandly named Southwater Brick, Tile, Terracotta Pipe and Clay Company. By 1981, after 1000 million bricks had been produced, the clay ran out and the works closed. In 1985, following extensive landscaping, conversion to the Southwater Country Park was complete.

Until recently, Downs Link walkers had to divert from the track into Southwater village. This is no longer necessary. Very shortly, go left up some steps and resume your course on the line of the old railway. After passing between a row of bollards, go ahead between the platforms of the former Southwater Station.

Ⓔ *From Southwater (grid ref. TQ 162 259), a reasonably direct series of field paths takes you east to Nuthurst where there is a welcome pub. From here, more paths allow you to head generally southwards to join the old railway at several points to the north of West Grinstead.*

Pass under a bridge, go forward on a narrow path between gardens, then ahead

across a field. Beyond a gate in the far field corner, cross a concrete drive and continue between fences. For a short distance, the path is less recognisable as an old railway, but soon re-establishes its character along a series of delightful wooded embankments. Just short of the next bridge over the track, a gate on the right provides access to the Bax Castle pub.

The Downs Link now approaches Christ's Hospital alongside the main Horsham-to-Portsmouth railway, with the playing fields of Christ's Hospital School to your right.

The school was founded in 1552, during the reign of Edward VI. It is familiarly known as the 'Bluecoat School' a name derived from the traditional costume, still worn by the boys, consisting of blue gowns, yellow stockings and knee breeches.

Join a metalled drive and follow it out to a road where you should go left and, shortly, left again over the railway. If you are finishing the day's walk at Christ's Hospital Station, go ahead instead of crossing the main line. After 200yds, fork left. The station is no more than a few minutes' walk away.

THE RAILWAY ORIGINS

The Downs Link owes its existence to two separate railway lines. The first of these was opened in September 1861. Originally a single-track line, but widened in 1879, the line was constructed and operated by the London, Brighton and South Coast Railway. A second line between Horsham and Guildford, single track throughout, started by the Horsham and Guildford Railway Company and completed by the London, Brighton and South Coast Railway, opened in 1865.

The two lines were linked by a short section of the Pulborough line, still in use today as part of the main through-route between London and Littlehampton. The two lines were never profitable, as grandiose plans to provide a through-route between the Midlands and the south coast failed to materialise. Both were closed when the Beeching axe fell in 1966.

Christ's Hospital

St Martha's Church

CHRIST'S HOSPITAL

CRANLEIGH

APPROX. 9³/₄ MILES/15.5 KM

OS Landranger 187
Start at grid reference TQ 146 288
Start point: At the point where an unclassified road crosses the main railway line at Christ's Hospital. Car parking at Christ's Hospital Station, ¹/₄ mile to the north. There is plenty of room at weekends, but it is very busy from Monday to Friday.
Christ's Hospital, conveniently placed near the half-way point of the walk, is the only intermediate point on the Downs Link served by train, though there is no Sunday service.

Walk along the station access road. Ignore a left fork and, shortly, join another road and go ahead. After 200yds, bear right over the railway, now on the Downs Link, which has to resort to quiet roads for the next mile as the track bed from Christ's Hospital Station is unavailable. At a road junction after ¹/₂ mile, turn right.

For a short diversion, take the field path ahead for ¹/₄ mile to the interesting church at Itchingfield, notable for an oak-framed belfry dating back to the 15th century. In the churchyard you will find a medieval timber-framed building, known as the Priest's House, built for visiting monks.

Back on the main route, after another ¹/₂ mile, where the lane bends to the left, turn right along the drive to Baystone House.

Cross the old railway and double back to the left down on to the track bed.

Towards Slinfold, the Downs Link crosses a road, where a faded advertisement on the brick wall of a house (now providing bed-and-breakfast) was clearly designed for train passengers. The village is ¹/₂ mile to the right here where the King's Head also offers accommodation. For anyone attempting to complete the Downs Link in two days, this is a good stop-over point with just over half the journey (18 miles) completed.

The site of Slinfold Station, ¹/₄ mile further on, has been converted to a caravan site with a car park beside the line. From here, a nature trail has been laid out through woodland typical of the Sussex Weald, a mixture mainly of oak and ash.

From this point northwards to Bramley, the land alongside the line, all in public ownership, has been carefully 'managed' in order to conserve a wide variety of wildlife. When the railway closed, the embankments reverted to dense scrub and woodland and many plants and animals declined or disappeared. Now a valuable 'wildlife corridor' has been restored.

After another 1¹/₂ miles you will come to the two-tier bridge over the River Arun which features on the Downs Link logo. The building of one bridge on top of the other was necessitated by the 19th-century railway inspector's requirement that the steep gradient up to Rudgwick should be eased.

Cross the busy A281 road with care as the traffic is fast. A few more minutes' walking brings you to the site of Rudgwick Station, where there is a small car park and easy access to the village street and shop.

Below *The Priest's House, Itchingfield*

GUIDE BOX

Places to visit
Slinfold Nature Trail, about 2 miles in length, uses part of the Downs Link and nearby woodland. A leaflet, describing the trail, is available from West Sussex County Council Planning Department, County Hall, Chichester, West Sussex, PO19 1RL.

Rudgwick, alongside the route, is an attractive village, strung out on either side of a long village street. The church dates mainly from the 14th century, with, near by, a fine group of tile-hung cottages.

Wonersh, a picturesque village, within half a mile of the Downs Link, as it passes Bramley, is worth a detour for its 17th-century half-timbered inn and the church which, although partly destroyed by fire in the 18th century, still includes work dating back to Saxon times.

Car parking
There are car parks at Slinfold and Rudgwick near the sites of the former railway stations. At Cranleigh, there is a large public car park. Further north, there are car parking areas on the route at the foot of Chinthurst Hill (grid ref. TQ 014 464), at Blackheath within ¹/₄ mile of the path (TQ 036 462), and to the east of St Martha's Hill (TQ 036 484).

Public transport
A useful bus service (scarce on Sundays) links Horsham, Rudgwick, Slinfold, Cranleigh, Bramley and Guildford. The Redhill-to-Guildford British Rail line passes through Chilworth, but not many trains stop there (none on Sundays).

Accommodation
Overnight accommodation is possible at Slinfold, Cranleigh, Blackheath (The Villagers Inn) and Guildford. The latest *Downs Link* route guide (available from West Sussex County Council, see page 68 under Detailed Guides) lists some of the addresses and telephone numbers of establishments providing bed-and-breakfast.

Ⓔ *A short distance beyond the next over-bridge, at grid ref. TQ 082 341, a signed field path, up three steps and over a stile on the right, leads directly to the King's Head pub, ²/₃ mile away, crossing a lane en route. From here a pleasant footpath may be followed back to Slinfold, via Hyes and Dedisham.*

Very shortly you will come to the barricaded entrance to Baynards tunnel. The Downs Link climbs a ramped path on the left. At the top, you have a choice of routes. Pedestrians may go to the right, over the top of the tunnel. Equestrians and cyclists must turn left. For a short distance the Downs Link coincides with the Sussex Border Path, which, for several miles both eastward and westward, follows the low ridge that forms the county boundary. After a few yards, turn right into Surrey and walk through woods to a road.

Turn right, cross a bridge and double back to the right down on to the old railway. At Baynards Station, the Downs Link skirts to the left of the buildings, in private ownership, and carefully restored to their former glory. Beyond the station, there is a small picnic area for Downs Link users, and

The Thurlow Arms pub is well placed beside the track (overnight accommodation).

After a little over a mile, at grid ref. TQ 063 372, a diversion may be made on a footpath that leads eastwards to Vachery Pond, once a hammer pond and a relic of the Wealden iron industry.

In a mile or so, the Downs Link reaches Cranleigh, with easy access to the town.

CRANLEIGH

ST MARTHA'S CHURCH

APPROX. 9 MILES/15KM

OS Landranger 187 and 186
Start at grid reference TQ 057 391
Start point: Knowle Lane, about 100 yds south of its junction with the B2128 at the western end of the village. Ample car parking in Cranleigh.

The path, narrow at first, but still on the line of the old railway, is well segregated from an industrial area on the right. Once clear of the town, the Downs Link runs on an embankment with the disused Wey and Arun Canal, here no more than an overgrown ditch, to the left. A low brick wall marks the point where the canal passed under the railway.

The third over-bridge north from here carries the Greensand Way (see pages 74-7) across the Downs Link.

Ⓔ *The 4-mile section of the Greensand Way westwards from here (grid ref. TQ 024 427) to Hascombe, provides a varied and attractive walk with a good pub at the end of it and various possibilities for circuits back to Cranleigh.*

Further on, approaching Bramley, the canal appears again, now on the right, partially restored and full of water. At Bramley, the Downs Link crosses the B2128. The village, with shops, pubs, and a good bus service into Guildford, is to the left. The walk goes ahead along the platform of the former Bramley and Wonersh Station, where the old station sign is still intact. After a short detour to the right, where a bridge has been demolished, resume your way along the track bed with a stream near by to your left.

Shortly, you will come to a double bridge. The lower arch across the Wey and Arun Canal has been incorporated into a newer bridge across the railway. The scene provides a graphic symbol of the eclipse of the canal by the railway and the final dominance of road transportation.

Turn right in front of the bridge, cross the lower arch and walk parallel to a lane on your left. Join the lane and shortly, at a road junction, go ahead on a roughly metalled drive which soon dwindles to a bridleway.

After ½ mile a path to the right leads up to the top of Chinthurst Hill, worth a visit if time permits. The Downs Link continues past a car park and out to the B2128.

Cross the road and follow a woodland path, opposite. At a drive, turn left. At Great Tangley Manor Farm, go ahead on a soft

sandy track which soon narrows and climbs between high banks. After a little over ½ mile, go straight over an oblique crossing track and follow the Downs Link waymarks carefully across Blackheath, crossing a lane at grid ref. TQ 032 463. (For the Villagers pub turn right, then left at a crossroads.)

About 30yds beyond the lane, fork right. Your next landmark is an isolated stone war memorial, on raised ground to the right of the track. From the memorial, you can just see St Martha's Church, over the trees.

A few yards past the memorial, go ahead over a crossing track, where the Downs Link way post is a little ambiguous. Shortly, cross the end of a drive and follow a narrow path to the right of the gateway to Lingwood House.

Descend into a valley, cross the railway and the A248 road and go ahead along a drive, with St Martha's Church now in clear view, perched high on the hill ahead. Beyond a footbridge, a detour along a narrow woodland path to the left leads to the ruins of Chilworth gunpowder mills, the only remaining signs of a once thriving local industry.

Shortly, cross the main Tillingbourne stream and, after another 300yds, turn right for the last ascent on to St Martha's Hill. Towards the top, a Downs Link logo, with the date 1984, set in stone, marks the end of the path at the point where it joins the North Downs Way. For the summit, a few minutes' walk, turn sharp left.

St Martha's Church, almost entirely rebuilt in 1848, stands on the site of a much

The final goal, St Martha's Church

older church, dating back to 1087. It has, for centuries, provided a place of sanctuary and worship for travellers on a much older long distance route, the Pilgrim's Way from Winchester to Canterbury. It is a fitting place to end the walk, with glorious views back across the Weald and along the Surrey Hills.

From here, the surest way to link with public transport is to follow the North Downs Way into Guildford (3 miles west). Infrequent trains stop at Chilworth (1½ miles south) and there is a bus service from Albury (2 miles east).

THE WEY AND ARUN CANAL

The Wey and Arun Canal, 18½ miles long with 23 locks, was opened for traffic on 29 September 1816 when a procession of four barges, sent on their way by two music bands, processed from Alfold to Guildford.

The canal, which linked the River Wey at Shalford with the Arun at Newbridge, was designed to carry an economical proportion of the London-to-Portsmouth cargo, but was never a success.

Floods in the Arun valley and lack of water at the summit level caused too many navigational delays. The final blow came with the construction of the two railway lines which now make up most of the Downs Link.

The canal was finally closed to traffic in 1871. Now, over 100 years later, a slow process of restoration is under way, thanks to the work of the Wey and Arun Canal Society. Although a long-term project, it is entirely feasible that London's 'lost route to the sea' may eventually be navigable once more.

Greensand Way

COMPLETE ROUTE
HASLEMERE TO HAM STREET
105 MILES/169KM

·

SECTION COVERED
WITLEY TO DORKING
23 MILES/37KM

THE idea for a long distance path along the line of the greensand hills in Surrey came from a local member of the Ramblers' Association and the route was developed with the support of the Surrey Amenity Council. A 12-mile section of the Greensand Way, linking Winterfold Heath with Dorking, was officially opened on Leith Hill on 15 June 1980. This section is maybe the finest on the entire route, and is certainly the most strenuous. The rest of the Surrey section was fully established by 1982, providing a 55-mile walk from Haslemere to Dorking. The Greensand Way in Kent was developed during the 1980s by the Kent Area of the Ramblers' Association and the final link, from Yalding to Ham Street, was officially opened in 1989.

In this book we cover the 23-mile section from Witley Station, just under 10 miles from the official start of the route at Haslemere, to Dorking. For walkers wishing to add the very attractive first section of the route to the journey described here, there is a direct railway link between Witley and Haslemere, and they will be rewarded by the exceptional landscape of Hindhead Common, Gibbet Hill and the Devil's Punchbowl.

From Witley, the Way crosses Hambledon

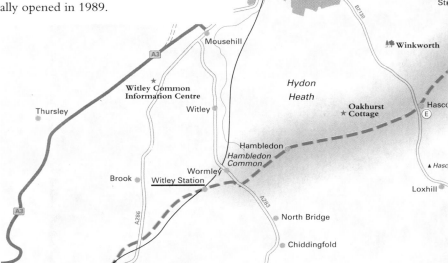

Detailed guides

The Greensand Way in Surrey describes the whole of the Surrey section of the route in detail, as well as five link routes between the Greensand Way and the North Downs Way, two of them from places on the section described in this book. It is available from Surrey County Council Planning Dept, County Hall, Kingston upon Thames, Surrey, KT1 2DT. The 50 miles of the Greensand Way in Kent are described in a guidebook available from Kent County Council, Planning Dept, Springfield, Maidstone, Kent ME14 2LX

Maps

OS Landranger 186, 187

Links

The Downs Link (see pages 68 – 73) crosses the Greensand Way near Shamley Green. The North Downs Way crosses Box Hill just north of Dorking and runs roughly parallel to the Greensand Way. A choice of linking paths makes it possible to design a series of circuits. The Wey-South Path crosses the Way near Grafham.

Common to Hambledon village. It then climbs gently across open heathland before dropping steeply to Hascombe, delightfully situated in a fold of the Surrey Hills. The path now heads north-eastwards through gently undulating, well-wooded countryside.

The Greensand Way, on level ground, then crosses, in quick succession, the A281 Guildford-to-Horsham road, the Downs Link path on the old Guildford-to-Horsham railway, and the disused Wey and Arun Canal, to reach Shamley Green.

A gentle climb on to Winterfold Heath marks the start of the finest section of the walk. Over the next 6 miles or so, the walker can enjoy a succession of spectacular summits as the Way picks a route along the main greensand ridge. Reynard's Hill (800ft/243m), Pitch Hill (843ft/257m) and Holmbury Hill (857ft/261m) follow in quick succession. After the descent to Holmbury St Mary, Leith Hill provides a final challenge. At 965ft (294m) above sea level, this is the highest point in south-east England.

From here, a long and easy walk north-

wards through woodland and along the Tillingbourne valley leads to Westcott and a last climb over the Nower to Dorking.

The Greensand Way has been comprehensively waymarked, using the GW logo superimposed on the standard yellow and blue Countryside Commission arrows. For most of the walk, route finding is easy. There are, however, one or two places where the waymarks are missing or less obvious. These ambiguous junctions are described in more detail in the route description on the following pages.

'Escape' from the later section of the route described here is easy – northwards to various points along the A25 road and the parallel railway line linking Guildford and Dorking.

The rocks of the greensand hills were first laid down about 130 million years ago when the Weald was one large shallow lake. Much later, the whole area was flooded by the sea and in turn clay, more greensand and finally a thick deposit of chalk was laid down. A combination of earth movements and

St Peter's Church, Hambledon

Leith Hill, as seen from Pitch Hill

erosion have led to the present geological formation. Of the chalk, only the South and North Downs remain. Between the North Downs and the clay of the central Weald, the lower greensand, less easily eroded, forms the highest hills in the area.

The Greensand Way is well named, because it is the nature of the soil which provides the landscape and the walk with its immediately recognisable character. For mile after mile, the walker is conscious of the sandy, well-drained soil underfoot, while on either side of the path, the recurring pattern of heath and woodland predominates. Although the acidic nature of the soil renders it relatively infertile, this is no waste land. A wide variety of trees flourish, including oak, beech, hazel and sweet chestnut as well as the pine and silver birch which are so characteristic of the open heath land.

The 'Greensand' label was first applied in the last century because of the presence of the mineral glauconite which does have a truly grass-green colour when first exposed to the atmosphere. Weathering, however, causes rapid oxidation, with the formation of black, brown, red and finally the yellow pigment which gives the sands of these hills their main colour.

Much of the area crossed by the Greensand Way in Surrey is managed as public open space by various organisations and it is possible to explore, with relative freedom, wide areas on either side of the 'official' path, notably on Winterfold Heath, Holmbury Hill and Leith Hill.

75

Witley
Dorking

OS Landranger 186
Start at grid reference SU 949 379
Start point: Witley Station on the Guildford-to-Portsmouth main line. There is an hourly train service from Guildford. There is a station car park.

Turn left along the station approach road. An enclosed path starts beside a road junction, almost opposite the Pig and Whistle pub. At the A283, turn left. After a few yards, go right and follow waymarks, embossed with the GW logo, soon crossing Hambledon Common, the first of a number of areas of open heathland which are a major feature of the greensand belt.

Descend to the road at Hambledon, a pleasant but rather scattered village. At a road junction, go ahead, signposted to Godalming. Shortly, beside the entrance to Rockhill House, fork right up steps and cross two fields to join a lane. Turn left, passing Hambledon Church.

St Peter's Church and the nearby Court Farm form an attractive group. The church contains a 14th-century chancel arch. In the churchyard stand two magnificent yew trees, the larger being 30ft in circumference.

Beyond the church, fork right and, at a T-junction, turn right again. After a few yards, a narrow path forks left along the top of a hanger before dropping down through the wood. After a short section, parallel to a lane, the route follows the foot of the hanger with wide views to the south.

At the next lane, turn left and after 50yds, go right up a sunken track to cross the wood and heathland of The Hurtwood, ignoring all side tracks. After ³/₄ mile go right and left, then drop down steeply between banks. Look out for a narrow, steep, descending path on the left, which can be slippery. A field path leads out to the road at Hascombe, opposite the White Horse pub.

Ⓔ *From Hascombe (grid ref. TQ 002 395) a visit can be made to Winkworth Arboretum (see Places to visit) and from there a well-linked series of paths leads along the Juniper Valley and over Hydon's Ball back to Hambledon.*

From Hascombe, an attractive village surrounded by wooded hills, a diversion is possible, to the 645ft (196m) summit of Hascombe Hill, jutting out southwards into the Weald, covered with fine beech trees and crowned by earthworks marking the site of an Iron Age fort.

The Greensand Way continues along Church Road, beside the pub, passing the beautifully kept village pond and the gothic-style church, rebuilt in 1864. Where the road ends, go ahead through a gateway and, shortly, enter an ascending sunken track.

A series of woodland tracks, well marked with the GW logo at all junctions, brings you to a lane. Turn right and, after a few yards, turn left along a waymarked path, beside a fence, through woods and across pasture beside another fence. In a dip fork left, uphill, beside a high fence. Cross a track and walk down across a field. In the bottom right corner, join a track, passing to the left of a barn and a wood.

Turn left along the drive from Gatestreet Farm. Beyond a house called 'Keepers', the drive loses its metalled surface. Fork right at a junction and, subsequently, turn left along a lane. Where the lane bears left, go forward across a cattle grid. A field path now leads to the A281. Turn left. After 150yds, turn right through Rooks Hill Farm. The Greensand Way now crosses the Downs Link, which

The view from the heights of Pitch Hill

follows the old Horsham-to-Guildford
railway line and is described on pages 68–73.

Ⓔ *The Downs Link (grid ref. TQ 024 428)
provides convenient access on foot either south to
Cranleigh or north to Bramley and Guildford.*

The path soon crosses the former Wey
and Arun Canal, no more than an
overgrown ditch at this point. A waymarked
bridleway continues to the B2128, south of
Shamley Green. Turn left along the road for
pub refreshment and a bus to Guildford.

SHAMLEY GREEN
DORKING
APPROX. 15 MILES/25KM

*OS Landranger 186 and 187
Start at grid ref. TQ 033 438*
Start point: Shamley Green on the B2128
Bramley-to-Cranleigh road. Bus from
Guildford. Limited roadside parking.

From the village green, walk southwards
along the B2128. Just past the church on the
left, turn left along an enclosed path. Join a
drive and, after 250yds, turn right along
another drive to 'Little Cuckrells'. Where
the drive ends, a good path continues to a
lane by Strouds Farm.

Turn right and, shortly, left along the
drive to 'Franklins'. By the house entrance,
go forward along a grassy path. Very shortly,
fork left, uphill through woodland. Climb
across an open area, passing a large new
pond, not marked on Ordnance Survey
maps. Re-enter woods and join a track.
Where this track veers right, downhill, go
ahead. Take care as there is no waymark
here.

Walk round the shoulder of the hill to a
meeting of six ways where you should go
ahead on a level track. Cross a lane and
climb steps, opposite. The Greensand Way,
waymarked at intervals, follows a path along
the scarp of Winterfold Hill, with a series of
views, glimpsed through the trees, out across
the Weald. The path eventually turns away
from the edge to join a road at the top of a
deep and dramatic gully. After a few yards
along the road, the Way diverges to the right
on a path, parallel to the road at first.

At a crossing track, turn right. Another
contour path follows the top of the scarp
slope to a viewpoint on the top of Reynard's
Hill, the first of a series of summit
viewpoints which are the main feature of the
next few miles. This is the westernmost
height of the Leith Hill range of hills and
offers a wide view to the south and west.
The bluff of Hascombe Hill stands out, with
Hindhead and Blackdown beyond and to the
left. On a clear day the South Downs are
visible on the southern skyline.

A path continues to rejoin the road, once
again for a few yards only. At a T-junction,
go ahead, soon passing Ewhurst windmill.
This brick post-mill was built in about 1820
and has been converted to a private
residence. Drop down beside a fence to cross

a road. In a few yards, turn right and climb
steadily to the top of Pitch Hill, also known
as Coneyhurst Hill. At 843ft (257m) above
sea level, this is another magnificent summit.
The village of Ewhurst is in the foreground.

Ⓔ *From the summit of Pitch Hill (grid ref. TQ
083 423) an escape can be made by a choice of
bridleways and footpaths leading north, to
Peaslake and then by quiet country lanes and
footpaths to Gomshall Station, on the Guildford-
to-Dorking line.*

Carry on round the edge of the hill with
views all the way. Your next challenge, the
summit of Holmbury Hill is prominent to
the east. About 60yds past a metal seat, fork
right down past the Duke of Kent School
and out to a road. A narrow path, opposite,
crosses the valley and climbs to the summit
of Holmbury Hill. The way is clear
throughout.

This third viewpoint, at 857ft (261m), is
perhaps the best of all. You can look back
across the successive ridges of Pitch Hill and
Hascombe Hill as well as forward to the
wooded heights of Leith Hill, our final and
highest summit. A large Early Iron Age fort,
with a double rampart and ditch, covers a
wide expanse of the summit area.

From the elaborate seat on the top, follow
the hill edge. Beyond a cricket pitch on the
left, fork right down to the village of
Holmbury St Mary. At the road, turn left,
shortly ignoring a left fork. Walk down past
the post office to a junction with the B2126.
The Way turns right here but the village is
about ¼ mile along the road to the left.

After a few yards to the right along the
B2126, the Greensand Way turns left. After

The Duke of Kent School

another 300yds, turn right into woodland on
a clear track. Beyond High Ashes Farm, go
right at a T-junction and after nearly ¼ mile
turn left up to a road. The track opposite
takes you for another ¾ mile up to the
summit of Leith Hill, at 965ft (294m) the
highest point in the south-eastern counties.

Go ahead, past the tower and steeply
downhill. At a National Trust notice,
'Duke's Warren', turn left on a crossing
track. Now descend for 1½ miles down a
long valley. At a road, turn right and,
immediately fork right again. Continue
along the valley with the Tillingbourne
stream near by on your left.

At the point where the track meets a lane,
the Greensand Way turns right on a path
parallel with and to the left of a track. Cross
another track and drop down through
woodland. Join, in turn, a track and then an
access drive out to the A25 road. A few yards
short of the main road, turn right up a
sunken path. Cross Westcott Heath and join
a path behind the houses of Westcott.

Cross a footbridge, turn left along a road
and, shortly, turn right up on to the Nower.
Follow waymarks up to 'The Temple' on
the highest point. Maintain direction, finally
bearing left down across grass to join a lane.
Turn right and then left into Dorking. The
bus station is near by, but the two railway
stations are nearly a mile on.

LEITH HILL TOWER (NT)

The tower on the summit of Leith Hill was
erected in 1764 by Richard Hull, who lived in
Leith Hill Place, at the foot of the hill. He was
buried beneath the tower – upside down, at
his request, so that he might 'face his Maker
the right way up'.

The tower was designed so that the top
reaches a height exceeding 1000ft (300m)
above sea level. By 1864, it had fallen into
disrepair and was filled with cement to prevent
complete collapse. To open it up again, an
external staircase was added.

Now under the care of the National Trust,
the tower is being painstakingly restored to its
former glory. From the top, the prospect is
magnificent, encompassing most of Surrey,
much of Sussex and parts of Kent, Hampshire,
Berkshire and counties north of the Thames.
In clear weather, Dunstable Downs, 50 miles
to the north, are clearly visible.

Open April to September, Saturdays,
Sundays and Bank Holiday Mondays.

Wealdway

GRAVESEND TO EASTBOURNE
80 MILES/129KM

THE idea for a long distance route linking the Thames Estuary with the English Channel goes back almost 20 years. The project was first conceived by a group of Kent ramblers. In 1973, Jim Carley, a member of the Meopham Footpath Group published a leaflet describing a route linking Gravesend and Tonbridge. In 1976, under the title of 'A Country Walk', the magnificent central section of the walk between Tonbridge and Uckfield was charted on a series of detailed strip maps, designed by Geoffrey King.

Further south there were many difficulties to overcome before any route description could be published. Years of neglect had left many rights of way in the Sussex Weald in very poor condition, often completely impassable. The route was surveyed in detail by members of the Ramblers' Association. Over 50 landowners were contacted, 70 new stiles erected and a comprehensive waymarking programme undertaken.

By 1980, all seemed set fair for publication of the first official guide to the entire route. Even then, all did not run entirely smoothly. Luddesdown Parish Council was unhappy about the route of the Wealdway through the beautiful valley known as the Bowling Alley, presumably fearing an invasion of inexperienced walkers. Ironically, two years later, the same Parish Council was glad to invoke the presence of the Wealdway to strengthen the arguments against use of the same valley by the Army to practise mine-laying, a much more serious threat. In the face of massive protests, the Ministry of Defence withdrew.

On 27 September 1981, the Wealdway was officially declared open by Derek Barber, the chairman of the Countryside Commission, at a simple ceremony on the top of Ashdown Forest. A commemorative plaque marks the spot at Camp Hill.

The Wealdway crosses the centre of the

Jevington Church and Willingdon Hill

Detailed guides
The 'official' guide is published by the Wealdway Committee of the Ramblers' Association, (Kent and Sussex Areas), and includes detailed 1:25,000 strip maps of the whole route (1991 edition). Contact Ramblers' Association (Sussex Area) 11, Old London Road, Brighton, Sussex, BN1 8XR. From the same source, you can obtain a list of establishments on or near the route providing bed-and-breakfast.

Maps
OS Landranger 177, 188, 198, 199

Links
The Wealdway briefly joins the North Downs Way and the Pilgrim's Way just east of Vigo. It also joins the Greensand Way west of West Peckham. The Eden Valley Walk starts at Tonbridge. The Sussex Border Path coincides briefly with the Wealdway a little south of Ashurst and the Forest Way crosses it about $2^1/_2$ miles west of Groombridge. The Vanguard Way runs parallel to the Wealdway for part of its route across the Weald and may be joined at several points. The Wealdway also meets or is concurrent with the South Downs Way, the Saxon Shore Way and the London Countryway.

overcrowded south-eastern corner of England, but the chosen route manages, for almost its entire length, to avoid the main centres of population. Although civilisation is never far away, much of the walk is quiet and remote, with only the occasional tiny village to interrupt a varied succession of woodland, arable field, river bank, heath, orchard and downland pasture.

The remarkable variety of the countryside through which the route passes is largely determined by the underlying geology. From the flat, largely arable land to the south of the Thames, the path soon begins to rise through undulating chalk hills and valleys, climbing steadily to the edge of the North Downs escarpment. It is well-wooded landscape, interspersed with sheep pastures as well as arable land.

At the foot of the scrub-covered scarp slope of the North Downs, a large sand quarry indicates the start of a wide belt of greensand. For the next few miles the Wealdway crosses patches of heathland, with well-drained sandy soil underfoot, before dropping into the fertile and intensively cultivated valley of the Medway. A 5-mile walk along the river bank brings the Wealdway into Tonbridge, the one major centre on the route.

To the south of Tonbridge, the route takes an undulating course, skirting to the west of Tunbridge Wells, through an area notable for a number of dramatic sandstone outcrops. The villages of Bidborough, Speldhurst and Fordcombe follow in quick succession.

After another crossing of the Medway, now in its upper reaches and little more than a stream, the Wealdway climbs steadily up on to the airy heights of Ashdown Forest, a mixture of wood and heathland with magnificent views southwards to the distant Downs.

From the outskirts of Uckfield, the way sets out across the heavily farmed clay soil of the low Weald. It is a surprisingly quiet and remote landscape. Between Wilmington and Jevington, a good track traverses the lower slopes of the South Downs before a final climb to join the South Downs Way, high above Eastbourne. The Wealdway officially ends about 2 miles short of the coast, but can easily be extended to the edge of the high chalk cliffs near Beachy Head, a fitting climax to the journey.

The Wealdway has been carefully waymarked, but the plastic yellow arrows, marked with the WW logo are vulnerable to vandals and it is easy to go astray, particularly in the cultivated areas between West Peckham and the Medway, and, further south, between Blackboys and Wilmington.

In spite of recent legislation designed to strengthen the law preventing the obliteration of field paths, many of the rights of way used by the Wealdway are ploughed out every year without reinstatement. Determined walkers usually ensure that a well-trodden path is quickly re-established: but not always. Summer growth can be a problem, too, as stiles and waymarks quickly become swallowed up by brambles and nettles, or buried in overgrown hedges.

The best insurance against wandering off the route, is to have to hand a copy of the latest edition of the definitive Wealdway Guide, which includes a detailed series of clear 1:25,000 strip maps, making OS Pathfinder maps unnecessary.

The Wealdway can be completed over a leisurely week or in four strenuous days. One runner managed to cover the whole distance in 14 hours. However you choose to tackle it, you will have sampled some of the finest countryside in south-east England.

The remains of Wilmington Priory

Gravesend (Tollgate)
Tonbridge

GRAVESEND (TOLLGATE)
WROTHAM HEATH
APPROX. 11½ MILES/18.5KM

OS Landranger 177, 188
Start at grid reference TQ 637 701
Start point: Tollgate, 2 miles south of Gravesend, where the A2 trunk road crosses the A227 Gravesend-to-Tonbridge road. There is a small car park beside the A227, just south of the road junction.

Coast-to-coast purists may wish to walk from the River Thames at Gravesend pier, but the Wealdway starts officially at Tollgate, alongside the A2, and over a stile to the east of the Tollgate hotel buildings. After a gate and a long diagonal field path, you should head southwards on a metalled track through a flat and featureless landscape for over a mile.

From Nash Street to Sole Street, the route is well waymarked and straightforward, though it is worth noting that the five stiles, marked in the official Wealdway guide as punctuating the path immediately beyond Nash Street, have all gone. Sole Street Station provides a useful alternative starting point for Wealdway walkers, omitting the rather dull first 3 miles of the route and the road walk out of Gravesend. There is a good train service from London.

If time allows, the delightful village of Cobham, about a mile across the fields from Sole Street, is well worth a diversion. The church dates back to the 13th century, and the half-timbered Leather Bottle Inn features in Charles Dickens' *Pickwick Papers*, as well as the *1992 Good Pub Guide*. Cobham Hall, a mile outside the village, is an exceptional

Elizabethan mansion. The garden is open on certain dates during the Easter and summer school holidays. In Sole Street itself a timber Tudor yeoman's house can be found only a few yards off the route of the Wealdway. The interior of the main hall can be viewed only by prior written application to the National Trust tenant.

From Sole Street, the Wealdway continues past the Railway Inn. After 200yds, turn left on a rough track (not through the gate into Camer Park). The track leads up on to Henley Down, the first of the chalk hills of the North Downs, where, beyond a copse, there is a sudden broad view over the Luddesdown valley.

The Wealdway is now well waymarked down to the hamlet of Luddesdown, a tiny but delightful group of buildings. Luddesdown Court (not, alas, open to the public) dates back, at least, to the 13th century and is said to be one of the oldest continuously lived-in houses in the country.

Beyond the church, walk between farm buildings and turn left on a superb path for over a mile along the valley known as the Bowling Alley. At a road, turn right, immediately forking right again to pass Great Buckland Farm. A fork left here, and another ¼ mile along the valley leads to the tiny church at Dode, parts of which date from Norman times (now locked and disused).

Ⓔ *For walkers looking for a circuit back towards Sole Street, a choice of paths to the west link Great Buckland (grid ref. TQ 670 642) with Priestwood and Meopham Green, then lead to the railway stations at Meopham or Sole Street.*

From Great Buckland, the Wealdway climbs steadily, overgrown in places, soon beside and then through Luxon Wood. After a short stretch of muddy bridleway, the route

Great Buckland, on the North Downs

crosses a paddock to a road. Turn left and where the road veers right, go ahead over a stile and shortly left over a second stile. Turn right to walk through two meadows and between barns to a road.

Turn right a few yards before going left through Whitehorse Wood. After ¾ mile, the path veers right and drops steeply down the North Downs escarpment. The spectacular view from the edge is partly obscured by foliage, but there are several good vantage points beside the path, providing tantalising glimpses of a spectacular Wealden panorama.

At the bottom of the hill, for a few yards, the Wealdway shares a track with the North Downs Way and also the much more ancient Pilgrim's Way from Winchester to Canterbury.

Ⓔ *Heading eastwards from here (grid ref. TQ 652 613), the North Downs Way provides part of another convenient circuit back to Luddesdown. In the other direction, the North Downs Way climbs to the top of the escarpment and passes through Trosley Country Park. The Wealdway can then be rejoined via the village of Trottiscliffe.*

The direct route of the Wealdway heads south into the Weald, with more good views. After 600yds, you will pass Coldrum Long Barrow, the remains of a Neolithic tomb. When it was opened in 1910, 22 skeletons were found, dating from about 3000BC.

Continue southwards on a concrete drive, forking left into Ryarsh Wood and on across fields to a road. Turn right and after 350yds, go left beside a sand quarry and under the A20 road, Immediately beyond the road tunnel, turn sharply right up a bank and along a path, beside the motorway fence at first. At Westfields Farm, turn left along a drive and, shortly, right on an unmarked path. At the next lane, turn right. After 1/2 mile, just beyond a large house on the right, turn right on a clear path, to reach the A20 at Wrotham Heath.

WROTHAM HEATH

TONBRIDGE

APPROX. 14¹/₂ MILES/23.5KM

OS Landranger 188
Start at grid reference TQ 633 581
Start point: The junction of the A20 and A25 roads at Wrotham Heath. The nearest British Rail station is at Borough Green, 2 miles to the west.

Start the walk along a drive to the right of the Royal Oak pub. It narrows to a path and passes under the railway. Ignore a left fork and, at the next lane, bear left. After 300yds, fork right on a narrow fenced path between rhododendrons. Ignore the many side and crossing tracks in this woodland, much depleted by the gales of 1987, but already regenerating well.

At the road on the edge of the village of Platt, turn right and, shortly, left into Potash Lane. For the centre of the village and the Anchor Inn, a few minutes away, go straight on from this point. Follow Potash Lane over crossroads and on to join a wider road. At another crossroads, go ahead between high hedges.

After 250yds, fork right. For the next 2 miles, the Wealdway heads south through Mereworth Woods, predominantly coppiced hazel, with a scattering of silver birch. Ignore all side and crossing tracks to reach a road at Gover Hill, a small National Trust area, with good views southwards over the valley of the Medway.

Cross a road and continue the walk along a track beside a white-walled cottage. Turn left, as waymarked. For the next mile, the Wealdway is also part of the Greensand

The River Medway at Tonbridge

Way, the continuation, in Kent, of the route described on pages 74–7. At a lane, turn left and, very shortly, fork right. A few minutes' walk brings you to West Peckham, where the church and the Swan Inn are delightfully set beside the village green.

Follow the road between pub and church. At a road junction, turn right on a path, enclosed at first. For the next 5 miles, south to the Medway, the Wealdway follows a series of field paths, subject to cultivation. Most of the paths are waymarked but there are one or two gaps. Care, plus a good 1:25,000 scale map, or the Ramblers' Association Wealdway guide strip maps, will ensure successful navigation.

On the first path, veer right in the third field. Cross the A26. The start of the next path, a few yards to the right, is not obvious. Cross the verge bank and go ahead on a roughly metalled track, a proposed diversion, and preferable to the official route. After 1/2 mile, turn right on a track which crosses two streams and continues to Peckham Place Farm. Follow the farm drive out to a lane and turn left.

The next path follows a straight southerly line through an orchard and across a field to a lane. Turn right. At Kent House Farm, a

massive converted oast, turn left along a narrow lane. After 1/2 mile, beyond an attractive house and garden on the right, turn right along the north bank of the River Bourne. Cross the river at the first opportunity, go ahead over a field to a second footbridge, and bear left across the corner of the field beyond to a third footbridge. Continue beside a field out to the road at Barnes Street, opposite a picturesque half-timbered house.

Turn right and, very shortly, go left along a track. Walk through an orchard, bearing slightly left, to find a wide grassy track leading onwards to the River Medway. Cross the river and turn right along the towpath. At East Lock, cross back over the Medway and follow the north bank for 4 miles into Tonbridge. It is quite a busy waterway and you are likely to encounter pleasure boats working through one of the four locks on this lovely stretch of the river.

On the outskirts of Tonbridge, cross the Medway once again, using the Cannon Road bridge. Continue beside the river, passing Town Lock, to reach Tonbridge High Street.

THE GARDEN OF ENGLAND

Until recent years, the fertile soil of the north Kent plain supported half of all England's apple orchards. As early as 1533, Richard Harrys, fruiterer to King Henry VIII, established the first Kentish orchards. The industry enjoyed its greatest success in the 19th century, when the arrival of the railway allowed the fruit to be transported efficiently into London. Even today, in spite of competition from cheaper Continental apples, the county still fully deserves its reputation as the centre of the 'Garden of England'.

Tonbridge

Camp Hill

TONBRIDGE

STONE CROSS

APPROX. 9½ MILES/15KM

OS Landranger 188
Start at grid reference TQ 590 465
Start point: The entrance to the grounds of Tonbridge Castle in the High Street about ¼ mile from the railway station. There is a large car park near by.

The Wealdway continues through the castle grounds beside the River Medway with the high castle wall to the right. The Norman castle was built on a prominent artificial mound, strategically placed to guard a ford over the river. It was constructed from local sandstone, but dismantled, like so many English castles, during the Civil War. The solid 13th-century gatehouse is still reasonably intact.

After 250yds turn left over a footbridge, signposted as the Eden Valley Walk, and then right past a miniature railway and a car park, a useful alternative starting point for walkers arriving by car (grid ref. TQ 588 468). The Eden Valley Walk, distinctively waymarked, runs beside the Medway and its tributary, the Eden, for 15 miles between Tonbridge and Edenbridge and for Weald-way walkers is a useful means of visiting Penshurst Place (see Places to visit).

The two long distance routes remain together for 2 miles, past playing fields,

under the railway, left over two footbridges and on beside the Medway for ½ mile.

Cross the river by the second bridge and bear right and left past a wood, replanted after the great gale of 1987. Beyond the railway, bear left and left again out to a road. Go ahead through Haysden, passing to the right of the Royal Oak pub. At Manor Farm, the Wealdway is waymarked across a field, under the A21, left for a few yards, and then right beside a hedge to a lane.

The path opposite marks the start of a gentle but steady climb out of the Medway Valley. Cross a field to join a track. After another ½ mile, a steeper climb through woodland brings you to the B2176. A bus service along this road links Tunbridge Wells and Penshurst.

The Wealdway now follows the road for ½ mile, with magnificent views northward across the Medway valley to the greensand ridge and the North Downs beyond. Look out for a narrow path on the left, signposted to Bidborough Church. (For the Hare and Hounds pub, carry on along the road.)

The small sandstone church at Bidborough occupies a superb site on high ground with views towards Speldhurst, the next objective. The Wealdway passes through the churchyard and descends a flight of steps to the lych gate.

Turn sharply back to the left, down Spring Lane and onwards through a quiet and secluded valley. After a steep climb, a woodland path cuts through a sandstone outcrop, a characteristic feature of the area, and then crosses high ground before

Tonbridge Castle, wrecked by Cromwell

GUIDE BOX

Places to visit
Penshurst Place, standing in wide acres of parkland, is an exceptionally well-preserved manor house, built for Sir John de Pulteney, four times Lord Mayor of London, and completed in 1337. The magnificent Great Hall remains almost as it was in the 14th century. In 1552, Penshurst Place came into the hands of the Sidney family. Sir Philip Sidney, Elizabethan poet and soldier, was born here.
Penshurst can be reached from the Wealdway either by bus from Bidborough or, on foot, using the Eden Valley Walk from a point on the Wealdway north of Haysden, a distance of about 4 miles. Gardens open March to October, Saturdays, Sundays. House open April to September, daily except Mondays.

Harrison's Rocks provide the most spectacular example of the many sandstone outcrops which are a prominent feature of the landscape in the Tunbridge Wells area. They can be found along the western edge of Forestry Commission woodland to the south of Groombridge, and are usually festooned with climbers at weekends. Groombridge and the rocks are most easily accessible from the Wealdway using the Forest Way along the old railway line from grid ref. TQ 492 363.

Two of the places described by A A Milne in his Christopher Robin books are within easy reach of the Wealdway. The bridge where Christopher Robin and Winnie-the-Pooh invented the game of Pooh Sticks crosses a stream at grid ref. TQ 470 338 and can be reached from the Wealdway at grid ref. TQ 483 355 by a footpath route of a little over a mile. The 'Enchanted Place' on the top of the forest is marked by a plaque, near Gill's Lap Clump at grid ref. TQ 469 321. From the Wealdway near Greenwood Gate Clump several tracks cross high ground to Gill's Lap.

Car parking
For Wealdway walkers, the most convenient car park in Tonbridge is at grid ref. TQ 588 467, to the north of the castle. There are no official car parks on the Wealdway for the next 15 miles, but it should be possible to find space at Modest Corner or in the villages of Bidborough, Speldhurst and Fordcombe.
On Ashdown Forest, cars are well provided for, with carefully labelled car parks at various locations. For the Wealdway, four are well placed, on the B2188 at TQ 474 308, at the junction of the B2188 and B2026 roads (TQ 472 301), and, for Camp Hill, at 'The Hollies' (TQ 463 287).

Public transport
There are British Rail stations at Tonbridge, Tunbridge Wells and Ashurst, 1 mile off the route. Bidborough, Speldhurst, Fordcombe, Stone Cross and Withyham offer an infrequent weekday bus service to Tunbridge Wells.

Accommodation
There is ample bed-and-breakfast accommodation within easy reach of the route in Southborough and Tunbridge Wells. The Wealdway Accommodation list (see page 78), lists two establishments in Fordcombe and one at Stone Cross. The Crown at Groombridge, 1 mile off the route, provides accommodation.

dropping down into another quiet valley.

The route now bears right along the edge of Southborough Common, an area of heath, criss-crossed by paths. At Modest Corner, the Beehive pub provides a welcome opportunity for refreshment.

Ⓔ *It is also a good point (grid ref. TQ 570 423) from which to 'escape' across the common to the A26 at Southborough, for a bus back to Tonbridge, or into Tunbridge Wells.*

If time permits, the spa town of Tunbridge Wells deserves a detour. The resort was developed and became fashionable after the discovery of a chalybeate (iron-bearing) stream in the 17th century. The Pantiles, a colonnade of shops and houses built beside the springs in about 1690, remains an elegant and carefully preserved pedestrian precinct.

At the bottom of the hill beyond the Beehive, the Wealdway joins a lane and climbs steeply. After ¹/₂ mile, an inconspicuous kissing-gate on the left marks the start of a field path which soon bears right in front of a garden and rejoins the lane ¹/₂ mile further on. The next path starts a few yards to the right, through the gateway to Forge House and drops down steeply across pasture.

Walk past a disused mill, where the rusting water wheel is still in place. Shortly turn right and climb the hill to Speldhurst. The Wealdway, as it did at Bidborough, picks a route through the churchyard. The church, although rebuilt twice after the original structure was destroyed by lightning in 1791, is not without interest. Dating from 1870, it contains some exceptional stained-glass windows by the Pre-Raphaelites, Edward Burne-Jones and William Morris. The George and Dragon Inn, near by, is a fine old pub, carefully restored.

Ⓔ *From Speldhurst (grid ref. TQ 553 415), there is a bus service, as well as several footpath routes, into Tunbridge Wells, still within comfortable walking distance.*

The Wealdway follows the Penshurst road. A wrought-iron gate on the left marks the start of a path through to Bullingstone Lane at grid ref. TQ 545 411. The next path, a few yards to the right along the lane, starts beside two picturesque 15th-century cottages and descends, forking right, into Avery's Wood. The stream crossing within the wood is a delectable spot, perfect for a picnic.

A clear path leads to a road and on for ³/₄

mile into the village of Fordcombe, all on the tarmac except for one short linking field path. Fordcombe is a pleasant village with a shop, pub and village green. The Wealdway continues beside the cricket ground and along a headland path across high ground for ³/₄ mile to the A264 at Stone Cross.

Ⓔ *From here (grid ref. TQ 522 390) Ashurst Station is just over a mile to the right along the main road. For a footpath alternative, carry on along the Wealdway and then follow the Sussex Border Path which goes directly to Ashurst Station.*

STONE CROSS

CAMP HILL

APPROX. 9 MILES/14.5KM

OS Landranger 188
Start at grid reference TQ 522 390
Start point: Stone Cross, on the A264 East Grinstead-to-Tunbridge Wells road, 1¹/₄ miles east of Ashurst.

From Stone Cross, the Wealdway is narrow and enclosed for a short distance. Then follows one of the finest sections of the walk, along a sloping, grassy hillside. Over the next ¹/₂ mile, the view ahead into Sussex steadily widens, with the heights of Ashdown Forest now clearly visible across the valley.

For the second time, the route descends into a valley carved by the River Medway. For ¹/₂ mile, the Wealdway and the Sussex Border Path coincide, marked by two solid wayposts. Over the stream on the Kent-Sussex boundary, a bridge, designed and built by local ramblers, stands in memory of one of their colleagues.

The Medway, crossed near Hale Farm is, in these higher reaches, little more than a modest stream. For the next mile, to the road at Summerford Farm, the Wealdway is never far from the river. Beyond the farm, the way is clear at first, along a cart track.

After ¹/₄ mile, watch carefully for a narrow, unmarked path which drops down left.

Shortly, cross the old railway, now the Forest Way, a 15-mile route linking East Grinstead with Groombridge.

Ⓔ *Groombridge is 2¹/₂ miles to the east from here (grid ref. TQ 491 363) and the track bed provides convenient access for Wealdway walkers. A footpath route continues via High Rocks into Tunbridge Wells. A mile in the other direction along the Forest Way brings you to the attractive village of Hartfield, a good place to break the journey, with two pubs and overnight accommodation.*

The tall shingled spire of Hartfield Church is a prominent landmark and the lych gate into the churchyard has been fashioned beneath a half-timbered house dating from 1520.

Continue through fields to the B2110 near Withyham, where you will find a shop, a pub and an occasional weekday bus to Tunbridge Wells. The church, on high ground beside the Wealdway, replaced an older building, destroyed by lightning in 1663. It contains various monuments to the Sackville family, many of whom are buried in a vault beneath the church. The Wealdway bypasses the village to follow the access drive to Fisher's Gate for over a mile. Then begins a long climb through Five Hundred Acre Wood on Ashdown Forest.

This is the countryside immortalised by A A Milne in *Winnie-the-Pooh* and *The House at Pooh Corner*. The wood is but a shadow of its former glory, destroyed by the 1987 storm, but the Wealdway, at one time difficult to follow, is now on a clear open track, marked by special wooden wayposts.

After 2 miles, the Wealdway reaches its highest point, at Greenwood Gate Clump. At 720ft (219m) above sea level, this is also the highest point on Ashdown Forest. From here to Camp Hill is a fine open walk with superb views.

Ⓔ *There is a good track, eastwards from the road near Greenwood Gate Clump (grid ref. TQ 476 309), for 3 miles into Crowborough, for a bus to Tunbridge Wells or Uckfield.*

ASHDOWN FOREST

Ashdown Forest is the name given to an area of heath and woodland, forming the central section of a broken High Wealden ridge of sandstone. The land rises to over 700ft (210m) at its highest point and is cut by a series of deep valleys, watered by streams.

In 1268 Ashdown Forest was created a royal hunting ground and surrounded by a pale, interspersed with a series of 'gates' or 'hatches', still identifiable today.

Much of the original 14,000 acres was enclosed in the 17th century, but over 6000 acres remain and have recently come into public ownership for the first time. The public may wander freely over the open forest, which is managed in its natural state by a Board of Conservators, who also maintain an extensive network of paths and forest rides.

Camp Hill

Horsebridge

CAMP HILL

BLACKBOYS

APPROX. 9 MILES/14.5KM

OS Landranger 188, 198, 199
Start at grid reference TQ 469 289

Start point: The nearest forest car park to Camp Hill, labelled 'The Hollies', is beside the Camp Hill–Nutley road at grid ref. TQ 463 287, about ¹/₂ mile west of the start.

Walk up to Camp Hill, passing to the right of the clump and to the left of a trig. point to reach the B2188 road. Follow the road, signposted to Crowborough, opposite. After a short but awkward section of road, the Wealdway bears right across open heathland to Crest Cottage, where there is a sensational view southwards to the distant South Downs.

From here to Oldlands Corner, route-finding requires some care and concentration. Waymarks and wooden posts indicate the line of the Wealdway but tend to be hidden by bracken, particularly in late summer. After a short distance along a track, go left over two stiles, join another track for a few yards and then drop down across another heathy area. Skirt to the left of a cottage at grid ref. TQ 474 280, and go ahead on a narrow path down through woodland to a stream crossing by Brown's Brook Cottage.

Follow the access drive from the cottage, keeping a lookout for a path to the right which crosses another area of open forest for ¹/₂ mile or so to reach the road opposite the entrance to Oldlands Hall.

After a short distance along the road, the path breaks away to the left through the bracken. The village of Fairwarp is ¹/₄ mile ahead along the road from this point and has a pub as well as two bed-and-breakfast establishments.

The Wealdway crosses a field and a stream before climbing through Furnace Wood. The brown colour of the water in the stream and the name of the wood are a reminder that this area was once at the centre of the Wealden iron industry. From Buxted, near by, came the first cannon to be produced in England, cast in 1543. Continue through this Forestry Commission area where a slippery scramble up one steep slope has been much improved by the provision of a flight of rough steps.

Beyond the wood, skirt to the left of a cottage and to the right of the prosperous-looking Hendall Manor. The Way now drops down across fields and climbs more steeply through the remains of Hendall Wood, before crossing a large field, once part of the wood, but clear-felled some years ago.

After a stile in the far field corner, the path traverses a patch of heath beside the busy A26, before crossing the main road at the start of the new bypass road at Five Ash

A fine example of traditional local building, Stonehill House, near Chiddingly

GUIDE BOX

Places to visit

Nutley Windmill, a mile to the west of Camp Hill and accessible via a direct footpath link across the open forest, is an open trestle post mill which, after many years of disuse, has now been restored to working order. Opening times are limited to the last Sunday of the month and summer Bank Holidays, but a good view of the mill can be obtained from the public footpath near by.

Sheffield Park Gardens (NT), 5 miles north-west of Uckfield, cover 100 acres, and were laid out by Capability Brown, with five lakes connected by waterfalls. The gardens are particularly splendid in the late spring when the rhododendrons and azaleas are in bloom, and during October for the colours of autumn. Open summer months, Tuesday to Sunday and Bank Holiday Mondays.

Car parking

There are clearly signed forest car parks to the east, west and north of Camp Hill, – at grid ref. TQ 473 297 on the B2026, at TQ 475 287 on the Crowborough road, and at 'The Hollies' on the Nutley Road (TQ 463 287). Uckfield has a large central car park. There is limited room to park on the roadside verge near the point where the Wealdway crosses the B2102, west of Blackboys, and there are village car parks at East Hoathly and Chiddingly.

Public transport

Buses to and from Camp Hill are few and far between. There is a railway station at Uckfield, offering a weekday service back to Buxted. A useful weekday bus service connects Uckfield, Blackboys, East Hoathly and Horsebridge. As with all country services, these are subject to change.

Accommodation

Fairwarp, ¹/₄ mile off the Wealdway along the lane from grid ref. TQ 473 267, is an attractive and well-placed stop-over point with two bed-and-breakfast establishments included in the latest Ramblers' Association accommodation list (see page 78). Other accommodation on or near the route is listed for Buxted, Uckfield, Blackboys (youth hostel), Chiddingly, Hellingly and Hailsham.

Down. There is a pub and post office down the road to the right, but the Wealdway continues beside a garage forecourt. A field path leads through to the A272 Maresfield-to-Buxted road. After ¹/₄ mile along this road, the Wealdway heads south through Buxted Park, passing the church and Buxted Park House, now a hotel and health farm. Bear left across pasture down to the edge of the River Uck, and go ahead beside the stream to reach Hempstead Mill and Hempstead Lane. Uckfield is ³/₄ mile along the lane to the right at this point (grid ref. TQ 483 217) and is a useful centre with all services, including a railway station and a good bus service.

The Wealdway turns its back on the town, crossing the River Uck. From the bridge there is an excellent view of Hempstead Mill. After a few more yards a stile on the left provides access to a field path which climbs out of the valley, crosses the railway in a deep cutting and continues to a lane near Highlands Pond.

The next path, from the lane at grid ref.

TQ 498 217, follows a stream along a remote and peaceful valley for over a mile to Tickerage Mill where a remarkable and quite unnecessary proliferation of notices discourages trespass from the track up towards Blackboys. It is an attractive spot, tempting the walker to linger and admire, in spite of written exhortations to keep moving.

For a short distance the route of the Wealdway coincides with that of the Vanguard Way, a roughly parallel long distance path across the Weald.

From the point where the route reaches the B2102 at grid ref. TQ 517 206, Blackboys is $^1/_4$ mile to the left. There is a shop, the 14th-century Blackboys Inn and, $^1/_2$ mile to the north of the village, the youth hostel at grid ref. TQ 521 215.

Ⓔ *From Blackboys (grid ref. TQ 521 205) the Vanguard Way provides a convenient return route via Buxted and High Hurstwood to the top of Ashdown Forest where it crosses the Wealdway again at grid ref. TQ 471 306.*

BLACKBOYS

HORSEBRIDGE

APPROX. 10$^1/_4$ MILES/16.5KM

OS Landranger 199
Start at grid reference TQ 517 206
Start point: The B2102 road, $^1/_4$ mile west of Blackboys. Bus service from Uckfield. Parking is possible on wide verge near the start.

The Wealdway uses the B2102 road for a few yards only before cutting through to the next lane. From the start of the path at grid ref. TQ 516 204, the South Downs come into view for the first time since the Wealdway descended the southern slopes of Ashdown Forest.

The route soon passes through the elaborately landscaped area surrounding New Place. Here, in sharp contrast to Tickerage, the track is open and unfenced and there are no unfriendly notices. From a large pond, a stream drops down a series of artificial cascades, a delightful sight, particularly in the spring when the surrounding area is a mass of daffodils.

The next 3 miles to East Hoathly are well waymarked and present few problems apart from the possibility of obstruction by growing crops. Access to the footbridge in a wooded dip at grid ref. TQ 523 183 is not obvious and, in the field beyond, the Wealdway makes a curious dog-leg turn beside a solitary tree before climbing across a large field, once part of Great Wood but clear-felled a few years ago, except for a remnant on the summit. At the other side of the wood, a wide downland panorama suddenly opens up ahead, now encouragingly nearer. The Wealdway arrives at East Hoathly through the churchyard, within a few yards of two pubs and a bus stop for buses back to Blackboys and Uckfield, or on to Horsebridge. Between East Hoathly and

Chiddingly, another 2 miles on, the route, for the most part, follows a designated bridleway and is therefore gated rather than stiled. It is clear and well marked, but may be muddy underfoot in places as this is an area of thick and sticky Wealden clay.

Chiddingly is a quiet and charming spot. On the way into the village, look out for the remains of Chiddingly Place, now incorporated into a farm building, to the right of the lane. Beyond the village shop and the Six Bells pub, there is a small car park.

Ⓔ *This is also another meeting point with the Vanguard Way (grid ref. TQ 544 142), providing a return route to Blackboys.*

The fine 130ft stone spire of Chiddingly Church is a conspicuous landmark for miles around. The church contains an Elizabethan monument to Sir John Jefferay, who lived at Chiddingly Place.

From Chiddingly to the A267, the Wealdway is, once again, well waymarked as it heads generally westwards across a gently undulating landscape, with frequent glimpses of the South Downs escarpment. From the point where the route crosses the road at Gun Hill, the Gun Inn (good beer and food) is a few minutes' walk to the north along the lane.

Approaching the A267, the Way descends through a lovely patch of woodland and climbs between high banks. After another dip, the path is a bit vague as it crosses an area of rough ground and the stile and steps giving access to the loop of old road at Lealands are well hidden.

A quiet lane leads to Hellingly, where the Wealdway passes diagonally through the churchyard, attractively and unusually lined by a row of tile-hung cottages. Follow the road over the Cuckmere River. The Sussex Martlet pub is a short distance ahead along the road, but the Wealdway bears right across a meadow to Horselunges Manor. A few years ago the landowners applied to re-

Chiddingly Church, visible for miles around

route this path away from the manor, but determined objections by local ramblers ensured that it is now still possible to obtain a reasonably close look at this magnificent 16th-century timber house, complete with a moat and drawbridge. Beyond the manor, skirt to the left of a row of garages. Another $^3/_4$ mile brings you out to the A271 through the entrance to Horsebridge Mill.

Ⓔ *From Hellingly (grid ref. TQ 581 112), it is possible to pick out a fairly direct footpath route back to Chiddingly, a distance of under 4 miles via Perryland Farm, Thunder's Hill and Muddles Green. You will need a good map as the paths are not all well defined.*

WEALDEN IRON

The iron deposits of the Weald were first extracted and smelted in Roman times and before. New techniques of smelting, introduced in the 15th century, led to a rapid expansion of the industry and the transformation of the area. Valleys were flooded to create strings of hammer ponds and vast areas of woodland were cleared, turning Ashdown Forest from thick woodland to open heath.

In 1574, 51 furnaces were recorded. By 1717, 14 furnaces and 10 forges remained active. Shortage of timber and competition from abroad led to further decline. By 1800, the last working furnace, at Ashburnham in Sussex, had closed down, but iron continued to be extracted on a small scale until as late as 1858.

The scars left by this thriving industry can still be sought out by the enthusiast. For the casual walker, only the evocative names, like Furnace Wood and Gun Hill, remain to remind us that this was once England's 'black country'.

A Sussex iron fire-back on display in Anne of Cleves' House in Lewes

Horsebridge

Eastbourne

HORSEBRIDGE

WILMINGTON

APPROX. 7³/₄ MILES/12.5KM

OS Landranger 199
Start at grid reference TQ 581 112
Start point: The entrance to Horsebridge
Mill on the A271 road to the north of
Hailsham.

To the south of Horsebridge, the Wealdway
has been diverted to find a way through a
housing estate. The new path is marked on
the latest edition of the Pathfinder map for
the area and in the 1991 edition of the
definitive Wealdway guide, but it is not
waymarked and is far from obvious on the
ground. Further diversions are possible as the
housing development progresses.

From the imposing entrance to
Horsebridge Mill, turn right along the A271
road. After about 100yds, turn left on a
rough track and, very shortly, go left again
along an estate road. Look out for a narrow
fenced path to the right running between the
houses.

A field path now heads south through
fields earmarked for an extension of the built
up area. Beyond the A22 dual carriageway, a
rather devious headland path makes its way
between cultivated fields. There are
waymarks and stiles at regular intervals but it
is easy to miss the way. Beyond an overgrown footbridge at grid ref. TQ 567 098,
the route crosses a large field with no clear
sight line to guide the walker.

After another ¹/₂ mile, the Wealdway
crosses the Cuckmere once more, using a
solid brick bridge. After a second bridge,
across the feeder stream for the moat surrounding Michelham Priory, a field path
continues to reach the road beside the village
store at Upper Dicker. To visit Michelham
Priory, use a short footpath which leaves the
Wealdway at grid ref. TQ 557 095. At the
road, turn left.

After about ¹/₄ mile along the road, the
next path starts almost opposite the Plough
Inn. After a low summit the Wealdway con-
verges on the Cuckmere and joins a bridleway to cross the river at Sessingham Bridge
(grid ref. TQ 544 082). After a few yards
along this enclosed track, a stile on the right
and a rising path across pasture leads on
towards Arlington's church spire.

The tiny flint church at Arlington has
Saxon origins but incorporates fragments of
earlier Roman material and later additions,
none more recent than the 15th century.
Near by, the Yew Tree pub provides a convenient refreshment stop, and there is a small
car park. The bumps in the field beyond the
church remind us that a much larger village
once stood on this site.

The waymark beside a footbridge on the

Michelham Priory, surrounded by a large moat

other side of this field incorrectly shows the
Wealdway bearing right. The official line
keeps straight ahead across rough ground and
on via an access drive to the road near
Chilver Bridge. The path to the right leads
over a footbridge to Arlington reservoir,
where there is another car park and a
pleasant perimeter path.

Ⓔ *The road over Chilver Bridge (grid ref. TQ 537 069) provides access via another field path to Berwick Station, a useful staging point for walkers using public transport and also another linkpoint with the Vanguard Way and a return route to Chiddingly.*

Beyond the road, the Wealdway continues beside the Cuckmere, with the first clear view ahead to the chalk figure of the Long Man of Wilmington, 2 miles away as the crow flies, on the steep slope of Windover Hill. A bridleway heads south, crossing the railway and then the A27, where you should follow the road, opposite, signposted to Milton Street. A well-trodden path on the left takes the Wealdway through to Wilmington village street.

For the Wilmington Arms, or a bus into Eastbourne, turn left out to the A27. The village car park is at the southern end of the village, beyond the church and priory.

WILMINGTON

EASTBOURNE

APPROX. 8 MILES/13KM

OS Landranger 199
Start at grid reference TQ 547 048
Start point: Wilmington crossroads on the A27 Lewes-to-Eastbourne road. If arriving by car, use the car park next to Wilmington Priory (grid ref. TQ 544 042).

Walk along the village street, lined by a variety of charming cottages. The church, much restored, has an attractive weatherboarded tower. Inside, hidden in a side chapel, it is worth seeking out the unusual Butterfly Window, dating from the 15th century. In the churchyard a massive, ancient yew, much propped up, still stands (just!) after an estimated life of almost 1000 years. Beyond the ruins of Wilmington Priory, the path to the Long Man starts opposite the entrance to the car park. It is not indicated in the official Wealdway guide, but avoids a narrow section of lane.

The Benedictine Priory at Wilmington was founded in the 11th century as a possession of the abbey of Grestain in Normandy. It was seized by the Crown during the wars with France and came into the hands of the Dean and Chapter of Chichester. After a period as vicarage and farmhouse, it was

given to the Sussex Archaeological Trust in 1926 and carefully restored.

The Long Man of Wilmington, standing 226ft high, is the largest hill figure in the country but very little is known of his origins. It is possible that he is a representation of Balder, the Norse god of spring. In 1874, the outline of the figure was carefully lined in white bricks and he is now, like the priory, in the good care of the Sussex Archaeological Trust.

From the foot of the Long Man, the Wealdway follows a fine, terraced path along the side of the Downs escarpment, high enough above the Weald to command a wide view, with the waters of Arlington reservoir clearly visible. After a mile, you will reach Folkington, with another tiny church, surrounded by trees, tucked under the Downs at the end of a quiet cul-de-sac.

A clear track, once an old coach road, follows an undulating route, still hugging the downland foothills, for another 2 miles to Jevington. The Wealdway follows the lane into the village as far as the Eight Bells pub, but, if time permits, it is well worth extending the walk to visit Jevington Church. Carry on along the lane and, very shortly, fork right on a narrow footpath, entering the churchyard through an interesting tapsell gate. The church, with a rare Saxon tower, occupies another idyllic downland setting.

The Wealdway continues up a flight of steps opposite the Eight Bells and climbs steadily along a ridge to reach the summit of Combe Hill, at 630ft (192m), where the low banks indicate the site of a Neolithic camp, dating from about 2500BC. The banks, laid out in concentric banks and ditches, indicate that this was a 'causewayed camp', one of only four, all in Sussex.

For the next 2 miles, the Wealdway follows an exhilarating high level route, with views across the Weald, back over Jevington to the woods of Friston Forest and, to the left across the built up areas of Polegate, Willingdon and Eastbourne.

Beyond Combe Hill a clear track sweeps round to the right, past the car parking area at Butts Brow and up on to Willingdon Hill (659ft/200m). By the trig. point on the summit (grid ref. TQ 577 009), the Wealdway bears left and continues with the scrub-covered slopes dropping away left.

After another ³/₄ mile, a choice is necessary. At the start of a golf course, near a brick seat, the official route of the Wealdway breaks away to the left across a fairway and drops downhill through scrub to finish at the A259 road beside Eastbourne youth hostel (grid ref. TV 588 991), where there is convenient off-road parking.

Having come so far, most Wealdway walkers will not wish to head for home without setting foot on the white cliffs of Beachy Head. To complete a true coast-to-coast walk, go ahead beside the golf course, using the South Downs Way. Cross the A259, near the club house. After another ¹/₄ mile, where the South Downs Way bears right, go ahead passing a trig. point and a dewpond.

Shortly, fork left along the upper edge of

Beachy Head, where the South Downs meet the English Channel

scrub and cross a road beside a junction at grid ref. TV 590 975. Now climb across open sloping downland with superb views across Eastbourne and eastwards along the coast towards Hastings. After a mile, walking parallel to the road which is a little way away on your right, you will reach Beachy Head. From the cliff-edge, there is an excellent view of the lighthouse, beneath the cliff and, from the highest point, a fine panorama along the line of the Seven Sisters, with the old lighthouse at Belle Tout a prominent landmark on the cliff-edge, 2 miles to the west.

At Beachy Head, there is a pub, café, shop, and a small wildlife exhibition, as well as a bus into Eastbourne. Another mile or so to the left along the cliff-edge leads down to Holywell at the end of the Eastbourne seafront, another point from which to pick up a bus to the railway station.

THE CUCKMERE RIVER

The Cuckmere is the shortest of the four rivers which have carved a route through the ridge of the Sussex Downs. It rises near Heathfield and for 6 miles between Hellingly and Arlington, it is never far from the Wealdway.

The Cuckmere is the only Sussex river without a port at its mouth. It has, however, had some commercial use. In the late 18th and 19th centuries, barge traffic could ascend the river with the tide as far as Alfriston, and on to Berwick, where there was a wharf at Sherman Bridge, the present A27 crossing point. The main cargoes were coal and sand from Newhaven, and sea shingle, used for road repairs. Navigation was difficult because of the many bends in the river and, in 1846, a new channel was cut between the mouth of the river and Exceat Bridge.

The last barge to be berthed at Alfriston wharf, made her final journey to the sea in 1915.

Ridgeway

OVERTON HILL TO IVINGHOE BEACON
85 MILES/137KM

FOR much of its route the Ridgeway Path follows part of an ancient track, the Great Ridgeway, which once ran from Dorset to Norfolk and which has been dubbed 'the oldest road' in Britain. In consequence of its importance through the centuries, the Ridgeway is like a magnet for historic sites of all ages and it is impossible to walk the track without experiencing the feeling that the division between past and present has been worn thin by the tramp of countless feet over the thousands of years of its use.

The Ridgeway near Hackpen Hill

Detailed guides
The following are available from The Ridgeway Officer, Countryside Service, Library HQ, Holton, Oxford OX9 1QQ: *Ridgeway Information and Accommodation Guide*; *Ridgeway Information Pack* – general interest leaflets; *Ridgeway Routes Pack* – circular walks and rides; *Let's Hear it for the Ridgeway* – family activity book by Elizabeth Newbery; *Public Transport Guide*. The National Trail Guide by Neil Curtis is published by Aurum Press in association with the Countryside Commission and the Ordnance Survey.

Maps
OS Landranger 165, 173, 174, 175

Links
A glance at the Ordnance Survey map shows that the ground crossed by the Ridgeway path is particularly rich in rights of way and it is not surprising therefore to find that there is a plethora of other recreational routes close to or linking with it.
The Wessex Way runs from Overton to Swanage in Dorset. The Icknield Way – the eastern end of the ancient highway of that name – runs from Ivinghoe Beacon to join with the Peddars Way in Norfolk. The Oxfordshire Way runs from Henley on Thames to Bourton on the Water in the Cotswolds. The North Bucks Way leaves the Ridgeway on Chequers Knap and runs to Wolverton. The Swan's Way and the Thames Path meet the Ridgeway at Goring and Streatley.

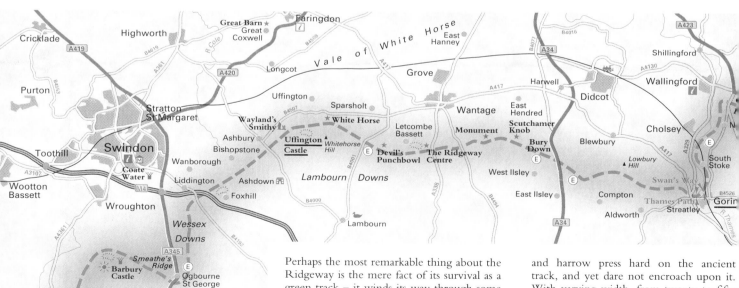

Perhaps the most remarkable thing about the Ridgeway is the mere fact of its survival as a green track – it winds its way through some of the most intensively farmed parts of England and yet is enormously wide. Even 100 years ago, so Richard Jefferies tells us, the Ridgeway was feeling the pressure of encroaching agriculture:

'It is not a farm track: you may walk for twenty miles along it over the hills; neither is it the King's highway... Plough and harrow press hard on the ancient track, and yet dare not encroach upon it. With varying width, from twenty to fifty yards, it runs like a green ribbon...'

One curiosity of this national trail (approved as such by the Secretary of State for the Environment in 1972) is that although the eastern end is clearly defined on the steep-sided spur of Ivinghoe Beacon – one literally runs out of ridge to walk along – no attempt seems to have been made to

The Ridgeway Path starts in a part of Wiltshire rich in exceptional ancient sites. An uphill climb a little west of the start point is rewarded with the West Kennet Long Barrow (above), one of the largest in Britain. Its burial chambers, have been fully excavated and can be entered by a passageway at the eastern end. Pottery found within it dates from about 3000 to 1600BC

easiest of the national trails for, although the Downs can take on a switchback appearance at times, the gradients are generally slight and the ground under foot either grass or a partially surfaced track. However, the mere fact that the route runs over chalk can create its own set of problems, especially after a period of heavy rain; there are few things as slippery as a mixture of wet chalk and clay, and the use of the track by vehicles leads to deep pot-holes which disguise themselves by filling with water. Ironically in such conditions one can also suffer from a shortage of drinking water – there are few dwellings alongside the western half of the Ridgeway, although the National Trail Guide recognises this problem by marking the position of the few water taps which do exist.

Accommodation, or the lack of it, can also cause some logistical headaches on the western section and if the walk is being tackled in one go, it is generally necessary to descend each evening into the villages along the base of the Downs in order to find bed-and-breakfast. The alternative, of course, is to camp and although official camp sites are few and far between, there is generally no objection to a tent appearing overnight on the wide verges of the track itself.

Parts of the Ridgeway Path are classified as byways and are available for public use on foot, horseback, bicycle or in vehicles. This can, of course, be a recipe for confrontation; irresponsible use of motor vehicles can disturb other users and cause damage to the surface of the track. For this reason a voluntary code has been agreed to discourage use by vehicles on the western part of the path on Sundays and Bank Holidays during the summer and after prolonged wet weather and to limit the speed and size of groups of cars or motorcycles. It may be that a legal ban will be made on recreational vehicles using the path on Sundays and Bank Holidays throughout the year.

The route is extremely well signposted and is generally self-evident.

The prehistoric hillfort, Barbury Castle

gives a more gradual approach to Avebury. Whichever choice is made, however, it would be a mistake to set out on the Ridgeway without first visiting Avebury.

The route of the path itself is better defined, initially following the northern edge of the Wessex Downs and then going on to finish on paths which run through the rolling and wooded Chiltern Hills. These two contrasting landscapes are divided by the River Thames, which cuts through the chalk hills at Goring, and the differences are further emphasised by the path following the banks of the river for some miles before climbing back into the hills.

The Ridgeway is by and large one of the

locate the western end of the path at a similarly physically defined point. The 'official' start of the path in Wiltshire is beside a busy road some 2 miles south-east of the extraordinary concentration of Neolithic monuments at Avebury. The only logical reason for this choice appears to be that it is actually on the line of the prehistoric Ridgeway route. Inevitably, alternative starts have developed, one popular one being to walk in from the railway station at Pewsey, which

Overton Hill

Uffington

OVERTON HILL

OGBOURNE ST GEORGE

APPROX. 9 MILES/14KM

OS Landranger 173
Start at grid reference SU 119 681
Start point: The north side of the A4 Beckhampton-to-Marlborough road on Overton Hill. Parking available.

The start of the Ridgeway is distinctly low-key – an unpretentious track running north from the busy A4 on Overton Hill. A signpost (made of recycled plastic) carries the long distance path 'acorn' symbol, the first of many to be seen along the route.

In fact, for those willing to sacrifice Overton Hill for a more romantic starting point, it is quite possible to start the walk within the great stone circle at Avebury and then join the Ridgeway path some 2 miles further on by means of an equally ancient track known as Herepath or Green Street.

If, on the other hand, the official start point has been chosen, before setting out for Ivinghoe Beacon cross the A40 to inspect the site of the Sanctuary – a double stone circle dating from 2000BC and destroyed in 1724, but which provides a good viewpoint for some of the Avebury monuments.

From the car park, the Ridgeway begins a steady ascent to the crest of the Downs to meet with Green Street as it climbs up from Avebury. A right turn here will lead you to Fyfield Down, a remarkable remnant of ancient downland which has been described as the 'best preserved accessible large tract of ancient landscape in Wessex'.

Ⓔ *To cut short the walk at this point (grid ref. SU 125 708), descend Green Street to Avebury and from there follow the footpath south to Silbury Hill before returning to Overton Hill by way of West Kennet Long Barrow and the Sanctuary. This pleasant 6-mile circular walk is one of the greatest archaeological adventures in Britain.*

The Ridgeway path itself continues its course northwards to meet the first crossing of a metalled road above the Hackpen White Horse, which tradition maintains was cut in 1838 by the parish clerk and a local publican to celebrate Queen Victoria's coronation.

The path begins to swing eastwards at this point and before long the ramparts of Barbury Castle, a hillfort with a long and violent history, rear up ahead. Probably built around the first century BC but later abandoned, the castle appears to have been refortified to face the threat of the advancing Anglo-Saxons. A great battle is reputed to have taken place here in AD556, in which the Anglo-Saxons crushed the remaining Romano-British resistance in the area and won for themselves a period of relative stability which allowed the foundations to be laid for what became the kingdom of Wessex.

Just to the west of the hillfort the Ridgeway path parts company for a while with the route of the prehistoric trackway and, preferring higher ground, goes over Barbury Castle before swinging south towards Ogbourne St George. Barbury Castle Country Park was opened in 1972 and provides toilet facilities, car parking and limited tourist information. Refreshments to wash away the accumulation of chalk dust are available.

The Ridgeway under snow, near Hackpen Hill

Ahead lies one of the most dramatic sections of the whole route, where the track undulates along the narrow back of Smeathe's Ridge, giving a feeling of unexpected airiness. The views to both sides are extensive; Liddington Castle to the north and the Downs stretching away into haziness to the south. Too soon a metalled road is reached where a right turn leads down to Ogbourne St George.

OGBOURNE ST GEORGE

UFFINGTON CASTLE

APPROX. 13 MILES/21KM

OS Landranger 173, 174
Start at grid reference SU 203 743
Start point: Park in the lay-by beside the telephone box in Ogbourne St George.

Since Ogbourne St George is not actually on the course of the Ridgeway path, it is necessary to make a short diversion to get back on to the official route. Turn right on to the old Roman road just under the bridge which carries the A345 bypass and at the 'No through road' signpost turn left uphill on a track to the Old Lime Works. Just after some commercial premises the route becomes a green lane which goes on to fork beside the entrance to a field. Take the left-hand branch which climbs to the north-east to join the Ridgeway path at grid ref. SU 214 744.

It is also possible to walk southwards along the main street of Ogbourne St George to join the A345. After some 200yds, alongside the main road, the Ridgeway path is signposted off to the left along a sunken track which climbs up on to the ridge of the Round Hill Downs.

In common with many sections of the route, the next few miles of track have clearly been subject quite recently to work to remove the worst of the ruts and improve surface drainage. The path is still climbing, but this is easy to forget as the views westwards open out and it is possible to trace the course of the route from Barbury Castle.

Ⓔ *If a shorter walk is required, turn left at the cross-tracks on Whitefield Hill (grid ref. SU 213 765) and leave the Ridgeway to follow a broad green lane towards a prominent mast. The track becomes metalled and spectacular views towards Barbury Castle can be enjoyed on the descent to the A345. At the road turn right and left after 100yds. When the course of the old Midland and*

South-West Junction Railway is reached, climb the ramp on to the old track bed. Turn left to return to Ogbourne St George. The entire round trip is about 5 miles in length.

About a mile away down the right-hand track on Whitefield Hill lie the remains of the village of Snap, a settlement which is known to have been well established in 1377 but which steadily declined and was finally abandoned early this century.

The Ridgeway path itself does not deviate to visit Snap but continues ahead towards Liddington Castle, an Iron Age hillfort beloved of Richard Jefferies, who was born at nearby Coate, and at 911ft (278m) the highest point on the path. Liddington may be reached by a permissive path from the Ridgeway.

From Liddington Castle it is only 2 miles by minor roads across the Wanborough Plain and over the M4 to the public house at Fox Hill. The Shepherd's Rest offers food and camping and is the last opportunity to obtain refreshments directly on the route until Goring – 26 thirsty miles away.

There is room for parking at the bottom of Fox Hill, where the Ridgeway shrugs off its coat of tarmacadam and strikes off with single-mindedness north-eastwards. Below this section of the ridge is the pretty village of Bishopstone, with its thatched cottages gathered around a large pond. The scarp

Above *Wayland's Smithy long barrow*

between the Ridgeway and the village carries a fine series of strip lynchets – contouring terraces formed over a long period of time by regular ploughing around the steep downland slopes. Just beyond Bishopstone a track runs off south towards Ashdown Park.

This section of the route lies slightly behind the northern edge of the Downs which, together with the almost continuous hedges, give an enclosed feeling to the walking so that, despite signposts to the ancient monument, it is almost possible to walk past Wayland's Smithy without noticing the presence of the barrow in a hanger of beeches some 50yds off the track. The first long barrow, constructed about 3700BC, was rebuilt some centuries later to make a larger, sarsen-faced chambered tomb. In folklore the cave-like tomb was to become the home of Wayland, the crippled smith-god of the Anglo-Saxons.

Beyond the Smithy lies one of the most familiar parts of the Ridgeway as it ascends on a chalk-surfaced track towards the ramparts of Uffington Castle. Some 600yds before reaching the castle, a track leads off to the left towards the car park on Woolstone Hill – but before finishing this section of the route, carry on up to the fort to experience spectacular views out over the Vale of the White Horse.

AVEBURY (NT)

Avebury straddles the A4361, 2 short miles west of the start of the Ridgeway and provides the focus for a series of Neolithic monuments which are unparalleled in Europe. The antiquary John Aubrey, who first brought the great stone circle to the attention of the public in 1648, claimed that Avebury excelled Stonehenge 'as a cathedral does a parish church'. The hundreds of 'sarsen' stones, some weighing more than 20 tons, were manhandled into their present positions between 2500 and 2200BC. Near by stands West Kennet Long Barrow (more than 1000 years older than the stone circle) and the mysterious Silbury Hill – the largest man-made mound in prehistoric Europe. Avebury is also home to the Great Barn Museum of Wiltshire Folk Life, housed in a great 17th-century barn (open all year, daily in summer, weekends only in winter).

Uffington
Goring

UFFINGTON
SCUTCHAMER KNOB
APPROX. 10¹/₂ MILES/17KM

OS Landranger 174
Start at grid reference SU 293 866
Start point: Uffington Castle car park,
signposted from the B4507, 7 miles west
of Wantage.

Before setting out on this section of the
Ridgeway, take the opportunity to explore
Uffington Castle and the famous White
Horse (visible from the road below the
Ridgeway but not on the Ridgeway itself).
Uffington was never a castle in the medieval
sense of the word, but is a hillfort of eight
acres encircled by a single bank and ditch.
The discovery of a silver coin dates its occupation to the 1st century BC. This coin is of
further interest because on one side it depicts
a horse similar in design to the great White
Horse cut into the turf close to the hillfort. A
horse was the emblem of the Dobunni tribe,
which suggests that the White Horse may
may be as old as the hillfort. Local tradition,
however, attributes it to King Alfred, who
had it cut to commemorate his victory over
the Danes at nearby Ashdown. The Castle
and White Horse Hill are in the ownership
of the National Trust and offer extensive
views northwards over the romantically
named Vale of the White Horse, studded
with small villages – among these Great
Coxwell, with its medieval barn.

Just outside the hillfort lie two oval
mounds, one of which proved to be a
Roman barrow containing 46 burials. Some

of the bodies had been placed in position
with coins in their mouths – the fee charged
by Charon the ferryman for their passage
across the River Styx.

The Ridgeway itself shuns the hillfort, as
if to make it clear that it is the greater antiquity, and continues its journey eastwards.

Ⓔ *Before long the opportunity arises for those*
wishing to cut the walk short and return to
Uffington to leave the Ridgeway at Sparsholt Firs
(grid ref. SU 343 852) by turning right along the
B4001. After 1¹/₂ miles, a grassy track branches
off to the right and runs down to Lambourn Seven
Barrows. The return to Uffington Castle is direct,
along a series of bridleways over Kingston Warren.
The walk, which gives a 7¹/₂-mile round trip, is
described in a leaflet available from Oxfordshire
County Council – one of a series of circular walks
based around the Ridgeway.

From the B4001 crossing, the Ridgeway
continues eastwards alongside racehorse
gallops with the natural ampitheatre of the
Devil's Punchbowl immediately below the
edge of the scarp. The village at its base is
Letcombe Bassett, the 'Cresscombe' of
Thomas Hardy's bleak novel *Jude the Obscure*.
Hardy wrote the book while staying in the
area and a number of the places passed on
this section of the Ridgeway appear there
with no greater disguise than a change of
name. In fact, a short way ahead, the
junction with the A338 marks the site of
Jude's ill-fated vision of the spires of Oxford.
A left turn along the A338 leads to the
Ridgeway Centre and Youth Hostel on
Court Hill. This section of the path is well
used by farm traffic and has been surfaced
accordingly, but the familiar grassy and

The Ridgeway from Uffington Castle

GUIDE BOX

Places to visit
Lambourn Seven Barrows Nature Reserve lies some 2
miles south of the Ridgeway close to B4001. As
well as being important for its chalk grassland,
this Site of Special Scientific Interest contains a
remarkable barrow cemetery dating from the
Bronze Age. The grassland surrounding the
barrows is believed never to have been ploughed
and is home to over 100 different plant species
including the fragrant orchid; the variety of
plants supports a rich butterfly population. The
site is managed by the Berkshire,
Buckinghamshire and Oxfordshire Naturalists
Trust.

The Ridgeway Centre stands amid beech woods on
Court Hill, ¹/₄ mile north of the Ridgeway. The
complex is housed in five formerly redundant
local barns which were dismantled and re-
erected on the site, which is itself a filled-in
chalk quarry. As well as housing a youth hostel,
the Centre has a picnic area, toilets and a display
room which are open to the general public. The
displays show in fascinating detail how the
buildings were moved and there are a series of
wall panels giving mile-by-mile information
about the Ridgeway.

Didcot Railway Centre is close to the A4130, just
to the north of the town and some 5 miles north
of the Ridgeway. The Centre shares a site with
the British Rail station and a few steps take one
back in time to the golden age of steam. Great
Western locomotives, an engine shed and
reconstructed station are open to the public on
weekends throughout the year and daily from
Spring Bank Holiday to the end of August. The
Centre has a refreshment room.

Car parking
The main sites for car parking may be found
below Uffington Castle (grid ref. SU 293 866),
Sparsholt Firs (SU 343 852), at the junction with
the B4494 near Yew Down (SU 418 841),
beside Scutchamer Knob (SU 458 850), at the
road crossing on Bury Down (SU 479 841), and
in Goring (SU 600 805).

Public transport
Goring and Streatley British Rail station lies on
the route of the Ridgeway path. The only other
station is at Didcot, 5 miles to the north.
Uffington, Sparsholt, Letcombe Regis, Wantage,
Chilton, the Ilsleys, and Compton may all be
reached by bus, but the frequency of services
does vary.

Accommodation
There is little accommodation on this length of
the Ridgeway but for those willing to leave the
route, bed-and-breakfast may be found at
Uffington, Wantage, Goring and villages close to
the route. There are youth hostels at Court Hill
(Ridgeway Centre) and Streatley.

slightly rutted surface of the track is not long
in returning and this leads on towards the
next crossing of a metalled road on Lattin
Down. Ahead rises the monument to Robert
Loyd-Lindsay, Baron Wantage, who was a
holder of the Victoria Cross and died in
1901. The inscription reads 'I will lift up
mine eyes to the hills from whence cometh
my help'.

The Ridgeway descends from the
monument and within the next mile or so
undulates three times. Ahead, in a group of

trees is Scutchamer Knob, a mutilated round barrow which would probably pass unnoticed were it not for its curious name which has aroused considerable speculation as to its origin. Old maps refer to it as 'Scutchamfly Barrow' or 'Scotchman's Hob'. One argument is that the name derives from the 'scutcher' who beat out the fibres from flax which had previously been softened by soaking. A second school of thought suggests that the name is a corruption of the Saxon 'Cwicchelmshlaew', the burial place of a Saxon king Cwicchelm who died in AD593.

At the end of the trees, just beyond Scutchamer Knob, there is room for parking at the head of the metalled road which climbs up from the A417 at East Hundred and marks the end of this section of the walk.

SCUTCHAMER KNOB

GORING

APPROX. 9½ MILES/15KM

OS Landranger 174, 175
Start at grid reference SU 458 850
Start point: To the east of Scutchamer Knob, at the end of the metalled road leading from East Hendred and the A417. Parking space.

The Ridgeway sets off eastwards alongside racehorse training gallops. Just to the north of this section of the path, at the base of the scarp, runs Grim's Ditch, one of three linear earthworks with this name which are passed during the course of the path. This particular Grim's Ditch stretches off and on for 8 miles but does not appear ever to have been continuous – those sections where the ground was either too steep or wooded being left. Its date is uncertain but it has been suggested that it may represent the boundary between two Iron Age estates.

The views from this length of the track are dominated by the presence to the north of the great cooling towers of Didcot Power Station. The power station operates on solid fuel and began operation in 1972. To the east of the power station lies the town of Didcot with its station and Railway Centre. Before long the path meets a minor road on Bury Down, where there is room for parking, and then presses on towards the roar of traffic on the A34. Fortunately one is spared having to attempt to cross this road for the Ridgeway dodges underneath by means of a tunnel, and continues to climb up on to Several Down.

Ⓔ *Just beyond the top of the Down the opportunity arises to leave the Ridgeway and return to the car at Scutchamer Knob by means of the villages of East and West Ilsley. Turn right on to a bridleway which heads off southwards from grid ref. SU 503 825 towards East Ilsley. From the medieval period to the early years of this century the village was famous (or perhaps infamous) for its sheep markets. Sheep were driven over the Downs from as far away as Salisbury and the annual fairs could see up to 80,000 penned*

alongside the village street. Droving was thirsty work and the village at one time boasted no less than 13 public houses. The atmosphere of the fairs has been summed up in verse:

> *Ilsley remote amidst the Berkshire Downs*
> *claims those distinctions o'er her sister towns*
> *far famed for sheep and wool though not for*
> *spinners*
> *for sportsmen, doctors, publicans and sinners.*

The road is followed from East to West Ilsley and here one can either return to Bury Down and thence back along the Ridgeway westwards or take a bridleway to the north-west which leads to Scutchamer Knob. The round trip is 8 miles.

The Ridgeway itself descends from Several Down and then bends sharply to the left, where another track continues straight on towards Compton and the field station of the Agricultural Research Council's Institute for Animal Health. The descent continues steeply on a wide track until the course of the dismantled railway. The next summit on the roller-coaster is Roden Down. To the left is the steep spur of Lowbury Hill, which according to the Ordnance Survey map is the site of a Roman temple. In fact excavations at the site failed to establish the exact

Above *The River Thames at Streatley*

purpose of the rectangular, banked enclosure and it is as likely to have been a farm as a temple. One grisly find from beneath the foundations of one of the walls was the skeleton of a middle-aged woman, a position which suggests a dedicatory burial.

The great traverse of the Downs is coming to an end and there is a sense of finality as the Ridgeway begins the long descent beside Streatley Warren towards the Goring Gap where the River Thames cuts through the chalk hills. The Gap itself is, in geological terms, a relatively recent feature and prior to its formation the Thames used to run northwards to join the sea near the Wash.

Just to the south of this part of the route lies the village of Aldworth, whose church is home to the Aldworth giants, nine huge effigies (dated 1300–1350) which represent members of the de la Beche family. Sir William de la Beche was tutor to the Black Prince. At Warren Farm the track becomes metalled and before long the A417 is joined and followed into Streatley where a left turn at traffic lights close to the youth hostel leads across the Thames into Berkshire and Goring.

THE WHITE HORSES

White Horses, formed by cutting away turf to expose the underlying chalk, are a feature of the Downs. The popularity for cutting hill-figures reached its height in the 19th century, but some are much more ancient. It is almost unbelievable that generations of local inhabitants have regularly scoured these older figures to keep them from fading back into the surrounding grassland, but their mere survival is proof that this has been the case. A fascinating leaflet entitled *A Tour of the White Horses* by J & M Young is available from local Tourist Information Centres and describes a tour by car of six Wiltshire White Horses, extended to include the unique Uffington Horse, believed to be 2000 years old and visible from the road below the Ridgeway.

The White Horse at Cherhill Down, Avebury

Goring
Chinnor

GORING

NUFFIELD

APPROX 10 MILES/16KM

OS Landranger 174, 175
Start at grid reference SU 600 805
Start point: The car park in Goring.

After the waterless expanse of the Downs, it is something of a surprise to follow the course of the River Thames. Note the distinctive swan's head and horseshoe way-markers for the Swan's Way, a long-distance bridleway route from Goring to Salcey Forest, which crosses paths with the Ridgeway on a number of occasions.

The path runs close to the railway line along this section and it is difficult not to contrast the various merits of different types of travel as the Intercity trains scream past and leave the walker to enjoy the leisurely route towards South Stoke.

At South Stoke the path draws away from the river to run through the village, before returning to the bank at a point where some maps mark a ferry. There is no sign of a ferry there today, but local rumour has it that if you shout loud (and long) enough, someone will come to take you across to the pub on the other side of the river.

Ⓔ *If a crossing is made, it is possible to cut the section short at this point (grid ref. SU 594 837) by returning to Goring along the west bank of the Thames. However, those whose patience or lungs are not up to this can continue along the*

Ridgeway until a World War II pillbox is passed in trees on the right (grid ref. SU 602 853). The Ridgeway Path runs along a track to meet the metalled road where a right turn leads past Littlestoke Manor to the bridleway signposted to the Portway, but just before meeting the A4074 turn right on to another bridleway. This meets a minor road where a right turn leads back to Goring. The round trip is 8 miles.

The path itself carries on through fields to North Stoke, where a visit to the early 13th-century church is well worth while. The ironwork on the door dates from the building of the church and inside are a number of 14th-century wall paintings. There is a curious sundial in the south wall. The Ridgeway leaves the village past the rushing race of the old mill and along a pleasant, tree-lined track which gives way to open fields on the approach to Mongewell Park.

Just beyond the buildings of Carmel College the path turns abruptly on to the line of another Grim's Ditch – if one were to carry straight on at this junction a path would lead in less than a mile to the pleasant town of Wallingford. The walk along Grim's Ditch (also known as Devil's Dyke) gets into its swing once the A4074 has been crossed. For the most part the path follows the top of the bank which runs to the north of the dyke, a position one would have expected to be exposed. In this case, however, the whole line of the ditch is well wooded so that the walk has an enclosed feel to it. There are occasional glimpses out at the surrounding countryside and, in the distance, the chalk-cut shape of the Watlington White Mark.

Below *Ancient Ewelme, just off the path*

Further on the path begins to cross from one side of the ditch to the other, sometimes running on the bank and sometimes weaving between fallen trees in the ditch bottom. This zig-zagging gives a good opportunity to look at the structure of the ditch as a whole and it is apparent from its lack of respect for the contours of the land it crosses that it was never intended to be defensive, but rather appears to mark a boundary.

hedges and over the next 3 miles passes below some of the finest chalk downland in the Chilterns. These north-facing slopes form part of the Aston Rowant Nature Reserve which can be visited from the Ridgeway by turning right over a stile just beyond the tunnel underneath the M40.

While there is no doubt that the motorway is an intrusion into this beautiful piece of countryside, as far as the Ridgeway is concerned, its impact is minimised by crossing at right angles and the sound of the traffic soon recedes into the background. Indeed, it has been said that the Icknield Way itself was the motorway of prehistoric England but it is interesting to contrast the modern route with its cuttings and embankments gouging its way between the vast conurbations that it serves and the natural lines of the ancient route, always so conscious of the terrain it is crossing, exploiting every easy slope and running with the grain of the landscape.

Above *The Icknield Way near Aston Rowant*

Ⓔ *A bridleway at grid ref. SU 679 899 gives the opportunity to cut this section short. A left turn here takes one on to join the Swan's Way whence another bridleway may be followed close to Potter's Farm to join the green road which runs parallel to, and appears to be an older course of, the A423. A left turn along this track brings one up to join the main road near the start point – a round walk of 5 miles.*

Route-finding along this part of the path could not be easier. The track varies in width, sometimes approaching in appearance the great grass swath which ran over the Downs west of Goring, but always it is bounded by hedges and bears steadfastly north-east. It is something of a shock to realise after a few miles that the fields on the other side of the hedges have been replaced by water-filled abandoned workings and that you are following a causeway through Chinnor cement works. Presently the path descends towards the Crowell Hill-to-Chinnor road, where there is ample parking on the edges of the track. Chinnor lies about a mile away to the left, down the road.

Suddenly the ditch disappears into farmland and the Ridgeway turns north once more, across a carpet of beech nuts, to meet with the road close to the 14th-century Nuffield Church, with its squat, square tower. Of interest to Ridgewayfarers will be the water tap on the outside of the tower and a seat on which to rest before the final leg of this section. In the churchyard is the unpretentious grave of the industrialist and philanthropist William Richard Morris, Viscount Nuffield, who founded Morris Motors in 1919.

The path goes on to cross the golf course on Nuffield Common, with the route clearly marked by a series of white numbered posts, and emerges on to the A423 beside The Crown public house.

NUFFIELD

CHINNOR

APPROX. 11 MILES/18KM

OS Landranger 175, 165
Start at grid reference SU 675 877
Start point: Beside the A423, at the top of Gangsdown Hill, 5 miles east of Wallingford. Parking in Nuffield.

The Ridgeway leaves the main road through a gate and descends through young woodland. This section of the walk is marked by the passing of two large houses, Ewelme Park and Swyncombe House. Ewelme Park is a ponderous mock-Tudor affair occupying high ground, its walls rendered a monotonous grey throughout. A couple of miles off route to the west, however, lies the village of Ewelme itself, which contains some gems of 15th-century architecture.

The path goes on to descend into the dry valley of Colliers Bottom.

The Ridgeway itself turns right at the junction with the bridleway and follows a track upwards through the Swyncombe estate to St Botolph's Church, a pleasant little building dating back to the 11th century. Above the church, the path crosses a minor road and begins the descent towards the route of the Icknield Way, an ancient trackway running across southern England from the Chilterns to Norfolk. Britwell House is visible in the distance.

One cannot help but feel a thrill to be stepping back on to the line of the ancient highway. At this point it is a flint-surfaced track, but it soon becomes a grassy lane whose hedges have grown up to form a tunnel. In places the track is sunken below the surface of the adjacent fields to produce a holloway which is invariably muddy. In this enclosed environment the miles speed by and soon after the crossing of the B480 beside Icknield House, a minor road is met where a left turn would lead down to the small town of Watlington with its fine central town hall, built by Thomas Stonor in 1664. Cut into the hillside immediately above this junction is the 270ft-high obelisk of the Watlington White Mark, carved by Edward Home in 1674 and said, when viewed from the vale, to look like a spire added on to the top of the tower of Watlington Church. There is a camp site at White Mark Farm, just off the road into Watlington.

The Ridgeway presses on between its

Chinnor

Ivinghoe

CHINNOR

WENDOVER

APPROX. 11 MILES/18KM

OS Landranger 165
Start at grid reference SP 760 002
Start point: About ½ mile from the centre of Chinnor, beside the road to Bledlow Ridge at the foot of Chinnor Hill. There is room to park on the edge of the Ridgeway itself.

Leaving the road, the Ridgeway path begins to ascend gradually beneath the wooded slopes of Wain Hill, at the same time taking the opportunity to show its cunning by contouring around the heads of the steep-sided combes which cut into the northern slopes.

For the last 10 miles the path has followed the course of the Upper Icknield Way, but at the edge of Thickthorne Wood there is a parting of the ways as the ancient route plunges straight across the valley towards Princes Risborough leaving the Ridgeway path to seek out a more interesting line across fields and to climb the grassy slopes of Lodge Hill. The view from the summit of the hill is far-reaching; on a clear day it is possible to make out the white triangle of Whiteleaf Cross in the distance. Nearer at hand is Lacey Green with its 17th-century windmill, which is believed to be the oldest surviving smock mill in Britain. The ridge from Lacey Green continues southwards towards Hughenden Manor and High Wycombe.

Ⓔ *If you wish to leave the Ridgeway at this point and return to Chinnor, turn right through a gap in the prominent hedge soon after the stile on the descent of Lodge Hill (grid ref. SP 797 001). A bridleway runs south-west and climbs to Rout's Green, where a right turn allows the Bledlow Ridge road to be followed back to Chinnor. This gives a round walk of 6 miles.*

The Ridgeway itself swings northwards to cross the High Wycombe-to-Princes Risborough railway line and join the Upper Icknield Way once more. Despite its size, Princes Risborough is passed by almost unnoticed on a pleasant grassy track before the path crosses a stile to begin the ascent to Whiteleaf Cross. This is one of the steepest climbs on the route but is well rewarded by the view from the grassy clearing above the Cross. Looking out westwards, it is possible to trace your route across the valley all the way from Chinnor, while in the distance the white towers of Didcot Power Station are clearly visible, with the line of the Wessex Downs behind.

Directly below where you sit are the deeply carved arms of Whiteleaf Cross itself. First recorded in 1742, the Cross may have been the work of monks in the 15th or 16th centuries. It is the oldest of the Chiltern hill-figures but its purpose is uncertain. One can speculate whether it was scoured as a landmark for travellers or perhaps to obscure a more obviously pagan figure which may previously have occupied the site.

Leaving the Cross, the path now descends steeply to the Plough public house at Lower

Princes Risborough, seen from Whiteleaf Cross

GUIDE BOX

Places to visit
Hughenden Manor (NT) stands within its park close to the A4128, some 5 miles south-east of the Ridgeway. The Manor is famous for being the home of Disraeli who lived there from 1847 until his death in 1881. The house contains many of his relics, including furniture, paintings and books. Disraeli is buried in the churchyard in the park. Open March, Saturday and Sunday; April to October, Wednesday to Sunday and Bank Holiday Mondays.

Ivinghoe Mills: there are two mills in the village open to the public:
Pitstone Windmill (NT), which stands just off the B488 ½ mile south of the village, is one of the oldest post mills in Britain. The mill has its origins in 1627, but may have been rebuilt since that time reusing some of the original materials. As the name suggests, the mill is built around a central post and whenever the wind changed direction, the whole mill had to be luffed or turned to face it once again. It was restored to working order in the 1960s by the Pitstone Windmill Restoration Committee and is now in the care of the National Trust. It is open to the public on Sundays and Bank Holiday Monday afternoons from May to September.
Ford End Watermill stands some 600yds from Ivinghoe Church, beside the road to Leighton Buzzard. There are records of a watermill in Ivinghoe in the 14th century, but we have to wait until 1798 for the first definite reference to a mill on this particular site. The mill was in regular use until 1963 and has recently been restored. Opening hours for the mill are similar to those for Pitstone post mill.

Whipsnade Wild Animal Park lies just south of the B4540. The White Lion cut into the chalk which marks its position can be seen from Ivinghoe Beacon. Whipsnade, which is the country home of the Zoological Society of London, was founded in 1931 and now contains more than 2800 animals in 600 acres of parkland. The park is open daily all year, with the exception of Christmas Day, and there are full facilities for visitors.

Car parking
The most useful car parks are to be found below Chinnor Hill (grid ref. SP 760 002), beside Whiteleaf Cross (SP 821 041), Coombe Hill (SU 852 063), near the library at Wendover (SP 870 079), and at the crossing of the Ringshall road below Ivinghoe Beacon (SP 955 149).

Public transport
This section is well served by British Rail stations at Princes Risborough, Wendover and Tring.
Chinnor, Princes Risborough, the Kimbles, Wendover, Wigginton, Tring and Ivinghoe all have bus services.

Accommodation
Bed-and-breakfast is available at Bledlow (½ mile off route), Princes Risborough, Great Kimble, Wendover, Wigginton and Tring. There is a youth hostel at Ivinghoe which has a camp site.

Cadsden before following a rare section of permissive path to enter the nature reserve of Grangelands and Pulpit Hill, which contains fine areas of chalk grassland. The Ridgeway leaves the reserve by climbing up steps over Chequers Knap and enters the grounds of Chequers where it goes on to cross the drive of the house. Chequers dates from the 16th century and was given to the nation in 1917 by Lord Lee of Fareham, as a country home for the prime minister.

There are good views of Chequers from the path and in the background rises Coombe Hill, with its golden-topped monument, which the Ridgeway goes on to climb, through an area of attractive beech woodland. On 29 September 1973 Coombe Hill was the site of the ceremony for the official opening of the Ridgeway path by Lord Nugent of Guildford. The open grassland around the monument is popular with local residents and there is a choice of routes downwards which lead directly to the attractive little town of Wendover.

WENDOVER
IVINGHOE BEACON
APPROX. 11½ MILES/18KM

OS Landranger 165
Start at grid reference SP 868 078
Start point: Car park adjacent to the library, Wendover, signposted from the town centre.

Turn right out of the car park in Wendover and follow Heron Path alongside the stream and out of the town, passing the 14th-century flint Church of St Mary the Virgin. The church contains a fine brass of 1537 to William Bradschawe, his wife and 32 children and grandchildren. The Ridgeway then climbs by means of Hogtrough Lane into Barn Wood and runs more or less level along the side of Cock's Hill.

Ⓔ *After a while a road is reached at grid ref. SP 989 074 where a left turn will lead back to Wendover, cutting the section short. A second, slightly longer way back is possible by following the road for about ½ mile and then taking a footpath northwards into Wendover woods, crossing over the spur of Boddington Hill, with its Iron Age fort, and so back to Wendover. The longer of these two escape routes gives a 4½-mile round trip.*

The Ridgeway plunges back into the woods and makes progress beside (or in, if you have wellingtons) a typical Chiltern holloway, sunken 6ft below the level of the surrounding ground and muddy in the driest of weather. There is a brief interlude over fields towards a radio mast and then more woodland before a minor road is followed to Hastoe Cross. Ahead, although not actually on the path, lies Wigginton, which has a shop and a pub.

From the trig. point on the outskirts of Wigginton you can see Ivinghoe Beacon clearly and, although it still seems a long way off, there is a feeling as you descend the path towards the valley – where the road, canal and railway rub shoulders as they squeeze through the gap to Berkhamsted – that the end of the walk is fast approaching. First, however, great care must be taken in crossing the A41, which follows the line of the Roman Akeman Street. This is probably the busiest road on the entire Ridgeway, and

the crossing point is situated on an unpleasant bend.

With Akeman Street safely behind you, it is not far to the Grand Union Canal and the Royal Hotel, adjacent to Tring Station, where fortification can be taken for the final assault on Ivinghoe Beacon. The Ridgeway intends to finish in style and begins the climb away from the narrow Bulbourne valley, back into the hills.

After ½ mile the path enters a nature reserve on Aldbury Nowers, which was opened by Queen Elizabeth the Queen Mother on 8 June 1991 and which is named after her. The reserve protects an important area of chalk downland, rich in wild flowers and butterflies. It then goes on to meet an earthwork with the by now familiar name of Grim's Ditch, although it is unlikely that this ditch is linked in any way other than by name to the ones followed earlier in Oxfordshire and Berkshire. The ditch lies to the south of the rampart, often on the uphill side, which suggests that it marks a boundary rather than having a directly defensive

At the end of the walk, Ivinghoe Beacon

purpose. The structure is generally accepted to be of Iron Age date.

The path emerges from woodland on Pitstone Hill and enjoys magnificent views to the west and north for almost all the remainder of the walk. Ivinghoe is clearly visible, with Pitstone windmill standing in isolation in a nearby field, while to the east the Whipsnade White Lion, cut in 1933 as an advertisement for the nearby zoo, stands out well on a clear day. It is not long before Ivinghoe Beacon is under foot and arrival at the trig. point indicates that the Ridgeway path is over.

While contemplating the 85 miles of the walk, spare a thought for those who raised the barrows visible on the hilltop and for their Iron Age descendants who fortified the hill in 700BC. Much of the route just followed would have been familiar to them and it is the remains of their temples, graves and fortresses which have helped make the walk so memorable.

THE ASHRIDGE ESTATE (NT)

Covering an area of 6 square miles of classic Chiltern countryside from Ivinghoe Beacon to Berkhamsted, the unspoilt commons, woods and open spaces of the Ashridge Estate are home to some 300 fallow and muntjac deer and a wide variety of other wildlife. Access by car is from the B4506 Ringshall-to-Berkhamsted road and there are numerous footpaths through the Estate. An information centre and tea kiosk is provided near to the granite monument which was erected 150 years ago to commemorate the 3rd Duke of Bridgewater, the great canal developer of the 18th century. A small charge is made for entry to the monument, which is open to the public from Easter to end October.

Oxfordshire Way

BOURTON-ON-THE-WATER TO HENLEY-ON-THAMES
65 MILES/104KM

THE Oxfordshire Way runs for 65 miles across the heart of England from Bourton-on-the-Water in the Gloucestershire Cotswolds to Henley-on-Thames in the south-east corner of Oxfordshire. It rambles along ancient rights of way, all of which existed long before they were thus joined together, passing through historic settlements and crossing the grain of the country. The route was devised in the early 1970s and developed from a dream of the Oxfordshire branch of the Council for the Protection of Rural England (CPRE) to create a 'walkers' link' between the Cotswolds and the Chilterns. By 1978 the actual route was ready. It is now maintained by Oxfordshire County Council.

The old tracks and field paths of the Oxfordshire Way lead the walker through the heart of England. These paths have been used for centuries. Some are prehistoric, some are Roman, many were first trodden in Saxon times. They link villages and hamlets mentioned in *Domesday Book* of 1086. The comfortable inns of these places usually provide food and accommodation, bed-and-breakfast can be found on or close to the route, and there are some camping sites. Village shops have survived in surprising numbers.

The Oxfordshire Way is no walkers' motorway. It passes through farmland and woodland, along valleys and over breezy hills. It can feel remote and, at times, lonely. Along the route are Iron Age earthworks, Roman antiquities, Saxon lanes and settlements and solid Norman churches. It passes the vestiges of two medieval royal forests, Wychwood and Bernwood, and goes through the ancient Chiltern beechwoods. It touches the old coaching routes at Wootton, Islip, Tetsworth and Henley. Everywhere there are memories of the Civil War.

There is virtually no road-walking, most of the way being along footpaths. Generally the route is easy to follow, signposted and waymarked by yellow or blue arrows on a white disc, superimposed with the monogram OW or with the words 'Oxfordshire Way', but at times the waymarks disappear, and the route is unsigned or simply marked as a public footpath. Go equipped with OS maps, preferably 1:25,000 Pathfinder, as the route does unexpected things and tends to wind about, going over stiles and round fields as if for the sheer pleasure of prolonging the journey.

There are hills to negotiate, but even so this is not strenuous walking, and the whole walk can be completed in less than a week. The two highest points of the walk, Wyck Beacon in the Cotswolds and Christmas Common in the Chilterns, are 812ft (247m) and 780ft (238m) high respectively, no great eminences, though commanding superb views.

Bus and rail services are infrequent, but this is more than compensated for by the good state of the paths, so that with the aid of an OS map you can plan a circular route, and some possibilities are mentioned here. The Oxfordshire Way itself gives you a choice of routes, and crosses the Ridgeway Path.

Looking across to Stoke Talmage

Detailed guides
Oxfordshire Way by Alison Kemp, published by Oxfordshire County Council (1985), is a new edition of the CPRE's 1978 Guide to the Oxfordshire Way. Available from Central Library, Westgate, Oxford OX1 1DJ, or from Oxfordshire County Council, New Road, Oxford.

Maps
OS Landranger 163, 164, 165, 174, 175

Links
The Oxfordshire Way meets the Icknield Way, the Swan's Way and the Ridgeway near Watlington. It meets the Thames Path at Henley.

The Oxfordshire Way can be walked safely at any season, though the lowland sections get very muddy in winter, but should it be walked from north-west to south-east or vice versa? The way from Bourton to Henley allows you to walk with, rather than against, the wind, gives you that superb vista ahead to the wooded Chiltern scarp, and follows the tributaries of the Thames, reaching the great river itself at Henley.

This is a route through differing landscapes, changing with the rock type beneath your feet. It starts in the Cotswold uplands, a landscape of stone. Stone lying on the surface of the fields, stone buildings, stone roofs; all blending and at one with the land itself. This sensation of stone is softened here and there by hedges, before the route falls to the clay vale and the drained fen of Ot Moor. Here there is not a stone in sight and the Way becomes marsh again after rain. The building materials used by our forefathers start to change so that timber, brick and tiles appear.

From Ot Moor the route mounts the Oxford Heights, and then heads down into the vale between them and the chalk bulwark of the Chilterns. This is a region of brick buildings, which slowly oust the stone, until flint starts to make itself felt. The whole flavour of the landscape has changed. This is lowland and south-eastern.

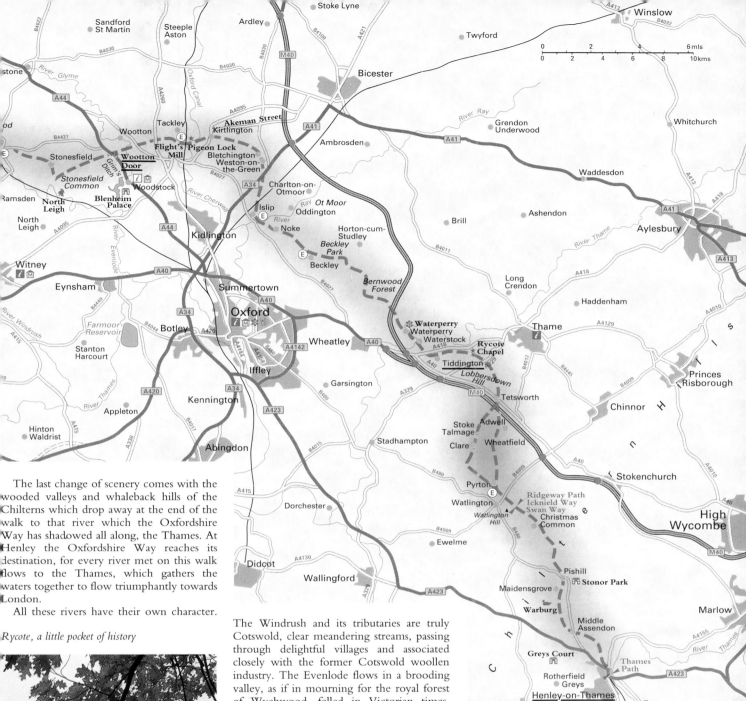

The last change of scenery comes with the wooded valleys and whaleback hills of the Chilterns which drop away at the end of the walk to that river which the Oxfordshire Way has shadowed all along, the Thames. At Henley the Oxfordshire Way reaches its destination, for every river met on this walk flows to the Thames, which gathers the waters together to flow triumphantly towards London.

All these rivers have their own character.

Rycote, a little pocket of history

The Windrush and its tributaries are truly Cotswold, clear meandering streams, passing through delightful villages and associated closely with the former Cotswold woollen industry. The Evenlode flows in a brooding valley, as if in mourning for the royal forest of Wychwood, felled in Victorian times, while the Glyme, though small and shy, blossoms into the stately lakes of Blenheim Great Park. The Cherwell is glimpsed briefly in the deep green valley which it now shares with the Oxford Canal; the River Ray drains lonely Ot Moor, and the Thame, last of the Thames tributaries on this walk, flows among luxuriant meadows.

These river valleys teem with water birds, like heron and kingfisher. The river banks are inhabited by water voles and the field boundaries contain many a rabbit hole. Foxes and badgers lurk in the woodlands, weasels and hares are by no means rare. You may spot a buzzard, and deer roam freely.

There is much to see along the route: a view to a great house here, a magnificent panorama there. In October the Chiltern beechwoods are golden and in April they take on a dream-like quality, carpeted with bluebells, while along the rivers in high summer flowers such as loosestrife and scabious bloom in profusion. Such is the Oxfordshire Way, thoroughly rural and full of surprises.

Bourton-on-the-Water

Wootton Door (A44)

BOURTON-ON-THE-WATER

ASCOTT-UNDER-WYCHWOOD

APPROX. 12 MILES/19KM

OS Landranger 163, 164
Start at grid reference SP 168 205
Start point: Bourton-on-the-Water, beside the River Windrush, 4 miles south of Stow-on-the-Wold, on the A429. There are two car parks for which a small charge is made.

The Oxfordshire Way begins in the Gloucestershire Cotswolds at Bourton-on-the-Water, a bustling centre on the grassy banks of the River Windrush. This town was founded on the wealth obtained from Cotswold wool, and in days gone by the land around echoed with the bleating of sheep. The walk passes along Moor Lane, where it is well-signed over a stile to the rough grass and massive earthworks of pre-Roman Salmonsbury Camp. Immediately the razzmatazz of Bourton is left behind, and the real countryside takes over, the 1½ miles to Wyck Rissington passing through water meadows and over little streams, Eye and Dicler, which flow to the Windrush.

Wyck Rissington snuggles into the Dickler Valley. The houses, mellow beneath their stone roofs, are idly clumped about a wide green of rough grasses. There is no hostelry or shop, but there is a village pond and a well, and beyond them the squat and solid Norman tower of the church. Gustav Holst had his first professional appointment here. He was organist in 1892-3, aged 17.

Passing through the churchyard, begin the ascent of Wyck Beacon. Throwing a glance back on the way up, there are magnificent views over the Windrush valley and across the Cotswold upland. You pass over 812ft (247m) Wyck Beacon, an exposed upland for all the veneer of verdure, where the trees lean away from the winds, bitten back by their keenness. Beyond the A424 you descend along the private road to Gawcombe, past huge parkland trees and ornamental lakes. Gawcombe is no more than a cluster of stone buildings about the main house, and once beyond them the way is open and exposed.

Some ¾ mile further on, the Oxfordshire Way turns left to saunter along the green banks of Westcote Brook before striking across fields into Bledington. Bledington Church escaped the fury of last century's church restorers. The porch is 700 years old, and there is a tiny chantry chapel separated from the chancel by an arch. The mottled stone houses and the King's Head, which provides accommodation as well as meals, are grouped about a peaceful green.

Ⓔ *You can leave the Oxfordshire Way here (grid ref. SP 249 223) and return to Bourton by turning left along the B4450 for about 1/4 mile and then left along a footpath via Pebbly Hill Farm to Icomb. Follow the road round and then turn right to Hill Farm and the A424. Cross the road and follow the bridleway over the hill to Wyck Rissington and the Oxfordshire Way back to Bourton. Alternatively, turn right along the B4450 for a mile, to Kingham Station.*

Bourton-on-the-Water, an important centre for touring the Cotswolds

The Oxfordshire Way enters the county after which it is named at the bridge over Westcote Brook, and then crawls shyly along the Evenlode valley to Bruern Abbey. Of this Cistercian religious house, founded around 1137, nothing remains. Here, on its site, is a yellowing grey stone mansion built for the Cope family in about 1720.

The River Evenlode is rarely visible, but its presence can be felt as you pass into Bruern Wood, and then out into the fields again to Shipton-under-Wychwood. Shipton formerly lay on the edge of the Wychwood

Forest, and Shipton Down, to the south of the village, was the scene of the Whitsuntide Revels, when local townsfolk had the right to hunt the king's deer. Today Shipton is a peaceful village of honey-coloured stone, with a shop and a choice of three hostelries. The Shaven Crown, a 15th-century building, is traditionally claimed as a guesthouse of Bruern Abbey.

The centre of Shipton is not on the Oxfordshire Way, and you must turn right at the road to reach it. The Oxfordshire Way turns left to cross the Evenlode and the railway line near Shipton Station with its huge old warehouse, built in the days of the reign of Cotswold wool. It then turns right to Ascott-under-Wychwood, a mellow stone village with a shop, a farm shop and one pub, the Swan, which serves food.

Ⓔ *Ascott Station (grid ref. SP 301 188) has morning and evening commuter services, but you can return to Bledington on foot by crossing the railway and river and following the bridleway on the left to the T-junction on the hilltop. Go straight along the road to Lyneham. Turn left and then right to follow the path via Lyneham golf course back across railway and river to Bledington.*

ASCOTT-UNDER-WYCHWOOD

· —

WOOTTON DOOR (A44)

APPROX. 11 MILES/17.5KM
(northern route, Ascott to Charlbury)

· —

APPROX. 10 MILES/16KM
(southern route, Ascott to Charlbury)

OS Landranger 164
Start at grid reference SP 301 188
Start point: Ascott-under-Wychwood Station. Limited car parking.

From Ascott-under-Wychwood to Charlbury, where a vestige of the medieval forest remains, the Oxfordshire Way is strongly aware of this former haunt of beasts of the chase. The Way offers two routes, one to the north and one to the south of the River Evenlode. The northern route is a mile longer and passes the grassy remains of

Ascott D'Oyley Castle, but the southern route has height above the river and goes through the tiny settlements of Chilson and Shorthampton and close by Charlbury Station, a listed building in Brunel's standard Italianate style.

Charlbury, which climbs up the hillside on a crook of the Evenlode, was a centre of the glove-making industry in the days when Cotswold wool reigned supreme. It has the distinction of being the birthplace of the first woman to preach publicly in London. She was Anne Downer, born in 1624. Charlbury has shops, a museum and four hostelries.

Ⓔ *It is easy to break the journey at Charlbury, as most InterCity trains stop at the station (grid ref. SP 353 194), and there is a bus service. You can walk back to Ascott-under-Wychwood by using the alternative route of the Oxfordshire Way.*

From Charlbury on to Stonesfield, famed for its slates, slabs of limestone split along the bedding planes to make a roofing material so splendid and so heavy that roofs had to be specially constructed to take the weight. The Romans quarried 'slates' here, and 'slates' continued to be cut until 1909. Interestingly, the 'slate beds' are full of fossils, from oyster shells to dinosaurs.

Take the longer route offered by the Oxfordshire Way, going down to the ford on the Evenlode and then up across Stonesfield Common. This passes the deserted 'slate' quarries, now a series of hollows and low green mounds and also provides the opportunity of visiting the Roman villa at North Leigh, just off the Oxfordshire Way.

At Stonesfield Common you join Akeman Street, the Roman road from Bath to Bicester, where it rises over the last long spur of the Cotswolds. Just beyond the Combe-to-Stonesfield road it passes the site of a Roman villa, the first to be discovered and recorded in this country. Little now remains to show that it ever existed.

Akeman Street enters Blenheim Park and crosses the Iron Age earthwork, Grim's Ditch. Here, on the edge of Woodstock, Henry I enclosed a deer park and built himself a hunting lodge. Henry II enlarged it, building a palace, and legend has it that he came here not just to hunt the deer but to visit his 'fair Rosamund'. He is said to have hidden her in a kind of pleasure garden in the midst of a maze where no one save himself could reach her. But, alas, the secret was discovered and Rosamund was poisoned by jealous Queen Eleanor.

The Palace of Woodstock was severely damaged during the Civil War, and the manor was granted during the reign of Queen Anne to the Duke of Marlborough, who built Blenheim Palace on the site. From the Oxfordshire Way there is a splendid vista down the north walk to Blenheim Palace, and then all the majesty is left behind as the Way passes out through Wootton Door, an actual door in the wall of the park, and leaves you standing on the verge of the busy A44. On the far side of this road, the Oxfordshire Way continues along Akeman Street, now a modern lane, but very sure of its Roman origins.

Breaking the journey here (grid ref. SP 435 185), you can turn left along the A44 for ³/₄ mile to catch a bus to Oxford or Stratford. A right turn leads to Woodstock, while a left turn down the minor road opposite takes you to Wootton on the steep banks of the River Glyme, where there is a shop and the King's Head.

BLENHEIM PALACE

Blenheim Palace, which is on the Oxfordshire Way, was built less as a home than as a national monument. It commemorates the nation's gratitude to John Churchill, Duke of Marlborough, to whom Woodstock was granted in 1704 following his famous victory over the French at Blenheim in Germany. Blenheim Palace was the birthplace of Sir Winston Churchill and there is a permanent Churchill Exhibition. The Marlborough Maze, the world's largest hedge maze, opened in 1991. There are fine tapestries, furniture and paintings; restaurants, cafeterias and shops, and boat trips on the lakes.

Blenheim is open mid-March to end October, daily. The park is open throughout the year, daily.

Wootton Door (A44)

Tiddington

WOOTTON DOOR (A44)

ISLIP

APPROX. 10 MILES/16KM

OS Landranger 164
Start at grid reference SP 435 185
Start point: Just off A44 opposite Wootton Door. Limited parking on a disused scrap of Akeman Street.

From the A44 the Oxfordshire Way continues along Akeman Street, initially along a lane, crossing the River Glyme, whose dammed waters make the majestic lakes of Blenheim before flowing to the Thames. Over the T-junction Akeman Street follows a raised cart track which rises up to give superb views. Glancing back, look across the Glyme valley to Blenheim, and across the clay vale to Didcot Power Station. Ahead the panorama encompasses all the ground between this last spur of Cotswold, the Oxford Heights, where the television transmission mast at Beckley acts as a good location marker, and Brill in Buckinghamshire.

Akeman Street reaches the A4260 opposite Sturdy's Castle, a hostelry which serves food, and beyond this descends into the Cherwell valley. Eventually it crosses a plank-bridge over a stream. Here you bid farewell to Akeman Street and turn right to a lane where the old stone house, Field Cottage, guards the humps and hollows of the now-vanished village of Old Whitehill.

The River Cherwell, where the Way crosses it

(E) *You can break the walk by turning left at the plank bridge (grid ref. SP 484 198) and heading into Tackley, where there are two pubs. Tackley Station is on the Oxford-to-Birmingham line.*

The Oxfordshire Way turns left at the lane, goes under the railway bridge and then turns right to cross two branches of the River Cherwell at Flight's Mill and reach the Oxford Canal at Pigeons Lock. Across the canal head along Mill Lane, reaching Kirtlington at a wide triangular green. This was a busy place in Saxon times. It lay on the frontier of Mercia, where Akeman Street crossed the Port Way and Aves Ditch, all important routes. Kirtlington still has an air of prosperity and the Oxford Arms and the Dashwood Arms both serve food. Go past a village pond and a shop before turning left at the entrance to Kirtlington Park, the mansion built between 1742 and 1746 for local worthy, Sir James Dashwood. It is not open to the public but is important for its 'monkey room', one of only two such *singeries* surviving in England, decorated in 1745 by the French artist J F Clermont. Monkeys are depicted disporting themselves in the landscape as elegant huntsmen.

Go across the park and through fields to Weston-on-the-Green. Here, down in the vale, are thatched cottages, a village shop and three hostelries. St Mary's Church was rebuilt in 1743 and gives the impression of being larger than it is. Inside, it is full of a sense of light. On the wall by the pulpit is a curious iron cross with an open centre. This is a strange relic indeed, a mast-head cross from a galleon of the Spanish Armada. Weston's Manor House, now a hotel, is on a site once belonging to Osney Abbey. The present facade dates from 1820, but hides

GUIDE BOX

Places to visit
The Oxford Canal was completed in 1790, and was used to carry coal to Oxford from the Midlands collieries. Today it is a playground frequented by pleasure craft. The Oxfordshire Way crosses it at Pigeons Lock, where the canal is running parallel to the River Cherwell in a deep valley. There is a rich vegetation and wildlife abounds.

Waterperry Gardens. The 83-acre estate of Waterperry House in the valley of the Thame, last of the Thames tributaries on the Oxfordshire Way, is justly famous for its gardens. There are magnificent herbaceous borders, shrub and heather borders, a rock garden, herb garden and fruit trees. The Georgian house was used as a horticultural college until 1970 and still offers day courses. Plants are for sale at the plant centre and there is an excellent tea shop. Open all year, daily.

City of Oxford. During this section of the walk, the Oxfordshire Way comes its closest to Oxford, city of the 'dreaming spires', of bustle, noise, college and university buildings. The college quads are open to the public on most afternoons, and there are a variety of galleries and museums to visit.

Car parking
Principal car parks on the route are at Weston-on-the-Green (grid ref. SP 532 186), Islip Station (SP 526 145) and Waterperry Gardens (SP 628 064). Space for roadside parking can be found opposite Wootton Door, just off the A44 (SP 435 186), in Kirtlington, by the green (SP 498 199), at the far end of Noke (SP 550 127) and at Tiddington in the lay-by near the Fox and Hounds (SP 648 052).

Public transport
The nearest British Rail stations are Tackley on the Oxford-to-Birmingham line and Islip on the Oxford-to-Bicester line. Wootton and Woodstock, Kirtlington, Islip, Horton-cum-Studley and Tiddington are on various bus routes.

Accommodation
Bed-and-breakfast and hotel accommodation is available at most of the villages along the route. There is a youth hostel in Oxford and a camping and caravan site off the B4207 at Diamond Farm, Bletchington, near Weston-on-the-Green. Detailed information is available in the booklet *The Oxfordshire Way, Accommodation Guide* (see Accommodation, page 100).

medieval and 16th-century work. Lord Williams of Thame acquired Weston Manor in 1540, and made the 16th-century alterations. This is the first of three houses on the Oxfordshire Way which are associated with Lord Williams. He was the trusted servant of four of the five Tudor monarchs, astutely keeping abreast of political and religious changes.

Leaving Weston along the lane opposite the church, pass through fields where the route is poorly waymarked and not easy to follow. Come to a halt at the busy, motorway-like dual carriageway of the A34: there is no bridge and no underpass. Take your life in your hands and cross it. On the further side the route takes the old road behind the garage and Little Chef, past Family Farm to Rowles Farm, where it strikes across fields and over the railway to

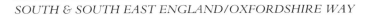
Ⓔ *You can break the journey at Islip (grid ref. SP 527 142), either by catching a train to Oxford or Bicester, or by walking back along Bletchington Road (B4027) for a mile to the A34 to catch a bus.*

ISLIP

TIDDINGTON

APPROX. 12 MILES/19.5KM

OS Landranger 164
Start at grid reference SP 527 139
Start point: Islip Bridge. There is no space for parking but there is a car park at Islip Station.

Islip, one of the 'Seven Towns' of Ot Moor.

You enter Islip past green mounds and hollows, all that is left of the palace where Edward the Confessor was born in 1004. The palace was built by the saintly king's father, Ethelred the Unready, in the days when Islip was a town and Oxford only a village. The Confessor gave Islip to the monks at Westminster when he began building the famous Abbey, and to Westminster the living of Islip still belongs.

Famous men of Islip include Simon, who became Archbishop of Canterbury in 1348 and John, Prior of Westminster in 1500, who built the Henry VII Chapel there. Two rectors spring to mind: Dr Robert South, who came here in 1678 and built the rectory, and Dr William Buckland, Dean of Westminster and a famous geologist, who became an outspoken supporter of the glacial theory in opposition to many other churchmen of his time. Dean Buckland, who died in 1856, was an eccentric and kept a menagerie. His son, Frank, was cast in the same mould, keeping a bear which wandered at will around Islip.

A right turn into Islip leads to the Red Lion and the Swan, both former coaching inns on the Worcester road, and Islip Bridge, scene of a Civil War skirmish in which Cromwell fought off a band of Royalists. The bridge, rebuilt in 1878, spans the formerly flood-prone River Ray.

Cross Islip Bridge and go uphill to take the path on the left. At last there is a glimpse of expansive Ot Moor, guarded by the church towers of its ring of 'towns'. Follow an old wake path into Noke, small, secluded and seemingly lost on the edge of the fen. Noke has no shop, but the Plough provides food and bed-and-breakfast. Then you head on to the flat floor of Ot Moor, which still retains something of its wild character. Beyond Noke Wood the route climbs the moor's southern rim to Beckley, on the Oxford heights. As you go upward, the chequerboard of this drained fenland spreads out beneath you, a great patchwork of colour.

Today Beckley makes its presence known by that symbol of modernity, its television transmission mast. But it is an ancient place, dating at least from Saxon times. In 1227 a palace was built here, of which only the moat is recognisable today. The Lord of the Manor had many rights over Ot Moor, including the appointment of a Moor driver to round up the cattle once a year and drive them into Beckley, where the owners were required to claim their beasts. Any left unclaimed became the property of the Lord of the Manor. There is no shop in Beckley, but the Abingdon Arms serves food.

Ⓔ *When the firing range is not in use you can return to Islip by heading out on to Ot Moor along the Roman road (grid ref. SP 566 113) for about 2 miles. Then turn left along the bridleway to Oddington and follow the road back into Islip.*

The Oxfordshire Way leaves Beckley on the lane at the eastern end of the village, and descends back on to Ot Moor. On the left is a moated mansion, Beckley Park, built in 1540 by Lord Williams of Thame, probably as a hunting lodge. The site once belonged to King Alfred, who excavated the moats.

At the bottom of the hill cross the drive to Beckley Park and follow the waymarks across meadowland to the road between Horton-cum-Studley and Woodperry (SP 589 118) where it is possible to break the walk and catch a bus from Horton-cum-Studley to Oxford. The Oxfordshire Way crosses the road and continues via Danesbrook Farm and Menmarsh Guide Post to the second shrunken medieval forest on this walk, the royal forest of Bernwood. Medieval kings hunted Bernwood from a hilltop palace at nearby Brill in Buckinghamshire. Pass its depleted remains at gloriously named Polecat End and Drunkard's Corner, to arrive at Park Farm. Turn right here and cross a field to the road at Ledell Cottage, by the M40.

Cross the bridge over the motorway and continue along the lane, lined with tall horse chestnut trees, to the crossroads and the little village of Waterperry. From here it is through the meadows, alongside the church and Waterperry Gardens, on to a well-used path to Bow Bridge over the River Thame.

Pass Mill House, and turn left into Waterstock. Just beyond the church, turn through a gate to go over the undulating fields to the A418. On the other side of the A-road, about 100yds to the left at the far end of the lay-by, the route turns right, crossing the disused railway line and going diagonally uphill before dropping to the village street at Tiddington. This village sits at a crossroads on the A418 where the Fox and Hounds serves food. It is a good place to break the walk, served by buses.

OT MOOR

Ot Moor was one of Oxfordshire's last wild places, an uninhabited fen covering 4 square miles, on which people of the fen-edge settlements had grazing rights. This common grazing land was poor and the excessive damp detrimental to the health of the animals. Its enclosure and drainage in the 1830s prompted the Ot Moor Riots, to which the militia had to be summoned. Today it is a jewelled patchwork of a plain, surrounded by its ring of 'Seven Towns', Oddington, Charlton-on-Otmoor, Fencott, Murcott, Noke, Beckley and Islip, whose church towers rise peacefully above the fields. Despite a MoD firing range and the M40, Ot Moor is still remote and full of wild birds. The Romans built a causeway across the fen from Beckley to the town of Alchester, just south of Bicester, and this old Roman road is a good means to explore the region.

Tiddington

Henley-on-Thames

TIDDINGTON

PYRTON

APPROX. 8¹/₂ MILES/13.5KM
(eastern route, Harlesford Lane to
Pyrton)

APPROX. 8³/₄ MILES/14KM
(western route, Harlesford Lane to
Pyrton)

OS Landranger 164, 165, 175
Start at grid reference SU 648 052
Start point: Lay-by on the A418, near the
Fox and Hounds, Tiddington.

From Tiddington village street, south of the
A418, the Oxfordshire Way follows the
footpath to Albury Church, which dates
from 1830 and serves both settlements. It has
a Norman font, re-cut at the top but with an
original lower band of zig-zag and roll
moulding. The route turns right on to a
broad track before descending to Rycote,
site of Lord Williams of Thame's great
mansion.

Rycote was originally a manor of the
Quatremains family, and they built the
chapel of 1445 which still stands. When Lord
Williams came here in 1539 he set about
building on a grand scale, in the same plum-
coloured brick that he used at Beckley Park.
Of his great mansion nothing remains save a
turret and a lonely farm among the parkland
trees above an ornamental lake. Rycote was
a splendid palace. Queen Elizabeth stayed
here frequently, so did James I; Charles I
visited Rycote in 1625 when the plague was
raging in London and Parliament sat at
Oxford. He came again in 1643, wearied by

the Civil War, his fortunes in decline. By
1745 the property was the home of the Earls
of Abingdon, and in November of that year
it burned down.

From Rycote, the Oxfordshire Way heads
to the A329 opposite a new golf course, and
now turns right along the road before taking
a path up Lobbersdown Hill so as to avoid
the flying golf balls. From here you can see
down to the M40 snaking across the land.
Then it is on to Tetsworth, emerging at the
large village green fronting the A40, the old
Oxford, Gloucester and Milford Haven
Road.

Tetsworth, which grew fat and self-
important during the coaching era, suffered
dearly with the coming of the railways in
1840. Now it has succumbed to the ultimate
indignity of rubbing shoulders with the
M40, bypassed by the modern world. The
Swan, that gracious old coaching inn dating
from Elizabethan times, now stands empty,
and the swan-shaped weather vane high on
the tiled roof swings idly to the changing
wind. What will become of the Swan? Time
will tell, but for the present, Tetsworth has a
village pub, the Lion on the Green, where
you can get food, and a collection of shops
including a post office. You can break the
walk here (grid ref. SP 686 018) and catch a
bus to Oxford or High Wycombe.

The Oxfordshire Way goes up Back Street
to Parkers Hill, crosses two fields and passes
under the motorway to Harlesford Lane.
Here there is a choice of routes to Pyrton.
The rustic western route begins with a right
turn along the lane and then a left turn across
meadows of sheep and cattle to Stoke
Talmage. From this tiny place continue over
open meadows to Clare, truly a lost village,
of which now remains but two farms and
half a handful of cottages. The rest lies
beneath the grass where peacocks pick their

The beechwoods of Chiltern Forest

GUIDE BOX

Places to visit
Rycote Chapel (EH), built in 1445, and attached
to Rycote Manor House, is now in the hands of
English Heritage. As large as many a church, it is
famous for its Jacobean carving including an
enormous canopied royal pew probably built for
Charles I. Open July to end September, daily.

Watlington Hill. This famous Chiltern viewpoint,
owned by the National Trust, stands 700ft
(213m) above sea level. It commands views over
most of Oxfordshire, is a good place for picnics
and has an interesting mix of vegetation that
supports an abundant wildlife. The 'white mark'
was cut on to the chalk hillside in 1764 on the
command of a resident of Watlington, so that
from his window the parish church would
appear to have a spire!

Henley-on-Thames. Apart from being the setting
of the famous regatta, held the first week of July,
Henley is a thriving town with an interesting
array of shops, attractive Georgian architecture
and a museum. Boats can be hired from Hobbs
& Sons Ltd.

Greys Court (NT), is close to the Oxfordshire
Way at Rotherfield Greys, 3 miles from Henley.
The Jacobean house and gardens are owned by
the National Trust. Open April to end
September, Mondays, Wednesdays and Fridays.

Stonor House, set in a private deer park, dates
from the 13th century. For 800 years it has been
owned by the Stonor family, who still live there.
It contains a medieval Roman Catholic chapel
where Mass was said even during the years of
Catholic repression, and was a hiding place for
Edmund Campion, the great Elizabethan Jesuit.
There is a shop and tea room. Open April to
September, certain days only.

Car parking
Principal car parks on the route are at Henley-
on-Thames (grid ref. SU 768 821 and 771 818),
Watlington Hill (SU 709 936) and Warburg
Nature Reserve (SU 720 879). Space for
roadside parking can be found in lay-bys at
Tiddington (SP 639 049 and 648 052), opposite
Harlesford Lane near the M40 flyover (SP 690
010) and on the old droveway north of the
B4009 (SU 696 951).

Public transport
The only British Rail station on this section of
the route is at Henley, at the end of the walk.
Buses serve Tiddington, Tetsworth, Pyrton and
Henley-on-Thames.

Accommodation
Bed-and-breakfast and hotel accommodation is
available at most of the villages along the route.
Detailed information is available in the booklet
The Oxfordshire Way, Accommodation Guide (see
page 100).

way among the leisurely herds. Beyond
Clare turn left and then right on to the
Chalgrove-to-Tetsworth road. Take the path
on the left opposite the drive to Golder
Manor where the great wooded wall of the
Chilterns dominates the scene, and head
downhill to a track leading to Pyrton.

The eastern route crosses Harlesford Lane
and rambles over meadowland to Adwell. A
right turn along the road leads to Wheatfield,
a lonely church and converted stable-block,
set amid magnificent parkland trees. The
church was renovated in the early 18th

century at the same time as Wheatfield House which, until its destruction by fire in 1814, stood between the church and the stable-block. In the church is an eastern window by Morris and Co., while the altar table has been ascribed to Chippendale. The walk skirts past the clump of beeches where Charles I breakfasted after a skirmish in the valley, and follows footpaths downhill towards the great Chiltern scarp, close to ancient Shirburn whose moated castle is hidden behind the trees. Then it turns right on to a bridleroad past Shirburn's West Lodge and so into Pyrton.

The Plough Inn provides food and the village basks in peace, a cluster of houses of brick and flint, some of them picturesquely thatched. In the little flint church on midsummer day 1619, John Hampden, that most fearless and fair-minded of Parliamentarians, married Elizabeth Symeon. She was a daughter of the manor house that stands half hidden among the trees.

Ⓔ *For a circular walk of approximately 9¹/₂ miles, leave the Oxfordshire Way here (grid. ref. SP 687 962) and return to Tetsworth by the other route of the Oxfordshire Way. Or, turn left at the B4009 to catch a bus to Thame.*

PYRTON
·
HENLEY-ON-THAMES

APPROX: 11¹/₄ MILES/18KM

OS Landranger 175
Start at grid reference SU 694 952
Start point: Pyrton, at the B4009. Limited roadside parking along the old droveway.

The Oxfordshire Way crosses the B4009 and heads along a bridleway under the gaze of the Chiltern Hills. This track is a medieval droveway which soon crosses ancient Icknield Way, one of the oldest trading routes in Britain, and here used by the Ridgeway Path. Beyond this you mount the steep Chiltern scarp on to Pyrton Hill. Watlington Hill, with its famous viewpoint, is on the right. There is gorse here, splashes of yellow against the green, the coconut scent of the blooms filling the air. The track skirts a great beech hanger and, as it gains height, the whole clay vale is spread out below, with Oxford itself hovering in the distance.

At the minor road turn right past the Fox and Hounds into Christmas Common. This place came by its name during the Civil War. Christmas 1643 found Royalist soldiers camping here and the local Roundhead force garrisoned at Watlington. They declared an unofficial truce, in true Christmas spirit, and celebrated the day together on the common.

Christmas Common is on the summit of the Chilterns, about 780ft (238m) above sea level, and the Oxfordshire Way has climbed about 375ft (114m) since crossing Icknield Way. From here it goes downhill to enter the Chiltern Forest, not a former royal forest but an ancient woodland, and winds along

The bridge over the River Thames at Henley, end of the Oxfordshire Way

the valley floor for about a mile, through beech woods.

Leaving the bridleroad and turning right up a path, emerge into the open and arrive at Hollandridge Farm. Cross the farm track to the path opposite and head obliquely downhill through College Wood. Then it is out of the wood and along the bottom of the steep-sided valley into Pishill. In this little hamlet, you can get food at the Crown Inn; while the flint and stone church, rebuilt in 1854, has a modern south-west window, of 1967, by John Piper, representing the sword and the gospel.

South-west of the church, behind the rectory, is a thatched barn built in flint and stone and partly weatherboarded, with a narrow blocked window dating from the 13th century. No one knows whether the window really belongs to the barn or not, or what the barn's original use might have been. It may be associated with a manor house at Pishill which belonged to the d'Oilly family in 1406.

From Pishill, the Oxfordshire Way goes through another beech wood to Maidensgrove. Stonor, with its great house and deer park lies down the road on the left. Cross the road and head uphill past Lodge Farm, where the line of sight extends across the Chiltern woodlands. Then it is downhill again, passing through the edge of the Warburg Nature Reserve, into Bix Bottom. A forlorn sight here is the ruin of a little Norman church, old St James's. It lies in a field where trees crowd round to claim it entirely, yet it was Bix parish church when most of that village lay low in the valley rather than exposed on the nearby hilltop. It was abandoned in 1875 and the congregation moved to a new church a mile away.

The Oxfordshire Way sweeps along the valley to cross the B480 at Middle Assensdon and go uphill along a grassy path heading for a noble line of Scots pines. It crosses the road and enters Henley Park along a lane,

continuing into Henley. Scene of the world-famous regatta, Henley looks to the Thames. It developed in the 12th century and later thrived as a port, supplying goods downstream to London. During the coaching era it grew further and when the railway arrived in 1857 Henley's expansion as a commuter town was assured.

The Oxfordshire Way ends at the bridge over the River Thames at Henley. Every river crossed on this walk pours its waters into the Thames, contributing to the great flood that flows downstream to London. And what a noble bridge this is! Rebuilt in 1786, its graceful arches skim across the river, while on the keystones are two masks carved in stone by Anne Seymour Damer, an eccentric sculptor of animal portraits. They show Father Thames looking downstream, his hair and beard matted, while Isis looks upstream, a picture of youth.

WARBURG NATURE RESERVE

This Site of Special Scientific Interest (SSSI) is the Berkshire, Buckinghamshire and Oxfordshire Naturalists Trust's (BBONT) largest reserve. It was bought in 1967 and covers 253 acres of chalkland dry valley system, comprising a number of different habitats, chiefly connected with the extensive Chiltern beechwoods but also mixed woodland, scrub and grassland maintained by annual sheep grazing. There are over 450 species of plants in the reserve, including many orchids, and a wide variety of animal and bird life such as purple emperor butterflies, lizards, woodcock, sparrowhawks, blackcaps, dormice, and fallow and muntjac deer. There is a well-marked Wildlife Walk which takes in the variety of habitats, and an interesting visitor centre.

Essex Way

COMPLETE ROUTE
EPPING TO HARWICH
80 MILES/130KM

· · ·

SECTION COVERED
EPPING TO DEDHAM
62 MILES/99KM

Detailed guide
The Essex Way, by Fred Matthews and Harry Bitten and available from Matthews/Bitten publications, Glen View, London Road, Abridge, Romford RM4 1UX, has sketch maps and a route description.

Maps
OS Landranger 167, 168

Links
The Essex Clayway meets the Essex Way at Coggeshall; the Camuplodunum coincides for a short stretch near West Bergholt, and the Three Forests Way coincides for the first part of the Way.

THE Essex Way was the first of the present network of long distance footpaths in Essex, established in 1971 as the contribution to 'Euro Conservation Year' by the Essex branch of the Council for the Preservation of Rural England (CPRE). The way finally adopted came about as the result of a competition between Essex schools to select the best and most interesting track for such a footpath. The route that was finally selected as the winning entry was the work of Chelmsford Technical High School, and was published by the East Anglia Tourist Board on behalf of CPRE.

Starting on the outskirts of London beside a far outpost of the London Underground network, the route winds its way through peaceful rural scenery in a north-easterly direction, connecting briefly with civilisation at the market towns of Ongar and Coggeshall, before arriving at Dedham Vale and Dedham in the very heart of Constable country. The route has since been extended to reach the coast at Harwich, adding another 20 miles to the stretch covered in this guide.

In Epping Forest, near the start of the Way

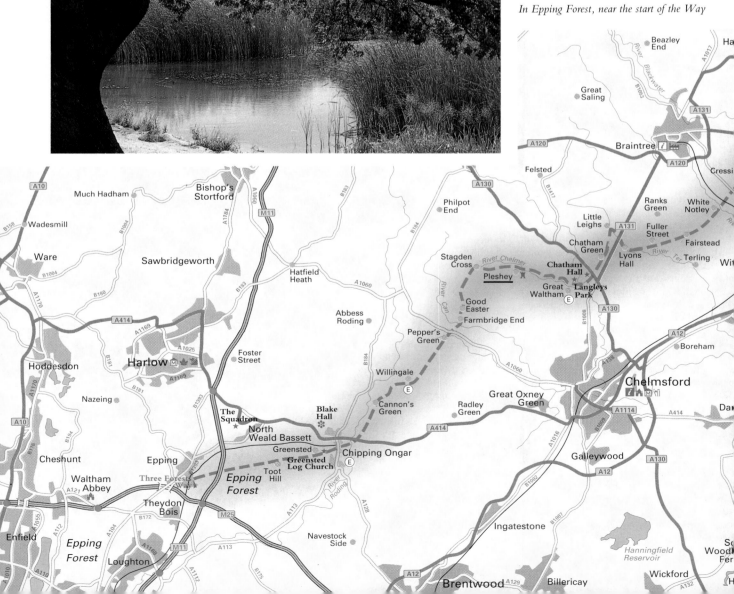

The walking is generally very easy and the terrain is almost completely flat throughout. Be warned that some stretches of the route can be quite overgrown in the summer months, and bare legs will suffer from the surfeit of nettles and thistles.

Due to the lack of a central theme for the walk (other than trying to get from one side of Essex to the other), the Way is somewhat unpredictable. The choice of route has been influenced by the desire to keep the walker off the road more than anything else, and at times the path indulges in some large-scale meandering, not really in a hurry to get to anywhere in particular. There is not a single occasion where the walker is subjected to unpleasant traffic.

Navigation is at times rather difficult. Much of the early section of the Way is well signposted, but the signs peter out in the later stages of the walk and so a map and guidebook are generally necessary. As so much of the route is around or across tracts of agricultural land, the walker is occasionally

The Cloth Hall, Dedham: the Way passes by many such early, traditional buildings

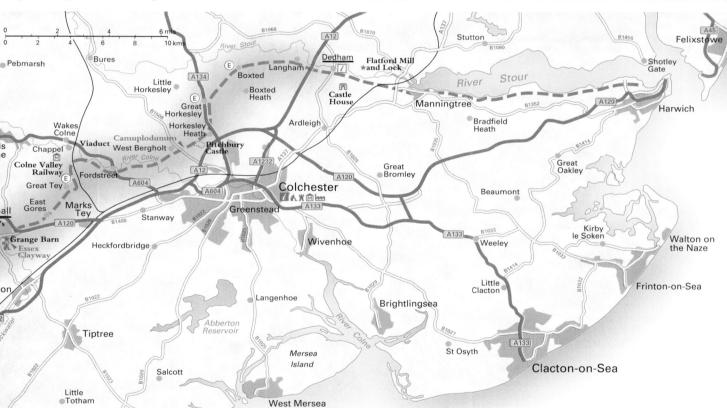

faced with acres of ploughed field and no sign of a footpath at all. The law requires the farmer to restore the right of way after disturbing the soil and the walker to follow the correct line, so, in these situations, the walker should march boldly across the field. A compass is sometimes useful in these situations.

While Essex has for many the reputation of being a land of commuters and slightly seedy seaside towns, the route of the Essex Way sees nothing of this, being almost completely confined to idyllic rural English countryside, with views that probably have not changed too significantly in the last 100 or so years.

The Essex Way is a walk very much about history, and it is the townships and buildings on the route which provide most of the interest along the path. While plenty of evidence of the Roman occupation of England remains in Essex, the route of the walk does not coincide with too much of this. There are some hints of medieval times – the wooden nave walls of Greensted Church date back to about 835 – but the history which can be seen today really starts with the Norman conquest of England in the 11th century. William of Normandy rewarded his faithful French barons with tracts of land, many of them in Essex, and the route passes right through a couple of

well-preserved motte and bailey castle sites.

From those days onwards, the rich industrial and agricultural promise of the Essex countryside has provided a legacy of buildings and barns for the walker to enjoy. Towns such as Coggeshall and Dedham were once the scene of extremely prosperous textile industries, and the clothiers of Coggeshall in particular have left many fine buildings.

The largely rural nature of the Essex Way provides plenty of opportunity for wildlife study, in particular when hitting the trail in early morning or evening. The route passes along the banks of many rivers, and close to a number of reservoirs both small and large.

Epping

Pleshey

EPPING

CHIPPING ONGAR

APPROX. 7½ MILES/12KM

OS Landranger 167
Start at grid reference TL 463 016
Start point: Epping Underground Station
(on the Central Line). Epping is just north of
the M25/M11 intersection. Car parking at
the station or in surrounding streets.

Once an important roadside town on the old
coach route from London to Norwich,
Epping had no less than 26 inns in its
heyday, and many tales abound regarding the
rogues and characters who frequented them.
The principal inn, 'Epping Place' (now a
private house), was said to have been visited
by O'Brien the Irish giant, who was over
eight feet tall and apparently caused many of
the doorways to be enlarged.

From the underground station exit, take
the footbridge to the eastern side of the track
and proceed down the residential street to a
main road. Cross to Bower Court, and
follow the footpath to the side of this
development. The path leads to open fields,
and continues through these to a road. Turn
left past some houses and then left again back
on to another footpath. After about ½ mile
this leads to another road and the Theydon
Oak Public House, where the walker should
turn right and then take the path on the left
just before the bend in the road. This stretch
of the route is dominated by the M11.

Up ahead is a large chunk of Epping
Forest. Its 6000 acres were declared a public
open space in 1878, and have since served to
educate many generations of children in the
sights and sounds of the countryside. The
path skirts around the south-east edge of this
part of the forest, past a school, and then
follows a wide track through the trees to a
footbridge over the motorway. The route
then proceeds via a straight track to the edge
of the forest, through pleasant countryside,
and up to the village of Toot Hill.

Following the road north through the
village, the path regains the countryside
when the road bears sharp left and it
continues straight ahead, behind a wooden
garage, into the field. The track follows the
hedge to the right and continues eastward for
another ¼ mile. It then turns to the north
and crosses four stiles in quick succession,
each clearly marked with the yellow acorn
waymark. However, the path being followed
then disappears into some buildings with not
a sign to be seen – the official route
continues north until reaching the road.

At this road the path turns sharply east
once again, and continues along the side of a
small wood to Greensted and its famous
church. St Andrew's is the oldest wooden
church in England and quite possibly the
world, and has long been a place of
pilgrimage. The nave is built of oak logs split
vertically in half, some dating back to the
mid-7th century. Tradition has it that the
body of St Edmund rested here in 1013 on
its way to Bury St Edmunds – Edmund
having led the Angles in their fight against
the Danes in the 9th century.

From Greensted the path continues due
east across a couple more fields to Chipping
Ongar, noted for its fine Norman motte and
bailey castle. While the impressive fortress
was demolished long ago, the earthworks
survive. Ongar was once the stronghold of
Count Eustace of Boulogne, one of William
the Conqueror's most prominent supporters
at the Battle of Hastings. He was later to
become the greatest lay baron in both Essex
and Hertfordshire.

Ⓔ *As Chipping Ongar (grid ref. TL 552 035)
is at the end of the Central Line, it is a simple
matter to return to Epping from here.*

GUIDE BOX

Places to visit
Waltham Abbey is 5 miles to the west of Epping.
This impressive Norman church was founded in
1066 by King Harold, who was later reputedly
buried here. The Crypt Centre houses an
exhibition on the history of the town and abbey.

The Squadron is located at North Weald airfield
just to the north-west of Epping and is an
impressive collection of historic and vintage
aircraft, dedicated to the various RFC and RAF
squadrons who were based at the airfield from
1916 to 1964. Open for special 'fly-in' days
during the summer months.

Blake Hall Gardens. These extensive gardens,
with both historical and botanical interest can be
found just to the north-east of Chipping Ongar.
There is also a well-preserved RAF operations
room to visit. Open Easter to September.

Car parking
Epping has many car parks, including one at the
underground station, although in weekdays this
is, not surprisingly, full with commuters' cars.
Both Chipping Ongar and Pleshey have car
parks and plenty of street parking is to be found.

Public transport
Epping and Chipping Ongar are both connected
to London via the Central Line, while the main
Chelmsford-Colchester-Harwich line runs more
or less parallel to the Essex Way, some 6 or 7
miles to the south.
Epping, Chipping Ongar, Willingale, Good
Easter and Pleshey are all served by more or less
frequent bus routes.

Accommodation
Epping, Chipping Ongar and Pleshey all offer
accommodation in both hotel and bed-and-
breakfast form. Accommodation guides are
available from the Essex Tourist Information
Centre in Colchester (see below). While the route
does not coincide with any official camp
sites, there are plenty of secluded corners for the
backpacker to enjoy an overnight pitch, with the
landowner's permission.

Below *Greensted's ancient church*

APPROX. 13½ MILES/21.5KM

OS Landranger 167
Start at grid reference TL 554 029
Start point: Chipping Ongar Church, by
the A113, some 7 miles north of Brentwood.
There are plenty of places to park within
the village.

For those with a nose for ecclesiastical
history, the Norman Church of St Martin of
Tours is worth a visit. From the church, the
path proceeds by the earthworks of the
motte and bailey, the moat now a very
pleasant border for a row of houses. The
wide grass track then zig-zags north, past
playing fields and a school to the main A414
Chelmsford-to-Harlow road. It is possible to
walk through the culvert at the bottom of
the field instead of crossing this busy road.

The culvert holds the water of the River
Roding, with which the walker now
becomes fairly well acquainted for the next
few miles. About as far removed from
civilisation as the Essex Way gets, there is
plenty of wildlife to enjoy here; moorhens in
the river, rabbits, hares and squirrels on the
river banks, and even the occasional deer
crashing through the undergrowth.

The Way crosses the second bridge over
the river, then follows a sunken and very
overgrown track up the hill towards
Cannon's Green. This track is one of the
many occasions on this walk where the right
of way is often just too overgrown to allow
passage and, Country Code notwithstanding,
the only feasible option is to walk in the field
adjacent to the path.

Towards the top of the hill, take the left
fork, leading along a field and eventually to
the road at Cannon's Green. The route
follows the road for a few hundred yards
north, and then proceeds straight across a
couple of huge fields. If these have been
recently ploughed there will be no sign of a
path anywhere, but it is a right of way, so fix
on Willingale Church tower up ahead and
march.

A quiet road leads into Willingale.
However, to avoid the tarmac it is possible
to turn left at the road, and continue straight
until reaching a farm track to the right,
leading downhill. This leads all the way to
the twin churches of Willingale – two
churches in the same churchyard, one
slightly more recent than the other.
Willingale is a pleasant little hamlet, with a
shop and a pub offering refreshments.

Ⓔ *From Willingale (grid ref. TL 596 074)*
there are regular buses back to Chipping Ongar.

From the churchyard the path crosses
straight over the main street, past the
sportsfield and then turns north, heading
towards the white house in the distance. The
next few miles follow well-marked tracks
through low-lying, fertile agricultural land to
reach civilisation at the small hamlet of

Peaceful days for Pleshey – but the walker may
contemplate on its more eventful past

Pepper's Green, and a track leading to the
main A1060 road.

Crossing this, the route follows a pleasant
track leading north-east and descending to
Farmbridge End, an attractive hamlet on the
banks of the River Can. On the other side of
the small valley, the path climbs gently
through a large field to the church of Good
Easter, with its 13th-century nave and
chancel.

A few yards of road-walking is now
necessary, to the main crossroads by the Star
public house (the only refreshments in
town). Turning north, the route then regains
the footpath behind the left-hand row of
cottages, and continues along this path to a
minor road, which it leaves again a few
hundred yards further on at the hard right
corner. This bridleway leads downhill into
trees and presently bears sharp left. At this
bend there is a gate on the right opening
into a long field, which eventually reaches
another bridleway on the left. This continues

for over a mile, passing a variety of horse
jumps and obstacles, to reach the small
hamlet of Stagden Cross.

The route from Stagden to Pleshey is well
signposted, following a long farm track to
Pleshey Grange, and then another clearly
marked path past the ramparts of Pleshey
Castle to reach Pleshey itself. Pleshey and the
surrounding 12,000 acres were given to
Geoffrey de Mandeville for his services to
William the Conqueror after the Battle of
Hastings. The town had an eventful history
from then on, including one particularly
black spot on Christmas Eve 1215, when
King John's forces sacked the castle and
surrounding lands.

The village is somewhat quieter nowadays,
but the castle is still an impressive remnant.
The outer rampart encloses the entire village,
some 40 acres in size – not easy to defend!

CHELMSFORD

Chelmsford Cathedral

Eight miles to the south-east of this part of the
route, the ancient borough of Chelmsford has
many attractions for the visitor. The county
town and seat of local government for the
whole of Essex, Chelmsford dates back to
Roman times. The cathedral dates to the 15th
century, and is noted for the unity of its
Perpendicular architecture, while the Bishop's
throne is a fine example of modern wood-
carving. The music festival during May is
particularly worth a visit. The large and
impressive Museum collection in Moulsham
Street gives an interesting insight into the
history of this area (open all year, daily), while
the nearby Moulsham Mill has been converted
by the Interface Association to house a variety
of craft workshops.

Pleshey
Coggeshall

PLESHEY
WHITE NOTLEY
APPROX. 13½ MILES/21KM

OS Landranger 167
Start at grid reference TL 664 144
Start point: Pleshey Church, about 6 miles north-west of Chelmsford. There is a reasonable amount of parking in the village.

The official route takes the walker through the very picturesque village of Pleshey to the slightly less picturesque sewage plant on the eastern side. From here the path heads due east across a number of low-lying fields beside a small stream, past a couple of small reservoirs, to the village of Great Waltham.

This pleasant settlement on the banks of the River Chelmer may be a good place to pick up provisions, as it is the only place for some time with any shops (except on Wednesday afternoons, when even these are shut). For those with an interest in historical inns the 14th-century Green Man in Howe Street may be a place to visit. There is something of a history of imbibing in Great Waltham – it used to be the site of a vineyard in Norman times.

Ⓔ *There are buses from Great Waltham (grid ref. TL 696 134) back to Pleshey.*

The path crosses the main road just north of the town, and then proceeds through the grounds of Langleys Park and Chatham Hall. Langleys is a large, brick mansion, still incorporating some of the original 17th-century building and standing in spacious grounds that run down to the river. Pause to read some of the inscriptions on the tombstones in the pets' graveyard by the main building.

This part of the path is well signposted, and continues north over pleasant fields to Chatham Green, up the road to Liberty Hall and then over more fields to Little Leighs, more or less parallel all the time to the busy A131 which runs along the course of an old Roman road. The church at Little Leighs is worthy of a visit, principally to admire the early 14th-century carved oak figure of a priest in cope, scarf and alb.

From the church, the route follows the road around the block to avoid walking any distance alongside the A131, and then crosses this main road to pick up the River Ter. It then follows the banks of the river south-east over more fields to Lyons Hall. Here the route leaves the riverside and proceeds in a north-easterly direction, along a track and then through open fields, to the village of Fuller Street.

From here there is some discrepancy between the official footpath guide and the OS map on where the route goes. The official route detours south-east into the small town of Terling, famous for its associations with the ubiquitous Friesian cow. The prefix Terling occurs frequently in the pedigrees of individuals of this breed, as a

Tombstones in a pets' graveyard in the grounds of Langleys Park

GUIDE BOX

Places to visit
Coggeshall Grange Barn (NT). This impressive National Trust property to the south of Coggeshall is open April to end October, Tuesdays, Thursdays, Sundays and Bank Holidays.

Fossil Hall in Witham, 4 miles to the south of the Way, is a museum housing accurate reproductions of over 2000 of the world's finest fossil specimens. It also contains Britain's largest specialist geological bookshop.

The Working Silk Museum in South Street, Braintree, is England's last handloom silk weaving company, operating on 150-year-old Jacquard looms, on the original site. With the prominence this whole area played in the early cloth and textile industry, this is of particular significance. Located just a few miles north of the Essex Way. Open all year, daily.

Car parking
Main car parking points on this section are in Pleshey (grid ref. TL 664 144), Chatham Green (TL 715 152), White Notley (TL 787 185) and Coggeshall (TL 854 230).

Public transport
White Notley is on the Witham-to-Braintree branch line off the main London-to-Harwich track, and the main line also stops at Kelvedon, which is 2½ miles south of Coggeshall. Pleshey, Little Leigh, Cressing and Coggeshall are all served by buses, some more frequently than others.

Accommodation
White Notley is one train stop away from both Witham and Braintree, each of which offer hotel and self-catering accommodation. Coggeshall also has a variety of accommodation to offer. There are no proper camp sites anywhere close to the route, but plenty of spots for the overnight backpacker to make a pitch.

reminder and tribute to the work of Edward Strutt of Terling, pioneer of modern milk production and, in the opinion of many of his contemporaries, the greatest agriculturalist of his day. (Strutt's brother, incidentally, was the 3rd Lord Rayleigh, the mathematician famous for his work on wave motion and vibrating systems.) The route marked on the OS map takes the walker north along the edge of Mann Wood to the road at Rank's Green, which does bring in a little tarmac-pounding. The quickest and easiest way is across country to Fairstead, whose church spire can be seen from some way off.

The various routes converge at Fairstead Church and then proceed uphill to the T-junction and south-east on the Terling road. About 300yds down this road, a farm track on the left passes Troys Hall and continues for about a mile, eventually reaching Maltings Farm, just south of White Notley. While it may be quicker to go straight up the road to the village, it is more pleasant to continue north-east along what appears to be a private drive, and then go over a field to the River Brain. The path then follows the river into White Notley, emerging at the road just below the railway station.

WHITE NOTLEY

COGGESHALL

APPROX. 7 MILES/11KM

OS Landrangers 167, 168
Start at grid reference TL 787 185
Start point: White Notley, just downhill from the railway station (Braintree-to-Witham line). There is limited parking in the hamlet.

While apparently out in the middle of nowhere, the proximity of the route to the railway makes a good start and/or finishing point for this section of the Essex Way.

Just downhill from the railway station is a track leading off to the north-east, which takes the walker through the farmstead of Fambridge Hall, where the ancient timber barns are worthy of a few minutes' contemplation. Beyond this farm, the track turns right and passes under the railway track, through a delightful old egg-shaped and echoing tunnel, and then continues to the Braintree-to-Witham road. A few hundred yards up this road, the route regains the fields and leads to Cressing Church.

Although now a sleepy hamlet, Cressing has an interesting history. It was the earliest English settlement of the military order of Knights Templar, who were given the Manor of Cressing in 1135. On their suppression by Pope Clement V, the military order of Knights of the Hospital of St John at Jerusalem replaced them in 1312. The Templar knights included farming among their activities, and the only surviving remnants of this era are two extraordinary wooden barns, one for wheat and one for barley, to be found about a mile to the south of the route in Cressing Temple. These 40ft high, aisled barns can be seen from some distance away, and are nowadays the site of more modern activities such as book fairs. They are certainly worth a visit.

From Cressing we must change OS maps, and follow the route as it zig-zags over very flat land through a number of fields. The route is at times difficult to follow along this stretch, but the walker should emerge at a small road, within sight and sound of large gravel workings up ahead. The official path

proceeds down the left-hand side of a lake to join the entrance track to these gravel workings, which leads to another road east of Bradwell Hall.

Ⓔ *Upon emerging from the gravel works (grid ref. TL 820 222), continue north on a track for 650yds to the A120 Braintree-to-Coggeshall road, where there are regular buses either way.*

After following this road to the east for a few hundred yards, the path is signposted off to the left, descending to the tree-lined banks of the River Blackwater. Then follows a pleasant stretch along the side of the river for ¹/₂ mile or so, to more gravel workings. After skirting these, the route climbs back up again out of the slight valley towards Curd Hall Farm, where it joins the farm drive and proceeds once again parallel with the river for almost a mile, eventually emerging by Grange Barn.

Grange Barn is the oldest surviving timber-framed barn in Europe and dates to the mid-12th century. It was originally part of the Cistercian Monastery of Coggeshall, and was restored to its present glory in the 1980s. It is now a National Trust property.

From here, about ¹/₄ mile south of Coggeshall, the walker has a number of options. It is possible to skirt the town centre and rejoin the footpath on the easternmost side of town. Alternatively, continue eastwards across the road from the barn to the remains of the abbey itself, founded by King Stephen and given over to the Cistercian order in 1148. The abbey is of particular architectural interest because of the

Timber clock-tower in Coggeshall

widespread use of brick in the 12th and early 13th centuries. From here the walker can backtrack to rejoin the road and proceed north into Coggeshall, crossing the bridge with its sign warning motorists to beware of ducks. Or, again, continue east across the river and then take the footpath north, eventually reaching Coggeshall town church.

Whichever way you enter the town, take the time to enjoy the amazing mix of architectural styles to be found here.

COGGESHALL AND PAYCOCKE'S (NT)

Located on the famous Roman Stane Street, Coggeshall is of great historical significance. Essex is reckoned to have been the site of the post-Roman rebirth of English brick-making, perhaps firstly in the 12th century at Copford and here at Coggeshall, long before brick became fashionable for Tudor mansions. In later centuries the town was an important cloth- and textile-producing centre, and as a result Coggeshall contains one of England's finest

timber-framed buildings, 'Paycocke's' in West Street, built by the village's leading clothier Thomas Paycocke *circa* 1500. The house has a very elaborate display of wood panelling and carving and was clearly built to impress. The large oriel windows would have made it much lighter inside than most contemporary buildings. Owned by the National Trust, open April to October, Tuesdays, Thursdays, Sundays and Bank Holidays.

Coggeshall

Dedham

COGGESHALL

WEST BERGHOLT

APPROX. 10 MILES/16KM

OS Landranger 168
Start at grid reference TL 854 230
Start point: Coggeshall Church, in Church Street. Coggeshall is just off the A120, 10 miles west of Colchester.

The impressive Church of St Peter ad Vincula was built all to one plan in the 15th century, and its large size and memorials to various clothier families reflect the prosperous medieval cloth trade. The church suffered severe bomb damage in 1940, the repairs to which can be clearly seen from the outside.

From the church the route proceeds east and then south for a few hundred yards, into areas of rather less architectural interest. A footpath soon leaves the road to the left, by the lamppost with 'Essex Way' stencilled on it. The path leads the walker into a field and soon to the Coggeshall bypass, which should be crossed with care.

The path makes its way eastward from the road, to run parallel with Stane Street through a number of flax fields, and passes to the south of the unusual buildings at Houchin's Farm.

After passing in front of two small reservoirs, the path turns north-east to cross a small road at East Gores. Do note the angle of the chimney on the house to your left. From East Gores the track turns more northwards to cross a number of fields and pass a small conifer plantation, running alongside a brook for some of the way. The route is not totally clear throughout this stage, but keep heading approximately north

and the great Norman crossing tower of St Barnabas Church in Great Tey should eventually come into view.

Upon reaching Great Tey, the official route meanders around three sides of a square to avoid the road. For the less hardy (or more lazy) walker, it is as easy to continue northwards along this quiet road to Pattock's Farm, and then rejoin the footpath from here.

Ⓔ *For those wishing to leave or join the walk via public transport, the railway station of Chappel and Wakes Colne is but a mile north of this point (grid ref. TL 895 290).*

From Pattock's Farm the path continues north-eastwards to cross the railway line, and then descends through Bacon's Farm to the banks of the River Colne. While walking downhill through these pleasant meadows, look away to your left to the elegant viaduct crossing the Colne Valley to Chappel Station, now also the home of a museum of railway artefacts (see Guide Box).

From here almost all the way to West Bergholt, the path is never far from the River Colne. Although in many places the official footpath is more direct than the river banks, out of consideration for the farmers' crops the path has over the years ended up following the line of the river until Fordstreet, where it passes along the river-ward side of a large nursery, eventually emerging by the A604 Colchester-to-Halstead road.

After crossing to the northern side of the river, the riverbank trail continues from the gardens of the Shoulder of Mutton public house. Fordstreet must have had some significance in times gone by if the number of public houses in such a small hamlet is anything to go by.

From Fordstreet the path once again hugs

A stretch of easy walking on this section

GUIDE BOX

Places to visit
Bridge Cottage at Flatford Mill (NT) contains an information centre and display regarding John Constable and his associations with the area. The property is located on the banks of the River Stour, and is now owned by the National Trust. Open April, May, September, October, Wednesday to Sunday; June, July, August, daily; November, December, Thursday to Sunday.

Castle House, less than 1 mile south-east from Flatford, was the home of Sir Alfred Munnings, famous for paintings of horses, who died there in 1959. Many of his paintings are on display. Open May to October, Wednesdays and Sundays.

The Colne Valley Railway Museum has a working steam locomotive and period rolling stock, which run on about a mile of track. There is also a large collection of locomotives and stock, plus various other railway memorabilia. Open March to December, Tuesday to Sunday plus Bank Holiday Mondays; steaming Easter to October.

The Dedham Centre, in the High Street, is an arts and craft centre housed in a converted church, plus an interesting toy museum. Wholefood refreshments are available. Open all year, daily, except Mondays in January, February and March.

Car parking
The three main ports of call on this stretch of the route all have car parks plus ample street parking. Elsewhere there are small parks at Boxted and Great Horkesley.

Public transport
The London-to-Ipswich line runs pretty much parallel to the route but a few miles to the south throughout; nearest main-line stations are at Kelvedon, Marks Tey, Colchester and Manningtree, while the Sudbury branch line stops at Chappel, about a mile to the north of the route.
Coggeshall, Great Tey, West Bergholt, Great Horkesley, Boxted and Dedham are served by buses, varying in frequency.

Accommodation
Bed-and-breakfast accommodation can be found in all three main townships along the route, while Coggeshall also has some self-catering accommodation to offer. Official camping sites are once again scarce, the nearest being either at Colchester, or a few miles to the east of Dedham at Bradfield.

the river banks fairly closely, including along one rather difficult stretch through heavy undergrowth and stinging nettles. After about ¹/₂ mile the route crosses a small road, but then meets with no interruption for the next mile, whereupon the path turns into a farm track, just after passing a ruined barn. This track leads uphill through Cook's Hall Farm, whence it turns north and continues uphill to West Bergholt Church. From there a path leads eastward across a field and into a housing estate on the outskirts of West Bergholt. New Church Road leads into the town centre.

WEST BERGHOLT

DEDHAM

APPROX. 10 MILES/16KM

OS Landranger 168
Start at grid reference TL 966 277
Start point: The junction between the B1508 and Armoury Road in the centre of West Bergholt, 3 miles north-west of Colchester. Parking in the town.

A great deal of this last section is on either roads or metalled pathways, but some fine views over the Vale of Dedham make up for this at the end. The route leaves town along the drive to Armoury Farm, and then goes into open fields. Due to the mildly undulating nature of the land in this vicinity, navigation across these fields can be somewhat tricky; if in doubt head for the very tall poplar tree which can be seen away in the distance.

Upon reaching the edge of a large orchard, the route connects with a track at Woodhouse Farm. Just to the west are the ramparts of Pitchbury Castle, defensive earthworks dating back to the Iron Age.

The farm track soon turns into a metalled lane. The next mile or so is all on tarmac, and follows for a brief period the A134 Colchester-to-Sudbury road towards Great Horkesley. Shortly before reaching the town, the route turns right along Ivy Lodge Road, and follows this for about ¹/₄ mile. At the bottom of the hill, a footpath on the left leads northwards along a grassy meadow to a couple of small cottages. From there the path becomes a proper track, and continues past two small reservoirs on the left.

After a right and then a left turn, this track reaches a road by some cottages. The countryside along this stretch is rather flat and featureless, offering no hint of the beautiful views into Dedham Vale waiting only a mile or so up the road.

Continuing north along Holly Lodge Lane, the route eventually passes by the farm of the same name. The official path goes through the farm buildings, and then turns right to follow a line of telegraph poles towards an orchard. This section of the route may well be across a ploughed field, making it rather difficult to know where to proceed. There is a track along the front of the orchard leading to a road on the right, which should be reached one way or the other.

The Essex Rose, Dedham: refreshment was served here back in the 16th century

A few hundred yards east along this road, a path leads north past the ruins of Carter's Farm, to arrive at another road. Directly opposite is a driveway leading to Boxted Hall. The route goes along the north side of the Hall and across a field to St Peter's Church at Boxted, noted for the reddish 'puddingstone' in the Norman tower.

Ⓔ *Both Great Horkesley and Boxted have a regular bus service into Colchester, from where it is possible to return to West Bergholt or to go on to Dedham.*

Passing the school on the northern side of the church, the route then joins a small road running through trees and past some pleasant houses. Suddenly the Vale of Dedham comes into view to the north, and one can immediately see why John Constable was so inspired to paint his pictures.

Where the road begins to descend, a track leads off into the trees on the left which takes the walker into a lush valley, with a large expanse of water on the left, especially picturesque when the sun is low in the west. The track then ascends to the fine estate of Rivers Hall, where some considerable effort has gone into routing the walker around its far reaches. From the top of the drive there is another ¹/₄ mile of road-walking, and then the route turns eastwards across the middle of some mighty fields – one instance where it is almost necessary to use a compass to be sure of the correct line. For a short interval the Way follows the driveway of Plumbs Farm, then there are more fields to cross as it descends very slowly into the Vale.

After following the base of an area of woodland, the track turns sharp right to climb to Langham Hall and thence to Langham Church, once one of John Constable's favourite haunts. It was from here that he painted 'Dedham Vale', which hangs in the National Gallery in London.

From the church a pleasant tree-lined drive leads to a road, which crosses over the

A12 main road to Ipswich. Shortly after crossing this busy trunk road, a left turn into the driveway of the Dedham Vale Hotel leads to a footpath that descends to the banks of the River Stour. Although merely a stream at this point, in just a few miles it opens out into a large estuary.

The final mile is along the riverside, and leads straight into Dedham itself, another old East Anglian wool town and considered to be the very heart of Constable country. Constable *aficionados* may recognise the Church of St Mary, the tower of which appears in a number of the artist's paintings. The magnificent flint and stone tower was built on the wealth of the clothier families in the 15th and 16th centuries.

The old grammar school at the side of the churchyard square, built in 1732, was attended by John Constable, who had been unhappy at school in Lavenham.

COLCHESTER MUSEUMS

The tremendous history of Colchester makes it an almost compulsory part of any visit to Essex, and much of interest from this heritage can still be seen. The five museums of Colchester are as good a place to start as any, in particular the magnificent Colchester Castle Museum, located within the largest Norman castle keep in Europe, which itself is built on the ground of a Roman temple. Evidence of the Roman occupation of this area is graphically displayed within, including tours of the Roman vaults, and the castle prisons. Open April to end October, daily; November to March, Monday to Saturday.

Colchester is only a few miles south of the later stages of this walk, and is also home to four other museums, covering the natural history of the area, town and country life over the last 200 years, arts and paraphernalia from the same period, and, last but not least, a collection of Colchester-manufactured clocks.

WALES
&
THE MARCHES

St David's Head, on the Pembrokeshire coast

Pembrokeshire Coast Path

COMPLETE ROUTE
AMROTH TO ST DOGMAELS
186 MILES/299KM

SECTION COVERED
BROAD HAVEN TO GOODWICK
52 MILES/84KM

THE Pembrokeshire Coast Path is a national trail following the Pembrokeshire coast through the Pembrokeshire National Park, from Amroth in the south to St Dogmaels, near Cardigan, in the north. The official distance is around 170 miles, but there are so many ups and downs and ins and outs that the real distance is impossible to measure and it is probably something closer to 200 miles. This 52-mile section offers three days' good walking, along some of the most spectacular scenery that the coast can offer.

The coast path was originally surveyed by the naturalist RM Lockley in 1951, statutorily designated the following year, but not officially opened until 1970. In between times the pioneers of this magnificent path had years of problems sorting out access rights with landowners, with the aim of running the path right by the sea whenever possible. In this way they were almost totally successful, a magnificent achievement.

However, there are a few parts of the walk where intransigent landowners have forced the route inland or on to the road, and nowhere more so than in the south-western section between Freshwater West and Stack Rocks, where the fine limestone cliffs of the coast are out of bounds due to military occupation, necessitating a 5½-mile deviation inland along minor roads. The walker also suffers, in other ways, from the presence of the massive oil refineries and terminals around Milford Haven/Pembroke.

To walk the whole length of the coast path usually takes 10 to 15 days, though the unofficial record was set by a fell runner in under three days! The three days' walking described here covers a much more modest distance – the north-west section of the path between Broad Haven in the southern corner of St Brides Bay, and Goodwick on the eastern side of Strumble Head. This includes much of the coast path's most magnificent scenery and gives plenty of variety, from the immense sandy beach of Newgale to the sheer cliffs and wild country of the northern coastline.

The distances to be covered may seem modest for a day's walking. However, the coastal path should not be underestimated. When it follows the cliff-tops it is frequently tortuous with ups and downs which can be steep and tricky underfoot. One's average speed is likely to be little better than 2mph, and even that will allow for fairly energetic walking. There are plenty of places to stop and many points of interest along the way, and the section described is certainly enough to give three very full and enjoyable days.

Obviously the walk can be extended at either end and, with this taster of the coast path, one will certainly want to experience more. Navigation on the route is mostly straightforward, with good signposting. Mostly one can see the next destination miles ahead, but because of all the ins and outs it can take a frustratingly long time getting there.

Newgale Sands: the Path drops down on to the magnificent two-mile stretch of beach

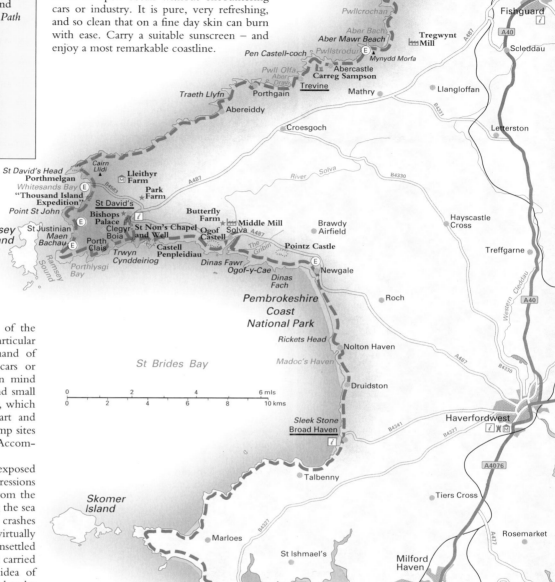

There are a few very wild parts of the coast path, and the whole of this particular stretch is largely unspoilt by the hand of man, with a minimum of roads, cars or buildings to mar enjoyment. Bear in mind that, with only isolated farmsteads and small villages, public transport is infrequent, which necessitates a fairly clear idea of start and finish points. There are occasional camp sites and bed-and-breakfasts (see under Accommodation, Guide Box, page 118).

This coastline is, of course, fully exposed to Atlantic weather systems, with depressions bringing lashings of wind and rain from the west. The wind is not so bad, making the sea look at its most magnificent as it crashes against the rocks below, but there is virtually no shelter from the rain, and in unsettled weather waterproofs should always be carried and the walker should have some idea of where and how to break the route and make for shelter. Strong shoes or boots should always be worn. The settled weather of summer may be the safest time to walk the coastal path, but it is very popular and the walker is unlikely to walk alone. For this reason spring or autumn is to be preferred, or a fine day in winter when the light is at its best, the cliffs are at their most striking and, on a weekday, there may be nobody else around.

The principal danger comes from the cliffs themselves. In places they are obviously crumbling and falling, and the 'Cliffs Can Kill' signs which are posted on stiles are serious and should be heeded. The walker is largely left to use his own sense and judgement, and care should be taken at all times. Some parts of the cliffs are particularly risky when walking with children or elderly

people, and if the behaviour of your dog is at all in doubt, it is safer to leave it behind.

A final word of caution concerns the possibility of sunburn. With the prevailing westerly winds, the air of the coast path is likely to be some of the least polluted in Britain, having come across hundreds of miles of open ocean without encountering cars or industry. It is pure, very refreshing, and so clean that on a fine day skin can burn with ease. Carry a suitable sunscreen – and enjoy a most remarkable coastline.

Porthgain, one of several harbours along the walk whose busy days are now over

Broad Haven

St David's

BROAD HAVEN

SOLVA

APPROX. 11 MILES/18KM

OS Landranger 157
Start at grid reference SM 861 135
Start point: The beach at Broad Haven.
Car parking in the village.

Most Coast Path guidebooks assume the walker will go from north to south, but on this stretch of coastline it seems preferable to go from south to north. Firstly, the prevailing wind is more likely to be behind; and secondly, this way the coastal scenery, after a comparatively tame start along St Brides Bay, becomes more and more magnificent and challenging.

Broad Haven is a sprawling village in a fine location, with a long sandy beach and all the usual amenities, including a youth hostel. It is easily accessible from Haverfordwest, with a regular bus service. The coast path starts at the north end of the beach, where it is clearly signposted up a track leading to the cliff-tops above Sleek Stone. It takes an easy route across grassy headlands as it follows a permissive path towards Druidston Haven, named after the Norman knight Drue, who invaded Ireland in the 12th century.

This part of the path is along one of many specially negotiated rights of way, but sadly it is forced to divert inland and join the road on the outskirts of Druidston, passing above the back of the hotel which, presumably, barred its passage. The beach at Druidston is

one of several encountered along this part of the walk as the path rejoins the coast above Madoc's Haven, leading on to Nolton Haven. This is a pretty little place, set in a valley, with the Mariners Inn, a shop, and a pleasant small beach – which all goes to make it a fine place to stop. From here the path heads steeply up along the side of the cliffs, passing above the unusual outcrop of Rickets Head, and then on down past a solitary chimney, a relic of the days when the Trefrane Cliff colliery operated here.

At the top of the next rise, Newgale Beach comes into sight. This magnificent 2-mile stretch of sand faces west and, not surprisingly, it is a favourite spot for surfers and windsurfers, and is also popular for family summer holidays. Facilities include cafés at either end and a pub. Rejoining the road, the path leads down to the beach and along Newgale Sands which is good, firm walking with shingle piled up by the unobtrusive road on the right. This is one of the few stretches of the coast path where fast progress can be made, but low-flying jets from the nearby RAF airfield at Brawdy may break your idyll.

The walker should join the road at the northern end of the beach by the last buildings, going a short way uphill before turning off on the coast path, which follows the cliffs to the left. Alternatively, if the tide is out and you do not mind risking wet feet, it is possible to continue along the beach to Pwll March, the more interesting end of Newgale Sands, where there are rock pools and caves. On the hillside above there is a small, cream-coloured building, and a track leads up past it to rejoin the path.

Solva, a port that once traded in limestone

Places to visit
St David's is the smallest city in the United Kingdom, a city the size of a village which is dominated by its Cathedral and Bishop's Palace (see page 121). It is a charming place which can only be seen on foot, and the Information Centre in the High Street can supply details of a walk round the city which covers about 2 miles and will take at least an hour. The centre of St David's is the 14th-century city cross, restored by Bishop Thirlwall in 1873. Until 1939 cabbage plants were sold from the steps on every St David's Day, and hot pudding eating competitions were also held here.

St Non's Chapel and Well. St Non was the mother of St David, and is said to have lived in a cottage on the site of St Non's Chapel, where St David was born in about AD500. A chapel was built here in the early 14th century, but was abandoned some 200 years later and is now a ruin. Near by, the Holy Well of St Non was regarded as one of the most sacred wells in Wales, with its water considered to have healing powers. It was restored by the Passionist Fathers in 1951, who also built the Shrine to Our Blessed Lady. The Chapel of Our Lady of St Non was built in 1934 by Cecil Hubert Morgan Griffiths, a Carmarthen solicitor. The architect was David Thomas of St David's, who used old materials to execute it in the ancient style.

The Woollen Mill, Middle Mill, 1 mile inland from Solva, has been in continuous production since 1907. Weaving can usually be seen in progress Monday to Friday, and daily in summer.

Car parking
Principal car parks are at Broad Haven (grid ref. SM 860 135), Nolton Haven (SM 860 185), Newgale Sands (SM 856 202, SM 853 210 and SM 851 218), Solva (SM 805 243), Caerfai (SM 759 243) and St David's.

Public transport
The nearest British Rail station is at Haverfordwest. Buses serve St David's, Newgale, Haverfordwest, and Broad Haven. Contact the Pembrokeshire Coast National Park Department, County Offices, Haverfordwest, Dyfed SA61 1QZ (tel. 0437 763 771) for details of a mini-bus service for walkers.

Accommodation
There is a youth hostel at Broad Haven, and Broad Haven, Solva, Newgale and St David's have hotels and bed-and-breakfasts. Contact the National Park Department (see under Public transport above) for an accommodation list.

Ⓔ *A return can be made to Broad Haven by following the network of minor roads south from Newgale (grid ref. SM 847 223). A return by public transport could be made taking a bus from Newgale to Haverfordwest, and then another on to Broad Haven.*

Here the coast path begins to bear westwards, with extensive gorse and heather on the hillside below, making towards the headland of Dinas Fach, where it follows steps down to the beach at Porthmynawyd. This is perhaps the most beautiful, secluded beach along the whole Pembrokeshire coastline, and accessible from the road only by bridleway from Pointz Castle – a hillock is all that remains of its 12th-century castle.

One soon discovers on the coast path that what goes down must also go up, and there is a comparatively steep climb on the other side to rejoin the cliff-top above Ogof y Cae, heading towards the splendid headland of Dinas Fawr. The site of a promontory fort which can now be reached by a solitary footpath, in good weather this is a wonderful spot for a picnic. The next beach is at Aberwest, which can be reached only by boat, and then the path passes the site of a Neolithic burial chamber before heading down a steep staircase to reach the valley beneath the Gribin, the ridge that leads to Solva.

Here the path crosses a stream by a hidden beach, before heading steeply up the side of the Gribin. This leads to a famous viewpoint above the Solva estuary, before following the ridge eastwards, high above the estuary, until it begins to head gently downhill into Solva. Near the bottom it passes old limekilns. Limestone was brought here by sea from Lawrenny, Milford, and West Williamston, but the trade died when artificial fertilisers became more economical.

The path emerges by the side of the River Solva, crossing in front of the pub, which will serve breakfast to passing walkers. This small village is now a popular tourist spot and, though somewhat dominated by its car park, is worth a good look round. There is hotel and bed-and-breakfast accommodation. The estuary is particularly charming, being completely sheltered from all quarters and drying out almost totally at low tide, leaving all its moored boats stranded. At this time one can walk along the sand to the head of the estuary, but care should be taken not to get caught by the incoming tide.

·
SOLVA
———— · ————
ST DAVID'S
———— · ————
APPROX. 6 MILES/9.5KM
———— · ————

OS Landranger 157
Start at grid reference SM 805 242
Start point: The west bank of the river, in the village of Solva. Public car park.

The path heads up the west side of the estuary, passing a terrace of houses in a fine position before joining an ivy-covered pathway which leads once more to the cliff-tops. The walking here is both easy and spectacular, with dramatic cliffs ahead, quiet farmland inland, and a view over the whole massive area of St Brides Bay, from Ramsey Island in the north to Skomer Island in the south, both noted as nature reserves. The cliffs themselves are quite forbidding, and evidence of their unforgiving nature can be seen in the rusting remains of a ship at Aberllong, one of three Greek tugs wrecked here while *en route* from Liverpool.

Passing through National Trust land, the path goes by the concentric ditches of the massive Ogof Castell hillfort, before dropping down to Porth-y-Rhaw, once a busy place with a woollen mill and factory which stopped working in 1915. Inland is Morfa Common, an area of heathland maintained by the National Trust. The path then leads to Caer Bwdy Bay, where one can see the purple sandstone that has been used over many centuries to build St David's

The coastline at Caerfai

Cathedral. The most recent quarry was reopened here in 1972. On the headland is Castell Penpleidiau, another Iron Age fort, in a most impregnable position. Then one comes to Caerfai, where the caravan and camp site intrudes upon the solitude of the cliffs, though there is a good beach in a dramatic setting, easily reached by a track down the side of the cliff. The Cambrian rocks here are dated at around 500 million years old, some of the oldest in Britain.

Round the next headland, at the head of St Non's Bay, one comes to St Non's Chapel, both old and new, sited in front of the rather austere-looking, solitary grey building which was originally established as a Passionist Monastery and now acts as a religious retreat. From here the road leads to the cathedral city of St David's, less than a mile inland.

COAL MINES OF THE COAST

Newgale, Nolton and Little Haven, south of Broad Haven, were three of the main coal-mining areas of the Pembrokeshire coastline, part of an industry dating back to the 14th century which went into decline only towards the end of the last century. By the early 19th century demand for Pembrokeshire coal outstripped the supply from mines that were said to produce the world's finest anthracite – Queen Victoria specified it for use on her royal yachts. Competition from the big inland collieries eventually brought about the demise of the Pembrokeshire mines, the last closing as late as 1948.

St David's

Trevine

ST DAVID'S

WHITESANDS BAY

APPROX. 8 MILES/13KM

OS Landranger 157
Start at grid reference SM 753 252
Start point: St David's City Cross. Nearest car park at The Pebbles.

In season St David's can become very crowded due to the attraction of its cathedral and Bishop's Palace. The limited number of car parks soon fill up, and it is advisable to find a space early. From the City Cross follow the road downhill, and then fork left along a road signposted to the Warlpool Court Hotel. The nearby Carn Warlpool is a gorse-fringed, rocky outcrop which gives views forward towards Ramsey Island and back towards the tower of St David's Cathedral. It also looks over Clegyr Boia, or Boia's Rock, to the west, and to the north to Carn Llidi, the highest point of the peninsula at 600ft (183m).

At the end of the road, a footpath leads down past the ruins of St Non's to rejoin the coast path, following the spectacular rocky

A view of Ramsey Island from Point St John

coastline westwards. Visible here is the wide colour range in the lichen-covered Cambrian rock structure which has been upended by volcanic activity. As one rounds the headland known as Trwyn Cynddeiriog (which can aptly be translated as the 'Furious Point'), small hollows alongside the path show where farmers quarried stone to build their field boundaries. As it winds its way along the coastline, the path affords wonderful views of the near vertical cliffs.

Past the next bay the path turns inland above Porth Clais Harbour. This picturesque inlet is a haven for a small fleet of fishing boats, the only habitation being two small cottages. A modern sea wall has been built on the remains of an old wall at the entrance, and at the head of the inlet a bridge crosses the River Alun, which flows into the sea here on its way from St David's. Porth Clais was the principal harbour for St David's from the 14th century, receiving building timber imported from Ireland and produce such as corn, malt and wool from as far afield as Barnstable, Bristol and Merioneth. Coal was brought to the harbour by boats well into the 20th century, but that trade has now completely disappeared. By the side of the river are restored limekilns, but the cottages which housed the lime-burners who looked after them are now ruins, and the pub which stood on the quay wall has also disappeared.

Past Porth Clais the St David's peninsula is flat and windswept, and the path moves away from the cliff-edges. Passing National Trust land, it drops downhill to cross behind the twin rocky beaches of Porthlysgi Bay, named after the Irish raider Lysgi who killed the Celtic chieftain Boia at Clegyr Boia, a mile inland. For a time it looks as if one has to walk round the end of Ramsey Island, but Ramsey Sound, which separates the island from the mainland, soon comes into view. This is a fearsome stretch of water where the tidal race called The Bitches can run at up to 20 knots. The island itself is about 2 miles long by 1 mile wide, with an area of around 600 acres. The Breton St Justinian built a cell on Ramsey in about AD500.

Round the headland the path once again follows the cliff-edges closely, passing ruined

GUIDE BOX

Places to visit
Lleithyr Farm Museum, near Whitesands Bay, is a National Park, award-winning museum of farm implements, tractors, carts, dairy utensils, tools and domestic bygones. Gift shop and tearoom. Open Easter to October, Tuesday to Sunday, and school holiday Mondays.

Rare Breeds Survival Centre, St David's Farm Park, is located on the St David's-to-Trevine coast road, and contains the most comprehensive collection of rare breeds on display in Wales. Fly fishing is also available. Gift shop, restaurant and art gallery. Open Easter to October, daily.

Thousand Island Expedition. Motorboat trips run along the coastline from Whitesands Beach, taking passengers through the whitewater rapids of The Bitches to view the wildlife of Ramsey Island and the coastal area. Easter to October. Contact Thousand Island Expeditions, Cross Square, St David's (tel. 0437 721686).

Car parking
Principal car parks are at St David's, St Justinian (grid ref. SM 724 252), Whitesands Bay (SM 733 272), Abereiddy Bay (SM 797 313), and in Porthgain and Trevine.

Public transport
A bus service runs along the A487 between St David's and Goodwick, just over 1 mile south of Trevine and about 2 miles south-east of Abereiddy. There is no public transport along the coastal road. See also under Guide Box, page 118.

Accommodation
There are hotels and bed-and-breakfasts in St David's, youth hostels at Llaethdy, near Whitesands Beach, and at Trevine, and numerous camp sites round St David's peninsula. See also page 118 for an accommodation list.

buildings as it heads northwards, and later the site of St Justinian's Chapel at Porthstinian. Apparently the luckless saint was beheaded and then walked, headless, across the Sound to place his head on the spot where the chapel was built some 1000 years later. A short way on, the lifeboat station at St Justinian dominates the coastline here. It is in an important position, servicing a large area, with a fleet of four inshore lifeboats moored in the lee of Ramsey Island, and a big, offshore lifeboat in a magnificent boathouse at the head of a high ramp. From here a daily boat service connects Ramsey Island to the mainland, and visitors may make day trips or stay overnight in bed-and-breakfast or self-catering accommodation. The island plays host to large numbers of deer, and at the southern end its cliffs and offshore stacks are nesting grounds for kittiwake, guillemot and razorbill, best viewed from the seaward side by boat.

Ⓔ *Minor roads and tracks lead directly back to St David's from Maen Bachan (2½ miles from grid ref. SM 721 241) and from St Justinian (2 miles from grid ref. SM 722 251).*

The path past St Justinian is perilously close to the cliff-edge, and has been moved inland in places due to erosion and cliff-falls. Round Point St John the path drops to the delightful small beach of Porthselau, which serves the reasonably well-hidden caravan park on the hillside above, and then goes on to Whitesands Bay, which, after Newgale, is the largest beach on this stretch of the coastal path. With a huge expanse of sand backed by cliffs at either end, it faces westwards and is connected to St David's by the B4583 which makes it popular in summer, but not over-commercialised, none the less. Dogs are not allowed on the beach in the main summer season. Just to the north-east of Whitesands, there is a small, youth hostel at Llaethdy.

Ⓔ *Footpaths and minor roads run east and south from Llaethdy (grid ref. SM 739 271) back to St David's.*

WHITESANDS BAY

TREVINE

APPROX. 10 MILES/16KM

OS Landranger 157
Start at grid reference SM 733 272
Start point: Whitesands Bay car park.

From the Whitesands car park the coast path continues northwards, gaining height and passing the beach at Porthmelgan close to St David's Head, the last beach that is accessible from the land until Abereiddy Bay. Inland the heather-covered headland is dominated by Carn Llidi, one of the Ordovician volcanic peaks of this wild area, which is mainly populated by seabirds, wild flowers, and other walkers. St David's Head sticks out to the west here, described by the ancient geographer Ptolemy as the Promontory of Eight Perils, because of its fatal attraction for early sail-powered shipping driven on to this unforgiving shore by relentless westerly winds. Here it is worth diverting off the coast path to follow a track on to the headland, where there is a stone barrier known as the Warrior's Dyke. The eight stone hut circles are among many prehistoric remains in this part of Pembrokeshire.

The route continues eastwards, following the cliff-tops all the way, with fine views along the coastline ahead. Here the path is a good way from the road, with few connecting footpaths and little habitation apart from the occasional inland farm. Past the banks of the three Iron Age forts at Caerau, the path drops to sea level once again at west-facing Abereiddy Bay, popular with the more adventurous holidaymaker who is willing to go further afield. Back on the cliffs, on the north side of the beach, pass the remains of a slate quarry which was operational until 1904, with ruins of the quarrymen's row, engine house and dressing sheds. Most impressive is the flooded quarry, cut deep into the cliff-face of the headland. It is now known as The Blue Lagoon, with a deep entrance wide enough for a single boat. The stone tower above may have been built to aid navigation in the 18th century, and is

Whitesands Bay, St David's peninsula

a useful landmark for walkers today.

The next beach is Traeth Llyfn, accessible via a steep path. The coast path follows the cliff-tops until it descends steeply to Porthgain, an inlet with a fascinating small harbour, once busily engaged in the export of slates brought by tramway from Abereiddy. After 100 years or so this trade ceased in 1931, and all that is left are the massive old brickworks and bins for the crushed stone. With a few fishing boats, a pub, an award-winning small restaurant, and a green with picnic tables, Porthgain has a welcoming air today.

On the far side of the harbour the coast path continues up past an old navigational tower, dropping to sea level once again at Aber Draw, where the path joins the road. Here the walker can continue downhill and

uphill along the road into Trevine, or better, turn off to the left to rejoin the coast path by a rather untidy small bay, passing a row of painted cottages to reach the next headland. From here a footpath heads inland to join a farm track which leads into Trevine. The path is fenced on both sides, but is not signposted so care needs to be taken to find it – if you go beyond the headland and start turning in towards the next bay at Pwll Olfa, you have gone too far. Trevine is an unexciting place to finish, but it has a pub, a camp site, a somewhat battered youth hostel and a shop that may serve those willing to sit outside with a cup of tea. Alternatively, some walkers may prefer to stop at Porthgain or push on to equally picturesque Abercastle.

ST DAVID'S CATHEDRAL AND BISHOP'S PALACE

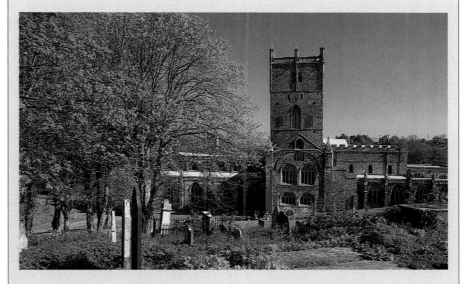

The Cathedral is in a wonderful position on the south side of the city, best seen first from The Pebbles (Y Popples) or Tower Hill on the hillside above. The first cathedral or church was built here by St David, but was burnt down in AD645. Its replacement suffered the same fate in 1088, and the basis of the building that we see today was started by the Norman Bishop Peter de Leia in 1180. Additions were made over the years, and in more recent times Sir Gilbert Scott

began restoration in 1863.

St David's Bishop's Palace, next to the cathedral, is now administered by Cadw: Welsh Historic Monuments as a magnificent ruin and is open throughout the year. The Palace was built between 1280 and 1350. It went into final decay in the 16th century when Bishop Barlow, the last bishop to live there, stripped the lead from the roof of the Great Hall to pay the dowries of his five daughters.

Trevine

Goodwick

TREVINE

PWILDERI

APPROX. 8 MILES/13KM

OS Landranger 157
Start at grid reference SM 840 325
Start point: Trevine, on the coast road, 3 miles north-west of Mathry on the A487. Roadside parking.

To rejoin the coast path from Trevine, walk past the modern houses on the north side of the village, joining a fenced track which heads towards the cliffs. The route continues along a permitted path on the cliff-side with farmland inland, passing above the rocky bay of Pwll Long, which can be reached by a steep path. It continues round the headland where the fine peninsula of Pen Castell-coch is connected to the mainland, with views opening out all the way to Strumble Head.

Turning inland, the path joins steep steps, heading down the side of the inlet which leads to the small port of Abercastle. Just past the stile near the bottom, a signpost points to the Carreg Sampson cromlech, a short distance to the west. Dated at around 5000 years old, it is considered one of the finest Neolithic burial chambers in Pembrokeshire, with a 16ft long capstone and six upright rocks. Abercastle is reminiscent of Porthgain, though it has neither pub nor restaurant. It was once a small port trading with Bristol and Liverpool, but now the only trade there is is that of a few fishing boats and the holiday letting firm, Coastal Cottages of Pembrokeshire, who have tastefully re-novated a quayside building. Before you leave Abercastle, look out for the old cannons acting as bollards and the limekiln.

The path continues up the other side of the inlet behind an attractive cottage, passing a dangerously ruinous granary in a fine position, with a sign saying 'Keep Out!'. Going along a permitted path with fields inland, the route winds its way slowly above the inaccessible bays below, sometimes passing very close to the cliff-edges. At Pwllstrodur it drops downhill to cross a stream by a small rocky cove, heading steeply uphill on the other side to continue round the next headland, past the Iron Age promontory fort of Castell-coch.

The path starts to head downhill towards Aber Mawr, parts of it being in a dangerous condition, with sideslip evident. The beach at Aber Mawr comes into sight, perhaps the most scenic of this walk, with perfect sets of waves rolling in from the north-west if there has been any wind. As they break they polish the beautiful stones of the shorelines to rounded perfection, the flattest ones at the top of the pile providing a pleasant walking surface. Inland there is an unspoilt reed valley with woods beyond, which makes a pleasant change from the monotony of farmland and affords an excellent windbreak for a picnic. The beach itself is connected to the outside world via a dead-end road, but is sufficiently isolated to remain totally unspoilt. It is also considered the most important Ice Age site in Pembrokeshire, with the remains of a submerged coastal forest that can sometimes be seen beneath the sand at low tides.

Ⓔ *For a return to Trevine (a walk of 3 miles from Aber Mawr), follow the bridleway at grid ref. SM 878 344, turning westwards inland of Mynydd Morfa, passing the farmstead at Carnachen-lwyd, and emerging on the road above Abercastle. The road then leads uphill to Trevine.*

Below *On a lonely stretch of coastline, the cliffs drop down to the bay of Pwllcrochan*

At the far end of the beach the path joins the road, near a small white building which was the transatlantic submarine cable terminus. The signposting is a little confusing here – either follow the coast round Pen Deudraeth, or continue along the road to a Coastal Path signpost pointing left. From here the path continues above the storm beach of Aber Bach and on past the rock and sand bay at Pwllcrochan, which is accessible with difficulty. This part of the coastline is very lonely, and is one of the best stretches to spot grey seals. Never approach a seal and keep dogs well away. Once a human has been close to a seal pup its mother may reject it. Seal Watch signs give emergency telephone numbers and explain what to do if a seal appears to be in difficulty. The cliffs have numerous seabird colonies, with guillemots and razorbills much in evidence.

As the path rounds Penbwchdy headland, the surroundings become rocky and wild. There is a convenient, walled circular shelter here, although in westerly winds it is better to find a place on the leeward side of the rocks, beyond which there is a grandstand view over the inland plain. The coast path here is magnificently wild, with hard volcanic cliffs over 450ft high. A bench provides a convenient viewpoint for those who walk up the road from Pwilderi.

The path joins the lonely road at Pwilderi, and comes to the back of a youth hostel high up on a windswept hillside, with a view southwards that must rate as one of the finest in Britain. Despite the usual Spartan accom-modation, this is an enviable place to stay. There is a memorial just near by to the Welsh poet Dewi Emrys, and behind the youth hostel is the dominating bulk of Garn Fawr, a most impressive hillfort.

OS Landranger 157
Start at grid reference SM 898 388
Start point: Pwilderi, on a minor road 4 miles west of Goodwick. Car park below Garn Fawr hillfort.

By the side of the youth hostel, the coast path goes downhill, passing the rocky outcrop of the fort Dinas Mawr, yet more evidence of the ancient Celts' extensive defence system. It can be reached by its own narrow track. The coast path continues through gorse and heather, winding high above Porth Maenmelyn and climbing on a crumbling path past a large, improbably sited house in the lee of the hillside to the right.

On the far headland there are the brick remains of ugly MoD buildings, which may have some use as shelter in wet weather, and then the path heads down and up through rounded hillocks of volcanic rock, passing the small, sheltered valley of Pwll Arian, or 'Treasure Cove', on the way. The lighthouse at Strumble Head is in view along this stretch of the path, a handsome building in traditional, turn-of-the-century lighthouse style, with its piercing light flashing by day and night. It was built in 1908 on Ynys Meicel one of a series of islets stretching westwards from Strumble Head. It is connected to the mainland by a footbridge, but since it is now automatic and unmanned one is unlikely to be able to look round it.

The path here joins the road, passing by a restored MoD building which is now mainly used by birdwatchers. Strumble Head is a breeding ground for herring gull and fulmar, though the principal interest is the passage of seabirds from breeding sites such as Ramsey Island *en route* to Cardigan Bay to feed. During the breeding season flocks of Manx shearwater can be seen going to and from these feeding areas, and in spring and autumn migrant birds such as sea ducks and divers can be seen off shore with the aid of binoculars.

The final 6 miles from Strumble Head to Goodwick are along a remote stretch offering excellent walking, with the view ahead looking all the way to Cemaes Head, the final headland before the coast path ends at St Dogmaels. The ferry may sometimes be seen making its daily crossing between Goodwick and Rosslare, in the Republic of Ireland, as the path passes above the bay of Porthsychan – where the headland of Carreg Gybi is named after St Cybi of Cornwall, an early Celtic saint. At Penrhyn there is a tiny holiday cottage in an enviably remote situation, and then the permissive path winds in and out along the cliff-tops, towards the extraordinary memorial stone above Carregwastad Point. This was erected in 1897, 100 years after the French invasion of 22 February 1797, when over 1000 men came ashore here, under the command of an American named Tate, bent on the

The view across the Bay from Goodwick to the ferryport of Fishguard

destruction of far-off Liverpool! They surrendered without resistance on nearby Goodwick Sands, two days after landing.

Just past here the path dives down into a hidden wooded valley at Cwm Felin, where a footpath leads to the small settlement of Llanwnda, before cutting off the headland of Pen Anglas to head across open country to Harbour Village on the hillside above Goodwick. Why the route should leave the coast path at this point is not clear, though it is probably due to the problems of getting past HM Customs, who are waiting on the quayside to receive passengers from the Irish ferries. The hillside descent offers a fine view over the long Goodwick breakwater, with Fishguard beyond, and the great mass of Dinas Head directly to the east, showing the route of the coast path continuing.

Once in Harbour Village there is no clear signposting. Head along a street of uniform houses, and then bear downhill on a road to join the road bridge over the railway line, coming to the main A40 roundabout, where there is a convenient harbourside car park. After the magnificent wildness of the Coast Path, the arrival into Goodwick is something of a come-down, but it has good public transport connections and for those with the time and energy there are another 28 miles of mainly very wild coastal path before reaching its official beginning/end at St Dogmaels, near Cardigan.

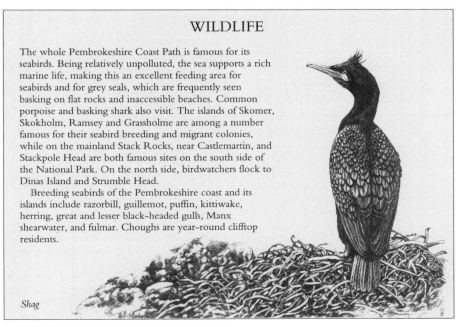

WILDLIFE

The whole Pembrokeshire Coast Path is famous for its seabirds. Being relatively unpolluted, the sea supports a rich marine life, making this an excellent feeding area for seabirds and for grey seals, which are frequently seen basking on flat rocks and inaccessible beaches. Common porpoise and basking shark also visit. The islands of Skomer, Skokholm, Ramsey and Grassholme are among a number famous for their seabird breeding and migrant colonies, while on the mainland Stack Rocks, near Castlemartin, and Stackpole Head are both famous sites on the south side of the National Park. On the north side, birdwatchers flock to Dinas Island and Strumble Head.

Breeding seabirds of the Pembrokeshire coast and its islands include razorbill, guillemot, puffin, kittiwake, herring, great and lesser black-headed gulls, Manx shearwater, and fulmar. Choughs are year-round clifftop residents.

Shag

Sirhowy Valley Walk

NEWPORT TO TREDEGAR
26 MILES/42KM

Detailed guide
The *Sirhowy Valley Map Pack* divides the walk into seven easy-to-follow stages with a mass of information on the area. It is available from Gwent County Council, County Hall, Cwmbran, Gwent NP44 2XF.

Maps
OS Landranger 161, 171

Links
The Sirhowy Valley Walk is crossed by the unofficial Cambrian Way near Mynydd Machen.

THE Sirhowy Valley Walk is a walk of contrasts, leaving the built-up fringes of Newport to follow the Sirhowy Valley northwards towards the Brecon Beacons. There are many reminders of South Wales' mining communities and of its importance during the Industrial Revolution. Some parts of the route are extremely beautiful; others have been destroyed by man. A keen walker could cover the route in a taxing day, or it can be spread over two days to make a pleasant weekend's rambling.

The start of the Walk, Tredegar House

Some of the route follows high ground, and the normal precautions for hill-walking should be followed. Plan the route carefully, use the OS maps with a compass, wear sensible boots and carry wet-weather gear. None of it is far from civilisation, but if the rain and mist come down it can be surprisingly difficult to find the way off the hills.

There is no reason to prefer walking south to north or north to south, and the excellent official guide gives a detailed route description in both directions. Newport is better served by public transport, but even then the official start at Tredegar House is some way out of town, requiring a bus or taxi journey from the railway station. Waymarking throughout is moderately good, but there are occasional problems with route-finding and it is necessary to have both the official guide and OS maps to find the way. To make a grand circuit of just over 50 miles, lasting three or four days, the walk can be combined with the Usk Valley Walk (see pages 128-31), which connects neighbouring Caerleon with Abergavenny.

Newport
Tredegar

NEWPORT
MYNYDD MACHEN
APPROX. 8 MILES/13KM

OS Landranger 171
Start at grid reference ST 290 849
Start point: Tredegar House Country Park. Ample car parking.

Tredegar House is on the south-western outskirts of Newport. It is worth taking time to look at the house and its grounds. The start of the walk is signalled by an information board in the car park.

Signposting through the urban fringes of Newport is good. Despite the built-up nature of the surroundings, there are plenty of points of interest. The route crosses the Ebbw River on an old bridge by the early 19th-century Mill House, passing under the A48. A short way on it makes its way uphill through a large housing estate, where it is easy to miss the left turn that brings you to a gate and a Sirhowy Valley signpost that leads on to open ground beneath the impressive Gaer Hill Iron Age fort. From the top there is a fine view, on a clear day, over Newport, Cardiff and the Severn Estuary on one side, and the mountains of the north on the other.

A path leads steeply downhill towards the M4. At the bottom the route leads through the Coed Melyn Park, close to the motorway. It is easy to stray off course here and end up in a maze of suburban side roads. Going upwards through the park, the route leads to the top of the ridge aptly known as the Ridgeway, and at last, after at least an

hour's walking, the built-up townscape is left behind and there is a fine view ahead over the area known locally as Little Switzerland.

The route continues downhill over farmland, crossing the Monmouth and Brecon Canal by an old bridge, and passing along the canalside through a tunnel which leads under the M4. As the motorway is at last left behind, the route follows the canal towpath to the north-west and becomes much more peaceful, passing the lock-keeper's house and going up by the side of an extraordinary series of 14 locks. A short way on is the Fourteen Locks Canal Centre.

The route continues along the canal towpath, but then turns off to the south-west, passing through Rogerstone by the Tredegar Arms public house, crossing the A467, and entering Ty Du Park, where the local cricket team plays on summer weekends. Three tall poplars lead the way to a metal bridge that crosses the River Ebbw, an impressive sight here when in full spate.

Truly rural from now on, the route heads uphill and skirts the village of Rhiwdern, going up across Fox Hill and into woods for a mile or so of easy walking through Coed Mawr. Coming out of these woods, the

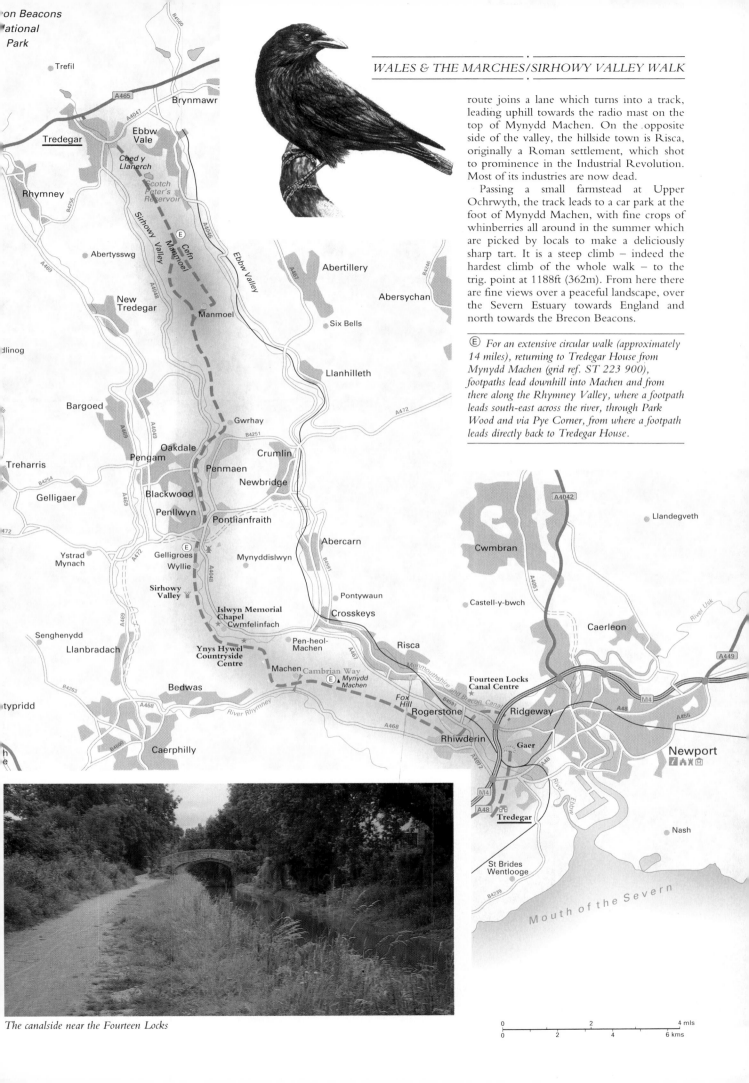

route joins a lane which turns into a track, leading uphill towards the radio mast on the top of Mynydd Machen. On the opposite side of the valley, the hillside town is Risca, originally a Roman settlement, which shot to prominence in the Industrial Revolution. Most of its industries are now dead.

Passing a small farmstead at Upper Ochrwyth, the track leads to a car park at the foot of Mynydd Machen, with fine crops of whinberries all around in the summer which are picked by locals to make a deliciously sharp tart. It is a steep climb – indeed the hardest climb of the whole walk – to the trig. point at 1188ft (362m). From here there are fine views over a peaceful landscape, over the Severn Estuary towards England and north towards the Brecon Beacons.

Ⓔ *For an extensive circular walk (approximately 14 miles), returning to Tredegar House from Mynydd Machen (grid ref. ST 223 900), footpaths lead downhill into Machen and from there along the Rhymney Valley, where a footpath leads south-east across the river, through Park Wood and via Pye Corner, from where a footpath leads directly back to Tredegar House.*

The canalside near the Fourteen Locks

MYNYDD MACHEN

BLACKWOOD

APPROX. 7 MILES/11KM

OS Landranger 171
Start at grid reference ST 232 898.
Start point: Car park below Mynydd Machen, reached via the minor road that connects Risca with Lower Machen.

From the top of Mynydd Machen a track leads downhill to the north-west skirting a wide band of woodland. The official guide appears to direct the walker to the west, which is misleading. The route continues along a springy grass track following the Rhymney Valley Ridgeway along the top of the hill. Close by to the left there is an enormous spoil tip from the Risca colliery, rapidly being covered by grass and undergrowth and looking for all the world like a giant's burial mound.

By Pen-heol-Machen the route leaves the track ahead and bears up the hill on a narrow path. Be careful to follow the yellow Sirhowy Valley waymarks here. For a time the Walk continues along the Rhymney Valley Ridgeway footpath (which eventually leads to Pontllanfraith), but then it bears off to the right and begins to zig-zag down the Graig Goch wooded hillside above the 1000-acre Sirhowy Valley Country Park where it joins a level forestry track. Here it heads downhill again to the Ynys Hywel Countryside Centre, passing a camping barn.

The Centre is a welcoming place for a Sirhowy Valley walker, and the camping barn, magnificently positioned on the hillside, is convenient and very cheap. A visit to the Islwyn Memorial Chapel, on the other side of the river in Cwmfelinfach, is also recommended; built as a Calvinist Methodist Chapel in 1827, it is now a memorial to the 19th-century Welsh poet 'Islwyn', the Reverend William Thomas.

The route continues along a narrow track a short way down the hillside from the Countryside Centre, going steeply downhill to join a disused railway line. Originally built as the Sirhowy tramroad in 1805 to carry iron ore from Tredegar to Newport, it was soon replaced by the railway. The last train ran in 1960.

The Sirhowy Valley route leaves the old railway line and heads quite steeply uphill on an overgrown path. At the top of the hill the route goes in and out of woodland and across bracken-covered trails. The waymarking is not all it might be here, leading to navigation problems, which may be compounded by mist on the hills. The route eventually leads down the hillside to join a track by a secluded house on the outskirts of Wyllie. The route next crosses an old railway bridge which was the scene of a famous incident in 1935: during the 'Stay Down' strike at nearby Nine Mile Point colliery, angry workers dropped a parapet stone on to a train passing underneath.

The route follows a path by the side of the River Sirhowy, leading to the 16th-century watermill at Gelligroes. This was once owned by radio ham Arthur Moore, who picked up distress signals from the *Titanic* on 14 April 1912. Sadly, no one believed him, convinced she was unsinkable.

Ⓔ *For a return to Mynydd Machen, take the country lanes leading eastwards from Gelligroes (grid ref. ST 177 947), to the village of Mynyddislwyn, where a footpath leads east and south along the side of Mynydd y Lan towards Newtown and back to Mynydd Machen, a circular walk of around 13 miles.*

From here the Walk leaves the river to follow the lane which was once the Penllwyn tramroad. Never replaced by rail, it functioned until the 1870s. It continues by the side of the South Wales Switchgear factory, passing the Greyhound pub on the outskirts of Blackwood, a meeting place for the Chartist political movement in the 1830s. The walk then rejoins the river as it passes through Blackwood.

Mynydd Machen: a steep but rewarding climb

BLACKWOOD

MANMOEL

APPROX. 6 MILES/10KM

OS Landranger 171
Start at grid reference ST 177 363
Start point: The car park at the Islwyn Civic Centre in Blackwood.

The route continues along a tarmac path by the side of the River Sirhowy, avoiding the town and leaving it by a park where it passes the Rock and Fountain Inn at a road crossing. This was originally the counting house for the Penllwyn tramroad. It continues along the line of the old tramroad but at the next road junction crosses the bridge in the valley and climbs uphill to the A4048. Opposite the Rock Inn it continues along another disused railway line. It served all the collieries in this part of the valley, the last of which closed in 1957.

Just by the overhead power cables a path

leads downhill towards the river. It is not waymarked, and the route directions in the official guide are confusing. Follow the path down to cross the river below the hamlet of Gwrhay, heading away from the river and joining a lane which heads uphill into open country, passing Penderi Farm on the right. A short way on the road bends right, and the Sirhowy Valley route goes straight ahead down a rough track, passing the extensive disused mine-working of Llanover Colliery. At the bottom of the track there is an old railway line with sleepers and track still in place, passing close by ruinous buildings.

The official route leads round the back of these buildings and away from the line, but it is easier and more pleasant to walk on the sleepers and follow the line straight ahead. It passes under and over a bridge, rejoining the official route, which then turns away from the line on a rough track that winds uphill with extensive forestry over to the right. Eventually it joins a tarmac lane, passing the farmstead of Twyn Gwyn on the left and then coming to a footpath on the right which leads across fields to Manmoel. Heading towards a solitary white cottage, it emerges at the road on a bend. The pub is down the lane straight ahead, opposite the tiny graveyard and chapel.

·
MANMOEL

·
TREDEGAR

·
APPROX. 6 MILES/10KM

·

OS Landranger 171, 161
Start at grid reference SO 179 034
Start point: The Manmoel Inn, in the village of Manmoel between Abertillery and New Tredegar. Parking on the roadside.

Here there is a choice of two routes to the finish. A 'short cut' route covers just over 5 miles and keeps along the high ground. The longer route is 6 miles and involves a longish downhill stretch followed by a longish uphill one, but neither is very taxing and this seems much the better option.

The route divides at a crossroads on the western outskirts of Manmoel. Here the short route follows a lane northwards, linking with the longer route after a mile or so for the ridge walk along the top of Cefn Manmoel. The longer route joins a track which leads alongside the woodlands of Coed y Llanerch, before heading steeply downhill through the woodland with fine views opening out of the valley to the left.

Near the bottom of the hill the track bears left towards the farmstead at Pont Gwaithyrhaearn, in an area which was the site of much activity during the Industrial Revolution, though no sign of this remains today. Just before the farm the route turns uphill, crossing a stream and climbing on a track by the side of stone walls. It should come out on to common land near the top, but the route guide is hazy here and it is easy to stray too far to the east and start heading down into the neighbouring valley. The route joins the single lane road which runs along the top of Cefn Manmoel.

Above *View of the valley from Coed y Llanerch*

Ⓔ *A return can be made to Manmoel via this road (which is the short cut route), a distance of some 4 miles (grid ref. SO 170 055).*

Further on the road deteriorates into a rough track as it heads north towards the Brecon Beacons. There are fine views over Tredegar to the north-west, a town which expanded rapidly, when the Sirhowy Ironworks were established in 1778 to exploit the local coal and ironstone.

The route continues past the radio masts above the forest on the left which surrounds Scotch Peter's Reservoir, continuing along a lane towards Sirhowy, on the eastern outskirts of Tredegar. At the A4047 the end of the walk is marked on the other side of the road by the three immense Aneurin Bevan Memorial Stones. 'Nye' Bevan represented the three principal towns of Ebbw Vale as an MP for 30 years. He was born in Tredegar in 1897, and was the pioneer of the National Health Service.

THE SIRHOWY TRAMROAD

The rapid industrialisation of the Sirhowy Valley area in the 19th century required an efficient transport system to replace the narrow cart tracks which had been used in the previous traditional farming era. Charcoal, coal and iron were at first transported by mule trains, but this proved too slow, and in 1802 Richard Fothergill suggested building a 24-mile tramroad between Tredegar and Newport with teams of horses used to pull the wagons. The project was shared with the Monmouth Canal Company, with the road starting at the Tredegar estate in Newport and finishing at the Tredegar Iron Company. The line was completed in 1805, and was an immediate success.

Usk Valley Walk

COMPLETE ROUTE
BRECON TO CAERLEON
50 MILES/80KM

SECTION COVERED
ABERGAVENNY TO CAERLEON
25 MILES/40KM

Detailed guides
The Usk Valley Walk Map Pack gives details of the full route from Caerleon to Brecon, on four separate cards. Available from Tourist Information Centres or Gwent County Council, County Hall, Cwmbran, Gwent NP44 2XF.

Maps
OS Landranger 161, 171

Links
The Cambrian Way meets the Usk Valley Walk at Abergavenny.

THE Usk Valley Walk originally linked Caerleon, on the eastern fringes of Newport, with Abergavenny, on the southern side of the Brecon Beacons. Recently it has been extended northwards to link with Brecon, in the heart of the Brecon Beacons National Park, following the route of the Monmouthshire and Brecon Canal and making the walk a full 50 miles. The southern section is described here, as it follows the meanderings of the River Usk, not so well known as the neighbouring River Wye but no less beautiful.

After rising on the northern end of Fan Foel in the Brecon Beacons National Park, the River Usk flows southwards through Gwent, becoming the county's mightiest river before it joins the sea via the Severn estuary at Newport, along with the neighbouring rivers of the Sirhowy, Ebbw Fach and Afon Lwyd. In fact, geographically the Usk Valley Walk is a very close neighbour of the Sirhowy Valley Walk (see pages 124-7), both walks following a similar north-south direction and being little more than 10 miles apart at any one time. However, their characters could not be more different, the Usk pre-

A display board shows what to look out for

dominantly being rural and in places even lyrical, while the Sirhowy has constant reminders of the locality's recent and not so recent industrial past. The two walks can easily be linked: there are regular buses from the outskirts of Tredegar to Abergavenny or, alternatively, taxis are relatively cheap and plentiful.

As with so many walks, there is no great advantage to be gained from following the Usk Valley Walk in one direction rather than the other; walking from north to south is the more natural route as it follows the flow of the river and brings the walker close to Newport with its excellent public transport connections, but as a finishing point the Usk

at Abergavenny is considerably more attractive than the Usk at Caerleon, and for those extending the walk northwards there is the added attraction of the Brecon Beacons as a final goal.

Generally the walk is easy to follow, plentifully waymarked by yellow plastic arrows and the words 'Usk Valley Walk'. There are occasional exceptions, in particular at the Caerleon end of the route, where it is possible to go off course on the last leg.

Apart from the climb up to Bertholey House, none of the route is high-level, and there should be no dangers from exposure or low cloud. However, in summer much of the riverside walking is along overgrown paths which can become wet and muddy, and waterproof walking boots and clothing are advisable unless the weather is particularly dry. Like the Sirhowy Valley Walk, the walk could be covered in a single day of around 12 hours' walking. Taken at a more relaxed pace over a couple of days, there would be time to look round Abergavenny, Usk and Caerleon.

Abergavenny

Caerleon

ABERGAVENNY

THE BRYN

APPROX. 6 MILES/9KM

OS Landranger 161
Start at grid reference SO 292 139
Start point: Usk Bridge on the south-western outskirts of Abergavenny. Public car parks in Abergavenny.

The walk appropriately starts from the fine road bridge that crosses the Usk, looking across fields towards Abergavenny and its 14th-century castle. At first the route heads westwards along the south side of the river, past a cemetery. It immediately leaves the road, passing under the A465 Heads of the Valley Road, skirting the village of Llanfoist, and then following a track uphill to the Monmouthshire and Brecon Canal.

The canal was originally built between 1797 and 1812 to connect the industrial southern parts of Gwent and the docklands of Newport with the farming country in the north. In more recent times 33 miles have been restored to make one of Britain's most attractive cruising waterways. The towpath can be followed as footpath along most of its length. However, while the northern part of the Usk Valley Walk keeps to the canal almost all the way to Brecon, the southern part follows it for only a couple of miles before leaving it to join the River Usk.

The turning off the canal towpath is not well signposted, but is marked by a bridge and a stile. The footpath heads downhill across a field towards the village of Llanellen, and the route then passes through a modern housing estate towards the conspicuous church spire. Passing by the side of the churchyard, it joins the main A4042 road close by the Llanellen Bridge over the Usk. The bridge needs to be crossed with care as there is no pavement, and then the route heads over fields, across a stile. This cuts a

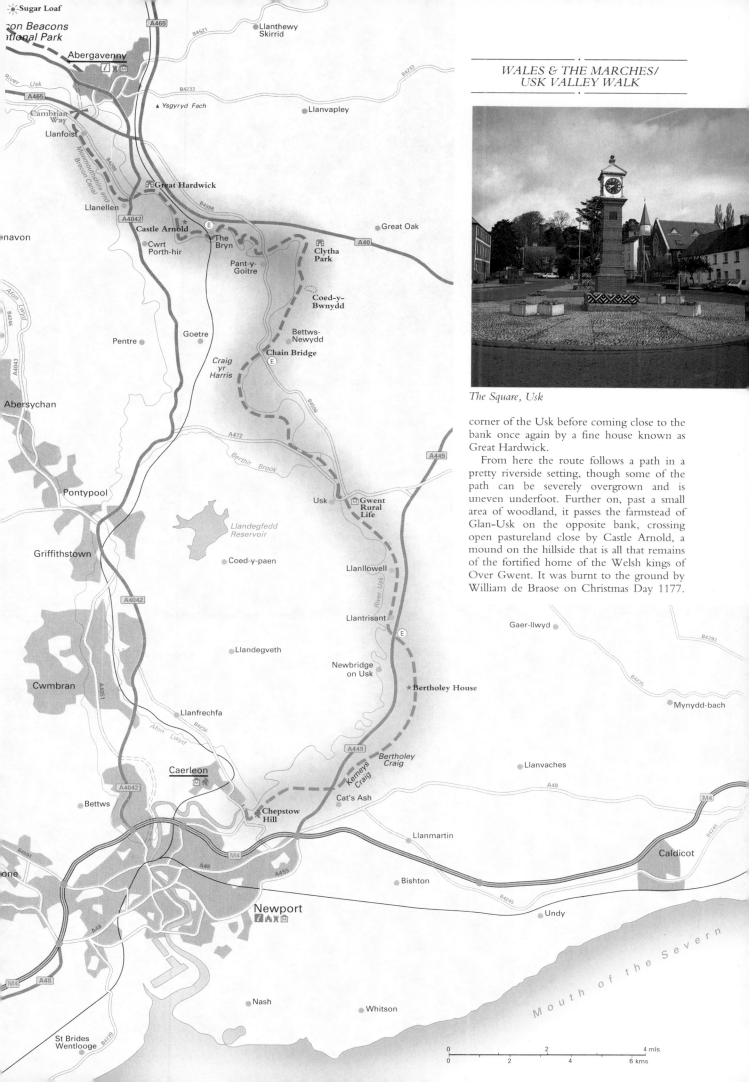

The Square, Usk

corner of the Usk before coming close to the bank once again by a fine house known as Great Hardwick.

From here the route follows a path in a pretty riverside setting, though some of the path can be severely overgrown and is uneven underfoot. Further on, past a small area of woodland, it passes the farmstead of Glan-Usk on the opposite bank, crossing open pastureland close by Castle Arnold, a mound on the hillside that is all that remains of the fortified home of the Welsh kings of Over Gwent. It was burnt to the ground by William de Braose on Christmas Day 1177.

Notwithstanding its grim past, the river here is very lovely, being tranquil, wide and at the same time obviously very powerful. Sadly the effect is to some extent spoilt by the noise of the nearby A40 dual carriageway.

The route continues to follow the river bank with open fields on both sides, passing a small settlement on a river bend, close by Cwrt Porth-hir, with characterful church and footbridge. It then passes beneath the railway near the small village known as The Bryn, where St Cadoc's Church boasts a Norman tower, nave and chancel. Two hundred years ago the river flowed right past this church, but its meanderings have now taken it some distance away.

Ⓔ *From The Bryn (grid ref. SO 332 099) there are two optional return routes to Abergavenny. Either follow footpaths northwards towards the conical-shaped hill known as Ysgyryd Fach or Little Skirrid (grid ref. SO 316 137). There are fine views from the summit, with waymarked paths leading down to the centre of Abergavenny (a circular walk of approximately 8 miles). Alternatively, cross the river beside the railway at The Bryn, following a footpath along the south bank and on towards Cwrt Porth-hir and Ochram Farm, where the footpath rejoins the canal towpath back to Abergavenny (a circular walk of approximately 11 miles).*

THE BRYN

USK

APPROX. 9.5 MILES/15KM

OS Landranger 161, 171
Start at grid reference SO 332 099
Start point: Roadside car parking at
The Bryn, on the A40, 3 miles south of
Abergavenny.

From The Bryn, the River Usk wiggles its way through quiet countryside, with the Walk pursuing a straighter course across fields towards the Pant-y-Goitre bridge. The waymarks need to be followed carefully here

The river as it approaches Abergavenny

as the river goes out of sight by trees, with the route passing a modern barn conversion to the left, near Manor House Farm. A fine-looking mansion comes into view – this is Pant-y-Goitre House, a neo-classical, 18th-century building, on the opposite river bank.

Bearing left, the footpath comes to the splendid Pant-y-Goitre bridge, crossing the B4598 (shown on the official route card as the A471 but now re-designated), and following an indistinct path (not marked as a public footpath on the OS map but waymarked as part of the route) along the side of a field towards a farmhouse. From here the route follows a quiet road for about ¹/₂ mile, coming close to the noisy A40 for the last time before bearing right on to an overgrown track beside a bus shelter. This joins a path which follows the Usk south.

Along this stretch the river is frequently obscured by trees and bushes. On the left side is Clytha Park (occasionally open to the public), an early 19th-century, neo-classical mansion faced in Bath stone. Further on, hidden in the wooded hillsides above, is Clytha Castle, a romantic crenellated folly built by William Jones, owner of Clytha Park, in memory of his wife in 1790. The route here follows the edge of fields, before the path climbs high above the river, passing through a delightful farmyard by Trostrey Lodge. Near by are the remains of a medieval forge on the hillside below. It made use of local charcoal supplies and harnessed the power of the Usk which swirls down through rapids at this point.

Dropping down towards the river once again, the route continues across parkland in front of an imposing 1920s house. A mile or so to the east is the Iron Age hillfort of Coed-y-Bwnydd, dated to around 400BC and accessible from the riverside via footpaths. For a time the path becomes slightly hard-going along the side of a hill between woods and a field, and then it goes into the woods to join a lane to the west of Bettws Newydd, dropping down to cross the river by the old Chain Bridge. Here it passes a large pub on the east bank, before turning immediately left on to a minor road on the west side of the river.

Ⓔ *To return to The Bryn, leave the Walk at the Chain Bridge (grid ref. SO 347 056) and continue west along the lane towards Nant-y-Derry. Turn off on to a bridleway/footpath that leads northwards to Highmead, joining the road by Pant-y-Goitre, and then following a footpath eastwards from the Pant-y-Goitre bridge along the south side of the Usk. Finally cross at the railway bridge to return to The Bryn.*

The route markers on the official route card are a little confusing here, implying that there is a left turn off the minor road before a stream. This would lead through a caravan park to nowhere. The correct turning is further up this road, by the side of the first house, leading along a grassy gated track and passing a modernised farmhouse. This emerges at a magnificent sweeping field, with the wooded hillside of Craig yr Harris on the right and the river to the left.

The route leads through the trees, and on to high ground with fine views across the plain, looking over the strangely named Kemeys Commander. Dropping downhill on to an overgrown trail, it passes a well-hidden pumping station – this is said to stand on the oldest rocks in Gwent, some 430 million years old. Just past here the route crosses a track, turning right on to an indistinct path with a waymark that is easily missed. This heads out across open fields as the river winds away to the east, going up and downhill to join a quiet lane a short way from Estavarney Farm. The land here was worked by Cistercian monks between the 13th and 15th centuries. A short way on, look out for a pair of fine ornamental iron gates.

Just past here the lane bears right downhill, and the route joins a track going straight ahead uphill on the left side. Crossing fields, it passes by the side of a thick belt of trees with the River Usk far below on the left side, while on the right an enormous field slopes down to the distant A472 in the valley, with Usk College of Agriculture coming into sight ahead. Keeping by the side of the woods, the footpath emerges on to a lane by an electricity sub-station. Here the route turns left towards the river, passing by a small estate of houses and coming to Prioress Mill. This was originally the site of a 16th-century watermill used for grinding corn, but it is now used for residential purposes, and the route as shown on the official route card has annoyingly been diverted away from the river. Instead it crosses fields, eventually rejoining the river by the Berthin Brook.

From here it is a pleasant riverside walk towards Usk, passing through a preserved wildlife area and on into recreational parkland known as the 'Island' picnic site, where there is an Usk Valley Walk notice board. Ahead lies the road bridge that leads into this attractive small town, with the river flowing cleanly below on its southbound way.

USK

CAERLEON

APPROX. 9½ MILES/15KM

OS Landranger 171
Start at grid reference SO 374 007
Start point: The Usk Bridge. Parking in the town.

Usk is a small town with a castle and a museum, worthwhile exploring. Sadly, from here on the footpath seldom comes right alongside the river until it reaches the finish at Caerleon.

From Usk there is a long 1½-mile stretch along a country lane going southwards, which comes to the outskirts of the hamlet of Llanllowell. As the road bends left to cross a bridge over a tributary of the Usk, the route follows a footpath on to a wooded track which bears right downhill. This leads on across peaceful meadows, hemmed in by trees on the east side with the river itself close by to the right. Passing to the left of a large public works building, the path bears left to cross a stream and joins the road at Llantrisant, where the pub and church are in a very attractive setting.

From here the route follows the road southwards for another mile or so. This is a quiet country lane which comes close to bends in the Usk at a couple of places,

Prioress Mill – its milling days are over

though here the river has become rather less pleasant and seems to attract litter as well as swimmers if the weather is sufficiently warm. Another problem is that the lane soon follows the path of the A449 dual carriageway, where the traffic thunders along only a short distance away. This makes the walk rather less of an idyll, and it is a relief to turn off the lane and under the A449 just past a farmstead, by the entrance to Llwynau Farm. Take care here to turn left under the second subway, not under the first which is part of the farmyard and acts as a storehouse.

Ⓔ *To return to Usk from here (grid ref. ST 388 953) turn off to the village of Newbridge on Usk. Cross the river here, and then follow footpaths and lanes northwards via Llangybi to Llanbadoc and Usk.*

By this stage it may seem that the quality of the walk has deteriorated, but a great surprise is in store as the route heads steeply up the hillside to pass Bertholey House. This is a wonderful ruin in a magnificent position. The views to the north are tremendous, looking over the Usk as far as Abergavenny with the Brecon Beacons beyond. The house itself was built around 1830 and burnt down by an accidental fire in 1905, becoming a charming and tragic ruin.

From here the path continues upwards, heading diagonally up an extremely steep field beneath the forestry of Bertholey Craig. The views from here are the best of the whole walk, making this a magnificent place to stop. The route then heads on into the woods, breaking into the open on a hard forestry track between uniform lines of plantation trees.

The woodland walk which follows via

Kemeys Craig bound for Caerleon is something over 2 miles, heading south-west. It starts well enough, but after a time the main forestry track disappears and the route continues along a path likely to be well laced with nettles and brambles in summer and very muddy if it has been wet. Worse, the A449 seems to become positively deafening, though one can never really see it. The only consolation comes from finding the occasional wild raspberry plant fruiting in July – until at last the path comes out of the woods on a narrow lane above Cat's Ash.

A short way along the road here, a narrow, stony and sometimes muddy track leads down to the hamlet of Cat's Ash. From there the route crosses the A449, going on for a mile or so along Chepstow Hill which, despite being on a road, offers relatively quiet walking. The final section of the route leads across fields via Cock-y-North Farm and downhill to the river, along the Bulmore Road. The official route guide appears to be inaccurate here and, at the time of writing, the correct turn-off for the public footpath joining the old Roman road, shown on the OS map close by the overhead powerlines, was unsignposted and unwelcoming, with no way obvious across the field ahead. The finish is by the Ship Inn on the banks of the Usk. By this stage the river has lost much of its charm and one's best bet is to cross the bridge and explore the old town of Caerleon or hop on a bus for Newport.

ISCA

The legionary fortress at *Isca* was one of three main military bases in Roman Britain. The second Augustan Legion, which boasted 5600 infantry, had its headquarters here for over 200 years, and the remains of their barracks at Caerleon are the best preserved in Europe. A Roman amphitheatre designed to seat 5000 people stands just outside the fortress walls, while the fortress baths, whose vaults once stood 60ft high, was one of the largest baths in the Roman province. A modern Legionary Museum in Caerleon High Street completes the collection of Roman remains at *Isca* (open all year, daily).

Wye Valley Walk

COMPLETE ROUTE
CHEPSTOW TO RHAYADER
110 MILES/177KM

SECTION COVERED
CHEPSTOW TO HAY-ON-WYE
75 MILES/120KM

Detailed guide
The *Wye Valley Walk Map Pack,* published by the Wye Valley Countryside Service, Hadnock Road, Monmouth, Gwent NP5 3NQ, includes route directions and transport/accommodation details. It is also available from local bookshops and Tourist Information Centres.

Maps
OS Landranger 148, 149, 162

Links
Offa's Dyke Path runs from Chepstow to Monmouth on the east bank of the Wye and meets the Wye Valley Walk again at Hay-on-Wye.

THE southern section of the Wye Valley Walk, a waymarked long distance route between the border town of Chepstow in Gwent and the market town of Hay-on-Wye in Powys, was developed in the mid-1970s, and has since seen considerable improvements. Despite starting and ending in Wales, this 75-mile section described here traverses mainly English soil, passing through the heart of the Wye Valley Area of Outstanding Natural Beauty. The lower Wye valley, between Chepstow and Monmouth, is perhaps the better-known section of the route as it parallels the most southerly part of the Offa's Dyke Path on the opposite side of the valley. The middle and upper sections, while less well frequented, are, however, equally charming and offer a splendid introduction to old Herefordshire.

A northern section, from Hay-on-Wye to Rhayader (some 35 miles) has been developed by Powys County Council, who produce a guide to the route (Powys County Council, Shire Hall, Llandridnod Wells, Powys LD1 5LG). This extends the walk into mid Wales, passing Glasbury, Builth Wells and Newbridge.

The appeal of the Wye Valley Walk is undoubtedly the variety of landscape

Tintern, romantic ruin in a romantic setting

through which it passes: the river in its upper reaches meanders gently through the red sandstone plains of Herefordshire, only to become increasingly dramatic in its lower reaches. This has come about because of an upward land movement resulting in the river carving deeply incised meanders and spectacular gorge-like channels in order to reach sea level at its estuary beyond Chepstow. The walk leaves the lush riverside meadows to climb the thickly wooded slopes of eastern Gwent, the undulating pastures of the Woolhope Dome and Herefordshire's high hill, Merbach. Paths through orchards, down green lanes, into churchyards and old quarters of borderland towns begin to unfold the subtle charm of the area which has barely been touched by industrialisation. Apart from in the more popular locations in lower Wye, the walker will share the route with few others. It is quiet and makes for a pleasant few days' rambling, whatever the season.

While the Wye Valley Walk can, of course, be walked in either direction, there is a stronger feeling of adventure and prospect when walking the route northwards, from Chepstow to the river's source.

Chepstow is a good starting point: as well as being served well by road, it has a daily rail service from Cardiff and Birmingham. Hereford also has trains from these places, as well as from Manchester and London. The other towns and villages *en route,* while no longer being served by rail, enjoy for the most part an acceptable level of bus services for a rural community, allowing a cut-off point almost anywhere. Sunday buses are a rarity, with links between Hay-on-Wye, Hereford and Ross-on-Wye only. Nevertheless, it is perfectly feasible to walk shorter sections of the route, particularly in the lower Wye, using local buses to ferry you between town and village or vice versa.

The walk, for the most part, avoids metalled roads but there is one exception where it follows a main road and then back lanes between Sugwas Pool and Byford, to the west of Hereford. This also happens to be gentle, open farming land which is pleasant but far less attractive than other parts of the route. Other than this, the remainder is guaranteed to bring interest to the walker, whether it be discovering the river as an

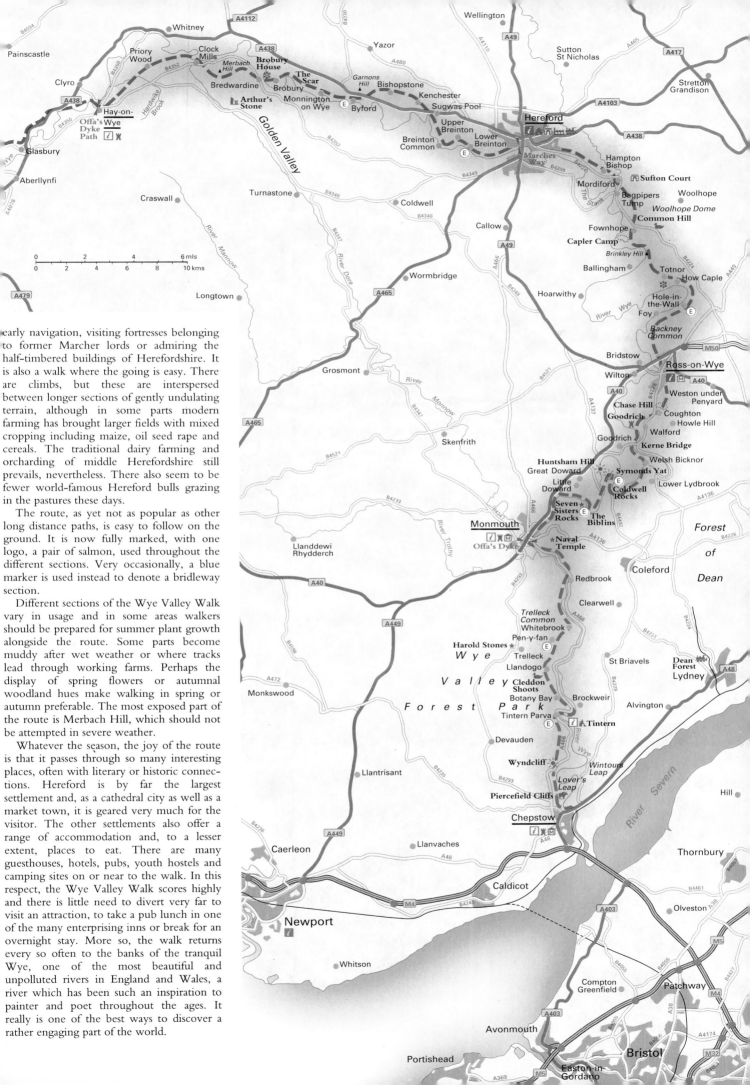

early navigation, visiting fortresses belonging to former Marcher lords or admiring the half-timbered buildings of Herefordshire. It is also a walk where the going is easy. There are climbs, but these are interspersed between longer sections of gently undulating terrain, although in some parts modern farming has brought larger fields with mixed cropping including maize, oil seed rape and cereals. The traditional dairy farming and orcharding of middle Herefordshire still prevails, nevertheless. There also seem to be fewer world-famous Hereford bulls grazing in the pastures these days.

The route, as yet not as popular as other long distance paths, is easy to follow on the ground. It is now fully marked, with one logo, a pair of salmon, used throughout the different sections. Very occasionally, a blue marker is used instead to denote a bridleway section.

Different sections of the Wye Valley Walk vary in usage and in some areas walkers should be prepared for summer plant growth alongside the route. Some parts become muddy after wet weather or where tracks lead through working farms. Perhaps the display of spring flowers or autumnal woodland hues make walking in spring or autumn preferable. The most exposed part of the route is Merbach Hill, which should not be attempted in severe weather.

Whatever the season, the joy of the route is that it passes through so many interesting places, often with literary or historic connections. Hereford is by far the largest settlement and, as a cathedral city as well as a market town, it is geared very much for the visitor. The other settlements also offer a range of accommodation and, to a lesser extent, places to eat. There are many guesthouses, hotels, pubs, youth hostels and camping sites on or near to the walk. In this respect, the Wye Valley Walk scores highly and there is little need to divert very far to visit an attraction, to take a pub lunch in one of the many enterprising inns or break for an overnight stay. More so, the walk returns every so often to the banks of the tranquil Wye, one of the most beautiful and unpolluted rivers in England and Wales, a river which has been such an inspiration to painter and poet throughout the ages. It really is one of the best ways to discover a rather engaging part of the world.

Chepstow
Monmouth

CHEPSTOW

TINTERN

APPROX. 5 MILES/8KM

OS Landranger 162
Start at grid reference ST 533 938
Start point: Chepstow Castle. There is a small car park here which can get busy in summer. Nearby Bank Street car park offers an alternative. Those arriving by train have a five-minute walk to the starting point.

The riverside town of Chepstow, or in Welsh Cas-Gwent, owes its existence primarily to its role as an early market town at a crossing-point on the tidal River Wye. It was the power-seeking Norman Marcher lords who brought military significance to the settlement when they set about building a castle of enormous proportions on the Welsh banks of the river and a wall around the town. In later centuries Chepstow flourished as the town became known as an importer of wines and yew and an exporter of wood products. Trade waned during the last century and in recent decades Chepstow has settled into the ways of a dormitory town, although it still retains considerable character and spirit of independence.

The Wye Valley Walk starts from Chepstow Castle, climbing through a delightful dell into Welsh Street. There is a tedious ten-minute walk up to a school and leisure centre where the path is coralled and littered to Alcove wood. The walk leads through the old Piercefield estate, woodland laid out for leisure purposes by Valentine Morris in the 18th century before his money ran out. The path keeps close to Chepstow racecourse, well-known for its National Hunt and Flat Racing Meetings, as it continues to curve left above Piercefield cliffs and beyond to Giant's Cave – a cave which has given rise to all manner of yarns, mostly spurious. Judging by the dimensions of the cavern, the giant must have been very cramped. The Walk proceeds to Lover's Leap and other such locations befitting the romantic walks devised for visitors 200 years or so ago. There are also views, between the tree cover, across a large loop in the Wye, to the ancient church at Lancaut.

The path climbs up to picnic tables between tall beech trees and by the A466. Cross here with extreme caution and proceed up an access track to another car park in what was an old limestone working, one of many such small workings in this area. The way is marked either to the left for those who seek the easiest ascent of Wyndcliff or to the right, up the 365 steps, which is far more of an adventure, even if negotiated at a steady pace. The path narrows and swerves left, soon to climb the stone steps originally built in 1828 and restored by army recruits in the early 1970s. The woodland is a remnant of a forest neither planted nor much-husbanded by humans through the centuries, despite its becoming a tourist attraction in the last century.

Climb to a viewpoint known as The Eagle's Nest and pause for breath – the ascent is something in the order of 700ft (200m). Here there are exceptional views

Chepstow Castle, set defiantly by the river

GUIDE BOX

Places to visit
Chepstow. The Castle (Cadw) is the main attraction in the town, standing majestically above the Wye. It is managed by Cadw: Welsh Historic Monuments and is open all year but hours vary. Opposite is the Stuart Crystal Visitor Centre (open all year). Chepstow is a compact walled town which is easily walked and the town's small Museum reflects mainly its maritime heritage. It is open from March to October.

Tintern Abbey. Built by monks of the Cistercian order in the early 12th century, the ruined abbey stands in what must be one of the prettiest settings imaginable. Open all year. Tintern also has its own Parva Farm Vineyard and shop, a restored Abbey Mill, which includes a craft shop (open all year), and the Tintern Old Station Visitor Centre (open April to end October). There are also several local walks written up in two leaflets available from the Tourist Information Centre.

Brockweir. There is a pottery in the Old Malthouse and Brockweir Glass at the Olde Post Office. Local walks to Tintern and surrounding areas are waymarked.

Monmouth. Monmouth is an attractive town to walk and The Castle and Regimental Museum (open all year, daily in summer, Saturdays, Sundays and Bank Holidays in winter) and the Nelson Museum (open all year, daily) give a history of the town's development. Agincourt Square, with its fine shire hall and contrasting statues of Henry V and Charles Rolls, is most attractive, with hotels and inns bedecked with flowers.

Car parking
Principal car parks are at Chepstow (grid ref. ST 535 943), Wyndcliff (ST 527 972), Tintern Abbey (SO 533 002), Tintern Old Station (SO 537 006), Monmouth (SO 508 128).

Public transport
Chepstow is served by British Rail. There is a regular bus service, except on Sundays, between Chepstow and Monmouth, calling at villages *en route*, such as Tintern, Brockweir and Redbrook. Monmouth is also served by a regular bus from Newport, except on Sundays.

Accommodation
There is ample accommodation at Chepstow, Tintern and Monmouth, as well as provision in the villages *en route*. Camp sites are available at Chepstow, Brockweir, Llandogo, St Briavels Common (off the route) and Monmouth. There are youth hostels at St Briavels and Monmouth. The *Wye Valley Walk Map Pack* includes a Camp Sites Supplement with up-to-date information about the availability of camping pitches along the route. See under Detailed Guide, page 132 for address.

down the Wye to cliffs named Wintour's Leap after Sir John Wintour, a Royalist who escaped capture by scrambling down the cliffs, Parliamentarians hot on his heels.

The going is easier, however, to Tintern. The path progresses through the appropriately named Minepit and Black Cliff woods, eventually emerging into a field which links the walk to Limekiln wood, where an old packhorse way, beautifully cool in summer, leads into Tintern opposite

Tintern Abbey. It was in these environs that William Wordsworth in 1788 wrote some of his loveliest lines and his contemporary JMW Turner captured the romantic dream of the abbey in a painting which is now in the Victoria and Albert Museum. The scene is almost the same today, 200 years on, and a visit to the abbey is obligatory.

Ⓔ *Some walkers may want to catch the local bus back into Chepstow from this point (grid ref. SO 533 001) or make their way back along the other side of the valley using Offa's Dyke Path, a walk of approximately 7 miles. From the abbey, walk into the village and, by an imaginatively restored abbey quay and mill, bear right across the old railway bridge (grid ref. SO 528 003). The path leads up the gorge to meet the national trail, where the walker bears right for Chepstow.*

TINTERN

MONMOUTH

APPROX. 11 MILES/18KM

OS Landranger 162
Start at grid reference SO 533 001
Start point: The entrance to Tintern Abbey, where there is a car park (often busy in summer) and Tourist Information Office. Those using the bus to travel to the start of this section will find that it stops by the abbey on the A466.

The walk bears right from the abbey through the village, between inns, guesthouses and shops, to cut off right, opposite The Wye Valley Hotel. It passes between houses and to Tintern Church before following the riverside for a short stretch to the old trackbed of the Monmouth-to-Chepstow railway, built in 1876 with great expectation on the part of the shareholders but in fact surviving less than 100 years. It is hard to imagine that Tintern was at one time the centre of a 16th-century iron-working business, some remains still being visible in the Angiddy Brook area. It was also the first British location to mould brass objects.

The path leads to the restored Victorian Tintern railway station and onwards to the village of Brockweir, where the path climbs up an embankment to the bridge. It is worth stepping across the bridge to Brockweir, at one time an ancient ferry point. It was also one of the main transhipment points for goods brought upstream on the tide by cargo vessels known as trows, to be transferred at the old quay to much smaller, flat-bottomed boats heading upstream or to carts for overland journeys. The quayside, pottery, glassworks and Brockweir Country Inn are all worthy of exploration.

The Walk crosses the A466 and enters woodland once again, up a steep zig-zag path to Coed Beddick plantation and on to Botany Bay, another reflection of the maritime influence of the Wye on these parts. The path exits on to a metalled road by a large house, only to leave it almost immediately by a camping ground and

Tintern's old railway station

activity centre, one of many which have grown up in these parts during the past ten years or so. The path descends to another road and then climbs up to the Whitestone picnic area, where there are toilets, children's play amenities and picnic tables provided by the Forestry Commission. The path continues through commercial woodland of mainly larch and spruce, above Cleddon Shoots nature reserve and the village of Llandogo below. The walk rises up through the woods to cross a lane by Orchard Cottage.

A detour can be made by turning left here to the village of Trelleck, to see the three standing stones known as the Harold Stones. There can be no plausible connection with King Harold. They may be Bronze Age marker stones, indicating an important overland route. The village also has a long-standing well, Virtuous Well, which draws from several chalybeate springs. The church dates mainly from medieval times or possibly earlier.

The Wye Valley Walk can be regained by following Greenway Lane, out of the village, then a bridleway through the wooded Trelleck Common, going ahead at the road and then right, down the Whitebrook valley.

Ⓔ *There are buses back from Trelleck to Monmouth or Chepstow, Monday to Friday.*

The main route continues onwards at Orchard Cottage as signposted to Pen-y-fan. This next section is particularly pleasant in spring when bluebells and primroses are out and maybe even the rare Tintern spurge.

Once through Cuckoo Wood, the path emerges on to a narrow lane. Be careful to follow the waymarks through the isolated hamlet of Pen-y-fan, threaded as it is with lanes. The descent to Whitebrook, where there were once several working mills, brings the path back to a metalled road, where a right turn is made for the short ramble down to the dismantled railway track on the left. Follow this along a narrow and pretty part of the lower Wye valley up to Redbrook, to go by the friendly Boat Inn and then over the footbridge to the village, which was at one

time a nucleus of industrial activity with a brewery, several mills and a foundry. At the main road turn left, passing the garage and café/restaurant before rejoining the river bank once again for the final 2¹/₂ miles to the Wye Bridge at Monmouth. Monmouth is the birthplace of Henry V and was home to such famous and disparate characters as the valiant Lord Nelson and the industrious Charles Rolls, co-founder of the Rolls-Royce organisation. Standing at the confluence of the Wye and Monnow Rivers, the town dates back to Roman times but gained its strategic position in early medieval days, when a castle and other fortifications were built (including the impressive Monnow Gateway, which can be seen at the far end of Monnow Street). Monmouth is not quite the market town it used to be, but it has a lively atmosphere on Fridays and Saturdays when stalls are set out in Agincourt Square, very much the centre of town.

THE WYE TOUR

From the mid-18th to the mid-19th century it became fashionable to explore wild and scenically beautiful areas of Britain such as Cumbria or Snowdonia. The lower Wye Valley was one such place and many writers made their voyage of discovery up river, sometimes on a boat with a guide, and this valued experience became known as the Wye Tour. Despite this growth in early tourist activity and the further impact of the railways in the mid-to-late Victorian period, the area has survived remarkably well, the only major intrusion by humans being the quarrying of limestone and dolomite.

The early traveller would have stayed in many of the old inns that survive today and would have marvelled at the same views as we do well over 200 years later. It is remarkable that so little has changed, helped during the past two or three decades by the fact that the valley was designated an Area of Outstanding Natural Beauty in 1971. Its conservation depends on co-operation between landowners, local authorities and of course ourselves, the visitors.

Monmouth
Ross-on-Wye

OS Landranger 162
Start at grid reference SO 513 128
Start point: The Wye Bridge. There are two main car parks near to the Walk, the larger being off Monnow Street.

At Monmouth the walker rejoins the Wye at the Wye Bridge, dropping down to the left by a boathouse and towards Dixton Church. The walk then passes through a succession of riverside meadows, sandwiched between the main A40 road and the river itself. Care should be taken as in places the river bank has been heavily eroded. After 2 miles the road rises and diverts to the left while the river bends eastwards into a deep and ancient landscape. Here the River Wye has cut a channel between the high hills of Little and Great Doward on the one side and The Slaughter on the other. The area contains many reminders of early cave dwellers who

The Wye valley at Symonds Yat

inhabited the higher reaches of these hillsides. King Arthur's and Merlin's caves, for example, are estimated to date from Bronze Age times and bones of long-extinct wild animals have been found in early excavations of the latter. These are now in the City Museum in Hereford. The cave names derive, so local folklore has it, from the prolific writings of 12th-century chronicler Geoffrey of Monmouth, who is said to have assembled the King Arthur legends when at Monmouth Priory. It has even been suggested that the Arthurian treasure is buried in these parts.

Pass Wyastone Leys House, in the near distance on the left, and then join a wooded section beneath Seven Sisters Rocks through to meadows leading to The Biblins, where there is a suspension bridge built by the Forestry Commission. Cross the river to the Forest of Dean side of the Wye.

Ⓔ *Those seeking a circular route (approx 7¹/₂ miles) to and from Monmouth can leave the walk at The Biblins (grid ref. SO 549 144), returning by way of Lady Park Wood and beneath Far Hearkening rocks to Hadnock and by metalled road to the Wye Bridge at Monmouth.*

The Wye Valley Walk rejoins the old track of the railway from Monmouth to

Ross-on-Wye beneath The Slaughter. The name is the subject of some speculation, not in that it suggests a battle in previous times, but as to which battle. Some antiquarians suggest it was Caractacus's last stand against the Romans, others that it was the scene of a bloody battle between Saxons and Danes.

The path enters Symonds Yat East near the Saracen's Head public house, where a rare river chain ferry can be hailed to Symonds Yat West for a short diversion to other inns, shops and attractions. In fact, Symonds Yat is the most commercialised tourist location on the route. There is also a very steep path up from Symonds Yat East to Yat Rock, a well-known and often extremely busy viewpoint. The views over Herefordshire are exceptional. There are also toilet facilities and a refreshment point near by.

Follow the Wye Valley Walk along the river bank to the upper ferry, which serves the Olde Ferrie Inne at Symonds Yat West.

The path dovetails back to a metalled road and soon begins to skirt the lower wooded slopes of Huntsham Hill. It then passes beneath Coldwell Rocks. Peregrine falcons nest here every year, and they may also be seen over Coppet Hill, in the near distance. Once again, the path joins the old railway route near the river and then moves closer to the river bank, heading for the old works at Lydbrook before crossing the river by way of the disused railway bridge. Bearing right, the route passes below the youth hostel at Welsh Bicknor, at one time a rectory to the isolated church near by.

Ⓔ *A good circular walk (approx 2¹/₂ miles) from Symonds Yat follows the Wye Valley Walk to Welsh Bicknor (grid ref. SO 587 177) and returns along the opposite bank to Huntisham Bridge, beneath Coppet Hill. The path passes near to a sad family monument to their boy drowned hereabouts in 1804. Bear left over Huntisham Bridge to walk along a fairly busy road for a mile back to Symonds Yat.*

Once more the walk secures a position alongside the tranquil and relatively unpolluted Wye, a favourite with fishermen in search of trout, Wye salmon and chad. The path follows the river bank beneath steep, wooded slopes to Kerne Bridge, which dates from 1828. Before this time there was a ferry a short distance upstream. One famous passenger was Henry IV on his way up from Monmouth. He was met at this point by a breathless messenger who had ridden hard to catch the monarch to announce the birth of his son, Harry of Monmouth, the future King Henry V. The king was so elated that he presented the ferry and all the revenues from it to the overawed ferryman. To the left of the bridge is the site of Flanesford Priory, the ruins having been incorporated into holiday apartments adjacent to Flanesford Farm. Beyond stand the gaunt, red sandstone towers of Goodrich Castle, one of the many fortresses which reflect the turbulent times in this border zone known as the Marches.

KERNE BRIDGE

ROSS-ON-WYE

APPROX. 5 MILES/8KM

OS Landranger 162
Start at grid reference SO 582 188
Start point: Picnic site and car park at Kerne Bridge.

The walk out of Kerne Bridge is a steep one and the way is easily missed. From the car park, cross the B4228 road to the left of the Kerne Bridge inn. Turn right into the steep lane and then immediately left up a driveway between cottages. The track continues to wind its way up Leys Hill, crossing others, until it eventually bears left into woodland, and descends towards Walford. Before it reaches the village it climbs away again up to Bull's Hill, on to a metalled road, goes left and soon right by houses, along a path which

leads up to the road at Howle Hill. Look for the track which climbs the edge of the hill, but the walk itself shortly bears left, to descend to farm buildings in Coughton. Coughton is situated in a deep valley which at one time would have been a large loop of the Wye, but is now drained by a small tributary brook. The walk leaves farm buildings to climb through fields to Chase Hill and wood, where the overgrown ramparts of an Iron Age hillfort remain. It passes by Hill Farm and then sweeps down from Penyard Hill to pass Alton Court, now the home of a major activity holiday company, to Penyard Lane. Look carefully for the yellow arrows guiding the walker

The Olde Ferrie Inne, near Symonds Yat

through the back of Ross-on-Wye to the main car park by Wilton Bridge, a 16th-century structure that (with some restoration) has weathered many a flood.

Many walkers will want to bear right, however, at Prospect Walk, laid out by 17th-century philanthropist John Kyrle, who gave so much to the town and became known as 'The Man of Ross'. This leads to the commanding Ross Church, with its plague cross near by, and to the town centre, nestled around the 17th-century Market House that stands defiantly amid 20th-century traffic.

THE FOREST OF DEAN

The Royal Forest of Dean, to the south-east of the River Wye, covers an area of approximately 40 square miles of woodland, mostly owned and managed by the Forestry Commission. In addition to the miles of coniferous cover, there are tracts of ancient woods to be explored and the Forestry Commission has improved access to many parts of the forest in recent years. For centuries, the forest was the preserve of the kings and queens of England and their favoured nobility as a hunting ground, and penalties

for those caught in the act of poaching on these vast estates were dire.

In more recent times the Forest of Dean has been a mining area for both minerals and coal and several of the older workings can be seen throughout the forest. There are several local attractions in the forest including the ancient iron mines at Clearwell, the Dean Forest Railway, The Dean Heritage Centre (open all year), as well as the market towns of Cinderford, Coleford and Lydney.

Ross-on-Wye
Hereford

ROSS-ON-WYE

FOWNHOPE

APPROX. 11 MILES/18KM

OS Landranger 162, 149
Start at grid reference SO 592 239
Start point: The main car park before the Wilton Bridge, on the B4260 (elsewhere in Ross parking can be difficult). Buses from Hereford and Gloucester stop by the car park.

The route leaves the car park by way of a short underpass to join the riverside, a popular spot for canoeists, fishermen and strollers. The walk soon leaves town to pass beneath the 20th-century portals of the A40 main road, shortly joining the old track bed of the Hereford-to-Gloucester railway line, a much-loved rural railway which failed to survive the Beeching closures in the 1960s. The landscape is flatter here, with large fields of cereal crops, potatoes or oil seed rape. A little further on, the walk pulls away to the right, to skirt a loop of the river at Backney Common where, evidently, the commoners still have the right to remove gravel from the river bank. The walk then follows a contour line above the flood plain to join a metalled

road. Here the walker bears left towards Hole-in-the-Wall, a hamlet where there is an activity centre specialising in canoeing. It is thought that some of the buildings in this area were built from the masonry of an early castle, now completely dismantled. A suspension bridge links the hamlet to Foy Church, on the opposite bank, which dates mainly from the 11th century and is well worth the short diversion.

Ⓔ *To return to Ross-on-Wye, cross the suspension bridge (grid ref. SO 605 284), turn left to Foy Church and then on to Backney Common, Bridstow and Wilton Castle. It is mainly on roads. The circular walk is approximately 8 miles in all.*

This section of the walk offers very pleasant road-walking, with wide green verges leading down to the river bank. The path cuts off left shortly, before a cattle grid, to rejoin a path through fields to the sleepy hamlet of How Caple, named after the Capel family. Bear left on the metalled road (unless visiting How Caple Court, in which case turn right here). Turn right again after a few paces, to join a bridleway to Totnor, a small settlement gathered around a mill on a brook. The way is to the left, along a metalled road, before shortly turning left along a bridleway through rich arable

A still evening at Ross-on-Wye

GUIDE BOX

Places to visit
How Caple Court. The Edwardian gardens of How Caple Court and How Caple Church are well worth the 1/2-mile detour from the walk. Open May to September.

The Woolhope Dome. The topography of this area to the south-east of Hereford has fascinated naturalists and geologists for well over a century and led in the 1850s to the formation of a well-respected group known as the Woolhope Club. The upward thrust of the older Silurian limestones and shales has been weathered to form this rounded dome, often exposing beds of fossils in old workings. Both Fownhope and Woolhope are good starting points for exploring the countryside of the Woolhopes on foot. Not all paths, however, are clear and local walking guides should be consulted to select the better routes. In the parishes of Much Marcle on the other side of the Woolhopes, a Big Apple Festival is held each autumn.

Hereford, while being a cathedral city that attracts visitors from all over the world to see the *Mappa Mundi* exhibition, is very much a market place for the Welsh borderlands – witness the crowds on a Wednesday at the Cattle Market or in the Victorian Butter Market, The pedestrianised areas around High Town and Capuchin Lane down to the cathedral are enticingly full of small book and specialist interest shops. There are attractions to suit all tastes, including a Cider Museum (open all year), the Jacobean Old House (open all year, Monday to Saturday), the Churchill Gardens Museum (open all year, Tuesday to Saturday, plus Bank Holidays and Sundays April to September) and the St John Medieval Museum (open Easter to September, daily except Mondays, Fridays). Those who enjoy industrial history will favour the Bulmer Railway Centre (open only selected weekends), or the Broomy Hill Engines at the Hereford Waterworks Museum (open on some Sunday afternoons).

Car parking
The principal car parks are at Brinkley Hill picnic site near Capler Wood (grid ref. SO 587 314) and near Mordiford Bridge (SO 568 378), but neither offers many spaces. Hereford has several car parks. One of the least crowded is just south of the old Wye Bridge but parking is not easy as the city is very congested at times.

Public transport
Buses are rare between Ross-on-Wye and Fownhope. There is a Monday to Saturday service from Fownhope to Hereford via Mordiford.

Accommodation
There is some accommodation available in How Caple, Fownhope and Mordiford, and plenty in and around Hereford. See also under Detailed Guide, page 132.

farmland to Brinkley Hill and on, past Capler Lodge, to Capler Wood and the ramparts of an Iron Age hillfort of the same name. The walk then descends by Caplor Farm to join the B4224. Bear left for a short distance, then climb once again into the rich and undulating farmland of the Woolhope Dome through Lea and Paget Woods.

The walk then continues to Common Hill by way of a green track, across a metalled road and shortly left on another series of tracks to Nupend Farm. Near by is a nature reserve and an unusual monument to son of Fownhope and one-time prize boxer, Tom

Spring, who fought his way through to the English championship in the early 1820s before retiring to become landlord of Booth Hall public house in Hereford (which exists to this day). Just before Nupend Farm the walk meets the Fownhope-to-Woolhope road. Fownhope is ¹/₂ mile away to the left, a settlement which grew up not only as an agricultural community but also engaged in bark stripping for tanning purposes. The bark was despatched by boat on the River Wye and several lanes lead down from the village to the riverside, where there also used to be local ferries to Ballingham.

FOWNHOPE

HEREFORD

APPROX. 7 MILES/11KM

OS Landranger 149
Start at grid reference SO 577 344
Start point: Fownhope village, at the crossroads with one turning to the old forge, The Forge and the Ferry Inn, the other to Woolhope. There is limited on-street car parking in Fownhope village.

Fownhope lies just off the Wye Valley Walk but is an excellent place for access, accommodation and refreshment. Walk the short distance from the village centre along the road signposted to Woolhope at the crossroads near the Green Man Inn. As the road bends right, ¹/₂ mile along it, look for the Wye Valley Walk waymark directing the walker to the left by Nupend Farm. The path rises gently through rich farming country in a very quiet part of the Woolhope Dome to isolated cottages and then follows a bridleway down to the large farm at Hope Springs. Once through the farm buildings, bear left to the clustered houses of Bagpipers Tump and then go between orchards to pass by a mill in the village of Mordiford. The village was at one time a hive of local industry, with tanning and milling near by. As at Fownhope, the river was an important means of distributing goods, and research suggests that the River Lugg was also used for navigation purposes, possibly as far as Leominster, although it is difficult to see how, even when the river is full.

The Wye Valley Walk crosses the road and uses old back lanes through to the bridge at Mordiford. Those seeking refreshment should turn right to visit the Moon public house at Mordiford and muse awhile about the legend of the Mordiford dragon, a people-eating monster who was killed by a cunning convict fighting for a pardon. He hid in a cider barrel and when the dragon came for its habitual drink the criminal dealt it a deadly blow with an arrow through an opening. The poor convict did not receive his reprieve, however, for the dragon breathed one last revengeful blast of fire at him before expiring!

Mordiford Bridge, overlooked by the parish church, is thought to be the oldest bridge for miles around, with a part of one

14th-century arch still remaining. A mile from here, on slopes reaching to the Woolhopes, is the impressive Sufton Court, set in parkland landscaped by Humphrey Repton. Alongside is Old Sufton, a manor farm which illustrates additional building through the ages. There is a splendidly restored 18th-century dovecot near to it. Unfortunately none of these buildings is open to the public on a regular basis.

From Mordiford Bridge (grid ref. SO 575 374), there is an excellent circular walk via the village of Clouds (approximately 1¹/₂ miles north-east), waymarked throughout as 'The Mordiford Loop' and offering a morning or an afternoon's exploration of the Woolhope Dome.

At the far end of Mordiford Bridge, the walk bears right to follow the flood levee, or embankment, to the edge of Hampton Bishop, a village with several listed half-timbered houses and a delightful church, dating mainly from the 12th and 14th centuries. The path joins a track on the left which meets a metalled road. Turn right here and walk through the village until a path is joined on the right to cut across a pasture to the B4224 road near to the Bunch of Carrots public house. Almost opposite is another path which leads up to another levee known as the Stanx, this time protecting farms from the Wye at times of flood (although it failed to do this during the floods of 1960 and had to be reinforced). The walk leaves this to follow the river bank

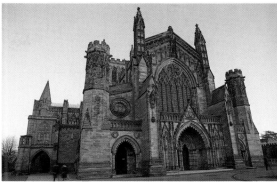

Hereford Cathedral: its treasures include the Mappa Mundi *and the Chained Library*

for a short distance before sweeping back to the main road on the outskirts of Hereford.

The Wye Valley Walk bears left along the B4224 to descend towards the city, passing by an old established public house, the Salmon. Once under the railway bridge it bears left down to Hereford and on to the edge of the Castle Green. Those diverting into Hereford should turn right here and then shortly bear left to pass by the Castle Pool and into St Owen's Street, where a left turn is made to St Peter's Square, where the Tourist Information Centre can be found. The Wye Valley Walk, however, bears left down to the Victoria suspension bridge over the Wye. Turn right on the opposite side and walk through the Bishop's Meadows to come out on to the old Wye Bridge.

Hereford

Hay-on-Wye

HEREFORD

BREDWARDINE

APPROX. 14 MILES/22KM

OS Landranger 149
Start at grid reference SO 508 396
Start point: The old Wye Bridge in
Hereford, where there are two car parks just
to the south.

The Wye Valley Walk sets out from
Hereford unceremoniously beneath the new
Wye Bridge and along a well-used riverside
route towards Hunderton. Here the walk
crosses a path known as Marches Way, an
unofficial borderland trail between Chester
and Cardiff. At the old railway bridge, climb
up the steps and cross over the bridge to
drop down the embankment on to the
opposite side of the river. Rejoin a riverside
path by playing fields and pass the distinctive
brick tower of Herefordshire Waterworks
Museum on the right. The path soon leads
into open countryside for a mile walk to the
very rural hamlet of Lower Breinton, where
the National Trust now owns a moated site
thought to date from the 12th century.
Adjacent is Breinton Church, dating from a
similar period but much restored in the mid-
19th century.

Ⓔ *For those seeking a short circular walk out of
Hereford to Lower Breinton, it is possible to return
from Breinton Church (grid ref. 472 395) along
quiet back lanes to Broomy Hill and the city.*

Walk through the National Trust car park
and look for a path on the left that cuts
through an orchard, across an access road and
by a house. The walk then bears left through

fields to meet a metalled road at Upper
Breinton. Go right, and then left at the
junction. The Wye Valley Walk then follows
a track by Manor House Farm on the left
which soon peters out into a path over fields
to Breinton Common, where it becomes an
enclosed lane again. It comes out by houses
and bungalows on to a metalled road.

Turn right here and follow this quiet road
to the A438, where the walk bears left to
pass by the traditional Kite's Nest public
house at Sugwas Pool. Continue along this
main road and at the next main junction turn
right along quieter lanes, to walk through
the hamlet of Kenchester, the site of the
Roman town *Magnis*. Remains of mosaic
floors and other artefacts have been found
and are now in the Hereford City Museum.
The walk follows a Roman road through the
village of Bishopstone to a crossroads,
continuing ahead past farms on the Garnons
estate. The parkland is the work of
Humphrey Repton again. The road bears
left beyond Home Farm to meet the A438
once more and then turns right for a short
distance before turning left into Byford, a
hamlet of half-timbered cottages, handsome
court and pretty church.

Ⓔ *It is possible to shorten the Hereford-to-
Bredwardine section of the route by catching a bus
out to Byford or back from there, but this requires
careful planning as the service is very limited.
Some walkers might prefer to catch a bus to Byford
and then walk through to Hay-on-Wye.*

Bear right after the church to follow a
bridleway through acres of cider apple
orchards cultivated by the world's largest
cider maker, HP Bulmer. Information boards
welcome the walker and explain modern
cultivation of cider apples. The bridleway
leads into the churchyard of Monnington

Francis Kilvert's grave, Bredwardine

GUIDE BOX

Places to visit
Brobury Gardens and Gallery. The walk passes by
Victorian Brobury Gardens, seven acres of formal
and semi-formal gardens stretching down to the
Wye. These are open from May to September
but the Court Gallery, which has a collection of
old and contemporary watercolours as well as
antique prints, is open all year.

Bredwardine. The church, situated near to the site
of Bredwardine Castle, is visited by many who
are intrigued by the writings of Francis Kilvert. It
stands very much as it would have looked when
Kilvert was the vicar here in the late 1870s,
before his untimely death. A leaflet is available in
the church with details about local places to visit,
including the Neolithic burial chamber at
Arthur's Stone (open all year).

Hay-on-Wye. This Welsh border town, nestled
on a slope between the Dulas Brook and the
River Wye, has remarkably retained its market
atmosphere – especially on Thursdays, when
there are stalls in the streets – despite the
overwhelming influence of books. The town has
become known as the second-hand book capital
of the world, with at least 20 shops offering all
manner of general and specialist texts. People
travel from all over the world to visit them. The
Castle, which dates originally from the 12th
century, has been a prominent feature in the
town. It has been ransacked and rebuilt many
times over the centuries and is now being
restored after a fire in the late 1970s. The narrow
streets of Hay fall away from the castle to the
riverside and give this little market town a rather
special feeling.

Car parking
There are no recognised car parks on the route
between Hereford and Hay-on-Wye except a
small area of parking provided by the National
Trust at Breinton (grid ref. SO 473 396). There
is limited street parking in some of the villages,
such as Bredwardine and Priory Wood.

Public transport
Hay-on-Wye is served by buses from Hereford
via the Golden Valley and from Brecon on
Mondays to Saturdays. On Sundays a special
leisure service runs between the same
destinations but by way of Bredwardine. It is
known as the Kilvert Connection, is very useful
for point-to-point walking on The Wye Valley
Walk (a leaflet is available at local Tourist
Information Offices).

Accommodation
There is a good accommodation base in
Bredwardine and Middlewood and to a lesser
extent on the rest of the route. Near
Monnington there is a youth hostel (at Staunton-
on-Wye). There is camping available near Hay-
on-Wye. See also under Detailed Guide, page
132.

Church and Court, the latter dating mainly
from the 17th century but having some
remnants of 13th- and 15th-century
building. It is not open to the public on a
regular basis. One previous dwelling on this
site is said to have been the last home of the
exiled, medieval Welsh Nationalist leader,
Owain Glyndwr. This may have been
possible, given that several of his daughters
had settled in these parts but whether he
lived here or not cannot be substantiated.
The woodwork of the church is exceptional
and is probably the craftsmanship of John

Abel, King's Carpenter to Charles I. He was also a capable designer, and historians suggest that he was architect of several major half-timbered buildings in the county. He is buried in Sarnesfield churchyard, a few miles away. Locals say that his tomb bears an inscription that he carved himself, aged 90.

Follow the green swath of path to a metalled road. Here bear left and then right to join the 1-mile avenue, Monnington Walk, between specially planted Scots pine and yews and probably the best surviving example in Britain. It ends at a metalled road at Brobury Scar. Bear left and left again at the next junction to drop down to redbrick Bredwardine Bridge where, on the other side, a little link path cuts off left through the old castle ramparts to Bredwardine parish church. This is the resting place of famous 19th-century diarist, Reverend Francis Kilvert, who unfortunately succumbed to peritonitis on returning home from his honeymoon, at the age of 38. He described life in Victorian times at nearby Clyro and here with such skill that his diary is rated as a minor classic. Some of his diaries were destroyed by his wife as they contained references to their courtship, and most of the remainder were disposed of by a descendant who also felt that some of the entries were of dubious moral value.

The walk follows the church drive into the village centre, to pass to the right of The Red Lion public house. There is a strenuous circular walk from Bredwardine, climbing Merbach Hill, then bearing left for Arthur's Stone, a Neolithic burial mound, before returning on roads to Bredwardine.

Sheep graze peacefully on the riverside pastures below Hay-on-Wye

BREDWARDINE

HAY-ON-WYE

APPROX. 9 MILES/14KM

OS Landranger 148
Start at grid reference SO 331 445
Start point: The Red Lion, Bredwardine. There is very limited street parking in Bredwardine.

The climbing really begins at Bredwardine, for within a mile or so is the highest point of the route, Merbach Hill. Standing at over 1040ft (317m), it offers views for many miles around. The road out of Bredwardine to the right of the Red Lion, becomes very steep. At the top of the first bank look out for an access road off to the right, the direction of the walk. Beyond the cottage, however, it climbs to the left, up to Woolla Farm beyond, to an isolated barn. The path soon reaches a bracken-clad hillside, where the walker has to bear right and very shortly left. This clear path leads to the right of the summit, but many walkers divert to the triangulation point to pause awhile, especially on a summer's eve when the sun is setting over the Wye below.

The path drops down to a lane which bears right near Croft Farm. This leads to the main B4352 road at Clock Mills, with the Castlefield public house to the right. The walk turns left and at Clock Mills Bridge bears right to skirt Clock Mills and Castleton Farms before joining the old track bed of the Golden Valley Railway, a very rural railway which survived until 1950, despite making chronic losses throughout its existence. It was at the time, however, a lifeline to the community, before the advent of the bus and car.

This soon brings the walker to a metalled narrow road where the walk bears left up to Priory Wood, an isolated and scattered hamlet named after a former Cluniac priory.

One of a score or so of secondhand bookshops in Hay-on-Wye

Within ¼ mile the walk cuts left up a path to a small common between roads. It then bears right on the higher road and, at the austere-looking chapel, cuts left across a paddock to another metalled road. Turn left to walk a few paces down to a junction and then walk along a narrow path adjacent to houses to pass by Priory Farm and on to another metalled road. The walk turns left, but look for a stile very shortly on the right. This leads through fields first above the Hardwicke Brook, then cross it and onwards towards Hay-on-Wye. It crosses a metalled road by a bungalow and then goes forward to another stile, leading to the Dulas Brook and into Wales – although the route from Bredwardine feels distinctly Welsh in its entirety. This is the heart of the Marches, where England meets Wales, where culture and custom change within a few short miles, regardless of county boundaries.

The path dips down to a ford and then rises up to a field. The walker heads slightly left here to the left of a house. The walk dips down to a bridge and up to a narrow road leading into Hay-on-Wye by way of Heol-y-Dwr, then left at The Black Lion to Oxford Road and right for Tourist Information and buses to Hereford and Brecon.

Hay-on-Wye has a number of local walks as well as being the meeting point of Offa's Dyke Path national trail. It is an excellent place to finish a walk.

HALF-TIMBERED HOUSES

The vernacular architecture of timbered and half-timbered housing is a distinctive part of the Marches, the frontierland between England and Wales. In Herefordshire, the tradition of constructing half-timbered buildings was very common in earlier centuries. Some date from medieval times and others from the last century, when the use of brick, whitewash and wood was very popular. The practice has continued into the 1990s as a few local companies have begun to convert barns, renovate old cottages and in some cases build new properties, using designs and styles from earlier periods.

Many of the villages in western Herefordshire have half-timbered houses and these have been dubbed 'Black and White'. There is a fascinating Black and White Trail through these settlements, and a walking trail book is available from local tourist information offices.

CENTRAL
ENGLAND
&
EAST ANGLIA

Staffordshire Way

COMPLETE ROUTE
MOW COP TO KINVER EDGE
92 MILES/148KM

SECTION COVERED
MOW COP TO ABBOTS BROMLEY
44 MILES/71KM

AMONG the many delights of the Staffordshire Way, not the least is the sheer variety of countryside it passes through, a spectrum which few of the long distance paths can hope to match. From the tough and demanding gritstone hills in the north, affording truly magnificent views across England, the Way passes through wooded valleys, by river, lake and canal, through quiet and beautiful nature reserves, across ancient pastureland and through seas of corn and plough. It is almost as though it is attempting to show the walker as many aspects of English scenery as possible along its length.

The Way was established by Staffordshire County Council, using public rights of way and paths on which access has been granted, and was completed in 1983. In its entirety it runs the whole length of the county, from Mow Cop to Kinver Edge, a distance of 92 miles, but here we confine ourselves to the northern half of the route, a 44-mile section from Mow Cop to Abbots Bromley. Staffordshire, like the Staffordshire Way itself, is a county of great variety, and it contains not only great and important industrial areas such as the Potteries but also some of the wildest and most lovely scenery in England. The Staffordshire Way confines itself to the rural areas, yet passes very close to urban ones, and it is a matter of some satisfaction that it is highly accessible to very large numbers of people who can leave the towns and cities and, in a comparatively short time, be breathing the fresh air and enjoying the freedom of the countryside.

Typical Staffordshire half-timbered buildings in Abbots Bromley

We have chosen to walk the Staffordshire Way from north to south for no better reason than that in doing so we are walking in the main towards the sun. There are a few steep climbs involved, particularly in the north, but nothing that should challenge the resolve of the average walker. On the whole the Way is well signposted by waymarks of a yellow or blue arrowhead incorporating the words 'Staffordshire Way' and the Staffordshire Knot symbol. For reasons of space, detailed directions are given only when considered necessary. Walkers who require more specific instructions are referred to the booklet *The Staffordshire Way* (see page 145), which is strongly recommended.

There is much of interest along the route. To begin with, the Way stretches north-east from Mow Cop, sandwiched between the towns of Congleton and Biddulph, with the vast sprawl of Stoke-on-Trent and Newcastle-under-Lyme not far to the south. It stays close to the county border, wandering briefly into Cheshire, as it follows the dramatic gritstone ridge of Congleton Edge eventually climbing to a height of 1100 ft (335m) at the pinnacle of 'the Cloud' hill. From here the views extend to Liverpool and the Welsh hills to the west and into the Peak District to the east.

The Way then turns south for the rest of its journey, descending at first through lovely country to a dismantled railway line which leads to Rudyard Reservoir, and then following the canal feeder which runs parallel to the River Churnet through quiet meadows and woods. Leaving the town of Leek to the east, it then rises and falls through Longsdon and Hollinhay woods before embarking on a fascinating and easy-walking section along the Caldon Canal, once an important commercial thoroughfare as various relics suggest, and now an attractive waterway for holidaymakers.

A steep and exacting climb from the canal takes the walker to old-fashioned farmland around the villages of Kingsley and Kingsley Holt before descending once again to the beautiful and unspoilt Churnet valley and from there to the romantic and wooded nature reserve of Hawksmoor, through Ousal Dale and up a sharp ascent through Toothill Wood to Alton, where the outlandish sounds of the amusement park mingle with the lowing of cattle and the bleating of sheep.

From Alton the Way follows an ancient packhorse route past Denstone and then continues to Rocester, after which it cheekily crosses the River Dove into Derbyshire for a short distance. Keeping to the eastern side of Uttoxeter, the Way then runs due south through Bagot's Park to its destination in the village of Abbots Bromley.

All along the route are reminders of the area's early involvement with the Industrial Revolution, be they flint mills, smelting works or other types of buildings, many now derelict and forlorn, some restored and open to inspection, and occasional ones never out of commission. There is also a wealth of wild flowers, trees, birds and wildlife to be observed, the species changing as the geology and countryside change. Access to the Way is easy, and accommodation can be found at most of the towns and villages. There are also many places of interest to be found both on and off the path, and these are detailed in the text.

There is something particularly satisfying about walking the Staffordshire Way. Attention has already been drawn to its great variety, but there is something more than this. In the heart of England, stretching from north to south of a busy, largely industrialised county, there is this wonderful route which rises and falls over the changing landscape, taking the walker back in time to a different and more peaceful world, offering fresh air and freedom, a certain amount of challenge, easy walking for most of the way, and above all the guarantee that whatever else the traveller may come across along the way, it will not be even a fleeting second's boredom.

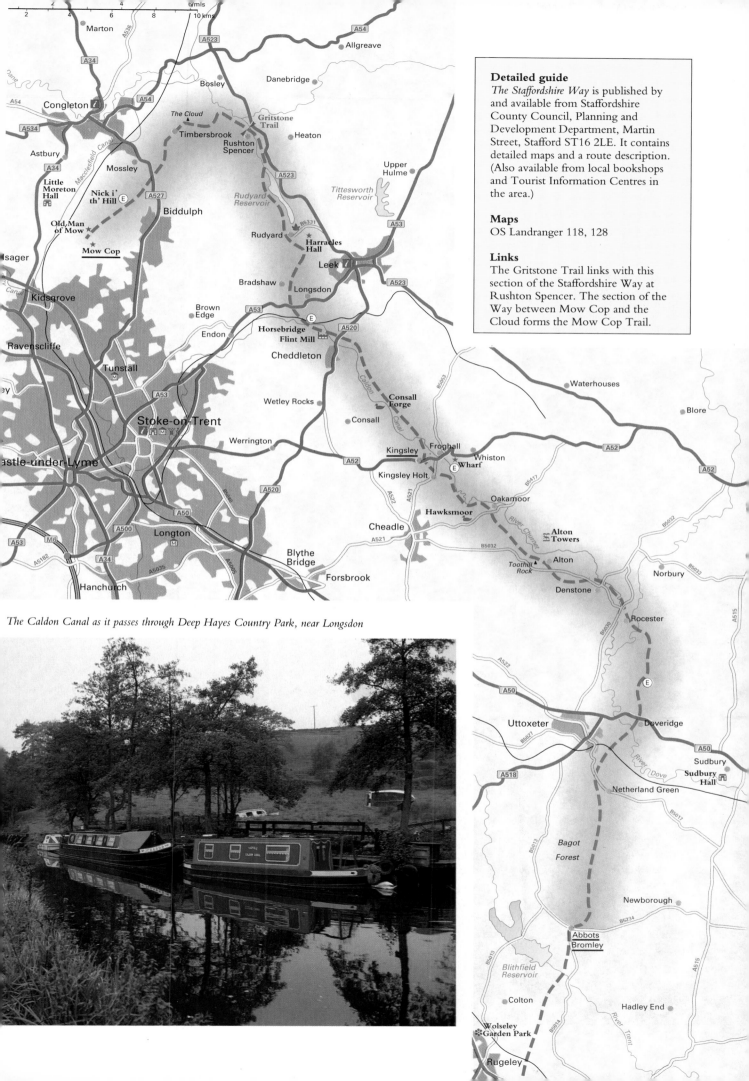

The Caldon Canal as it passes through Deep Hayes Country Park, near Longsdon

Mow Cop

Kingsley

MOW COP

RUDYARD

APPROX. 12½ MILES/20KM

OS Landranger 118
Start at grid reference SJ 857 572
Start point: The car park at Mow Cop, for which there is a modest charge. Ample space is available.

The first section of the route, between Mow Cop and the Cloud, is also known as the 'Mow Cop Trail', and is waymarked by arrows with the letter M. It basically follows the boundary between Cheshire and Staffordshire, straying into each of the counties in turn. Mow Cop Castle is a very early example of a folly, built in 1754 by Randle Wilbraham, to be admired from nearby Rode Hall. Mow Cop is also the birthplace of the Primitive Methodist movement, founded at the beginning of the 19th century by Hugh Bourne, a carpenter, and William Clowes, a potter, who organised open air meetings here. The local types of stone, millstone grit and whetstone, have both proved valuable in the past for a variety of industrial uses. There are magnificent all-round views from the trig. point (1099ft/335m) above the Old Man of Mow, as the pillar of rock that survived the quarrying all round it is called.

Indeed this part of the Staffordshire Way is hardly short on views, demonstrated by the walk along Congleton Edge on path and road. This gritstone ridge is the western boundary of the Pennines, and on a clear day it is possible to see right over Cheshire and as far as Merseyside and the Welsh mountains.

After the viewpoint at Cheshire's Close the road swings round to the left and the Way continues straight ahead along Edge Hill, through Willocks Wood, descending to Nick i' the Hill after ½ mile.

(E) *A circular walk of some 6 miles back to Mow Cop may be taken from Nick i' the Hill. Leave the route at grid ref. SJ 876 599, taking lanes and footpaths to Gillow Heath. Follow the lane to Towerhill Farm, turn right, take the second footpath on your left, and turn right along the road for the short distance back to Mow Cop.*

From Nick i' the Hill the Way now descends via Whitemore Farm to the disused railway which runs parallel to the A527. The track crosses the main road after ¾ mile, and then crosses Reade's Lane. The Way leaves the railway after another ¼ mile and approaches the Cloud by a series of footpaths and charmingly named lanes – Brook, Weathercock, Acorn and Gosberryhole. Just before the plantation on the Cloud itself (the trees obscure the remains of an Iron Age hillfort, while a short distance to the south, at Bridestones, there is an impressive Neolithic burial chamber) bear left where the paths divide and make for the summit (1125ft/343m), where once again the views are superb. To the north-west can be seen the giant reflector of the Jodrell Bank radio telescope.

From the Cloud take the south-easterly path downhill to the road to Ravensclough

The sham ruin known as Mow Cop Castle, built as a folly in the 18th century

GUIDE BOX

Places to visit
Froghall Wharf is situated on the Caldon Canal at Foxt Road, Froghall, near Stoke-on-Trent. From here, twice a week in summer months, three-hour trips aboard a traditional narrow boat are run through the beautiful Churnet valley, and a great deal about the history of the canal can be seen and learnt.

Little Moreton Hall (NT), 4 miles south-west of Congleton on the A34, is one of the most perfect examples of a half-timbered house in the country. Surrounded by a moat and built round a cobbled courtyard, it boasts a wainscoted long gallery, early plasterwork and wall paintings. Open April to September, Wednesday to Sunday; October, Saturday and Sunday.

Rudyard Lake is a 2-mile long reservoir of 180 acres situated just 3 miles north of Leek, off the A523. It is the site of much sailing activity, and a boat hire service, aimed specifically at beginners, is now available.

Tittesworth Reservoir, near Leek, covers an area of 188 acres, and the land surrounding it provides a haven for many species of flora and fauna. The general public are encouraged to walk along the 4½-mile nature trail, taking about three hours.

Car parking
Principal car parks along the route are at Mow Cop (grid ref. SJ 857 572), at Cheshire's Close (SJ 868 588), at Rushton Spencer (SJ 936 626), at the northern end of Rudyard Reservoir (SJ 938 611), and two at the southern end of Rudyard Reservoir (SJ 952 582 and SJ 958 579), at Deep Hayes Country Park (SJ 962 534) and at Consall Nature Park (SJ 994 484).

Public transport
The nearest British Rail stations to this part of the route are at Congleton, Kidsgrove, Stoke-on-Trent, Longton and Blythe Bridge. Places on or near this part of the route served by bus include Mow Cop, Rudyard Reservoir, Leek, Cheddleton, Kingsley, Churnet and Froghall.

Accommodation
Most of the towns and villages along or near the route offer accommodation in the form of bed-and-breakfasts, pubs, guesthouses or hotels. There are also a limited number of camp sites, camping barns and youth hostels. The pamphlet *The Staffordshire Way* and, especially, the brochure *Staffordshire Moorlands in the Southern Peak District* have detailed information about all sorts of accommodation. Both are issued free, by Staffordshire County Council and Staffordshire Moorlands District Council respectively, and are available at Tourist Information Centres.

Farm and then down through beautiful Ravensclough Wood, over the stream and across the water meadows in the valley of the River Dane, until the Way joins the southerly route of the now dismantled Churnet Valley Railway. Past Rushton Spencer and to the right, a footpath leads to the charming little church of St Lawrence, standing by itself in the fields, with its weatherboard bell-turret. It dates from the 17th century.

The Way then leads to Rudyard Reservoir, passing by on the west side. The lake was created in 1831 to supply the Caldon Canal to its south and has become not only a famous beauty spot but also a

Rudyard Reservoir: the Way passes alongside

favourite place for sailors and water sports enthusiasts. Walkers are well catered for too, there being a 5-mile circular walk around its shores. The writer Rudyard Kipling was named after the lake, where his parents met for the first time in 1863. His father, John Lockwood Kipling, was an architectural sculptor who had a hand in designing the Wedgwood Memorial Institute in Burslem. The potter Josiah Wedgwood founded the famous firm that still bears his name (the Wedgwood Visitor Centre at Barlaston is well worth a visit) and the influence of the family is everywhere in these parts. Half-way along the lake, indeed, the Way passes by Cliffe Park Hall, an interesting gothic house built for the Wedgwood family in about 1830.

At the southern end of the lake the path becomes a track giving access to various houses. Turn right into Lake Road and then turn left after 100yds at the footpath sign down the path to the dam, and then right along the canal feeder, emerging on to Rudyard Road at Rudyard village.

RUDYARD

KINGSLEY

APPROX. 10³/₄ MILES/17KM

OS Landranger 118, 128
Start at grid reference SJ 958 579
Start point: From the more southerly of the two car parks at Rudyard, just off the B5331.

The next section of the Staffordshire Way is for the most part very easy walking, with rises and falls at both ends, and extremely enjoyable. From the B5331 the route follows the canal feeder past delightful meadows and the twin nature reserves of Cowhay and Longsdon Woods. The path can be muddy at certain times of the year. Harracles Hall, a Georgian home of the Wedgwood family, is situated to the north-east of Cowhay Wood. Just to the east is the town of Leek. Leek is an ancient settlement which became increasingly industrialised from the 18th century onwards but has managed to remain a reasonably sized market town, enhanced by the fine country around it. The canal engineer, James Brindley started out as a millwright here.

At the A53 the Way crosses the feeder and continues up through the southern tip of

Longsdon Wood, past some cottages, left along the lane, left along the A53 for a short distance, and right into Mollatts Wood Road. It then continues down past Hollinhay Wood, on to the road at Horse Bridge, across the Leek Arm canal bridge, over the railway bridge and down on to the Caldon Canal at the next bridge, turning left (east) along the towpath.

Ⓔ *For a circular walk of some 10 miles back to Rudyard, leave the prescribed route at grid ref. SJ 964 548, continuing straight across the lane on the footpath, rather than turning left towards the A53. Turn right on to the A53 when the footpath ends, continue over the crossroads and take the footpath to your right, past the church. Continue to Bradshaw then follow the footpaths· in a north-easterly direction back to the canal feeder, where you turn left back to Rudyard.*

The Way itself continues along the canal. Anybody thinking that a canal section of a walk may become monotonous will soon have their illusions dispelled, for this part of the route is perhaps the most interesting of all. The Caldon Canal runs for 17¹/₂ miles between Etruria, the site of the factory opened by Josiah Wedgwood in 1769, and Froghall, and the Staffordshire Way takes in some 5 miles of this. Near Horse Bridge is Deep Hayes Country Park which offers circular walks in the most attractive surroundings.

By the beginning of the 1960s, its commercial use having been superseded by other methods of transport, the canal had fallen into a sorry state of neglect and decay. After much work by the Caldon Canal Society, however, backed by various bodies, it was reopened in 1974 and is now very popular for the hire of narrow boats and other craft.

After a mile along the towpath, the walker comes to Cheddleton Flint Mill, now a museum of great interest. The Red Lion public house is just across the canal in Cheddleton. From the Mill, the walker passes two locks and so comes to Basford Bridge, where the Churnet Valley Railway joins the route of the canal. Various industries were once established along the banks

CHATTERLEY WHITFIELD MINING MUSEUM

Britain's first underground mining museum at Tunstall, Stoke-on-Trent, opened in 1979 and is on the site of the former million-ton-a-year Whitfield Colliery. Established to preserve and present the story of coal mining in North Staffordshire, Chatterley Whitfield's purpose has broadened with British Coal's decision in 1989 to place their national collection of mining artefacts there. The museum now offers tours, led by retired miners, which include pit cage and manrider locomotive rides, and retired pit ponies can be visited in their underground stalls. On the surface visitors can take refreshments in the site's 1930s pit canteen. The museum is open all year, daily.

of the canal here, all now defunct, including many limekilns in the hillside.

In another mile the Way passes a restored, wooden drawbridge, and then the canal falls to the same level as the River Churnet at Oakmeadow Ford Lock. Beyond, Consall Forge was where the iron from nearby foundries was once forged, and up to 2000 men are thought to have worked in the valley. There is a tremendous atmosphere of history here, and it is quite easy to close one's eyes and imagine the scene of activity and noise that would once have held sway. The canal, river and railway lie alongside each other at the Black Lion Inn. A splendid footpath crosses the valley at this point. Consall Nature Park, with a visitor centre giving information about the history of the valley, is near by.

The towpath continues past Flint Mill Lock, across a 'trickle ridge', where the water flows across the towpath, between Booth's and Hazles Woods, and so to Cherry Eye Bridge. Here the Staffordshire Way at last leaves the canal, ascending steeply the side of the valley via path and steps, past a falconry to the fields above Banks Lane. The Way then crosses the fields towards the village of Kingsley.

Froghall Wharf, near Kingsley

Kingsley

Abbots Bromley

KINGSLEY

ROCESTER

APPROX. 9 MILES/14.5KM

OS Landranger 128
Start at grid reference SK 014 469
Start point: The war memorial on the A52 in the village of Kingsley. Roadside parking.

From Kingsley the Way continues towards the smaller settlement of Kingsley Holt to the south-west, crossing a recreation ground and some fields and heading for the landmark of the tower of the Methodist Church, opposite which there is a useful shop. Cross the A521, turn right for a few steps, and turn through a stile on your left. The Way now leads down through ancient pasture land, past Hag Wood and Lockwood Waste, to the Churnet valley.

Ⓔ *Near here a circular walk of about 5 miles back to Kingsley can be taken. Leave the prescribed route at grid ref. SK 032 455 and double back along the footpath to cross the River Churnet at Ross Bridge, then taking the footpath and lane to Eavesford. Cross the railway and river at Whiston Bridge, and follow the footpaths through Banktop and the northern end of Kingsley Holt back to Kingsley.*

The Staffordshire Way itself follows the Churnet for a short while and then leads over a stile and up a bank. Note the series of large stones standing in the line of hawthorn trees on the other side of the river. The Way makes for a stone post near the river, through a stile beyond it and so into Hawksmoor Nature Reserve and to East Wall Farm.

Avoiding going through the farm itself, and keeping to its right by two stiles, the Way joins the track leading to Hawksmoor, taking the right-hand fork when the track divides. The Hawksmoor Reserve's 250 acres is owned by the National Trust and has many interesting species of flora and fauna. There are several nature trails to follow. The Way passes between Hayes and Hawksmoor Woods, coming out on the road by Hawksmoor Cottage, leading left along the road for a short while and then turning off right at the footpath sign. After an uphill stretch of 100yds, take the right fork and descend steeply between Sutton's and Lightoaks Woods. Oakmoor is to the north-east, at the centre of one of the most thickly and variedly forested districts in the county, and it is surprising to recollect that until 1962 it was the site of a huge copper works, which badly polluted the area.

At Stoney Dale the Way turns right and then left, and so into Ousal Dale. The Ranger Youth Hostel is close at hand. At the far end of the pond is a disused mill. Built in the mid-18th century, it originally smelted lead ore from Ecton, and it then became a corn-grinding mill. There was once quite a little community living around it in the dale. The path comes out on the road at the Ramblers Retreat Café and then runs parallel with, and then follows, the road to Alton, eventually diving off at the footpath sign marked 'Alton ½ mile', climbing steeply through the wood, under a crag and so to the marvellous viewpoint of Toothill Rock. Go back through the stile and into Alton.

Alton is a village of great interest. St Peter's Church, the Old Coffee Tavern, and the rare Italianate design by HA Hunt for the old station (North Staffordshire Railway) are all worthy of inspection. So too, of course, are Alton Castle and the Hospital of St John,

The old station at Alton

GUIDE BOX

Places to visit
Stoke-on-Trent City Museum and Art Gallery, one of the most modern in the country, concentrates on the area of the Potteries, its products, people, arts and atmosphere, housing one of the largest collections of pottery and porcelain in the world. Its Staffordshire wares are unrivalled. Open all year, daily

The Staffordshire Moorlands Cycle and See scheme has a cycle hire centre at Waterhouses, between Leek and Ashbourne. There are five recommended circular tours of between 18 and 30 miles, with various longer options and shortcuts. More information is available from Leek Tourist Information Centre (see below).

Sudbury Hall (NT), Sudbury, is 6 miles east of Uttoxeter on the A50. Formerly the home of Lord Vernon, it is a most individual and richly decorated late 17th-century house, with superb plasterwork ceilings, fine wood carvings by the celebrated Grinling Gibbons, and decorative paintings by Laguerre. There is also a Museum of Childhood in the former servants' wing, while the coach house provides refreshments and teas. It is open from Easter to end October, Saturday to Wednesday.

Wolseley Garden Park is 2 miles north of Rugeley at Wolseley Bridge, off the A51. Created by Sir Charles and Lady Wolseley on land that has been in their family for over 1000 years, the 45 acres includes a Spring Garden, a walled Rose Garden, a Scented Garden, a Cathedral Garden, and lakeside walks, a cafeteria and a museum. Open May to October, daily.

Car parking
There is ample free parking in most of the villages and towns on or near this section of the route, at Kingsley, Kingsley Holt, Oakamoor, Alton, Denstone, Rocester (grid ref. SK 109 393), Uttoxeter and Abbots Bromley.

Public transport
The nearest British Rail stations to this part of the route are at Longton, Blythe Bridge, Uttoxeter and Rugeley. There are bus services to Alton Towers, Cheddleton, Deep Hayes, Gladstone Pottery Museum, Leek and elsewhere.

Accommodation
See Accommodation section on page 146.

the work of the great Victorian Roman Catholic architect AWN Pugin, on the site of a medieval castle. Across the river, also partly by Pugin for the Earls of Shrewsbury, is the massive shell of Alton Towers, whose pleasure ground and gardens are now one of the biggest tourist attractions in the country. As you leave Alton through the fields, the sounds of the largely unseen rides and crowds sound almost ghostly.

The Way threads through the village and then heads into the country again down Saltersford Lane. This ancient track was once, as its name suggests, part of a long-distance saltway used to bring salt to the Midlands from Cheshire by packhorse. The Way then skirts Denstone via Quixhill Bridge, where a former entrance to Alton Towers can be seen, and so south along the Churnet, over the junction of the B5031 and B5030, and into the village of Rocester.

ROCESTER

ABBOTS BROMLEY

APPROX. 11¾ MILES/19KM

OS Landranger 128
Start at grid reference SK 109 393
Start point: The car park in Rocester.

Rocester is used by the great Victorian lady novelist George Eliot, whose real name was Mary Anne Evans, as the setting for the novel *Adam Bede*. She renamed it 'Rosseter'. Rocester was originally a Roman settlement on the old Roman road of Ryknild Street which ran from Derby to Chesterton and possibly into Lancashire. The old Roman fort lay in the area near the church.

The Way runs through the town past Tutbury Mill across the bridge over the River Dove, and then through a stile, across three fields bordering the river, and through the left of two stiles in the field corner. It then follows the track bordering Abbotsholme School playing fields and on past Sedsall Rough, past Sedsall Farm, past Eaton Dovedale Farm and so to Eaton Hall Farm.

Ⓔ *At this point a circular walk of some 8 miles may be taken back to Rocester. Leave the prescribed route at Eaton Hall Farm (grid ref. SK 106 363), turning right (west) along the track which first crosses the county border back into Staffordshire and then the River Dove. Turn right at the footpath which leads to the B5030 at Brookend, turn right on to the road and then right again along the footpath that heads back to the B5030 at the lakeside on the outskirts of Rocester.*

The stretch of the Way east of the Dove is firmly in Derbyshire, the river forming the county boundary. The noise of shotguns will here assail the ears, as members of the Doveridge Sporting Club fire at clay pigeons. Walk through the club car park, up the track, turn right along the field edge and so eventually downhill and across the water meadow to Dove Bridge. Near by is the pretty village of Doveridge with its fine church. Dove Bridge itself dates from the 14th century and brings the walker back into Staffordshire. Cross the A50 and turn right. Go to your left after 200 yards through a metal gate into a field, pass to the left of the electricity pylon to the kissing-gate at the corner of the field, go over a stile and turn right towards the farm buildings. Go right along the farm track for a few yards and then through a stile on your left. Cross this field and the next, then cross the disused railway line. The track to your right soon joins Brookside Road, near Uttoxeter Station.

Uttoxeter is a thriving town, complete with livestock market and racecourse, at the heart of a piece of country that has long been renowned for its dairy farming. The town has experienced two disastrous fires in the past, in 1596 and 1672, while in 1642, during the Civil War, Prince Rupert put the torch to the houses of certain civilians who would not join the king's cause. The tower

The River Churnet at Rocester

of St Mary's Church, however, survived all these trials and tribulations. It was built by Henry Yevele, architect of the naves of Westminster Abbey and Canterbury Cathedral, and son of a Uttoxeter man. In the market place is a monument marking the spot where Dr Johnson paid penance for his boyhood sin of refusing to help his father with his bookstall by standing for a long time bare-headed in the rain.

The Way now crosses the railway bridge, passes through a stile on the right, climbs the bank into Bank Close, turns left into Leighton Road and right into West Hill. It then continues straight ahead past Field Head, Knightsfield and Knightsland Farms, continuing then past Hanging Wicket Farm, across Scounslow Green and so down the track through Marlpit House Farm and into Bagot's Park.

Bagot Forest is just about all that remains of the old royal forest of Needwood and wild fallow deer are still to be seen here. It was also, from as long ago as the 13th century, the site of furnaces for the making of glass. It is named after the ancient

Staffordshire family of Bagot, still resident at nearby Blithfield Hall. The Way passes through the 815 acres of Bagot's Park, following for some distance the line of the Story Brook, before zig-zagging its path south towards Abbots Bromley, entering the village by a housing estate, Swan Lane, Schoolhouse Lane and finally ending in the market place.

The walker of this northern half of the Staffordshire Way has now reached his destination after as fine a hike across the English countryside as can be found anywhere. And Abbots Bromley is a splendid place to end up. The village is famous for its annual Horn Dance, performed in early September, so called because the villagers dance around the village bearing six sets of reindeer horns which have been proved to date from the 11th century. It is thought that the dance may originally have been devised to celebrate the villagers' rights in the forest of Needwood. Abbots Bromley is an attractive village with welcoming pubs and shops.

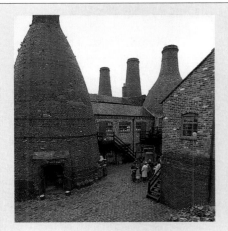

GLADSTONE POTTERY MUSEUM

This pottery has been preserved as the only example in the Potteries of a 19th-century pottery factory, with its cobbled yard, original workshops and huge bottle-shaped kilns. There are exhibits of all kinds of ceramics and the techniques of production, and you do not have to have specialised knowledge to enjoy a rewarding visit. The shop sells a range of gifts from the Potteries, including items made in the Pottery Museum's own workshops in the traditional way. Situated on the Uttoxeter Road at Longton, Stoke-on-Trent, the Museum is open March to October, daily; November to February, Tuesday to Saturday.

Limestone Way

MATLOCK TO CASTLETON
26 MILES/42KM

THE Limestone Way is a delightful walk through the Peak National Park. Despite the hilly nature of the terrain, its 26 miles are not over-taxing; the ambitious could accomplish the whole walk in a long day, though extending it over two days is much more relaxing. Established by the Matlock Rotary Club in 1986, the route follows the limestone plateau of Derbyshire's White Peak, with fine views and constantly changing scenery, and visits some interesting hamlets and villages on the way. There are also constant reminders of Derbyshire's lead mines of the 18th and 19th centuries, and of its agricultural past, a criss-cross pattern of white drystone walls dominating much of the landscape.

Detailed guide
The leaflet giving details of the route, transport and camping barns/youth hostels may be obtained from the Planning Officer, Derbyshire County Council, Town Hall, Matlock, Derbyshire DE4 3NN.

Maps
OS Landranger 110, 119

Links
The Bakewell Circular Walk and the Limey Way both meet the Way, the former near Monyash and Winster, and the latter at Youlgreave. The Monsal Trail crosses at Miller's Dale.

Unlike many long distance walks, the Limestone Way has no official guide and at the time of writing only a sheet giving very basic details of the route was available. In addition to the OS Landranger 1:50,000 maps listed below, the OS Outdoor Leisure 1:25,000 maps may be useful (24, The Peak District – White Peak area and 1, The Peak District – Dark Peak area). These have more detail on them than the 1:50,000 Landranger maps, and indicate the route of the Limestone Way, but are, by comparison, clumsy to use. Alternatively, there is the single 1:63,360 OS Tourist Map Peak District which covers the whole walk.

The route is waymarked by signs of the Derbyshire ram, the Limestone Way's logo, but some of the waymarking is poor at the Matlock end and care needs to be taken to stay on the correct route.

Much of the Limestone Way crosses high ground and, even in summer, mist and poor visibility may be encountered on the hills. Although the route is never far from civilisation, all the usual precautions should be taken with strong footwear, waterproof clothing, and use of maps and a compass. The most obvious dangers are the many disused mineshafts along the Way. Most have been capped, but walkers are advised to keep well clear of all of them.

Matlock is well served by public transport, while at the other end of the route there are bus services from Castleton, and Hope (2 miles distant) has a British Rail station. In the high summer season both Matlock and Castleton become very busy and car parking can be a problem in the Matlock area. Generally, starting and finishing this walk with the aid of public transport is easier than being hampered by a car.

Following the Limestone Way from south to north has several advantages. The route almost immediately leaves the crowds of Matlock behind, soon entering countryside which is remarkably quiet and unspoilt and which stays that way for the 26 miles to Castleton. The views improve as the Way heads north, and the finishing stretch down Cave Dale and past Peveril Castle is a fine way to enter the town of Castleton. Despite its popularity, it is a pleasant place to look around before heading back home.

A dramatic sight, Norman Peveril Castle

Matlock
Castleton

MATLOCK
MONYASH
APPROX. 13 MILES/21KM

OS Landranger 119
Start at grid reference SK 298 602
Start point: Matlock Bridge, crossing the River Derwent at the junction of the A6 and A615. In summer car parking is difficult. The nearest park is at the railway station.

Matlock Bath, approximately 1½ miles south along the A6, has numerous tourist attractions, and the route can be joined from there instead by climbing directly up the Heights of Abraham and joining a footpath signposted to Bonsall.

From Matlock Bridge the route follows the minor Snitterton road westwards, climbing steeply and bearing left on a footpath to cross fields towards Masson Lees Farm. Keeping right along field boundaries over Masson Hill, the route joins a narrow walled lane which leads down into Bonsall, the first of several delightful villages. Like many Derbyshire villages, Bonsall takes part in the annual well-dressing ceremony during the summer. Believed to be an early Christian custom based on pagan worship of water gods, it has now become highly specialised, with well-dressings being set in large wooden trays lined with clay and using flowers, foliage, berries, mosses, bark, cones, vegetables, wool and other suitable organic materials. Nothing synthetic is used. The wells are then blessed at a special service, and remain dressed for several days.

Past Bonsall the route follows a narrow,

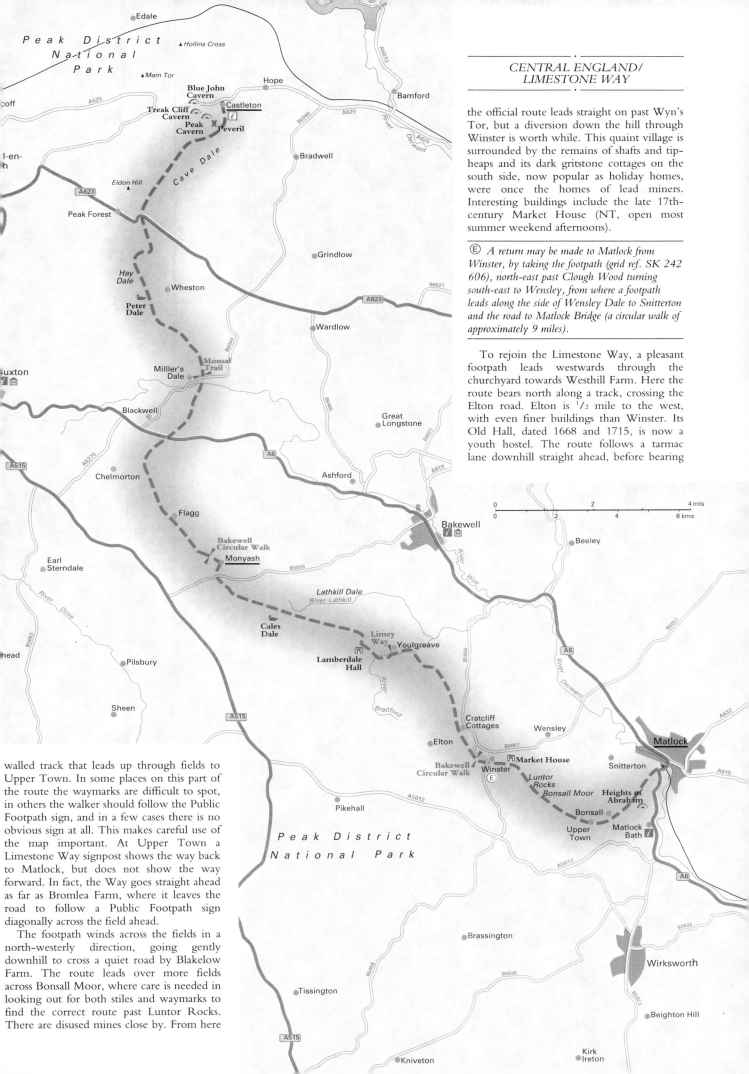

the official route leads straight on past Wyn's Tor, but a diversion down the hill through Winster is worth while. This quaint village is surrounded by the remains of shafts and tip-heaps and its dark gritstone cottages on the south side, now popular as holiday homes, were once the homes of lead miners. Interesting buildings include the late 17th-century Market House (NT, open most summer weekend afternoons).

Ⓔ *A return may be made to Matlock from Winster, by taking the footpath (grid ref. SK 242 606), north-east past Clough Wood turning south-east to Wensley, from where a footpath leads along the side of Wensley Dale to Snitterton and the road to Matlock Bridge (a circular walk of approximately 9 miles).*

To rejoin the Limestone Way, a pleasant footpath leads westwards through the churchyard towards Westhill Farm. Here the route bears north along a track, crossing the Elton road. Elton is ¹/₂ mile to the west, with even finer buildings than Winster. Its Old Hall, dated 1668 and 1715, is now a youth hostel. The route follows a tarmac lane downhill straight ahead, before bearing

walled track that leads up through fields to Upper Town. In some places on this part of the route the waymarks are difficult to spot, in others the walker should follow the Public Footpath sign, and in a few cases there is no obvious sign at all. This makes careful use of the map important. At Upper Town a Limestone Way signpost shows the way back to Matlock, but does not show the way forward. In fact, the Way goes straight ahead as far as Bromlea Farm, where it leaves the road to follow a Public Footpath sign diagonally across the field ahead.

The footpath winds across the fields in a north-westerly direction, going gently downhill to cross a quiet road by Blakelow Farm. The route leads over more fields across Bonsall Moor, where care is needed in looking out for both stiles and waymarks to find the correct route past Luntor Rocks. There are disused mines close by. From here

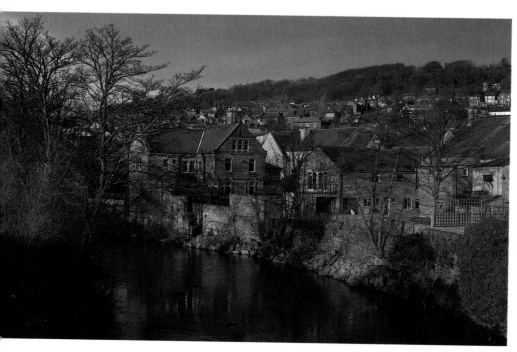

Matlock, a resort on the Derwent

left on a track at the bottom just before the B5056. This track bears left uphill, away from Cratcliff Cottages, then climbs through the natural gap between Robin Hood's Stride, an impressive pile of limestone by the woods at Cratcliff Rocks.

Beyond the rocks the route crosses two fields to reach the road ahead. The direct route here is straight on, along the footpath that skirts Harthill Moor Farm, but the Limestone Way takes a prettier if slightly longer route, turning right along the road to turn left on to a woodland trail, before rounding the next hillside to resume the north-westerly direction. This leads down across fields to cross Bleakley Dike, reaching the lane ahead on the outskirts of Youlgreave, which sits on the ridge between Bradford and the Lathkill Dales. This is another village well known for its well-dressings. Its 15th-century church has one of the best towers in the Peak District.

The Limestone Way does not go into the village, but crosses the River Bradford and then turns along its north bank to follow a pretty route upstream, passing remains of 19th-century weirs. The route crosses to the south bank on a clapper-bridge, just by a tea house on the hillside. It then follows the river to an old stone bridge where it crosses once again, climbing through the woods on a zig-zag track to join the road by Lomberdale Hall. Another footpath leads uphill across the Hall's parkland, crossing fields to eventually reach the car park and picnic site at Moor Lane.

From here the footpath leads on to the north-west, using a well-defined track that goes straight across a wide expanse of fields which are sown with cereals, a comparative rarity in this area. Skirting a patch of woodland, a diversion leads round the side of Calling Low Farm. The path then heads steeply downhill, with fine views of the countryside ahead and Lathkill Dale over to the right. At the bottom it follows steps steeply down into the wildlife preserve of Cales Dale. On the far side a less steep path leads uphill by caves, and soon reaches One Ash Grange Farm, where a camping barn is a convenient place to stay, after some 11 miles of walking.

The route follows the side of fields and drystone walled paths to the roadside on the outskirts of Monyash. Turn right for the picturesque village green with its solitary, welcoming inn named The Hobbit, which also offers overnight accommodation. This simple and unpretentious village was chronicled in *Domesday Book,* with its market and fair recorded in 1340. It has a pleasing collection of typical White Peak cottages, originally built for the lead-mining community. The area now depends on farming.

·
MONYASH

CASTLETON

APPROX. 13 MILES/21KM

·

OS Landranger 119, 110
Start at grid reference SK 150 666
Start point: The green at Monyash. Small roadside car park to the north.

From Monyash the character of the walk changes as the views grow more impressive. Heading out of the village on the lane that goes north, look out for a noticeboard on the left giving some interesting historical pointers about the village. Carry on past footpaths on the left into the bottom of a dry valley, where the route is clearly waymarked. Following drystone walls, the route skirts Knotlow Farm, joining a tarmac track by the hamlet of Flagg, where it meets the road.

Flagg is a quiet, unremarkable place with the road leading to the north-west for the longest on-road section of the Limestone Way (about 2 miles). There are few cars around and, once the route crosses the Bakewell-to-Chelmorton road, it feels as if the straight lane ahead is seldom if ever used by traffic. To the west, Chelmorton is famous for its pattern of narrow enclosure walls, a classic illustration of medieval farming practice.

A green lane leads northwards, and soon gives the first really fine view of the Limestone Way, over the A6 in the valley to the hills beyond. The A6 is one of only two major roads to be encountered on the 26 miles of this walk, and a track zig-zags down the hillside to cross it by the Waterloo Inn, close by a blind brow. Once past here, the route follows a pretty cart track downhill by the side of Blackwell Dale. Overgrown with wild flowers in summer, it is a reminder of the way many of our roads used to be.

At the bottom, join the B6049, going downhill into Miller's Dale, a charming small place carved out of bedded limestones by the side of the River Wye. The road passes under the formidable viaduct, built to carry the old railway line that has now become the Monsal Trail. Miller's Dale was famous for its lime, and the remains of 19th- and 20th-century kilns can be seen near the station.

From Miller's Dale the route goes north, forking uphill past the church and then doubling back up a steep track which zig-zags past Monksdale Farm. A walled track leads on across fields to a quiet lane near Monksdale House, where the route turns downhill to follow a path through delightful Peter Dale, preserved as a site of wildlife interest. Past Dale Head Farm, the route continues along Hay Dale before turning uphill on a walled track, passing a sheep-wash on the way to the long, straight lane which crosses the track ahead. From here it is just under a mile to the A623, where the route turns left for about 150yds – one can walk on the grass verge for safety. The right turn is among trees by the side of Mount Dale Farm, on to a disused railway track.

Down in the next valley a minor road

Mam Tor towers above Castleton

leads up to the Cop Farm on the hillside ahead, with the route passing over a stile on the right with the first footpath sign for Castleton. A field path joins another walled track above the forested clump of Oxlow Rake to the left – 'rake' being the common name for a large vein of lead in the Peak area. Indeed, there are many signs of disused mine-workings around here. The first modern limestone quarry which intrudes upon the landscape is to the west, at Eldon Hill, one of a number of quarries serving the vast Hope Valley Cement Works to the east of Castleton, an eyesore for visitors but a major local employer.

Rowter Farm comes into sight on a far hillside ahead with a large quarry, where blasting may be heard, over to the right. Here the route crosses a track, passing through two gates on to a faint path over springy turf, with upland sheep grazing on the hillsides above Castleton. The path goes downhill, passing the remains of a waymark signpost, where it bears right through an old metal gate to join the path going down the side of Cave Dale. This turn can easily be missed, taking you over the hill rather than down the dale.

Cave Dale is a water-cut limestone dale formed in the Ice Age, and now completely dry. The path is sometimes steep and rocky and better suited to sheep, but the view of Peveril Castle in a fine position on a ledge ahead makes it worth while. It was built by William Peveril, an illegitimate son of William the Conqueror who was made Steward of the Royal Forest of the Peak, an important hunting area. With a curtain wall, it was one of the earliest Norman stone-built castles in England, mentioned in *Domesday Book* and sited in an almost impregnable position between Peak Cavern and Cave Dale. Past the castle the path leads down to Castleton's small square, and the end of the Limestone Way. There is a good selection of pubs, tea houses and cafés to choose from in this pleasant place.

From Castleton there is a magnificent ridge walk between Mam Tor (grid ref. SK 128 835, height 1700ft/517m) and Hollins Cross (SK 136 845), which can be approached via footpaths that pass Blue John Cavern and Treak Cliff Cavern, returning via Dunscar Farm (approximately 5 miles).

MONSAL TRAIL

Monsal Viaduct

The Monsal Trail, which can be enjoyed by walkers and in parts by horse-riders and cyclists, runs for 8½ miles from Blackwell Mill Junction, near Buxton, to Coombs Viaduct, near Bakewell, crossing the Limestone Way at Miller's Dale. It uses part of the disused Midland Railway. The line was completed in the mid-19th century and was used to carry passengers and freight such as milk, coal and locally quarried lime. The line connected with services to London and Manchester, with a shuttle service used to transport people into the spa town of Buxton. It was finally closed in 1968, and in 1980 the Peak National Park negotiated with British Rail to put the line to new use.

Peddars Way
& Norfolk Coast Path

KNETTISHALL HEATH TO CROMER
93 MILES/150KM

THE Peddars Way and Norfolk Coast Path became the Countryside Commission's 13th long distance route on its opening in 1986. It begins at Knettishall Heath just over the border into Suffolk, passes through the fascinating Breckland of Norfolk, continues through the remote and lonely north-west of the county, and then turns east at the sea and follows the line of one of the most unspoilt and beautiful coasts in the country.

As the name of the route suggests, it is in fact two long distance paths put together. The first, the Peddars Way (there is no satisfactory explanation for the name), follows in the main the line of the old Roman road towards the north-east tip of the Wash. There is some likelihood that it may have been built after the defeat of the rebellion of the Iceni led by Boudicca in AD61. The original road may even have started as far south as Colchester, and it has been suggested but never proved that it follows the line of a far older, prehistoric track.

Whatever the truth, there is no doubt that the Peddars Way casts a spell of antiquity over the walker along much of its distance. At various stages it crosses or is crossed by other ancient tracks, and though the only village of any importance it takes in is Castle Acre, it passes through and near many sites of great historic interest. It also takes the walker through lovely and out-of-the-way countryside for long stretches at a time, so that the

rigours and stresses of the 20th century can be happily forgotten for many hours on end.

The satisfaction of walking a route which has for so long been walked by man is equalled by the pleasure of passing through areas into which one would not normally venture. At Brettenham Heath, for example, one gets a glimpse of what large portions of the wilds of the Breckland would once have looked like, while in the military training area north of East Wretham the forests and fields have a lonely and untamed aspect that is particularly pleasing in a county that has suffered more than some from the excesses of modern agricultural methods.

The North Norfolk Coast is justifiably famous for its harsh beauty and remoteness. It is designated an Area of Outstanding Natural Beauty and much of it is luckily and strictly protected by various organisations, including the National Trust and the Royal

Sand dunes and pine trees at Holkham Gap

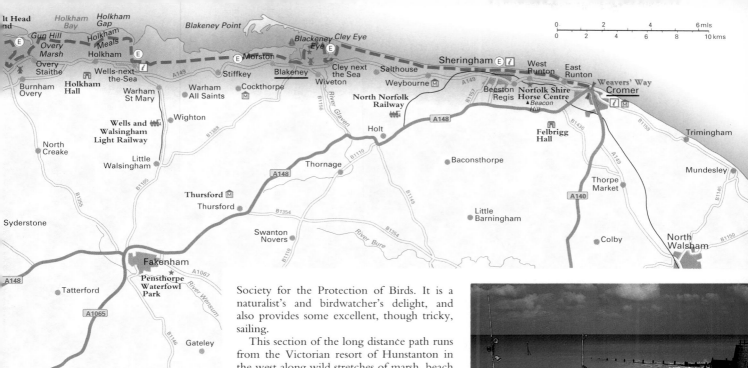

Society for the Protection of Birds. It is a naturalist's and birdwatcher's delight, and also provides some excellent, though tricky, sailing.

This section of the long distance path runs from the Victorian resort of Hunstanton in the west along wild stretches of marsh, beach and cliff, interspersed with a few attractive villages and small towns either on the route or near by, and ends at the attractive town of Cromer, famous for its fishing boats, crabs and pier. It crosses the wild and vast expanse of Holkham beach, visits the still-working harbour of Wells-next-the-Sea and passes along the quays of such delightful villages as Morston and Blakeney, the latter with its famous seal colony at Blakeney Point. Always the North Sea stretches to the horizon, sometimes a mile or two away beyond the marsh and sand when the tide is out, sometimes close at hand. Always the wide Norfolk skies, full of the sound of lark's song, give the walker a sense of openness and freedom.

Throughout the whole of the Peddars Way and Coast Path there is an abundance of wildlife. The coast is famous for its wonderful variety of birds, often very rare ones, especially in the protected 25-mile stretch between Holme and Salthouse, and the walker is likely to meet a birdwatcher or two at the most isolated spots. The Peddars Way, too, offers a large range of flora and fauna, particularly in the Breckland area, where the walker is quite likely to spot roe deer in the woodlands.

The entire route is exceptionally well signposted, either by wooden fingerposts or by green, yellow and white discs. It also affords very easy walking. While Norfolk is not, as Noel Coward described it, very flat, it seldom does more than pleasantly undulate, and though the path passes by the highest point of the county at Beacon Hill, this high point is a mere 346ft (105m) and, indeed, the lowest high point of any county in Britain. Parts of the route can become muddy during wet weather, however, and while Norfolk benefits from a great deal of sun and not much rain, it does suffer at times from extremely cold winds from the north and east.

The path passes near or through various places where refreshment, supplies and accommodation can be found, though it is sometimes necessary to divert slightly from the prescribed route. It can of course be walked in either direction and there is much

Fishing boats at Sheringham

to be said for travelling from Cromer to Knettishall, particularly as, on the southward journey along the Peddars Way, the walker will be walking towards the sun for much of the time. Most walkers, however, prefer to walk it northward and eastward as described here, and there is certainly something stirring in the sensation of walking towards rather than away from the sea. Whichever way the walker approaches it, there are good connections, including the railway at both Thetford in the south and Cromer in the north.

Detailed guides

The Peddars Way and Norfolk Coast Path, by Bruce Robinson, is published by Aurum Press in association with the Countryside Commission and The Ordnance Survey (1992). *A Guide to the Norfolk Way,* by David Kennett (Constable), covers part of the walk described here. The Peddars Way Association, 150 Armes Street, Norwich NR2 4EL, publishes *The Peddars Way and Norfolk Coast Path: a Guide and Accommodation List for Walking the Peddars Way and Norfolk Coast with Weavers' Way.*

Maps

OS Landranger 132, 133, 144

Links

The Path meets the Angles Way and the Hereward Way at Knettishall Heath, and the Weavers' Way at Cromer.

Knettishall Heath

North Pickenham

OS Landranger 144
Start at grid reference TL 944 808
Start point: Knettishall Heath Country Park on the unclassified Euston-to-Hopton road east of Thetford. Free car park directly opposite start of Peddars Way.

Knettishall Heath Country Park is a particularly attractive place to set off on the Peddars Way, the start of which is clearly marked by a wooden post with an acorn sign directly opposite the car park. For a short distance, until the Little Ouse River which is the county boundary, the Peddars Way is in Suffolk. The path leads gently down for 650yds to the bridge over the river at Blackwater, and into Norfolk.

A short distance to the east is Riddlesworth Hall girls' school, once attended by the Princess of Wales, while to the west is the small village of Rushford, where in 1342 Edmund Gonville, founder of Gonville and Caius College at Cambridge, established a college for a master and five priests which lasted until the Dissolution. Still further to the west lies the substantial town of Thetford, the power-base in Saxon times of the king of the East Angles and in 1737 the birthplace of the influential radical writer and politician Tom Paine, whose statue stands in the town. Despite the ravages of modern development, Thetford is still worth a visit.

After the bridge, continue along the path, skirting the wood to your left and passing a magnificent old oak tree until you come on to a straight section of Roman road leading up to the A1066. Following a line of trees to the left and a wide arable field to the right, this section is now a very charming footpath. Watch out for a peculiar, half-buried stone with 'Rs' clearly carved on its surface.

Cross the A1066 and, shortly afterwards, the road to East Harling. The route of the Peddars Way along the old agger, or embankment, is now clearly visible alongside the footpath. Shadwell Park estate, with its

Typical Breckland habitat, Brettenham Heath

GUIDE BOX

Places to visit
Kilverstone Wildlife Park is Britain's only zoo specialising in South American animals. Just off the A11 near Thetford, it has over 1000 mammals and exotic birds, including some of South America's rarest wildlife, and is well known for its collection of Falabella miniature horses. Open daily.

Grime's Graves, off the A1065 between Brandon and Mundford, are fascinating 4000-year-old flint mines, one of which is open to the public, set amid a large area of chalk grassland in Thetford Forest, to much of which the public is allowed access. Open all year, daily, except Mondays in winter months (tel. 0842 810656).

Banham Zoo and Monkey Sanctuary is just west of Banham on the B1113, There are snow leopards, zebras, maned wolves, camels, fur seals, pelicans, flamingos and excellent collections of owls and monkeys. There is also a 'woodland walk', a monkey jungle island, a deer park, a reptile and insect house, a farmyard corner, a macaw lawn and bird garden. Food and drink available. Open all year, daily.

Oxburgh Hall (NT) is 7 miles south-west of Swaffham at Oxburgh on the Stoke Ferry road. The Hall is a moated house built in 1482. There is a magnificent Tudor gatehouse and rooms furnished in many periods from medieval to Victorian. The fine grounds include a charming parterre garden of French design. Open April to end September, afternoons, Saturday to Wednesday; weekends only in October.

Cockley Cley Iceni Village and Museums offers a reproduction of an Iceni settlement of the 1st century on an original site of such a village. There is also a nature trail, a carriage collection, one of the oldest churches in the country (AD630), the East Anglian Museum – historical and archaeological exhibits – and a collection of farm implements and engines. Open April to October, daily.

Car parking
Principal car parks along the route are at Knettishall Heath Country Park (grid ref. TL 956 807), at the junction of the Peddars Way and the Thetford-to-East Harling road (TL 945 832), and at the junction of the Peddars Way and the A11 (TL 934 870).

Public transport
The nearest British Rail stations to this part of the route are at Thetford, Harling Road and Downham Market. This section is not well served by buses.

Accommodation
There is accommodation available in many of the villages and towns along the route, in pubs, hotels, guesthouses and bed-and-breakfasts. There is a Forestry Commission camping and caravan site, in very pleasant surroundings, near Thorpe Farm (grid ref. TL 943 840). See also the Peddars Way Association Accommodation List under Detailed guides on page 155.

huge Victorian mansion (not open to the public) is some way away on the left, and the path borders copious woodlands to the right. A good circular walk is clearly marked along this section. The footpath then crosses an attractive meadow, turns right along the bank of the River Thet and crosses it by a wooden bridge at Droveway Ford.

As a prominent 'No Fishing' sign would

suggest, the River Thet is teeming with fish, and in summer months this lovely spot is a perfect place to linger. This is ancient country, and feels so. Downstream there is an Anglo-Saxon burial ground at Brettenham and various early remains. Upstream the nomenclature Thorpe Woodlands embraces the sites of three abandoned medieval villages. Beyond is the location of an Iron Age riverside settlement at Micklemoor Hill.

Cross the Brettenham road past an open pig farm to the right and skirt a delightful wood. To the left, where once heathland would have been undisturbed, there is now a wide area of agricultural land. The path continues on the old, raised embankment and then leaves it to cross a fence by a stile.

You are now on Brettenham Heath, a nature reserve in the hands of English Nature, and the view to the left gives a splendid impression of what much of the Breckland landscape would have been like before the intrusion of the modern world. This is now the territory of thousands of rabbits and their predators. To the right, the forest protects the walker from the east wind and assails the nostrils with the smell of pine.

Ⓔ *For a circular walk of about 9 miles leave the Peddars Way at grid ref. TL 936 864, turning right along the small road to High Bridgham. From Bridgham Church (near Hall Farm) follow footpaths to Thorpe Woodlands and Dolphin Farm, and turn left on to the A1066. Then, taking the first right, follow the lane over the Little Ouse River and so back to Knettishall Heath Country Park.*

The Peddars Way crosses the minor road to Bridgham and then the busy A11. This is now Bridgham Heath, where it is thought that Sweyn and the Danes defeated Ulfcytel and the Saxons at the bloody battle of Hringmara (perhaps modern Ring Mere) in 1010. A short length of metalled road leads to the Norwich-to-Ely railway crossing, then the path continues through the pines of Roudham Heath, past a gas pipeline service station, and alongside the dismantled Thetford-to-Watton railway to the village of Stonebridge or East Wretham. Roe deer are occasionally seen here, and there is a circular walk clearly marked just before the abutments of the old railway bridge.

There is a Post Office shop (closed Sunday) and pub, the Dog and Partridge, in the village. Turn left after the pub to continue along the Peddars Way. This next section is as wild and lonely as any; wild and lonely, that is, as long as the military are not on manoeuvres, for much of it is a Ministry of Defence training area, and it is important

not to stray into the protected zones off the path. The country on both sides is heavily forested and unspoilt. Deer abound, as do small, semi-wild flocks of sheep. The names of the wooded areas have a resonant ring: Broom Covert, Woodcock Hill, Cranberry Wood, Blackrabbit Warren and, more ominously, Madhouse Plantation.

Opposite the last-named is Thompson Water, a beautiful lake created in 1854 by the damming of a tributary of the River Wissey. This and the adjoining Thompson Common are now in the hands of the Norfolk Naturalists' Trust and both are open to the public. The path continues through an area of wood and heath, over a crossways completed by a track to the Stanford Battle Ground to the left and the road at Sparrow Hill to the right, and then continues north alongside fine woodland on the right and bordering the estate of Merton.

This property is owned by Lord Walsingham, who did much to open up this part of the Peddars Way to the public. The fine Jacobean hall, for long the home of the ancient de Grey family, was burnt out in a calamitous fire in 1956.

Edward Fitzgerald, the translator of *The Rubáiyát* of Omar Khayyam, died at Merton Rectory in 1883, while nearby Wayland Wood, south of Watton, is said to be the scene of the old Norfolk ballad 'The Babes in the Wood'. North of Home Farm the path turns left and then right until it meets the B1108 Bodney-to-Watton road east of Threxton Hill.

THREXTON

NORTH PICKENHAM

APPROX. 6¼ MILES/10KM

OS Landranger 144
Start at grid reference TL 892 000
Start point: Junction of the Peddars Way with the B1108 Bodney-to-Watton road. Limited roadside car parking.

The next section of the Peddars Way is along metalled roads. Turn left on to the B1108 to Little Cressingham, making use of the verges and the signposted path that runs along the north side of the road. In the village of Little Cressingham turn right opposite the White Horse pub and continue across a stream and a crossroads towards South Pickenham through an attractive, undulating landscape.

Ⓔ *For an 'escape' route of about 6½ miles turn left off the Peddars Way (at grid ref. TL 866 027) at the lane to Great Cressingham, go through the village and turn left again up the lane past Chalkhill, and then take the second turn left down the lane to Little Cressingham and so back to your starting point along the Peddars Way (B1108) to Threxton.*

Shortly before South Pickenham village you will see handsome Pickenham Hall, rebuilt in 1904, to your left and, to your right, the smaller but lovely Hall Farm, now sadly unoccupied. The church in the estate village contains an ornate organ case by Pugin.

Across the road the path continues at the side of the road and then to the left of the hedge, though at the time of going to press it was obliterated by what seemed to be clearance for new drainage. Then it zig-zags across fields, over the River Wissey, towards the village of North Pickenham and the 350ft high British Telecom relay tower beyond. It has been claimed that this was the route used for centuries by pilgrims on their way to Walsingham, and certainly there is an old feel to this part of the walk, emphasised perhaps by the pleasure of once more being away from the road. In North Pickenham turn right on to the road and then left at the junction to continue your route. There is a pub, the Blue Lion, and a Post Office stores in the village.

BRESSINGHAM LIVE STEAM MUSEUM AND GARDENS

Bressingham, on the A1066 west of Diss, is where nurseryman Alan Bloom offers rides on three steam-hauled trains, a steam museum, visits to locomotive sheds, a collection of vintage fire engines, and a Victorian 'Gallopers' roundabout, as well as a plant centre and six acres of gardens, with 5000 species of perennials and alpines. There is also a shop, restaurant and picnic area. Open daily. There are special 'Steam days' on Thursdays, Sundays and Bank Holidays between April and October, plus Wednesdays in July and August.

North Pickenham

Fring Cross

NORTH PICKENHAM

RHUBARB COTTAGE

APPROX. 10¹/₂ MILES/17KM

OS Landranger 144, 132
Start at grid reference TF 862 066
Start point: North Pickenham village. Car parking in the village.

From North Pickenham the Peddars Way runs along the road going north-west until it meets the road to Swaffham, where it crosses over and, passing through a disused railway bridge, becomes a pleasing, broad grassy track known as Procession Way. It may have been called this after the ceremony of 'beating the bounds' that used to be practised along it, but more likely because of the number of religious processions that may have followed this part of the route on pilgrimage to Walsingham. In wet weather it can become fairly muddy.

After a mile, you reach a crossways of paths, the left-hand of which leads to the interesting and still largely unspoilt market town of Swaffham, with its fine Georgian houses, market cross and legend of the pedlar's dream. It is said that a pedlar, John Chapman, dreamed that if he went to London Bridge he would hear something to his advantage. There he met a shopkeeper who told him that he had dreamed that in the garden of a certain John Chapman in Swaffham were buried two pots of gold. Chapman hurried home and literally found his fortune. With some of the gold he rebuilt much of the fine parish church of St Peter and St Paul, famous for its especially magnificent double hammer-beam roof. In Georgian times Swaffham became a social and sporting centre. On Saturdays there is an extensive open-air market and public auction that is well worth attending.

After another 100yds meet the hurly-burly of the A47. This is a good example of how, along the Peddars Way, one can lose oneself in a sort of timewarp, for much of the route has doubtless been walked by man since time immemorial, and the occasional reminders of the hustle and bustle of the late 20th century only serve to reinforce one's enjoyment.

Thankfully leaving the A47 behind, now make your way down a metalled farm lane, across the old Swaffham-to-East Dereham railway line, then go right and left past a row of cottages, past Palgrave Hall on your left and on to the farm at Great Palgrave. Between here and Little Palgrave Hall to the north is the site of the medieval villages of Great and Little Palgrave, deserted since the terrible ravages of the Black Death. A certain melancholy still lingers here. Near by is the particularly attractive village of Sporle.

The route now leaves the original Peddars Way and follows metalled roads across high country, down to the ancient crossroads with the A1065 at Bartholomew's Hills.

The 11th-century priory at Castle Acre

GUIDE BOX

Places to visit

Swaffham is an excellent example of the old-fashioned Norfolk market town. The wide market place is dominated by its fine market cross. The church of St Peter and St Paul is one of the finest in East Anglia, while Swaffham Museum, in the Town Hall, has a good variety of exhibits.

Houghton Hall is a fine Palladian house in beautiful parkland, built for Sir Robert Walpole. Open Thursdays, Sundays and Bank Holidays, Easter to end of September.

Sandringham House is the Norfolk seat of the Royal Family. It was bought in 1862 by Queen Victoria for the Prince of Wales (later King Edward VII) for £220,000. The estate was then 7500 acres but has since been increased to 20,000. Much of the house and grounds are open to the public. The flower garden, opposite the east entrance, should not be missed, and there is an attractive mile-long scenic drive through the woods. Open April to end of September, Sundays to Thursdays. Closed for a few weeks in July and August.

High Farm, Dersingham, is situated on the old road through the village of Dersingham towards Hunstanton. The farm creates the peaceful atmosphere of the past, and there are daily demonstrations of Suffolk Punch heavy horses pulling old-fashioned farm implements, while a haywagon ride round the farm reveals the wealth of nature and wildlife to be found in such surroundings. Light refreshments are available. Open Easter to end of October, Thursday to Sunday and Bank Holidays.

Great Bircham Windmill is the only working windmill in the area. The interior can be explored. Freshly baked bread and rolls are available from the old-fashioned bakery with its coal-fired oven. Teas and lunches are served, and bikes may be hired, with suggested routes available. Open daily (bakery and café closed Saturday) from 20 May to 30 September and on Sundays, Wednesdays and Bank Holiday Mondays from Easter to 20 May.

Car parking
Cars may be parked in most of the villages and towns, in particular at North Pickenham, Castle Acre, Great and Little Massingham and Fring.

Public transport
The nearest stations to this part of the route are at Downham Market and King's Lynn. Swaffham is served by buses from King's Lynn and Great Massingham is on a bus route from King's Lynn to Fakenham.

Accommodation
There is bed-and-breakfast, hotel and pub accommodation in most of the villages and towns along the route and Swaffham Tourist Information Centre (see below) maintains a list. See also under Detailed guides, page 155.

Ⓔ *For a 12-mile circular walk back to North Pickenham, leave the Peddars Way route (at grid ref. TF 818 132) turning right on to the A1065 for a few yards and then right again along the track leading past Little Palgrave Hall. Keeping right, turn right at the crossroads to Sporle, where you pick up a track by the church which takes you right, left and right again, across the A47 and so back to North Pickenham.*

The Peddars Way now goes up and then down again, past South Acre to Castle Acre in the valley of the Nar, affording fine views of the priory. The original Peddars Way is likely to have continued its straight course over Hungry Hill towards Castle Acre.

Castle Acre is a charming and fascinating village and it is well worth spending a little time here. Granted to William de Warrenne by the Conqueror, it was he who built the castle, of which the fine bailey gate still guards the entrance to the village, and his son who founded the Cluniac priory. The earthworks of the now mainly vanished castle are considered by some to be the most impressive in the country, and are certainly some of the largest, while the magnificent remains and attachments of the priory should on no account be missed. Until the Dissolution, one of the priory's greatest treasures to attract pilgrims on the Walsingham Way was what was claimed to be the arm of St Philip. There are now various pubs, restaurants and bed-and-breakfast establishments in the village to cater for a more modern sort of sightseer.

From Castle Acre the Peddars Way turns left out of Stocks Green and follows the road to Great Massingham. It must be said that this stretch of the route is not the most exciting, for, after a stretch of footpath behind a hedge, the walker is forced to walk on the gradually ascending road for well over 2 miles. Large agricultural estates, farmed with maximum efficiency, border both sides, and it is with some relief that one continues straight on, when the road eventually bends right at Shepherd's Bush, and descends a pleasant, broad track to the junction with the B1145 by Rhubarb Cottage and Betts Field Barn.

RHUBARB COTTAGE

FRING CROSS

APPROX. 10 MILES/16KM

OS Landranger 132
Start at grid reference TF 791 211
Start point: Junction of Peddars Way and B1145, 3 miles west of Rougham, approx. 9 miles east of King's Lynn. Limited car parking on the track on both sides of the junction.

For this section of the Peddars Way the route is a wide, sometimes stony, sometimes grassy, cart-track affording easy walking and always gently rising or falling through one of the loneliest parts of Norfolk. Much of the land is arable and, except in small parts, there is little sign of the forest which would once have held sway. Yet all along the way there are fine views on both sides of distant villages, farms and churches and there is a pleasing sense of solitude and calm.

From the junction of the B1145 the Way crosses in fairly quick succession three small roads south-west from the pretty villages of Great and Little Massingham. The former once boasted an Augustinian priory, fragments of which remain, and was the

The Peddars Way near Fring

home of the late-Elizabethan physician Stephen Perse, who founded the Perse School at Cambridge. It is an attractive village, with a large pond and two greens at its heart. There was once both a market and a fair here.

The Way leads downhill to cross the busy A148 at Harpley Dams. The former house of the crossing-keeper of the old railway line is now the 'Paradise Dogotel'.

Ⓔ *For an 8³/₄ mile circular walk returning to Rhubarb Cottage , leave the Peddars Way at grid ref. TF 771 255 and take the lane to the right to Little Massingham (you can walk some of the way along the abandoned railway line running parallel). Turn right at the end and walk through the villages of Little and then Great Massingham. Past the second pond in Great Massingham, go straight on along the road to Castle Acre, and then branch off on the first right. Take the footpath on your left at a bend in the road. This leads you to the B1145. Turn right here and walk the short distance back to the junction with the Peddars Way at Rhubarb Cottage.*

The Way then climbs up towards Harpley Common. Several Bronze Age barrows are clearly visible here on the walker's right, one just before Bunker's Hill wood. There are also some 50 18th-century marl pits on both sides of this section of the Peddars Way (marl being a fertiliser made of clay and carbonate of lime). To the east, beyond the woods, is the great Palladian house, the biggest in Norfolk, Houghton Hall, built for Sir Robert Walpole, chief minister to the first two King Georges. Built of Yorkshire stone, it was designed by Colin Campbell with a fine interior by Kent, and was completed in 1735 (see Places to visit). The Way then crosses a small road to Anmer, a village on the 20,000-acre Sandringham Estate, beyond which is Sandringham itself, the Norfolk home of the Queen and Duke of Edinburgh. The lovely gardens and grounds are often open to the public. The area of scrub to the left of the Way after the crossroads is known as Anmer Minque, and after the next crossroads, with the B1153, the profile of Great Bircham Windmill can be seen to the north.

The Way continues its straight course, passing between the villages of Great Bircham to the east and Shernborne, whose fine church was splendidly rebuilt by the Prince of Wales (later King Edward VII) at the turn of the century, to the west. Near Fring it crosses two roads before descending past two woods to the footbridge and road to Sedgeford, where a beautiful torc from the Iron Age was unearthed, at Fring Cross. To the west is Snettisham where several important Iron Age hoards have been unearthed in the last few decades, some as recently as the late 1980s. This part of north-west Norfolk was evidently rich and prosperous then as now.

The walker who has followed the Peddars Way from its start has now traversed a wide variety of Norfolk scenery. This section of the route, crossing thousands of acres of abundant farm land, passes through one of the least populated areas of England. It is easy to bemoan the detrimental influence that modern farming methods may have had on the landscape, but there is no doubt that the fields of corn, flint-built farm-buildings, fine churches and sleepy villages have a special magic of their own.

CASTLE RISING

The village of Castle Rising, near King's Lynn, situated on the holiday route to the North Norfolk Coast and the beginning of the Coast Path at Hunstanton, is well worth a detour. The castle itself (EH) was built by William d'Albini, 1st Earl of Arundel and son of the steward of William the Conqueror. Queen Isabella was confined here after the execution of her lover Mortimer in 1330 and was visited here by her grandson, the Black Prince. It is set within some impressive defensive earthworks and is approached across a deep ditch and then through the gatehouse, set in a massive earth bank (open all year, daily except Mondays). The village of Castle Rising is one of the most attractive in Norfolk, and Bede House, given to it in 1614 by Henry Howard, Earl of Northampton, is particularly worth visiting.

159

Fring Cross/Hunstanton
Burnham Deepdale

FRING CROSS or HUNSTANTON
THORNHAM

APPROX. 10¹/₄ MILES/16.5KM or APPROX. 7 MILES/11KM

OS Landranger 132
Start at grid reference TF 728 356 (Fring Cross)
or TF 672 410 (Hunstanton)

Start point: *Either* Fring Cross, where the road from Fring to Sedgeford crosses the Peddars Way. Limited roadside car parking. *Or* Hunstanton. Ample parking in the town and its car parks.

From Fring Cross the Peddars Way rises to Dovehill Wood, changes to the other side of the hedge and then turns left and right and past some cottages to Littleport at the junction with the B1454. Turn right for a few yards along this road and then left at the distinctive Sedgeford Magazine House, said to have been built by the royalist Sir Hamon Le Strange as an armoury in the time of the

Civil War. Two and a half miles further on along the B1454 is Burntstalk, a huge workhouse built in 1836 and intended to house some 500 paupers.

The Way continues past Magazine Farm and crosses the line of the former railway from Heacham to Wells-next-the-Sea. To the west, Heacham is the centre of the Norfolk lavender trade. Until 1941, when the Hall was destroyed by fire, it was also home to the ancient Rolfe family. It was a John Rolfe who married the celebrated and beautiful Indian princess Pocahontas in Virginia in 1613, and she returned to live at the Hall with him until dying of the old-world disease of consumption.

After turning left and right, descend towards the village of Ringstead. Just to the west, the Icknield Way ends its long journey at Ringstead Downs. Courtyard Farm, to the east, is owned by the former president of the Ramblers' Association, Lord Melchett. He encourages walkers on the estate and has devoted much of it to conservation purposes. There is both a pub and a shop in Ringstead village.

Hunstanton's red and white chalk cliffs

Ⓔ *For an enjoyable circular walk of a little over 7 miles, returning to Fring Cross, leave the Peddars Way at Ringstead (at grid ref. TF 707 403) and, head back due south along the lane to Sedgeford. Turn left in the village and then right at the war memorial, following the lane back to Fring Cross.*

The main route continues through the village and turns right and left towards Holme next the Sea. The sea is now visible in the distance and there is a sense of excitement that one has walked from the southern border to the north coast of one of Britain's biggest counties. Just after Ringstead Mill the Peddars Way turns left and right along the boundary of a field, descends between hedges across the A149 and finally arrives at its destination, the pleasant little village of Holme next the Sea. Continue along Seagate, past the car park and towards the sea. Walkers who began at the start of the Peddars Way will now have travelled some 46 miles to its northern end and now make their way eastward along the Norfolk Coast Path.

Others may prefer to walk the Coast Path from its beginning in Hunstanton. Hunstanton (pronounced 'Hunston' locally) was developed as a seaside resort in Victorian times by Hamon Le Strange, whose family held the manor for eight centuries until 1948. Little remains of their hall at Old Hunstanton but there are fine family memorials in the church. One of the most interesting Le Stranges was the long-lived Sir Roger (1616-1704), who unsuccessfully attempted to win back King's Lynn from Cromwell's forces in 1644, was sentenced to death for his troubles, eventually escaped to the Continent, returned to England at the Restoration and began a busy career as pamphleteer and writer. He is now perhaps best remembered as the translator into English of Aesop's *Fables*.

The Coast Path begins at the central green near the Golden Lion Hotel and the Pier Entertainment Hotel (the pier no longer exists) and follows the road towards the Garden of Rest (dedicated to East Anglians who lost their lives in World War I). On the walker's left is the Wash, and on decent days here are fine views of the Lincolnshire coast and the unmistakable outline of Boston Stump (the church at Boston). Ahead lies a disused lighthouse, and just before this on the right the few remains of St Edmund's Chapel can be made out.

This is St Edmund's Point, where the Saxon King of East Anglia is said to have landed after his journey from Germany. Walk through the car park on the cliffs (this is another good place from which to begin) and take a little path down to the beach at the far left. Walk through the dunes and beach huts for a short time until you meet a sandy track leading up from the beach between a small shop and the lifeboat house. At the junction by Le Strange Arms Hotel turn down the rough lane with houses on both sides that leads to the golf club house. Follow the road by the links and turn left at the edge of them by the Linksway Hotel. Now skirt the links along the path by a small stream. Continue alongside a small caravan site and turn left towards the sea at the bridge. Here the Coast Path meets the northern tip of the Peddars Way.

Passing Beach Cottage, turn right before the dunes along a track and boardwalk leading out to Gore Point, passing alongside Holme Dunes Nature Reserve, a haven for all manner of flora and fauna. Access is on application to the warden, and there are hides and a nature trail. At Gore Point and beyond there is an exhilarating sense of wildness and isolation as the walker leaves all traces of humanity behind. Then, at Broad Water corner, the path turns inland along the sea bank and heads past Thornham Creek, with its pleasing jumble of boats, and eventually to Thornham village.

In common with most of the villages and towns along this coast, Thornham is no longer a commercial port and, apart from a fishing boat or two, all the craft are now used for leisure purposes. Indeed, the last commercial vessel, the *Jessie Mary*, was sailed in by the merchant Nathaniel Woods in 1914. The village is a delightful spot and has shops, three pubs and accommodation.

THORNHAM

BURNHAM DEEPDALE

APPROX. 6 MILES/10KM

OS Landranger 132
Start at grid reference TF 734 434
Start point: Thornham. Limited car parking in the village.

The Coast Path now makes a brief detour inland. Walk east through the village of Thornham towards Titchwell and turn right up the lane signposted to Choseley. The walker is now faced with a steady climb of 1¼ miles until the familiar Coast Path sign points left off the road by a small plantation. To the west is Beacon Hill, occupied since Neolithic times and once a Roman signal station. Continue along the edge of a couple of fields and soon the Path becomes a broad track.

Ⓔ *For a circular walk of approximately 7 miles, leave the prescribed Coast Path at grid ref. TF 764 422, turning right along the southbound lane. Turn first right along the lane to Choseley Farm. Keep right at the junction here, and so head north-east along the lane back to Thornham.*

The Path continues over the crossroads and then over a second small road to Titchwell and then itself turns left towards the coast again. Now there are skylarks singing overhead, and once more there are fine views of the sea beyond Titchwell, where the Titchwell Marsh Nature Reserve, in the safe hands of the Royal Society for the Protection of Birds, boasts many fine and rare species of bird and plant life. The Path itself descends past ancient barns to Brancaster.

At Brancaster the Path crosses over the main road and then makes its way along the edge of the marsh – conditions can be wet

Sand dunes at Brancaster

and muddy along this stretch – towards the site of the Roman fort of *Branodunum*. The Dalmatian cavalry was garrisoned here in the times when the harbour was one of the main bases for Rome's British fleet. The National Trust has acquired the site, which is open to the public and can be reached from the Coast Path. Brancaster is also the site of a fine golf course, part of the Royal West Norfolk Golf Club, and the path to the course affords fine views of the creeks.

The next point of interest is the village and harbour of Brancaster Staithe, once the focal point of a busy trade in coal and grain before the harbour became inaccessible to big boats, and now a highly popular centre for sailing. Mussels are still bred, sorted, riddled and cleaned here, and the path runs between fishermen's huts and past the cleansing pools.

Brancaster Staithe runs almost imperceptibly into the small village of Burnham Deepdale, the first of five, once seven, villages with the prefix Burnham, and before embarking on the next stage of the journey, the walker is advised to investigate the fascinating Saxon Church of St Mary's with its superb and famous font, whose carvings illustrate the months of the year by depicting life on the land.

BUTTERFLY PARK, LONG SUTTON

The Park, at Long Sutton near Spalding, is within access of the north-west section of the Peddars Way and North Norfolk Coast Path and well worth a visit. The Butterfly House contains hundreds of the world's most colourful butterflies flying freely around, and they can be observed and photographed at all stages of their life-cycles. There is also a wealth of tropical, Mediterranean and temperate flowers and foliage set around ponds, streams and waterfalls. An Insectarium contains scorpions, tarantulas, giant stick insects and other extraordinary creatures, safely housed behind glass, while a nature trail passes by conservation ponds through wildflower meadows and old orchards. Newts, frogs, dragonflies, ducks and over 30 species of aquatic plants may be observed. There is also an animal centre, an adventure playground, a tea room and garden and a falconry centre, with live displays twice a day, while children are allowed to handle some of the birds. Open March to end October, daily.

Burnham Deepdale

Blakeney

BURNHAM DEEPDALE

WELLS-NEXT-THE-SEA

APPROX. 10 MILES/16KM

OS Landranger 132
Start at grid reference TF 804 445
Start point: Burnham Deepdale village.
Limited car parking available in the village.

From Burnham Deepdale the Coast Path curves out on the sea bank towards Scolt Head Island and its nature reserve. Once more the walker is alone in a world of creek, marsh, birds, sand, sea and sky. Facing Gun Hill, the Coast Path turns again inland, bordering creeks, and winds round to the village of Burnham Overy Staithe. As it does so, it affords magnificent views of the coastal villages and landmarks such as Burnham Overy Mill. This is one of the prettiest sections of the whole route, and some might say that Overy Staithe is the most satisfactory of all the coastal villages.

It is off this tricky coast that Britain's greatest naval hero, Horatio Nelson, may have learned to sail. He was born in 1758 at nearby Burnham Thorpe, where his father was rector, though sadly the rectory no longer stands, and it is there that he wished to be buried, though his posthumous fame after Trafalgar assured him of a grander resting place in St Paul's Cathedral. There are various memorabilia of Nelson in the church, and the pub, the Lord Nelson, is a veritable treasure trove of objects, prints and paintings associated with the great hero, collected by the knowledgeable landlord Les Winter and displayed with pride.

From Overy Staithe the Coast Path follows the sea bank along Overy Marsh and Creek and out towards Gun Hill and the dunes to its east. Cross through the dunes and emerge on to the wide expanse of Holkham Bay. This is one of the finest beaches in the country and so large is it that, despite its popularity, it never feels crowded. When the tide is out the sea can be a long way away, and it comes in and goes out at quite a rate. The walker now has a wonderfully airy 2½ mile walk across the beach towards Holkham Gap, identified as the point where the line of pine trees dips momentarily only to rise again eastwards. Alternatively, walk along tracks in the pinewoods covering Holkham Meals.

Just inland is one of the great houses of Norfolk, Holkham Hall. This grand Palladian mansion was built by Thomas Coke, 1st Earl of Leicester, of local brick to the designs, inside and out, of William Kent. Both house and grounds are open to the public. Coke's great-nephew, another Thomas Coke, inherited the estate in the 1760s. He became famous as 'Coke of Norfolk', on account of his far-sighted and far-reaching ideas for agricultural reform and improvements. Made 1st Earl of Leicester of the Second Creation by Queen Victoria, he died in 1842.

At Holkham Gap the walker follows the boardwalk towards Lady Anne's Road and the car park, turning left at the edge of the trees and continuing along a track bordering the woods to Wells. This leads past a lake, a caravan site and a car park and joins the beach road near the lifeboat station. This was all once part of the fishing boat harbour. Turn right here and walk along the top of the bank for a mile into town. In summer months the tired walker can take a ride on the miniature railway.

Wells-next-the-Sea is the only working port left on the north Norfolk coast. Although its trade is by any standards only small, dealing mainly in animal feeds, it still retains the charm and atmosphere of a working port. Several fishing vessels still work out of it too. In summer this quiet little town is swelled by an influx of tourists, many from the Midlands, and it takes on a carnival atmosphere. There are no big hotels

Monumental Holkham Hall

Places to visit
Holkham Hall is an 18th-century Palladian mansion with sumptuous state rooms containing old master paintings. There is a fine park, a pottery and a garden centre. Open end May to end September, Sunday to Thursday, plus Bank Holiday Sundays and Mondays, Easter to late summer.

Little Walsingham is a medieval village and an important centre of pilgrimage, now and as it has been since 1061. There is a great deal to see and do. There are the ruins of the Augustinian Priory, the site of the original shrine to Our Lady of Walsingham, ancient inns, half-timbered houses and narrow alleyways. Much visited are the Anglican shrine and the Roman Catholic shrine, and the tranquil walk of the Holy Mile links them together. There are also tea rooms, restaurants and shops. Many medieval monarchs visited Walsingham, including Henry III, Edward I and Henry VIII, who is said to have walked there from the manor house at East Barsham.

Cockthorpe Hall Toy Museum is situated at Cockthorpe Hall in the village of Cockthorpe, near Stiffkey. It contains a fascinating range of toys dating from 1860 to 1965, some 3000 items in all. Cockthorpe Hall itself is a fine 16th-century brick and flint house and was the birthplace of Admiral Sir Clowdisley Shovell (1650-1707). The museum specialises in dolls, dolls' houses, teddies, novelty toys, transport toys, games and puzzles, lead figures and soldiers, and theatrical and optical toys. Open all year, daily.

Car parking
There are car parks along this section of the route at Burnham Overy Staithe (grid ref. TF 845 444), at Holkham (TF 892 447), at Wells-next-the-Sea beach (TF 913 454), on Wells-next-the-Sea quay (TF 919 437), at Stiffkey (TF 965 440), at Morston (TG 006 442) and at Blakeney (TG 027 442).

Public transport
The nearest British Rail station to this section of the route is at Sheringham.
A very infrequent bus service connects the villages on this section.

Accommodation
There is plenty of accommodation on offer in villages and towns along this section of the route, in hotels, guesthouses and bed-and-breakfasts. There is a camp site at Stiffkey. See also under Detailed guides, page 155.

– most visitors stay in camp sites or bed-and-breakfast accommodation – and Wells avoids undue sophistication or pretentiousness.

At times of high tide, Wells is susceptible to flooding. It was particularly badly hit in the great floods of 1953, and a coaster was stranded on the quay as recently as 1978. All in all, it is a charming little town and well worth investigating. The walker anxious to get on his way turns left at the quay, walks along it and then along the road continuing by the sea, eventually passing a few workshops and thus gaining the sea bank beyond the town.

Ⓔ *For a circular route of about 7¹/₂ miles, leave the Coast Path at grid ref. TF 836 438 and take the path which leads from the gate to the left of the mill and to the main A149 road. Turn left on to the main road and walk up it a short distance almost immediately turning right up a farm track and so into a lane leading to Burnham Overy Town. Walk through the village, cross the River Burn, turn first right, then left along a path beside the school. Continue along it, over the B1355 and past Burnham Norton Church and along the edge of a field until turning right on to the road back to Burnham Deepdale.*

WELLS–NEXT–THE–SEA

BLAKENEY

APPROX. 7¹/₂ MILES/12KM

OS Landranger 132, 133
Start at grid reference TF 917 437
Start point: The quay at Wells-next-the-Sea. Car parking on the quay (for a small price in summer) and elsewhere in the town.

From Wells-next-the-Sea the Coast Path runs along a lonely stretch of salt-marsh towards Stiffkey. These marshes are flooded on the occasion of really big tides, but usually the sea is only a distant glimmer beyond the marsh and, at low tide, tempting, wide, open areas of sand. These marshes are a haven for all sorts of birds. That great

delicacy samphire grows in abundance in the summer, and the sands hide great profusions of cockles, known locally as 'Stewkey Blues' ('Stewkey' is an old pronunciation of Stiffkey), that used to be gathered by the women of the village. Now the only people seen out on the sands are the occasional diggers for bait worms.

Indeed, it is unusual to meet anyone else on this section of the walk. The marshes have a rare, mournful beauty that is enhanced in July and August by the blue of the sea lavender. At various places a series of footbridges leads out towards the sea and the marshes can be explored by those with waterproof boots or bare feet. Care should be taken not to wander out too far and become cut off by a rising tide.

Ⓔ *For a circular walk of about 8 miles, leave the Coastal Path at the second of the two tracks leading inland between Wells-next-the-Sea and Stiffkey, known as Cocklestrand Drove (grid ref. TF 949 438), walk up to and cross the A149 and descend the lane to Warham. Turn right at The Horseshoes pub, an excellent and old-fashioned establishment, and take the small lane at the bend in the road by the church. Cross the B1105 and then the miniature railway and continue on to the junction at Gallow Hill on the edge of Holkham Park. Turn right here, and so back to Wells and the Coast Path.*

There are a pub and shop at Stiffkey, to which three separate tracks give access. Part of the (private) Hall built by Sir Nathaniel Bacon at the end of the 16th century remains. He was the half-brother of the great essayist and philosopher Francis Bacon. The author and naturalist Henry Williamson came to live in the village in the 1930s and was, indeed, briefly interned at Wells police station at the beginning of the war for his political views. The village also gained notoriety in the 1930s for its rector, Harold Davidson, who became known as the 'prostitutes' parson' and, after being un-frocked, died after a mauling by a lion while making a living as an attraction at a Blackpool fair.

Shrimp boats at Wells-next-the-Sea

The Coast Path continues past the Freshes Creek, a lovely spot where a few boats are moored, past Morston Quay with its fine views of Blakeney Point, and on towards Blakeney, whose tall church tower has been a landmark for much of this section of the route. Once a thriving port, Blakeney contents itself now as a focal point for holidaymakers, sailors and tourists, and its bustling quay and two pretty streets leading down to it are certainly very attractive. Here the walker will find everything required in the way of supplies.

WELLS & WALSINGHAM LIGHT RAILWAY

The Wells and Walsingham is the longest 10¹/₄ inch gauge steam railway in the world and is pulled by a specially built Garratt locomotive. It runs from the holiday town and working port of Wells-next-the-Sea, through lovely countryside to the famous place of pilgrimage, Little Walsingham, passing through the villages of Warham St Mary and Wighton. Open from Easter to end September, daily, with between four and six return journeys each day.

Blakeney

Cromer

BLAKENEY

WEYBOURNE

APPROX. 8½ MILES/13KM

OS Landranger 133
Start at grid reference TG 027 441
Start point: Blakeney quay. Car parking available at a reasonable price, and elsewhere in the village.

After the bustle of Blakeney, the Coast Path leads north away from the village towards Blakeney Point before turning in an easterly direction along the coast. This part of the route is popular with holidaymakers staying in Blakeney, and the long distance walker may not be unaccompanied. There are wonderful views of Blakeney and its neighbouring village, Cley next the Sea, with its prominent windmill. At Blakeney Eye the few remnants of 13th-century Blakeney Chapel may be discerned in a field, and at this point the walker turns right at the end of the fence and heads inland towards Cley.

(E) *For an enjoyable circular walk, leave the Coast Path just before Cley next the Sea (at grid ref. TG 042 438), turn right along the coast road for a short distance, and then left into Wiveton. From Wiveton you can either take the road directly back to Blakeney or, if you wish to walk further, take the lane towards Langham and turn right at the first crossroads and so back to Blakeney by Ruberry Hill, a distance of about 6 miles.*

Now cut off from the sea, Cley, along with its neighbour Wiveton, whose church can be seen in the distance, was once a prosperous trading port. As the walker approaches the village, the basin of the old harbour, now a mass of reeds and rushes, can clearly be seen. Cley now offers other attractions in the form of a couple of good food shops and pubs.

The Coast Path runs parallel with the A149 for a short distance as it crosses the River Glaven, affording good views to the south along the Glaven valley. Turn left at the village for a few yards. Just past a telephone box on the right-hand side of the street, find a narrow alley on your left. Take this and turn right at the end. Now follow the path along the old quay wall, up some steps and to the windmill (open to the public at times, and offering accommodation).

The Path now leads out along a sea bank towards the sea again. The car park at the end of the road is the place to set off on a rewarding exploration of Blakeney Point. Here the Path turns right and follows the coast for some miles. There is no disguising the fact that this part of the long distance route is the hardest of all. The walker can walk most of the way to Weybourne either along the beach or on the landward side of the steep sea bank (walking on top of the sea bank causes erosion and is not recommended). The beach route has obvious attractions, with the waves crashing in, the vast expanse of the North Sea, a fresh breeze, and the diversion of groups of shore fishermen with their long rods and lines. The problem is that the beach is shingle, and deep shingle at that, and the walking is

Cley Marshes, a Mecca for birdwatchers

GUIDE BOX

Places to visit
The Thursford Collection, at Thursford Green, near Fakenham, houses a fine collection of road engines, mechanical organs and fairground rides. There is a demonstration of the mighty Wurlitzer organ each day, steam train rides and other attractions. Open Easter to end October.

The Muckleburgh Collection at Weybourne houses tanks, armoured cars and other armour, vehicles and exhibits from World War II and other periods. The collection comes from all over the world but also focuses on the history of Weybourne and of the Suffolk and Norfolk Yeomanry. Open Easter to end October, daily, and then Sundays until Christmas.

The North Norfolk Railway, often known as the 'Poppy Line', is a steam train service from Sheringham to Holt and back again that is extremely popular with visitors to the coast. It runs from March to November. Some special services are also available, like the East Coast Pullman dinner service which operates each Saturday evening.

The Norfolk Shire Horse Centre is at West Runton, just off the A149 coast road between Sheringham and Cromer, and offers a collection of heavy horses (seen at work), native ponies, foals, farm animals, poultry and other livestock. There are special demonstrations on certain days, a museum of farming equipment and riding stables. Open from Easter to end of October (closed Saturdays except Bank Holiday weekends).

Felbrigg Hall (NT), 2 miles south-west of Cromer is one of the finest houses in north Norfolk. Built in 1620 for Thomas Windham, it has a brick wing added in the late 17th century by the architect William Samwell. At the northern end is the room by James Paine, the Cabinet, which still displays pictures bought by William Windham on his Grand Tour. There is a large walled garden with a dovecot, and the orangery has a spectacular display of camellias. The church is famous for its brasses. House and garden open end March to end October, daily except Tuesdays and Fridays.

Car parking
Principal car parks along this section of the route are at Blakeney (grid ref. TG 027 442), at Cley-next-the-Sea beach (TG 048 853), at Salthouse beach (TG 082 444), at Weybourne beach (TG 117 436) and at Cromer (TG 215 420).

Public transport
The nearest British Rail stations to this part of the route are at Sheringham, West Runton, Cromer and Roughton Road. A very infrequent bus service connects Blakeney and Sheringham.

Accommodation
Most of the villages and towns on this section offer a variety of accommodation. See also under Detailed guides, page 155.

extremely hard going. The landward side can be tough too, especially in wet weather, but is less so. It is a little frustrating to be so near the sea and not see it. On the other hand, the walker has the compensation of fine views inland.

The Path slowly passes the village of Salthouse, and there are paths to each end of it. Salthouse too was once a port (the main

164

road approximately follows the old shoreline) and, as its name suggests, was for many centuries the centre of a trade in sea salt. The sea continues to cause problems, even in modern times, in that the village is susceptible to floods.

It is with some relief that the walker approaches hillier ground towards Weybourne and then the beginning of cliffs. RAF Weybourne is on the right, and the walking becomes easier. This has always been an area of the coast that an invader might exploit, due to deep water inshore. This was a fear even in Elizabethan times, and it was then that this saying was coined:

He who would old England win
Must at Weybourne Hope begin.

Walkers wishing to visit the pretty village of Weybourne and refresh themselves can do so by taking either one of two lanes to it. Those who don't, can pause at the car park at the beginning of the furthest lane and congratulate themselves on having accomplished the hardest part of the Peddars Way and Norfolk Coast Path.

WEYBOURNE

CROMER

APPROX. 8½ MILES/13KM

OS Landranger 133
Start at grid reference TG 117 436
Start point: The pay-and-display car park at Weybourne beach.

From Weybourne, the walking becomes easier. The coast is now one of crumbling cliffs, slowly losing their battle with a treacherous sea. There are fine views inland and in both directions along the coast. The walker, nearing the end of the 93-mile route, feels a spring in the step, aided and abetted by a fresh breeze and the wide expanse of the sea. A steam train clanks along the old Sheringham-to-Holt railway line. The woods and farmland eventually give way to an extensive golf course.

At Skelding Hill, climb steeply to the coastguard lookout hut at the top. Pause here. There is a certain satisfaction to be had by looking back westward along the coast. On a clear day, the lifeboat house at Wells-next-the-Sea can be discerned in the far distance, and even on a dull one, Blakeney Church, that great coastal landmark, is clearly visible. The curve and shape of a good portion of England's coastline presents itself. To the east, the bustling seaside resort of Sheringham is laid out, with Beeston Hill, or 'Beeston Dump' as it is known locally, in the distance.

Descend Skelding Hill and walk into the town. Sheringham has the knack of being a jolly and friendly place in summer and winter, and there are various good pubs, shops and cafés. Originally a small fishing village, it was developed as a holiday resort at the end of the last century, but lobsters, crabs and other fish are still landed here by the handful of fishing boats remaining.

The North Norfolk Railway runs between Sheringham and Holt, close to the Path

A splendid 9¾-mile circular walk can be taken by following the Coast Path from Sheringham to Cromer and then walking back along the cliffs.

Walk along the front, past holidaymakers either basking in the sun or huddling in corners away from the sharp wind. Eventually there is a sign saying 'Beeston Hill'. Mount steps and continue past a putting green towards the summit. Here there is another spectacular view of the coast. Ahead lie the villages of West and East Runton, and, beyond them, the town of Cromer and journey's end. Descend Beeston Hill towards a rough meadow, which in July is a dazzling blaze of poppies, reminding you that this is indeed 'poppyland'. At the end of the meadow turn right by the entrance to a caravan site and skirt the meadow. Cross the single-track railway line, and then the coast road, continuing on the other side, soon turning right on to a track that leads past Beeston Hall preparatory school and on and up towards some attractive woodland.

This is National Trust property, and the Path leads up through the woods towards Roman Camp. Near by is the highest point in Norfolk at 346ft (105m). Roman Camp is somewhat of a misnomer. Roman pottery has been found hereabouts, but there is no certainty that the unexcavated earthworks are in fact Roman. What is sure is that the many ancient pits, mainly concealed by the woods, are the remains of iron smelting carried out between the 9th and 12th centuries. Cross the clearing and take the left of the two paths ahead, then turn left down an unmade road to a camp site. Keep straight ahead here, past the entrance, and continue down a path which skirts the site. Cross the fields towards Manor Farm and then take the track which leads under the old railway line and eventually past houses to emerge on the A148 Cromer-to-Holt road. From here it is a question of walking downhill, past the burgeoning new stores and warehouses, and into the town of Cromer.

There was once a village called Shipden-juxta-Mare here, but it had lost its battle with the ravaging sea by 1400 and Cromer

took its place. It remained a small fishing village until the early 19th century when it began to gain a reputation as a bathing place. It grew in fashionableness and prosperity throughout the century until it reached a pinnacle in the Edwardian era. Nowadays it is famous principally for its crabs that are caught in pots in the shallows. The pier was built in 1899 and has a theatre and, at its tip, a lifeboat house. The famous cox, Henry Blogg, commanded the crew for half a century (he died in 1954) and during his courageous and distinguished career saved the lives of some 873 people. He was awarded the George Cross among other honours.

The 93-mile route from the Suffolk border is now ended, and the walker has traversed a fascinating range of shifting scenery, from Breckland and heath, to marsh and cliffs, and will have gathered more knowledge about the character of Norfolk than could ever be gained in such a short time by any other means.

BLAKENEY POINT

The spit of land which comes out from Cley and lies along the coast off Blakeney and Morston is known as Blakeney Point. Owned by the National Trust, it is a nature reserve of wild and desolate feeling and is well worth a visit. It can be approached either on foot from Cley or Blakeney, or by boat from Morston or Blakeney Quays. The advantage of this latter method is that a boat trip enables one to get fairly close to the celebrated colony of seals that lives on the tip of Blakeney Point, as well as giving a splendid view of this lovely coastline, and some idea about the treacherous nature of the tides, currents and sandbanks hereabouts. The boat trips are organised by John Bean of 12 The Street, Morston (tel. 0263 740038) and by John Temple of Quay Lane, Morston (tel. 0263 740791), and one or the other must be contacted for up-to-date information. Car parking is available on the quays for a modest charge.

Weavers' Way

CROMER TO GREAT YARMOUTH
56 MILES/90KM

THE Weavers' Way was created by the Norfolk County Council, making use of footpaths, dismantled railway lines and minor roads. It is aptly named. Not only does it weave a genuinely circuitous route through north-east Norfolk, seldom content with a straight line when a loop or a diversion can be found, but it also passes through that area of the county which for many centuries was renowned as a centre of the weaving trade. Its 56 miles, connecting two of Norfolk's larger towns, present extremely easy walking through a variety of different types of country and take the walker past or near to many places of great interest. The clear and consistent waymarks make detailed directions unnecessary except in a couple of cases.

There is no pressing reason why the Weavers' Way should be walked from north to south, as detailed here, except that by doing so the walker will make the most of the sun. The Way links at Cromer with the Norfolk Coast Path, which in turn links at Holme next the Sea with the Peddars Way. The walker with time on his or her hands is thus presented with the enticing prospect, by making use of all three long distance routes, travelling 149 miles of Norfolk's footpaths and byways, of experiencing the best and most contrasting scenery that this huge county has to offer.

Starting at the busy and attractive town of Cromer, still a fishing village at heart despite its annual influx of holidaymakers, the Weavers' Way soon leaves the bustle behind, passing through quiet countryside towards Felbrigg Hall, the famous 17th-century mansion, before retreating into even more unspoilt scenery. This part of Norfolk, around Metton and Hanworth, is as sparsely populated as any, and the feeling of peace and solitude continues as the walker progresses via Thwaite Common and Erpingham towards Blickling Hall, one of the greatest of all Jacobean jewels.

From the quiet market town of Aylsham, the Way makes use of a stretch of disused railway line that leads towards North Walsham, another largely unspoilt town, and across an ancient battlefield before running roughly parallel to the old canal to Honing. This is all part of the area which gives the route its name: Aylsham, North Walsham and Stalham were all important centres in the weaving trade, a largely cottage industry which finally collapsed at the beginning of the 19th century.

From Stalham, the Way passes through the celebrated Norfolk Broads. The Broads will come as a revelation to those who have not visited them before. Discard all notion that they are too crowded and touristy. Certainly the main centres like Wroxham and Potter Heigham attract their fair share of visitors, but even at the height of August there are areas that are remote, lonely, beautiful and unique. You have to know where to go, of course, and the Weavers' Way does.

There can be few districts of the British Isles which combine the often opposing concepts of leisure and concern for the environment as successfully as the Broads. For the walker, they are pure joy, with easy paths leading past reed-fringed broads where wildlife abounds, or along beautiful rivers where pleasure craft and sailing boats strain against the wind, and windmills, both ruined and restored, dot the skyline. The final part of the route crosses low-lying farmland from Halvergate, past the famous Berney Arms windpump, and then beside Breydon Water to the thriving town of Great Yarmouth.

All along the Weavers' Way there is easily available accommodation of various sorts, from smart hotels to the most humble bed-and-breakfast establishments. All of the route is also painlessly accessible for the car driver wishing to walk only a part of it. This is Norfolk, a county which has hidden from the modern world more successfully than most, at its finest. Here are the vast skies and calls of the birds for which it is famous. Here also are the east winds which can make even a good spring feel like the Arctic, and the fine, dry Septembers and Octobers which often make East Anglian autumns spectacular.

The Way seeks out some of the older and more evocative landscapes – common and broad, pastureland and lane – so that much of the route retains an ancient feel to it so beloved of the modern-day walker. It is well served by two railway lines, one to Cromer

All in all there is much to enjoy along the Weavers' Way and little to disappoint. Its character is one of quiet secretiveness rather than great spectacle. If you were forced to pick out one particular section as the most entertaining, you would probably select that which runs through the Broads between Stalham and Acle Bridge, if only because there is nowhere else in Britain quite like it, and certainly nowhere else where you can see, or think you see, boats gliding across field and lane, their sails spread out above the reed beds, with apparently no need for such a mundane element as water.

Detailed guides
The Peddars Way Association (150 Armes Street, Norwich NR2 4EG) publishes a guide and accommodation list that covers the Weavers' Way: *The Peddars Way and Norfolk Coast Path: A Guide and Accommodation List for Walking the Peddars Way and Norfolk Coast with Weavers' Way.* Norfolk County Council publishes *The Weavers' Way,* a guide in three sections available from The Planning Department, County Hall, Martineau Lane, Norwich NR1 2DH.

Maps
OS Landranger 133, 134

Links
The Weavers' Way connects with the Norfolk Coast Path at Cromer. It meets the Angles Way at Great Yarmouth.

and North Walsham, the other to Yarmouth, both emanating from Norwich, and there are various bus services too. Some sections of the route can become boggy at certain times of the year, especially in the Broads and the marshes east of Halvergate.

Hickling Broad, one of the largest

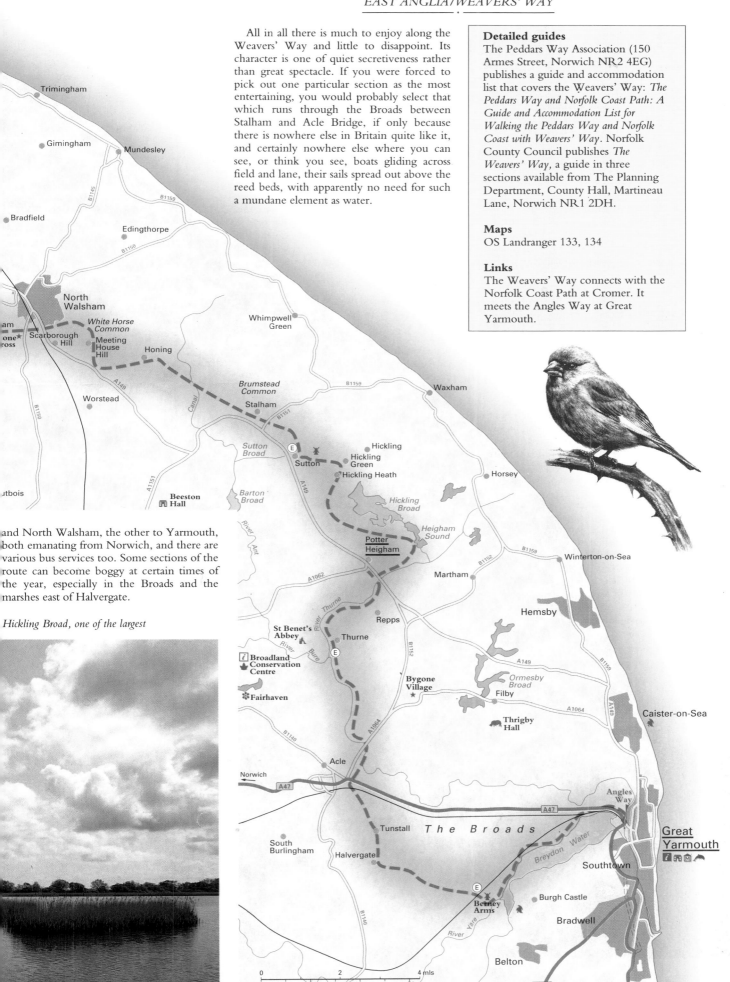

Cromer

Aylsham

CROMER
HANWORTH
APPROX. 7½ MILES/12KM

OS Landranger 133
Start at grid reference TG 217 421
Start point: The car park in Cromer, near Cromer Methodist Church. A modest charge is made.

The Weavers' Way begins in the car park in Cromer and heads out of town along the road past Cromer Hall for ⅗ mile before ducking off to the right and leading through fields and over the railway line. This branch line mercifully escaped the Beeching axe of the 1960s, and a small diesel train still plies its trade between Norwich and Sheringham on the coast. Do not take the track to your right after the railway, but keep straight ahead along the edge of the field. Do not continue straight across at the minor road, but go right for a few yards and then left. The Way comes out on the B1436 at Felbrigg and turns left at the Cross to pass by Felbrigg Hall and its park, in which there are several delightful walks.

Ⓔ *For a circular walk of some 7½ miles, leave the Weavers' Way (at grid ref. TG 199 396) in Felbrigg Park and carry straight on passing alongside the Hall to the Lodge on the minor road. Turn right here, along the Lion's Mouth, cross the A148 and take the minor road leading to Beacon Hill and Roman camp. At the crossways near the television mast turn right and then left along footpaths waymarked as the Coast Path back to Cromer.*

Felbrigg was left to the National Trust by the writer and scholar RW Ketton-Cremer. It was built by Thomas Windham in about 1620 and enlarged later in the century and again in the 1750s by James Paine. Equally worthy of inspection is the Church of St Margaret, easily reached down a path from the Weavers' Way. The church, which stands alone in the park, the medieval village having disappeared, is famous for its very fine collection of brasses, particularly the one to its builder, Sir Simon de Felbrigg and his wife.

The Way continues past Felbrigg Church, through woods and across fields to the hamlet of Metton. There is a sense of great age here, as indeed there is for the remainder of this section of the route in this remote part of north Norfolk. Roman pottery has been found at Metton and there is evidence of a substantial settlement at the nearby village of Gresham. The early 14th-century church has a brass to Robert Doughty and his wife (1493) and the manor is Elizabethan or Jacobean.

After Metton the Way continues across and around arable fields until it reaches a stile leading on to pastureland. The Way is not waymarked here. The walker should not carry straight on but should turn right through the gap and follow the track to the field gate in the far side of the field, coming out eventually in the village of Hanworth. There is a feeling of great peace and solitude here. The village stands round a common where animals graze and the very fine Hall, which dates from the early 18th century, stands away from the rest of the village facing the 14th-century church. The church at the nearby village of Roughton is also notable, particularly for its Saxon, semi-fortified round tower. There are a number of

The sun goes down behind Cromer

GUIDE BOX

Places to visit
The Pavilion Theatre, Cromer, is perched on the end of the pier and is quite literally the last of the end of the pier shows in the country. It is thus the final example of a tradition which has entertained the British public since Victorian times. Open during the summer months.

Felbrigg Hall (NT), a splendid house dating from the 17th century. Housed in the handsome rooms are paintings which have been there since the 18th century. Large park and a walled garden. Open Easter to end October, daily except Tuesdays and Fridays.

Alby Craft Centre is near Erpingham, on the A140 between Aylsham and Cromer. Displays and features include a lace museum (closed Saturdays), studio craft workshop, a bottle museum, a bee garden, a touch wood showroom, and meadow gardens. Open March to mid December, daily except Mondays.

The Black Sheep Farm Store at Ingworth, an ancient and charming village near Aylsham, sells a variety of jerseys, tweeds, etc made from the wool of the flock of Black Welsh Mountain sheep that can often be seen grazing near by on the meadows of the River Bure. At the shop in Penfold Street, Aylsham, it is possible to see the jerseys being knitted. Shop open normal shop hours, while the Farm Store is open between Easter and Christmas, Tuesday to Sunday, plus Bank Holiday Mondays.

Wolterton Park, near Erpingham, was opened to the public by its owner, Lord Walpole, as recently as 1991. Originally designed by Bridgeman and Ripley, it has many interesting features and is also home to the Hawk and Owl Trust. Open all year, daily.
The Hall, built for Horatio Walpole, brother of Sir Robert Walpole, England's first Prime Minister, was designed by Ripley and built in the early 18th century. It is open to the public only for special events.

Car parking
There are public car parks in Cromer and Aylsham. Parking in Hanworth (grid ref. TG 204 349) and Erpingham (TG 192 319) villages.

Public transport
The nearest British Rail stations to this part of the route are at Cromer, Roughton Road, Gunton, North Walsham and Worstead. Various bus services are available.

Accommodation
There are hotels, public houses, guesthouses and bed-and-breakfast establishments of all sorts in Cromer and Aylsham. The Buckinghamshire Arms at Blickling has a few bedrooms. For a detailed list, see page 167, Detailed guides.

prehistoric barrows on Roughton Heath.

Across the A140 from Hanworth, standing in its own grounds of lake and woods, is another great house, Gunton Hall. For long the seat of the Harbord family, it was built in two stages by Matthew Brettingham and James Wyatt in the 18th century and became a favourite haunt of the Prince of Wales (later King Edward VII) until gutted by fire in 1882. It has recently been restored. The fine classical Church of St Andrew was built by Robert Adam in 1769.

HANWORTH

AYLSHAM

APPROX. 7½ MILES/12KM

OS Landranger 133
Start at grid reference TG 204 349
Start point: Hanworth Church, just off the
A140 south of Roughton. Limited parking
in the village.

The Way leads south past Hanworth
Church, bears left where the track divides,
passes through Manor Farm, and comes out
on the minor road leading to Aldborough.
Here it crosses the road by the church and
soon comes to Thwaite Common. This is an
attractive spot, and rights of pasture mean
that there are usually several horses and
donkeys grazing peacefully on the ancient
grassland.

Ⓔ *For a circular walk of some 7½ miles, leave
the route at Thwaite Common (grid ref. TG 203
324) and follow minor roads and footpaths to
Aldborough and from the church there take a track
and footpath to the minor roads that lead back to
Hanworth Church.*

The Way leads over Thwaite Common
and comes out at Erpingham by the Ark, one
of the best restaurants in Norfolk, which also
offers bed-and-breakfast facilities. The family
of Erpingham were prominent landowners
hereabouts from the time of the Norman
Conquest on and gained royal favour by
their support of John of Gaunt, whose son
Bolingbroke acceded to the throne as Henry
IV. Sir Thomas Erpingham commanded the
archers at Agincourt. 'Lend me thy cloak, Sir
Thomas,' says the King in Shakespeare's
Henry V on the eve of the battle, and, so
disguised, he mingles among his men.

Erpingham almost imperceptibly merges
into the hamlet of Calthorpe at its west end.
The Way passes through the two, and takes a
left turn down the lane just past Calthorpe
Church and Manor Farm. It then leads down
to a couple of cottages. Some maps suggest
that here it crosses the big field beyond. This

is incorrect. The walker keeps on down the
twisting lane, past a footpath sign to the
Saracen's Head pub, till Weavers' Way signs
point down a footpath to a footbridge over
the River Bure. This is a place to take your
time and linger awhile before taking the lane
past the beautiful mill and, after a short
distance, turning left into Blickling Park.
Blickling is the best known of several great
houses in the area and there are various
delightful walks in the grounds. The
Weavers' Way emerges at the
Buckinghamshire Arms and then takes the
walker past the celebrated front aspect of the
Hall itself. Ghosts are said to abound at
Blickling, including that of Anne Boleyn,
second of Henry VIII's six wives, who met
her end at the hand of the executioner.
Blickling belonged to her family for a time,
and the headless queen can apparently be
seen approaching the Hall in a carriage
driven by a headless coachman and drawn by
a headless horse.

Other great houses near by include
Wolterton Hall, the home of the Walpole
family, and the moated and beautiful
Mannington Hall. The latter was also owned
by the Walpole family for many years and is
a fascinating house, dating from 1640 and
open by appointment. It was substantially
altered by the Earl of Orford in 1864. His
eccentric inscriptions can still be seen. 'A
tiger is something worse than a snake,' reads
one of them, 'a demon than a tiger, a
woman than a demon, and nothing worse
than a woman.' The grounds are delightful
and are open for much of the year. There are
fine rose gardens and several countryside
walks and trails.

From Blickling, the Way leads to the
hamlet of Silvergate, along the edges of
fields, down a broad green avenue towards
the very fine Aylsham Old Hall, and then, by
means of a dismantled railway line and minor
roads, crosses the River Bure again and skirts
the north side of Aylsham. This charming
town is well worth a visit, if time allows. In
the Middle Ages it relied mostly on linen-
weaving for its prosperity. Then in 1372 the
manor came into the hands of John of
Gaunt, Duke of Lancaster, and the town

began to concentrate on the weaving of
woollens and in particular the making of
worsted stockings, waistcoats and breeches,
an industry which kept it prosperous until
the great industrial changes of the late 18th
century.

Everywhere in the town are examples of
this Georgian wealth and the wide Market
Place is as attractive as any in the county.
Markets and auctions are held every
Monday, bringing an added zest to the town.
The Church of St Michael is sizeable and
handsome and dates from the 14th century.
It is said to have been refounded by John of
Gaunt. In the graveyard is the tomb of the
great landscape gardener Humphrey Repton,
who had many connections with the locality
and had a hand in the design of the grounds
of several big Norfolk houses. His self-
composed epitaph reads:

> Not like Egyptian tyrants consecrate,
> Unmixed with others shall my dust
>   remain;
> But mold'ring, blending, melting into
>   Earth,
> Mine shall give form and colour to the
>   Rose,
> And while its vivid blossoms cheer
>   Mankind,
> Its perfumed odours shall ascend to
>   Heaven.

It is pleasant to note that his rose-covered
grave is carefully tended by the Aylsham
Society. He died in 1818.

BLICKLING HALL (NT)

One of the finest Jacobean houses in the
country, Blickling Hall was built in the early
17th century by Robert Lyminge for Sir
Henry Hobart, the previous house having
been owned by the Fastolf and Boleyn
families. Now owned by the National Trust,
this magnificent redbrick hall is particularly
famous for its Long Gallery and its Peter the
Great Room. The gardens too are very
impressive, especially the Parterre, the Secret
Garden, the 18th-century Orangery and the
yew hedges planted in the 17th century. The
park and woods offer several miles of footpaths
and feature a lake and the pyramidal
mausoleum of the Earl of Buckinghamshire.
Blickling is situated 1½ miles west of Aylsham
on the B1354. Open Easter to end October,
Tuesdays, Wednesdays, Friday to Sunday, plus
Mondays and Thursdays in July and August.

Aylsham

Potter Heigham

OS Landranger 133 or 134
Start at grid reference TG 192 276
Start point: Where the Weavers' Way (at this point following the dismantled railway) crosses the road to Ingworth from Aylsham. Park the car in Aylsham and walk the short distance out of town on the Ingworth road.

From the start point, the Weavers' Way makes use of minor roads (well waymarked) in order to skirt the north side of Aylsham and cross the A140, after which it settles down for a spell along the dismantled railway line which used to run between King's Lynn and Great Yarmouth (opened in 1883 and closed in 1959). This is easy walking, if not the most exciting part of the Way, and many different varieties of plants, shrubs and trees can be seen along the route. The cutting before the road leading to Felmingham is a butterfly nature reserve and it is quite likely too that there may be an adder or two basking in the sun here (they are quite harmless unless interfered with). This whole section of the route can become extremely hot in fine summer weather.

Ⓔ *For a circular walk of some 11 miles back to Aylsham, leave the Weavers' Way at the junction with the Felmingham road (at grid ref. TG 252 286), taking minor roads to Tuttington and then following a small road back to Aylsham.*

Not long after the Felmingham road, the Weavers' Way divides, and the walker has the choice of going into North Walsham or avoiding the town by keeping to its south via Stone Cross, Scarborough Hill, and White Horse Common. Both routes have their advantages, both are well waymarked and there is little difference in terms of distance.

North Walsham is well worth a visit for those with a little time to spare. For many centuries it was a centre of the weaving and worsted trades, and it still remains a prosperous community, with a market on Thursdays. The ruined tower of the church was once the highest in Norfolk, at 147ft, while the attractive market cross was rebuilt after a fire in 1602. In 1606 Sir William Paston, of the great Norfolk family, founded a grammar school to instruct the young to 'become good and profitable members in the Church and commonwealth'. The Paston School moved to its present site in 1765 and among several famous pupils passing through its portals over the centuries none was more so than the future admiral, Horatio Viscount

A decorated screen in North Walsham Church

GUIDE BOX

Places to visit
The Bure Valley Railway runs steam trains on a narrow gauge line between Wroxham and Aylsham (where there is a coach link with nearby Blickling Hall). The 9-mile journey passes by villages such as Brampton, Buxton, Little Hautbois, Coltishall and Belaugh and gives travellers a good look at this popular but largely unspoilt area of Norfolk between Aylsham and the Broads. Trains run at varying intervals for much of the year.

The East Anglian Falconry Centre is at Skeyton, set beside the ancient Goat Inn and is open all year, daily. It keeps and cares for over 100 birds of prey, many of which may be handled. Some have been injured in the wild and have been taken in to save them from certain death. Their young are released back to the wild to ensure the species' futures.

Beeston Hall, the property of Sir Ronald and Lady Preston, is signposted 2¼ miles from Wroxham off the A1151 to Stalham. It was built by the family in the Gothic style in 1786. Besides furniture and portraits associated with the family and the locality, there are objects of interest brought back from Russia by Sir Thomas Preston, British Consul at Ekaterinburg in 1918. Home-made teas are served in the Orangery and on the lawns and there is a woodland walk to the lake and Ice House. Open Easter to mid September, Fridays, Sundays and Bank Holidays, plus Wednesdays in August.

Sutton Mill is a famous corn windmill, the tallest surviving in the country, and was built in the 18th century. In use until 1940, it then fell into a period of neglect. In the last few years it has undergone prolonged restoration work and is now open to the public. The views over the Broads and to the coast from the top stage are breathtaking, and the milling machinery is also on show. The Broads Museum, incorporated in the Mill's buildings, has many displays of great interest. Open April to September, daily.

Car parking
Principal car parks along this section of the route are at Aylsham, on the Weavers' Way just south of Felmingham (grid ref. TG 287 249), at North Walsham and at Stalham.

Public transport
The nearest British Rail stations to this part of the route are at North Walsham and Worstead. Aylsham is served by buses running between Cromer and Norwich.

Accommodation
Accommodation of all sorts is available in the towns and villages along the route. For a detailed list, apply to the Peddars Way Association (see Detailed guides, page 167).

Nelson, a Norfolk lad born and bred, who studied here between 1768 and 1771 and is said to have scrambled down into the headmaster's garden one night by means of knotted sheets to steal pears.

The Way leaves town by the old Yarmouth road, follows the footpath and turns left into the minor road. It turns right at the crossroads into Holgate Lane and then takes the first right to Meeting House Hill.

The alternative route follows a more rural course. It skirts substantial woodland as it makes it way to Stone Cross, set up to mark the site of a battle of 1381, part of the Peasants' Revolt against the poll tax, when a band of rebels led by John Litester, a dyer from nearby Felmingham and self-styled 'King of the Commons', was crushed by the fearsome and high-living Henry le Despenser, Bishop of Norwich. The latter was described as entering the fray 'grinding his teeth like a wild boar, and sparing neither himself nor his enemies . . . stabbing some, unhorsing others, hacking and hewing'. Not surprisingly, the peasants turned tail and ran. The unfortunate Litester was hanged, drawn and quartered, the four parts of his body being sent to Norwich, Yarmouth, King's Lynn and back to his own village.

South of Meeting House Hill, the Way meets the A149 and takes again to the disused railway line. To the south is Worstead, which gave its name to the famous cloth, with its huge 'wool' church, St Mary's, whose 109ft tower is a local landmark. The Way continues across the disused North Walsham and Dilham Canal, never a great success and now peculiarly melancholy, to the village of Honing, a quiet backwater with an 18th-century Hall whose grounds were laid out by Humphrey Repton. After Honing, the landscape and atmosphere of the countryside becomes more and more that of the Broads, especially around Brumstead Common, and the Way eventually leads to Stalham, a bustling little town which supplies the many holiday-makers making use of Barton and Sutton Broads and the River Ant. The Way leads along the High Street. Note Stalham Hall towards the east end. It is a delightful and much admired house of the late 18th century.

STALHAM
POTTER HEIGHAM
APPROX. 10 MILES/16KM

OS Landranger 134
Start at grid reference TG 249 378
Start point: From outside Stalham Hall in Stalham High Street. There is sufficient parking in the town.

The Weavers' Way heads east out of Stalham from the Hall along the road towards Hickling, eventually turning right and then left past Sutton Hall, and then taking the footpath to the right that leads to Sutton Mill.

Ⓔ *For a circular walk of some 8 miles, instead of turning right down this footpath to the Mill (at grid ref. TG 395 242) continue along the minor road, past a junction to the right, and take the footpath on the left to Whinmere Farm. Take the road to Calthorpe Street and on to Ingham Church. Take the minor road south, past the mill, to the junction with the road back to Stalham.*

The Way now continues along minor roads through Hickling Green and Hickling Heath until finally leading round to the south side of Hickling Broad and becoming footpath again. Apart from Breydon Water, Hickling Broad represents the largest area of water in the Broads. Swallowtail butterflies can be seen here in some abundance, but the once common marsh harriers and bitterns are now sighted extremely rarely. There is, however, still a huge variety of birds to be spotted – warblers, tits, flycatchers, reed buntings, redshanks, snipe, sandpipers, kestrels, and any number and type of ducks

The swan is a common sight on the Broads

and geese – and much of Hickling Broad, and the Broads in general, is a nature reserve. As so often is the case, it is the walker who is able to get to the more remote areas, and who is able to experience more than his fellow man the essence and true nature of a place. Certainly walking the Weavers' Way along the edge of Hickling Broad and Heigham Sound, or for that matter along any of the numerous paths and nature trails hereabouts, down paths through the reeds, with the occasional glimpse of sail and water, and with the songs and the cries of the birds in one's ears, is an experience not to be missed.

From Heigham Sound, the Way takes a straight track south-west, almost parallel to the River Thurne, crosses the A149 and turns left on to the minor road that leads into the bustle of shops and boatyards that surround the lovely old bridge at Potter Heigham, which probably dates from the late 14th century. Potter Heigham is a centre of the huge holiday industry that now threatens to engulf the Broads, and a good many of the 100,000 or so people who have their own boats keep or bring them here. Some 200,000 more hire boats on the Broads for holiday cruises. The village itself was since Roman times the home of potters making beakers and urns from the local deposits of clay.

THE BROADS

Peaceful out of season, broads such as Hickling bristle with holidaymakers in summer

Draw lines from Mundesley to Norwich and from Norwich to Yarmouth. The area to the east and north of these lines is Broadland, an extraordinary and enticing region of waterway, marsh, fen, windmill, church, wind, woods and sky. It was always thought that the Broads were originally remnants left by a retreating sea, but it is now known that they were created between the Norman Conquest and the 14th century by medieval man digging for peat to fuel Norwich and the big monasteries. Then a rising sea came to flood the dug-out pits. Few of them, large or small, are more than 12ft deep.

Until late Victorian times Broadland was a remote and isolated region where people lived a quiet life and the majestic, clinker-built Norfolk wherries plied their trade along the waterways. Then suddenly the Broads were discovered as a holiday paradise, and now hundreds of thousands of people each year take their pleasures here. The result has been a desperate struggle to balance the conflicting needs of leisure and nature and, none too soon, Broadland was recently designated a National Park.

Potter Heigham
Great Yarmouth

POTTER HEIGHAM BRIDGE

HALVERGATE

APPROX. 10 MILES/16KM

OS Landranger 134
Start at grid reference TG 420 185
Start point: The bridge at Potter Heigham.
Car parking is available near by.

The Weavers' Way crosses the ancient bridge at Potter Heigham and sets off on the south bank of the Thurne River in the direction of Thurne itself. For some time the path runs behind an extraordinary assortment of holiday huts, chalets and cottages, many with boats moored alongside, that are crammed together along both banks of the river. Some are quite unsightly, some rather charming and some are plain eccentric. All along this stretch of the river proud boat owners, jaunty yachting caps on heads, perhaps paintbrushes in hands and pipes in mouths, move slowly and contentedly around their crafts, always finding something to do while giving a good impression of doing nothing much in particular. There is little the Englishman on holiday enjoys more than simply 'messing about in boats'.

Meanwhile the river itself is host to all sorts of vessels, from large and expensive cruisers to tiny sailing dinghies, all jostling for their fair share of the water. The most attractive to look at are the flat-bottomed, wooden Broads sailing boats, often with galley and three or four berths, that are a feature of these waters. Many were built

earlier this century and, maroon or white sails aloft, still afford a great deal of fun and excitement to their crews. It is not uncommon to see sailing races in progress, with many boats of similar build straining into the wind, tacking from one reed-lined bank to the other.

As the walker leaves Potter Heigham behind, the chalets die out and the path becomes increasingly lonely and the landscape increasingly beautiful. To the left cattle graze contentedly in the low-lying meadows and the twin windmills of Thurne are visible around the bend in the river. Eventually the walker approaches the village. A few boats are moored up alongside the banks of the river, and the pub is probably doing good business, but Thurne is a wonderfully unspoilt place, cut off as it is and only approachable by car on small roads.

To the west across the river are the remains of St Benet's Abbey. This was an early foundation and was endowed with three manors by King Canute in 1020. It withstood attack by John Litester's rebel peasants in 1381 and prospered until the Dissolution when it fell into ruins. An 18th-century windmill was built inside the gatehouse, and now little remains. The Bishop of Norwich, who also retains the title of Abbot of St Benet's, arrives by boat at the Abbey once a year to conduct an open-air service amongst the ruins.

The walker now makes his way through a farm, across a couple of fields, past the 14th-century church and so across country and back to the river, which has now become the Bure, the Bure having met the Thurne just south of the village.

Thurne Dyke Windpump

GUIDE BOX

Places to visit
The Fairhaven Garden Trust is a beautiful woodland and water garden at South Walsham. Open Sundays in April and September; Wednesdays to Sundays, plus Bank Holidays, May to early September.

The Bygone Heritage Village is just off the A1064 at Fleggburgh. There are a collection of craft workshops, rare and unusual steam engines, fairground organs, a narrow gauge railway, a pump museum, an adventure playground, a putting green, farm animals, fishing and a daily recital on the 'Mighty Compton Organ'. Open all year, daily, with facilities restricted on Saturdays and off season.

The Broads can be visited on various tours organised by Broads Tours, the Bridge, Wroxham. All weather day launches are for hire by the hour, half-day or day. Alternatively it is possible to book various tours, ranging in length from one and a quarter hours to three and a half. The latter would take passengers to Wroxham Broad, Salhouse, Horning village, Ranworth Broad and back along the River Bure to Wroxham.

Berney Arms Windmill (EH) is accessible only on foot, by boat from Great Yarmouth or by train to Berney Arms Station. Seven storeys high, it dates back to the 19th century. Open Easter to end September, daily.

The Kingdom of the Sea can be found at the Marine Parade, Great Yarmouth. Multi-level viewing allows the visitor to enjoy spectacular displays of the underwater beauty and fish of the ocean, from sea anemones to sting rays, while the Ocean Tunnel houses a collection of tropical sharks that can be viewed at close quarters. Open all year, daily.

Car parking
There are car parking facilities at all the towns *en route* - Potter Heigham, Acle and Great Yarmouth.

Public transport
The nearest British Rail stations to this part of the route are at Worstead, Wroxham, Acle and Great Yarmouth. Various buses serve the area.

Accommodation
Accommodation of all sorts is available in the towns and villages along the route. For detailed information apply to the Peddars Way Association (see under Detailed guides, page 167). There is a camping barn at Tunstall on the edge of Halvergate Marshes near Acle which must be booked in advance.

Ⓔ *For a circular walk of some 7¹/₂ miles, leave the Weavers' Way at Thurne Church (at grid ref. TG 405 156) and instead of crossing over the minor road, turn left along it, taking the first proper turning left again along the road past Ashby Hall and on into the village of Repps. Turn left in the village and right along the River Thurne, back to Potter Heigham Bridge.*

The path along the east bank is delightful, and once again one feels that there can be no better way of getting to know the countryside than by walking it. At Acle Bridge cross the A1064 and then take the path along the other side of the river for a while before turning right by a boatyard towards Acle. Acle is a busy little town, standing as it does at the junction of two main roads and complete with a railway station. The church of St Edmund is well worth visiting. It contains graffiti thought to date from the time of the Black Death, referring to the 'brute beast plague that rages hour by hour'. The Way does not go into Acle, however, but turning south, crosses the A47 and then the railway line to Yarmouth, before setting off on a thoroughly enjoyable stretch by woods and pastureland to the hamlet of Tunstall, and from there to Halvergate.

HALVERGATE

GREAT YARMOUTH

APPROX.7 MILES/11KM

OS Landranger 134
Start at grid reference TG 420 069
Start point: Where the Weavers' Way meets the road in the centre of Halvergate. Limited car parking in the village.

From Halvergate the Way strikes east, following the minor road out of the village and taking the track at the sharp bend in the road. This is now marsh country, intersected with hundreds of ditches and sparsely populated. The rich pastures between the Rivers Yare and Waveney were once famous for their cattle. Daniel Defoe, the author of *Robinson Crusoe,* visited the district in the 1720s and reported that the preferred Scottish-bred cattle were doing well. 'These Scots runts, so they call them,' he wrote, coming out of the cold and barren mountains of the Highlands in Scotland, feed so eagerly on the rich pasture in these marshes, that they thrive in an unusual manner, and grow monstrously fat.'

It has to be said that there is a desolate atmosphere about these parts, especially in the winter when the winds blow from east and north. The Weavers' Way now becomes footpath again and offers the walker two alternatives. Either walk due east towards Breydon Water past two mills on South Walsham Marshes or, a more interesting and longer route, take the footpath which leads south-east, crosses the railway line at Berney Arms Station and takes you to Berney Arms Mill. Built in the mid-19th century, it was originally designed to grind cement but soon became a pumping mill. There is a pub and shop near by.

A few hundred yards downstream the River Yare and the River Waveney, which forms the border with Suffolk for much of its length, meet in Breydon Water, which is effectively their estuary, though a land-locked one.

Ⓔ *For a circular walk of some 11 miles, take the northern alternative of the Weavers' Way (where the footpaths divide at grid ref. TG 435 066) as far as the railway crossing at Breydon Water and then return to Halvergate by the southern alternative via Berney Arms Mill.*

Sailboats on the Thurne, a typical scene

The Way runs along the north side of Breydon Water. Great Yarmouth is visible in the distance, looking not so much like a popular English coastal resort as part of some sprawling industrial American town. To the south-west is Burgh Castle, nowadays a Mecca for campers and caravanners, but once the proud Roman fort of *Gariannonum,* an area of six acres surrounded by an impregnable wall 15 – 20ft high and 9ft thick, built in the 3rd century AD to keep out the Saxon raiders. Much of it still exists. After the departure of the Romans there was a monastery here, founded in about AD635 by St Fursa, the Irish missionary, but this too fell foul of the changing circumstances of history after only 250 years and was destroyed, probably by Danish invaders, towards the end of the 9th century. Indeed, this whole area was settled by the Danes.

The Way continues along the lonely north shore of Breydon Water. Much of it is a nature reserve and a haven for birds. Eventually the Way meets the A47 and together they journey the short distance towards Great Yarmouth. To the north is Caister-on-Sea. Though now mainly a holiday suburb of Yarmouth, Caister has two glorious links with the past. As its name suggests, it was originally a Roman settlement, begun most likely in the 1st century AD and then developed over the years. It may eventually have become a Roman town for retired seamen. English Heritage now looks after the Roman remains. The Saxons made use of the massive defences in later centuries. Many 'boat burials' have been discovered outside the walls and a number of Saxon huts inside. Caister's other fascinating site is the castle (see below).

The Weavers' Way's final destination, Great Yarmouth, suffers from its modern reputation as the Blackpool of the east coast, and it is true that much of the modern development in pursuit of the holiday trade has done the town no favours. However, Yarmouth has a long and proud history, and for many centuries was an extremely important port, trading in everything from cloth to coal, but above all in herrings. As recently as the first quarter of this century the herring industry was at its peak, and fisher-girls from Scotland would flock to the town in the autumn to demonstrate their skills of cleaning and gutting the herrings at the rate of a cran (1200 – 1500 fish) an hour. Yet as early as the 18th century Yarmouth acquired a reputation as a fashionable resort, and the Victorians capitalised upon this. Now, late in the 20th century, it is the holidaymaker, not the herring, which provides the town's prosperity.

CAISTER CASTLE

Sir John Fastolf, on whom Shakespeare modelled his Falstaff, was prominent in the English army at Agincourt and enriched himself during the French campaigns. In 1432-5 he built Caister Castle, one of the finest 15th-century castles in the country, and no expense was spared. Now partly ruined, it was furnished in the height of contemporary luxury, and even the servants are said to have had feather mattresses. Here Fastolf lived out his retirement days in great comfort. The castle passed to the Paston family on his death, but not before many disputes, all detailed in the Paston Letters, which give considerable insight into how life was lived in Norfolk in those far-off times. Nowadays, visitors can also enjoy the Veteran and Vintage Car Museum on the same site. Open mid May to end September, daily except Saturdays.

173

THE NORTH COUNTRY

On the shores of Derwentwater, Cumbria

Ribble Way

LONGTON TO GAVEL GAP
72 MILES/115KM

Detailed guides
The Ribble Way, by and available from Lancashire County Council Planning Dept, PO Box 160, East Cliff County Offices, Preston PR1 3EX (tel. 0772 264132).
The Ribble Way by Gladys Sellers (revised edition, 1992) is published by Cicerone Press.

Maps
OS Landranger 98, 102, 103

Links
The Pennine Way, the Abbott's Hike and the Yorkshire Dales Centurion Walk link with the Ribble Way near Horton in Ribblesdale. The Dales Way joins the Ribble Way near Gearstones.

FOOTPATHS have ever laced the lovely Ribble valley, but not until 1 June 1985 was a middle distance way opened that extended from the salt flats at the Ribble's mouth to its lonely source on the slopes of Gayle Moor. The walk sews up a number of local paths, many of which have been upgraded, and some existing rights of way have been diverted, thus establishing harmony between walkers and those whose livelihood comes from the land. The Ramblers' Association first proposed it and Lancashire County Council, North Yorkshire County Council and the Yorkshire Dales National Park Authority maintain it.

The Ribble estuary is not an impressive seaboard although its long range of sands and spreading dunes has a charm of its own. Inland, a rich agricultural country, dotted with many pleasing villages, spreads eastwards to the edge of the industrial area. But turn upstream from the mouth of the Ribble and you enter a valley of rare and increasing beauty.

At Walton-le-Dale, on Preston's southern outskirts, the Ribble is joined by the river Darwen, which along its course from the moors flows past the spur crowned by Hoghton Tower, where James I was lavishly entertained in 1617. At Walton, in Leland's day, was 'the great stone bridge of Ribble having five great arches'.

Above Preston the river winds in expansive curves to Ribchester, an ancient riverside village built on the site of *Bremetennacum*. The ancient parish church and churchyard cover most of a temple built there by the Romans to the goddess Minerva. Up the valley from Ribchester, in sight of the gentle, green slope of Longridge Fell, the river leads by lovely Sale wheel, where it swings northwards on escaping from a cramped channel between well-wooded banks.

Hurst Green, across the fields from Dinckley Ferry, is the home of Stonyhurst College, a world-famous Roman Catholic public school, set in extensive parkland with two large ponds that were excavated in 1686. The college houses a wonderful museum collection, including private seals of James II and Sir Thomas More's embroidered cap. A superb library has many priceless volumes, including the oldest English bound book in existence, a 7th-century copy of the gospel according to St John, and books printed by Caxton.

The outlook up the valley from Hurst Green is a beautiful one into the Craven country and towards the Pennines. Across the valley is a gap in the spur of Pendle Hill down which the River Calder descends from east Lancashire to join the Ribble at Hacking Ferry.

Whalley Abbey once stood on the banks of the River Calder. This splendid Cistercian monastery was founded towards the end of the 13th century. John Paslew, the last abbot, was hanged in 1537 at Lancaster for his part in the Pilgrimage of Grace.

Drystone walls criss-cross the pastures above Horton in Ribblesdale

Following the Dissolution, the monastery was ruthlessly despoiled and nothing remains of the grand, conventual church.

Further up the valley Clitheroe's Norman castle keep crowns a limestone crag high above the town and, east of this stronghold of the de Lacey's, rises Pendle Hill which, at 1831ft (558m), is one of Lancashire's most famous landmarks. This level-browed mass rises from the valley in a grand sweep to give extensive views, which include the wild fells of Bowland and the whole length of Ribblesdale from the Yorkshire heights of Ingleborough, Whernside and Pen-y-ghent down to the coast.

Downham, probably the prettiest village in Ribblesdale, lies at the foot of Pendle Hill. Here lived the 17th-century, roistering Puritan, Nicholas Assheton, whom Harrison Ainsworth featured in his *Lancashire Witches,* a fitting reminder that the Forest of Pendle was the reputed home of the Lancashire witches.

The River Hodder, which drains the

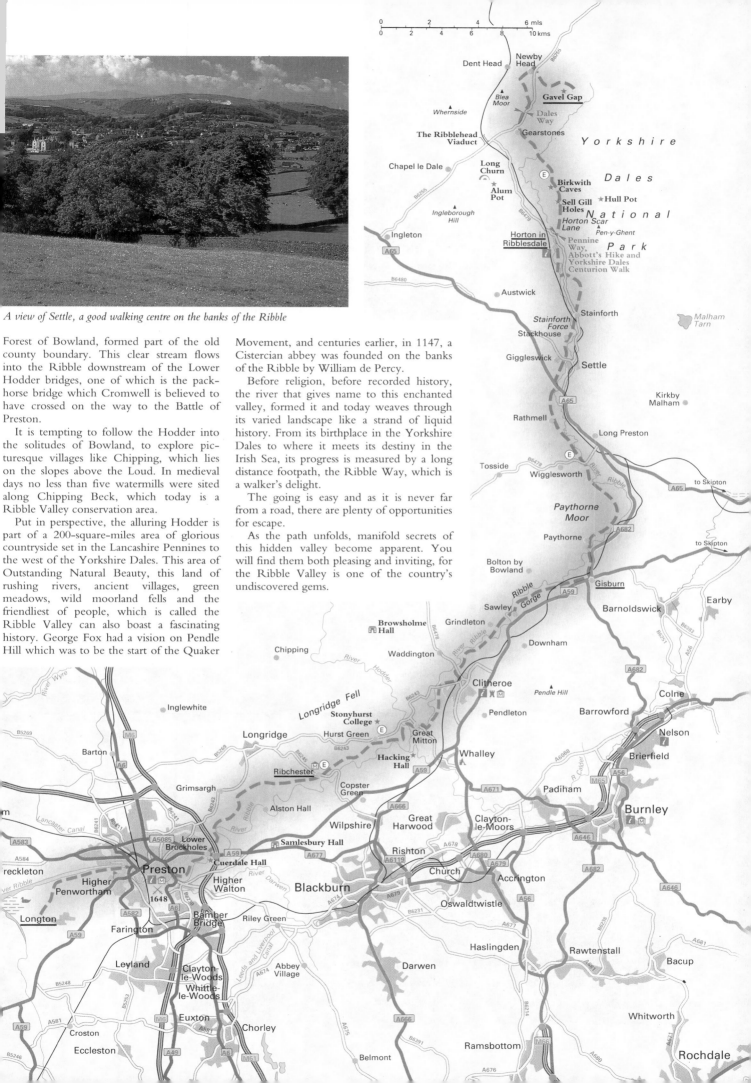

A view of Settle, a good walking centre on the banks of the Ribble

Forest of Bowland, formed part of the old county boundary. This clear stream flows into the Ribble downstream of the Lower Hodder bridges, one of which is the pack-horse bridge which Cromwell is believed to have crossed on the way to the Battle of Preston.

It is tempting to follow the Hodder into the solitudes of Bowland, to explore picturesque villages like Chipping, which lies on the slopes above the Loud. In medieval days no less than five watermills were sited along Chipping Beck, which today is a Ribble Valley conservation area.

Put in perspective, the alluring Hodder is part of a 200-square-miles area of glorious countryside set in the Lancashire Pennines to the west of the Yorkshire Dales. This area of Outstanding Natural Beauty, this land of rushing rivers, ancient villages, green meadows, wild moorland fells and the friendliest of people, which is called the Ribble Valley can also boast a fascinating history. George Fox had a vision on Pendle Hill which was to be the start of the Quaker Movement, and centuries earlier, in 1147, a Cistercian abbey was founded on the banks of the Ribble by William de Percy.

Before religion, before recorded history, the river that gives name to this enchanted valley, formed it and today weaves through its varied landscape like a strand of liquid history. From its birthplace in the Yorkshire Dales to where it meets its destiny in the Irish Sea, its progress is measured by a long distance footpath, the Ribble Way, which is a walker's delight.

The going is easy and as it is never far from a road, there are plenty of opportunities for escape.

As the path unfolds, manifold secrets of this hidden valley become apparent. You will find them both pleasing and inviting, for the Ribble Valley is one of the country's undiscovered gems.

Longton

Ribchester

LONGTON

A6 PRESTON

APPROX. 9 MILES/14KM

OS Landranger 102
Start at grid reference SD 458 254
Start point: The Dolphin Inn, Marsh Lane, Longton. Parking space is available near by.

From the Dolphin Inn turn west along Marsh Lane and right along the tidal embankment overlooking Longton Marshes.

Longton Marshes form a small part of the Ribble Marshes National Nature Reserve, 5689 acres of saltmarsh and intertidal flats on the south side of the River Ribble. It protects the habitat of waders, ducks, geese, gulls and terns. It is a staging point for Arctic migrants, and oystercatchers, grey plover and redshank winter there.

At Longton Brook the path bends sharply to the right, leaving the track by a stile in the hedge to the right. Continue along the official waymarked path, crossing a series of stiles, and Longton Brook. Follow the path around a field boundary, northwards and, after crossing a lane and another field, rejoin the embankment.

The path turns right, to follow the south bank of the River Ribble for 3½ miles to Preston. After a while it goes downhill and crosses a beck. Continue over a stile to the left of a padlocked gate to rejoin the embankment. Follow the path past Higher Penwortham Golf Course and the site of Penwortham Power Station into Holme Road. Continue along it to the Liverpool Road (A59). Cross the road and follow a riverside footpath directly opposite. Turn left on to Leyland road (A582) and left again to cross Penwortham Bridge. Descend steps at its northern end, turn right into Riverside and follow a tree-lined, riverside avenue in Miller and Avenham Parks.

The starting point for Ribble wayfarers

This district of Preston, the area south of Fishergate dominated by Winckley Square, where Georgian streets run into landscaped Miller and Avenham Parks, is the towns's visual pride and joy. The many fine 19th-century buildings include the Harris Museum and Art Gallery, deservedly known as 'The Jewel in the Town'. The building is one of the most notable examples of the Greek Revival in the country. It dominates the town centre and its 'Story of Preston' gallery attracts thousands of visitors.

Preston's past is Roman and medieval. It was granted its first charter in 1179. The lowest crossing of the River Ribble was at Preston and this aided its development. Spinning and weaving began there in the 16th century. Arkwright, a Preston man, born in 1732, developed a spinning or water frame. The first cotton mill was started in 1777. Every 20 years a local festival, 'Preston Guild', relates the town's history with processions and many associated events.

Pass the end of the horse-drawn tramway bridge. Climb slightly, curving right, along a tree-lined avenue adjacent to the river bank and continue along the Boulevard. Across the river is the confluence of the Ribble and Darwen at Walton Flats.

Ribchester Church, mainly 13th-century

GUIDE BOX

Places to visit
The Harris Museum and Art Gallery, Market Square, Preston, houses, in addition to temporary exhibitions, fine collections of British 19th- and 20th-century paintings, sculptures, costume and decorative art. Open all year, Monday to Saturday.

The Guildhall/Charter Theatre/Shopping Centre, Lord Street, Preston, offers ballet, music, opera, plays, and variety shows – all sweet counterpoint for walkers using Preston as base.

Samlesbury Hall (NT). The first Samlesbury Hall, close to a ford over the Ribble and on the line of a raiding route from Scotland, was constantly attacked during the 13th and 14th centuries and in 1322 the Scots fired it. A new one was built, this time in deep woodland. Today these woods have gone and the nearby farmland has been levelled for Samlesbury Aerodrome.
There are collections of antiques, paintings and crafts, and changing exhibitions. Open all year, daily except Mondays.

Longridge is a shopping and social centre commanding fine views of the Ribble Valley, the Fylde Plain, the Welsh mountains, the Isle of Man, Ingleborough, and the Loud valley. Cromwell's army passed through it *en route* to the Battle of Preston.

Car parking
Parking space is available near the Dolphin Inn, Longton. There are 10 car parks in central Preston. Ribchester has a car park and parking space.

Public transport
The nearest British Rail station to the start of the Ribble Way is Preston. The best means of reaching the Way from Preston by public transport is from the central bus station using Zippy mini-bus Z28.

Accommodation
Preston Borough Council's *Accommodation Guide* gives details of hotels and guesthouses in and around Preston. The *Ribble Way* booklet, (see page 176) gives details of serviced accommodation, self-catering accommodation and camping/caravan sites along the route.

A6 PRESTON

RIBCHESTER

APPROX. 10 MILES/16KM

OS Landranger 102
Start at grid reference SD 552 287
Start point: The London Road, A6, where it crosses the Ribble.

Cross London Road (A6) and follow a track between the bridge parapet and the Shawe Arms. Soon, just beyond a small bridge leave the track by a stile on the right, go back to the river and keep close to it around a long loop. Mete House and its associated farm buildings are seen on the left.

On reaching the entrance to Melling' Wood, which climbs an escarpment, descend some riverside steps, continue through the

wood and turn right at its end, edging a golf course to rejoin the river bank and follow it to Brockholes Bridge. Cuerdale Hall is seen near the south bank of the River Ribble. There, in 1840, workmen discovered 10,000 early silver coins and some silver ingots, believed to have belonged to an invading Scandinavian army. The coins were minted between AD815 and 930. Most of the Cuerdale Hoard is now in the British Museum.

In pre-turnpike days, travellers between Blackburn and Preston crossed the River Ribble at Brockholes on an ancient ferry. A temporary structure, built in 1826, superseded the ferry and had a halfpenny toll. Today, slightly upriver, the M6 motorway spans both the A39 and the River Ribble near a ford that, centuries ago, brought history to this part of the valley.

Cross Brockholes Brow (A59) and follow a farm track immediately opposite, bearing right, along a fenced track on the approach to Lower Brockholes, edging the river and going under the motorway.

On the river's south bank, slightly to the east, lies 14th-century Samlesbury Hall. It was extensively altered in Tudor times to a moated manor house, and much of the existing building dates from that period. Now National Trust property, it houses collections of antiques and paintings. Exhibitions are held there throughout the year.

The Ribble meanders through its valley near Ribchester

The track turns sharp left and veers northeast, crossing meadows, to the site of Higher Brockholes. Here cross a stile and turn left along a field boundary to enter Red Scar Wood along a well-defined, climbing path. Where the path forks at the hilltop, turn right, along the back of a wood, and cross a field. At the end go right, through woodland, to join another path. Continue along it round the back of Red Scar Wood. Follow the fenced track to the edge of the woodland and, where it veers off in a northerly direction, cross a stile on the right and then cross three fields on a clear path, keeping roughly parallel to the wood on your right. The path cuts across the corner of the fourth field to enter Tun Brook Wood. Go down steps to cross Tun Brook. Climb steeply up the other side, out of the wood, cross a meadow and turn left on to a metalled lane. After a short distance turn left, into Elston Lane, follow it for $^1/_2$ mile and turn right, on to a track which passes Marsh House. Cross a stile at the end of the track and continue alongside a hedge. Cross a large field to join Alston Lane on the north side of Alston Hall Cottages. Turn left on to the

road and take the footpath almost opposite, signposted to Hothersall Lane. The path crosses meadows and several small streams before descending to the bottom right-hand corner of King Wood, where it crosses a bridge and leaves the wood, going uphill over a meadow alongside the wood. Continue north-easterly, following field boundaries, and turn right into Hothersall Lane. Just beyond Hothersall Hall, leave by a stile on the right. Continue along the top of

Red Bank Wood and descend to a gate to reach a riverside track which leads into Ribchester.

Here, in the churchyard, a motto carved on a sundial gives food for thought:

I am a shadow, so art thou;
I mark time, dost thou?

Ⓔ *From Ribchester there is a bus service back to Preston.*

THE CIVIL WAR IN THE RIBBLE VALLEY

In 1648 Preston and the Ribble Valley saw decisive action in what was to be the final battle of the Civil War. The last of Charles I's Scottish supporters, under the leadership of the Duke of Hamilton, invaded England to be met in August by Cromwell and some 8500 men in the Ribble Valley. Proceeding along the north bank of the river, Cromwell passed through Gisburn Park, Hodder Bridge and Stonyhurst Hall before the

Battle of Preston started on the site of some allotments close to Cromwell Road. The 21,000 Scots retreated south, with more fighting taking place at Ribble Bridge, close to the confluence of the Ribble and the Darwen, and finally surrendered to Cromwell near Warrington. Charles's attempt at fomenting a second civil war was thus speedily crushed: he was brought to trial and beheaded in January 1649.

The Battle of Preston rages at Ribble Bridge, 17 August 1648

Ribchester

Gisburn

OS Landranger 103
Start at grid reference SD 649 350
Start point: Anchor Holme, on the riverside, near Ribchester Museum. There is a car park in Ribchester.

Ribchester, 'the walled town by the Ribble', was a major Middle Bronze Age settlement that was occupied through the Iron Age. The Romans recognised its importance and established the cavalry fort of *Bremetennacum* there, at the hub of five great roads. It remained an active cavalry fort on Julius Agricola's military highway linking Chester and Manchester with Hadrian's Wall. Roman pillars, intended for temples, now hold up the porch of the White Bull Inn.

From Anchor Holme follow the riverside path along the Ribble, turn left along Duddle Brook to Greenside, then turn right, on to the Blackburn road. Follow this to where it turns sharp right across Ribchester Bridge and continue straight on along the west bank of the river to Dewhurst House.

From Dewhurst House farmyard turn right towards the river, cross a small meadow and turn left, along the river bank, to Haugh Wood. Follow the path round the bend of the river and on leaving the wood turn left and continue around a field boundary. When close to the bottom left-hand corner of the field go left, uphill, to the top left-hand corner of the next field, between Hey Hurst and a country house. Cross a farm track, continue round another field boundary alongside Clough Bank Wood and cross Starling Brook. Continue eastwards, alongside field boundaries to a fenced track. Follow this to Trough House farmyard, then along Lambing Clough Lane to Hurst Green. Trough House takes its name from Trows Ferry; resembling a pair of troughs lashed together, it was dragged by ropes across the Ribble between Dinckley and Hurst Green.

Ⓔ *Anyone wishing to return to Ribchester from Hurst Green may do so by taking the Longridge road (grid ref. SD 684 379) to St John's Church and turning left, along a farm track to Merrick's Hall, thence over field paths to Bailey Hall, continuing via rights of way past Dutton Hall and Low Dutton to Ribchester Bridge.*

Turn right on the main road and immediately after the Shireburn Arms turn right, passing petrol pumps on your left, and continue along a short lane into a field. Follow the hedge on your left, downhill, and continue alongside a small stream on your left to enter Raid Deep Wood. Descend the clear path and on leaving the wood follow the riverbank for 1½ miles, passing Jumbles Farm and Hacking Ferry boathouse.

A tablet on the side of the front door of Jumbles Farm dates the house to 1723. Built in the late Stuart style, it takes its name from Jumbles Rocks, an ancient ford that links the two Bronze Age sites of Winckley Lane and Brockhall Eases. The two large mounds near Hacking Ferry boathouse are man-made. The one beside a barn, excavated in 1894, contained a cinerary urn of circa 1250BC, with a cremated body and the skulls of a young man, a boy and a child. The burial was one of an important person, probably a local chieftain. The larger mound, known as Loe Hill, is also man-made. It is thought that it was built after the Battle of Billington in AD798, at a time when the Anglo-British kingdom of Northumbria was fraught with internal conflict. A third mound once stood across the river at Brockhall Eases. During the summer of 1836 the farmer at Brockhall, while levelling the earth mound, discovered

GUIDE BOX

Places to visit
Museum of Childhood, Church Street, Ribchester. An award-winning museum that houses a nostalgic collection of toys, dolls' houses, games etc. Open all year, Tuesday to Sunday, plus Bank Holiday Mondays.

Clitheroe Castle Museum is sited on Castle Hill at the junction of Castle Street, Moor Lane and Parson Lane. Emphasis is given to the geology and the history of the Ribble Valley. Open Easter to end October, daily.

Browsholme Hall, 5 miles north-west of Clitheroe. Historic home of the Parker family, who have lived there for nearly 500 years. It was chosen by Granada TV for their series *History Around You.* Open Bank Holidays, Easter weekend and Saturdays June to August.

Car parking
There is a car park in Ribchester. In Clitheroe there is car parking at North Street, Holden Street, Queensway, Whalley Road and Chester Avenue, which is also suitable for coaches. Street parking in Gisburn.

Public transport
British Rail passenger service almost non-existent. The Ribble Bus Company's Skipton-to-Preston service runs through Gisburn, Clitheroe and Longridge. The closest it gets to Ribchester is 1¾ miles. The Blackburn-to-Preston service runs through Ribchester.

Accommodation
There are a variety of places to stay on this section. See under Accommodation, page 178.

a stone-lined cist. It was said to have contained human bones and the rusty remains of some iron spearheads. All crumbled to dust when exposed to the air.

Hacking Hall, on the Ribble's eastern bank near the confluence of the River

The view over Clitheroe towards Pendle Hill

Calder, is a magnificent Jacobean mansion with a five-gabled, many-mullioned frontage. Follow the river bank to where the River Hodder joins the Ribble as the latter turns sharp east. Continue up the Hodder, through a gate, along a road past Winckley Hall Farm and through the wooded grounds of Winckley Hall. The Hall's most notable occupant was Dorothy Winckley, who, it is claimed, is the 'White Lady' who walks the lanes around the Great Hall at Samlesbury.

When the drive curves left, around Winckley Hall, go right, through a kissing-gate on the right and continue along a field path, parallel to Spring Wood, aiming to the right of Stonyhurst College, seen ahead. On reaching the Longridge-to-Clitheroe road at a junction, turn right along it, using the footpath, and cross Lower Hodder Bridge, slightly upstream of Cromwell's Bridge.

This medieval bridge with three segmental arches, one of the prettiest over the Hodder, is so named because it was there, in 1648, that Oliver Cromwell decided to advance westwards, along the Ribble to cut off the Scots. The Battle of Preston was the result.

Continue along the roadside, now using the verge, for 1/2 mile and turn right to Great Mitton. Cross Mitton Bridge and, just beyond the Aspinal Arms, turn left over a stile. Follow a path along the line of the river, joining a track near where a pipe-bridge crosses the Ribble. Follow the track to Henthorn Road. Take this, edging a wood on the left. Opposite 'Langdales' turn left along a track for 30yds. Turn right and in a few yards cross a stile and follow the boundary of the field ahead to its far corner. Turn right, following a riverside path past a caravan site and picnic area to reach Edisford Bridge, on the outskirts of Clitheroe.

Clitheroe lies at the heart of the Ribble Valley. A bustling market town, it is dominated by a huge limestone rock crowned with the Norman keep of Clitheroe Castle. This proud town has accommodation, a range of shops and plenty of character.

CLITHEROE

GISBURN

APPROX. 10 MILES/16 KM

OS Landranger 103
Start at grid reference SD 726 415
Start point: Edisford Bridge, Clitheroe.
Several car parks in the town.

From Edisford Bridge turn right along Edisford Road, then left, along a metalled path, passing the right side of the Ribbleside Pool, continuing to a riverside path. Turn right along it, soon to curve right away from the river to go between houses into Low Moor, Clitheroe.

Bear left into High Street, which turns right and, just past Union Street, on your right, bear right, past a former Wesleyan School. Follow a fenced track and go over a field to cross a stile. Follow a fence on your right and continue to the edge of Boy Bank Wood. Descend through it and follow the

The river making its way through meadowland near the village of Sawley

riverside to Brungerley Bridge. Turn right, along Waddington Road, and left, as signposted, into Brungerley Park. Follow a wooded riverside path, leaving the park where the river bears left to follow it to the Bradford Bridge. Cross the Bradford road and follow the river bank to a wooded escarpment, 'Bond Hurst', and continue above it into a field. Cross this and climb two stiles into Ribble Lane. Turn left, along it, to Grindleton Bridge, which cross. Follow the riverside path signposted 'Rathmell Sike' and after the first field continue along a flood bank. When the river curves right, leave it over a ladder-stile in a wall to your left and climb two meadows to a road at Foxley Bank (SD 768 460).

Turn right to Sawley and, where a meadow lies between road and river, follow a footpath diagonally right across it to Sawley Bridge. Cross and go into Sawley. The village is known mainly for its ruined Cistercian abbey. Turn left, along the river bank at the Spread Eagle Hotel, continue through the gates of Sawley Lodge and along a metalled drive to another set of gates. On reaching sheep-dipping pens on the left, go through them and follow the line of the fence on your right, crossing it at points, to the river at Hartsails Wood.

To protect farming and fishing interests along this part of the walk, picnicking is not allowed.

Follow the riverside upstream through the Ribble Gorge, where beautiful Rainsber Scar is passed. On reaching the upstream end of Steep Wood, follow a clear uphill track (SD 803 485), climbing the embankment and keeping above woods.

The path bears right, following two sides of a field and crossing a stile on the right. Turn right along a field boundary east of Wheatley Farm and continue along a farm track towards Higher Laithe. Just before it, go left, over a stile, descend to cross Wheatley Beck and continue through a shallow wood and across a field to a farm road left of Coppice Cottages, with Coppice House on your left. Turn right, into Mill Lane, follow it to the A59 on the edge of Gisburn and turn left into the village.

THE GREY HERON

The grey heron is one of the most proficient of Ribble fishers. Standing sentinel-like in the shallows, it embodies the very spirit of this beautiful river, being equally at home in all its reaches.

Solitary and of sober plumage, it is one of the largest and most impressive-looking birds in Europe, having a wing span of about five feet.

In flight it appears slow and ponderous, but head and long neck tucked in, wings arched and legs trailing, it can maintain 30mph for long distances.

For hundreds of years anglers attributed the heron's superior fishing technique to a special oil exuded by its feet which is irresistible to fish. It is in fact just an abundance of patience.

The heronries are in woodland close to water, and herons returning to them spiral down in breathtaking aerobatic displays. Silhouetted against a golden sun, roosting herons are an unforgettable sight.

Gisburn

Horton in Ribblesdale

GISBURN

SETTLE

APPROX. 12 MILES/19 KM

OS Landranger 103, 98
Start at grid reference SD 828 488
Start point: The Post Office/village store,
Gisburn. Street parking.

Gisburn, which sits astride the busy A59, is very old and possesses many attractive buildings, one of the best being the Ribblesdale Arms, dated 1635. The village is the venue for a weekly auction and an annual steeplechase. Parts of Gisburn Church date from Norman times.

From Gisburn Post Office follow the A59 through the village and turn left along the Settle road at the churchyard. Follow it for 1¹/₂ miles and, as the road bends right, turn left, as signposted. Continue diagonally right, to the top right-hand corner of the field. Pass through a fenced enclosure to the right of Castle Haugh, continue alongside a fence and down a path through Bridge Wood. Turn left, over Paythorne Bridge, and follow the road uphill to Paythorne village.

Annually, on the Sunday nearest 20 November, hundreds of spectators congregate on and around Paythorne Bridge, hoping to watch salmon spawning on the sandy gravel river bed. This is one of the two main spawning areas for Ribble salmon, the other being at Nappa Flatts. When opposite the Buck Inn, turn right into Bow Hill Lane, signposted 'To Nappa', and, just before Broach Laithe, turn left as signposted, along

a track. Continue along the edge of a field and turn right along the raised right-hand side of an ancient way, 'Ings Lane'. At its end enter Paythorne Moor over a stile and continue across the left-hand side of the next field as signposted to another stile. Keep in the same direction, signposted at regular intervals, and cross a slab-bridge to a step-stile. Now cross to the top left-hand corner of the next field to a stile alongside a hawthorn. Turn left up the field to a gate.

The boundary between Lancashire and North Yorkshire crosses the Ribble Way at the eastern end of Paythorne Moor. Keep ahead to a road, turn right along it to Halton West and, just before Town Head Farm, turn left along a broad track signposted 'To Deep Dale'. On reaching Low Scale farmyard, skirt the farm, going left then right, and continue ahead, passing a barn and crossing two stiles. Turn right over a third stile and go left towards the left-hand end of a wood and follow metalled Todmanlaw Lane to the B6478 where turn right, briefly, to turn left over a stile before Cow Bridge.

Ⓔ *An 'escape' can be made from Cow Bridge (grid ref. SD 570 827), by crossing the Ribble and following the B6478 for 1¹/₂ miles to Long Preston, which is on a bus route between Settle and Skipton.*

Follow the right-hand bank of a drain and continue along the left-hand side of Wigglesworth Beck. On approaching Wigglesworth Hall go right, in front of a house, cross a bridge and turn left, away from the Hall.

Looking west across the valley, over road and railway, towards Giggleswick

GUIDE BOX

Places to visit
Bolton by Bowland is a charming little village with a green, a stone cross and old stocks. The church contains a tomb dating from 1500 which shows the arms of the Pudsey, Percy, Tempest, Hammerton and other families. The Pudsey tomb has an engraved figure of Sir Ralph Pudsey in full armour with the figures of his three wives and 25 children.

Stainforth Force is a majestic series of limestone steps into a deep pool where, in spate, the Ribble has a 'mile long voice'. Above it, the old packhorse bridge was built in the 1670s by Samuel Watson to replace an earlier ford.

Car parking
Public car parks at Settle and Horton in Ribblesdale. Street parking in Gisburn.

Public transport
The Settle-to-Carlisle British Rail service stops at Horton in Ribblesdale. The Pennine Bus runs between Settle and Skipton. The Ribble bus runs between Skipton and Preston, via Gisburn.

Accommodation
Gisburn, Settle and Horton in Ribblesdale all have places to stay. See Accommodation, page 178.

Wigglesworth Hall, a haven of peace, overlooks an area of uncultivated wetland where the Ribble performs a succession of ox-bows that overflow every winter. This forms an important habitat for a variety of birds including grey heron, curlew, lapwing, redshank, oystercatcher and pied wagtail.

Hereabouts the Hammerton family reigned supreme over many centuries. One of their seats was Hammerton Hall, above Slaidburn, and much of the River Hodder was theirs. They also lived at 14th-century Wigglesworth Hall, with its own chapel; and, to protect their dependants when raiding Scots swept through the Aire Gap, they built a pele tower at Hellifield. They worshipped in Long Preston Church where the hammer heads of their family crest are carved on their tombs. The Hammertons were a bold family with a proud boast that 'From Bowland to the Plains of York we ride over our own ground'. The family fortunes, however, were broken when Sir Stephen Hammerton joined the ill-fated Pilgrimage of Grace and was executed for his pains. It is said that his son, on hearing of his father's death, died of a broken heart. Until destroyed by fire in the 1950s, the tithe barn at Wigglesworth Hall was one of the largest in England.

Cross a cattle grid, bear right over a footbridge and climb to a large ash at the right end of some trees. Continue in the same direction over a series of stiles to join a track leading from farm buildings. Where it bends sharp left, continue ahead, on rising ground, to the right of a ruined barn, guided by a post ahead to a stile.

Turn left, alongside a wall on your left and bear right to a wood. Just before it, turn right downhill, cross Hollow Gill Beck and skirt a large enclosure to follow a farm track to a road. Turn right towards Rathmell.

Celtic Rathmell, with its windbreak of sycamore and ash trees, sits on a hillside because the valley bottom was once a vast uninhabitable swamp. It is an unpretentious village of closely gathered stone-built cottages and farmhouses, all of which share fine views that embrace long, blue fells, the flat 'Ings' of the valley floor and the towering scars and mountains at the dale's head. A Rathmell farmer, so the story goes, climbed on to a haystack to sleep, following a heavy drinking session. While he slept a storm broke at the dale's head and the rising waters of the Ribble lifted the haystack, which was floated downstream for some considerable distance before being deposited on the river bank. The following morning the farmer woke to find himself surrounded by enquiring strangers in what was to him unknown country. When asked where he had come from the farmer shouted, 'I come fra Rothmell – Ra'mell in England'.

Dr Richard Frankland's Non-Conformist Academy, one of the earliest Congregational centres, was founded at Rathmell in 1670.

After 150yds turn left to Far Cattle Side Farm. Continue past the farmhouse and, on approaching woodland, cross a stile on your right and continue left to a signposted stile. Cross a field towards a cricket field and go over the road, edging it at its left-hand corner. Continue along an unsurfaced lane and continue to meet the wood on your right at a tangent. Descend, through it, to cross Rathmell Beck and turn right, along a walled lane. Where it turns right continue ahead, following arrows. Within 30yds turn right, along a smaller track to a stile marked RW. Continue close to a wall on the right and where it ends keep ahead to a facing wall-stile, with Rathmell over on your right. Keep ahead, using a large sycamore tree as a guide. A stile beneath it leads to a road entering Rathmell. Turn left, as signposted, and turn right at a signposted stile near the road's summit. Cross a lawned paddock and keep straight ahead to a large barn. Pass it and in a field corner on your right, near some dwellings, go through a gap-stile. Turn right, along an unsurfaced track, past some buildings and through two gates into a field. Continue diagonally left, downhill, to a stile near its bottom corner. Cross a stile and continue between buildings. Turn right, along a track towards the river, then left at a metalled road for 60yds and right over a stile signposted 'To Settle'. Continue northwards, cross a bridge and a stile and join the river bank. Follow it upstream to Brigholme Barn

The packhorse bridge at Stainforth, built in 1670 and beautiful in its simplicity

Riverside Helwith Bridge Hotel, near Horton in Ribblesdale

and, 220yds beyond the farm buildings, veer left as the river curves right. Go over a field to a road. Cross and continue along a narrow passage between bungalows. Cross part of a housing estate, as signposted, to return to the riverside. Follow it upstream to Settle Bridge.

To the left is Giggleswick, a delightful village with a gurgling beck, the Tems, cawing rooks, a quiet green, delightful cottages and lots of back lanes and paths. The name Giggleswick could have had a double derivation; Norse Farmer Ghikel had a farm or 'wick' and it was sited near a bubbling or 'gugglian' spring. To the right is Settle, which has a station and several places to stay, as well as many buildings of interest.

SETTLE

HORTON IN RIBBLESDALE

APPROX. 8 MILES/13 KM

OS Landranger 98
Start at grid reference SD 813 633
Start point: Settle Bridge, on the western side of Settle. Public car park.

Settle, which received its market charter in 1249, is surrounded on three sides by impressive limestone uplands. Located where stock-rearing, uplands farming meets the mixed farming of the south, it has prospered from both. Later, 18th-century development reduced the town's reliance on farming and today tourism plays an important part in its economy.

Impressive Giggleswick Scar, which lies on a major fracture in the earth's crust, the South Craven Fault, is just west of Settle. It forms the edge of the limestone upland of the Yorkshire Dales National Park through which the Ribble Way passes.

Follow the riverside path, signposted 'Stackhouse', past a sportsground and over fields to Stackhouse Lane. Continue right,

along it, and turn right into a lane at a white house. At the river turn left, along a clear stiled path, past Stainforth Force to Stainforth Bridge. Cross the bridge, continue along the lane and turn right on to the B6479, then left into Stainforth, passing the church. Pass the war memorial, turn left beyond Stainforth House along a short lane, cross a field diagonally left to a stile and, ignoring the obvious path, go diagonally right, uphill, to a field corner stile. Continue uphill, with a wall on your left, cross a ladder-stile and continue uphill, gradually bearing right, to a facing ladder-stile on the horizon. Follow the clear, stiled path ahead to Moor Head Lane and turn left along it. Descend steeply to the B6479. Turn left on to it briefly, and right at the junction. Cross Helwith Bridge, the hotel car park and field. Turn right into a narrow road and, where it bears left, go through a gate, under the railway line and along a walled lane. Follow the river bank to the New Inn Bridge, Horton in Ribblesdale.

EDWARD ELGAR'S RIBBLE DELICACY

Charles William Buck, son of a Settle solicitor, was born there in 1851.

Edward Elgar, second son of the owner of a music business, was born at Broadheath, near Worcester, in 1837.

Buck was educated at Giggleswick Grammar School on the Ribble's west bank. He studied medicine in Manchester and London, became a doctor and established a practice in Settle in 1876.

Elgar was educated at various Roman Catholic schools in and around Worcester, ending his formal education aged 15 years.

The two met at a musical soirée in Worcester in 1882, becoming great friends. In the years ahead Elgar visited Dr Buck's home many times and the friends spent many halcyon days along the River Ribble, being especially attracted to Stainforth Foss and, on its tributaries, Catrigg and Scaleber Falls.

In old age Elgar recalled a local delicacy he tasted on his first visit to Settle – potted Ribble trout.

Horton in Ribblesdale
Gavel Gap

HORTON IN RIBBLESDALE

GEARSTONES

APPROX. 6¹/₂ MILES/10 KM

OS Landranger 98
Start at grid reference SD 807 727
Start point: New Inn Bridge, Horton in Ribblesdale. Public car park in Horton.

From New Inn Bridge, Horton in Ribblesdale, go through the Crown Hotel car park to join the Pennine Way and follow its route along Harber Scar Lane.

At Horton in Ribblesdale the lush valley that takes the mature Ribble to the sea is far behind. Horton in Ribblesdale, as its name implies, is not in the Ribble valley; it is in Ribblesdale, where the mountains of West Yorkshire cradle the infant river. The Ribble valley and Ribblesdale may be synonymous but there are many differences.

Historically, the Ribble has been a natural boundary between Celtic Cumbria and Scottish Strathclyde, between Northumbria and Mercia, when there were three kingdoms and, before Lancashire existed, between Eurwicshire and Chestershire. South of Swanside Beck and east of the Ribble, walkers encounter brooks, cloughs, moors and barns. North of Swanside Beck, Anglican and Danish names are left behind and their Scandinavian and Norse equivalents, ghyll or gill, foss or force, fell and bield, become the new language.

The lead on the roof of the Norman church at Horton in Ribblesdale looks new, but it pre-dates the warring years of the Reformation and the Civil War. Thanks to its out-of-the-way situation, the church escaped the roof-stripping that happened to other churches on main travel routes.

A strange story lies behind a mysterious inscription on a brass plate brought in from the churchyard to protect it from the weather. It reads:-

Sacred to the memory of Richard Thornton, a short time ago schoolmaster here for the district, an honest man, fleeing from the Law, anxious to prove his innocence, and also Elizabeth, his wife. Catherine, their only daughter, erected these tombstones at her own expense as a token of appreciation of the life of her dead parents. Died 29th August, 1744, 57 years.

Nobody knows why the honest teacher was fleeing from the Law. The enigma remains to tantalise.

Close to Horton in Ribblesdale lie famous Alum Pot, Long Churn Cave, Hull Pot, Penyghent Hole and Ginger Pot, names honoured by caving people and reminders that this area is singularly rich in potholes and caves. Alum Pot is 130ft long by 40ft wide and Alum Pot Beck hurls into its depth of 292ft, dropping sheer for over 200ft. Just 150yds away is Long Churn Cave from where a stream and a passage enter Alum Pot's main shaft. Penyghent Pot, which does not look impressive at ground level, is a frightening 500ft deep, making it one of the deepest pots in Yorkshire. Hull Pot is 300ft long and as deep as it is wide, some 60ft.

Horton is a starting point for people attempting the famous circular Three Peaks challenge over Pen-y-ghent, Whernside and Ingleborough. Pennine Way and other long distance walkers use it as a base, as do cavers and pot-holers. The Three Peaks are the best-known of the Yorkshire Dales and their shapes are perhaps the best-loved of all the Dales mountains. Whernside to the north-west is the highest at 2418ft (737m), to westwards Ingleborough rises to 2373ft

The churchyard, Horton in Ribblesdale

GUIDE BOX

Places to visit
The Three Peaks countryside around Horton in Ribblesdale. This part of the National Park is rich in natural limestone treasures. Some of the finest limestone pavements in the country are to be found to the west of Horton in Ribblesdale. They were formed 12,000 years ago at the end of the last ice age when glaciers scraped the land surface down to bare rock. Rainwater draining down cracks and joints in the rock widened them, dissolving the rocks to form grykes. The rocks between the grykes are clints.

The Ribblehead Viaduct is one of the most impressive of the Settle-Carlisle Railway. Work was started on this most scenic of England's railways in 1869 by the Midland Railway Company. Shanty towns were built along the route to house the 5000 navvies who carried out the arduous construction work in harsh and often dangerous conditions. Many who died during the railway's construction are buried in Chapel le Dale churchyard, almost within the shadow of Batty Moss Viaduct, the structure's correct name, although it is known locally as, and is usually called, Ribblehead. For many years following the Beeching report of 1963 the line was under threat of closure. Now that threat has been removed and its future looks secure.

Horton Scar Lane is a typical example of a 'green road', an ancient trackway still in regular use by local farmers and walkers. It connects Horton in Ribblesdale with Halton Gill in Littondale.

Horton Church A delightful Dales church, it is built of locally quarried slate and limestone and the lead on its roof was probably mined locally. One of its stained-glass windows contains an ancient fragment showing the mitred head of Thomas à Becket. All the pillars lean to the south, and have done so for generations. At no other Dales church does the whole interior lean like it does at Horton.

Car parking
A pay-and-display car park at Horton in Ribblesdale. Roadside parking at Ribblehead/Gearstones.

Public transport
This section is not on a bus route. British Rail's Settle-to-Carlisle service stops at Horton in Ribblesdale.

Accommodation
There is a choice of places to stay in Horton in Ribblesdale. See Accommodation on page 178.

(723m), to eastwards and just 100ft (30m) lower, is Pen-y-ghent at 2273ft (693m). In 1887 two Giggleswick school teachers, Canon J R Wynne-Edwards and D R Smith, walked over Ingleborough to have tea at the Hill Inn, Chapel-le-Dale. Whernside beckoned and they decided to tackle it. From its summit Pen-y-ghent lured them on, to complete the three. So the golden age of peak bagging in the Dales began and the Yorkshire Ramblers was born.

In 1897 four of its members started and finished the Three Peaks in 10¹/₂ hours from Gearstones. Today 12 hours is considered a reasonable time in which to 'do' them, clocking in and out at the Pen-y-ghent Café in Horton in Ribblesdale. Because of erosion the present route has been extended to 25 miles with 5,000ft (1524m) of ascent.

Just past Sell Gill Holes (SD 812 744) turn

left, away from the Pennine Way, go through a small gate and behind a barn. Continue over stiled fields and at the far end of a long field pass through a gate below a disused limekiln, pass to the left of a water-tank and enter another long field, soon to cross a deep valley. Climb through a series of limestone outcrops to join a track which passes over Birkwith Cave. Continue along the track and turn left at the first junction. Turn right at the second junction, signposted 'Nether Lodge'.

Ⓔ *The walk can be shortened by taking a farm lane south from High Birkwith (grid ref. SD 800 768), through New Houses, back to Horton.*

To continue on the Ribble Way, where the track turns right, up the hillside, leave it and follow the wall on the left to God's Bridge over Brow Gill Beck (SD 798 776). The grassy path bears left and becomes a clearly defined track as it descends to Nether Lodge. Just past some buildings turn left to Gearstones, as signposted. Continue along the bottom of the hill on your right and cross a ladder-stile in a fence that soon comes into view. Keep forward to Back Hools Barn, which soon appears between drumlins. There are many drumlins along this section of the Ribble Way. Deposited by retreating ice sheets, these mixtures of broken rock debris called boulder clay are clearly identified, rounded hills, frequently shaped like the half of an egg that has been sliced lengthways. The more pointed tail ends of the drumlins point in the direction of the moving ice.

Continue past Back Hools Barn and alongside a wall on your right to Thorns, a cluster of isolated farm buildings. This is home to the Swaledale sheep and its variant the Dalesbred. Other breeds are the Rough Fell and the Wensleydale.

Turn right into a walled lane and at its far end follow the wall round to the left and over the hill to Thorns Gill. Cross a footbridge and bear left along a faint track to the Ingleton-to-Hawes road (B6255) at Gearstones.

GEARSTONES

GAVEL GAP

APPROX. 5½ MILES/9 KM

OS Landranger 98
Start at grid reference SD 779 799
Start point: Gearstones, on the B6255 Ingleton-to-Hawes road. Roadside parking.

Two centuries ago, thousands of head of cattle were gathered annually on Newby Moor and Gearstones where the autumn sales were held.

In the 1870s, the solitude of the wilderness around Batty Moss was shattered by gangs of tough navvies building the Settle-to-Carlisle railway through this wild, inhospitable countryside. An incident in May 1873, shook Gearstones Inn, a roadside hostelry near Ribblehead, to its foundations.

A Ribble wayfarer's view of Pen-y-ghent

A railway labourer drinking there threw a compression cap on to the fire. A loud explosion followed and the oven and the fireplace grate were dislodged. A clock, part of a window frame and 15 panes of glass were broken. Otherwise damage to the inn was less severe than expected. The labourer was committed to the Assizes and the Gearstones Inn entered local folklore.

Turn right along the road and soon after it bends to the right, turn left, along a track signposted 'to Denthead'. Here the Dales Way is joined. Continue past Winshaw, climb steeply alongside a wall and swing right, contouring to the top side of the fell wall. On reaching a footpath sign (SD 787 817) bear left along a more obvious track, climbing slightly, and ignoring a track branching off to the right. Continue ahead, following a clear track and cross into Cumbria at a fence. Cross some duck-boarding and follow the bottom of Blea Moor Hill. Turn right on to the road to Newby Head, leaving the Dales Way. When the Ingleton-to-Hawes road is reached turn left, along it, for about 110yds and turn right on to a moorland footpath signposted 'to Gavel Gap'. Go southwards, past a derelict circular sheepfold, and continue up past a small building. Descend slightly and continue up Long Gill with the beck on your right. Cross it at a junction of streams and follow the right-hand one, Jam Sike, passing a small cairn. Soon the path reaches a wall which once marked the boundary between the old West Riding and North Riding counties. This is Gavel Gap (SD 813 832) and the

concrete block seen in the wall at this lonely spot marks the end, or the beginning, of the Ribble Way.

There being no right of way between Gavel Gap and Cam High Road – the route of both the Pennine Way and the Dales Way, about ½ mile away to the south-east – steps must be retraced for 1½ miles to the Ingleton-to-Hawes road at Newby Head, an ideal support party pick-up point.

RIBBLE HEAD

Of all the railway lines in England the Settle-Carlisle line, opened in May 1876, was the most difficult to build. It remains the highest and probably the most scenic. It is certainly supreme in matching the triumph of its construction with the grandeur of its surroundings. From Settle to Ribblehead, where Ribblehead Viaduct, with its 24 arches, carries the track 165ft above Batty Moss, this most beautiful of main lines follows the River Ribble between Ingleborough and Pen-y-ghent.

Work on the line began in 1869 and was carried out for the London Midland Company by 5000 navvies, housed in shanty towns along the route. Many who had worked abroad in rough areas agreed that never had they worked in as harsh a place as Batty Moss and under such harsh and dangerous conditions.

Some never left when the work was completed. They are buried in the churchyard at nearby Chapel le Dale. Nothing worthwhile comes easy.

Dales Way

ILKLEY TO BOWNESS-ON-WINDERMERE
81 MILES/130KM

THE Dales Way is one of Britain's longest established and most popular recreational long distance footpaths. It was created by the West Riding Area of the Ramblers' Association in 1968 as a way of enjoying a continuous riverside walk, largely using existing rights of way along three of the most beautiful rivers in the Yorkshire Dales, the Wharfe, the Dee and the Lune. With the route coming close to the old Westmorland boundary at Crook of Lune, in the Lune Gorge, however, it seemed logical to link the two National Parks, the Yorkshire Dales and the Lake District, by crossing through the green foothills of southern Lakeland and partially following the banks of the Rivers Mint, Spring and Kent to reach the shores of England's largest natural lake, Windermere.

Since its inception in 1968, the Dales Way has become one of Britain's best loved trails, now on a short list for consideration as a national trail. One reason for its popularity is the variety of the landscape through which it passes, from rich, fertile valley bottoms in central Wharfedale or along the Lune, to the heads of valleys where the rivers are little more than sparkling moorland streams. Although essentially a low-level route – as its name implies, it takes advantage of natural passes formed by steep, often glacier-carved river valleys through the central Pennines – it does have high-level sections, most notably above the watershed of the Wharfe and the Dee on Cam Fell, and along high-level limestone pastures and terraces in upper Wharfedale.

Another reason for its popularity is its accessibility. From the very beginning, the Dales Way was seen as a route that people would want to walk, and so it does not lose itself in remote and hostile places away from all human civilisation and creature comforts. It goes through a number of villages offering pubs, shops, bed-and-breakfast cottages, and youth hostels. There is also good farmhouse accommodation to be found along much of the Way and in recent years a number of specially adapted barns provides clean but basic bunkhouse accommodation.

The Dales Way is also a route which can be easily walked in stages, using good public transport links along almost its whole length – frequent trains run from Leeds and Bradford to the start of the route at Ilkley, whilst at Windermere a branch line feeds into the InterCity service at Oxenholme. The central parts of the route are served by the newly reopened stations at Ribblehead and Dent on the Settle-to-Carlisle railway. There are also useful bus services in upper Wharfedale and local rail services at Burneside and Staveley on the Windermere branch.

Riverside walks are always rich in interest and the Dales Way is no exception. The wildlife, of course, is fascinating in any season. The banks in both the Dales and the Lake District are rich in wild flowers in spring, and there is rarely a stretch without some birdlife. The Wharfe is also a particularly fine river for trout, while the Lune is a salmon river.

The Dales Way is also a walk full of history and legend. There is an Augustinian priory, a deep cataract which has claimed scores of lives, a hunting lodge which became the home of a lord who grew up in hiding as a Cumberland shepherd, a forest chapel, a Roman road, lead-mining villages, the birthplace of one of the greatest geologists of the 19th century whose friendship with Queen Victoria was to result in the renaming of a Dales chapel, and isolated communities who, in the 17th century, took part in the birth of Quakerism.

Most Dales Way walkers follow the route from south to north, if for no other reason than that Ilkley, on the edge of the West Yorkshire conurbation, is so easy to reach by public transport and yet signifies the point where the true Dales country begins. The Lake District is an inspiring destination.

Most of the Dales Way is very well signposted and waymarked, and easy to follow on the ground but there is no consistent waymark symbol yet in use (one is currently

Linton Falls, south of Grassington, used in times past to power a textile mill

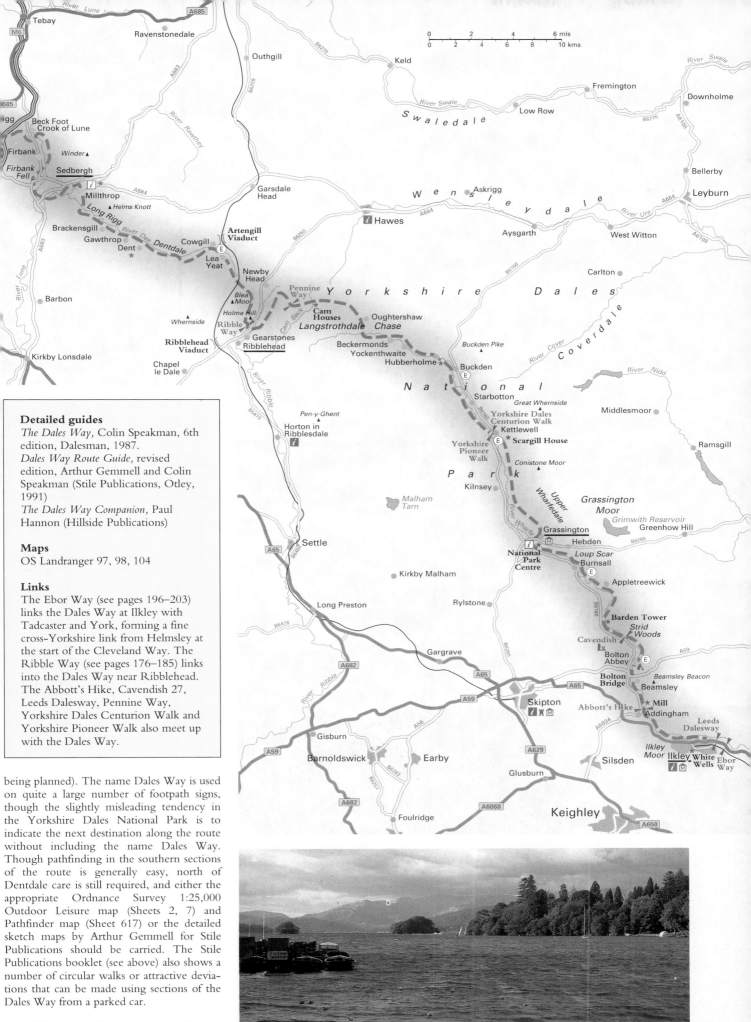

Detailed guides

The Dales Way, Colin Speakman, 6th edition, Dalesman, 1987.

Dales Way Route Guide, revised edition, Arthur Gemmell and Colin Speakman (Stile Publications, Otley, 1991)

The Dales Way Companion, Paul Hannon (Hillside Publications)

Maps

OS Landranger 97, 98, 104

Links

The Ebor Way (see pages 196–203) links the Dales Way at Ilkley with Tadcaster and York, forming a fine cross-Yorkshire link from Helmsley at the start of the Cleveland Way. The Ribble Way (see pages 176–185) links into the Dales Way near Ribblehead. The Abbott's Hike, Cavendish 27, Leeds Dalesway, Pennine Way, Yorkshire Dales Centurion Walk and Yorkshire Pioneer Walk also meet up with the Dales Way.

being planned). The name Dales Way is used on quite a large number of footpath signs, though the slightly misleading tendency in the Yorkshire Dales National Park is to indicate the next destination along the route without including the name Dales Way. Though pathfinding in the southern sections of the route is generally easy, north of Dentdale care is still required, and either the appropriate Ordnance Survey 1:25,000 Outdoor Leisure map (Sheets 2, 7) and Pathfinder map (Sheet 617) or the detailed sketch maps by Arthur Gemmell for Stile Publications should be carried. The Stile Publications booklet (see above) also shows a number of circular walks or attractive deviations that can be made using sections of the Dales Way from a parked car.

Lake Windermere, a fitting end to the walk

Ilkley

Grassington

ILKLEY

BARDEN

APPROX. 11 MILES/18KM

OS Landranger 104
Start at grid reference SE 112 481
Start point: Ilkley. There are several car
parks in the town centre.

The official start of the Dales Way is at Ilkley
Bridge – not the Edwardian Middleton
Bridge carrying the road across the River
Wharfe, but the narrow, hump-backed,
17th-century stone structure about 400yds
upstream. For many years this was the only
bridge across the Wharfe between Otley and
Bolton Bridge, a distance of some 12 miles.

Ilkley is a town with a long history. It was
originally a Celtic settlement, *Llecan,* within
the kingdom of Brigantia. After the Roman
Conquest it became a small military camp,
Olicana, guarding the river crossing and a
junction of important campaigning roads.
Warriors of a later age anglicised *Olicana*'s
name to Ilkley and left behind three
magnificently carved Anglo-Viking crosses,
probably grave-markers, which are kept
inside the church. For centuries Ilkley was
nothing but a quiet village. Then the
discovery of the healing properties of its
moorland springs – on Ilkley Moor of Baht
'At fame – led to its growth during the
Railway Age as the Heather Spa, famed for
its hydropathic cures, bracing air, comfortable hotels, and elegant shopping parades
which have survived into the 1990s to greet
a new clientele.

A signpost by Ilkley Bridge confirms the
start of the Dales Way. The route follows a
riverside track behind gardens to a drive to a
sports centre. A kissing-gate on the left leads
to a path across low-lying fields, heading to
the riverside and squeezing between gardens
and river before crossing more pastureland
and emerging in the old road to Addingham.

The Dales Way follows the riverside to a
lane, right, which leads into Addingham
Low Mill, an interesting adaptation of a
former textile mill and early Industrial
Revolution cottages. A stile leads out of the
cul-de-sac lane into another tarmac lane just
beyond which a narrow path, through a stile
on the left, leads over a tiny hump-backed
bridge to Addingham's fine medieval church,
its size reflecting the importance of this early
industrial settlement from the Middle Ages
onwards. The Way crosses to another footbridge and cottages to the road, Bark Lane,
where 200yds to the right, just by the suspension bridge over the Wharfe, the riverside path begins again.

A popular Dales Way diversion which
takes in some splendid views is reached
directly through the village past Highfield
and Haw Pike to Bolton Bridge, but most
Dales Way walkers keep to the riverside path
past High Addingham Mill (another former
watermill converted for residential use). The
path curves towards the B6160 road to
return almost immediately on to a lovely
stretch of riverside path, dominated by the
view of Beamsley Beacon.

The path once again reaches the road and
to avoid an extremely dangerous stretch of
narrow main road without a footpath, the
Dales Way walker must turn left for 50yds to
the entrance of Lob Wood Farm, going

The Wharfe rampaging through the Strid

GUIDE BOX

Places to visit
Ilkley Moor. An extensive area of ancient
common land and heather moor, rich in
archaeological remains, just south of the town.
White Wells (grid ref. SE 118 467), on the
centre of the Moor and an easy walk from Ilkley,
is an 18th-century bath-house built over one of
the original moorland springs where infirm and
gout-ridden patients would be carried on
donkeys to be immersed in the ice-cold waters.

Manor House Museum, Ilkley. A Tudor manor
house, close to Ilkley Church, which now
houses the town's museum and art gallery, and
contains extensive archaeological remains of
Ilkley's Roman past, as well as exhibitions
illustrating the town's development as a
Georgian and Victorian Spa. Open Tuesdays to
Sundays and Bank Holiday Mondays (tel. 0943
600066).

Barden Tower. Ruins of a medieval hunting
lodge, restored in the 17th century. Open to the
public at all times.

Car parking
There are public car parks in central Ilkley, at
Bolton Abbey (grid ref. SE 072 539), Cavendish
Pavilion (SE 078 552), Strid Woods (SE 059
563), Barden Bridge (SE 053 574), Burnsall (SE
033 611). There is a small car park for access to
Barden Tower only at the Tower (SE 051 573).

Public transport
Frequent British Rail/Metro services from Leeds
(InterCity) and Bradford Forster Square to Ilkley,
Sundays included. Yorkshire Rider bus to Ilkley,
from Leeds and Bradford. Addingham, Bolton
Abbey, Barden and Burnsall are also served by
bus routes.
For full details of bus and rail services within the
Yorkshire Dales National Park see *Dales
Connections,* from National Park Centres or by
post from Elmtree Publications, The Elms,
Exelby, Bedale, North Yorkshire DL8 2HD.

Accommodation
Wide choice of bed-and-breakfast
accommodation in Ilkley and Grassington.
Limited bed-and-breakfast accommodation in
Bolton Abbey, Burnsall. Bunkhouse barn,
Barden Barn. Youth hostel at Linton (2 miles off
Dales Way).
For full details of accommodation on the Dales
Way see the West Riding Ramblers'
Association's *Dales Way Handbook* (available from
27 Cookridge Avenue, Leeds, LS16 7NA) or
Great Northern Walks Where to Stay (Leading
Edge Press, Hawes).

along the track past the farm before reaching
a field path to Lob Wood which descends
underneath an old railway viaduct on the
former Ilkley-to-Bolton Abbey railway
closed in 1965. Reach the road at a stile
turn left and 200yds on the right, past the
lay-by, a stile leads over a footbridge to a
path alongside the stream which emerges at
Bolton Bridge on the A59.

Steps at the far side of the bridge lead to a
path close to the riverside. The large expanse
of pasture on the right is reputed to be the
cornfield where Prince Rupert spent the
night before his defeat at the hands of
Cromwell's Ironsides in the Battle of
Marston Moor, near York, in 1642.

For the next few miles pathfinding is easy
Bolton Priory is soon reached (Bolton Abbey

the name of the village). The Dales Way crosses the Wharfe by a footbridge (stepping stones can be used if the river is low) and takes the path up the steps that leads through the woods, with magnificent views back to the priory.

Ⓔ *From the footbridge (grid ref. SE 074 542) a return to Ilkley can be made along paths and minor roads on the east side of the river (approx. 5 miles).*

The path eventually joins a lane where soon after a ford over Pickles Gill, the Dales Way heads for the riverside where a path leads over the wooden bridge to Cavendish Pavilion, a welcoming café and restaurant, open most days of the year.

Now follows one of the most romantically beautiful parts of the Dales Way through Strid Woods, a magnificent riverside walk rich in natural history. The woods are mainly beech and the area is noted for its variety of lichen, fern and fungi, as well as birdlife. The well-waymarked nature trails provide interesting variations to the main path. The paths converge at the terrifying Strid, a narrow sandstone chasm through which the entire force of the River Wharfe plunges, carving out deep underwater caverns. The name 'Strid' is derived from 'stride': many of those who have attempted the deceptively difficult leap have paid with their lives, the most famous being the Boy of Egremond, heir to the great de Romille Estates in the 12th century.

The riverside path climbs rather thrillingly between crags (some care is needed) to descend to the path leading past the Edwardian aqueduct that carries waters of the Upper Nidderdale Reservoir to Bradford, before reaching the lovely, traditional stone bridge at Barden.

BARDEN

·

GRASSINGTON

·

APPROX. 7 MILES/11KM

OS Landranger 104 and 98
Start at grid reference SE 052 574
Start point: Barden Bridge just east of the B6160, 6 miles north-east of Skipton. There is a small car park.

Barden Tower, about 120yds above Barden Bridge, was originally a hunting lodge built for the Cliffords, Lords of Craven. According to legend, in 1461 when 'Butcher' Clifford, the scourge of the Yorkists, was killed at the Battle of Towton, his widow, Margaret, left her eldest son, Henry to be raised in secret by the family of a Cumberland shepherd. Years later, after Richard III perished at the Battle of Bosworth in 1485, the estates were restored to Henry Clifford, but the 'Shepherd Lord' chose to live at Barden Tower rather than in his great castle in Skipton. Taught by the Canons of Bolton Priory, Clifford became a considerable scholar as well as a wise and just leader. There is a bunkhouse barn near by.

The medieval bridge at Grassington

Between Barden and Grassington the Dales Way is easy to follow, along the north side of the river, from Barden Bridge, past Drebley Stepping Stones, curving into the lane at Howgill Bridge and then returning to the riverside path through a wooded gorge, past a series of white-water rapids. Soon the path passes camp sites by Appletreewick, a village once known for its onion fairs. It has some charming 17th-century cottages and two pubs. Another wooded section of route follows, the path traversing the gnarled roots of trees by the water's edge before crossing to Woodhouse Farm, and open pasture to Burnsall.

Burnsall is a jewel. It is a village in an almost perfect setting, within a great fold of heather-covered fells. There is a superb 17th-century bridge, a medieval church with Viking 'hog-backed' gravestones, and a pub with rose-covered walls offering real ale.

Ⓔ *Burnsall is served by a bus service, useful for an escape back to the start of the walk.*

The route to Grassington starts at the riverside between the Red Lion and the bridge, and soon passes a dramatic geological feature, Loup Scar, a limestone cliff above rocky rapids. This is the result of the great Craven Fault which crosses Wharfedale at this point. From Ilkley the predominant rock has been acid millstone grit; north of Burnsall is the Carboniferous limestone country of the Dales, creating a softer, gentler, landscape with more fertile pastures,

more wild flowers, and drystone walls which gleam grey white in sunlight – or moonlight.

The Dales Way crosses a low, limestone headland before returning to the riverside along a newly reconstructed stretch of path. At Hebden the river is crossed by an elegant little suspension bridge. The path now follows a gentle section of riverside, along a fine avenue of chestnut trees, going over stiles to another great curve of the river where, on the far bank, the long, low profile of Linton Church will be seen. This handsome church, sometimes called the Cathedral of the Dales, dates from the 12th century, and can be reached, when the river is low, by an ancient parishioners' way across worn stepping-stones.

Otherwise the Dales Way turns right through a kissing-gate along Mill Lane, past Grassington's old manorial corn mill (now a trout farm), the powerful spring clearly visible in the fish ponds.

A stile on the right some 50yds above the mill gives access once more to the riverside path which leads to Linton Falls, a series of spectacular rapids and waterfalls over water-carved limestone, another manifestation of the Craven Fault. The footbridge over the river at this point provides a fine viewing platform for the falls. Dippers are usually to be seen in and out of the water. A narrow, enclosed path to the right, known as Snake Walk, leads to the main Grassington car park and National Park Centre.

BOLTON PRIORY

This was a priory of Augustinian Canons (Black Monks) who came here from Embsay in 1154. The nave of the priory church, restored in 1864, is still in use as the parish church, while the evocative ruins, superbly situated on a headland above a bend in the Wharfe, have long attracted poets, painters and writers – Wordsworth, Turner, Landseer and John Ruskin are among the most celebrated to have been inspired by the special sense of place. Open daily, throughout the year, except when services are taking place.

Grassington
Ribblehead

GRASSINGTON

BUCKDEN

APPROX. 12 MILES/19KM

OS Landranger 98
Start at grid reference SE 003 637
Start point: Grassington, on the B6265, 9 miles north-east of Skipton. Parking at the National Park Centre, Hebden Road.

The Dales Way leaves the pretty village of Grassington along its main street, turning left in front of the town hall along Chapel Street. Almost at the bottom of this street is Town Head Farm, a lovely Jacobean farmhouse with mullioned windows. The Dales Way goes through the farmyard past barns, and then alongside a wall to the right across Lea Green.

The wood visible from here on the left is Grass Wood, an exceptionally fine nature reserve, nationally known for its orchids.

But the main line of the Dales Way now crosses upland pasture, the path marked by stiles. There are some superb exposed limestone beds in the crags above Dib Scar. In spring the wild flowers include yellow mountain pansies and the lovely pink and yellow bird's eye primrose, an alpine plant remarkably common on the limestone pastures of the Yorkshire Dales.

The path crosses broad fields, the line of route marked by stiles, soon approaching more scars, this time the top of Conistone Dib, a deep limestone ravine. The Dales Way goes along the top of the Scar, crossing an ancient monastic track known as Scot Gate or Bycliffe Road. This is one of its most spectacular sections – superb, high-level walking, past ancient enclosures and medieval ridge-ploughing terraces or lynchets. There are magnificent views into and across the valley below, past the confluence of the River Wharfe and its tributary the Skirfare which forms Littondale. A notable landmark to the south is Kilnsey Crag.

As the Dales Way reaches an area of woodland just before Scargill House, it bears down a crossing track to join the lane to Kettlewell just before Scargill House.

Scargill House is an Anglican study retreat, and the tall, Scandinavian-style roof of its chapel makes a notable landmark. A narrow path on the right marked by stiles crosses fields into Kettlewell.

Kettlewell, a compact village of grey stone houses and cottages in a dramatic setting of green fields, takes its name from a Norse invader, Ketel. It is another popular tourist and walkers' centre, with a choice of pubs, shops and café.

Ⓔ *Anyone wanting to return to Grassington can do so by bus.*

From Kettlewell the Dales Way is once again a riverside path, the route starting from the far side of the bridge over the Wharfe. The path follows a narrow ledge along the river bank, eventually leading to a broader, partially enclosed path never far from the river, and along a valley whose sides become ever steeper, a classic U-shaped glaciated valley with a flat bottom which is often, after heavy rain or melting snows, flooded to form a series of shallow lakes.

The next village is Starbotton, reached from the Dales Way across a footbridge. This is another compact Dales village with a village pub.

The Dales Way heads north-westwards, again on an easy-to-follow route soon leaving the river and following another narrow enclosed way before joining an estate track through handsome, ornamental woodlands. Just after the point where the river comes close to this track, the Dales way bears to the right to join and follow the river floodbank to Buckden Bridge. Two hundred

and fifty yards along the lane to the right is Buckden village.

Ⓔ *Buckden is also served by buses, for a return to Grassington.*

BUCKDEN

RIBBLEHEAD

APPROX. 12 MILES/19KM

OS Landranger 98
Start at grid reference SD 942 775
Start point: Buckden Bridge. National Park car park.

Buckden is the site of a former hunting lodge in the medieval reserve of Langstrothdale Chase, its name literally derived from the hunt – the wood of the buck or deer. As the last village of Wharfedale, it still has the feeling of an outstation, with an attractive village green, a pub, the Buck Inn, and the last shop and post office until Dentdale. This is yet another former lead-mining community with lead mines deep into Buckden Pike, the hillside which climbs steeply above the village. It is also the terminus of the upper Wharfedale bus.

From Buckden Bridge the Dales Way continues along the west bank of the river via a field gate on the right, again crossing to the river and following it as it loops round to re-emerge in the lane below Hubberholme. This is about the point where upper Wharfedale changes its name to Langstrothdale, a name with strong Viking associations, like other hamlet names along this valley, indicating the settlement pattern of the Vikings who came to northern England via Ireland and Dublin in the 10th century and settled in many of the heads of valleys in the western Dales.

The first of such communities is Hubberholme with its sturdy church, like many in the Dales, built to give a degree of

Upper Wharfedale, near Kettlewell

protection against marauding Scots in the 13th century. It is also one of the few churches in England to have a rood loft, a pre-Reformation screen above the altar, said to have survived because Cromwell's men never reached remote Langstrothdale. The ashes of the great Yorkshire novelist, playwright and broadcaster J B Priestley lie scattered in the vicinity, Hubberholme being one of Priestley's favourite places.

The Dales Way continues behind the church, soon following the riverside once again. In Langstrothdale the Wharfe is now little more than a turbulent stream. As you pass the hamlet of Yockenthwaite with its handsome bridge, it runs in a rocky gorge. Not far beyond Yockenthwaite, on the right, are the remains of a Bronze Age stone circle, its purpose and origin unknown, but quite possibly a place of worship on an already cross-Pennine trade route.

Beyond Deepdale Farm, with its series of stiles, the path crosses to the other side of the river, which is now a number of shallow waterfalls between grassy banks, a popular picnic place on summer afternoons. Beckermonds is soon reached, and for a time the Dales Way has to join the Hawes road, which can be busy in summer, climbing the narrow gorge past a little roadside spring before descending again past Oughtershaw and into Oughtershaw itself. The former school building on the right was originally designed, in Venetian style, by John Ruskin.

The Dales Way now bears off to the left along a lonely farm track. Ahead is Nethergill and, beyond, Swarthgill Farm, a remote sheep farm with its scatter of trees looking like the end of the world. But the Dales Way continues to climb slowly upwards, over rough pasture, towards Breadpiece Barn ahead. The tiny stream to the left, now known as Oughtershaw Beck, is in fact the source of the River Wharfe, and on the hillside opposite, on Oughtershaw Moss, is the moorland spring where this great river emerges, little more than a narrow sike. Only a few yards to the west lies the source of Cam Beck, a tributary of the River Ribble which flows into the Irish Sea – whereas the Wharfe flows into the North Sea. This is the watershed of all England.

Breadpiece Barn owes its name to its curious shape, like a loaf. The route climbs past it over bleak gritstone moorland, but the ascent is soon rewarded – in clear weather – by views of all three of Yorkshire's famous peaks, Ingleborough, Pen-y-ghent and Whernside, in magnificent profiles.

At one of the highest farms in the Dales, Cam Houses, Dales Way walkers can usually find welcoming refreshment and, by prior arrangement, bed-and-breakfast accommodation and a bunkhouse barn.

From Cam Houses the route climbs up through a forestry plantation, eventually reaching a track on the summit of the ridge of Cam Fell at a cairn. This is part of the old Roman Road between Ribchester and Bainbridge built by Julius Agricola in the 1st century AD to tame the warlike Brigantes. It also carries the 250-mile Pennine Way

Kettlewell, a former lead-mining village

between Derbyshire and Scotland.

The views from the Cam Fell High Road are breathtaking, and include not only a splendid panorama of the Three Peaks but also the great multi-arched Ribblehead Viaduct on the Settle-to-Carlisle railway, a magnificent engineering feat on a scale that matches the epic grandeur of the landscape.

The Dales Way follows the Cam Fell High Road to Cam End, a cairn where the Pennine Way bears off to the left, and then continues steeply down to Gayle Beck. Here a ford and footbridge crosses Gayle Beck, leading to a track up to the main Ingleton road. Turn left along the road for Gearstones and Ribblehead where there is a railway station and pub.

GRASSINGTON

With its ancient cottages and shops crowded around a cobbled Market Square, Grassington is one of the most picturesque tourist villages in the Yorkshire Dales. Its past, however, was very different.

The village we see today reflects a 17th- and 18th-century industrial community which arose as a result of the rich veins of lead ore which for centuries were worked and smelted on Grassington Moor, high above the village.

The decline and eventual closure of the mines towards the end of the last century probably helped prevent dramatic change to the cluster of former miners' cottages around narrow courts, or folds, which today gives Grassington much of its charm. The coming of the Yorkshire Dales railway in the early 20th century brought the village its first tourists, numbers of which increased greatly in the era of the motor coach and car, so that Grassington is now a focal point for visitor activity. Shops, cafés, pubs, and a choice of accommodation make it a popular starting point for a range of moorland and riverside walks. There is a National Park Centre in the main car park on Hebden Road, and there is the excellent Upper Wharfedale Museum in the Square.

Ribblehead
Sedbergh

RIBBLEHEAD (GEARSTONES)

DENT

APPROX. 9 MILES/14KM

OS Landranger 98
Start at grid reference SD 764 793
Start point: Informal car park area near crossroads.

The scattered communities between Ribblehead and Gearstones can hardly be said to constitute even a hamlet. In both the 18th and the 19th centuries, however, the situation was very different. At Gearstones there was an inn, part of which still survives as a roadside farmhouse offering bed-and-breakfast and camping facilities. This was one of the most important drovers' inns in the north of England, where Scottish drovers would spend the night while bringing down huge herds of cattle on foot along the drove roads from the Scottish uplands (mainly Galloway and Ayrshire) to the cattle markets of the English Midlands. Many were too poor to afford a room in the inn, but would sleep rough, wrapped in their great tartan plaids, entertaining themselves in the evenings around camp-fires with eating, drinking and dancing. The trade ceased abruptly when the Settle-to-Carlisle railway was opened in the 1870s, though the inn lingered on until World War II.

Activity of a very different kind was seen on Batty Moss around what is now Ribblehead Viaduct, about a mile down the valley, when, in the 1870s, the mighty Midland Railway was pushing its main line northwards to Scotland. Here developed a series of shanty villages housing a vast army of navvies to build the great 24-arch, 165ft high viaduct and the adjacent 2629yds long Blea Moor Tunnel. Many of the workers were Irish but others came from Devon, Scotland and from the Dales lead-mining communities which were already declining. Traces of the villages, which had Wild West, biblical or military names such as Jericho and Sebastopol, can still be seen on the moor together with the tramways used in building the viaduct. Over 1000 lives were lost through accidents and disease in one of the last major railway schemes in Britain to be built almost entirely by manual labour.

One fine variation of the Dales Way at this point is to follow the old Craven Way, a medieval packhorseway from Ribblehead Viaduct which climbs the shoulder of Whernside to run along a narrow, limestone shelf before descending into Deepdale towards Dent. Another popular variation for rail enthusiasts is to follow the line of Blea Moor Tunnel, the path marked by great spoil-tips and brick ventilation shafts across the empty moor.

The main Dales Way route, however, starts from a lay-by just at the unenclosed section of the main road. It follows a track past Holme Hill and goes up around the outside of enclosed land above Winshaw and High Gayle Farms along the edge of Blea Moor, before crossing Gayle Moor to join the road from Newby Head, where it turns left down the lane under Dent Head Viaduct, just beyond the mouth of Blea Moor Tunnel. This impressive viaduct is built of 'black' limestone (which is ordinary Carboniferous limestone with a high carbon content) and is 100ft high and has ten arches along its 197ft length. The lane is a favourite vantage point for photographers taking shots of the occasional Steam Special, as well as the modern blue and grey Super Sprinter trains crossing the viaduct.

The Dales Way follows the lane alongside the little River Dee into Dentdale, soon passing Denthead Youth Hostel. Walking on tarmac (the road is usually quiet) is here

Ribblehead Viaduct strides over Batty Moss

GUIDE BOX

Places to visit
Dent Church dates from Norman times and has a Norman doorway (now blocked), but is mostly late Perpendicular (early 16th-century). Its square 18th-century tower was heavily restored in the 19th century. The pulpit is partially 17th-century and there are some 17th-century pews. There are memorials to Professor Adam Sedgwick (1785-1873) and other members of his family.

Car Parking
Car parking around Ribblehead crossroads (grid ref. SD 765 793), public car parks in Dent off the main street (SD 705 872), in Sedbergh on Dent Road (SD 658 920) and off Joss Lane (SD 660 923).

Public transport
Good train services to Ribblehead and Dent Station (to reach Ribblehead from the south passengers must travel to Dent Station to catch the next southbound train from Dent to Ribblehead). Dent Station is 4½ miles east of Dent.
Limited bus service from Dent to Sedbergh or to Dent Station or Garsdale Station. Limited bus service also operates to Kendal from Sedbergh.

Accommodation
Limited accommodation at Gearstones/Ribblehead. Youth hostel at Denthead. Camp site, bed-and-breakfast provision in Dent. Bunkhouse at Cat Holes, near Sedbergh. Bed-and-breakfast accommodation in Sedbergh.

simply compensated by the intimate beauty of the valley, with river, trees and quiet farms sharing the narrow gorge, the railway high above along the fellside. Just above the junction with the path from Artengill (the old track from Widdale and Hawes), is another fine piece of railway architecture, crossing a narrow gill. Also built of black marble, Artengill Viaduct has 11 arches and is 117ft high.

Just below the Artengill Viaduct is the site of a long-vanished water-powered marble works. Dentdale black marble was highly prized last century for use as an ornamental stone for table-tops and fireplaces, its many fossils gleaming a pale grey when polished. A young Tyneside engineer known as William Armstrong came on a walking holiday to Dentdale with his wife in the 1830s and, fascinated with the waterwheel, conceived the idea of creating a more efficient form of harnessing that power – the turbine. Armstrong went on to found the great Newcastle engineering and shipbuilding dynasty that bore his name, the turbine principle perhaps being one of the most significant engineering discoveries of all time.

The Dales Way continues past the 18th-century Sportsman's Inn (which sells locally brewed Dent bitter).

Ⓔ *At Lea Yeat (grid ref. SD 761 868), where in former times there was a Quaker Meeting House, a lane to the right zig-zags up a 1-in-4 hill to Dent Station, England's highest mainline railway station, at 1150ft (350m) above sea level, and a useful starting or finishing point for anyone walking the Dales Way in stages.*

The main path, however, takes the stile to the left of the little bridge, and follows a rocky, narrow path on the south side of the river. Much of the river here and further along the valley runs dry in the summer or after a period without rain, the stream following subterranean passageways and cave systems through the water-carved limestone, only to re-emerge with spectacular energy after heavy rainfall.

The chapel with a small bell tower across the river, by the trees, is Cowgill Chapel, the cause of a curious dispute in the 1860s. Professor Adam Sedgwick (1785-1873), the great Victorian geologist who was born in Dent, wrote a booklet known as *The Memorial by the Trustees of Cowgill Chapel,* which claimed that through an administrative error the chapel had been wrongly named Kirkthwaite. Queen Victoria, a close personal friend of Professor Sedgwick from the time when Sedgwick had worked with Prince Albert on university reforms, intervened in the dispute and an Act of Parliament was passed to restore the ancient name of Cowgill.

Sedgwick wrote a subsequent pamphlet, like its predecessor, filled with notes on local geology and history and personal anecdote.

Together, the two pamphlets constitute a remarkable record of a Yorkshire dale as it was in Sedgwick's boyhood at the end of the 18th century, a time when new factories in the West Riding were destroying the cottage hand-knitting industry and the 'terrible' (i.e. fast and furious) knitters of Dent were soon to be no more.

The Dales Way rejoins the lane at Ewegales Bridge before once again taking a lovely, meandering footpath across pasture past Rivling Farm, through a conifer plantation to Little Town and on past scattered farms, some now converted to second homes, at Coat Faw, Clint and High Laithe. Being an old Viking settlement, Dentdale was originally divided in Norse, democratic fashion into long, narrow farms, each containing its share of good bottom meadow land and higher poor pasture. Hence, there are few villages hamlets, but isolated 'statesman's' or yeoman farmsteads.

Beyond High Laithe the Dales Way leads back to the lane before crossing to the riverside at Nelly Bridge, a footbridge across a rocky gorge of the Dee where there are fantastic limestone formations to be seen. It then follows the riverside to Tommy Bridge (who Nelly and Tommy were is lost in history), before crossing the pasture to Mill Bridge. At the farm here, in the early 19th century, there was a 'knitting school' where local children learnt the techniques of hand-knitting. Both men and women knitted the rough but hardwearing local wool from Swaledale or Herdwick sheep when tending flocks or undertaking housework, or on winter evenings around the peat or fell coal fire, supplementing otherwise meagre incomes. Most of the vast quantity of woollen gloves, hats and stockings were sold at Kendal market, sometimes supplying the military with winter gloves.

The riverside path continues from Mill Bridge along flood banks above Deepdale Beck to its confluence with the River Dee, then alongside the Dee itself to Church Bridge below Dent. Dent is well supplied with cafés, two pubs, and shops, including an outdoor shop for walkers.

OS Landranger 98
Start at grid reference SD 704 872
Start point: Dent, 4¹/₂ miles west of Dent Station. Public car park off the main street.

The Dales Way leaves Dent by the riverside, conveniently reached by turning down a narrow path to the right some 50yds beyond the car park. The path follows the flood embankment, rejoining the road for a few yards before again following the riverside to Barth Bridge. The Way continues along the same side of the river across stiles and a footbridge, the River Dee here being more sluggish, lined with willows.

The Dent Fault crosses the valley about here, the typical Carboniferous limestones and sandstones of the Yorkshire Dales yielding to the older, harder Silurian slates and shales of the Lake District, a difference which is soon apparent in building style and drystone walls. The colour, form and even vegetation of the landscape change noticeably as you pass the line of Fault. A certain instability on the hillside, including landslips, is caused by the Fault line, roughly marked by the road from Barbon and by Helms Knott, the round hill to the north.

The riverside path eventually emerges in the narrow lane at Ellers, and the Dales Way follows this farm road up past Rottenbutts Wood to Brackensgill to cross the river. The Way then crosses the main Sedbergh road, climbing up to a grassy track across the edge of Long Rigg where there is a spectacular panoramic view of the town of Sedbergh. The track winds down the hillside, through the hamlet of Millthrop and into Sedbergh.

For a less steep route to Sedbergh, stay on the south side of the river at Brackensgill, and go via Cat Holes and Birks Mill.

The old grammar school

DENT

Dent Town, to give it its correct name, is one of the loveliest and least spoiled of all Dales villages, with its narrow, winding cobbled main street, and colour-washed cottages which once had balconies where local people would knit and chat to each other across the road. In the village centre is the fountain of pinkish grey Shap granite, memorial to Adam Sedgwick, a great benefactor to his native dale. The inscription giving his name and dates was only added later, because everyone who mattered in the dale knew who he was and did not need a reminder. There is also a memorial to Sedgwick and other members of his family (Sedgwick is still a common Dentdale family name) in the church. The little grammar school, where Sedgwick was taught by his father, the vicar, before going on to complete his studies at Sedbergh School and Trinity College, Cambridge University, survives behind the church.

Sedbergh
Bowness

SEDBERGH

BURNSIDE

APPROX. 15 MILES/24KM

OS Landranger 97
Start at grid reference SD 657 921
Start point: Sedbergh town centre. Public car parks in Sedbergh.

Sedbergh enjoys a magnificent position immediately below the southern ramparts of the Howgill Fells, with one particular hill, Winder, dominating the town. Though most of the town is relatively modern, some old parts of the town remain, notably some old Tudor shops and courtyards off the Main Street, where, down quiet alleyways, weavers' galleries are still to be seen.

That the town once had a strategic importance is revealed by the fact that a grassy mound immediately behind the town is the site of a Norman motte-and-bailey castle which guarded what was an important pass across the Pennines, now followed by the A684 between Kendal and Richmond. The little National Park Centre in Sedbergh (open daily in summer) occupies a former wool shop which, according to a reputable source, was patronised by playwright George Bernard Shaw because it was the only shop he knew in England that would supply socks, one to fit his left foot and one his right.

It was to Sedbergh that George Fox, son of a Leicestershire weaver, made his way in 1652 after his great vision on Pendle Hill, Lancashire. Soon afterwards, having stayed overnight with his friend Richard Robinson, Fox preached an inspirational sermon to over 1000 'Seekers' on nearby Firbank Fell, standing on a rock still marked as Fox's Pulpit. These Seekers were told to spread the word far and wide, and it was from this moment that the Quaker Movement or Society of Friends, as it came to be known, was established. Despite much suffering and persecution the Quaker faith became strongly established in both Britain and the United States and has an enormous, still continuing influence.

Sedbergh is also celebrated for its Sedbergh School, the village grammar school which during the 18th and 19th centuries expanded to become a major public school. The buildings and playing fields now dominate much of the town.

The Dales Way makes its way out of Sedbergh past these grounds along a path which leads down towards Millthrop Bridge. It continues along the narrow riverside past Birks Mill and bridge and a beautiful stretch where the Rivers Dee and Rawthey meet at a point not far short of where they both join forces with the Lune.

An interesting variation can be made by taking the field path which leaves the riverside before Birks and which crosses to Brigflatts, an unusual early Quaker Meeting House dating from 1675 – a time when the Friends were suffering persecution and, being too poor to fit a ceiling, lined the roof with moss for warmth. The gallery was added in 1711.

The main Dales Way follows the A683 for a short distance before taking a field path across to High Oaks Farm, and then a narrow, grassy track past Luneside Farm, eventually meeting the A684 at Lincoln's Inn Bridge. The name recalls a long-vanished drovers' inn by what was then a ford, Mr Lincoln being the landlord.

Now follows a lovely section of Lonsdale. The Dales Way passes the remains of the Lune Viaduct, on the long-vanished and much lamented Ingleton-to-Tebay railway,

The Friends' Meeting House in Brigflatts, Sedbergh

GUIDE BOX

Places to visit
St Andrew's Parish Church, Sedbergh is a particularly fine Dales church, with work from many different medieval periods – Norman, 13th- and 14th-century work predominating. There is a memorial to John Dawson, the Garsdale shepherd mathematician who was one of the finest teachers of mathematics of his day and tutor to Adam Sedgwick.

The Friends' Meeting House, Brigflatts, Sedbergh is a beautiful late 17th-century Quaker Meeting House with a library and a small garden.

St Martin's Parish Church, Bowness is notable for its magnificent east window filled with 14th- and 15th-century glass, and an unusual 300-year-old carved figure of St Martin, who shared his cloak with a beggar.

Car parking
Public car parks in Sedbergh on Dent Road (grid ref. SD 658 920) and off Joss Lane (SD 660 923), and several in Bowness. Street parking available (with care) in Burneside (SD 505 956) and Staveley (SD 470 983).

Public transport
Limited bus services from Kendal to Sedbergh and from Garsdale on the Settle-to-Carlisle line, summer only. Good train services with InterCity connections at Oxenholme to and from Kendal, Staveley, Burneside, Windermere Town. Hourly bus service along main A591 via Staveley and Burneside between Lancaster, Kendal and Windermere.

Accommodation
Moderate choice of bed-and-breakfast and small hotel accommodation in Sedbergh. Limited accommodation in upper Lonsdale, Grayrigg, Burneside, Staveley. Good choice of all kinds of accommodation including youth hostel in Kendal. Excellent choice of accommodation in Bowness and Windermere.

before taking a series of linking farm and field paths up the valley below Firbank Fell - Low Branthwaite, Bramaskew, Nether Bainbridge, Hole House, Ellergill and Crook of Lune. Compared with the early, better known parts of the Dales Way, this is little known countryside, quiet and peaceful.

Ahead is the Crook of Lune Bridge, the narrow, stone bridge which once marked the most north-westerly point of the old West Riding of Yorkshire at its boundary with Westmorland, (now part of Cumbria). The Dales Way goes under the fine, disused brick viaduct of the Tebay line to Beck Foot where a grassy track and field paths lead to farm bridge across the roaring M6 Motorway to Lambrigg Head. A field path crosses a series of stiles past Holme Park, a fine country house. The route now cuts in front of Moresdale Hall to a lane where, after right then left turns, a bridlepath leads across the high-speed electrified West Coast main railway. Care is needed to cross the tracks.

The Dales Way is now entering the foothills of the Lake District with the route bearing right across pasture to Green Head and Grayrigg Foot on the A685, before taking a meandering path across the River Mint to Shaw End and Patton Bridge.

The route continues past Biglands Farm across fields, marked by stiles, heading past little Black Moss Tarn, to reach a good farm lane and keeping straight ahead past farms with Skelsmergh Tarn visible on the right.

The Way now crosses the A6 and passes below Burton House Farm and over a little stream before crossing more fields by stiles to bear right past Oak Bank Cottages and across to the banks of the little River Sprint and the lane at Sprint Bridge, then turning into Burneside village.

Burneside is notable for its fine pele tower, Burneside Hall, passed on the Dales Way. This is one of several such fortified houses in Cumbria, dating from the 14th century and built as defence against raids by marauding Scots. It has an impressive crenellated tower and gateway. It is now a farm and there is no public access.

There is limited bed-and-breakfast accommodation in Burneside, which also has good rail and bus services into Kendal for a wider choice of accommodation, including a youth hostel and public transport.

BURNESIDE

BOWNESS

APPROX. 9 MILES/14KM

OS Landranger 97
Start at grid reference 508 959
Start point: Burneside, 2 miles north of Kendal. Street parking in Burneside, using consideration.

Between Burneside and Staveley the Dales Way is easy to follow, starting to the right of Burneside Mill, around by a tall fence, to the River Kent and continuing upstream past the weir to Bowston and then turning right along the main road past bungalows. It then picks up the line of an old industrial railway between bungalow gardens and on to Cowen Head Paper Mill, going through an attractive hamlet of mill cottages with another weir and on along a pretty stretch of riverside. This is another good area for birdlife, with mallard and swans usually to be seen. Past Hagg Foot Bridge, the Dales Way eases its way below Cockshoot Woods and soon after crosses the boundary of the Lake District National Park. This stretch of riverside path makes its way on narrow and awkwardly sloping stones, but the attractive views and wooded areas more than compensate for the tricky features of the path. Soon, past the trees, the path once again comes along narrow fields into the village of Staveley, now mercifully by-passed and free of heavy traffic.

Though not a tourist centre, Staveley has shops, an inn and café, and both a railway station and good bus services.

Ⓔ *A return can easily be made from Staveley to Burneside or Kendal by rail or bus.*

A popular and quite spectacular alternative to the Dales Way from Staveley is to take the lane to Kentmere from Staveley where, past

the mill reservoirs, a track leads to Kentmere village (4 miles). From here a superb ancient track, the Garbun Pass, crosses over to Troutbeck, between Windermere and Ambleside, with footpath links into Windermere town.

From Staveley the Dales Way uses a combination of quiet farm tracks and roads and linking field paths through countryside of impressive beauty, as the hills get increasingly steep and more craggy approaching Windermere. A track past Field Close Farm leads to the tarmac track by New Hall to Waingap, a name which evokes old farm wagons lumbering through a narrow pass between the hills. A short way to the right on this lane, and the Dales Way once again plunges along a green lane, now taking a twisting route past a wood and over a lovely area of gorse before climbing to Crag House Farm. From here, the Dales Way winds past cottages known as Outrun Nook and an isolated farm, Hag End, on the shoulder of Grandsire Hill.

Now follows a gentle climb to a low saddle between the hills where there is a sudden, magnificent view, a vast panorama of Lakeland fells unfolding around you. Directly ahead is the long, dark tree-covered valley which contains Windermere, lush, rich and romantic.

The last few miles have a feeling of pleasant anticipation as the Dales Way descends along School Knott, bearing left along the track to the B5284 near Cleabarrow, then along the drive towards Cleabarrow itself, before bearing left along a lovely footpath across parkland by Matson Ground. The well-waymarked path passes mature trees, crosses a farm drive, and bears left by woods and across pasture on the side of the Brant Fell before bearing right to

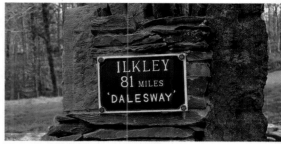

The end of the Way, marked at Bowness

where there is a magnificent view across Windermere itself, usually white with sails, the wooded backcloth of hills shimmering in the water.

Ahead is a fine slate seat on which there is a plaque with the legend 'For Those Who Walk the Dales Way'.

Though this is now the official end of the Dales Way, most people are likely to continue down through the kissing-gate ahead and down Brantfell Road into the centre of Bowness and across to the shores of Windermere itself, England's largest natural lake and a fitting symbol for the end of a walk which enjoys remarkable contrasts of landscape and goes through fine and not always well-known parts of two of Britain's National Parks.

Though Bowness is a busy tourist metropolis, it has its older, and more interesting, side with a fascinating medieval church, Britain's only steam launch museum, some really old pubs, and some excellent shops and cafés. Minibuses link the town centre with Windermere Railway Station, whilst Lake steamers run to Ambleside and Lakeside. The ferry to the western shore leads to Hawkshead and the link path to the Cumbria Way for Carlisle.

THE WINDERMERE STEAM BOAT MUSEUM

This museum on the lake shore has a unique collection of Victorian and Edwardian steam launches, which illustrates the nautical history of the lake from the 18th century to the present day. The examples of both steam- and motor-powered craft, all in full working order, include the steam launch *Dolly,* reputedly the

oldest mechanically powered boat in the world. Twice a year a model boat regatta is held (mid-May and mid-August) and there are other special events and exhibitions during the summer months. Steamboat trips are on offer subject to availability and weather. Museum open Easter to end October, daily.

Ebor Way

HELMSLEY TO ILKLEY
70 MILES/112KM

THE Ebor Way was created in 1975 by Ken Piggin and the Ebor Acorn Rambling Club. The intention was to offer walkers a linking route between the Cleveland Way at Helmsley and the Dales Way at Ilkley. The Cleveland Way is a 110-mile walk that follows the western and northern edges of the North York Moors National Park and then continues down the coast along a clifftop path to end near Filey Brigg. The 81-mile Dales Way (see pages 186–95) follows the River Wharfe through the Yorkshire Dales National Park to its source, then crosses the watershed, descends through Dentdale to Sedbergh and continues to Kendal, finishing on the banks of Lake Windermere at Bowness. This combination of three walks offers 263 miles of walking or, with the Wolds Way (see pages 204–11) some 340 miles of walking.

Detailed guide
Ken Piggin's *The Ebor Way: a 70-mile walk from Helmsley to Ilkley through the ancient City of York* (1990) is a pack of laminated cards with route description and sketch maps, published by Northern Leisure Publications.

Maps
OS Landranger 100, 104, 105

Links
The Ebor Way links the Cleveland Way at Helmsley with the Dales Way at Ilkley. It also links or coincides with the Minster Way, the Leeds Dalesway, the Yoredale Way, the Abbott's Hike, the Centenary Way, the Bounds of Ainsty, the Foss Walk and the Sheriff's Way.

The route chosen for the Ebor Way was not the most direct path but it does pass through some interesting countryside. From Helmsley it heads south, crossing the Howardian Hills to Sheriff Hutton, and on along the banks of the River Foss into York. The route along the city's ancient walls gives good views of York Minster and passes three of the four main bars or gateways. The Way continues south beside the River Ouse to Bishopthorpe, with views of the Archbishop of York's Palace by the river. The line of a Roman road is followed to Tadcaster and the walker meets the River Wharfe for the first time and continues westwards, rejoining it again at Wetherby and Harewood. The final 15 miles is through parkland and along the Chevin, with extensive views. Ilkley Moor is crossed before descending to finish in Ilkley, the start of the Dales Way.

The route the Ebor Way follows is not a high-level path. Its highest point is on Ilkley Moor at about 1000ft (300m) above sea level. This means that there is a rich variety of wild flowers in the lanes and woods on the walk. The Way passes close to the nature reserve at Strensall Common, a mixture of dry and wet heath and a breeding ground for nightjar. Throughout, the mixture of deciduous woods and mixed farmland offers an interesting variety of birds including blackcap, yellowhammer, finch, skylark and pheasant.

The area through which the walk passes is rich in history. The Brigantes had a settlement at Tadcaster, the Romans established York (*Eboracum*) as their northern military base in AD71, the main building being on the site of York Minster. Ilkley was the Roman *Olicana* and Tadcaster was

The broken ruin of 12th-century Helmsley Castle stands on its craggy outcrop

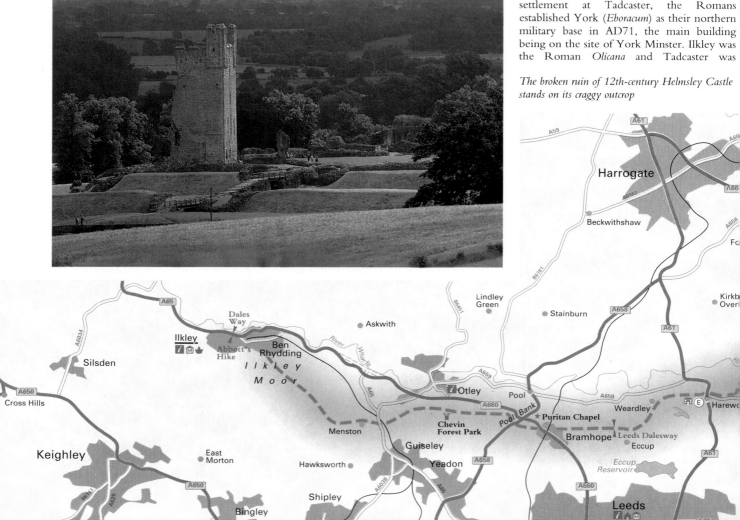

Calcaria, forts which protected river crossings and trade routes. There were other Roman sites at Newton Kyme and Hovingham.

There is a wide variety of interesting churches along the route. Hovingham Church has a Saxon tower and Norman stonework, while Sheriff Hutton Church contains a monument to Edward, Prince of Wales, the son of Richard III. York has many fine churches including the Minster, of course, and All Saints' Church in North Street, both of which have beautiful displays of medieval stained glass. All Saints' Church in the Pavement has a lantern tower which was used to guide travellers through the Forest of Galtres, along the line of the Ebor Way. Bramhope has a Puritan church built during the Commonwealth period, while Ilkley's All Saints' Church stands on the site of the Roman fortress.

For the castle-lover, the Ebor Way offers Helmsley, which was besieged and captured during the Civil War, and Sheriff Hutton, which belonged to the powerful Neville family. The walk around York's medieval walls ends at Baile Hill, the site of one of York's two castles. The other, a motte crowned by a stone keep, stands across the river. Harewood Castle stands at the top of a hill on the outskirts of the village and commands an extensive view over the valley of the River Wharfe.

Various parts of the walk show evidence of the Industrial Revolution. The River Foss was made navigable to Sheriff Hutton Bridge, the work having started in 1794. Wetherby was a busy town during the peak years of the coaching era, serving the stage coaches racing between London and Edinburgh. At Otley, below the Chevin, is an unusual memorial to the navvies who built the railway tunnel that cut through the ridge on which Bramhope stands.

The Ebor Way is well waymarked between Helmsley and York with wooden signboards at road junctions and blue or yellow waymarking arrows on the field

Low Petergate, at York's ancient heart —

routes. Between York and Ilkley there are numerous markers and often a public footpath sign will carry an extra sticker to indicate it is used by the Ebor Way. Field routes and woods which are less well way-marked are covered in detail by the text that follows here, as are routes through towns and villages.

The walk is a relatively easy one, with many points where public transport is available for a return to base. Initially, the section from Helmsley to Strensall has the poorest choice, but there are bus services to Hovingham and Oswaldkirk Bank Top. A convenient service operates from Strensall through York to Copmanthorpe providing a good day's walking and an easy return. Tadcaster is on the regular Leeds-to-York bus route and as you travel westwards there is also the opportunity to use the British Rail services that operate between Ilkley and Menston.

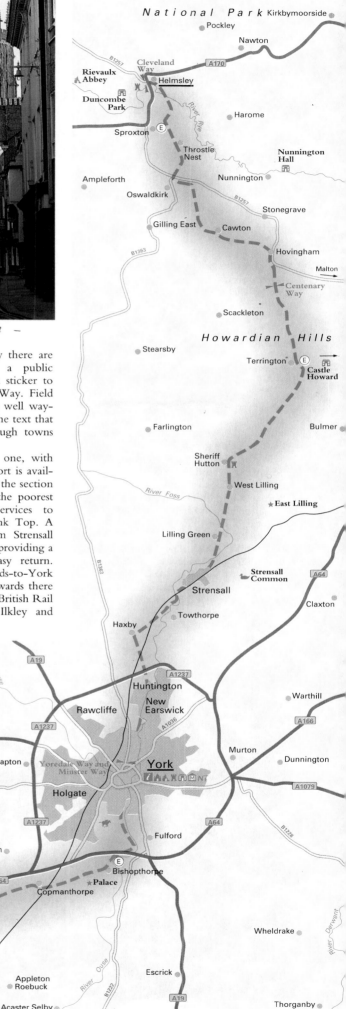

Helmsley

York

HELMSLEY
HOVINGHAM
APPROX. 8 MILES/13KM

OS Landranger 100
Start at grid reference SE 612 838
Start point: The old market cross, Helmsley
Market Place. There is parking in the Market
Place and in Cleveland Way, Helmsley.

The small market town of Helmsley stands
near the River Rye under the southern edge
of the North York Moors. Stone buildings
surround the Market Place and close by is
the castle.

From the Market Place walk down Bridge
Street and just before the bridge turn right
along Ryegate and after 100yds turn right
again into Sawmill Lane. At the end the
track turns right. At the next junction turn
right and then left on a broad track that
becomes a riverside path. Eventually it bears
left towards a gate, passing some yellow flag
irises in a bog. Bear right beside the river to
Moorland Trout Farms. Turn right over a
footbridge, cross the field, then turn left. A
stile and two gates lead to a climb passing
Low Parks Farm. The farm access road
crosses a wooded valley to a track just east of
Sproxton.

Ⓔ *For a 4¹/₂-mile circular walk, continue
straight ahead from here (grid ref. SE 620 814)
into Sproxton village. Turn right along the road
back into Helmsley.*

The Ebor Way turns sharp back left
towards Throstle Nest. Pass through a wood
and then turn right to follow the edges of

the fields. Cross a footbridge, climb to a
tarmac farm road and turn right. Climb
towards Oswaldkirk Bank Top, a wide view
opening up behind across Rye Dale.

At the road turn left for ¹/₂ mile and just
beyond Laysthorpe turn right. There was
once a village at Laysthorpe but it had
diminished in size even by the time of the
Norman conquest. Pass through the yard to a
gate on the right. The Ebor Way descends
and then crosses the valley to the Cawton-
to-Gilling East road. Turn left, pass through
Cawton, a hamlet of stone-built farms and
cottages, and carry on along the track to Spa
House, a large stone house set amongst trees.
The spa was commercialised in the 19th
century.

Continue along the track, heading for
Hovingham's church tower. Cross the
second bridge over a stream in Hovingham
and turn right past the church and the
entrance to Hovingham Hall.

HOVINGHAM
YORK
APPROX. 18 MILES/29KM

OS Landranger 100, 105
Start at grid reference SE 667 755
Start point: The centre of the village, on
the B1257 Helmsley-to-Malton road.

Hovingham nestles under the edge of the
Howardian Hills. The church retains a Saxon
tower with walls 3ft thick. There is an 8th-
century stone altar frontal used as a reredos,
and parts of a 9th-century stone cross. Near

Sproxton Church, just off the Way

GUIDE BOX

Places to visit
Helmsley Castle (EH) stands on a small outcrop of
rock, its defences strengthened by massive
earthworks. It was defended during the Civil
War by Colonel Crosland who only yielded the
castle after a three-month siege. There are still
plenty of remains to be seen. Open Easter to end
September, daily; October to Easter daily except
Mondays.

Duncombe Park, Helmsley. The original mansion
was built for Thomas Duncombe in 1713. Two
disastrous fires destroyed the building, in 1879
and 1895, but the house has now been restored
to its former grandeur. The rooms contain
English and Continental furniture and family
paintings. The house stands in a 300-acre park,
containing a 30-acre landscaped garden. Open
April, Sundays plus Easter weekend; May to end
October, Sunday to Thursday plus Bank Holiday
Saturdays.

Rievaulx Abbey (EH) lies 3 miles to the west of
Helmsley. The extensive remains of the
Cistercian Abbey lie close to the River Rye in a
picturesque setting. Founded in 1131, it is the
earliest Cistercian Abbey in Yorkshire. Open all
year, daily.

Nunnington Hall (NT) nestles under the steep
ridge of Caukley's Bank, beside the River Rye.
It is about 2 miles north of Hovingham. There is
a magnificent hall, and the panelled room is
reputedly haunted. On display are 22 miniature
rooms, decorated in the styles of different
periods. Open Easter to end October.

Sheriff Hutton Church. The nave and tower date
from the 12th century with later additions. Inside
is a tomb with an effigy of the son of Richard
III, Edward the Prince of Wales, who died in
1484 aged 11 years. Close to the church is the
old Glebe conservation area, set around the
mound of a castle.

Car parking
There are public car parks in Helmsley and
York. Roadside parking in Hovingham (grid ref.
SE 667 755), Sheriff Hutton (SE 655 664) and
Strensall (SE 633 608).

Public transport
The nearest British Rail stations are at Malton
and York. Bus services operate from Helmsley,
Hovingham, Strensall, Haxby, New Earswick,
Huntington and York.

Accommodation
There is a youth hostel in Helmsley. Details of
other accommodation are available from the
Tourist Information Centre, Helmsley (see
below), which also operates a bed-booking
service.

by is Hovingham Hall, built by Thomas
Worsley, a friend of George III, in the
middle of the 18th century. Occasionally the
gardens are open to the public. The hall was
the home of Katherine Worsley, the present
Duchess of Kent, before her marriage.

Leave the village on the road to Malton
and just after the sharp bend turn right on to
the road to York. After 200yds turn left up a
lane which in summer supports a mixture of
wild flowers. The lane leads into South
Wood and soon joins the Centenary Way,
an 80-mile walk from York Minster to Filey

Brigg opened in 1989 to celebrate the centenary of Yorkshire County Council.

Bear left in the wood, follow 3ft-high marker posts for ¹/₂ mile to a gate. Continue to a bridge and turn left through a gate and follow waymarkers. Turn right to go past Howthorpe Farm and along its access road, cross over the hill and at the bottom turn right through a gate. Cross a footbridge and continue over the fields to Terrington. Bear right, then left round a walled garden, passing a sportsground with views back over the Howardian Hills. Turn left into the village, passing All Saints' Church whose herringbone stonework is typical of the Saxon period from which the church dates.

Ⓔ *A return can be made to Hovingham by taking the road opposite the church. Turn right along a lane at grid ref. SE 668 707, pass Rose Cottage Farm and go through a wood. At the far corner of the wood bear left to meet a road. Turn right back into Hovingham (a circular walk of about 4 miles).*

The Ebor Way continues into the village of Terrington to the road junction where there is a village pump opposite. The attractive houses stand back from the road; in 1896 one lucky householder found a tin of 100 gold sovereigns while repairing his roof. Turn right, then left along Mowthorpe Lane, continuing past the cemetery to a stile on the right. As you cross the stile there is a distant view of the stark ruins of Sheriff Hutton Castle on the skyline.

Cross the field at the third stile and turn right downhill, past the former Primrose Farm. Cross the stream at a bridge and continue on the path, crossing two more bridges. Bear right across a racehorse gallop before turning left on to a lane that leads to a road. Turn right, then left on to a field route to Sheriff Hutton Church (see Places to visit). Before reaching the church, turn right through a yard and along the village street. Look out for a pair of stocks on the spacious green near the Castle Inn.

Down the entrance to Castle Farm there is a path that turns right along the side of the castle ruins. Ralph Neville, Earl of Westmorland, rebuilt and enlarged the castle in the early 15th century. In 1471 the castle passed to Richard of Gloucester, later Richard III, who had married Warwick's daughter, Ann. The castle now became politically important. Edward, Earl of Warwick and Elizabeth of York, niece of Richard III and later Queen of Henry VII, both stayed here in safe keeping from the Lancastrians. It achieved great importance during the reign of Henry VIII, who sent his illegitimate son Henry, Duke of Richmond, to live in it as Lieutenant-General of the North in 1530. The castle later declined and was in ruins by the reign of Charles I.

The Ebor Way continues to the road junction. Turn left. After 100yds turn left before the village hall, to join a path to West Lilling. Turn left at the village street, then in 25yds turn right along a quiet unsigned tarmac lane out of West Lilling.

The lane crosses a road and continues as a broad track to Lilling Green. A tubular bridge takes the path over the River Foss. Continue, turning right through a nature reserve and alongside the lane beside the railway into Strensall.

Before the level-crossing, turn right through the village. Turn right along the road just before the Ship Inn, cross the bridge over the Foss and turn left along the river bank. The riverside path leads to Strensall New Bridge, the last surviving bridge built by the Foss Navigation Company in 1796. The creation of the Foss Navigation from York meant improved communications for 50 years for the villages of Huntington, Strensall and Sheriff Hutton.

The route continues beside the river, going under a railway bridge, to Towthorpe Bridge. The path now bears right across the field to a road, where the route turns left into Haxby. Just after the sharp bend in the road turn down Landing Lane. After passing some old railway trucks, turn left on a waymarked path and turn right along the river bank. Pass Lock House, a delightful place with water lilies growing on the site of the lock. Cross at a footbridge and return to the west bank at the next footbridge.

Strensall New Bridge spans the River Foss

Pass under the York outer ring road and continue beside the river to Huntington Church. The church was built in 1874 but contains a fine Jacobean pulpit. Robert de Skitherby, an Augustinian friar, collected tolls from travellers at Huntington to be used for making a safe way through the Forest of Galtres. This royal forest covered the area through which the walk passes to York.

Continue beside the river until you join a road at Lock House, New Earswick and then bear left after a short distance, when the river veers away from the road. Your nose indicates the next point of interest: as you pass close to the Nestlé Rowntree factory you will notice the sweet, pleasant smell of chocolate. The path turns right to join a road near traffic lights. Turn left along Somerset Road, cross over a bridge and turn right through a playing-field to rejoin the River Foss which continues to Heworth Green, York. To the right is the roundabout that leads to Monk Bar.

CASTLE HOWARD

Castle Howard lies 3 miles east of the Ebor Way as it passes through the village of Terrington. One of the most palatial stately homes in England, it was designed by Sir John Vanbrugh for Charles Howard, 3rd Earl of Carlisle, whose descendants still live here. The building, completed in 1737, is notable particularly for its cupola, unique at that time on a domestic building.

Familiar to many as the setting for the TV series *Brideshead Revisited*, the rooms are filled with fine furniture and paintings and the house is set in a 1000-acre park and overlooks the Great Lake. There is a large collection of period clothes, and an adventure playground for children. It is open from Easter to the end of October, daily.

York

Wetherby

YORK

TADCASTER

APPROX. 12 MILES/19KM

OS Landranger 105
Start at grid reference SE 608 525
Start point: Monk Bridge roundabout, York on the A1036. There is parking at grid reference 610 526.

From the roundabout walk along Monkgate, then pass under Monk Bar, one of the four main gateways into the city in medieval times. Turn right to climb the staircase inside the bar that leads on to the city walls. There are excellent views of the Minster and the Treasurer's House as you walk to Bootham Bar and descend into Exhibition Square. Walk on past the Theatre Royal and turn right along Museum Street to cross Lendal Bridge. Immediately after crossing the river turn right, back on to the walls, to walk to Micklegate Bar. In medieval times it was on this bar that the barbaric custom of sticking the heads of traitors on poles was practised. Sir Henry Percy, known as Hotspur, and the Lancastrian leaders captured at the Battle of Towton met this fate, and the last victims were Jacobites from the 1745 Rebellion.

Continue on the city walls over Victoria Bar, an opening cut in the walls in 1838. When the opening was cut, a former gateway from medieval times was discovered. This part of the walk ends when you descend to the road below Baile Hill. This hill was the site of one of William the Conqueror's early castles which defended the River Ouse. Turn right and cross over the busy road at the pedestrian crossing and turn left down to the river beside Skeldergate Bridge.

The Ebor Way turns right along the western bank of the Ouse. There is a camping ground about 200yds further on. On the opposite bank is the Minster Way, a 51-mile footpath linking York and Beverley Minsters. The Ebor Way follows the river bank passing under the York bypass. As the path approaches Bishopthorpe, the palace comes into sight beside the river. At one time there was a custom whereby vessels passing the palace gave a salute and a can full of ale was lowered to the deck for the crew. The palace was originally built in the 13th century by Walter de Grey as a residence for the Archbishops of York, but many changes have taken place over the succeeding 700 years. Shortly before Bishopthorpe the path turns right to reach the road.

Ⓔ *To walk back into York turn right on entering Bishopthorpe from the river (grid ref. SE 596 478), cross over the bypass and skirt the Knavesmire, a large open space used for York's horse-racing. When you reach the A1036 turn right to pass through Bootham Bar into the city (a circular route of about 6 miles).*

On reaching Bishopthorpe the Ebor Way turns left, passing the palace grounds near to the gatehouse. The gardens are occasionally open to the public. Turn right beyond the palace and walk through the village, passing three inns. At the junction bear to the right of the school along Copmanthorpe Lane and at the end of the road continue straight on to a small footbridge. Turn right, then left along the edge of the fields, following a line of poles. This leads to the main railway line. Warning of approaching trains is given by red and green lights beside the track.

Cross the railway with care, turn left beside the line and take the third street on the right, Sawyers Crescent, then the second street on the right off Farmers Way – a short street that soon turns into a stoned path. After a gate fork left, join a road, then eventually turn right past the shops to the Royal Oak on the corner. Turn right, then left along School Lane, then right on Manor Heath and finally left on Colton Lane to leave Copmanthorpe. The Way is now on the line of an old Roman road.

Skeldergate Bridge, York, opened in 1881

GUIDE BOX

Places to visit
York offers a wide range of places to visit, from the magnificent Minster to the award-winning Jorvik Viking Centre, where visitors are taken back in time to visit Viking Age York, reconstructed on the original site. There is also an interesting Museum of Automata and the Castle Museum, which includes Victorian and Edwardian streets and offers a fascinating look at everyday life in this and earlier centuries. 'The York Story' has displays on York's medieval and modern history. In addition there are many fine buildings in the city including the Treasurer's House and Fairfax House, a masterpiece of classical architecture, containing a fine collection of mid-18th-century English furniture and clocks.

Two of the halls belonging to York's medieval guilds still survive, the Merchant Adventurers' Hall and the Merchant Taylors' Hall. Standing on a mound close to the river is the keep of York Castle, known as Clifford's Tower, which offers a splendid view over the city. Close to the Ebor Way is York City Art Gallery with its fine collection of British and European paintings. The walk passes the Museum Gardens which contain St Mary's Abbey and the Yorkshire Museum with its archaeological exhibition and where there is often a large feature exhibition.

Marston Moor Battlefield. An obelisk marks the site of the 1644 Civil War battlefield near Long Marston, 5 miles north of Tadcaster. After raising the siege of York, Prince Rupert rode out with his men to meet the Parliamentary forces. It was a confusing battle which the Royalists finally lost.

Towton Battlefield, 3 miles south of Tadcaster, is the site of the bloodiest battle of the Wars of the Roses, in 1461. Close to the B1217 is Lord Dacre's Cross, marking the Lancastrian line, while the Yorkist forces were near the village of Saxton. In the ensuing carnage the Lancastrian forces were trapped beside the River Cock. Many soldiers were buried around the small Lead Church. Lord Dacre's tomb is in Saxton Church.

Bramham Park, 3 miles south of the Ebor Way, beside the A1. The large house was completed in 1710 for Robert Benson, the Lord Treasurer to Queen Anne. The interior contains an excellent display of fine furniture, paintings and porcelain. The formal gardens are designed in a style similar to Versailles.

Car parking
There are two convenient car parks in York (grid ref. SE 610 526 and SE 605 512). There is a public car park in Tadcaster (SE 496 433) and in Wetherby (SE 397 484).

Public transport
There are British Rail services at York. Bus services operate from York, Bishopthorpe, Copmanthorpe, Tadcaster, Thorpe Arch and Wetherby.

Accommodation
There is a camp site beside the Ebor Way as you leave York on the riverside walk. There is a youth hostel at Clifton, York. The two Tourist Information Centres in York (see below) operate a room-booking service.

After about a mile the road turns sharp left. The Ebor Way follows the old Roman road straight ahead, through a small gate and beside a hedge, eventually passing behind a building to reach a road. Turn right to the

main road and cross carefully to the other side of the dual carriageway. Turn left, passing the Little Chef restaurant and bear right down a lane. This leads to a minor road on the outskirts of Tadcaster. Turn left, then right to walk into the centre of a town noted for brewing ale.

TADCASTER

WETHERBY

APPROX. 8 MILES/13KM

OS Landranger 105
Start at grid reference SE 487 436
Start point: The bridge over the Wharfe in Tadcaster. There is a large car park in the middle of the town.

Cross over the bridge coming from York and turn right beside the River Wharfe. It was to the centre of Tadcaster Bridge that kings were escorted by the mayor and bailiffs of York, this being the limit of their control.

Tadcaster saw the remnants of the Lancastrian forces pass by after their defeat at the Wars of the Roses Battle of Towton Moor in 1461, the bloodiest battle fought in Britain with between 28,000 and 38,000 men killed out of some 76,000 on the field.

The walk beside the river passes Tadcaster Church on the left. The church was taken down and reconstructed in 1877 to reduce the risk of flooding from the nearby river. Inside are some interesting Art Nouveau furnishings which were made locally. It is a pleasant riverside walk for the next 2 miles.

The route to Wetherby coincides with the 44-mile Bounds of Ainsty Walk beside the Rivers Nidd, Wharfe and Ouse. When the riverside path approaches Newton Kyme the Ebor Way turns left away from the river, around the boundary of Newton Kyme Hall, to reach a road. On the way there are good views of both the church and Newton Kyme

Hall. Turn left down the road, passing the pretty stone cottages and further on pass the old tithe barn.

Ⓔ *When you reach the A659 (grid ref. SE 455 447), for a 3-mile walk back to Tadcaster, cross straight over the road, pass under a bridge and turn left along Rudgate, an ancient trackway. After ³/₄ mile turn left along a bridleway, past Smaws Farm, to a road. Take the path opposite to the river bank and turn right to return to Tadcaster beside the river.*

For the Ebor Way, turn right for ¹/₄ mile along the A659, then turn right again along a signposted path to the river, where the Way turns left. At this point there is an ancient crossing over the River Wharfe. On the Newton Kyme side of the lane is the site of a small Roman fort and the prehistoric Rudgate trackway leads down to it.

Follow the riverside path – one of the finest stretches on the walk – until it passes along the edge of Boston Spa and reaches the bridge into Thorpe Arch. On the approach to the bridge, pass the spa which gave the town its name; it was discovered in 1744 and the saline spring was believed to be beneficial in treating rheumatism.

Turn right on to the narrow bridge over the River Wharfe into Thorp Arch. A story goes that a traveller staying at an inn near by watched the workmen building the bridge. He ordered beer and food to be sent down to the men at his expense, but early the fol-

The River Wharfe at Tadcaster

lowing morning he left the inn without paying his bill. He left a letter to the innkeeper, wishing him health and prosperity, and from then on the innkeeper did indeed prosper and stayed in good health.

The Ebor Way continues through the pleasant village of Thorpe Arch, which is mentioned in *Domesday Book* as Torp. All Saints' Church was rebuilt in 1871 by the noted architect GE Street, and it retains its Norman south doorway. The walk passes the Pax Inn, an unusual name probably taken from the racehorse which won the Ebor Handicap at York in 1860.

Continue along the road for ¹/₂ mile beyond the village, then turn left along a signposted track. Turn right to pass along the top edge of a wood and bear left to Flintmill Grange Farm. The flint mill used to be on the other bank of the river and flint powder was used as a whitening agent by the pottery trade in the 18th century. The walk continues between the farm buildings and across the fields to the A1 road. Turn right and cross over the road bridge into Wetherby.

THE COACHING AGE

Wetherby was within a mile of being halfway between London and Edinburgh on the Great North Road. The two main coaching inns in the town were the Angel Inn and the Swan and Talbot Inn. In 1750 the roads were in a bad state – wet, deeply rutted and sometimes impassable due to flooding and the journey from London to Edinburgh took 12 days. By 1830 this time had been cut to 45 hours: the carriages were better, the roads had been turnpiked and improved, coaches travelled through the night, and a team of horses could be removed and a fresh team fitted in two minutes.

The Angel carried a stock of over 100 horses and the Swan and Talbot Inn over 60. You can imagine the flurry of activity when the posthorn heralded the arrival of the Mail Coach.

Wetherby

Ilkley

WETHERBY

BRAMHOPE

APPROX. 13 MILES/21KM

OS Landranger 105, 104
Start at grid reference SE 404 480
Start point: The bridge over the River Wharfe in Wetherby. There is a public car park ½ mile west, near the river.

Cross the bridge over the River Wharfe and turn right to the swimming pool car park. Turn right to the riverside path, then turn left and walk round to the footbridge. Cross this and turn right, then left. Cross the park to a stile and go over the golf course to the road. Turn left into Linton, a pretty village set above the River Wharfe. Just before you reach the Windmill Inn turn right along a tarmac road, signposted to Woodall. The minor road climbs, passing a number of 'sleeping policemen' in the road.

There are extensive views across the valley to Collingham and Bardsey. The village of Bardsey on the ridge-top has the site of the oldest inn in Britain. There are records of ale being brewed on the site of the Bingley Arms in the 10th century. Known at that time as the Priest's Inn, it also served as the local court in the 11th century. Bardsey is the birthplace of Restoration playwright, William Congreve.

The tarmac road leads to a small wood, where you turn right, following field boundaries to Sicklinghall House.

Ⓔ *For a 6-mile circular route, turn right at Sicklinghall House (grid ref. SE 367 474) along the road into Sicklinghall village, then turn right along the road back to Wetherby.*

To continue along the Ebor Way from Sicklinghall House, turn left to pass the Wood Hall Hotel. Signs indicate the route to the right and then the left, down a grassy path to the iron bridge over the River Wharfe. The path turns right, then left to reach the A659 road, where you turn right.

Take care walking along this busy road and take a right turn (north), opposite the next (south) turn to East Keswick. The signposted path follows first the hedge, then a green lane down to the River Wharfe, where you turn left along the river bank. After about 2 miles Harewood Castle can be seen on the hilltop. The castle may date back to the middle of the 12th century. The bulk of the castle ruins that can be seen today were built for Sir William Aldburgh. In the time of Edward II the Scots marauded this area, the castle being the only place to withstand the invaders.

From the banks of the River Wharfe

climb up a track to join the road into Harewood, an interesting estate village worth exploring. From Harewood turn right on the road marked with a public bridleway sign, beside the shop and before the Harewood Arms Hotel. Pass the police house and carry straight on along the private road. The road passes through a wood which may well be alive with birds and animals early in the morning. On the left of the road a track leads to Harewood Church, 15th-century in origin. The medieval alabaster monuments inside include one to Sir William Gascoigne, a Lord Chief Justice.

After the cattle grid an extensive view opens out across the River Wharfe to Armscliffe Crag on the skyline. Further ahead you can see the Chevin above Otley, still some 8 miles of walking away. At the junction of tracks take the road to the left.

Ⓔ *A short circular walk back to Harewood can be made by turning right at the junction of tracks (grid ref. SE 306 451). Eventually cross the A659 to reach the riverside path near the road bridge and turn right, continuing for nearly a mile before climbing back up to Harewood on the broad track used by the Ebor Way.*

To continue on the main route, from the junction of tracks where you turned left on to the tarmac road, cross a cattle grid and pass the buildings of Home Farm. Note how the windows are set upright while the building is on a steep slope, looking altogether rather odd. Continue along the road, passing over a stream, then climb steeply before descending to go through two gates across the road. Turn right on the track which climbs to an empty house. Look back for a view of Harewood House and the fish pond over the tree-tops.

When the estate was created, four former villages disappeared – Stockton, Tonehouse, Stubhouse, which were already only very small hamlets, and Lofthouse, which stood to the west of the Leeds-to-Harrogate road, near the entrance to the present estate. The new Harewood village was built in the 1760s and the inhabitants of the four hamlets probably moved into it.

Pass to the right of the empty building and continue on the track into the woods. Turn right twice on the broad track that passes through the wood and joins the road from Eccup to Weardley. Eccup reservoir, to the south, is popular with birdwatchers in winter. Weardley was the birthplace of John Nicholson, who was born in 1790 and became known as the Airedale poet.

Turn left up the road and at the first

junction turn right, before reaching Burden Head Farm. Descend Bedlam Lane and take the second turn left at a public bridleway sign. The track passes Bank Side Farm and Bank Top Farm before reaching a road, where you continue straight ahead. On the outskirts of Bramhope look out for a stile on the right. Cross the stile and turn left along the road into the village. At the junction with the A660 there are old milestones at each side of the road on which the distances to local places are given in miles and furlongs.

BRAMHOPE

ILKLEY

APPROX. 11 MILES/18KM

OS Landranger 104
Start at grid reference SE 256 430
Start point: On the A660 Leeds-to-Otley road, at Bramhope crossroads. Roadside parking.

Walk into the centre of Bramhope, where there is a former market cross that now acts as both a lampost and a signpost. The road to the right leads down to the Puritan Chapel, but the Ebor Way continues straight ahead. At the end of the village turn right on a signposted footpath to Pool Bank. Cross straight over the road at Pool Bank. The signposted path passes through a squeeze-stile beside a gate and the track leads into a wood. Keep the wall on the left until the path meets a broad track. Turn right. There are several routes through the wood but the third track on the left leads through the Chevin Forest Park to a car park. Another lower route gives extensive views over Wharfedale, then climbs back to the same car park beside the Otley-to-Cookridge road.

From the car park turn right down the road and take the second public footpath on the left, signposted West Chevin Road. The broad track climbs on to the top of The Chevin, a ridge offering an exhilarating walk and some superb views. Set below is Otley,

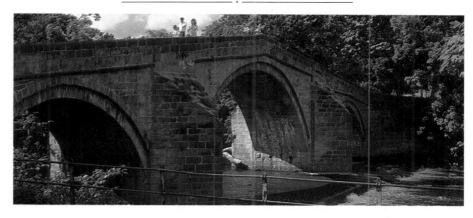

The packhorse bridge at Ilkley, end of the Way

the birthplace in 1718 of Thomas Chippendale, the master furniture-maker and designer. The Way reaches a wood. Keep the wood to the right, then turn left down to Yorkgate. Turn right down the road, turning left and then right to reach the Chevin Inn.

Walk into the car park and bear left, passing a new barn on the right, and descend to a track. Turn left and after 200yds turn right. Keep the hedge to the right, then turn right beside the railway to cross a bridge into Menston. Go straight ahead along Station Road and turn left up Cleasby Road, opposite the railway station. Turn right along Main Street. Pass the Menston Arms and at the top turn right, on the signposted footpath to Burley Woodhead. Sweep left past the houses and follow the lane to reach the entrance to a former bleach mill.

Take the path to the left of the entrance. The route is nearly straight passing to the right of a farm to reach a road. At the top of this road is the Hermit Inn, named after Job Senior, who used to frequent the local inns. He became known for his remarkable range of songs, often singing to earn a drink, and used to appear in local theatres. He married his wife when she was 80, much to her relatives' disapproval – indeed, when she died they pulled down their house in anger. From then on he lived the life of a recluse in the

Climbers on Cow and Calf Rocks, Ilkley Moor

ruins of the house and became a popular sight for travellers.

The Ebor Way carries straight on at the foot of the road, across the fields, to turn left up the next road. At the top turn right down the road, then left on a track which climbs to Barks Crag. The next section of the walk, over the famous Ilkley Moor, is magnificent and heads for the large outcrops called the Cow and Calf Rocks. There are extensive views over Wharfedale, with Ilkley now in sight. From the rocks, head over the moor to the trees, where a footbridge leads to the outskirts of Ilkley. Walk down into the town, crossing straight over the main road to reach the River Wharfe. Turn left through a park and walk along the riverside to the old packhorse bridge. This is the end of the Ebor Way and the start of the Dales Way.

THE RAILWAY NAVVIES

During the vast expansion of the railway network in the 1840s the decision was taken to build a line from Leeds to Thirsk, from where the route would continue on to Newcastle and Edinburgh on existing lines. A major obstruction was the long Chevin ridge (used by the Ebor Way) and it was decided to build a tunnel beneath Bramhope some 2 miles and 243 yards long. Between 1846 and 1849 about 2300 men and 400 horses were used to dig the tunnel and remove rock. During the tunnel's construction 23 men were killed and they were buried in a communal grave in Otley churchyard. The contractor paid for a huge gravestone in the shape of the northern portal of the tunnel to be erected over their grave.

Wolds Way

HESSLE TO FILEY BRIGG
79 MILES/127KM

THE Yorkshire Wolds form an arc of chalk uplands swinging north and east across from the River Humber to end abruptly on the coast between Filey and Bridlington. It is an area unkown to many walkers outside the former East Riding of Yorkshire, although it offers some delightful walking. Even on Bank Holidays it is possible to walk on the Wolds without meeting crowds of people. Typical features of the Wolds are the dry valleys without rivers or streams, making firm walking conditions which would be the answer to a walker's prayer on the Pennine Way.

Detailed guides
The Wolds Way by Roger Ratcliffe (Aurum Press in association with the Countryside Commission and the Ordnance Survey) has a full route description with 1:25,000 OS maps. David Rubinstein's *The Wolds Way* (Dalesman) was the first guide to the walk (now out of date in some places).

Maps
OS Landranger 100, 101, 106, 107

Links
The Wolds way connects near Filey with the 112-mile long Cleveland Way. To the south, the Wolds Way connects across Humber Bridge with the Viking Way, and at Thixendale with the North Wolds Walk. It also coincides with the Minster, Centenary and Derwent Ways.

The Wolds Way, which is well signposted throughout, starts at Hessle Haven and passes under the Humber Bridge. At North Ferriby it turns north along the western edge of the Wolds passing through Goodmanham and Nunburnholme. The route then continues above Millington to Fridaythorpe and Thixendale, to reach Wintringham where it turns east towards the coast at Filey Brigg. The western and northern edges of the Wolds drop away steeply and offer excellent views to the walker. On the eastern and southern edges there is a more gradual descent into Holderness.

This area has a rich history. In prehistoric times it was inhabited by the Parisii, the area around Arras, through which the walk passes, being particularly rich in finds of their culture. Garton Slack to the south-east of the Wolds Way was the site of several Iron Age chariot burials. Prehistoric routes crossed the Wolds and later the Romans built their road from Brough to Malton over the Wolds rather than in the softer lowlands.

The rise and fall of the population of the Wolds is best seen at Wharram Percy. This is the most thoroughly researched deserted village in Britain. The various sizes of the church are marked on the ground as it grew and then contracted due to the change from arable to sheep farming which was less labour-intensive. In the 18th-century came more scientific farming. The Sykes family of Sledmere, with others, changed the Wolds to the rich farmland we see today.

One of the problems for farming the Wolds used to be shortage of water. Around the beginning of the 19th century, however, the problem was solved by fitting new farm buildings with tiled roofs and gutters to take the rainwater into cisterns for pumping out when required. For the animals in the fields, dewponds were constructed. These consisted of a cone-shaped depression dug into the chalk on sloping ground. The hole was lined with layers of clay and straw and was then coated with small stones. Once filled with water, the ponds hardly ever dried out. A number can be seen on the walk.

There are several interesting churches to be seen on or close to the walk, from Goodmanham, which stands on the site of a 7th-century church, to the 19th-century churches designed by GE Street and built at the expense of the Sykes family.

The chalk uplands offer a rich variety of plants including field scabious, rough and lesser hawkbit, salad burnet, crosswort and the delicate harebell. Close to the walk are two nature reserves at Wharram Percy and Rifle Butts Quarry, Goodmanham. The River Humber supports a rich variety of birds, especially waders on the mudflats in

Looking east down river to Humber Bridge

Rowley Church, one of several on the Way

winter. Filey Brigg at the other end of the walk is a landing ground for migrating birds in spring and autumn. The extensive bird list at Filey includes many rarities blown off course during migration.

The Wolds Way owes its origin to the East Riding area of the Ramblers' Association. The name had originated with that doyen of Yorkshire walkers, A J Brown, in the 1930s but the idea for the present route was put forward in 1968 by the Ramblers' Association. It was accepted by the East Riding County Council and the Countryside Commission in principle. Then began a long fight to establish new rights of way and reclaim others which had been omitted from the draft map of rights of way published in 1953. Vast stretches of the route were opposed by landowners and the difficulties of walking the original route are told in the first edition of David Rubinstein's book *The Wolds Way* published in 1972.

Public transport and accommodation can be difficult without walking off the route into nearby towns and villages. The easiest way to complete the walk is either to arrange to be dropped off and picked up in a car, or to set up a vehicle at end each end of a day's walk.

Hessle
Goodmanham

OS Landranger 106, 107
Start at grid reference TA 033 256
Start point: The Ferry Boat Inn, Hessle Haven, 4 miles west of Hull. Parking available.

The Wolds Way starts at Hessle Haven, one of a number of places from which ferry boats used to cross to the southern side of the Humber. Across the creek which forms Hessle Haven there is still shipbuilding, a trade that has gone on for over 400 years. On 30 March 1693 John Frame launched the 80-gun warship *Humber* at Hessle.

Cross over the road from the inn and take the gravel path past the telephone box. This turns right along the river bank and heads towards the Humber Bridge. The towers which support the suspension wires are 533ft high and the span between the towers is, at 4626ft, the longest in the world. After passing under the bridge look for an old whiting mill on the right, in the Humber Bridge Country Park. It was built in the early 19th century to replace a horse-

Beechwoods on Brantingham Dale

powered mill and was wind-powered until 1925, when a gas engine was used. Chalk was quarried near by, crushed at the mill and passed through settling pits. The resultant whiting was used in the manufacture of paints and putty.

Continue for 2¼ miles beside the River Humber, whose mudflats are a rich feeding ground for wildfowl and waders in winter and for birds in passage in spring and autumn. On the approach to North Ferriby, pass a former brickyard pond that is now a conservation area attracting tufted duck, sedge warbler, reed warbler, reed bunting and shelduck. There is also an interesting variety of plants. At North Ferriby a set of steps leads to a car park where instructions are given for an alternative route through the town if the next section of the walk is impassable due to exceptionally high tides. Otherwise, continue on to another set of steps, which gives access into Long Plantation. Continue through the plantation to the busy A63 road. If it seems dangerous to cross the road here, there is a footbridge 600yds to the left.

The route continues through Terrace Plantation to a road where you bear right to a metal gate near quarry buildings. Pass to the south of the large quarry, with views over the River Humber. When you reach a lane, turn left and descend into Welton, an attractive village with a duck pond and the Green Dragon Inn. It was here that Dick Turpin was captured and details are recorded inside the inn. Most of his crimes were committed in the London area where he had been a cattle thief, smuggler and robber. With a price on his head, he headed north, changed his name and took up horse dealing. He was apprehended after threatening to shoot someone during a dispute. Eventually his identity was discovered and he was hanged at Tyburn, York in 1739.

Descend Chapel Hill, taking the first turn right up Dale Road that leads into Welton Dale, the first of many attractive Wolds valleys. After 1¾ miles the path emerges from a wood. Cross the concrete road and turn right along the field side, turning left to Wauldby Manor Farm. This is the site of a deserted village, one of a number on the Wolds, but only the farm and church remain. The path continues, turning right to

join a lane, where you turn left to a road.

Continue straight ahead along the road opposite and when it turns left carry on along a green lane, which eventually becomes a surfaced road. Approaching Brantingham village there are extensive views over the plain and the River Humber.

Ⓔ *For a 6¹/₂-mile circular walk back to Welton, or the main road, take a path to the left at grid ref. SE 947 298, through a plantation, which leads into Elloughton Dale, where you can turn right down to the outskirts of Elloughton and then left along the minor road to Welton.*

For the Wolds Way, watch for an arrow on a pole that indicates a right turn and descend the field to Brantingham Church. The church is picturesquely set at the foot of conifer-clad Brantingham Dale. There is a Norman doorway and font, but the church was one of a number restored by G E Street for Sir Tatton Sykes.

Walk up the dale for nearly ¹/₂ mile, then turn left up a track into the wood. Descend a lane and turn right above Woodale Farm. Climb to Mount Airy Farm and take the access lane down to the road where you turn left towards South Cave. The Wolds Way turns right 100yds down the road.

SOUTH CAVE

GOODMANHAM

APPROX. 11 MILES/18KM

OS Landranger 106
Start at grid reference SE 930 317
Start point: The Wolds Way path just over ¹/₂ mile north-east of South Cave on the unclassified road to Beverley, off the A1034 Hull-to-York road. Roadside parking.

Walk up the road from South Cave and turn left along the signposted Wolds Way path. This path climbs to a lane. Turn right along the edge of Little Wold Plantation. There are extensive views to the south and east over South Cave, which stands on the line of the Roman road from York to Lincoln. All Saints' Church, South Cave was restored in the 17th century after a fire.

At the top turn right along the track until the Wolds Way turns left into Comber Dale. After 500yds turn right along the disused railway track in Weedley Dale. This railway line between Hull and Barnsley was built to break the monopoly of the North-East Railway Company in carrying coal to Hull for shipment from the docks. The construction of the line, which was opened on 20 July 1885, required 4900 workers. The biggest project was the 1¹/₄-mile long Drewton Tunnel, driven through the chalk wolds from the end of this cutting to Little Weighton. The last train ran on the line in 1959.

The Wolds Way turns left out of the cutting, up some steps, at a signpost and into the mixed woodland of West Hill Plantation. Bear left up East Dale and, on emerging from the wood, continue to the B1230 North Cave-to-Beverley road. Follow the path opposite to a minor road and turn right, pass over a crossroads and then turn left. The route descends and turns left into Swin Dale,

The Wolds Way signposted at Brantingham

leading to a road ³/₄ mile east of North Newbald.

North Newbald has two inns. The church is the most complete example of a Norman church in East Yorkshire, the central tower being raised in the 13th century.

Ⓔ *Those wishing to return to South Cave can pass through South Newbald and along the A 1034 Roman road to South Cave.*

The Wolds Way turns right along the road and left just beyond a farm, up a broad track that rises to another road. Turn right for 200yds, then turn left up another wide track. Just over ¹/₄ mile up the road is the Northern Shire Horse Centre at Flower Hill. This intensively farmed area is an appropriate place to maintain these magnificent animals.

The broad track leads eventually to a road,

continues ahead passed Hessleskew and over a crossroads, then bears left along a track to Arras. This area is noted for its 5th-century BC cemetery, which has yielded information on what has become known as the Arras culture. There are estimated to be up to 200 small barrows surrounded by small ditches in the area. The burials can be compared with similar ones in northern France, indicating that there was probably an influx of people from that area at this time.

The path crosses fields to reach a road junction. Go ahead, passing a disused railway track which offers an easy route into Market Weighton, where there are inns and other services. The Wolds Way continues along the road into Goodmanham, where there is another inn, below the church.

CROSSING THE HUMBER

The broad river had proved an obstacle for centuries until the Humber Bridge was opened in 1981, at a cost of £91 million. The earliest known plank-built boats in Europe were discovered at North Ferriby in 1937. Built about 1500BC, they consisted of bevelled oak boards held together with yew withies and caulked with moss. Later, the Romans were to set up a 'Great Ferry' service between Winteringham and Brough and since then ferry services have operated in a number of places. In 1814 the first steam-powered boat appeared on the Humber operating from Hull to Gainsborough. The last steam ferry ceased working across the river in 1978. Schemes had been suggested for both a tunnel and a bridge for many years before the Humber Bridge was finally built.

Goodmanham

Wintringham

GOODMANHAM

FRIDAYTHORPE

APPROX. 16 MILES/26KM

OS Landranger 106
Start at grid reference SE 890 432
Start point: Goodmanham Church, 1¹/₂ miles north-east of Market Weighton, off the A1079 York-to-Hull road. Roadside parking.

All Saints' Church, Goodmanham, probably built on the site of a pagan temple, has Norman work with later additions, and an ornate carved font. The pagan temple was destroyed by Coifi, the high priest, after King Edwin of Northumbria was victorious in battle – the king had promised his queen he would become a Christian if he was successful and, true to his word, on Easter Day 627 he was baptised in York, on the site of the present York Minster.

The Wolds Way passes the top side of the church and continues under the former Driffield-to-Market Weighton railway. The path then climbs to the A163 Bridlington-to-Selby road at Towthorpe Corner, where there is a large car park and picnic site. Just over 2 miles to the east is the racecourse on which the Kipling Cotes Derby is run. Dating back to the 16th century, this is believed to be the oldest horse race in the world. It is always run on the third Thursday in March and one year, 1947, the Wolds were still covered in snow from the harsh winter. The only entrant was a local, Fred Stephenson. The Clerk of the Course read the rules and away Fred went on Londesboro Lad. He made detours around the worst snowdrifts, but even so, had to dismount at one point and lead the horse through a 4ft drift. It took him an hour and 20 minutes to complete the 4-mile race, the slowest ever.

Cross the road and continue through the parkland of Londesborough Hall. A castellated building was built about 1589 by Francis, Lord Clifford which was enlarged in about 1670 by Richard Boyle, 1st Earl of Burlington. The estate passed to the Duke of Devonshire, who pulled the house down in 1818 to build farmhouses. In 1845 the estate was bought by George Hudson, the Railway King. A more modest Londesborough Hall, built in brick, can be seen as you pass through the parkland into the village.

Ⓔ *A waymarked path leads from Londesborough to Market Weighton. This offers a 7¹/₂-mile circular route back to Goodmanham when coupled with Hudson Way, a walk on a disused railway line named after the Railway King.*

All Saints' Church, Londesborough

The Wolds Way continues straight ahead in the village, turns left at Warrendale Farm and right at the crossroads. After a mile, at the T-junction, turn right, then left through Partridge Hall, pass above a wood and eventually turn left to descend into Nunburnholme, which takes its name from a vanished Benedictine nunnery. The church is partly Norman and contains the shaft of an Anglo-Saxon cross. The rector from 1854 to 1893 was Reverend F O Morris who wrote a six-volume book on British birds.

Turn left past the church, then right around a field to the road where you turn left. Fork right up a steep track through Bratt Wood to Wold Farm, cross the Warter-to-Pocklington road and continue with Kilnwick Percy below to the left, pass Warrendale House Farm and eventually turn right up a track beside Warrendale Plantation, and along the wold top above Millington. The path crosses two valleys before climbing out above Pasture Dale.

For a short while the Wolds Way coincides with the Minster Way, a 51-mile walk between York and Beverley Minsters. It then continues over the Wolds to a point north of Huggate, where you turn left on the road towards Northfield House. On the roads in the vicinity are some curious quasi-'Roman' milestones and markers bearing pseudo-Latin inscriptions that were erected earlier this century.

The Wolds Way continues over the fields to reach an earthwork running along the top of the valley. These earthworks are some-

GUIDE BOX

Places to visit
Pocklington nestles under the edge of the Wolds. On an outside wall of the 12th-century church is a plaque to Thomas Pelling, a professional acrobat. In 1733 he attempted to fly from the church tower to a nearby inn, using an aerial ropeway, but unfortunately he collided with the church wall and was killed in front of a large crowd. Housed in the former cinema in the Market Place is Penny Arcadia, a fascinating collection of mechanical amusements operated by pennies (open May to September, daily). On the outskirts are the noted Burnby Hall Gardens, which contain a national collection of water lilies and a museum with hunting trophies. At Canal Head, beside the York-to-Hull road, is a picnic site and a walk alongside the Pocklington Canal.

Malton dates back to Roman times and the foundations of the Roman fort lie under the Orchard Fields on the Old Malton road. The early history of the area is explained in the museum in the Market Place. There are also changing exhibitions on the area's more recent history and crafts. The museum is open from April to end October, daily, and on Saturdays in November and December.

Eden Camp, Old Malton was a World War II prisoner-of-war camp. The site, close to the bypass, has been restored and the 30 huts contain an interesting look both at aspects of World War II and the social conditions of the 1940s. Themes covered range from the rise of the Nazi movement and the Home Guard to a walk through a blitzed street and the inside of a submarine being depth-charged. There are also military vehicles, a tank and a full size replica Spitfire. Open from February to December, daily.

Eden Farm Insight, Old Malton. Near Eden Camp is a working farm that is open to the public. There are farm walks of up to 2¹/₂ miles and a Pet's Paddock for children. Farm machinery, old and new, is on display, including a combine harvester stripped down to a skeleton, to show how it works. Among displays are a blacksmith's shop and a wheelwright's shop. There is a farm shop and picnic area. Open from Easter to end October, daily.

Car parking
Parking is not a problem in any of the Wolds villages. There is a car park and picnic site at Towthorpe Corner (grid ref. SE 878 439), a car park with access to Wharram Percy (SE 860 643), and also at Wintringham Church (SE 887 731).

Public transport
The nearest British Rail stations are at York and Malton. Bus services operate from Market Weighton, Fridaythorpe and along the A64 from Malton to Scarborough.

Accommodation
There is a youth hostel at Thixendale and the Tourist Information Centre at Malton (see below) offers a bed-booking service.

thing of an enigma: they may have been built to mark boundaries in prehistoric times, and here, set at the top of the valley, they would make a defensive mound – especially with a palisade. Descend into Horse Dale and bear left into Holm Dale, the name being all that is left of the vanished village of Holme Archiepiscopi, the seat of a York prebend. In 1295 there was a manor house, chapel and nine tenants and the outline of the row of houses with their garths can be seen on aerial photographs of the fields.

The path continues into Fridaythorpe, a village set on the A166 York-to-Bridlington road. It was the home of a man called Wellburn, an expert at making the dewponds that were used to water animals all over the riverless Wolds.

FRIDAYTHORPE
WINTRINGHAM
APPROX. 14½ MILES/23KM

OS Landranger 100, 101, 106
Start at grid reference SE 875 591
Start point: The centre of Fridaythorpe on the A166 York-to-Bridlington road.

The route out of the village is along the Thixendale road, which turns left off the main road at the Manor House Inn. After 400yds bear left on the signposted path just before Northern Nutrition Ltd. This leads to a path that descends into West Dale, then climbs more gradually to Gill's Farm. At the road turn right, then left after 100yds to the top of a valley. The path swings left down the hillside, then right towards Thixendale.

At this point the Wolds Way coincides with the North Wolds Way, a 20-mile circular walk covering the high wolds and valleys. Turn left on the road through Thixendale. Set in these remote valleys, the village is easily blocked off by winter snowfalls. There is an inn, and the former village school now doubles as a youth hostel and village hall. The church, like the former school, was designed by GE Street at the expense of Sir Tatton Sykes.

The Wolds Way leaves Thixendale up a broad track on the right at the end of the village. Cross over Cow Wold and descend into a valley with an earthwork along the bottom. Climb out along another earthwork and turn right, passing North Plantation to reach a minor road from Wharram le Street to Thixendale. At this point you are on the same route as the Centenary Way. This 80-mile walk from York to Filey Brigg was opened in 1989 to celebrate the centenary of the founding of Yorkshire County Council. As well as Wolds Way signs there are Centenary Way signs and yellow waymarkers with CW. In a few places the Centenary Way route to Filey Brigg varies from the Wolds Way route.

Immediately after joining the road, the Wolds Way turns left and before reaching Bella Farm passes a small grassy car park. This is the parking place for visitors to Wharram Percy, a deserted village set in the valley bottom. Close to Wharram Percy is Burdale Tunnel, where the Malton-to-Driffield railway cut through the Wolds. The 200 navvies who built the tunnel lived a hard and rough life in temporary lodgings, much of their wages being spent in the beer shop. In 1849, to improve their spiritual life, it was decided to employ a missionary for six months, at a cost of £39 6s 8d.

The Wolds Way passes Bella Farm and eventually continues over the fields into Wharram le Street, where you turn right to the road then left through the village, where accommodation is available. Just beyond the end of the village, when the road bears left, carry straight on up a track to join the North Grimston-to-Duggleby road. There is a superb view from here as the Wolds drop away towards Malton, the Derwent valley and the Vale of Pickering.

Cross straight over the road along a track then turn left down to Wood House Farm. A climb past High Bellmanear leads to Settrington High Street, probably a prehistoric ridge route. Near by is the site of Settrington Beacon, set up to warn of the threat of the Napoleonic invasion.

The approach to Wintringham

Slightly to the right, the Way continues on a path through the trees to turn right and then left to descend off the northern edge of the Wolds. The route continues straight ahead for a mile before turning right over the fields to cross a footbridge and enter Wintringham. Just over a mile down the road, to the left, is the Malton-to-Scarborough road, with a good bus service into Malton (where there is accommodation). The Wolds Way bypasses Wintringham, but both the village and church are worth exploring. The Way turns left at the road then sharp right to head over the fields towards Wintringham Church, where there is a car park.

WHARRAM PERCY

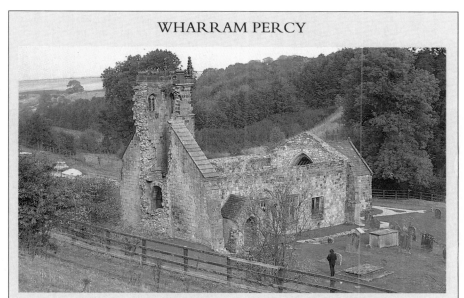

An interesting diversion can be made off the Wolds Way (grid ref. SE 867 644) down into the valley bottom, to the site of Wharram Percy village. People had lived and worked in the valley for 2000 years before the village was deserted in about 1500. The landowners switched from arable farming to sheep-rearing, thus gaining more profit but requiring fewer workers. If the farm workers did not move elsewhere, they found themselves evicted. In 1517 records show that a case was prepared for the prosecution of the landlord for evicting families.

In 1950 excavations began on the site and continued every July for the next 40 years, making Wharram Percy the most intensively researched deserted village in the country. Apart from the ruined church, the foundations of earlier churches can be seen, as well as the foundations of a 13th-century village and manor house, old field systems and a reconstructed pond.

Wintringham
Filey Brigg

WINTRINGHAM

GANTON

APPROX. 9¹/₂ MILES/15KM

OS Landranger 101
Start at grid reference SE 887 731
Start point: The car park near
Wintringham Church, 2 miles south of the
A64 Malton-to-Scarborough road.

From the car park, facing the church, turn
right and walk to the bend in the road. Turn
right, then left at the Wolds Way signpost.
Cross the field and begin climbing steeply
through the wood. From the top there are
views northwards across the Vale of
Pickering to the North Yorks Moors. An
earthwork leads to a lane, where you turn
right past West Farm. Then turn left and
right above Knapton Wood.

Rising out of the wood is a chalk hill
named Staple Howe. In the early 1950s the
noted local archaeologist Tony Brewster
became aware of prehistoric pottery on the
site and subsequent excavations revealed an
Iron Age settlement of three buildings, and a
wooden palisade defending the hilltop.

The Wolds Way continues on the ridge-
top until a right turn leads to a road above
West Heslerton.

Ⓔ *For a 6-mile circular walk you can turn right
along this quiet road (grid ref. SE 911 748) over
West Heslerton Wold to grid ref. SE 916 726,
where you turn right down a track to a road in the
valley. Turn right, back to Wintringham.*

To continue on the Wolds Way, walk
along the track opposite and turn left at the
end of the wood. A right turn leads back on
to the plateau top. As the path climbs, the
view opens out down to East and West
Heslerton. Between the two villages an
extensive archaeological dig has been
recently undertaken on an Anglo-Saxon site.

Continuing eastwards, the walk passes
above East Heslerton whose prominent
church was another designed by GE Street
and built in 1877 at the expense of Sir
Tatton Sykes. Walk eastwards until a right
turn leads to a minor road at the top of
Sherburn Brow. Turn left down the road for
a mile, then either follow the Wolds Way by
turning right at the signpost or continue the
short distance into Sherburn, where there are
two inns and a frequent bus service to
Malton and Scarborough.

Ⓔ *For those who wish to break the journey and
return to Wintringham, there is the option of
taking the Malton bus from Sherburn (grid ref. SE
958 767). Alight at Wintringham Lane End and
walk back into the village.*

To continue on the Wolds Way, follow
the signposted path to the Sherburn-to-
Weaverthorpe road and turn right. In front
of you as you reach the road is High Mill
Farm. High Mill ground corn, and a dam on
East Beck retained the water to power the
wheel. A little further downstream was Low
Mill which was also used for grinding corn.

When the road forks, bear left up the
Foxholes road. At the end of the first field
turn left on a signposted path which leads
into Brow Plantation, then descend and turn

Below *The Wolds Way passes Ganton Hall, on
the outskirts of the village of Ganton*

right into the hamlet of Potter Brompton.
Take a right turn along the road, then left
over the fields into Ganton. The Way is now
running beneath the Wolds, which rise to
your right. When you reach the road, turn
left and walk the short distance down to the
main road, where there is an inn and a
regular bus service to Malton and
Scarborough.

GANTON

FILEY BRIGG

APPROX. 15 MILES/24KM

OS Landranger 101
Start at grid reference SE 986 776

Start point: The crossroads in Ganton, on the A64 Malton-to-Scarborough road. There is parking in a lay-by near the inn.

Walk up the road towards Foxholes and turn left along Main Street. Continue over the stream and along the track, passing the church on your left. The Way continues straight ahead, then turns right just beyond a plantation and climbs back on to the Wolds. A series of left and right turns crosses the familiar open countryside to reach the B1249 Scarborough-to-Driffield road. Four hundred yards to the left is the picnic site at Staxton Brow which offers an excellent viewpoint.

Take the road opposite which leads to RAF Staxton, a radar defence station which first opened in 1939. The track eventually turns right over Staxton Wold, then left above Cotton Dale.

Earlier this century the Wolds had a large group of itinerant workers called the Wolds' Rangers. They were always available to farmers during the busy periods such as harvesting. At other times some may have moved on to another district, but many stayed on the Wolds all the year round. Most were hard-working and appreciated by the farmers; a few were not against a bit of stealing — usually of game or other food. A custom prevailed with the farmers of never refusing to help them and barns were left open to provide shelter. Sir Tatton Sykes had a bell fitted to the back door of Sledmere House and any Ranger who rang the bell received a meat sandwich and a cup of tea. Many had unusual names: Cut Lip Sam was an excellent worker, there was Bungey Twist and Horse Hair Jack, Well Well carried his belongings in a cart, and Cloggie

Sam sold trinkets to the farmers' wives.

Cross two valleys to reach the minor road from Flixton to Fordon, turn right for 400yds then left on a track to pass above Raven Dale on your right. Cross Camp Dale and climb the small dale opposite. The route then turns right, descending back into grassy Camp Dale and swinging left to a valley junction. At this point the Centenary Way turns right to find a different route to Filey, while the Wolds Way turns left up Stocking Dale. At Long Plantation the path turns right, passing Stockendale Farm to reach the Flixton-to-Hunmanby road.

Continue straight ahead on a route with extensive views along the coast. The end of the walk is now in sight. After about ¹/₂ mile the Wolds Way turns right, crossing over the fields to reach the A1039 Staxton-to-Filey road, on the outskirts of Muston. There is a pub in the village. In 1886 a wooden Wesleyan chapel was moved bodily from South Cliff, Scarborough and set up in Muston. It was placed on a special carriage and hauled the 9 miles by traction engine.

Pass through the village and just after the road takes a sharp left turn, bear left below a triangular green (the path is indicated at the right end of the terrace of houses in front of you). Follow the path over fields to the busy A165 Scarborough-to-Bridlington road. Cross straight over and walk through the long field to a footbridge, where you turn right to the main road into Filey.

Turn left and walk down the road and over the railway crossing to a roundabout. The most pleasant way to reach Filey Brigg is to turn left at the roundabout and bear slightly right at the next junction along Church Street. In Queen Street, to the right, is the Filey local history museum, housed in a 17th-century cottage. Over one of the doorways is an interesting carved stone, probably erected when the house was built.

The route to Filey Brigg continues down Church Street and crosses a ravine on a footbridge. Ahead is the church where Reverend

THE WALKING PARSON

Canon AN Cooper (1850-1943) was the vicar of Filey for 55 years. He first came to the notice of the people outside this area when he set off after service one Sunday and walked to London in six days. He arrived at the Bank of England by 2.00pm and returned by train for the following Sunday service.

In 1887 he set off and walked from Filey to Rome, a distance of 743 miles, in six weeks. Although he walked for pleasure he wrote a number of books on his walks, reaching a larger audience than his lectures. He also undertook walks across France, from Dieppe to Monte Carlo, 601 miles; from Hamburg to Budapest, 600 miles; and from Filey to Venice, 653 miles. Also he undertook walks in Holland, Portugal and Norway.

A N Cooper, known as the 'Walking Parson', was vicar for 55 years.

Turn right on the path alongside the churchyard wall, to keep the wooded ravine on the right. Follow the top path and swing left along the cliff-top. Steps lead across the small valley, a popular place for birdwatchers spotting rare migrants. The Filey North Cliff Country Park is to the left as the clifftop path follows round to Filey Brigg.

Here there is a decision to be made. For the purist, the Wolds Way continues along the cliff-top towards Scarborough for another 1¹/₄ miles and then, at a stile set on the old North Riding-East Riding county boundary, the Wolds Way ends and the Cleveland Way begins. For many the prospect of taking the path down the Brigg and easing their feet in the sea will be more appealing. A return to Filey can be made either along the beach, if the tide permits, or along the cliff-top again.

Filey Bay: fishermen's cobles and, at the far end, the rocky reef, Filey Brigg

Cumbria Way

ULVERSTON TO CARLISLE
76 MILES/122KM

Detailed guide
John Trevelyan's *The Cumbria Way*, published by Dalesman, has a route description and sketch maps.

Maps
OS Landranger 90, 96

Links
The Furness Way crosses the Cumbria Way near Skelwith Bridge.

JOURNEYS are explorations and the Cumbria Way is unsurpassed in the rewards it offers discerning walkers. It begins quietly enough in Ulverston, an unpretentious town described by one of its most famous sons, Lord Birkett, as 'a family town. Everyone knowing everyone; everyone rather friendly'. The sea is virtually on its doorstep and from the swelling uplands on its outskirts there are breathtaking all-round views. The vast expanse of Morecambe Bay lies to the south. Westwards is the Duddon estuary, with Black Combe beyond: the Pennines spread along the distant, eastern horizon. Coniston Old Man and its attendant fells soon loom large to the north, a stunning background to the long, lovely reach of Coniston Water, lying almost due north to south.

From Coniston's eastern shore Grizedale Forest extends to Windermere, the 'Winandermere' of the Lakeland poets and the largest of the lakes. It provides an arboreal wonderland, embroidered with nature trails. Each misty autumn the forest explodes in a riot of glorious russet, lemon and red.

Coniston village sits darkly beneath the Coniston Fells that rise steeply almost from the back doors of the houses, the rugged Yewdale Crags prominent among them. Until about 1916 several small tarns were dotted about an area of marsh to the east of the Coniston Fells. Then a landowner, James Marshall, built a dam and converted them into one. He planted various clumps of conifers around it and in so doing turned the place into a beautiful, if somewhat alien, Lake District feature. Its name, Tarn Hows, is taken from a nearby farm and is not really appropriate because a 'how' is a hill. Perch, roach and rudd live in this exquisite gem.

Great Langdale, with Windermere's head in its mouth, is one of the most spectacular of the Lakeland dales, hence its popularity. Lingmoor Fell separates it from Little Langdale and both meet at Elterwater,

overlooked by the twin towers of Pike of Stickle and Harrison Stickle. All the drama of Lakeland lies in these vales where, on gentle days, pliant nuances of light delight painters. But this wild landscape is fickle, constant only in inconstancy. When the mood takes it, placidity is swept aside by ill-humoured fury within the compass of a few minutes.

North of the Langdales, Sergeant Man, 2414ft (736m), marks the geographic heart of the Lake District – but this is a tenuous distinction, for Lakeland's heart is in the eye of the beholder. For some it is a honeypot like Keswick, Ambleside or Bowness; while others favour the exquisite arabesque of the Jaws of Borrowdale and Grizedale. To mountaineers and fell-walkers, cruel bastions like Great and Green Gable, Haystacks, Helvellyn, High Street, the Pillar Saddleback, Scafell Pike and Skiddaw, the lakes they dominate and the passes that cross the high ridges, offering challenge, excitement and the opportunity for valiant spirits to soar, are the real Lakeland. For those who find contentment in the companionship of mountains, that rare,

Coniston, from across the Water

proud breed of solitary fell wanderers, it is in the northern fells 'back o' Skidda' that the pulse of Lakeland is strongest.

In friendly hostelries – and Cumbria is bursting with them – convivial company, flowing ale and fine fare draw out another important aspect of Lakeland life through talk of farming, fox-hunting, fishing and famous folk long dead.

Collectively the Lakeland fells present a formidable array of peaks, pinnacles and summits that are overwhelming in their complexity. But they can be split into a dozen groups or ridges and this aids identification. Anti-clockwise from the Coniston Fells, in the south lie the Scafell Fells and north of them the Great Gable group, flanked by the Pillar group to the west and the High Rise and Central Fells to eastwards. Then come the High Stile and Dale Head ridges, north of which is found the Grasmoor group. Furthest north is the Skiddaw group. To the east lie the Helvellyn ridges with the Fairfield Horseshoe south of them and, lastly, the far eastern High Street Fells. Keswick, superbly situated close to the shores of Lake Derwentwater and sheltered on its northern side by Skiddaw, England's third highest mountain, is an excellent centre for exploring some of Lakeland's loveliest corners. Walks radiate from it through beautiful countryside, much of which is owned by the National Trust.

Both Samuel Taylor Coleridge and Robert Southey lived at Greta Hall, Keswick, and its associations with the 'Lake Poets' are surpassed only by Dove Cottage and Rydal Mount. William and Dorothy Wordsworth were frequent visitors, Charles and Mary Lamb were entertained there, as were Hazlitt, De Quincy, Shelley and many other literary giants.

Keswick's literary links, however, are not confined to Greta Hall. John Ruskin's associations with the town are legend. Shelley and his young bride spent their honeymoon on Chestnut Hill, Keswick. James Spedding of Mirehouse, on the eastern shore of Keswick's other lake, Bassenthwaite, was the foremost authority of his day on the works of Sir Francis Bacon. He included among his friends Tennyson, Carlyle, Monckton Milne and Edward Fitzgerald, the translator of Omar Khayyám. They and other eminent mid-Victorian writers and poets visited him at Mirehouse. Of all the lovely places in England's green and pleasant land, the Lake District is justly called beyond compare. With its mountains, high fells and hidden valleys, its literary associations, its fickle moods and ever-changing aspects, it is truly the land of romance, a magical place.

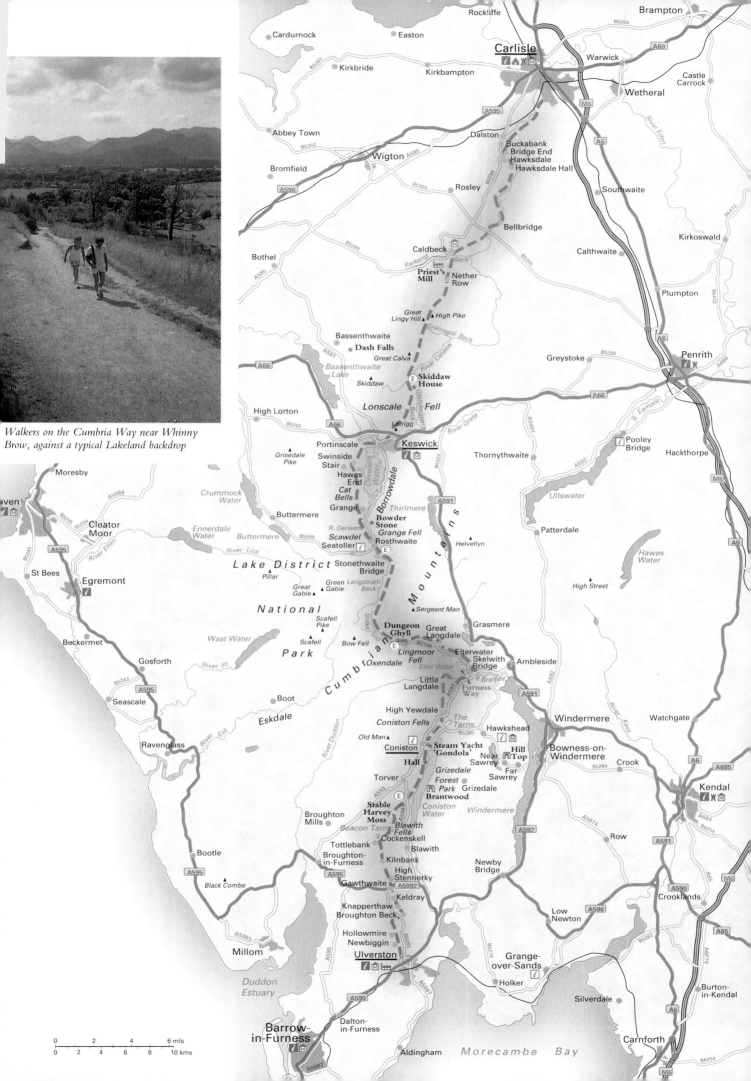

Walkers on the Cumbria Way near Whinny Brow, against a typical Lakeland backdrop

Rockliffe
Brampton
Easton
Cardurnock
B6264
Carlisle
Warwick
A69
Kirkbride
Kirkbampton
Castle
Carrock
Wetheral
Abbey Town
Dalston
A595
Buckabank
Bridge End
Hawksdale
Hawksdale Hall
B5302
Southwaite
Wigton A595
Rosley
Bromfield
A596
Bellbridge
B5305
Kirkoswald
Bothel
Caldbeck
Calthwaite
Parkend
Beck
Priest's
Mill
Nether
Row
B5299
Plumpton
A595
Great
Lingy Hill
High Pike
Grainsgill Beck
Greystoke
Penrith
Bassenthwaite
Dash Falls
Great Calva
River Caldew
B5288
A591
Bassenthwaite
Lake
A66
Skiddaw
Skiddaw
House
R. Eamont
Pooley
Bridge
Hackthorpe
High Lorton
Lonscale
Fell
Glenderaterra Beck
Latrigg
River Greta
Thornythwaite
A591
Keswick
Ullswater
A592
Portinscale
B5322
Patterdale
A6
Grisedale
Pike
Swinside
Stair
Derwent Water
Borrowdale
Hawes
End
Cat
Bells
Grange
Thirlmere
Helvellyn
Hawes
Water
Crummock Water
Bowder
Stone
Grange Fell
Rosthwaite
High Street
Buttermere
B5289
R. Derwen
Scawdel
Seatoller
Ennerdale
Water
Lake District
Stonethwaite
Bridge
Pillar
Green
Gable
Langstrath Beck
River Liza
River Ehen
National
Great
Gable
Scafell
Pike
Sergeant Man
Cleator
Moor
A5086
Moresby
A595
Park
Scafell
Dungeon
Ghyll
Great
Langdale
Grasmere
Egremont
B5295
Bow Fell
Lingmoor
Fell
Elterwater
Skelwith
Bridge
Ambleside
St Bees
B5294
River Ehen
Wast Water
Oxendale
Elter Water
Furness
Way
R Brathay
A593
Beckermet
Eskdale
Little
Langdale
A591
Windermere
Watchgate
River Irt
High Yewdale
The
Tarns
Hawkshead
Gosforth
B5343
Coniston Fells
B5285
Bowness-on-
Windermere
Crook
Boot
Old Man
Steam Yacht
'Gondola'
Near
Sawrey
Hill
Top
A6
A685
Seascale
Coniston
Far
Sawrey
River Esk
Hall
Grizedale
Forest
Grizedale
B5284
Kendal
Ravenglass
Torver
Park
Brantwood
Coniston
Water
Windermere
A5074
Stable
Harvey
Moss
Bootle
Blawith
Fells
Cockenskell
Newby
Bridge
Row
Broughton
Mills
Beacon Tarn
Blawith
A595
Tottlebank
Broughton-
in-Furness
Kilnbank
A592
Low
Newton
A590
Black Combe
A5095
High
Stennerky
Gawthwaite
A5092
Keldray
Crooklands
M6
Knapperthaw
Broughton Beck
A684
A65
Hollowmire
Newbiggin
Low
Newton
B5278
Grange-
over-Sands
A590
Burton-
in-Kendal
Ulverston
A5093
Duddon
Estuary
Millom
Holker
Silverdale
A6070
Barrow-
in-Furness
Dalton-
in-Furness
A5087
Aldingham
Morecambe Bay
Carnforth
B6254
M6

0   2   4   6 mls
0 2 4 6 8 10 kms

Ulverston
Coniston

OS Landranger 96
Start at grid reference SD 284 785
Start point: The car park at the western end
of the Gill, Ulverston.

Beyond the ring of small towns circling Lakeland is an outer ring of larger ones, where contact is made between the dales and the farming and industrial lands. Ulverston is one such town which, while becoming industrialised in the final decade of the 18th century, still carried out its function as a market town. When Rennie built a canal connecting it with the sea, Ulverston became a port for the Furness iron industry. The town thrived and by 1840 its population numbered over 5000. The advent of the railway in 1850, however, and the discovery of the famous Park iron ore deposits led to the rapid expansion of nearby Barrow, while Ulverston's industry declined. Ulverston's once-important blast furnaces have been demolished and replaced by a penicillin factory and today this grey and white town remains astonishingly unsullied, having about it the gentility of a minor spa town.

From the car park follow the beck which, when Ulverston was a textile centre, provided the water power. After about ¼ mile cross the beck and climb a walled lane. At its end turn right along a field track, signposted to Old Hall Farm. Cross the farmyard, pass the farmhouse and immediately cross a stile on your left. Just beyond the farmhouse garden, cross another stile on your left and go diagonally right, past the corner of a wood on your left and continue uphill to cross a corner step-stile. Turn right, then left uphill, to a gap-stile in a wall corner. The prominent monument seen on Hoad Hill, overlooking Ulverston, is a 100ft replica of the Eddystone Lighthouse, erected in 1850 to commemorate Ulverston-born John Barrow, writer, traveller, Arctic explorer and, for 40 years, Secretary of the Admiralty. He was born in 1764.

Contour a hillock, cross a depression and then a field to Higher Lath Farm. Continue right, along the road to Windy Ash and follow a CW signpost along a short, grassy track to Newbiggin to go through the farmyard and along a surfaced road. When the road turns right, leave it through a gate and head across fields.

Keep to the right of Stony Crag Farm and do not enter the farmyard. Instead, turn left, through a gate and immediately turn right behind the farm, following a wall on the right and continue alongside a beck to Hollowmire. Turn right, through the farmyard, follow a farm road to a junction and turn left for 200yds, then right through a kissing-gate. Take the field path past the church ahead and turn right, along a road to Broughton Beck.

Scafell and Scafell Pike can now be seen to the north-west, while closer to hand buttercups, oxeye daisies and a constant splurge of wild roses brighten lush hedgerows. Leave the village along a track and on reaching a beck turn left into a field. Head left across it, to a not very obvious step-stile mid-way along the wall section of a

Ulverston, one of The Lakes' larger towns

GUIDE BOX

Places to visit
The Laurel & Hardy Museum is in Upper Brook Street, Ulverston, and houses the largest collection of Laurel & Hardy memorabilia in the world. Laurel – his real name was Stanley Jefferson – was born in Ulverston in 1890 and teamed up with Oliver Hardy in 1926, to become pioneers in cinema comedy. Open all year, daily.

The Renaissance Theatre, Fountain Street, Ulverston, is a venue for touring theatre and music groups from across the country.

Ulverston Point, The Old Cornmill, Mill Street, Ulverston, is a good craft gallery.

Coniston Water. The lake is approximately 5 miles long and ½ mile across at its widest. At some points the depth exceeds 180ft. Wintering wildfowl and nesting birds use the lake and the shore and these conservation areas should be avoided. The Lake provides for sailing and racing, windsurfing, canoeing, diving, swimming and angling.

Steam yacht Gondola (NT). Cruise on Coniston Water in Victorian style. Up to 86 passengers can enjoy opulent travel in the National Trust's renovated steam yacht, *Gondola* which, when launched from Coniston Hall for service on Coniston Water in 1859, was described as 'a perfect combination of the Venetian and the English Steam Yacht'. Piers at Coniston and Park-a-Moor, at the south-east end of the lake. April to end October, daily.

Brantwood, John Ruskin's Coniston house is one of the most spectacularly sited houses in England. There are exhibitions of local interest and a good café. Open all year, mid-March to mid-November, daily; winter season closed Mondays and Tuesdays.

Car parking
The best Ulverston car park is in the Gill, but there are others. Roadside parking in Blawith (SD 288 833) and in Torver (SD 285 942), a mile off route. There is a large car park in Coniston village.

Public transport
Ulverston is on the British Rail Furness Line, between Lancaster and Barrow. There are good bus links to Barrow, Coniston and Newby Bridge, with connections from the latter to Grange, Kendal and Windermere.

Accommodation
There is a youth hostel in Coniston. An Accommodation Guide giving details of hotels, guesthouses and bed-and-breakfast farms in and around Ulverston is available at the Tourist Information Centre (see below). Details of camp sites throughout the Lake District are available from: The Regional Public Affairs Manager, The National Trust, Hollens, Grasmere, Ambleside, Cumbria LA22 9QZ, and from the Lake District National Park Visitor Centre, Brockhole, Windermere LA23 1LJ.

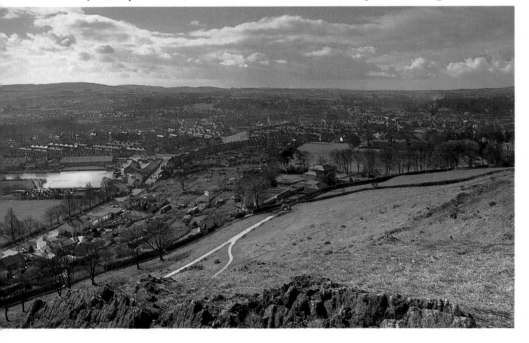

mix of wall and hedgerow. Veer left across the next field, bridging the beck in its middle, and go upstream, using a series of stiles, to an unsurfaced road.

The distinctive-looking grey heron fishes these parts and may be seen, sometimes in flight, its long neck tucked against its body and its legs stretched far beyond the tip of its tail, sometimes standing motionless at the beck's edge waiting to pierce an incautious fish or frog.

Just past Knapperthaw, turn right at a Y-junction and left at the next one to follow the track to Keldray. Pass to the left of it and climb to a wall-stile near an electricity pole. Continue ahead, past Keldray, and cross the A5092 to Gawthwaite village.

The A5092 is the southern boundary of the Lake District National Park, which, at 866 square miles, is the largest of the National Parks. Unlike similarly designated areas in some other countries, the National Parks are made up of land that is not publicly owned.

Climb sharply out of the village along a road that soon levels out. At the third gate turn right along a gravel road to High Stennerley. Turn left here, around the back of the buildings, on to a minor road. Turn right along it for 35yds and then enter a field on the left. At a minor road, go left along it for ¹/₂ mile.

The Cumbria Way leaves the road at a sharp bend (grid ref. SD 277 871) for Kiln Bank, but anyone wishing to break the journey here can do so by continuing along the road for a further mile to Blawith, on the A5084, where church, pub and roadside parking are available.

BLAWITH

CONISTON

APPROX. 8 MILES/12.5KM

OS Landranger 96
Start at grid reference SD 288 884
Start point: Blawith, on the A5084 Coniston-to-Ulverston road. Roadside parking.

From Blawith the Cumbria Way may be joined at Beacon Tarn by going left at the north end of the village, along a lane to Picthall, continuing along a path to Greenholme Farm and turning left along a lane at the end of which a path leads to Beacon Tarn.

The Way itself continues from Kiln Bank (grid ref. SD 274 873). Where the track splits, just beyond the farm, take the right-hand, higher route to a surfaced road (grid ref. SD 272 880). Go left towards Tottlebank.

From March to October, annually, migrating wheatears are much in evidence around this climbing road, the white rumps of both sexes a complete give-away. Once served up as delicacies on Victorian dinner tables, today's delightful wheatears are definitely not for human consumption.

At a CW sign marked on slate turn right along a rising green track through bracken. It is a joy to walk, the views are terrific, and it soon descends to Cockenskell. Pass to the left of it, bridge a beck and climb the fellside ahead along a clear, meandering track to lonely Beacon Tarn. Follow its western shore, crossing some marshy areas, and climb a spur of Blawith Fells, to descend steeply to a marshy area.

Gondola under full steam on Coniston Water

This is glorious walking, through rough grass, bracken and rocky outcrops, with the mountains beginning to loom ahead at the entrance to this empty valley. It's a great feeling. The track is typical of lakeland fells country, sometimes smooth and grassy, sometimes rough and rocky.

The route curves eastwards, skirting Stable Harvey Moss to join a minor road at a bend. Turn left along it, uphill, for 125yds to a point where a bridleway leads westwards. After ¹/₂ mile, it crosses a beck on the left and here the Way bears right, goes over another beck and follows a clear track along the western side of the valley to cross first a footbridge and then the A5084.

Ⓔ *Anyone wishing to terminate this section can do so by turning left at grid ref. SD 288 927 along the A5084, for 1 mile to Torver, where there are both inn and phone. But do so only as a last resort because the thrilling climax of this section lies ahead and is highly recommended.*

The Way continues along the track sign-posted 'Coniston via Lakeshore', which leads to the lake and then goes along the shoreline for 3 magnificent miles on a path, partly wooded, that is one of the pleasantest in Lakeland. Brantwood, home of John Ruskin from 1872 to 1900, can be seen clearly on the other side of the lake and the Way then passes Coniston Hall, with its splendid chimneys, and leads nicely along a well-used track into Coniston.

JOHN RUSKIN

John Ruskin (born 1819, died 1900) was one of the greatest writers of the Victorian age and nobody has surpassed him in his descriptions of mountain scenery. Artist and critic, he was also a social revolutionary who challenged the moral foundations of 19th-century Britain. A pioneering conservationist, he railed against industrialisation and its effects. His ideas came to shape much of our thinking today and his words are as relevant now as they were in his own lifetime. Many great thinkers have been inspired by Ruskin, and the world still has much to learn from him.

Tolstoy said of him: 'Ruskin was one of the most remarkable of men, not only of England and our time but of all countries and all times. He was one of those rare men who think with their hearts, and so he thought and said not only what he himself had seen and felt, but what everyone will think and say in the future.'

Ruskin's Lake District home from 1872 until his death in 1900, Brantwood, on the eastern shore of Coniston, is a fascinating memorial to a remarkable man.

Coniston

Keswick

CONISTON

DUNGEON GHYLL

APPROX. 13 MILES/21KM

OS Landranger 96, 90
Start at grid reference SD 303 976
Start point: Coniston car park

Coniston has a strong industrial background that goes back to Roman times, but it was not until the 16th century that miners from the Mines Royal at Keswick were brought to work the copper mines here. The area is rich in copper and iron and was once an important charcoal producing area. When the mining industry declined, its place in the local economy was taken by slate quarrying. The area around Church Beck is still known as Coppermine valley.

Coniston used to have good transportation links with the outside world, none as delightful as the route of the Cumbria Way, which makes a brilliant start and maintains it all the way to Keswick, where this section ends in splendour.

Leave Coniston along Tilberthwaite Avenue, turn left along a road signposted to Ambleside and, opposite Coniston AFC ground, cross a beck on your right and follow a footpath signposted to High Yewdale. Pass a ruined byre with a castle-like front and climb to a wood. From here the retrospective views of Coniston Water are excellent.

Leave the wood by a stile and after 300yds

veer left through a gateway. Cross the field ahead and take a track towards Low Yewdale Farm but do not cross the stone bridge over Yewdale Beck. Instead, cross a stile on the right and follow a path parallel to the beck to a wood. Continue along an uphill track through the wood, coming out at Tarn Hows Cottage and turning right on a track that leads to the Tarn Hows Road. Turn left, soon to reach this Lakeland jewel.

The tarn is well worth circling so, having done that, leave along its left-hand side and descend to a marshy area with some facing fir trees. Here turn left, crossing the marsh on a clear path which leads over a stile to a rough road. Turn left along it to the Coniston-to-Ambleside road and turn right along that for ¹/₄ mile, turning left along a road signposted to High Park Farm. From here follow a waymarked route to a wood and descend through it to the Little Langdale road at Colwith Bridge. Do not cross the bridge but instead turn right along the road and soon cross a stile in the wall on the left to follow a clear, woodland path to the Coniston-to-Ambleside road. Turn left along it, briefly, and cross Skelwith Bridge. A path leads left, between slate workshops, and then continues as a wide track squashed between the River Brathay and the main road, passing impressive Skelwith Force.

The riverside route continues through fields where two exciting things happen: the Langdale Pikes loom ahead and the river swells into Elterwater Lake. At Elterwater village cross the bridge and continue upstream for ¹/₄ mile along a surfaced road. At a sign follow a riverside path to a

Tarn Hows, a famous but unspoilt beauty spot

GUIDE BOX

Places to visit
Beatrix Potter Gallery, Main Street, Hawkshead, houses an award-winning exhibition of Beatrix Potter's original drawings. The exquisite display tells the story of her life as an author, artist, farmer and conservationist. Open April to end October, Monday to Friday.

Hill Top (NT) at Near Sawrey, Ambleside, is the cottage where Beatrix Potter wrote many of her children's books. Open April to beginning November, daily except Thursday and Friday.

Keswick Museum and Art Gallery, Fitz Park, near the town centre, is old-fashioned, ramshackle and charming, prowling around and peering into dark corners being *de rigueur*. It is informative and great fun. Open April to end October, daily except Saturdays.

Cumberland Pencil Museum, Southey Works, Keswick. This fascinating museum contains the world's largest pencil and explains all you need to know about pencils. Open all year, daily.

Keswick Spa, Station Road, Keswick, has an indoor pool, waterslide, café, shop, restaurant and space-invader machines. Not 'Lake District', but a boon to harassed parents when it rains.

Derwent Launches run clockwise and anti-clockwise circuits of Derwentwater at regular intervals, daily, all year round. There are numerous landing points, making it possible to disembark, walk between landing stages and catch a later boat back to Keswick. This is a good way to see the surrounding fells.

Car parking
There is a car park in Rosthwaite, and at Tarn Hows (grid ref. NY 996 327) and Old Dungeon Ghyll Hotel (NY 284 062). Of the several public car parks in Keswick, the best one is down by the lake.

Public transport
Good bus connections from Keswick to Ambleside, Carlisle and Windermere. Reasonable ones for Penrith which connect with British Rail at Penrith. Regular bus service to Seatoller, via Rosthwaite. The Mountain Goat runs a service to Buttermere via Stair.

Accommodation
There are more bed-and-breakfasts in Keswick than in any other town of its size anywhere in the country. Accommodation in the lower price ranges is no problem. The more expensive Keswick hotels tend to be large and impersonal, but outside the town the prospect is much better. There are youth hostels at Longthwaite and Keswick. For details of camp sites, see page 214.

footbridge. Cross to a road and go left along it for 50yds, passing the Wainwright Inn, to a rough track on the left.

Follow this track past Thrang Farm, bridge the Brathay, and take a riverside path to the former farm of Oak Howe. Contour and then descend to Side House Farm and beyond here re-cross Great Langdale Beck to the main road. Turn right to the New Dungeon Ghyll Hotel and follow the rough path, left, behind the hotel and above an intake wall. Take a fairly level route to the Old Dungeon Ghyll Hotel which, mid-way on this section, is an ideal stopping place.

Ⓔ *Should the weather be adverse, end the walk here (grid ref. NY 284 062), for the next section is tough, exposed and should not be attempted in bad weather. There is an infrequent bus service to Ambleside. Alternatively, a return can be made to Skelwith Bridge by walking along the minor road that leads south and east from here through Little Langdale.*

The waterfall behind the New Hotel is well worth a visit and an obvious path leads along Stickle Gill, which has two waterfalls.

DUNGEON GHYLL

KESWICK

APPROX. 16 MILES/25.5KM

OS Landranger 90
Start at grid reference NY 284 062
Start point: Old Dungeon Ghyll Hotel, off the B5343, 7 miles west of Ambleside.

The route west from the Old Hotel is along the wide, flat bottom of Mickleden, skirting a wall of rock nearly 2000ft (610m) high, which is topped with Pike O' Stickle.

At the head of the valley, where the path forks at a marking stone, turn right and zig-zag up the very steep, glaciated valley side. At the top, cross an upland hollow full of glacial moraines. From the 'hause' or pass, descend the deep trough of Langstrath, edging Stake Gill and zig-zagging down 500ft (150m) in less than ¼ mile. At the bottom take the level but rough track with Langstrath Beck on the left. After about 2 miles the beck turns sharp left as Greenup Gill joins it. At this point bridge Greenup Beck and turn left for another 1¾ miles. Pass Stonethwaite Bridge after a mile and, after another ¾ mile or so, cross a second bridge to reach Rosthwaite.

Ⓔ *At grid ref. NY 263 138 an escape may be made from the route to Longthwaite Youth Hostel (about 1 mile north-west) by crossing Stonethwaite Bridge, turning right in the hamlet, following a lane to a junction and then taking a short permissive path to the hostel and public transport.*

Leave Rosthwaite along a road opposite the Post Office that leads to the River Derwent. Either bank can be followed to New Bridge. Beyond New Bridge go right, keeping close to the river, and then soon go

Dawn mists near Skelwith Bridge

left, around a knoll, to return to the river and enter High Hows Wood. Where the path forks go left, through an old slate quarry, to turn right at a T-junction and descend to the river at the entrance to the famous Jaws of Borrowdale. At a junction with a bridleway, turn right along what soon becomes a rough track. At the end of the wood turn left towards Hollows Farm, beyond which a stony track leads north through fields.

The Jaws of Borrowdale, where Grange Fell on the east and Scawdel (Castle Crag) on the west almost meet, mark Borrowdale's northern end. The Bowder Stone lies in the Jaws like a hazel in a nutcracker.

On reaching a conifer plantation turn left, up the skirt of Cat Bells, and where the track splits, take the right-hand path, contouring for 1½ miles and descending to a minor road, which the Way crosses. Follow a road downhill, continue along a lane (passing close to Hawes End outdoor pursuits centre), and turn right at a signposted junction to Portinscale. In the village, turn right by the Derwentwater Hotel, cross the Derwent on a suspension bridge, and after 100yds go right on a path through fields to Keswick.

SAWREY

Far Sawrey and Near Sawrey are two small villages about 2 miles south-east of Hawkshead. Beatrix Potter lived at Far Sawrey and her home, Hill Top Farm, still furnished as it was in her lifetime, is now owned by the National Trust and is open to the public (see Places to visit). Just across Windermere in the Old Laundry Visitor Centre, Bowness, The World of Beatrix Potter Exhibition brings to life the settings for some of her famous stories (open all year, daily).

It was from the proceeds of *Peter Rabbit* that Miss Potter was able to buy Hill Top, and Mrs Tabitha Twitchit, Jeremy Fisher, Tom Kitten, Jemima Puddleduck and Samuel Whiskers were all born there. When she married William Heelis, they moved to Castle Cottage in the village, but kept Hill Top as it was. By the time she died, in 1943, Beatrix Potter had become a successful farmer.

Hill Top Farm

Keswick

Carlisle

KESWICK

CALDBECK

APPROX. 16 MILES/25.5KM

OS Landranger 90
Start at grid reference NY 264 235
Start point: Keswick. Several car parks, the best being by the lake.

Keswick, the busiest town in Lakeland, claims to be the metropolis of the lakes. An ancient place, it was granted a market charter in the 13th century and in the 16th century became a trading centre for the wool produced in Borrowdale. In 1565 Goldscope copper mine was opened in the Newlands valley and 50 German miners were brought over for their expertise (Goldscope is a corruption of the German name for the mine, 'God's gift'). Within two years of the mine opening, Keswick became a thriving industrial town and within the next 150 years huge tracts of woodland were felled to provide charcoal for the furnaces. In the 18th century the romantic age of tourism began and Keswick became a popular resort. Today climbers, walkers and tourists rub shoulders in the narrow streets. The famous Keswick

The Cumbria Way climbs Latrigg

Convention, held every July, brings the town literally to its knees. Evangelical Christians gather from all over the world for prayer and bible study.

Leave Keswick along Station Road, crossing the River Greta and turning sharp right to pass under a railway bridge. Turn right, up Spooney Green Lane, a rough track that soon bridges the Keswick bypass (grid ref. NY 269 243). The track now curves left, gently climbing Latrigg. After a mile, meet a metalled road and turn right and, almost immediately, left along a fenced path. Below the monument, fork right along a descending path to Whit Beck.

Latrigg, Skiddaw's cub, was once wooded and the dead stumps of former trees can still be seen on its summit and upper slopes. It has a nicely shaped head and the Greta meanders about its foot. The most popular ascent of Skiddaw from Keswick is by Latrigg; but people climb Latrigg mainly for the superb views it offers, especially across Derwent Water.

The path now contours Lonscale Fell for $^{1}/_{2}$ mile, giving good views ahead and to the south, before turning left along the narrow valley of Glenderaterra Beck, contouring mid-way up its steep side. At the head of this lonely valley, where a watershed is passed, cross Salehow Beck to reach solitary Skiddaw House. Set within a vast expanse of open moorland and protected by conifers, Skiddaw House was originally built for use by shepherds. It is now open as a youth hostel, having been renovated, and is a welcome sight for fell wanderers, especially at the onset of bad weather.

Ⓔ *From here (grid ref. NY 287 291) an escape route goes westward past Dash Falls to Bassenthwaite. It is also an alternative bad weather route on to Caldbeck, joining roads near Bassenthwaite.*

Past the front of Skiddaw House turn right along a spongy track, cross the infant Caldew and follow the track close to the river for about 3 miles to the point it becomes surfaced and Grainsgill Beck is bridged. Once over the bridge turn left, pass Wolfram mine buildings and continue up Grainsgill Beck, climbing. There is no reasonably clear track but a hut on the skyline is your immediate destination. At the head of the valley turn right, away from the beck, over boggy ground to the hut (grid ref. NY 312 336), a welcome shelter in bad weather. From here a clear track leads past Great Lingy Hill towards High Pike, but not to its summit. However, 1 mile from the hut, leave the track and follow a clear path to the summit, which, at 2159ft (658m), is the most northerly fell over 2000ft (610m) high in the Lake District. From its flat top the view towards Carlisle and the Pennines is extensive – and, just as important, it boasts a seat!

The correct way down High Pike is by retracing your steps to the track and follow it, curving anti-clockwise, descending the fellside. In practice, the easy way is down the slope ahead until the original track is regained. It leads to an enclosed lane as the Way approaches Nether Row. Continue north from Nether Row, directly over crossroads and right, after 200yds, across fields and a footbridge on to a path that leads to a road. From here the middle of Caldbeck is in view.

218

CALDBECK

CARLISLE

APPROX. 15 MILES/24KM

OS Landranger 90, 85
Start at grid reference NY 325 395
Start point: Caldbeck, on the B5299, 12 miles south-west of Carlisle. There is a parking area outside the Oddfellows Arms.

Caldbeck was an agricultural settlement until the discovery of minerals in the Caldbeck Fells during the 18th century brought about a gradual change of character. Riverside mills were built to provide water power, corn was ground, wool spun and paper manufactured. Lead, copper and coal were mined, limestone was quarried and, with such prosperity, pubs were built. By 1829 there were six in the village. Two famous people lie in the churchyard: Mary Robinson, the Maid of Buttermere; and John Peel, born in 1777, who lived in Caldbeck, was Master of the local hunt, died in 1854 and was immortalised in the song 'D'ye ken John Peel?'.

Leave the village along a walled path, passing the church on your right. Cross Parkend Beck, turn right, pass a sewage farm

The tombstone of Caldbeck's most famous son, John Peel

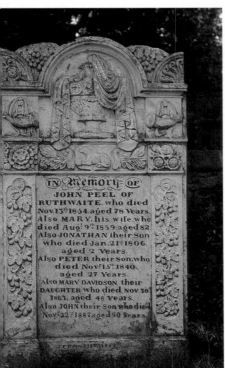

and go through Parson's Park Wood. Where the path splits, go left, uphill and then levelling out for a mile or so, about 100ft (30m) above the Beck. Where the forest ends, maintain height, across open pasture for ¹/₂ mile (there being no clear track). Enter the woodland ahead at the top left-hand corner and then follow posted directions where a vast landslide has swept away the original path. Continue through the forest, contouring along a broad ridge which crosses the top of the slip. Just past it, where the ridge curves left, continue ahead, following a descending path through conifers. Cross a field, continue uphill and turn left through a gate alongside a garage.

The clear track leads to a lane from the vicarage to the church. Opposite the church turn left, along a lane, keeping to the right of the Hall grounds and descend to a road at Bell Bridge.

Cross the bridge and turn right to follow the river bank past Bog Bridge and Rose Bridge until the river swings right. Keep straight ahead, on rising ground and through a kissing-gate, to a track near Holm Hill on the right. Turn left, cross a tarmac road, go through a kissing-gate and along a track. At a gate turn right to Georgian Hawksdale Hall. Turn right and follow a track northwards, through fields, to reach the B5299 and Bridge End. Cross the bridge into Buckabank.

Where the road divides, turn right, curve left past a mill, keep forward at a crossroads to go alongside a millstream and through a mill before crossing White Bridge and following the road to Dalston Green.

In the centre of Carlisle, a stone's throw from the station, the Citadel stands on the site of the English gateways to the city

Once clear of Dalston the way ahead follows a railway line, going under it when it bridges the Caldew. It then crosses the river on a footbridge, reaching Carlisle along the other bank.

This superb walk ends in the city centre.

CARLISLE

The ancient city of Carlisle, which first developed as a Roman frontier town when Hadrian's Wall was built, is now the county town of Cumbria and Britain's largest city, covering 347 square miles. Its boundaries run along the Scottish border, down by Northumberland, the North Pennines and across the Eden Valley to the Solway Firth. No other city offers such varied landscapes or compelling history. Places to explore include Carlisle Castle, where, within the massive Norman keep, an exhibition covers the Border Wars in which the castle played a part over 600 years; Tullie House Museum and Art Gallery in Castle Street, which takes the visitor on a journey of discovery through Cumbria's history; and the 12th-century cathedral, noted for its painted ceiling and the stalls with painted backs. Other sights include a medieval town house, St Cuthbert's Church, the 15th-century tithe barn, the Citadel and the City Walls. Carlisle's pedestrianised shopping centre includes The Lawes, an award-winning complex, and the Sands Leisure Centre plays host to national orchestras, bands and touring theatre companies.

Pennine Way

COMPLETE ROUTE
EDALE TO KIRK YETHOLM
256 MILES/412KM

SECTION COVERED
ALSTON TO KIRK YETHOLM
78 MILES/125KM

THE first and the most famous long distance footpath in Britain began in the 1930s as the dream of one man, Tom Stephenson, a journalist and campaigning rambler. It took 20 years for mounting public interest and pressure to be translated into ministerial approval, and another 20 years for access wrangles and bureaucracy to be ironed out, but in April 1965 the Pennine Way was officially opened at a ceremony near Malham in North Yorkshire.

The Pennine Way follows an uncompromising line, seeking out the most dramatic ridges and sweeps of moorland, beginning at Edale in Derbyshire and ending across the Scottish border at Kirk Yetholm. The whole national trail is just over 250 miles long, a perfect introduction to remote scenery and still a major challenge to any walker. However, continual use has caused some severe erosion problems and this has contributed to an uneasy feeling that the Pennine Way is turning from a 'long green trail', into an endless peaty groove. This is certainly true on some of the Peak District stretches, where heather moors and sphagnum bogs have been pounded into rivers of cold black sludge. There are also problems in the Yorkshire Dales, where popularity has worn Pen-y-ghent almost bare. Fortunately things are very much better further north. The 78-mile section of the Way described here receives only a fraction of the pressures associated with the corresponding southern third of the route. This has nothing to do with either the quality of the landscape or the difficulty of the terrain; the Cheviot traverse includes a host of spectacular views and was Tom Stephenson's favourite walking country. Any lack of appreciation of the top third has more to do with the shortage of roads and villages, for access, accommodation and pubs, the absence of towns within easy motoring distance, and the convention of starting the walk at Edale. Many Pennine Way novices fall by the wayside long before they have reached the Yorkshire-Cumbria border and comparatively few walk the trail in reverse from Yetholm, or sample the best sections over weekends rather than in the traditional three-week slog. Starting at Alston allows the route to be enjoyed as it was intended, as an adventure over the most extensive, wild and challenging uplands in England.

The stone-built market town of Alston

Detailed guides
The National Trail Guide, *Pennine Way North* by Tony Hopkins (Aurum Press in association with the Countryside Commission and the Ordnance Survey, 1989) covers the section from Bowes to Kirk Yetholm. Wainwright's *Pennine Way Companion* (Westmorland Gazette, 1968) is a classic but out of date. Also of interest is *A Guide to the Pennine Way* by CJ Wright (Constable, 1987).

Links
The Pennine Way joins Hadrian's Wall from Greenhead to Housesteads and footpaths allow the Wall to be followed eastwards. A complete Hadrian's Wall national trail is in preparation by the Countryside Commission.

Maps
OS Landranger 74, 80, 86, 87

The greatest hazard to anyone planning a Pennine walk is the climate. The conditions that created blanket bog and moorland, and shaped a whole system of rugged hill-farming, are hardly likely to be easy on walkers. It rains a lot and the ground is often very soft. Good outdoor clothing, and especially footwear, is essential, as is a basic level of fitness and an ability to find your way by map and compass. In most places the route is waymarked, but over some of the very worst ground, over featureless moors and in poor visibility, it is all too easy to get lost. What had been the beauty of the open hills is then your worst enemy: you are alone and the nearest farmhouse or road may be several miles away. Good preparation, knowing the escape routes down into the nearest valley, and being properly equipped when caught out by the weather, will turn any such mishap into an adventure rather than a disaster.

Very few people get into real trouble on the Pennine Way; blisters are the commonest cause of failure.

Heading north from Alston, the Way follows an easy route on the shoulders of the River South Tyne, never far from the A689, but near Lambley it rises suddenly to cross Blenkinsopp Common, a reprise of the North Pennines, then drops down into the Tyne-Solway gap. Hadrian's Wall, and Northumberland National Park, is joined near the village of Greenhead, and the Way turns eastwards for several miles to follow the Wall and the ridge of the Whin Sill, one of the most famous landscape features in northern England. When molten magma was pushed up between existing sediments some 300 million years ago, it solidified as dark crystalline rocks, which later were eroded to form the impressive, almost vertical crags of the Whin Sill.

Just before Housesteads the Way turns north, crossing wide open pastures and forest plantations before dropping down into the North Tyne valley at Bellingham. From here the route rises again, following a broad ridge of heather moorland to enter the Border

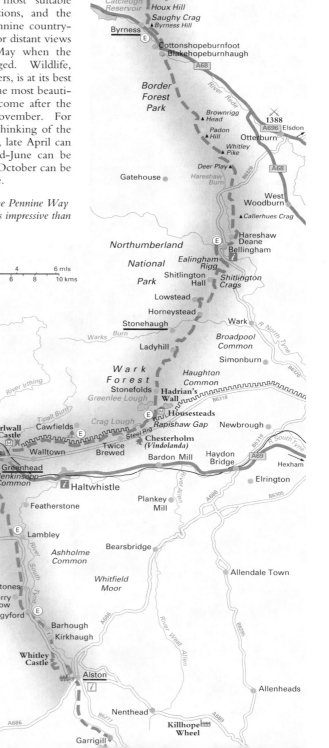

Forest Park, then drops into Redesdale. The tiny village of Byrness is the last easy access and provision point before the stiff climb to the start of the long border ridge and the Cheviot massif. This is an exhilarating and inspiring route linking some fine hills such as Windy Gyle (2032ft/619m) and there is a short detour for those who wish to set foot on the summit of The Cheviot (2674ft/815m). Generally the ground is firm and grassy, but on the tops there is wet peat. Eventually the Way leaves the border ridge near White Law and descends into the Bowmont valley to arrive at the village of Kirk Yetholm. The sense of achievement is remarkable; you have become part of a tradition and have walked in the footsteps of Tom Stephenson and Wainwright.

The most popular time of year for walking the whole Way is in July and August, a compromise between available holiday time of three or four weeks, the most suitable weather and walking conditions, and the amount of interest in the Pennine countryside. Ideal weather and light for distant views often comes in April and May when the ground is most waterlogged. Wildlife, notably upland birds and flowers, is at its best from late May to mid-July. The most beautiful colours in the landscape come after the frosts of October and November. For anyone with an open diary, thinking of the Alston to Kirk Yetholm walk, late April can be the most magnificent, mid-June can be the most interesting, and late October can be the prettiest of times to choose.

The Cheviot: a detour leads off the Pennine Way up its slopes, but its summit is less impressive than it looks

Alston
Greenhead

ALSTON
SLAGGYFORD
APPROX. 5½ MILES/9KM

OS Landranger 86
Start at grid reference NY 715 462
Start point: A signposted track beside the bridge of the A686, over the River South Tyne at the southern edge of Alston. Car parking is possible along side-roads or in the town centre.

Prosperity for the little cross-Pennine town of Alston came and went with lead mining. Alston had been at the hub of a rural community for centuries and had a sort of heyday when it was in the possession of the Radcliffe family. Unfortunately the Radcliffes chose the wrong side in the Jacobite rebellions and it took another century after their demise, and the arrival of the London Lead Company, to wake the town up. After a period of rapid expansion, the mining industry collapsed and Alston was back where it had started – serving farmers and wagoners and waiting for better times. Tourism has become the latest panacea and all sorts of quaint shops have appeared, but the character of the place remains as it ever was, solid with a hint of eccentricity.

Alston makes a good starting point for a walk, self-contained and with all essential services. The Pennine Way crosses the bridge at the southern edge of the town, having completed the long descent from Cross Fell. From the bridge, the route turns right, off the A686 and along the A689 for a few yards, then right along a track and through a gate beside a white house. There are good views east, over the river towards the town as the path heads north to Harbut Lodge. The Way is signposted to the left of the house, then around the edge of the pasture to a stile on to a track. The 'inbye' fields are full of sheep in the spring, gathered off the hills to lamb on the better pasture around the farms. The usual breed these days is the Swaledale, but there are still some Blackface about, as well as a sprinkling of blue-faced Leicester and Suffolk for breeding purposes.

After crossing the A689 the Way heads westwards, past a byre and uphill over rough pasture. Elaborate ladder-stiles then mark the route north-west across marshy ground, inhabited by snipe and redshank, to a little footbridge over a burn. After crossing the burn, the Way climbs up to the shoulders of the open fell, bearing to the left of the knoll encircled by shallow grassy ridges. This is Whitley Castle, the site of a Roman fort which once protected an important link-road known as the Maiden Way. It was probably constructed in the days of Agricola. The Pennine Way descends to a farm called Castle Nook and crosses the A689 again, then bears to the right around Dyke House and follows the South Tyne valley, through Kirkhaugh and parallel with the old railway line. On the far bank of the river is Barhaugh Park and Barhaugh Hall, which is now a field studies and holiday centre. Below Lintley Farm, the Way turns right, to follow a burn beneath a five-arched viaduct, then arcs around a pasture and drops down to the banks of the South Tyne. The river is shallow and stony, the home of dippers and grey wagtails. Wych elms once shadowed the riverside path but these are mostly dead and any woodland is now hazel, ash, oak and sycamore. The path meets the road close to a footbridge, and the Way continues along the verge and into the village of Slaggyford.

Ⓔ *On Mondays to Saturdays a bus runs from Slaggyford back to Alston.*

SLAGGYFORD
GREENHEAD
APPROX. 11 MILES/17.5KM

OS Landranger 86
Start at grid reference NY 677 524
Start point: Slaggyford village, on the A689, 4½ miles north of Alston. Ample parking around the village green.

Slaggyford is a bright little cluster of houses, including a post office but no shop, spread loosely around a green and penfold. The Pennine Way turns left off the A689 on a side road, then bears right of the old Methodist chapel and heads along a marshy lane beside damp fields of marsh marigolds. The old South Tyne Railway line, which closed in 1976, is down to the left. The Way descends through some attractive woodland, awash in their season with wild flowers such as primrose, wood anemone, early purple orchid and wood cranesbill. After crossing a footbridge, the Way goes under the railway embankment, and across a field to Merry Know. The route is confusing here, as is so often the case around working farms. Go through the gate and between the buildings, then out of a gate and right to a stile in the

GUIDE BOX

Places to visit
Alston is an important little town, serving a scattered community of farmers as well as tourists. The town is compact, has cobbled streets and interesting alleys and shops, and retains its aura of being a one-time lead-mining capital of the high Pennines.
A section of the South Tyne Railway has recently been re-opened, so that it is possible to take a short steam-train ride from Alston Station.
About 3 miles south-east of Alston is the village of Carrigill, from where it is possible to walk to Cross Fell.

Car parking
Alston is the principal market town in the area and there is usually ample parking space in the town centre (grid ref. NY 718 465). Along the South Tyne Valley there are several access points to the route, with car parking at such places as Slaggyford (NY 674 524), Burnstones (NY 675 544) and at Lambley where there is a lay-by at grid ref. NY 666 586, close to where the route crosses the A689.

Public transport
The nearest British Rail station to this section of the Way is at Haltwhistle. Buses run between Alston and Haltwhistle, calling at villages *en route*, most on or near the Pennine Way (Monday to Saturday).

Accommodation
Alston is the only reliable base with small hotels and bed-and-breakfasts, but there is usually bed-and-breakfast available at the smaller villages such as Slaggyford, Lambley and Halton Lea Gate, or at farmhouses. The Tourist Information Centre at Alston (see below) provides a helpful book-ahead service.
Useful accommodation guides are produced: from the Pennine Way Council who issue a regularly updated *Accommodation and Camping Guide* (available for a small charge from 23 Woodland Crescent, Hilton Park, Prestwich, Manchester, M25 8WQ), and from Leading Edge Publishing (The Old Chapel, Burtersett, Hawes, North Yorkshire, DL8 3PB), who have published a little guide to accommodation on the major northern routes called *Great North Walks: Where to Stay*.

wall. This brings you out again on to pasture and, although there is no clear path to follow, route-finding is quite easy, across a stile to a tumbled-down wall and towards the viaduct at Burnstones. Just before the viaduct, drop down to the Thinhope Burn and go under the first arch of the viaduct and out on to the road. Go along the road to beyond the viaduct then turn left, up the drive towards the big house and bear right, steeply uphill and on to the shoulder of a wide expanse of open moorland.

The dome of the moorland to the left is Glendue Fell, part of Geltsdale and one piece in a giant jigsaw of sandstone blocks at the edge of the North Pennines. High rainfall and poor drainage has encouraged the formation of peat, which is usually wet and acidic and stops most vegetation from growing. The result is a whole panorama of heather, cotton-grass and sphagnum moss and a specialised collection of birds and insects. Red grouse and curlew are the commonest of the larger breeding birds, but there are a few pairs of short-eared owls and merlins. The green hairstreak butterfly is on the wing here in late April and May.

After following the shoulder of the moor for a mile, the Way drops down to cross the pretty Glendue Burn, then climbs again to contour the side of another dome of dark moorland at the edge of Hartleyburn Common. The route shadows the Maiden Way and it is quite easy to visualise cohorts of Agricola's all-conquering army heading north to reinforce the wooden forts on the Stanegate. The distant views are excellent, east over the wooded South Tyne Valley to Ashholme Common and Whitfield Moor, south to the plateau summit of Cross Fell, the highest ground in England.

The A689 is joined for the last time just west of the village of Lambley, the path turning left on the descent to the road to cut off the corner and minimise road-walking. However, it is worth noting for future visits that by turning right along the road and

The Way at Castle Nook, north of Alston

LEAD MINING

Lead mining and farming were the most important industries in the North Pennines; often they were inseparable and most of the dwellings that now grace the lonely Pennine dales were built during the heyday of miner/smallholders in the late 18th century. Grass-covered dead-heaps and remains of old workings all testify to the widespread dominance of mining operations until the collapse of the entire industry around the turn of the present century. However, it is still difficult to appreciate how deep an impression the mining industry made on the culture and landscape of the region. The best way to see how things were is to visit the Killhope Wheel Lead Mining Centre, 7 miles east of Alston on the A689. As well as looking at the layout, buildings and machinery of one of the most prosperous mines of its day, complete now with its restored 34ft-high Great Wheel, it is possible to work a jigger on the washing rake and sort your own ore! The centre is open March to October, daily, and has its own shop and restaurant.

taking a footpath south of the village it is possible to get down to the river and see Lambley Viaduct, an elegant nine-arch span to carry the old South Tyne Railway.

Ⓔ *From grid ref. NY 666 586 a return may be made to Slaggyford by dropping down into Lambley and either taking the bus (Mondays to Saturdays) or using lanes and footpaths that follow the east bank of the River South Tyne.*

The Pennine Way crosses the road and heads north-west over boggy ground with no obvious path, past old mine workings and seeking the higher ground via hummocks and ridges to a derelict barn at High House. Hartley Burn is then crossed at a footbridge and, after following the burn as it angles left, a grassy path climbs out of the valley and leads through green pastures to Batey Shield. This is a typical farm-steading of the region, a tidy group of buildings each with a purpose but no longer thriving. Rural depopulation has left the landscape looking poor. Quickset hawthorn hedges, planted with care early last century, are now moribund and the field drains are blocked. This is still good livestock country, but for how long? Further on, across a footbridge and a road, the Way passes to the left of Greenriggs, then begins a long steady climb culminating in a stile and a sudden view over the north side of Hartleyburn Common.

Having only clipped the sides of the big moors so far, it is a surprise to come on this vast expanse of open country. The route is vague, sometimes clear on the ground and sometimes quite invisible. It is a good idea to use a compass and head north-west making for the left side of Round Hill, then continue in the same direction for a mile over Blenkinsopp Common. Few people would describe this country as pretty, but it is undoubtedly impressive. You will probably be the only human for miles around; even sheep are few and far between. At first the rolling plateau has no landmarks, but a triangulation column comes into view at Blade Hill and the Way makes for the right of this. There is at last a real view to the north, over the Tyne Gap with the busy A69 road below. To avoid road-walking again, the route zig-zags downhill, through old mine working, along old tracks at Todholes ('tod' means fox; this is still ideal fox country) and under electricity pylons. The Carlisle-Newcastle corridor is a major cross-country link, not only for road and rail but also for power and communication. Hence a clutter of pylons, masts and cables.

Down on the A69, the contrast after the open moorland is startling as cars and lorries hurtle past. If you intend completing the day at Greenhead then cross the road and turn right along it as far as the start of the bypass, then left on a side-road into the village. The Pennine Way follows a different course, crossing the road and climbing the embankment the other side, then heading north-east over fields and by the golf course, dropping down to meet the B6318 just north of the village.

Greenhead
Stonehaugh

GREENHEAD

STEEL RIGG

APPROX. 6¹/₂ MILES/10.5KM

OS Landranger 86 or 87
Start at grid reference NY 650 654
Start point: Greenhead village, off the A69, 3 miles west of Haltwhistle. Ample free car parking.

Greenhead used to be a very noisy little place but the bypass has transformed it, and it is now worth more than a passing glance. Most of the buildings are made of honey-coloured sandstone. There is a youth hostel, garage and hotel, and outside St Cuthbert's Church there is a war memorial and an old ornamental fountain planted up with flowers. On the west side of the village is the B6318 Blanchland road and by walking along this to a terrace of redbrick cottages the Pennine Way is reached.

The route leaves the road at a gate beside the cottages, crosses the Newcastle-to-Carlisle railway line and a footbridge over a little burn, then follows an old hedge-line beside the Tipalt Burn. The stream is attractive, lined with sallows and sycamore beneath which grow primroses, anemones and butterbur. The pasture to the left is usually inhabited by an assortment of sheep breeds, including local specialities such as the Border Leicester. Hadrian's Wall crossed the gap of the Tipalt Burn at this point but nothing is visible; most of the stone was used in medieval times in the construction of nearby Thirwall Castle. The route meets a track and turns right at Duffenfoot, over a footbridge. Once across the Tipalt and climbing the winding walled track on the other side, it is possible to look back for a romantic view of the ruins of Thirlwall Castle. It was in its prime in the reign of Edward I, who stayed here on one of his campaigns against the Scots in 1306.

At the top of the track, with a line of beech trees on the left, the Way crosses a stile by a gate and heads uphill beside a deep grassy ditch. This is the ditch excavated by the Romans on the north side of the Wall to hamper any attack by the Caledonian tribes. The Wall itself has again been dismantled; an ordinary drystone wall marks its course.

At the top of the hill it is time to stop to orientate yourself by the views. If the air is fresh it should be possible to see Blenkinsopp Common and Cross Fell (the radio transmitting station in Great Dun Fell is distinctive; beside it is Little Dun Fell, then the more extensive low dome of Cross Fell at 2930ft/893m). Looking eastwards, it should now be possible to see the dark grey cliff-face of the Great Whin Sill. Hadrian's Wall follows the crest of this famous igneous intrusion for several miles, making the most of its daunting scarp slope. Beyond the field on the right as the Way continues eastwards is the Museum of the Roman Army and the unexcavated remains of one of Agricola's forts called *Carvoran*. This was built to protect the east-west road known as the Stanegate but was later employed as a garrison fort for the Wall.

The route meets a road and turns left

Hadrian's Wall, and the Pennine Way, at Cuddy's Crags, on the brow of the Whin Sill

GUIDE BOX

Places to visit
Hexham is the main centre for anyone exploring the Wall country. The busy market town is 12 miles east of Steel Rigg and is most notable for its abbey, which contains a fine Saxon crypt.

The Museum of the Roman Army at Carvoran is the only one of the many museums and excavations specialising in Roman history that lies adjacent to the route of the Pennine Way. Carvoran is opposite Walltown and less than a mile from Greenhead. Open February to October daily; November weekends; closed December and January.

Vindolanda, at Chesterholm about a mile north of Bardon Mill on the A69, and therefore about 1¹/₂ miles south-east of the Pennine Way when it reaches Steel Rigg, is probably the most fascinating of the sites to visit. Not only is there a short reconstruction of the Wall but also an excavated civilian settlement associated with the fort of *Vindolanda*, where work is still in progress and some exciting finds are still being made. The museum contains a wealth of beautiful and interesting artefacts. Site open all year daily. Museum open March to October, daily; February and November weekends; closed December and January.

Housesteads (EH/NT) lies about 2¹/₂ miles east of Steel Rigg, only ¹/₂ mile east of where the Pennine Way strikes north at Rapishaw Gap. It is accessible by car from a car park and small visitor centre on the B6318; a ¹/₂-mile uphill walk to the Roman fort is unavoidable. The fort is well laid out and is superbly sited on the brow of the Whin Sill. A small museum close to the ruins contains some of the finds (open all year, daily).

Allen Banks (NT), signposted south off the A69 a mile east of Bardon Mill, is by way of contrast to the wide, wild landscape of the Wall. A broad, level footpath alongside the River Allen leads through very attractive woodland and across a little suspension bridge to Plankey Mill.

Car parking
The major car parks giving access to Hadrian's Wall are off the B6318, the Military Road. These are at Greenhead, where the B6318 leaves the A69, at grid ref. NY 660 654; at Walltown, where a side-road opposite Carvoran leads to a small car park close to the Wall (NY 677 663); at Cawfields (NY 713 667); at Steel Rigg, where there is a car park allowing the easiest pedestrian access to the Wall (NY 755 677); and at Housesteads (NY 795 684). North of the Wall there are few roads and no suitable parking places close to the Pennine Way except at Stonehaugh (NY 792 761).

Public transport
British Rail's Newcastle-to-Carlisle line has stations at Hexham, Haydon Bridge, Bardon Hill and Haltwhistle. Greenhead is served by a bus route that runs from Newcastle to Carlisle through Hexham and Haltwhistle. In school summer holidays a National Park bus runs along the route of the Wall through Greenhead and Housesteads.

Accommodation
There is ample bed-and-breakfast in the towns and villages of the Tyne valley, from Greenhead to Hexham. Close to the route, many farms do bed-and-breakfast, there are youth hostels at Greenhead and Once Brewed (south of Steel Rigg), and there is some camping, most notably at Hotbank, off the B6318 between Steel Rigg and Housesteads. See p.222 for available lists.

along this, then left around the outside of the extensive Walltown Quarry. What was once a dreadful eyesore, extracting dolerite for roadstone and slicing away a section of the Whin Sill and any Roman remains, is now a picnic site. Beyond the quarry the path meets a road, with some attractive marshy woodland on the right where roe deer and woodcock hide and wait for dusk. After following the road over a cattle grid, the Way at last bears left, uphill to the crest of the Sill, to follow an impressive section of Hadrian's Wall.

Dramatic countryside sometimes needs little description, and this is perhaps true of the next 3 or 4 miles along the Whin Sill. Route-finding is easy – simply follow the Wall. In places the remains stand at head-height, but even here there is only a hint of how daunting the military barrier must have been; when it was built the Wall would have been three times taller.

The rock is cut by deep gaps, created by meltwater at the end of the Ice Age, and the Wall switch-backs and snakes along the best line of defence. The going is firm but never easy because of the undulating nature of the ridge. Jackdaws and wheatears nest among the columns of dolerite and among the sandstone boulders of the levelled turrets and milecastles. After Great Chesters Farm, and the grass-covered ruins of the cavalry fort of *Aesica*, the route drops down, crosses a road and passes another little quarry picnic site at Cawfields.

Ⓔ *A return to Greenhead may be made from Cawfields (grid ref. NY 713 667): in the school summer holidays a National Park coach service runs along the route of the Wall. Otherwise, follow roads or paths (approx. 2 miles) to Haltwhistle for a regular bus service to Greenhead.*

The Way then rises again for Cawfield Crags, where the Wall is especially fine and the *Vallum* - the system of ridges and trenches which marked the Roman military zone – is easily visible to the south.

After Caw Gap, the Whin Sill rises to its highest point at 1132ft (345m), with views west across the Solway to the Galloway hills. It then descends again to Steel Rigg, where there is a car park. A right turn along the road soon leads down to Once Brewed, where there is a visitor centre and youth hostel. Nearby is the Twice Brewed Inn.

STEEL RIGG

STONEHAUGH

APPROX. 8 MILES/13KM

OS Landranger 87, 80
Start at grid reference NY 751 677
Start point: Steel Rigg, National Park car park, ½ mile north of the B6318, 3 miles north of Bardon Mill. Free.

The view of the Whin Sill is excellent from the car park; in the distance, at the foot of the cliff, is Crag Lough, one of the shallow lakes scooped out by moving ice during the

The path at Crag End, near Greenlee

Ice Age and now being filled in slowly by reeds and silt. From the car park the route actually follows a path along the top of Hadrian's Wall for a short distance, then drops down beside it. There is then a sequence of gaps and crags rising eventually to Highshield Crags above Crag Lough. The Wall, and its associated turrets and milecastle, are in good condition on this most famous stretch of the monument. Further on, the route climbs again quite steeply past Hotbank farm. From Hotbank Crags four loughs are visible and ahead lies the familiar picture-postcard view of Cuddy's Crags.

The Pennine Way leaves Hadrian's Wall at Rapishaw Gap, just before Housesteads (*Vercovicium*) Roman Fort. The excavated ruins, almost too neat and tidy, are worth a special visit as, of course, are the other forts and features on the Wall.

Ⓔ *A return may be made to Greenhead from Housesteads (grid ref. NY 790 688) by taking tracks and lanes south to Bardon Mill to pick up a bus back to Greenhead. In the school summer holidays a National Park coach may be taken from Housesteads back to Greenhead.*

The route turns north and heads out over marshy pasture inhabited by black Galloway cattle, then follows an indistinct path through rolling heather country with the air full of the cries of curlews and the songs of skylarks. To the left is Greenlee Lough, recently bought by the National Park as a wildlife refuge. To the right, in the distance, are King's Crags. Ahead lies the forest.

The path rises to the right of Stonefolds then drops down to meet a track and enter Wark Forest. This is Forestry Commission land, part of the Border Forest Park, and there has recently been extensive felling and re-planting. The paths and rides are more open, there are wider views, and deciduous trees have been planted along the watercourses. In places it may look dull now, but it was very much worse before the Commission's change of attitude. The Way stays on the main track for a while, then turns off to the right along a path. Most of

the trees are spruce, so the wildlife interest is limited. Roe deer are very numerous, as are foxes. The tree-tops sometimes resound to the calls of crossbills, and willow warblers seem to have adapted to the young conifers quite well.

A wide sweep of moorland comes as a refreshing change as the Way clips the corner of Haughton Common. The path makes for an isolated sheepfold in which stand a few stunted pines and birches. The views south and east, over miles of purple moor-grass, are memorable for anyone who had hoped to get away from civilisation. However, this is just an interlude and the Way is soon back in forest, descending to a road a mile east of Stonehaugh at Ladyhill.

HADRIAN'S WALL

Building a frontier across the narrow neck of northern England was a monumental task, even for the Romans. It was necessary because of the constant risk of uprisings from Caledonian tribes; Hadrian's intention in AD122 was to set the bounds to his empire and keep the peace. The Wall was in use for nearly 300 years. It stretched from Wallsend, east of Newcastle, to Bowness-on-Solway in Cumbria, a total distance of about 72 miles. It took eight years to build and in its final form it used over a million cubic yards of stone, stood 16ft high and was probably whitewashed to make it look even more daunting to the 'barbarians'.

Most of the stonework from the Wall was robbed in the 18th and 19th centuries for use in other local building work. The best surviving fragments lie beside the Pennine Way. In addition to the Wall, the Roman defences included a ditch and bank just to the north, a system of mounds and ditch called the *vallum* to the south which probably marked a civilian exclusion zone, and a series of turrets and milecastles built at regular intervals between the forts. At first glance the landscape may seem to bear little trace of its imperial past; in fact it is remarkable how much has survived.

Stonehaugh
Byrness

STONEHAUGH
BELLINGHAM
APPROX. 7 MILES/11KM

OS Landranger 87, 80
Start at grid reference NY 792 761
Start point: Stonehaugh village, 5 miles
west of Wark. Car parking in the village.

From the little Forestry Commission village
of Stonehaugh, the Pennine Way is met
either by returning to the road at Ladyhill or
by walking along a forest drive eastwards for
just under a mile. From the road the route
turns north opposite Ladyhill and soon
crosses two forest drives from Stonehaugh.

The forest ends at another block of
moorland, the side of Broadpool Common.
The path is indistinct but follows the flank of
a burn, past a pretty waterfall and downhill,
then up beside a wall and over the brow into
the valley of the Warks Burn. The route
descends by an old hedge, then turns right,
through a gate and past a hay barn before
dropping down between rocky clefts to cross
the attractive Warks Burn.

The character of the land begins to change
now, less open moorland and more green
pasture as the route climbs through damp
woodland and across a field to Horneystead,
then from field to field and farm to farm.
Behind the farmhouse at Horneystead stand
the ruins of a 'bastle', a fortified farmhouse
with massively thick walls, built at the time
of border troubles in the 16th century. Past
The Ash and Leadgate and across a side-road,
the Way leads to Lowstead which
incorporates two bastles into its structure.
The route then follows an access track above
the Blacka Burn opposite Linacres Farm,
then keeps to a quiet side-road with a block
of marshy woodland on the left. Snipe and
woodcock abound in such places.

At a junction the route turns left and

A wide, wild prospect, from Padon Hill

GUIDE BOX

Places to visit
Hareshaw Dene lies just to the east of Bellingham.
A footpath leads through attractive pasture and
ancient woodland to the waterfall of Hareshaw
Linn.

Otterburn, on the A696, is the site of one of the
most famous battles between the English and the
Scots, in 1388. The spot where the Earl of
Douglas is reputed to have fallen is marked by
Percy's Cross, accessible from the road.

Elsdon, on the B6341, 3 miles east of Otterburn
and about 6 miles east of the Pennine Way, is
the most interesting village of Northumberland.
Its houses are gathered around a wide green;
there is a 14th-century church, a pele tower and
one of the finest Norman motte-and-baileys in
the country.

The Pennine Way crosses sections of the *Border
Forest Park* and *Northumberland National Park:*
both have their own atmosphere and attractions.

Car parking
Stonehaugh, at grid ref. NY 792 762, is
accessible by driving along side-roads westwards
from Wark. After the town of Bellingham (NY
839 833) there are few proper car parks,
although the route does cross two roads, near
Hareshaw Head and south of Padon Hill. Main
access points with car parking are
Blakehopeburnhaugh (NY 784 003) and
Byrness.

Public transport
Bellingham is served by buses from Hexham and
Otterburn, which is on a bus route serving
Jedburgh and Newcastle.

Accommodation
Bellingham is the only town with a full range of
facilities, including small hotels and a youth
hostel. There are official Forestry Commission
camp/caravan sites at Stonehaugh and
Cottonshopeburnfoot and a youth hostel at
Byrness, but otherwise accommodation is limited
to farmhouse bed-and-breakfast, which is in turn
limited by the scarcity of farms. See p.222 for
available lists.

passes a small grassed-over quarry and an
outstanding example of cord-rigging (narrow
ridge-and-furrow ploughing) over the
pasture on the left. There was a Romano-
British settlement here; the ruins are thinly
covered and are easy to make out and the
fields were intensively cultivated. The farm
produce, probably barley, was sent to feed
the occupying Roman army.

At the next road junction the route crosses
a stile straight ahead and follows the edges of
the fields over the hill and down to the
Houxty Burn. Over the footbridge close to
Esp Mill, the Way then heads up a track to
the farm at Shitlington Hall, then down a
track on the left before turning right to
follow the field-edge again all the way up to
Shitlington Crags. The sandstone outcrop is
easy to climb via a short flight of rough-
stone slabs; the path is clear once you have
spotted it from the track just below. The
views, all the way down to Hadrian's Wall
and beyond, are very fine if the light is with
you. From here the route is clear, uphill
again over moorland, making for the wall at
the very top of the ridge, to the left of the
radar mast. Again, the views are excellent.

After crossing a stile in the wall the route turns right, along a track and past the radar mast. To the left is Ealingham Rigg, a ridge of heather moorland where emperor moths fly and adders sun themselves. The route crosses a stile by a gate, then continues along the track for a short distance before turning left across the moorland and heading for a marker post. There is no visible path now but the orientation is easy; north-east and down into the North Tyne Valley to a road, then left off the road at a stile and downhill to meet the B6320. The Way turns left to follow the road, over the North Tyne and into the town of Bellingham.

Ⓔ *A bus runs from Bellingham, south to Wark, from where lanes and paths may be followed westwards to the Pennine Way near Stonehaugh.*

BELLINGHAM

·

BYRNESS

APPROX. 15¹/₂ MILES/25KM

OS Landranger 80
Start at grid reference NY 839 833
Start point: Bellingham town centre. The market town lies on the B6320, 13 miles north of Hexham. Ample car parking.

After making the most of the shops and services in the town, follow the West Woodburn Road, below the old Border Counties Railway line and on for ¹/₂ mile, then turn left along a track to Blakelaw Farm. The grass-covered mounds by the road are old spoil-heaps from the Hareshaw iron works. The iron produced here was used in the building of the famous High Level Bridge in Newcastle. From the farm the Pennine Way climbs up an open pasture, following posts, and eventually makes for a ruin to the right of a block of pines. Through the gate by the ruined barn the Way is soon on to open moorland below Callerhues Crag. The original Pennine Way made for the higher ground but a much better path is now signposted and can be followed northwards above the Hareshaw Burn and below Hareshaw House. The ground is usually marshy and there are old coal workings littered around the hillsides. The route continues for 2 miles to cross the B6320, after which it rises through heather moorland making for the stone cairn on the top of the distant hill called Deer Play. There is a strong sense of wilderness about the heather country, enhanced by the wide views and the occasional lack of a clear path. From the stone post on the brow of Deer Play, the Way drops down over boggy ground and past some shake holes to make for the top of Whitley Pike, a fine-featured hill to the north-west. It then drops down to a minor road.

A wire fence makes the next few miles of the route very easy to find, past Grey Mare rock and up to the ridge of Padon Hill. Its bell-shaped monument, to the right of the fence, is visible for miles around. The

monument commemorates Alexander Padon, a Scottish Covenanter, who held services here in the 18th century.

After Padon Hill, and still following the fence, the Way heads north-west, then north-east, to the next open hilltop of Brownrigg Head. There are fine views of Redesdale and the Cheviot Hills, and of Otterburn, where one of the most famous border battles was fought in 1388. Turning left, north-west again, the route now enters forest plantations and a long walk begins through dull conifer country. There are occasional views out on to moorland, and glimpses of deer, red squirrels and sparrowhawks, but few walkers enjoy the forest except in very bad weather.

Eventually the track descends into Redesdale. Past the Forestry Commission settlement at Blakehopeburnhaugh, the Way turns left along the east bank of the River Rede and meanders with it past picnic places and sallow groves to Cottonshopeburnfoot. These are the longest place-names in England! After crossing to the west bank of the river, the route follows a forest drive then drops down to the right, across the river again and past tiny Holy Trinity Church.

The village of Byrness, built by the Forestry Commission for its workers in the days before mechanised harvesting, lies a few hundred yards along the A68, reached by turning left after the church. The road is fast and busy, leading up to Carter Bar and the border. Byrness village is the last provisioning point before the border ridge; there are no shops between here and Kirk Yetholm, 27 miles away. Apart from a post office/shop there is also a youth hostel and bed-and-breakfast accommodation, so many walkers stay here overnight.

Ⓔ *A bus runs through Byrness (grid ref. 764 028) to Otterburn, where another bus can be caught back to Bellingham and Hexham.*

Catscleugh Reservoir, just west of Byrness

UPLAND BIRDS

Peregrine

Meadow pipits are the winged mice of the Pennines. During the summer they are everywhere, easily outnumbering any other small birds such as skylarks and wheatears. Of the larger birds the waders and gamebirds are the most characteristic of the uplands. Both red and, in smaller numbers, black grouse occur on the heather moorland of Northumberland, and on the inbye fields the grey partridge is still quite common. Curlew, lapwing, snipe and golden plover make up the complement of waders.

Carrion crows, known locally as corbies, are the scavengers of the moors and are more widespread now than ever before. Of the birds of prey, the aristocrats of the uplands, the sparrowhawk is probably the most numerous but the peregrine has increased dramatically in recent years. The merlin is scarce, but Northumberland is one of its strongholds; its main prey is the lowly meadow pipit. Almost any other species of raptor can be seen from time to time; hen harrier, goshawk, even red kite and golden eagle.

227

Byrness

Kirk Yetholm

BYRNESS

CLENNEL STREET

APPROX. 13 MILES/21KM

OS Landranger 80
Start at grid reference NY 764 028
Start point: Byrness village, on the A68.
Parking in the village.

This last section, from Byrness to Kirk Yetholm, is a long hard walk, with escape points being few and far between. It is important that walkers note the information given on accommodation and car parking in the Guide Box.

From the village centre, walk along the A68 for a short distance and turn left off it, close to Holy Trinity Church, up a tarmac track and through a gate beside Byrness Cottage. A path then climbs steeply up to Byrness Hill, from where there are impressive views over Redesdale. The Way is now on to open hilltops and never again goes through forest. The route heads north, from Saughy Crag to Houx Hill, then above Windy Crag to Ravens Knowe. The land to the east is owned by the Ministry of Defence, part of the 'dry training area'. Views are far-reaching and exciting.

From Ravens Knowe the route makes for Ogre Hill and follows a clear but often boggy path downhill alongside a forest plantation to a fence and stile at the headwaters of the River Coquet. This rather undramatic feature marks the Scottish border and it is very satisfying to climb over the ladder-stile and set foot on Scottish peat. The Way sets out north, straight out uphill as if heading for the Highlands, but in fact the route is simply avoiding the worst of the mires of the Coquet watershed and it soon turns right to follow the valley eastwards, descending gradually to a wicket-gate beside the gathering stream.

A scatter of grass-covered earthworks, extensive and difficult to interpret, lies beyond the gate on the rising ground. This is Chew Green, a Roman marching camp, used for centuries as a stop-over *en route* to the wild north. A road runs just the other side of the Coquet and there is a small car park. It is a long drive anywhere from here; left heads along Coquetdale to Alwinton, right is an MoD road leading to Redesdale; it is only open at certain times or by special arrangement.

From Chew Green, the Way follows the grassy course of Dere Street up to the border ridge, to the right of Brownhart Law. Continuing north, Dere Street soon disappears beyond Gaisty Law towards Woden Law, where the Romans practised battle and siege tactics. The route heads north or north-east, following a path away from the border fence, linking cairns on the hilltops. The ground is peaty and often boggy but there are some bridges or boardwalks over the worst sections. Vegetation on these exposed hills is thin, usually mat-grass with some heather and drifts of purple moor-grass which bleaches white in the winter and spring. After about a mile the route bears right and heads eastwards at the head of the Rennies Burn.

Past the Grassy Loughs the route meets up again with the border fence and keeps with this for many miles, so that route-finding is no longer a problem. It is easy to become disorientated in the Cheviots. The views seem to go on for ever. After a sharp turn left in the border fence the route leads to one of the Pennine Way shelters at Yearning Saddle. Although far from comfortable, the shelter offers a respite if the weather has closed in. To be benighted here is better than to die of exposure in a June blizzard.

Lamb Hill is the next summit, then Beefstand, then Mozie Law. They are all excellent vantage points and the Way links them like pearls. To the north, the distinctive hills in the middle distance are the Eildon Hills, close to Melrose. On the descent the eye is caught by a very obvious path off to the right, following a grassy ridge. The path is called the Street, an ancient border crossing once used as a drove road.

Ⓔ *It is possible to follow the Street (grid ref. NT 835 150) down into Coquetdale as an escape route or in an emergency; there are a few scattered farms in the valley but nothing else. It is also possible to make this part of the Way a circular walk out of Coquetdale by parking at Barrow Burn (grid ref. NT 867 108).*

The Pennine Way heads eastwards, brushing the border fence at Plea Knowe at the head of the Street, then cutting the corner at Foul Step. Ahead now rises Windy Gyle, and the Way leaves the border fence to climb to its summit. Windy Gyle is certainly one of the finest features on the whole Pennine Way and from the top the panorama is breathtaking. At 2030ft (619m), there is a view over most of the Cheviot massif. The big hills to the left of Kidland Forest are Bloodybush Edge with Cushat Law behind. To the north-east are the even higher summits of The Cheviot and Hedgehope.

GUIDE BOX

Places to visit
The Cheviot Hills are remote and difficult to penetrate except along the major valleys of the Coquet, the Breamish, the Harthope and the College Burn. Alwinton is the main village in upper Coquetdale, with the pretty town of Rothbury (close to the Cragside estate) further downstream. The Breamish is the most visited valley, with a National Park visitor centre at Ingram. The Harthope valley lies above the market town of Wooler, and the College valley lies upstream of Kirknewton but is only accessible by vehicle along a private road for which a permit is required.
From Kirk Yetholm the attractive border towns of *Cornhill-on-Tweed* and *Kelso* are within a short drive of 7 miles each. *Etal* and *Ford* are interesting villages with castles and craft shops, 11 or 12 miles to the north-east. Close to the village of Branxton, 8 miles north-east from Kirk Yetholm and close to the A697, is the site of the *Battle of Flodden*. There is a small car park and interpretative panel.

Car parking
There is parking in Byrness village and in Kirk Yetholm, at the end of the walk, but no roads cross the border ridge and few approach to within easy walking distance. There is a small car park at Chew Green (grid ref. NY 794 084). Further down the valley towards Alwinton, it is possible to park on the road verges at such places as Windyhaugh, to walk to the border ridge around Windy Gyle. Road access to the head of the College valley is possible by permit from College Valley Estate via their agent G Sale of Wooler. Parking is then possible along the verge around Mounthooly or Fleehope, around grid ref. NT 88 23.

Public transport
Kirk Yetholm and Byrness are served by buses but the service is limited.

Accommodation
There is very little accommodation of any sort along the final section of the Way. However, there is some bed-and-breakfast at farmhouses at such places as Uswayford (grid ref. NY 886 145) and this is certainly the best option. Kirk Yetholm has a youth hostel and a small hotel. See p.222 for available lists.

The massive pile of boulders on the top of Windy Gyle is a Bronze Age burial mound. It was such an obvious landmark that it became a meeting place for the Wardens of the Marches during the unsettled and lawless centuries of the border troubles. In 1585 Lord Francis Russell was killed here after being double-crossed at a Wardens' Meet and ever since the pile of stones has been called Russell's Cairn.

For a little while the Way descends north-eastwards on the Scottish side of the fence but it soon crosses back and heads down the ridge to meet another cross-border drove road called Clennel Street.

ⓔ *There are escape routes either way (from grid ref. NT 872 161), north-west down to Cocklawfoot and south-east to Alwinton. Cocklawfoot is closer but is nothing more than a farm. Alwinton makes a good start point for a strenuous walk. Bed-and-breakfast is available at Uswayford.*

CLENNEL STREET

KIRK YETHOLM

APPROX. 11 MILES/17.75KM

OS Landranger 80, 74
Start at grid reference NT 872 161
Start point: Access to any point along the border ridge is impossible by car; there are no roads. Clennel Street and the crossing point, Border Gate, mark the more convenient break in the route on the ridge but require a stiff 7-mile climb from Alwinton, which is the nearest village.

The cleft of the border crossing place is often shrouded in mist. This was once the heart of the Badlands, a place for dark deeds. The route follows the border fence along a broad ridge called Butt Roads, then rises to King's

Below *Domed giants: The Cheviot and, offering excellent walking and fine views, Hedgehope*

Above *The view from Auchope*

Seat, where there is nothing but a triangulation point and wide acres of windswept heather. The ridge on the English side drops away to Usway Burn (pronounced Oozy or Uzzy). Several small streams drain the ridge eastwards, including Murder Cleugh and the Inner Hare Cleugh, where Black Rory the Highlander established one of his illicit stills 200 years ago.

Above King's Seat there is a long pull north-eastwards, by Green Gair and Crookedsike Head, and the ground is often boggy. As the route climbs even more steeply towards Cairn Hill there is a tumble of rocks on the brow to the right called the Hanging Stone, another place of ill-repute which marked the boundary between the Middle and East Marches. The top of the hill is peaty and gives a foretaste of The Cheviot; an optional detour leads off to the right over Cairn Hill to the summit of The Cheviot which, at 2674ft (815m), sounds impressive but has poor views and a covering of deep liquid peat. Most people avoid it. The main route heads sharp left, at a stile and over boardwalks across very wet ground to Auchope. There is then a descent, past another refuge hut, at a strategic place where conditions can be treacherous and there is no easy escape route. In good light the views are excellent; in the foreground to the right is the Hen Hole, a hanging valley by which the College Burn leaps and rushes down through the andesite and heads north to join the River Glen at Kirknewton. The hills are the haunt of wild goats and peregrines.

The Schil is a shapely summit and one of the most beautiful links along the whole chain of border hills. The views are breathtaking, as is the climb. On its northern side there are several rocky tors; tors of baked andesite are small but important features of the inner Cheviots.

An exhilarating descent along the border fence from the Schil leads to a dip, with the next hill, Black Hag, ahead.

ⓔ *There are escape routes here (grid ref. NT 863 233), left by a lowland path to Kirk Yetholm via Burnhead, and right into the College*

valley to Mounthooly. Either path can form part of a circular walk; the Mounthooly circuit, via Dunsdale and the Bizzle or Goldscleugh and Bellyside, offers one of the best options for an ascent of The Cheviot.

The Pennine Way crosses into Scotland but follows the border for a little while longer. There is one more memorable stretch after Black Hag as the Way rises to Steerig Knowe and then sweeps along the crest of Steer Rig with the basin of the Trowhope Burn to the right and the twin-peaked summit of Coldsmouth Hill ahead. White Law is magnificent, offering the last panorama, across to the Tweed and to Flodden where the Scots were finally defeated in 1513, and into the Cheviot foothills.

North of Whitelaw Nick the route turns left and quits the border ridge, following a track at first towards the dome of Green Humbleton, then left to follow the Shielknowe Burn. After crossing Halter Burn, the Way turns right along a quiet road; the last mile into Kirk Yetholm gives you a chance to come to terms with the end of the walk. The village has all the necessary services, including a youth hostel and the Border Hotel.

THE CHEVIOT LANDSCAPE

The Cheviots are 'white land'; although there is some heather on the high ground and there are attempts to encourage its rehabilitation – mainly in the interests of grouse management – most of the hill slopes are covered with grass which is bleached by winter winds. The Cheviot grasslands look white in spring whilst heather moorland looks black. A few inches below the surface lies andesite, an igneous extrusive rock and the solid evidence that the Cheviots were created by a vast volcano that choked itself on seas of lava. Beneath the andesite and showing at the surface at a few places is a core of granite. Where the hot granite met the existing andesite a hardened 'aureole' was created. Tors on the otherwise smooth slopes are the weathered skeletons of the Cheviot aureole.

SCOTLAND

The Pass of Glencoe in the West Highlands

West Highland Way

GLASGOW (MILNGAVIE) TO FORT WILLIAM
95 MILES/152KM

THE West Highland Way was the first long distance route to be officially designated in Scotland. Opened in 1980, it takes the walker from the northern suburbs of Glasgow through some of the most splendid loch and mountain scenery in Scotland to its finish in Fort William. Along the Way you walk much of the eastern shore of Loch Lomond, cross the western fringe of Rannoch Moor and pass through Glencoe. The Way uses military roads, drove routes and lochside paths in its varied progress.

Detailed guides
The official guide, *The West Highland Way* (written by Robert Aitken, published by HMSO, available from all main bookshops) is strongly recommended. Not only is it full of interesting historical and topographical information, it contains its own 1:50,000 maps, which obviates the need for buying five separate Landranger maps.

Maps
OS Landranger 41, 50, 56, 57, 64

Links
There are no officially recognised linking Paths.

The West Highland Way has proved popular ever since it was opened. It is most often walked from south to north, and is described that way here. There are several advantages to walking it this way: the sun will most often be behind you, the wind will be at your back or your left flank, and above all, the scenery grows steadily more splendid and wild as you make your way northwards, until the final crescendo delivers you through the magnificence of Glencoe and the Mamores to the foot of Ben Nevis, Britain's highest mountain.

The West Highland Way has its attractions at all times of year, but spring and autumn have a certain edge. In July and August, the weather is uncertain, midges can be a pest, and accommodation fully booked. In spring the days are long, the weather often clear and the visibility sharp. First leaf on the trees and last snow on the higher hills make a supremely beautiful combination: and the midges are still hibernating. Autumn is also a fine time for walking, with a different colour contrast, of dying leaf and flowering heather; this time it is the snow which is fresh. Days are shorter but there are fewer people about and the birdlife is excellent.

Although the Way is waymarked through-out, with the symbol of the former Countryside Commission for Scotland (now Scottish Natural Heritage) of a thistle within a hexagon, it travels through exposed and wild country, and walkers must be prepared. You will be very lucky to walk the whole Way without getting wet at some point: the Fort William area has an average of 100 inches of rain a year! Higher parts of the Way are subject to mist, and the ability to navigate with map and compass is a prerequisite. It is understandably impossible to walk from Glasgow to Fort William without a considerable amount of ascent and descent being involved. There are few genuinely steep sections on the Way but plenty of up-and-down, for which you should again be prepared.

The going underfoot varies, as you would expect. The initial section is on minor roads and good tracks, but along Loch Lomondside the going is much slower, the narrow path forcing its way along the hillslopes that fall towards the loch. Many walkers have found this part of the Way difficult and tiring. After Crianlarich, things improve, with extensive use of established tracks and easier going underfoot. The final pull up through the forest before the end can seem as hard as anything on the route.

Because of the nature of the country through which it passes, accommodation is scattered along the Way, and for substantial sections there is little or nothing. In recent years, a number of bunkhouses have opened, and details are given on the following pages. Main settlements such as Crianlarich, Tyndrum and Kinlochleven offer a variety of accommodation, but in the intervening stretches you are thrown back on your own resources. Many people choose to camp, which gives considerable freedom as well as the ability to vary your day to suit your own requirements.

On the following pages, the West Highland Way is broken down into five stretches of roughly 20 miles each, but for most people a week to ten days is a more usual time for completing the whole walk. This gives you the chance to see some of the things along the way and perhaps to climb one or two of the superb hills that flank the route.

The law in Scotland regarding rights of way differs from that in England. Contrary to an often-expressed view, the offence of trespass does exist, but it is a civil not a

The view across Loch Lomond from the west, towards Inversnaid

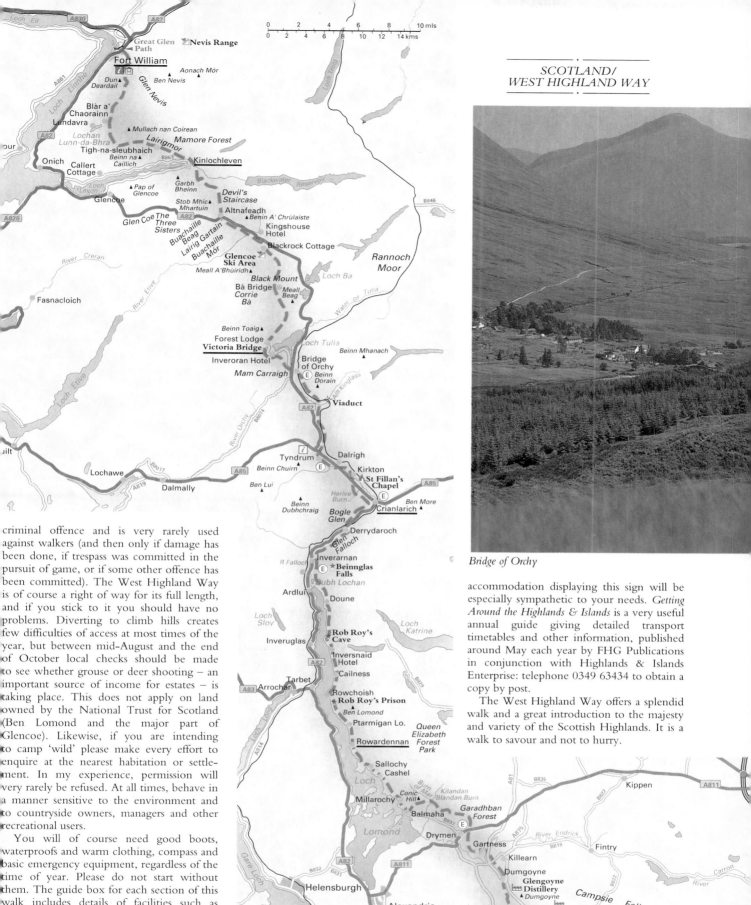

Bridge of Orchy

criminal offence and is very rarely used against walkers (and then only if damage has been done, if trespass was committed in the pursuit of game, or if some other offence has been committed). The West Highland Way is of course a right of way for its full length, and if you stick to it you should have no problems. Diverting to climb hills creates few difficulties of access at most times of the year, but between mid-August and the end of October local checks should be made to see whether grouse or deer shooting – an important source of income for estates – is taking place. This does not apply on land owned by the National Trust for Scotland (Ben Lomond and the major part of Glencoe). Likewise, if you are intending to camp 'wild' please make every effort to enquire at the nearest habitation or settlement. In my experience, permission will very rarely be refused. At all times, behave in a manner sensitive to the environment and to countryside owners, managers and other recreational users.

You will of course need good boots, waterproofs and warm clothing, compass and basic emergency equipment, regardless of the time of year. Please do not start without them. The guide box for each section of this walk includes details of facilities such as shops and banks en route.

Because there is relatively little accommodation along the Way, it may be worth booking ahead, especially between Easter and October. A free accommodation leaflet is available from Scottish Natural Heritage, Battleby, Redgorton, Perth PH1 3EW. Along the Way a 'Walkers Welcome' scheme operates, and you can be sure that

accommodation displaying this sign will be especially sympathetic to your needs. *Getting Around the Highlands & Islands* is a very useful annual guide giving detailed transport timetables and other information, published around May each year by FHG Publications in conjunction with Highlands & Islands Enterprise: telephone 0349 63434 to obtain a copy by post.

The West Highland Way offers a splendid walk and a great introduction to the majesty and variety of the Scottish Highlands. It is a walk to savour and not to hurry.

Milngavie

Rowardennan

MILNGAVIE

BALMAHA

APPROX. 12 MILES/20KM

OS Landranger 64, 57, 56
Start at grid reference NS 557 745
Start point: Milngavie Station, north of Glasgow (frequent services from Queen Street or Charing Cross in Glasgow). Car park at the station. Milngavie has shops, banks and cafés.

The official starting point of the West Highland Way is the railway station at Milngavie, north of Glasgow. It is an appropriate place for several reasons. Within a very short distance, you are into pleasant countryside; the train link to Glasgow is excellent; and Milngavie is one of those places associated with the great outdoor movement of the depression years in the 1930s, when hundreds of unemployed men journeyed into the countryside to find solace in walking and climbing.

A word about the name: it traps the unwary, for the pronunciation is 'mull-guy', and indeed it appears on some old maps as Milguy. Its origin may be Gaelic *muileann-gaoithe,* 'a windmill'. You will come across many names with Gaelic origins on this walk, and even the briefest study of them will yield a rich harvest of understanding which will add immeasurably to your appreciation of the land and its history.

From the railway station, follow the signs under Woodburn Way and along Station Road into Douglas Street. Here you will find shops, banks and cafés – it is the last such shopping centre on the route until Fort William, so make the most of it! From Douglas Street, follow waymarks over the Allander Water and along to an attractive tree-lined lane, on the line of a former railway serving one of the long-defunct mills in the area. The Allander Water is rejoined for ¼ mile or so before a right turn, uphill, takes you on to the birch and gorse moorland of Allander Park.

From here to Loch Lomondside the Way passes through the ancient lands of Lennox. The Earldom of Lennox was created by King Malcolm IV in 1153 and by the late 14th century the lands of Lennox extended to the north end of Loch Lomond. In medieval times, the earldom passed to the Darnley Stewarts, one of whom was briefly married to Mary Queen of Scots, then to the Dukes of Richmond, and finally to the Grahams, Dukes of Montrose.

Southwards is Glasgow, westward the Kilpatrick Hills, and north the Campsies and the approach to Loch Lomond. Most of the area is set on the Clyde plateau lavas, laid down 350 million years ago during the Lower Carboniferous period. The walk continues along the former drive of Craigallian House to enter Mugdock Wood, with a fine variety of trees and many lovely wild flowers in spring and summer. Mugdock was gifted to the people of Glasgow in 1980 by Sir Hugh Fraser, and is now run by the local authorities as one of the 40 country parks in Scotland, providing many thousands of people with an invaluable recreational lung.

Leaving Mugdock, the Way follows a track beside the Allander Water to reach Craigallian Loch, a favourite weekending place for generations of Glaswegians. Some of the holiday huts built decades ago, and lovingly cared for ever since, can be seen in this area. From Craigallian you can see Dumgoyne, the stubby hill at the western end of the Campsies, which dominates this part of the walk – and is itself a splendid viewpoint and an easy climb.

The Way continues, entering the Tinker's Loan, an old track as the name indicates, and crossing the ·low watershed dividing the Glasgow basin from the Loch Lomond lands; it too is a fine viewpoint, with Ben Lomond prominent, urging you forward. For the next few miles the Way follows an old railway line through Strathblane, passing Dumgoyne (and its distillery, which can be visited). As you walk the old railway, Glasgow's water is flowing under your feet, along a 60-inch pipe from Loch Lomond to the city.

GUIDE BOX

Places to visit
Mugdock Country Park, the former estate of the Frasers of Allander, was given over for public use in 1980. Visitor centre, car parks, trails, lochs, castle ruins. Open all year.

Glengoyne Distillery has been a malt whisky distillery since 1833. Conducted tours April to November, Monday to Saturday (check times locally). Reception area and shop open all year.

Car parking
Principal car parks are at Milngavie Station (grid ref. NS 557 745), Balmaha (NS 421 909), Milarrochy Bay (NS 410 925), Rowardennan (NS 380 957).

Public transport
Buses from Glasgow and Stirling to Drymen; from Glasgow to Strathblane and Killearn. Limited service from Drymen to Balmaha.

Accommodation
There are hotels and guesthouses in Milngavie, Strathblane, Drymen, Balmaha and Rowardennan, a youth hostel at Rowardennan (open February to October), a bunkhouse at Balmaha and camp sites at Drymen, Millarochy and Cashtel. For an accommodation leaflet from Scottish Natural Heritage, see page 233.

The Way passes within a mile of Killearn and finally leaves the old railway to take to quiet lanes, crossing the River Endrick – a fine salmon stream, where herons are commonly seen – near Gartness and climbing, with more fine views, to approach Drymen. It does not pass through the village, but a short diversion will take you there.

Ⓔ *Drymen (little ridge in Gaelic) has shops, cafés and hotels, and bus services back to Glasgow. It also has the last bank on the Way before Kinlochleven, so ensure your wallet is fed here as well as your stomach. Leave the Way at grid ref. NS 482 885.*

The Way itself passes east of Drymen into the Garadhban Forest, owned by the Forestry Commission, and home to many woodland birds including finches, siskins and crossbills. At the forest edge a stile is crossed to an open moor, a great contrast with the enclosed woodland. To your left is Loch Lomond and ahead is the bulk of Conic Hill, which the path climbs. Here you truly pass into the Highlands, for the hill is on the line of a great geological fault that crosses Scotland from west coast to east.

Take care crossing the moorland: the waymarks can become almost buried in bracken in high summer, though the path itself is generally clear enough. It crosses two burns, the splendidly named Kilandan Blandan and the Burn of Mar, where dippers may be seen. The top of Conic Hill is some 700ft (215m) above, and a sharp climb it is too. The reward is a superb panoramic view of loch, hills and islands. Although Conic Hill is roughly conical, the name probably comes from the Gaelic *A'Coinneach,* meaning 'moss' or 'bog', so it is the hill above the bog. The hill is a steep-sided ridge of conglomerate rock with some erratic boulders deposited by glaciation near its top.

From Conic Hill there is a sharp descent to the car park at Balmaha, a busy place in summer with its marina and cafés, and the start of the long traverse along the east bank of Loch Lomond.

Clouds gather over Dumgoyne and Strathblane

Loch Lomond at Balmaha

BALMAHA

ROWARDENNAN

APPROX. 7 MILES/12KM

OS Landranger 56
Start at grid reference NS 420 909
Start point: Balmaha (infrequent bus service to Drymen from where there are more frequent services to Glasgow). Large car park, cafés, shop, toilets.

Loch Lomond is the largest sheet of inland water in Britain. It is 23 miles long, has a maximum depth of over 600ft (180m), and covers over 20 square miles. Facts cannot convey its beauty: that has to be seen, and walking its banks is the best way to do it. The West Highland Way follows the loch for nearly 20 miles of changing views, fine woodland and superb mountain scenes.

The loch alters its character markedly as you travel north. This southern section is broad, relatively shallow, and has numerous islands – well seen from Conic Hill. The north end is narrower, more confined by mountains, and also much wetter. The botanical interest is remarkable – some 25 per cent of all known British flowering plants and ferns can be found here.

Little wonder that the loch has found such fame. Ask any visitor to Scotland to name three places in the country and Loch Lomond is likely to be one of them. It is a major tourist attraction, with peak summer weekends drawing perhaps 40,000 visitors. Despite this, its future remains uncertain. It was designated a Regional Park in 1988, but many feel its conservation should be enshrined in stronger terms. Time will tell.

The Way wanders along beside the loch. Its path from Balmaha to Rowardennan is somewhat tortuous, and those in a hurry have been known to abandon it for the road. That would be a pity, for it winds in and out of attractive woods, down to little bays,

round small promontories and through plantations. Above Balmaha, pass the cairn marking the official opening of the Way in 1980, on a 'dreich' autumn day. The car park at Milarrochy Bay is passed and at this point the path enters the Queen Elizabeth Forest Park, which covers much of the Trossachs.

At Cashel, where there is an excellent camp site, the road is joined for a short way before it is left again for the oakwoods of Sallochy. These woods once provided timber for housing and also charcoal for iron smelting, carried out on a small scale at 'bloomeries' in the woods. The Way goes past a field centre at Ross and climbs steeply into Ross Woods, before further meanderings end on the road just south of the Rowardennan Hotel. Here there is a large car park, the favourite place to start the climb of Ben Lomond, a pier for the loch steamer and, a little further on, a youth hostel.

ROB ROY

Robert Macgregor, known as Rob Roy ('Red Robert') was born in 1671, the second son of Lt-Col Donald Macgregor of Glengyle. As a young man he worked as a grazier, later purchasing from his nephew the estate of Craigroyston and Inversnaid on the east bank of Loch Lomond. It was a time of raiding and plunder, and Rob gathered his own band of followers, working as a cattle drover and demanding rent or 'black mail' in return for guaranteeing safe passage of the beasts.

In about 1712 his fortunes declined. In debt to the Duke of Montrose, his lands were seized and his family turned out of their home in winter. Then began the adventures for which Rob gained fame as he waged war on the Dukes of Montrose and Atholl. Rob had assumed his mother's name of Campbell and enjoyed the support of the Campbell chief, the Duke of Argyll. He survived many adventures and died at his home, Inverlochlarig, in 1734. He is buried in Balquhidder churchyard. Rob's life was romanticised by Sir Walter Scott in his novel *Rob Roy,* published in 1818.

235

Rowardennan
Crianlarich

OS Landranger 56
Start at grid reference NS 360 983
Start point: Rowardennan (hotel, youth hostel, car park). Pier for loch steamers. Seasonal ferry across loch to Inverbeg. No other public transport.

The east bank of Loch Lomond can provide a glorious traverse through splendid oakwoods with a wide variety of birds, plants, mammals and other trees to delight the eye, plus the changing vistas across the water; or it can be a tortuous struggle through what the Scots aptly call 'glaur'. This part of the walk is undoubtedly best done in dry conditions, for here the path is at its most fragile and considerable erosion has occurred. During or after wet weather (a not unknown phenomenon in these parts) it can be unpleasantly muddy and slippery. Unless you are very fortunate or have infinite time to spare, you will have to take it as you find it; even in adversity there is pleasure in thinking ahead to the better going once Glen Falloch is gained.

Do not be put off by these words of warning, rather be prepared. If you are ready

The Falls at Inversnaid, inspiration for poets Wordsworth and Hopkins

for the worst, anything better will be a pleasant surprise, and if you catch the fickle Scottish climate at its best, you will enjoy a memorable walk in unparalleled scenery. But first you have to break clear of the crowds and their cars at Rowardennan. This is achieved in only a few hundred yards; most people are either picnicking by the lochside or climbing Ben Lomond, and once past the excellent youth hostel you will meet few. You may, these days, encounter mountain-bikers, who on much of the Way are not a problem, given the firm nature of the path. Some consider that the section to Inverarnan is simply unsuitable for them, but they are determined characters and there may be some struggling along here.

Opposite the youth hostel, on the right of the track, is the site of a large bloomery, now occupied by a number of chalets. The track continues for $\frac{1}{2}$ mile or so to Ptarmigan Lodge, named from the shapely outlier of Ben Lomond high above, itself named after that most distinctive bird of the high tops, which with luck can still be seen (and more often, heard) on these hills.

Just after Ptarmigan Lodge, a choice of routes presents itself. Either continue on the broad track or descend steps to a lochside path, which is slower going but gives much better views. About a mile further on is a crag known as Rob Roy's Prison, where it is said the outlaw kept hostages in a natural rock cell. The facts are difficult to unearth, but he certainly operated in these parts.

From here northwards you can see across the loch, through the Tarbet gap, the hills affectionately known to climbers as the Arrochar Alps, the distinctive overhanging crags of The Cobbler standing out among them. The pass from Tarbet to Arrochar was used by the Viking King Haakon in 1263 to drag boats through, in order to mount a surprise attack on the Lennoxes. Tarbet means 'isthmus' in Gaelic.

The next building on the Way is Rowchoish Bothy, restored as a memorial to William Ferris, who worked tirelessly for walkers for much of his life through the Scottish Youth Hostels Association, the Scottish Ramblers' Federation and the Scottish Rights of Way Society. You may

well have the bothy to yourself if you stay overnight here; 200 years ago there were nine families at Rowchoish, a typical example of the way the Highlands have been depopulated.

After Rowchoish the two routes combine into a lovely path through the woods to the farm cottage at Cailness. The footbridge here has been washed away twice in recent years by sudden spates down the steep burn. Woodland birds likely to be found on this stretch include jays and woodpeckers and perhaps the little treecreeper looking for insects in the tree bark. The path continues to Inversnaid, celebrated in verse by Wordsworth and especially the Jesuit poet Gerard Manley Hopkins, whose poem 'Inversnaid' has become famous as a plea for wild places:

This darksome burn, horseback brown,
his rollrock highroad roaring down,
In coop and in comb the fleece of his foam
Flutes and low to the lake falls home.

What would the world be, once bereft
Of wet and of wildness? Let them be left,
O let them be left, wildness and wet;
Long live the weeds and the wilderness yet.

Those words have never seemed more appropriate. At Inversnaid there is an elegant and unexpectedly large hotel, dating from Victorian times, a ferry pier, and the end of the road from Aberfoyle. And of course the falls, crashing down under the bridge.

Inversnaid was a garrison for a time in the 18th century, and some of the buildings are still there, up on the hill. Down here, once away from the hotel, all is peaceful by the loch: as well to take a break here and gird the loins, for the next few miles are among the roughest on the whole walk. The hillslopes fall steep and broken straight into the loch and are heavily wooded, and the path has to fight a way through, with a fair amount of up-and-down and scrambling over rocks and tree-roots. Normal time allowances go out of the window on this stretch. The really fainthearted can catch the ferry (summer only) across the loch to Inveruglas and walk up the road on the west side to rejoin the Way at Inverarnan.

Rob Roy's Prison is followed here by the Cave; since his time the view across the loch has been marred by the enormous pipes feeding Loch Sloy power station. The walker might prefer not to know that Loch Sloy holds the Scottish rainfall record for a 24-hour period – over nine inches on 17–18 January 1974.

As the Way crosses the Allt Rostan it passes from Strathclyde to Central Region; shortly after this a very steep slab is crossed by a rather precarious bridge, where care is always needed. But in another ¹/₄ mile or so you emerge at the bay south of Doune, and difficulties are over. Doune is also a bothy. The path continues past the lovely little Dubh Lochan (*dubh* meaning 'dark') and at last the north end of the loch, companion for so long, is reached. The path enters Glen Falloch, and in a further mile a diversion can be, and often is, made along the short distance to the old drovers' inn at Inverarnan for a well-earned refreshment.

Ⓔ *From Inverarnan (grid ref. 318 185) an 'escape' may be made back to Glasgow by walking the 2 miles along the A82 to Ardlui, where there is a station on the Oban/Fort William-to-Glasgow line.*

INVERARNAN

CRIANLARICH

APPROX. 6¹/₂ MILES/10KM

OS Landranger 56, 50
Start at grid reference NN 318 185
Start point: Inverarnan Inn on A82 (hotel, car park). Buses to Glasgow and Fort William/Oban; British Rail station at Ardlui, 2 miles south.

From the Inverarnan Inn there is a superb view of the splendid Beinnglas Falls, crashing down the hillside above Beinn Glas Farm. It is an easy walk up to the falls from the farm and one well worth taking; after heavy rain the noise is terrific and the force of the water is exceptional.

The Way now runs up Glen Falloch, a much more pastoral scene than hitherto, following the east bank of the River Falloch for 3 miles to Derrydaroch. (From the Inverarnan Inn, walk up the A82 for a short way and cross the river by the bridge to Beinn Glas Farm to rejoin the Way.) The Falloch tumbles over a succession of rapids, small falls and waterslides, maintaining interest all the way. Geologists have

suggested that the river originally flowed north to Crianlarich and is still adjusting to its 'new' course after a mere 10,000 years.

You pass through several fine groups of trees, including oak, alder and birch on this stretch, and although the road is never far away, it is surprisingly secluded down here. The railway from Glasgow to Oban and Fort William is just the other side of the road. On the same slope is the Clach-na-Briton, said to mark the ancient boundary between Brythonic, Scots and Pictish territories.

Derrydaroch means 'the oak grove', though these trees are less numerous nowadays and there are as many pines. The river is crossed here and the path takes the other bank for ¹/₂ mile before passing under the railway through a 'cattle creep' in which it is best to take your pack off and carry it low down. The A82 road is crossed (take care) and the path strikes uphill to join the line of the old military road, built in 1752–3 after the Jacobite Risings as part of the

Crianlarich, a good break point for walkers

London government's plans to quell the rebellious Highlanders.

There are fine views along this stretch of hills to either side; the Cruach Ardrain group to the east, outliers of Ben Lui above you, and Strath Fillan hills ahead. The path passes Keilator Farm, whose name may mean 'the nook on the slope', and enters a delightful small glen called Bogle Glen; a bogle is a Scots word for a ghost or ghoul.

You are now above Crianlarich, at roughly the half-way point of the full walk. The path passes west of the village, but most people elect to stop here, as there is a choice of accommodation including a hotel, several bed-and-breakfast places and an excellent new youth hostel.

Ⓔ *Crianlarich (grid ref. 385 250) has a station and is on a bus route from Glasgow.*

WEST HIGHLAND WILDLIFE

The West Highland Way passes through a great variety of scenery, and the wildlife varies accordingly. The southern part of Loch Lomond is a National Nature Reserve and holds many waterbirds, especially in winter. The oakwoods beside the loch are also rich in birdlife and you may see foxes and deer here. Once past Crianlarich the country becomes wilder and more open; deer are common, though they keep to the higher ground in summer. Birds include red grouse, curlew and buzzards, and if you are very lucky you may see an eagle. There are a few pairs in the area, and they make a thrilling sight soaring high above the mountain peaks.

The latter part of the walk passes through several areas of forestry, notably between Kinlochleven and Glen Nevis, and here the birds include short-eared owls, kestrels and other raptors. Ravens are also quite common, their harsh 'cronk' a characteristic sound of hill areas. Pocket guides and small binoculars are well worth taking on the walk.

Crianlarich
Victoria Bridge

CRIANLARICH

TYNDRUM

APPROX. 6¹/₂ MILES/10KM

OS Landranger 50
Start at grid reference NN 384 251
Start point: Crianlarich railway station
(Glasgow-to-Oban/Fort William line: daily
service, though fewer trains on Sundays).
Daily buses on same route. Café at the
station, shop in village.

From Crianlarich to Tyndrum the West
Highland Way follows a much more
meandering course than the A82 road, which
shakes itself out of Crianlarich in a dog's tail
of bends and then zooms uphill, arrow-
straight, as if in a hurry to pass through this
lovely valley. Hurry is inexcusable here: not
only is the valley itself full of interest, the
hills to either side repay in orders of
magnitude whatever time is spared to gaze
upon them.

Climbing them is even better, if there is
the time to spare and the energy and
enthusiasm available. But these are not hills
to be taken lightly, even in summer. The
area is ringed with Munros of high quality,
including Ben More and Stobinian, highest
hills of the Southern Highlands at over
3800ft (1158m), and Ben Lui, felt by many
to be amongst the shapeliest of Scotland's
mountains.

But back to the Way itself. Pick it up just
west of Crianlarich, or from the railway
station, from where it is waymarked as it
dives into the new forest. This plantation and
the Way arrived here more or less together,
so the path was created as the planting took
place. There is a good variety of tree species
and enough breaks to enjoy the views.

The path crosses the Herive Burn and
joins a forest road to run down to the
railway line (the Oban branch), passing a
lively waterfall. The A82 is crossed (again,
take care) and a path squeezed in beside the
road leads to the bridge over the Kirkton
Burn and the lane to Kirkton Farm, one of
two farms operated as experimental units by
the West of Scotland College of Agriculture.
Walkers are especially requested not to use
this section if they have a dog with them,
keeping to the road until the Way recrosses
it past Auchtertyre Farm.

Kirkton is notable for the remains of St
Fillan's Chapel almost hidden in the trees.
Fillan came from Ireland. He is said to have
been the son of St Kentigern, who died on
Inchcailloch Island on Loch Lomond in 734
and (as St Mungo) became the patron saint
of the City of Glasgow. Fillan himself was
engaged on missionary work in the area you
are walking through; the chapel was a
monastic establishment, probably established
in the 12th century, and raised to the status
of a priory by Robert the Bruce, who is said
to have received a message or sign of support
from St Fillan on the eve of the Battle of
Bannockburn in 1314.

From here walk along to Auchtertyre, the
other experimental farm, and back to the
A82. Having safely crossed it, meander along
the west side of the road through more
forestry plantings towards Tyndrum.

The area where the Way crosses the road

GUIDE BOX

Car parking
The principal car parks for this section are at
Crianlarich (grid ref. NN 385 251), Tyndrum
(NN 330 301), Bridge of Orchy (NN 299 396).
Roadside parking at Victoria Bridge (NN 271
422).

Public transport
Crianlarich and Tyndrum are on the British Rail
line from Glasgow to Oban and Fort William;
Bridge of Orchy is on the Fort William line.
Daily service, though fewer trains on Sunday.
Daily buses on the same routes also stop at these
places. No public transport at Victoria Bridge.

Accommodation
There are hotels at Crianlarich, Tyndrum,
Bridge of Orchy and Inveroran; guesthouses and
bed-and-breakfasts at Crianlarich and Tyndrum;
bunkhouses at Tyndrum and Bridge of Orchy, a
camp site at Tyndrum.

Facilities
General stores at Crianlarich and Tyndrum;
outdoor shop at Tyndrum selling clothing,
boots, maps etc.

is called Dalrigh ('the king's field'), marking
this time a defeat for the Bruce, in 1306 at
the hands of the MacDougalls of Lorne.
From here you have an excellent view of
Beinn Dubhcraig and Ben Lui. The bare
patch of ground by the river just before
Tyndrum is a remnant of the former lead
mining industry which was started here by
Sir Robert Clifton in 1741 and continued to
1862. Over that period about 5000 tons of
ore were extracted. Now Tyndrum is again
the focus of an exploration for riches; in this
case it is gold, a source of which has been

*Beinn an Dothaidh and Beinn Dorain, seen from
Bridge of Orchy*

found on Beinn Chuirn, above Cononish Farm. At the time of writing the price of gold had dropped and work had stopped, but the company, Ennex, may be back. A condition of their being granted rights to mine here is that they restore the land as far as possible, once mining has ceased.

Part of Tyndrum is still called Clifton, after the man who set up the mine and the workers' village here. Today Tyndrum exists largely to service tourists, standing as it does at the junction where the roads to Oban and Fort William divide. There is accommodation here, and several cafés, and Tyndrum must be the smallest place in Britain to have two railway stations: the lower serves Oban and the upper, 1/4 mile or so away, is on the Fort William line. Tyndrum means 'the houses on the ridge', and Scotland's main watershed is a little west of the village. It was on one of the main droving routes in former times, so it is used to catering for travellers of all kinds. Queen Victoria called it 'wild and desolate' which, especially in winter, it certainly can be – but it has a fairer face too.

Ⓔ *From Tyndrum (grid ref. NN 328 306) a return may be made by rail to Glasgow, or an intermediate station.*

TYNDRUM

VICTORIA BRIDGE

APPROX. 9 MILES/15KM

OS Landranger 50
Start at grid reference NN 328 306
Start point: Tyndrum village. Cafés, shops, parking. Trains and buses to Glasgow, Oban, Fort William.

The West Highland Way marches up the hill out of Tyndrum as if eager to see what lies ahead – and indeed another mountain treat is in store. The line of the Way here follows the old military road again. Originally constructed by troops under Major Caulfeild, successor to the better-known General Wade, in 1750-2, it was later used as a motor road until the latter route was redesigned in the 1930s. Now it is again the province of the walker (and mountain-biker).

The track is clear, broad and easy as it climbs past Tyndrum's water treatment plant. As it reaches the top of the rise, Beinn Dorain comes into view ahead. From this angle, Beinn Dorain looks like every child's picture of a mountain; an almost perfect cone, rising steep-flanked to a pointed summit. In fact, like so many similar hills, what you are seeing is the end of a ridge, but it is no less fine for that. You have now, by the way, recrossed – for a short time – into Strathclyde Region.

Beinn Dorain is associated with the great Gaelic poet Duncan Ban Macintyre (1724-1812) who lived for most of his life in this area and composed many verses and songs about it – written down by others, for Duncan himself was illiterate. His songs do

Loch Tulla: the Way passes alongside

not translate particularly well, but some of the feeling comes over, as in this verse from 'Cead Deireannach nam Beann' ('Final Farewell to the Bens'): 'Blithely would I set out for stalking on the hill passes, away to climb rough country, and late would I be coming home; the clean rain and the air on the peaks of the high mountains helped me to grow, and gave me robustness and vitality.' Sentiments many of us will share as we walk amongst these hills today.

The Way tracks the railway line as far as Auch Farm, where the latter swings right to cross the Allt Kinglass by a fine viaduct. There is an excellent view up Auch Glen to Beinn Mhanach ('hill of the monk'), a Munro detached from the main group here and for that reason a splendid viewpoint itself. The railway is recrossed and the broad path followed to the station at Bridge of Orchy, where trains pause for breath before starting the long climb across Rannoch Moor to the remote halt at Corrour – a journey every rail enthusiast should take. The hotel at Bridge of Orchy has a bunkhouse; inside the main building you can see pictures of times when they have been completely snowed in here in bad winters, with even trains buried under massive drifts.

Ⓔ *Bridge of Orchy railway station (grid ref. NN 301 394) provides an escape route by rail.*

The next short section offers a choice of routes: after walking down the road to cross the rushing Orchy by a fine old bridge, the path disappears into the woods over Mam Carraigh. The climb does allow excellent views, but the path is often very muddy and the road walk round to the Inveroran Hotel is not at all unpleasant, passing the pines of Doire Darach and walking beside lovely Loch Tulla. Those who take the hill path are rewarded with a fine panorama of the Blackmount Hills ahead, Stob Ghabhar ('peak of goats') prominent among them, while eastwards the vast expanse of Rannoch Moor stretches away to the horizon.

There has been an inn at Inveroran for over 200 years. William and Dorothy

Wordsworth had breakfast here in 1803. Those who stop here today are most unlikely to be served, as they apparently were, with 'butter not eatable, the barley-cakes fusty, oat-bread so hard I could not chew it, and four eggs which they had boiled as hard as stones', in Dorothy's words. The present building dates from about 1830 and was for long a droving inn, until the 'stance' was moved to Bridge of Orchy on the insistence of Lord Breadalbane, who took his case all the way to the House of Lords in 1844 so that he could keep the land for stalking.

In more recent years, Inveroran has become popular with walkers, climbers and anglers, and remains so today, the last hostelry before you tackle the section leading over to Glencoe. The true start of this is a mile or so further on, at Victoria Bridge.

WADE AND HIS ROADS

In 1724, the London government, worried by reports of further unrest, sent Major-General George Wade north to investigate. He reported that one of the main difficulties was 'the want of good roads and bridges'. Wade was appointed Commander-in-Chief, North Britain, and set out on the work of improving lines of communication – the military roads. He stayed in Scotland until 1740, pioneering routes over the Corrieyairack Pass between Fort Augustus and Strathspey, a road which rises to 2500ft (762m) and is a superb walk today, and many others, including the route from Stirling to Fort William partly followed by the West Highland Way.

From Victoria Bridge to Blackmount the Way follows the old motor road, itself largely following Wade's line, but the most impressive section is undoubtedly the Devil's Staircase rising above Altnafeadh in Glencoe in a series of finely engineered zig-zags starting the long descent to Kinlochleven. It is fascinating to trace the old military roads on the ground today. Many, although labelled as 'Wade's Road' were in fact overseen by his successor, Major Charles Caulfeild, but Wade was the great pioneer.

Victoria Bridge

Kinlochleven

VICTORIA BRIDGE

ALTNAFEADH

APPROX. 10 MILES/16KM

OS Landranger 50, 41
Start at grid reference NN 271 422
Start point: Victoria Bridge. No facilities or public transport. Roadside parking.

The next section of the Way continues to follow either the old military road or the first motor road over to Glencoe. The track is excellent all the way, but for 8 miles there is virtually no shelter of any kind, and the track reaches well over 1000ft (300m). In poor weather conditions it is a considerable test: and the average annual rainfall here is around 120 inches. There are no escape routes, so once you have started you must either press on or turn back. That said, in good conditions this is a magnificent walk, to be relished for the superb scenery, the sense of wildness, and the history around you and under your feet.

If climbing the stile by Forest Lodge seems like starting an adventure, it is a feeling that has been shared by others – among them the Marchioness of Breadalbane. Her book, *The High Tops of Black Mount,* written nearly 100 years ago, is well worth reading for the vivid descriptions of long days in the hills. She was the first honorary president of the Ladies Scottish Climbing Club when it was formed in 1908.

There is a long, steady pull up from Forest Lodge to the top of the rise between Beinn Toaig, on the west, and the smaller Meall Beag to the east, and here you pass from Strathclyde into Highland Region for the rest of the walk. You also cross a watershed: the waters ahead of you flow east into the Tay system rather than west.

As the Way continues, a large corrie opens up on the west (left). This is Corrie Ba ('corrie of the cattle') and magnificent it is, especially when viewed against the vast expanse of Rannoch Moor to the east. On a good day there can be few finer places than

Ba Bridge to stop for a rest and a brew-up. To the west is the corrie, with the Blackmount Hills soaring above it, and to the east the river gurgles down towards Loch Ba in the heart of the moor. The colouring is subtle and the sense of wilderness glorious: odd to reflect then that this was the route of the motor road up to the mid-1930s.

In the autumn here the awesome and thrilling sound of red deer stags at the rut can be heard. Their deep and powerful roar carries for long distances and prickles the hair on the neck. The Way continues past Ba Cottage, once a drovers' stance but long since abandoned, to the summit of this section at 1450ft (442m). Above the track is a memorial to Peter Fleming, former owner of the estate and himself a great traveller, adventurer and writer, who died of a heart attack here in 1971. He is less well-known than his brother Ian, creator of James Bond, but his books are minor classics of travel literature.

It is all downhill now, round the flanks of Meall a'Bhuiridh ('hill of roaring' – another reference to the stags) to the neat whitewashed Blackrock Cottage, a climbers' hut. Meall a'Bhuiridh has been developed for piste skiing, and the summit area is consequently spoiled, but it is a fine hill none the less, with a truly splendid rocky ridge on its west linking it with Creise, another fine Munro. The walk continues down the road serving the skiing car park to cross the A82 – last seen at Bridge of Orchy – and over to the Kingshouse Hotel.

The Kingshouse was once just that – a changehouse set up by the Crown for travellers. The inn now offers every modern comfort, and has a bunkhouse for walkers and climbers, but it seems things were not always thus, for here we again encounter Dorothy Wordsworth complaining that she

GUIDE BOX

Car parking
Principal parking places on this section are Victoria Bridge (roadside) (NN 272 423), Glencoe Ski Area (White Corries) car park (NN 265 525) (1 mile south of route), Altenafeadh car park (NN 222 562), Kinlochleven.

Public transport
The daily Glasgow-to Fort William bus passes through Glencoe and will stop on request. A bus runs from Kinlochleven to Glencoe Village or Fort William (Monday to Saturday only).

Accommodation
There are hotels at Kingshouse (Glencoe) and Kinlochleven; bed-and-breakfast in Kinlochleven; a bunkhouse and camp site at Kinlochleven. Off-route, there are hotels, bed-and-breakfast, a youth hostel and camp site in or near Glencoe Village (8 miles down the glen from Altnafeadh).

Facilities
Seasonal café and toilets at White Corries ski car park, Glencoe (¹/₂ a mile off route). Shops and a bank in Kinlochleven.

never saw 'such a miserable, wretched place'. She cannot have been talking of the landscape, which is dominated by the craggy splendour of Buachaille Etive Mor – the great herdsman of Etive, one of Scotland's premier rock and ice climbing mountains and irresistible to any photographer.

If there is the time and energy, a scramble up behind Kingshouse to the summit of Beinn a'Chrulaiste will give the best view of 'the Buachaille' as the hill is affectionately known. Beinn a'Chrulaiste (simply 'the rocky hill') stands apart from the other Glencoe hills and thus provides a superb view of them, especially the Buachaille. It can be climbed without difficulty from either Kingshouse or Altnafeadh, which is where the path is now heading.

There are alternative routes there. Either

A climbers' hut on Meall a'Bhuiridh

walk on the route of the old military road, under the hill, or go down by the River Coupall. Each way has its attractions. The riverside walk gives a closer view of the Buachaille, and climbers may be seen on one of the classic routes such as the Crowberry Tower or Great Gully.

Either way, arrive at Altnafeadh – a new house, replacing the older building burned down only a few years ago. From here there is a view down much of Glencoe, a glen redolent in history and rich in wild scenery. The story of the infamous Glencoe Massacre, its 300th anniversary marked in 1992, need not detain the walker here: it is amply documented. Glencoe itself is in the care of the National Trust for Scotland.

ALTNAFEADH

KINLOCHLEVEN

APPROX. 7 MILES/12KM

OS Landranger 41
Start at grid reference NN 222 562
Start point: Altnafeadh. No facilities. The daily Glasgow-to-Fort William bus will stop here on request. Car park.

Leaving Altnafeadh, you face the long haul over the Devil's Staircase, built by Caulfeild's troops in 1750. The zig-zags are still there; please walk them and do not take short cuts – that way this fine old route will be preserved.

Take your time on the ascent: the views back across and down Glencoe are superb, the Three Sisters rising into full view and the two Buachailles, Mor and Beag, dominant

either side of the deep trench of the Lairig Gartan. This is a place to avoid in early May if you like peace and quiet: it is used most years as a stage of the Scottish Six Days Trial when 300 or more scrambler motor bikes tackle the Staircase as part of their endurance week.They have been coming since 1907 so they should be tolerated, but they are certainly noisy.

At the summit of the pass (and of the whole walk, at 1800ft/549m) there is a cairn; a short climb to the west on to Stob Mhic Mhartuin gives an even better prospect of the area, especially the whole new aspect to the north, with the glorious serrated peaks of the Mamores framing the unmistakable hunchback shape of Ben Nevis itself. Your final target is within sight.

Below to the east is Blackwater Reservoir, built early this century by 3000 navvies. Tales of those days relate of hard living and hard drinking, of death and disappearance, of ten-hour drilling shifts – a different world. The reservoir feeds the aluminium works in Kinlochleven, which itself dramatically transformed a tiny Highland village into a

The Pass of Glencoe

town. Blackwater is nearly 8 miles long and its dam is over 80ft high.

The feeder pipes accompany the walker down towards Kinlochleven, with Garbh Bheinn (appropriately, 'rough hill') to the west. It too is a fine climb with a magnificent panorama, but not to be undertaken lightly. All this country was used by Robert Louis Stevenson in *Kidnapped,* and a finer setting for an escape would be hard to find.

The path passes through birchwood to meet the great pipes and runs down with them into Kinlochleven. In recent years the labour force at the aluminium smelter has declined in numbers and the West Highland Way has provided a welcome boost to the local economy. Despite the splendour of its surroundings, no one would pretend that Kinlochleven itself is very attractive, but it does provide a chance to shop, eat (it has one of the best fish and chip shops in the West Highlands), and perhaps stay overnight before tackling the final stage of the journey.

HARNESSING WATER FOR POWER

The first commercial application of hydro-electric power generation in Britain was for the British Aluminium Company's plant at Foyers, on the east side of Loch Ness, in 1896. Ten years later the same company opened a major plant in Kinlochleven, transforming a small Highland village into an industrial town. To provide the power, the Blackwater Reservoir, 4 miles to the east, was created. It holds 4000 million cubic feet of water and is fed by the copious rains that fall on this area.

This is a standard hydro-electric scheme, the power of the water coming down the great pipes

seen on the hillside above Kinlochleven turning the turbines that generate the electricity. In the 1940s and 1950s a number of very large hydro-power schemes were set up in the Highlands, including those based on the Tay-Tummel system and around Glen Affric. Since 1960 there has been much less development, the notable exception being the pumped storage scheme at Ben Cruachan, Argyll, in which water is pumped back up to the holding reservoir during the low demand period at night so that a constant supply is available during the day. There is a visitor centre at Cruachan.

Kinlochleven

Fort William

KINLOCHLEVEN

LUNDAVRA

APPROX. 7½ MILES/12KM

OS Landranger 41
Start at grid reference NN 187 620
Start point: Bridge in Kinlochleven (weekday bus service to Glencoe Village or Fort William, shops, bank). Park considerately in the village.

On leaving Kinlochleven, there is a definite feeling of entering the last lap of a long journey. If you are using the official guide, you are on the last map section; and you are entering Lochaber – like Lennox, where you started, one of the old provinces of Scotland (the name is still used in local government). Lochaber is a region of long lochs cutting deep into the interior, and of dramatic hills rising steeply, almost from the waterside. There are only 14 miles left, but there is still much to savour.

From Kinlochleven, the path climbs steadily through shady birchwoods, crossing the road up to Mamore Lodge. From here to Lundavra the Way is still on the line of the old military road, and of a long-established right of way, the Lairigmor, the name meaning 'the big pass'. For the fit and ambitious, there are temptations either side which are not easily ignored. To the right is the magnificent Mamore range, containing 11 Munros in all. Two or three of them can easily be savoured as a high-level alternative.

The hills to the west should not be discounted just because they are of lower height. Their position apart from the main hill groups makes Beinn na Caillich ('hill of the old woman') and Man na Gualainn ('pass of the shoulder') particularly fine viewpoints, looking not just north to the great Lochaber hills but also west, out towards the sea, and across Loch Leven to its Pap – Sgorr na Ciche in Gaelic.

These are for a fine day (but not during the main autumn stalking season). Access is by stalking tracks, which you will find on many Scottish hills. Superbly well engineered for ponies as well as men, they always take the best line and if you can find one, use it. The soldiers making the Lairigmor track were also looking for the best line, though their task was simpler. The track reaches about 800ft (240m) and then levels off to carry on through the broad glen. This can be a dreich place indeed in rain or mist.

Lundavra, at the end of the Lairigmor pass

GUIDE BOX

Places to visit
Ben Nevis Exhibition, High Street, Fort William. Exhibitions and models depicting topography, wildlife and history of Britain's highest mountain. Open Easter to November, daily.

West Highland Museum, Cameron Square, Fort William. Fascinating displays on local history clans, tartan, Jacobite relics (secret portrait of Bonnie Prince Charlie etc), natural history and industry. Open all year, Monday to Saturday.

Aonach Mor, 3 miles north-west of Fort William on A82. Scotland's newest ski resort. Gondola (open all year) goes to mountain restaurant at over 2000ft.

Car parking
There are parking places at Kinlochleven, Blar a'Chaorainn (grid ref. NN 100 666) and in Fort William.

Public transport
Buses run on weekdays to Glencoe and Fort William from Kinlochleven; daily to Glasgow and Inverness from Fort William. There is a daily train service (fewer trains on Sunday) to Glasgow and Mallaig from Fort William.

Accommodation
There are hotels, guesthouses and bed-and-breakfasts in Kinlochleven and Fort William; a youth hostel in Glen Nevis (closed November and Tuesdays October to March); bunkhouses and camp sites in Kinlochleven and in Glen Nevis.

Facilities
Shops and a bank in Kinlochleven. Full range of shops, banks, supermarket, cafés etc in Fort William.

Just over the summit you pass Tigh-na-Sleubhaich ('the house by the gully'). By turning right and climbing steeply (though always on grass) here, the Mamores ridge can be gained at a point where the rock type changes literally in a step, from grey schist to pinkish granite and by continuing over the easy Munro Mullach nan Coirean ('summit of the corries'), the Way can be picked up again lower down.

The path over the Lairigmor passes the eponymous ruin, where the right of way to Callert on Loch Levenside diverts left, and drops down into a forestry plantation. Beyond it lies Lochan Lunn-da-Bhra. The meaning of this name is obscure, but it is one of those lochs said to hold the *each uisge,* 'the water-horse', which came out of the water, tempted young men on to its back, and then galloped under the waves with them.

Emerge from the trees at Blar a'Chaorainn ('field of rowans'), where there is a small car park, and face a choice. The path goes right, climbing up and over the extension of the

Mamores ridge to drop into Glen Nevis; this is the actual route of the West Highland Way. In poor weather, an alternative is simply to continue along the switchback road which leads you straight into Fort William. Either way, you are now faced with the very last section of the walk.

LUNDAVRA

FORT WILLIAM

APPROX. 6¹/₂ MILES/10KM

OS Landranger 41
Start at grid reference NN 100 666
Start point: Blar a'Chaorainn car park. No other facilities or public transport.

Whether on the road or the path, in clear conditions there is a superb view of Ben Nevis, and of the many other fine hills surrounding it. From Blar a'Chaorainn, the path climbs to the right under a power line, partly following the line of a dyke (wall) which would formerly have marked the boundary between the better ground lower down and the rough grazing on the upper slopes.

As the path climbs, more of Ben Nevis comes into view: impressive more for its vast bulk than for any beauty of form. It hunches its shoulders way above the surrounding hills, rising to a rough plateau at 4406ft (1343m), the highest point in Britain.

The path enters forestry once more, contouring round to pass the site of Dun Deardail, an ancient fortified site possibly dating back to the Iron Age. It is one of many such sites in Scotland, and if you take the trees away in your mind's eye you will realise that it commands an excellent position above Glen Nevis, for long an important through-route on foot between the west coast and the hinterland. The name Deardail might mean 'fort on the stormy hill', which would be appropriate in view of the high rainfall levels experienced hereabouts.

Not long past the fort, the path joins a forest road which gives easy walking down to the glen. Partway down, a branch to the right leads to the excellent youth hostel and other facilities in the glen itself. The main path continues to meet the Glen Nevis road about a mile from Fort William, the largest settlement since Milngavie.

Fort William was established as such in the 17th century, named after King William III. Its Gaelic name, An Gearasdan, is linked, meaning the garrison. The original fort has disappeared, but the importance the town assumed with its strategic location has remained. It is the local administration and shopping centre, a tourist centre, and a rail and bus terminus (or more properly junction, since the separate rail line to Mallaig, one of the finest journeys in Britain, starts from here). As you would expect, there is a wide range of accommodation.

For those going on to climb Ben Nevis, a word on the ascent may be in order here. The usual route is from Achintee, accessed from the large car park in lower Glen Nevis

(grid ref. NN 125 729): a branch path from the youth hostel joins the main path partway up. The Ben Nevis path is well defined all the way to the top, for it was made when the summit observatory was constructed in the late 19th century (at that time, walking up cost you sixpence: today it is free). The path rounds the shoulder of Meall an t-Suidhe to cross the Red Burn and start up the notorious zig-zags before reaching the summit plateau, where you will find the ruins of the observatory, a variety of cairns commemorating events wholly unconnected with the mountain, and an emergency shelter. It is not a prepossessing place, but it is the roof of Britain.

The ascent needs preparation at any time of year. It is a long way and a rough one, and many underestimate it simply because there is a path. In mist (very frequent) the summit can be confusing, and it is all too possible to lose the path. There are cliffs on the north and east. Snow comes early and lingers late. The Ben is busy all year round, but one notable date is the first Saturday in September when 400 or so hardy souls tackle the Ben Nevis race to the summit and back (the record, believe it or not, is just under 90 minutes for the round trip). The descent is far worse than the climb. If you do climb the Ben, you can be pleased with your achievement, but you will be glad to get back down.

The West Highland Way is a journey not just through distance but through evolving landscapes and through history: a fine walk which one visit is unlikely to satisfy. Haste ye back.

A magnificent last lap, Glen Nevis

BRITAIN'S HIGHEST MOUNTAIN

At 4406ft (1343m) Ben Nevis is the highest mountain in Britain, and for that reason alone is climbed by many thousands of people who probably never tackle another hill. The usual route is the 'tourist track' starting from Achintee in lower Glen Nevis, where there is a car park and visitor information centre. The return trip is 10 arduous miles, and although there is a path all the way it should not be undertaken lightly. The overall average summit temperature hovers around freezing and the weather can change dramatically within an hour.

There was an observatory on the summit from 1883 to 1904, when it closed through lack of funds. The weather observers lived at the top

all year round, supplies going up by pony along the same path used today. The recordings made at that time are now being analysed by computer. The summit area is a plateau with a rather unsightly litter of cairns, the observatory ruins, and a small emergency shelter.

The famous Ben Nevis race takes place on the first Saturday in September each year. Up to 500 runners set out from Town Park to race to the top and back, the winner taking only about 90 minutes for the return trip. Because of its status, Ben Nevis is also used for many charity climbs: cars have been up it several times. On its north-east face are tremendous cliffs holding major rock climbs.

Speyside Way

SPEY BAY TO TOMINTOUL
47 MILES/75KM

Detailed guides
There is no full guidebook available. A *Speyside Way* leaflet can be obtained from Moray District Council, District Headquarters, High Street, Elgin (tel. 0343 545121). There are Speyside Way information boards at Spey Bay, Fochabers, Boat o'Brig, Craigellachie, Aberlour, Carron, Tamdhu, Ballindalloch, Glenlivet and Tomintoul. A countryside ranger is based at Craigellachie (tel. 0340 881266).

Maps
OS Landranger 28, 36

Links
No other officially recognised paths link with the Speyside Way.

THE Speyside Way was the second long-distance footpath to be officially designated in Scotland. The northern section of the Way, from Spey Bay to Ballindalloch, opened in July 1981, just nine months after the West Highland Way was inaugurated. It was intended that the Way would continue beside the River Spey to the Glenmore Forest Park, near Aviemore, but difficulties with obtaining access have led to this section being placed in abeyance. Instead, an inland spur has been added, taking the Way to Tomintoul.

There is a particular attraction in riverside paths, and the concept of a walk linking the foothills of the Cairngorms with the coast, largely following the course of the Spey, Scotland's second longest river, was an enticing one. Unfortunately, it was not possible to bring the original concept to fruition due to an unresolved dispute over access to the former railway line south of Ballindalloch.

Most walkers start the Way at its northern end, at Spey Bay on the Morayshire coast. This gives two days of relatively easy walking before tackling the final section through the hills to Tomintoul. From Spey Bay, the Way follows paths and a minor road for 5 miles to the attractive planned village of Fochabers. Paths are then followed to Ordiequish, where a minor road is joined all the way to Boat o'Brig.

This first section illustrates very well the tantalising nature of the relationship between path and river. The very first Speyside Way signpost at Spey Bay points away from the river and, until Craigellachie is reached, the Spey is often within sight but rarely your close companion. There are compensations in wide views and varying scenery, notably between Boat o'Brig and Craigellachie when the Way rises on forest tracks and viewpoints provide superb panoramas of the lower river valley and coast.

At Craigellachie the track bed of the former Strathspey Railway is joined, and for the next 14 miles it provides a firm, broad path with neither gradient nor other difficulty to contend with. Excellent progress can be made on this section, though there is always the lure of the Tamdhu Distillery visitor centre to stop walkers in their tracks.

The Speyside Way is in whisky country for most of its length. If the Dufftown spur is included, no fewer than 11 distilleries are either passed or sighted; two actually on the route, Tamdhu and The Glenlivet, have full visitor facilities, and a tour around them is a fascinating experience. Whisky is a very important industry in this area and makes a major contribution to the economy of Speyside.

After Ballindalloch, the nature of the Way

Tomintoul, one of Scotland's highest villages and a fitting end to the walk

changes abruptly. The Spey is left behind and for its final 15 miles the path passes through the Avonside hills using old tracks with some new linking sections. This section is a much stiffer challenge to the walker, rising to a high point of nearly 1900ft (570m) on Carn Daimh before descending through forest and over a mossy moor to Tomintoul, another planned settlement, which at 1160ft (352m) claims to be the highest village in the Highlands.

The description 'nearly 1900ft' for Carn Daimh underlines another curious characteristic of the Way: variability of information. There is no full guidebook. Moray District Council issues a very helpful leaflet giving basic information such as car parks, camp sites etc and showing the route of the Way (though not in sufficient detail to follow it on the ground). However, the leaflet gives the metric length of the Way as 58km instead of 75km and the height of Carn Daimh (which it spells Cairn Daimh) as 589m, which translates to 1937ft. This contradicts the sign at the summit which gives the height as 1866ft (567m). Unfortunately no spot height is given on the OS 1:50,000 map so the matter will have to be left intriguingly unresolved!

There is, in fact, no difficulty in following the Way on the ground. It is very well waymarked throughout with the symbol of the former Countryside Commission for Scotland (now Scottish Natural Heritage), a thistle within a hexagon. The path itself is very clear apart, perhaps, from a section of the descent into Tomintoul over the Feithmusach peatmoss, where it could be lost in conditions of poor visibility. It is essential not just to carry the appropriate OS maps (1:50,000 sheets 28 and 36) and a compass, but to know how to use them.

Logistically, the Speyside Way presents few problems in the summer, as from June to September the excellent Speyside Rambler bus trundles up and down the route twice a day on Mondays, Wednesdays and Sundays, stopping at all significant points between Spey Bay and Tomintoul. Outside this period there are more problems, for neither terminus is particularly well served by public transport and a little ingenuity may be needed if, for example, you have left a car at

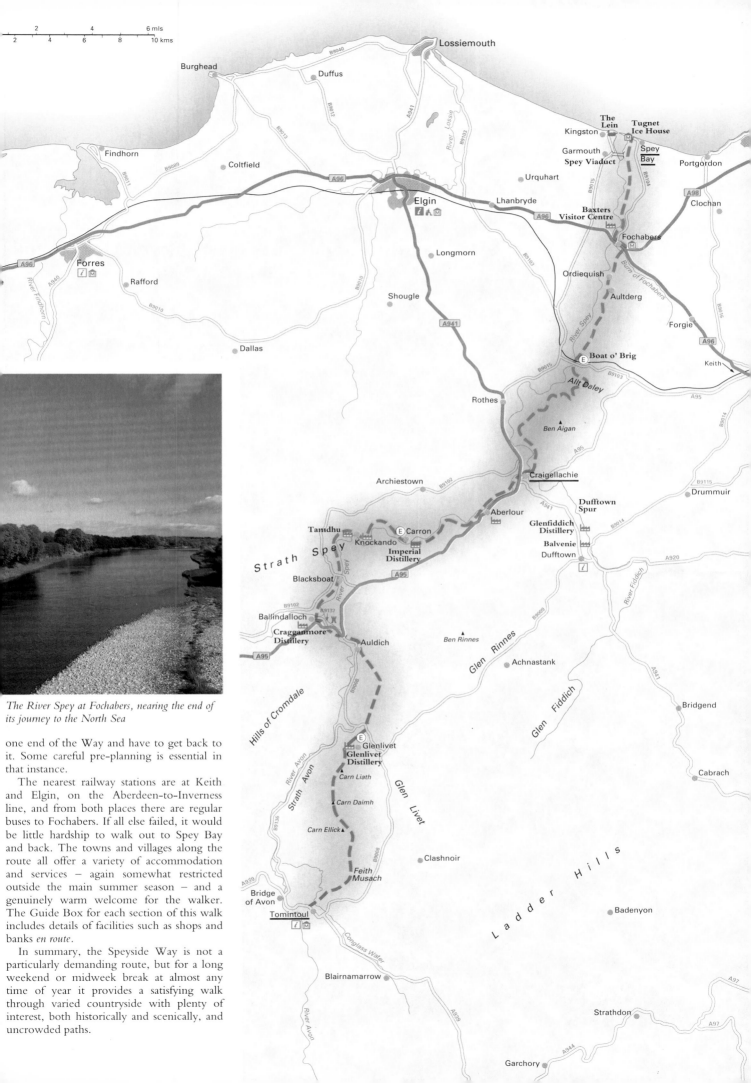

The River Spey at Fochabers, nearing the end of its journey to the North Sea

one end of the Way and have to get back to it. Some careful pre-planning is essential in that instance.

The nearest railway stations are at Keith and Elgin, on the Aberdeen-to-Inverness line, and from both places there are regular buses to Fochabers. If all else failed, it would be little hardship to walk out to Spey Bay and back. The towns and villages along the route all offer a variety of accommodation and services – again somewhat restricted outside the main summer season – and a genuinely warm welcome for the walker. The Guide Box for each section of this walk includes details of facilities such as shops and banks *en route*.

In summary, the Speyside Way is not a particularly demanding route, but for a long weekend or midweek break at almost any time of year it provides a satisfying walk through varied countryside with plenty of interest, both historically and scenically, and uncrowded paths.

Spey Bay

Craigellachie

SPEY BAY

BOAT O'BRIG

APPROX. 10 MILES/16KM

OS Landranger 28
Start at grid reference NJ 348 655
Start point: Tugnet Ice House, served by Speyside Rambler bus from June to September. Car park and toilets.

The Speyside Way starts at the mouth of the river, at a car park beside the Tugnet Ice House, which is well worth a visit. It was the largest of its kind in Scotland, built at a time when the best way to store perishable foodstuffs was to pack them in layers of ice inside thick stone walls. The Tugnet Ice House dates from 1830.

Across the river is Kingston, named after their home town by two entrepreneurs from Kingston-upon-Hull who leased the large Glenmore Forest, between Aviemore and Grantown, from the Duke of Gordon in the 18th century and floated timber in rafts down the Spey to this point. Some of the timber was used for boatbuilding, and at one time there were seven shipyards between Kingston and Garmouth. The industry declined with the coming of iron-clad vessels, and no trace remains today.

Beyond Kingston is The Lein, a Scottish Wildlife Trust reserve. The shingle system at the mouth of the Spey is the largest in Scotland and is second only to Chesil Beach, Dorset, in the whole of Britain. Its habitats range from marsh to heathland, supporting many orchids and other interesting plants. The birdlife is excellent too, with a good variety of waders and seabirds to be spotted at most times of the year.

The Way turns away from the river for a short distance before taking a track leading south in a mile to the Spey Viaduct, a vast construction dominating the landscape. The viaduct, which carried the Great North of Scotland Railway branch line from Elgin to Portgordon, was designed by Patrick Barnett and opened in 1886. Its great length – 317yds – and size were necessary because of the power of the river in flood, and its frequently shifting flow pattern through sandbanks. The viaduct has ornate castellated portals and is supported by huge piers which actually drop to 52ft below the river bed, showing how the engineers respected the force of the Spey, one of Scotland's fastest-flowing rivers. There is a path from the Way across the viaduct to Garmouth.

The Way continues, partly through woodland, sometimes veering away from the

The shingle beach of Spey Bay, one of the longest in Britain

GUIDE BOX

Places to visit
Tugnet Ice House, Spey Bay. Exhibition on the River Spey, its salmon fishing and wildlife, in the large 1830 ice house. Open June to September, daily.

Fochabers Folk Museum, High Street, Fochabers. Fascinating collection of photographs and other memorabilia telling the story of the village, including the original 1776 plans, housed in a former church. Upstairs there is a collection of horse-drawn vehicles. Open all year, daily.

Baxters Visitor Centre, on the A96, 1 mile west of Fochabers. The factory of the famous food manufacturers and processors can be toured and there is a visitor centre, a reconstruction of the original Baxters village shop, and a Victorian kitchen. Restaurant, gift shop, woodland, picnic area open March to December, Monday to Friday, plus summer weekends; closed for staff holidays.

Car parking
Principal car parks are at Tugnet Ice House (grid ref. NJ 348 655), Fochabers (NJ 342 594), Boat o'Brig (318 517) and Craigellachie (NJ 293 453).

Public transport
The Speyside Rambler bus makes two journeys a day between Spey Bay and Tomintoul, June to mid-September, Mondays, Wednesdays and Sundays. Regular bus services from Aberdeen, Inverness, Elgin and Keith to Fochabers. Bus services from Rothes, Elgin, Dufftown and Grantown to Craigellachie.

Accommodation
There is one hotel at Spey Bay, hotels and guesthouses in Fochabers, three hotels in Craigellachie and a camp site in Fiddich Park, Craigellachie.

Facilities
There is a bank at Fochabers, shops at Fochabers and Craigellachie.

river, sometimes close to it, until it joins the B9104 for a mile to the outskirts of Fochabers. On the left here are the policies (estate) of Gordon Castle, former home of the Dukes of Richmond and Gordon (not open to the public). The Way passes under the A96 road into a pleasant riverside path. Across the Spey here is the Baxters Visitor Centre (see Places to visit).

Fochabers is a planned town, one of many in Scotland. In 1776, the 4th Duke of Gordon wished to enlarge his policies and castle. The village of Fochabers was in his way, so he engaged the architect John Baxter to lay out a new town on the present site. As is commonly the case, the basic street pattern is a grid-iron and there is a handsome central square, which holds the fine Bellie Church. The history of the town is very well told in the Folk Museum on High Street. The Speyside Way does not actually pass through Fochabers, but it would be a pity to miss out the town, and a short diversion around it, including the Folk Museum, can easily be taken. Fochabers has a good range of shops.

From the riverside park, the two bridges crossing the Spey here can clearly be seen. The older bridge is based on a design by the famous engineer Thomas Telford. Built in

1806, it was a victim of the great flood of 1829, when the river flooded the whole of the surrounding area. An eyewitness account dramatically describes the bridge falling 'with the cloud-like appearance of an avalanche' and the river 'rushing onwards, its thunderous roar proclaiming its victory, and not a vestige of the fallen fragments to be seen'. The bridge was rebuilt in the 1850s, but has now been supplanted by the modern road bridge alongside it.

The Way again turns away from the river to follow paths beside the Burn of Fochabers and then south for a mile to join a lane near the farm of Ordiequish. From here to Boat o'Brig the Way follows a minor road, giving very easy walking. There is rarely much in the way of traffic to trouble the walker.

At Aultderg (meaning 'red stream') a Forestry Commission car park has a path leading to a good viewpoint above the river, but for most of this section the Spey is out of sight as the road winds either through or alongside forest, high above the river plain. After a junction is passed, the road drops, gradually at first and then more steeply around a zig-zag of bends, to reach Delfur Lodge and Boat o'Brig, where there is a small Speyside Way car park beside the river.

The river is spanned here by road and rail bridges. The former carries the B9103 which leads east to Keith and west to Rothes. The Speyside Rambler bus stops at Boat o'Brig. The railway bridge was designed by another great Victorian engineer, Joseph Mitchell. His 1858 approach arches are still there, but the river is now crossed by a later steel truss, erected in 1906. It would be nice to think that in time ScotRail might be persuaded to provide a halt for walkers at Boat o'Brig.

The name Boat o'Brig is said to have derived from the fact that there was originally a bridge here. When it collapsed a ferry was provided – the 'boat of the bridge'. The curious small building with the Doric columns was a toll house.

E *Roads lead from Boat o'Brig to Keith, where buses can be caught to Fochabers; or (in summer) use the Speyside Rambler bus.*

BOAT O'BRIG
CRAIGELLACHIE
APPROX. 7 MILES/11KM

OS Landranger 28
Start at grid reference NJ 318 517
Start point: Boat o'Brig car park on the B9103. The Speyside Rambler bus service stops here.

The Way climbs up behind the toll house to join a track leading to Bridgeton Farm. A notice advises that dogs must be on a lead, and that, if the gate is closed, walkers should wait as stock is being herded. The Way passes through the farmyard (often quite muddy) and swings left and then sharply right to enter the forest on the western slopes of Ben Aigan.

The old railway station at Fochabers

The path passes close to the Speyside Gun Club's range: firing is taking place if red flags are flying. The path itself is quite safe, which is something of a relief. The next section of path is along the forest edge, giving good views, before entering the forest and climbing steadily to join a broad track for a substantial diversion around the deep side valley of the Allt Daloy.

Two further, smaller side valleys are rounded. Between them a short diversion leads to a seat at a viewpoint giving a magnificent and somehow unexpected panorama of the whole of the lower river valley and the coast. It is a lovely scene with a mixture of farmland and woods, the Spey winding through and the sea beyond. In very clear conditions you can pick out the mountains of Sutherland and Caithness.

In time, the track heads steadily downhill to join a minor road which is followed for nearly 3 miles to Craigellachie. This is part of the Arndilly Estate which was noted for its splendid trees, both conifer and broadleaved. Arndilly House is passed, with a double row

of neat stone toadstools lining the drive. The house was built in the 1830s by David McDowal Grant, one of the great land 'improvers' of the time.

The Spey is regularly seen but not approached on this section, which ends by crossing the River Fiddich at the Fiddichside Inn, to enter Fiddich Park. A small camp site for walkers is provided here, and there is a triple-arm signpost showing the start of the Dufftown Spur (see page 248, Guide Box). There are toilets here (Easter to October). The main path swings right under a bridge to reach the ranger's house at Boat o'Fiddich. There is a small exhibition on the Spey and the Way here (open May to September, Monday to Saturday), and the ranger is always glad to help walkers.

The Way then enters Craigellachie, a popular centre for fishermen. It has three hotels, which offer tea and coffee as well as alcoholic and other drinks, and the Way's first distillery – not open to the public.

Aultdearg Pillars, on the banks of the Spey

THE RIVER SPEY

The Spey is Scotland's second-longest river, running for 98 miles from its source high in the Monadhliath Mountains to Spey Bay. Only the Tay is longer. The Spey is a noted salmon river, its fast run leading to the creation of many pools where fish lie up. Main settlements on the river include Newtonmore, Kingussie, Aviemore with its year-round holiday centre and Grantown-on-Spey. The Grant family have been major landowners in the area for centuries, and were responsible for laying out several towns and villages, including Aberlour and Grantown itself. Near the village of Boat of Garten is the RSPB reserve of Loch Garten, famous for its ospreys. The Spey flows through much fine scenery from the wild moors of its upper reaches to the extensive forestry lower down.

Craigellachie
Ballindalloch

Thomas Telford's graceful iron bridge over the Spey at Craigellachie

CRAIGELLACHIE
CARRON
APPROX. 6 MILES/10KM

OS Landranger 28
Start at grid reference NJ 293 453
Start point: Fiddich Park, Craigellachie (camp site, toilets). Buses from Elgin, Keith, Grantown and Dufftown. The Speyside Rambler bus stops at Craigellachie (June to September only).

Craigellachie should not be left without making the short diversion to see Telford's bridge over the Spey. This is the oldest surviving iron bridge in Scotland. Built in 1814, it is the work of a genius, for Telford was using a new material and allowed his imagination full rein in taking every advantage of the lightness and airiness possible in an iron bridge. The result is a graceful, elegant structure, its appearance enhanced by the frowning cliff above it on the west bank of the river (Craig Ailichidh, the original spelling, means 'strong rock'). The iron was cast in Wales by Telford's favourite ironmaster, William Hazledine and the bridge, which cost £8,200, has castellated towers at each end.

The bridge inspired the noted local fiddler Will Marshall to write a strathspey dance called Craigellachie Brig. Mention of this brings us to the vexed question of what to call the river valley the Way passes along. It is the Speyside Way but Strathspey is used by the local authority higher up and in some ways is more accurate.

From here to Ballindalloch the Speyside Way follows the track bed of the former Strathspey Railway (illustrating the point!). Between Craigellachie and Aberlour the path goes through the only tunnel on the line, a short affair some 150yds long with clear visibility, and continues more or less beside the river, with the A95 close by to the left, to enter Aberlour.

The village – Charlestown of Aberlour, to give its full name – is another planned settlement, established here by Charles Grant of Wester Elchies in 1812. It has a broad, handsome main street and a small square holding the church, which has an unusual castellated tower. Aberlour is a noted salmon fishing centre; its distillery, on the southern edge of the town, can be visited. The village shop, in the High Street, has been maintained partly in 19th-century style.

The Way passes behind houses close to the river to reach the former station, happily preserved and open as a café in summer, selling excellent local produce at very reasonable prices. The café is manned on a voluntary basis by the ladies of the village, all the proceeds going to charity, so it is well worth patronising. The station is now part of the attractive Alice Littler Park, named for the wife of Sydney Littler, a noted local benefactor. A graceful suspension footbridge crosses the river here, and the banks are favoured by anglers.

From Aberlour the Way continues on the old railway. The plentiful tree cover and frequent cuttings mean that views are somewhat limited on this stretch, but it is easy walking. The path joins a minor road for a short distance to cross the Spey on a bridge which gives good views not only along the river but down into it! This was in fact the last cast-iron bridge made in Scotland. It dates from 1863 and features a lattice construction. It is worth going down to the river to look up at the bridge and appreciate its lightness.

The Way runs alongside the road into the

GUIDE BOX

Places to visit
Aberlour Distillery, off the A95 at the south end of village. Open all year, Monday to Friday.

Tamdhu Distillery, on the Way near Knockando. Open Easter to May, Monday to Friday; June to September, Monday to Saturday. Distillery tours, tasting, visitor centre, café, gift shop, picnic area.

Cragganmore Distillery, off the B9137 at Ballindalloch. Open all year, Monday to Thursday. Tours, tasting, gift shop.

The Dufftown Spur. From Craigellachie a 4-mile spur path follows another old railway line beside the River Fiddich to the attractive town of Dufftown, where it passes three distilleries – Balvenie, Convalmore and Glenfiddich. The last-named has full visitor facilities (open all year) and in its grounds is the ruin of Balvenie Castle. The spur makes a pleasant half-day diversion.

Car parking,
The main car parking places are at Craigellachie (grid ref. NJ 293 453), Aberlour old station (NJ 265 428), Carron (NJ 221 415), Tamdhu (NJ 188 418) and Ballindalloch old station (NJ 168 367).

Public transport
Speyside Rambler bus June to September, twice a day in each direction, stops at Craigellachie, Aberlour, Carron, Blacksboat and Ballindalloch. Buses to Grantown and Elgin from Aberlour and Ballindalloch.

Accommodation
There are hotels and guesthouses in Aberlour; the Carron Inn does bed-and-breakfast and there are several bed-and-breakfast places in the Knockando and Ballindalloch area. There is a hostel at Ballindalloch Station (open all year: must be pre-booked by telephoning 0540 651272).

Facilities
There is a bank at Aberlour, and shops at Craigellachie, Aberlour, Carron and Ballindalloch.

For a short stretch, the Way disappears into the old Strathspey Railway tunnel

small village of Carron, passing the entrance to the Imperial Distillery, home of Black Bottle Whisky (not normally open to visitors). The Carron Inn welcomes walkers and offers meals and accommodation.

Ⓔ *From Carron a minor road leads back to the A95 and buses to Craigellachie.*

CARRON

BALLINDALLOCH

APPROX. 8 MILES/13KM

OS Landranger 28
Start at grid reference NJ 221 415
Start point: Car park, Carron village. No public transport except for the Speyside Rambler bus in summer.

Leaving one distillery, the Way heads firmly off towards two others, still on the old railway line, elevated above the river but with little in the way of distant views.

The river curves in slow loops here and the path largely follows it towards Knockando, 3 miles from Carron. The Way passes directly behind Knockando Distillery, the aroma either overpowering or inspiring, according to taste. The distillery was founded in 1898 and has attractive stone facing with a smart carved sign. It is not normally open to the public.

Tamdhu is, however, and after crossing the Knockando Burn the path reaches the visitor centre at the former station. The distillery was built here in 1896, partly because of the railway line and partly because of the pure waters of the Knockando Burn. A road had to be built to serve it. It bottles its own single malt, which can be tasted after taking the distillery tour and looking at the exhibits in the visitor centre. Admission is free and there is a tea room, café and toilets. The Cardhu Distillery, 1¹/₂ miles away off the B9102, is also open to visitors.

From Tamdhu the path runs close to the Spey most of the way to Ballindalloch.

The suspension footbridge at Aberlour

There is generous tree cover and rabbits and pheasants are almost certain to be seen on this stretch – maybe even roe deer. These lovely small animals bound gracefully along in a way humans can only envy; they are often sighted by a flash of white rump.

In 2 miles from Tamdhu the Way reaches Blacksboat, where the station building survives. Picnic tables have been provided here. The bridges over the railway and river were completely rebuilt in 1991 to eliminate a very awkward double bend in the road. The name is thought to have come from two brothers, John and James Black, who farmed here and operated a ferry in the 18th century – 'Black's Boat'.

Another easy 2 miles in pleasant surroundings leads to the fine viaduct spanning the river at Ballindalloch. The engineer, G

McFarlane of Dundee, proudly gives his name at each end – and why not, for this sturdy bridge, built in 1863, is a fine piece of work, as strong today as when it was first opened. The viaduct leads to the former station at Ballindalloch, now a hostel used mainly by groups of canoeists. Walkers can use it, but it has to be pre-booked (see Accommodation).

From the station, a right turn leads in ¹/₄ mile to the Cragganmore Distillery, open to visitors all year, Monday to Thursday. Admission is free. The Way, however, goes left on the B9137, which must be one of the shortest numbered roads in Britain. It leads in ¹/₂ mile to the A95, the Avon and the start of the final, very different part of the Way.

THE SALMON – KING OF FISH

The salmon provides superb sport for anglers, a livelihood for net fishermen in estuarial and coastal waters, and a wonderful food for all of us. Fishing for salmon has long been regarded as one of the finest forms of angling. The fish are caught by several methods, including spinning and fly-fishing. Spinning is generally used in the early season (January to April) and flies later on in late summer and autumn when the water is warmer.

Salmon fishing is carefully controlled. All fishing rights in Scotland (except in Orkney and Shetland) basically belong to the Crown, and are granted or leased to other parties. Salmon and sea trout have a separate status from other freshwater fish. It is illegal to fish for them without a permit, and fishing is also banned on Sundays. The regulations are

controlled by District Salmon Fishery Boards and enforced by water bailiffs.

Salmon go through several stages. When they are young they are called parr. The next stage is the smolt; neither is generally sought by the angler. Kelts are migratory fish which have spawned. Salmon return upriver to spawning grounds each year and can sometimes be seen 'leaping' waterfalls.

Net fishing for salmon takes place in tidal waters between February and mid-August. Salmon netting can still be seen around the mouth of the Spey, and the story of this industry is told in the Tugnet Ice House. There has been considerable concern in recent years that net fishing has reduced the salmon stock, and a number of nettings have been bought out by fish conservation groups to try to safeguard the future of the wild fish.

Ballindalloch

Tomintoul

BALLINDALLOCH

GLENLIVET

APPROX. 7 MILES/11KM

OS Landranger-28, 36
Start at grid reference NJ 168 367
Start point: Speyside Way car park,
Ballindalloch Station. The Speyside Rambler
bus calls here in summer; it is a ¹/₂ mile walk
from the A95, served by buses from
Grantown-on-Spey and Aberlour.

From Ballindalloch Station the Way heads
up the B9137 road to join the A95. A
tempting sign informs you that the
Delnashaugh Inn is 150yds ahead, but don't
be fooled: it is a good ¹/₄ mile, up a steep
brae, with only a narrow footpath.

It crosses the River Avon (pronounced
'A'an' and simply meaning a river, so the
name is 'river river'). A short diversion leads
down to the old bridge, below and
somewhat dwarfed by the bulky road bridge
above it. On the far side is the ornate gate to
Ballindalloch Castle, the seat of the
MacPherson-Grant family since 1546. It is
open on Sunday afternoons in summer. The
Avon is here at the end of its turbulent
journey from Loch Avon, deep in the
Cairngorm Mountains below Ben Macdui.

The Delnashaugh Inn – the only hostelry
on this stretch of the walk – is an elegantly
furnished hotel catering for sportsmen and
general tourists. Walkers are made welcome
and excellent bar meals are served, but it
might be as well to take your boots off
before entering.

Leaving the inn, pass the war memorial at
the road junction and turn right on to the
B9008 above the Avon. The road curves
round, giving tempting views southward,
before the Way leaves it in about ¹/₂ mile to
take the track past the farm of Auldich
(Aldich on the OS map), which has a
splendid row of gnomes on its garden wall.
The track continues beyond the farm,
surfaced for a further ¹/₄ mile to reach a
rubbish dump and a small car park with
information board.

There is a definite feeling here of a change
of mood. The Spey has been left behind; to
the left, Ben Rinnes, the area's highest hill,
rises to 2760ft (840m); and the whole
atmosphere is wilder and, to the mountain
lover, more alluring. The track leads
enticingly ahead, rising steadily. It can be
seen crossing the shallow valley leftwards: the
route to Tomintoul, however, leaves it a
mile beyond Auldich to go right on a
moorland path, still quite clear and with
waymarks at intervals. Here Landranger sheet
28, your companion since the start of the
walk, is at last exchanged for sheet 36.

As the brow of the hill is reached, the
view southwards opens out to reveal Glen
Livet and Strath Avon, with the Hills of
Cromdale away to the right. The variations
in light and shade can be quite stunning,
enhanced by the patchwork nature of the
landscape, many darker forestry plantations
alternating with lighter-coloured farmland
and the rich hues of the heather moor. It is a
particularly fine scene in spring, with the last
of the snow on the distant tops, and in
autumn when the heather is at its best. Red
grouse are very likely to be seen on this
stretch – and heard, urging you to 'go back,
go back'.

From here to Glenlivet the Way crosses

Deskie Farm, and a new route has been
established. The path is reasonably clear, and
further use will settle its line even more, but
the waymarks need to be watched carefully,
and lower down in particular it takes several
frustrating twists before depositing you at the

*The Way crosses the peatmoss of Feith Musach,
below Carn Ellick*

roadside by the telephone box outside Glenlivet Village Hall.

On the lower ground a neat variation of the squeeze-stile is encountered – a metal gate on chains that swings open at the top and is easily closed to prevent livestock getting through. At the road, the Way goes left for a short distance and then right up a lane to join the distillery road, but if you have time, the rightward diversion to see the Old Bridge of Livet – a triple-span, now grassed over – is worth taking.

Ⓔ *From Glenlivet, buses can be caught back to Ballindalloch.*

GLENLIVET

·

TOMINTOUL

·

APPROX. 8 MILES/13KM

·

OS Landranger 36
Start at grid reference NJ 200 297
Start point: Glenlivet Village Hall. The Speyside Rambler bus stops here in summer, and a regular service between Tomintoul and Aberlour also passes.

For whisky-lovers, one of the high points of the walk is now in sight: The Glenlivet distillery, visible throughout the descent to the village. This was the first distillery to be licensed after the laws were changed in 1823 to stamp out illicit whisky production and smuggling. The distillery tour takes an hour and is well worth the stop.

Fortified by the free dram, continue up the lane past Blairfindy Lodge Hotel to turn off on a track leading past abandoned farmhouses. Above them a new path has been made at the edge of a forestry plantation. At its top gate a much better, broader path is joined, rising to a pass below Carn Liath (grey hill) and contouring round the hill on a wonderfully well-graded track giving excellent walking. Carn Daimh, the highest point of the walk, is now clearly visible ahead.

For the whole of this section there are superb views back to Ben Rinnes, a notable landmark with its rock tors or Scurrs prominent. It is a superb climb if you have time to spare either during or after the walk; but for the moment the target is Carn Daimh (pronounced 'carn dye' and meaning 'hill of stags'). The path briefly worsens through a diversion before markedly

Glen Conglass, near Tomintoul

improving all the way to the summit. Just before the final climb there is a three-way signpost indicating a path down to Tomnavoulin (and yet another distillery).

Carn Daimh commands a splendid panorama. To the west are the Hills of Cromdale, topped by Creagan a 'Chaise. South is Strathavon, leading the eye further on into the Cairngorms, up to Ben Avon itself – like Ben Rinnes topped by rock tors. As you look back, Rinnes dominates the north-east sector, while a little further west, if conditions are right, the distant sea, left behind two days or more ago, is visible.

It is a place to savour, but it can be wild and windy too, and the last lap lies ahead. From Carn Daimh the Way descends easily to enter forestry on Carn Ellick. This is another new stretch of path, and being based on peat, it can be a good-going glaur in wet conditions. After a rather tedious trudge through the trees, the Way emerges to face a fine vista of moorland and woods.

The long descent across the peats of Feithmusach demands care in bad weather. The path is not well defined but there are regular waymarks and a bearing just west of south keeps you on course. The extensive peatmoss here is commercially worked at its eastern edge, by the B9008 road, where a display explains the process.

The Way wriggles tortuously in, around and through small plantations before descending (more metal squeeze-stiles) to a lane which is followed for ¼ mile. The Conglass Water is crossed by a fine new footbridge and a short stretch on a broad grassy track leads to the A939 at the north end of Tomintoul.

This is another planned village, set up with the encouragement of the 4th Duke of Gordon. The first houses were occupied in 1780 and the village developed steadily over the following decades, with three long streets on a north-south axis joined by short lanes.

The central square has three hotels and the tourist information office (Easter to October), which includes a local history museum. The name derives from Gaelic *Tom an t-sabhail* meaning 'barn knoll'.

It is a fine place to end a walk and to sit and reflect on the wide variety of scenery encountered since leaving Spey Bay: the walk has gone from the estuary of Scotland's second-longest river to one of its highest villages, taking in whisky, woods and wildlife. It provides an excellent introduction to the area, whetting the appetite to return and explore further the straths, glens and hills of one of Scotland's most attractive areas.

THE GLENLIVET DISTILLERY

Whisky was made in the Glenlivet area long before 1823, but in that year the laws were changed to try to stop both illicit production and smuggling. With the encouragement of the Duke of Gordon, George Smith built a new distillery in Glenlivet; he was the first to take out a licence under the new laws. A pair of pistols he kept by his side to guard against smugglers who saw the new distillery as a threat can be seen today in the visitor centre. The business flourished and continued to grow under the guidance of George's son John Gordon Smith and then Captain Bill Smith Grant.

Such is the attraction of the Glenlivet name that a number of other distilleries add it to their own, but this is the only one able to call itself simply 'The Glenlivet'. The malt whisky it produces, light in colour and with a distinctive, delicate flavour, is world-famous. It is the leading malt in the USA and is exported from the glen to over 100 countries. The distillery tour explains the process and offers a free tasting, and there is a well-stocked souvenir shop.

Fife Coast Walk

COMPLETE ROUTE
NEWBURGH TO INVERKEITHING
94 MILES/152KM

SECTION COVERED
ST ANDREWS TO INVERKEITHING
59 MILES/96KM

Detailed guides
No full guidebook exists. A series of booklets on the coast walk has been produced by the Wemyss Environmental Education Centre, The Primary School, East Wemyss, Kirkcaldy, Fife KY1 4RN.

Maps
OS Landranger 59, 66, 65

Links
No officially designated paths connect.

WALKING the Fife Coast is still something of an adventure. Although the Regional and District Councils have developed some stretches in recent years, putting in bridges and stiles and supplying information boards, the path has no official status and waymarking is at a minimum. There are parts where there is to all intents and purposes no path, and beach-walking is the only option; at other times the walker is forced inland on to roads. In several places unbridged burns must be forded or a considerable diversion taken to find a bridge.

The walk is still very much worth undertaking. The section included here runs a total distance of about 60 miles from the university town of St Andrews to the railway station at Inverkeithing, in the shadow of the two great Forth Bridges. It includes superb stretches of sandy beach, wild headlands, fantastic offshore rock formations, and a considerable number of small towns and villages of great charm and character.

Fife was for many centuries a place apart: indeed, it considered itself to be a 'kingdom'. The wide Firth of Forth, crossed by ferry, separated it from Scotland's capital, and it was a journey not undertaken lightly, especially in winter. The first bridge over the Forth was 20 miles west, at Stirling. Fife developed its own industries and traded extensively with the Continent even in medieval times. Traces of those industries,

The extensive ruins of St Andrews Cathedral

notably salt and coal, will be seen on the walk.

Fife contains many notable historic buildings. The walk starts at the ancient cathedral of St Andrews and passes a number of castles in various states of repair, fine old churches and much splendid vernacular architecture. The 'East Neuk' of Fife is noted for houses with red pantile roofs and crow-stepped gables, while on the shore fishermen's cottages often have an outside stair. Fishing has long been a vital industry, and its history is commemorated in the Scottish Fisheries Museum at Anstruther; one of the main leisure activities, golf, is an almost constant companion from the start, near the world-famous Old Course of St Andrews.

Modern industry is not absent, and the coast has to be left to pass the oil platform construction yard at Methil, Dysart's colliery and the tanker terminal near Aberdour. A modern industry of a different kind – tourism – has developed steadily in Fife, helped by good communications including excellent train and bus services which cover most parts of the coast.

These make the walk logistically easy, and the many settlements mean that an 'escape' is rarely more than 3 or 4 miles away. The walk can thus easily be done in a series of days out, but it also makes a fine single expedition over four or five days.

As on all coastal walks, the birdlife is superb, with many seabirds and waders in evidence, and the constant interplay of sea and land is an endless source of interest. In sum, this is a walk of considerable character, a challenge to the walker, giving a sense of real satisfaction when it is completed.

Note

While indication is given in the following pages of any diversions or difficulties on the path, space does not always allow detailed directions.

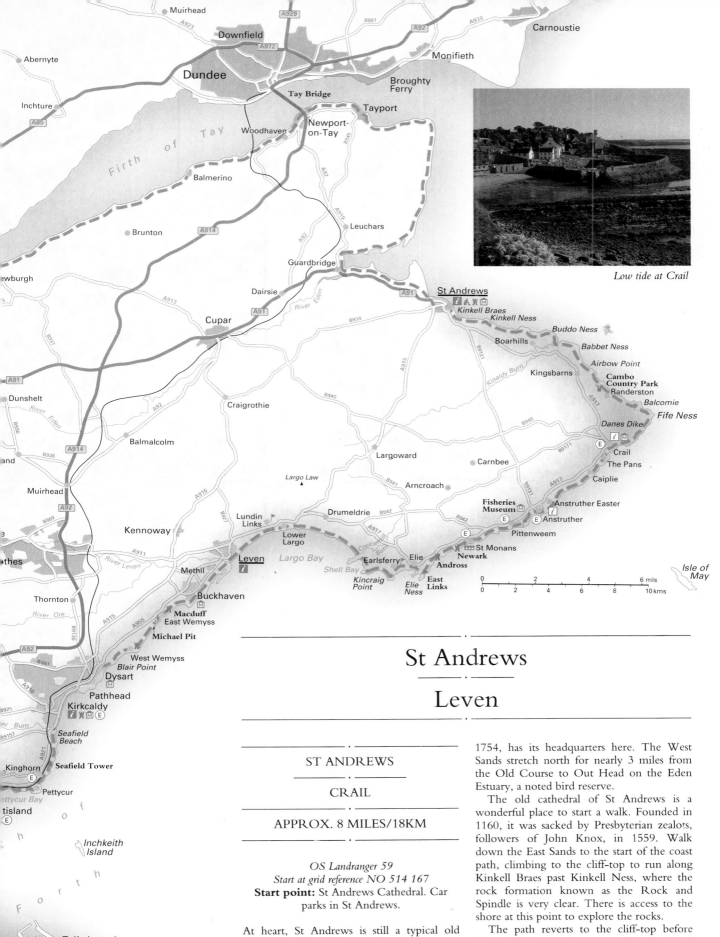

Low tide at Crail

St Andrews
—— · ——
Leven
—— · ——

—— · ——
ST ANDREWS
—— · ——
CRAIL
—— · ——
APPROX. 8 MILES/18KM
—— · ——

OS Landranger 59
Start at grid reference NO 514 167
Start point: St Andrews Cathedral. Car
parks in St Andrews.

At heart, St Andrews is still a typical old
Scottish burgh, with narrow wynds, courtyards and closes. The town has grown
substantially and is now a major holiday and
golfing centre as well as holding Scotland's
oldest university, founded in 1410 by the
Augustinian priors at the cathedral. The
Royal and Ancient Golf Club, founded in
1754, has its headquarters here. The West
Sands stretch north for nearly 3 miles from
the Old Course to Out Head on the Eden
Estuary, a noted bird reserve.

The old cathedral of St Andrews is a
wonderful place to start a walk. Founded in
1160, it was sacked by Presbyterian zealots,
followers of John Knox, in 1559. Walk
down the East Sands to the start of the coast
path, climbing to the cliff-top to run along
Kinkell Braes past Kinkell Ness, where the
rock formation known as the Rock and
Spindle is very clear. There is access to the
shore at this point to explore the rocks.

The path reverts to the cliff-top before
dropping down again to pass the mouth of
the deep, overgrown gully known as
Kittock's Den, continuing along the shore –
quite rough going at times – to Buddo Ness,
beyond which is the eroded natural arch of
Buddo Rock, an extraordinary formation.

The first potential difficulty, the Kinaldy

253

Earlsferry beach, with Elie beyond

(known locally as the Kenly) Burn, is now ahead, across a damp saltmarsh area. The burn can usually be crossed with care, though the rocks are very slippery; if it is in spate a substantial detour through Boarhills will be necessary, adding 3 miles to the walk.

The coast walk continues past an old salmon-fishing bothy on the south side of the Kinaldy Burn to Babbet Ness and the long sandy beach of Airbow Point before reaching the car park and picnic site at Kingsbarns. The nature of the walk is already becoming clear, with the path varying from excellent to non-existent. The scenery and varied birdlife more than compensate; this is not a walk to be hurried.

Beyond Kingsbarns the path is more developed, as it passes through part of Cambo Country Park, with a visitor centre at the former farm-steading a little way in from the coast. Passing one of the few plantations on this walk, the path continues to Randerston, where raised beaches can be seen, and then to Balcomie golf course.

Beyond Balcomie, Fife Ness is rounded – a real turning-point, leading from the North Sea into the broad Firth of Forth. The Dane's Dike, an ancient boundary which once ran right across the headland, is crossed, and the walk continues past the former Royal Naval air station – called HMS *Jackdaw* during World War II – to reach the beautiful fishing village of Crail, with its late 17th-century Customs House, Mercat Cross, and almost unbelievably picturesque harbour.

Ⓔ *Buses run back to St Andrews from Crail.*

CRAIL

· ·

ST MONANS

· ·

APPROX. 7 MILES/11KM

OS Landranger 59
Start at grid reference NO 612 074
Start point: Crail harbour. Car Park.

There is a good path all the way on this section. Leaving Crail – which deserves much more space than it can be given here – the path runs along the shore, with superb

---

views of the Isle of May, a nature reserve purchased in 1989 by the Nature Conservancy Council (now Scottish Natural Heritage). It has one of the oldest lighthouses in Scotland; summer boat trips run from Anstruther.

In a mile or so from Crail the path goes through the area known as The Pans. This is one of number of sites on the Fife coast where salt was collected, an important trade in former centuries. In a further mile the path reaches another set of fantastically eroded sandstone pillars and arches, called the Caiplie Caves. They can be reached only on foot. This is a place to linger, to enjoy the sea views and the birdlife and the strange shapes carved by wind and water.

The path leads into Anstruther Easter through Cellardyke – named from cellars built here by the fisherfolk for their tackle. At Anstruther Harbour (the name is pronounced more like 'Enster' by locals) is the Scottish Fisheries Museum, full of interest and well worth a visit, and here is moored the former North Carr Lightship, also sometimes open to view. The parish church of Anstruther Easter dates from 1634. Around it are narrow wynds with old buildings including Melville's Manse.

There is much to explore in Anstruther, but the coast beckons, and leaving through Anstruther Wester, the path passes along beside another links golf course to enter Pittenweem. The name means 'place of caves'. The old kirk here dates from 1588, and in the High Street is the 16th-century Kellie Lodge.

Pittenweem harbour is usually busy with fishing boats. It has a covered fish market and the fleet holds a gala day each summer. A further 2 miles of splendid coast-walking lead to the equally attractive village of St Monans, passing the site of the Newark Coal and Salt Company. An information board gives details of the twin industry which flourished here from 1772 until the 1820s. There were nine salt panhouses here; production was continuous but salt could be sold only between sunrise and sunset. St Monans has been a burgh since 1621. It has fine old fishermen's cottages, very well restored by the national Trust for Scotland and the then Town Council in the 1960s and 1970s.

Sun and sea at Elie

GUIDE BOX
———— · ————

Places to visit
St Andrews' numerous attractions include the ruined cathedral, a fine old castle with a superb bottle dungeon, the Sea Life Centre at The Scores, the British Golf Museum and the Old Course just across the road. In the summer tours of the University are offered.

Crail Museum, Marketgate, Crail, has interesting local history exhibits. Open March to May, weekends; June to September, daily.

Scottish Fisheries Museum, The Harbour, Anstruther, tells the story of the fishing industry over the centuries. Open all year, daily.

Car parking
Principal car parks are at St Andrews, Kingsbarns, Crail, St Monans, Leven.

Public transport
Regular buses run to St Andrews from Dundee and Leuchars, the nearest British Rail station. Frequent buses from St Andrews, Kirkcaldy and Leven serve the towns and villages on this stretch.

Accommodation
There are hotels and guesthouses in St Andrews and most of the villages *en route*.

Ⓔ *Buses can be caught back to St Andrews from Anstruther, Pittenweem and St Monans.*

· ·

ST MONANS

———— · ————

LEVEN

———— · ————

APPROX. 11 MILES/18KM

———— · ————

OS Landranger 59
Start at grid reference NO 526 015
Start point: St Monans harbour. Car park.

Leaving St Monans harbour, the way passes attractive cottages with outside stairs before crossing the burn to the superb old church.

Started in 1326, it has seen several restorations, the most recent in the 1960s. There is a Sailor's Loft in the north gallery and from the ceiling hangs a full-rigged model ship.

The walk continues by steps cut into the rock outside the church wall and along the coast for ¼ mile to the ruin of Newark Castle. Built by the Sandilands family in the 16th century, it was later owned by General David Leslie (the first Lord Newark), who defeated Montrose at the battle of Philiphaugh, near Selkirk, in 1645.

A good path continues to, and through, the even older ruin of Ardross Castle and on past Elie's East Links golf course to Elie Ness and the Lady Tower, built for Lady Janet Anstruther in 1679 as a summerhouse. She often came here to bathe in the sea.

Elie spreads round its rocky bay. The name may come from 'Eilean', meaning 'island'. It is worth going up to the main street of Elie to see the church, built by Sir William Scott of Ardross in 1638 and with a bell-tower added a century later. Elie leads into Earlsferry, one of many places from where boats plied across the Firth. The offshore rocks are called East and West Vows.

The walk continues on the seaward side of Earlsferry golf course to the foot of the cliffs at Kincraig Point. Here there is a choice of route. A steep climb leads to the clifftop path, which goes over the headland, or you can take the Chain Walk round the cliffs. It does indeed have chained sections, and passes several caves. It should only be attempted when the tide is low, and is unsuitable for dogs or small children.

Either way you will reach Shell Bay with its fine sweep of sand. Take the road and track skirting the large caravan park and cutting through plantations to reach another potential obstacle, the Cocklemill Burn. It is rarely more than calf-deep and with a sandy bottom can easily be waded. The alternative is a 2-mile detour to a bridge at West Muircambus farm.

Beyond the burn is the long, lovely curve of Largo Bay. There is no real path and the beach can be slow-going, but the views and birdlife, as ever, are more than sufficient compensation. Inland rises Largo Law, a volcanic stub reaching just under 1000ft (300m) and a superb viewpoint.

Nearer Largo the path improves. Lower Largo – the name meaning a sunny slope – was the birthplace of Alexander Selkirk, the inspiration for Defoe's *Robinson Crusoe*. He ran away to sea, rebelled and was placed on the island of Juan Fernandez in the Pacific, where he remained for four years entirely alone before being rescued. There is a statue of Selkirk in Main Street.

Past the Crusoe Hotel – a former granary with an amusing signpost saying 'Juan Fernandez Island 7500 miles' – the walk continues through Lundin Links, locally dubbed the 'Scottish Riviera', and on along a glorious stretch of sand towards Leven, with the view dominated now by Methil Power Station. The whole stretch between Lundin and Leven has golf courses by the shore. Continue by Leven Links and along the promenade to the River Leven, in the shadow of the power station chimney.

Leven

Inverkeithing

LEVEN

KIRKCALDY

APPROX. 10 MILES/16KM

OS Landranger 59
Start at grid reference NO 381 005
Start point: Leven bus station. Public car park.

From Leven to Buckhaven the coast is not accessible. Cross the River Leven by the A955 bridge, on the site of the former 'Bawbee Bridge', so called because of the toll (bawbee) payable, and turn left to walk through Methil past the large RGC oil platform construction yard. Oilrigs are often anchored off shore here. Continue into Buckhaven, turning left at College Street and taking the next small road left to the shore.

Walk round a headland and continue towards East Wemyss: the shore is quite rough-going on this stretch. In a mile the site of the former gasworks is reached, with the first of a series of impressive caves eroded into the sandstone cliffs. Some of the caves contain wall drawings: several can be explored with care (and a torch).

Just past Jonathan's Cave (named after a nailmaker who lived here for some years in the 18th century) a diversion up the cliff path leads to the ruin of Macduff Castle, the oldest part of which dates from the 13th century. In East Wemyss itself, at the primary school, are the offices of the Wemyss Environmental Education Centre, which has much interesting material on the caves.

The coast walk continues past further caves. Little has been done to make the caves accessible or offer any form of interpretative presentation. A local history society is trying to get some action but meantime the caves continue to suffer vandalism.

Unless the tide is out you must walk through the Michael Pit, between East and West Wemyss. There has been a great deal of coal mining in this area over the centuries. The Michael Pit closed after a tragic accident in 1967 when nine miners died in an underground fire. Continue along an old railway siding and then by woodland to reach the imposing Wemyss Castle, started in the 14th century. The name Wemyss comes from the Gaelic *uamh*, 'cave'.

The path continues past St Adrian's Church into West Wemyss, with its fine 16th-century Tolbooth. From West Wemyss, a lane and then path leads to the 15th-century St Mary's Chapel, disused for the past 200 years. Another inland diversion

GUIDE BOX

Places to visit
Buckhaven Museum, College Street, Buckhaven, has displays on the fishing industry and local life. Open all year, Monday to Saturday.

John McDouall Stuart Museum, Rectory Lane, Dysart, is the birthplace of the explorer John McDouall Stuart (1815-1866), the first to cross Australia on foot. Open June to August daily, afternoons only.

Kirkcaldy Museum and Art Gallery, next to the railway station, is an award-winning museum of local history and crafts, with many fine paintings. Open all year, daily.

Burntisland Museum, High Street, Burntisland, houses local history displays and recreation of 'Edwardian Fair'. Open all year, library hours.

Inchcolm Abbey is on the island of Inchcolm. There are boat trips from Aberdour.

Car parking
Car parks in Kirkcaldy, Kinghorn (Pettycur Bay), Burntisland, Aberdour Station, Inverkeithing.

Public transport
Regular train services from Edinburgh and Dundee to Kirkcaldy, Kinghorn, Aberdour, Burntisland and Inverkeithing. Regular bus services from Edinburgh and Dundee to Leven. East Wemyss and all the above towns.

Accommodation
Hotels and guesthouses in Leven, Kirkcaldy, Kinghorn, Aberdour, Burntisland, Inverkeithing.

is now needed around the Frances Colliery. From Blair Point steps lead up towards the pithead and thus to the A955 road. After the railway crossing, walk down through Dysart to the shore at Pan Ha, an attractive area with finely restored houses.

From Dysart harbour the walk continues through Ravenscraig Park, with the ruin of Ravenscraig Castle, to Pathhead Sands. The road must again be taken to pass round Kirkcaldy harbour and reach the superb long sands for which the 'Lang Toon' is rightly renowned. The famous Links Market is still held here each April, lasting a week and with all sorts of stalls and fairground attractions. Kirkcaldy is an administrative and business centre with excellent shopping facilities. It has grown substantially in recent years.

Ⓔ *The bus and railway stations are easily reached from the shore. Trains go to Leuchars, with a bus connection to St Andrews.*

KIRKCALDY

ABERDOUR

APPROX. 11 MILES/18KM

OS Landranger 59, 66
Start at grid reference NT 278 915
Start point: Kirkcaldy bus station. Public car parks in the town.

After enjoying the splendid walk along Kirkcaldy's promenade (or on the fine sands), cross the Teil Burn by the road bridge and take the lane down to Seafield Beach (past the bus garage). Ahead is the site of Seafield Colliery.

From here the walk runs parallel to the railway line for nearly 3 miles to Kinghorn, passing the ruined 15th-century Seafield Tower. Seals can often be seen on the offshore rocks on this stretch. Remains of limekilns are passed, as is a large cave (near Abden Home) which can be explored at low tide. A path leads up from the metal bridge over the cave – take care as there is a substantial drop to the rocks below.

Abden Home, a former poor law house, is now converted into flats. The path continues round a grassy bay and improves as it reaches the outskirts of Kinghorn, a name which may mean 'head of the corner'. The coast does take a swing from south to west here, round Pettycur, once a very important trading harbour. Another diversion is needed at Kinghorn: take the path between the caravan park and the railway line, pass under a railway viaduct and go through a playpark to the road leading back to the shore.

Kinghorn has an attractive small harbour and excellent views of Inchkeith Island in the Firth. Take the road through Pettycur. From the far side of Pettycur Bay, it is best to follow the A921 into Burntisland. The shore can be walked at low tide but it is slow-going. The road walk is not uninteresting. The views are excellent and you pass the tall statue of King Alexander III, killed here in 1286 when his horse stumbled

in the dark and he fell over the cliff.

Burntisland gets its name from times when the land was indeed burnt, to improve its productivity. Walk along the promenade and follow the sea wall through the dockyard or go through the town to reach Burntisland Station.

From the station, turn west along Sailors' Walk. Go up steps to Castle Wynd and then turn under the archway to Rossend Castle, built in the 16th century. Go right, downhill, left to some garages, and right on a path to cross under the railway again and walk along beside the aluminium works.

From here to Aberdour there is a good path all the way, first on the landward side of the railway past Carron Harbour and then recrossing it to the seaward side, passing the Starley Falls. The area is noted for its liverworts, flat seaweed-like plants.

The path continues through woodland to Silversands Bay, a popular picnic area, then up Hawkcraig Cliffs with good views of Inchcolm, another of the Forth islands. Walk round the attractive harbour at Aberdour, cross the Dour Burn and continue to the railway station.

Ⓔ *To return to Kirkcaldy or St Andrews (via Leuchars and bus connection) trains may be taken from Kinghorn, Burntisland and Aberdour.*

ABERDOUR

INVERKEITHING

APPROX. 9 MILES/15KM

OS Landranger 65
Start at grid reference NT 191 854
Start point: Aberdour Station. Car park.

From Aberdour to Dalgety Bay (3 miles) the coast is largely out of reach, due to rocks, a golf course, and the Braefoot oil terminal. From the station follow the main road round a double bend and turn left on the road

leading in a mile to St Colme House. The house, built in 1835 for the Commissioner of the Moray Estates, is now converted to flats.

Past the turning to the house, walk under the road serving the oil terminal and in a further 300 yds turn left down stone steps to walk beside a field to another minor road. Turn right towards Dalgety Bay. In 1/2 mile, where the road bends right, divert to the shore to see St Bridget's Kirk, dating originally from the 13th century.

From the kirk continue along the shore path. To the right are the houses of Dalgety Bay. The path goes through Crownhill Wood; off shore, seals may be seen and there is a good variety of birdlife. Pass a Sailing Club to reach Donibristle House. Its central part was destroyed by fire in 1858. The wings remain, now converted into flats. Between them is a superb wrought-iron gateway, said to have been a gift from William of Orange to the Earl of Moray, whose home this was.

The path continues past Donibristle Chapel, and some new houses, to cross Downing Point and then Hopewood Point to reach St David's Bay, once a busy port exporting coal from mines at Fordell, just inland. Seafield House, built in the mid-19th century for the Fordell Estate manager, is passed, and then a large boundary cairn.

The Forth Bridges are visible and the end of the walk is near. Go through the former Preston Quarry, which produced greenstone, and swing right into Inverkeithing. The town has a number of interesting old buildings including the town hall of 1770 and the Mercat Cross, with a stone commemorating the Battle of Inverkeithing in 1651, when Cromwell's troops defeated the Scots. Inverkeithing Museum is in the 14th-century Friary, which has lovely gardens. The walk ends at Inverkeithing Station. It has encompassed a great variety of scenery from deserted bays to industrial sites, and has been full of interest and character: a description that sums up Fife itself.

Ⓔ *From Inverkeithing a return can be made by train to Aberdour, Burntisland, Kington, Kirkcaldy or St Andrews (via Leuchars and bus connection).*

THE FORTH BRIDGES

The two splendid bridges crossing the Forth, well seen from the closing stages of the walk, both celebrated notable anniversaries in 1990. The Rail Bridge marked its centenary. The powerful cantilever design so familiar today was not the original concept, but after the Tay Bridge disaster in December 1879, no chances were taken by the designers, John Fowler and Benjamin Baker. The bridge contains 8 million rivets and 57 workmen were killed during its construction. Beside it is the Forth Road Bridge, carrying the A90 road linking Edinburgh with Fife and Perth and opened in 1965. The bridge, an elegant and fitting companion for its sturdy neighbour, is one of the longest suspension spans in the world. It is possible to walk across the road bridge but not the rail bridge; a train journey over the latter is still a great experience.